1983

THE
BOOK OF CALIFORNIA WINE

THE

UNIVERSITY OF CALIFORNIA / SOTHEBY

BOOK OF CALIFORNIA

WINE

editors

DORIS MUSCATINE

MAYNARD A. AMERINE

BOB THOMPSON

UNIVERSITY OF CALIFORNIA PRESS / SOTHEBY PUBLICATIONS

BERKELEY   LOS ANGELES   LONDON

1984

FIRST PUBLISHED IN THE UNITED STATES & CANADA IN 1984 BY THE
UNIVERSITY OF CALIFORNIA PRESS, BERKELEY AND LOS ANGELES,
AND SIMULTANEOUSLY IN GREAT BRITAIN FOR SOTHEBY PUBLICA-
TIONS, BY PHILIP WILSON PUBLISHERS LIMITED, RUSSELL CHAM-
BERS, COVENT GARDEN, LONDON WC 2E 8 AA. ©1984 BY THE REGENTS
OF THE UNIVERSITY OF CALIFORNIA. LIBRARY OF CONGRESS CATA-
LOG CARD NUMBER 83–47666. INTERNATIONAL STANDARD BOOK
NUMBER, AMERICAN: 0–520–05085–1; BRITISH: 0 85667 185 1.

LIBRARY OF CONGRESS CATALOGING IN PUBLICATION DATA

Main entry under title:

The University of California / Sotheby book of California wine.

Bibliography: p.   Includes index. 1. Wine and wine making—California.
I. Muscatine, Doris. II. Amerine, M. A. (Maynard Andrew), 1911–
III. Thompson, Bob. IV. University of California (Berkeley)
V. Sotheby & Co. (England) V. Title: Book of California wine.
TP557.U64   1984   641.2'22'09794   83–47666
ISBN 0–520–05085–1 (U. of Calif.)

PRINTED IN THE UNITED STATES OF AMERICA
1   2   3   4   5   6   7   8   9

ACKNOWLEDGMENTS

by THE EDITORS

The idea for this book began in London in the spring of 1980, when Anne Jackson and Philip Wilson of Sotheby Publications and Patrick Grubb of the Sotheby Wine Department felt the need for a book that would explain the rising worldwide importance of California wine. They approached James Clark, Director of the University of California Press, to suggest a collaboration between the two publishers. When the Press and Sotheby turned to us for advice, we agreed that such a monumental subject would require the skills and knowledge of many people. To those forty-four contributors to this volume, and to the many other friends, colleagues, and experts who gave generous assistance, we express our warmest gratitude.

Particular thanks go to Dr. Robert K. Adamson, Joseph Arenas, Burton Benedict, Elizabeth Boardman, Esther Born, Robert Brown, Katherine Caldwell, Sucheng Chan, George Cooke, D. Steven Corey, Lois C. Farrell, Susan ffrench, Rabbi Alvin Fine, Jonathan W. Fleming, Alfred Fromm, William A. Garnett, Judith Gilbert, Jeffrey Granett, Gladys Hansen, Paul A. Harrell, Stanley Hock, Joan V. Ingalls, Julius Jacobs, J. R. K. Kantor, Robert H. Kozlowski, Donald Kunitz, Ralph E. Kunkee, Susan Lawson, Timothy Leahy, Marty Lee, Wendell Lee, James R. Lucas, John W. McConnell, John W. Mamer, Jill Mann, the late Ernest G. Mittelberger, Irene Moran,

▶

v

ACKNOWLEDGMENTS

Charles Muscatine, Chuck O'Rear, Allan R. Pred, Donn P. Reisen, Belle Rhodes, Gloria Rigazio, René Rondeau, Alan Ross, Alison Seidel, Rabbi Malcom Sparer, Ted Streshinsky, Jeanne Sugiyama, Harolyn Thompson, Alan Tobey, Rabbi Jacob Traub, Jean Valentine, and A. Dinsmoor Webb. Two people should be singled out: Peter Dreyer, for his unusually meticulous copyediting; and Marilyn Schwartz, of the University of California Press, for her masterful and sympathetic orchestrating of the entire production.

Our appreciation also goes to the staffs of the Wine Institute, San Francisco; the Wine Museum, San Francisco; the Bancroft Library, the General Reference Service of the Main Library, and the Natural Resources Library at the University of California, Berkeley; the Special Collections Department of the library at the University of California, Davis; the Napa Wine Library, St. Helena; the San Francisco Room and Archives of the San Francisco Public Library; and the library of the Wine Institute.

Our designer, Ernest Born, was a true collaborator in the making of this book. We feel privileged to have been able to work with an artist whose creative genius extends far beyond matters of design and typography. A very special thanks must also go to William J. McClung, the Sponsoring Editor for the Press, for his high standards, steady and benevolent attention, equanimity in times of crisis, and good company over several memorable bottles of wine.

D.M. *Berkeley*
M.A.A. *St. Helena*
B.T. *St. Helena*

vi

FOREWORD

One year during the harvest at our Napa vineyard, my partner Marijke and I gleaned some second-crop Zinfandel and Petite Syrah that had not ripened in time for the general picking and piled it, glistening and purple, in the back of the small, green Datsun for the drive to the cellar where we make our annual stash of house red. On the way down the hill, we stopped along the Silverado Trail at Clos du Val, the winery that was then buying our first-picked Zinfandel, in the hope of getting some yeast for the fermentation.

Bernard Portet, the winemaker, had learned his skills at Château Lafite during the time when his father had been the cellarmaster. Obligingly he gave us enough of a Champagne strain to get things started and, when he walked us back to the car, plucked off a few of the grapes we had just picked and tasted the juice. "Good sugar—about 23.4," he grinned, and reaching for a sample from a far lug, asked, "What's the Petite Syrah?—About 24.2. You'll have a good big wine." We who had not had the advantages of growing up in Bordeaux at the side of a master winemaker had measured the sugars in a hydrometer. They had been 23.4 and 24.2.

He wanted to know how we were going to crush the grapes. By foot, of course, we joked. "Good," he said again, ignoring the facetiousness; "it's the best way." And suddenly we were seriously committed. Rigging some chicken wire over a rudimentary wooden frame that had once formed the sides of a

▶

lug, he showed us a gentle way to destem—"the berries fall through and most of the stems are left behind." He told us how to punch down the cap that forms during the fermentation without assaulting the berries, another gentle technique respectful of the grape. Later that day, we rolled up our jeans and, purple-footed, crushed the grapes in two thirty-gallon green plastic garbage cans—the University of California's recommended equipment for home winemaking. When we finally drank the wine those uncomplicated methods had helped to shape, it was, everyone who tasted it agreed, the best we had ever made.

Savoring it, we realized that what Bernard had given us that day was more than some hints about how to improve our winemaking technique. He had shared with us a tradition of pleasure in and veneration for the grape that has endured for over 4,000 years. It was an implicit part of his own French culture and of California's since the earliest days of its settlement. In California, however, Prohibition had interrupted and almost destroyed that tradition. Now, after half a century of strenuous rebuilding, California wine once again excites our enthusiasm, enriches our lives, and commands a new respect and appreciation abroad.

D.M.

CHAPTERS

CONTENTS

CONTENTS

Contents

III

GEOGRAPHY, CLIMATE, AND VINTAGES

IV

CULTIVATING THE VINE IN CALIFORNIA

V

WINEMAKING STYLES AND TECHNIQUES

Contents

VI

SOME REFLECTIONS ON THE WINES

▶

VII

ART, ARTIFACTS, AND SOCIETIES

Contents

X

APPRECIATIONS AND EVALUATIONS

BACK MATTER

✳

DIAGRAMS

FIGURES

ILLUSTRATIONS

TABLES

MAPS

INCIDENTALS

ILLUSTRATIONS

DIAGRAMS

FIGURES

Illustrations

TABLES

MAPS

▶

INCIDENTALS

M. F. K. FISHER

A
PREFACE

Wine Is Life

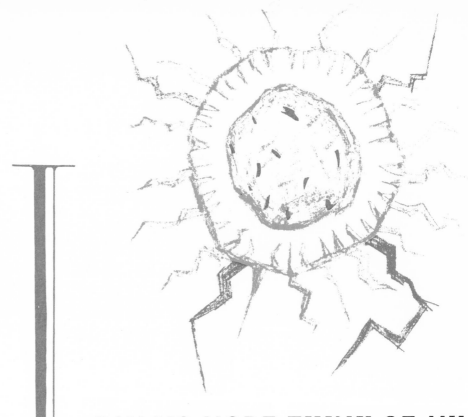

I CAN NO MORE THINK OF MY OWN LIFE WITHOUT THINKING OF WINE AND WINES AND WHERE THEY GREW FOR ME AND WHY I DRANK THEM WHEN I DID AND WHY I PICKED THE GRAPES AND WHERE I OPENED THE OLDEST PROCURABLE BOTTLES, AND ALL THAT, THAN I CAN RE-MEMBER LIVING BEFORE I BREATHED.

In other words, wine is life, and my life and wine are inextricable. And the saving grace of all wine's many graces, probably, is that it can never be dull. It is only the people who try to sing about it who may sound flat. But wine is an older thing than we are, and is forgiving of even the most boring explanations of its élan vital.

In some ways there is nothing much more encouraging about

man's stumbling progress than his growing deftness in making good wine better and then getting it to the mouths and minds of more people. On the other hand, perhaps it has lost some of its mystery and luster in its new availability. The leap from a high priest's sacramental flagon on a marble altar to the plastic container in a motel icebox is shorter than we care to ponder.

Myself, I am glad that people almost everywhere can find potable and honest wines more easily than they used to, even in supermarkets. It was impossible to buy anything alcoholic in Whittier, where we went when I was about four, because it was a town founded by and for the Quaker way of life. My father Rex respected this aim, but as a non-Quaker he did not subscribe to it, and some of the best times of my young life were spent driving into the beautiful hills and hidden quiet valleys of southern California with him to buy house-wines. I loved the cold smell of wine cellars as much as I did the fine whiff of ink and fresh paper at the daily NEWS.

It never surprised me that the ranchers always seemed glad when we drove up their roads in our open Model-T. The women would put tumblers and a long loaf of their last baking, and cheese or a dry sausage, on the kitchen table or under the grape arbor "out back." When the men came with two or three bottles from the old barn or hillside cellar where the casks were stored, they would eat and try the wines and talk. The women and I stayed carefully apart, and I was always given a seed-cake or a piece of bread and jam. Finally the jugs Rex had brought along were filled, and sometimes he took older bottles for special days ahead, and we drove away gently so as not to jiggle them too much.

The wines were probably crude and dirty, compared to what we can buy everywhere today. They were unpasteur-ized, unfiltered, unfined, not made to last long. Although I know that now and then I was given some at the little ranches, well watered to a sickly pink, I cannot remember anything except that I loved the bouncy rides and the fair countryside, and my father for taking me along with him.

My anglophile mother liked to serve heavy brownish sherries occasionally with desserts, and I was always given a ceremonial sniff or sip, which I still associate with the com-munion wine I did not taste until after I was twelve, of course, in our small Episcopal church. By then, Prohibition had been in effect for over a year, and we were firmly known in Whittier as the only so-called religious group in town that deliberately flouted the law and served "liquor" from its altar rail. This was, I learned later, because my father, as a respected vestry-man, refused flatly to invest in the barrel-washings that were then called sacramental wines, and managed somehow to have a comparatively fine imported sherry sipped from the St. Matthias chalice. It always made our empty stomachs rumble at the Early Service, but at least it was decent stuff, and al-

though Rex himself only went to church on Christmas and Easter mornings, he felt it his duty to protect his elected brethren from what he mildly referred to as Volstead Swill.

Until 1919 and Prohibition, though, I really enjoyed beer more than I did wine as a day-to-day tipple. Before World War I, I went often with Father to Anaheim, where we filled the back of the Ford with fresh bottles from two or three of the small German breweries there. As I now understand it, this was almost as easy in southern California as it had been in Albion, Michigan, where my parents had run a smaller newspaper than the NEWS and had started a family. There, and then in the little Quaker town, my father put the paper to bed by about three o'clock, six afternoons a week, and walked home to sit on the front porch or by the fire and drink a bottle of beer with Mother. And I got to carry the empty bottle and two glasses to the kitchen and tip back the last few delicious drops of bitter dead brew. (If for no other good reason, this early sampling taught me the mighty difference between real beer and the pale foamy water we now mass-produce in the United States.)

All during Prohibition we kept two decanters on the dining room sideboard, half filled with fairly good sherry and a mediocre port, mostly used to make an occasional Tipsy Parson when our teetotaller grandmother was out of town. We never drank at the table when she was in residence, out of re-

spect, but that was a time of frequent church gatherings for her, so that almost any birthday or fiesta, sacred or profane, meant a good bottle on the table. We children always had a sip or two in our own glasses but seldom drank them. And Cresta Blanca is the only wine name left in my mind, for a round rich red. The others were unlabeled, from a little vineyard off the Workman Mill Road, or Futelli's over near Cucamonga, or Old Man Johnson's back of Corona. They had to be honest to be good, and good meant drinkable.

We moved down Painter Avenue and into the country when I was eleven, and as money flowed faster in the decade before the Crash of 1929, the family served dependable bootleg liquor to their friends, and the wines came oftener and tasted more exciting. The two decanters still stayed on the sideboard, and it was understood that if we young ones wanted to drink in our own home, Father would gladly offer what he had to our guests, as long as they knew how to behave. We never accepted this tacit invitation, but as a clear result of it and of our complete lack of any need to find forbidden fruits, my younger sister and I emerged from our Prohibition teens with our livers intact and our palates unscarred by the poisons our dates carried in flat silver flasks to all the football games and dances. The flesh-warm booze was literally impossible for us to swallow, because we already knew what good drink tasted like, and we were young and healthy and had no need for extra stimulants. Other girls told us we must drink with our dates or have none, but we danced blandly past the Crash of '29 and into the Depression, learning a lot about the drinking patterns of our times, but always backed by what we had been taught unwittingly since our youngest days. There was good wine if we cared to look for it, or good beer–gin–whiskey–brandy. And the best was none too good!

In 1929, I started to learn more seriously about winemaking and winetasting when I married and went to live in France, mostly in Burgundy, for three years. We were lucky to live there with the Ollagniers first and then the Rigoulots, who were as different as two middle-class French families can be but who shared a genuine zeal for learning how to live intensely. They used all their physical senses steadily and deliberately, like musicians or surgeons training their fingers, and they studied and talked and polished all their wits like artisans honing their tools.

When Paul Ollagnier, a municipal architect, had to inspect the attic beams in an old château down the Côte d'Or near Gevrey-Chambertin, for instance, he took us along, and we saw how to use the little silver tâte-vins and stand like polite awed sheep, in the cellars or courtyards, while the men went through their long obligatory tastings after the business at hand was over. The smell of ice-cold stone and wine and mildew was good. We were learning, *with every cell and pore in our young minds and bodies.*

On Sundays the Ollagniers took us on rough endless walks with the Club Alpin, and we ate and drank our ways through endless enormous meals in village cafés that seemed to live for our annual treks, and then we snoozed for endless train-rides back to Dijon and bed and the next week's classes. And all week we discussed with the family the dishes and wines we'd absorbed on Sunday, as if they were Corneille or Voltaire or the futur indicatif *of the verb "to understand."*

M. Ollagnier had a cousin in Belley in the Ain, who occasionally sent him a gamey pâté or some long-necked bottles of pale rosé or straw-wine from his vineyard farm, so I learned about Brillat-Savarin's country and started then and there my "continuing delight" in that old man's good company. I read the Ollagnier copy of his PHYSIOLOGY OF TASTE and was as surprised then as I still am that few Frenchmen knew of it.

And then the Rigoulots rented us along with the Dijon house and for many more months taught us a completely sensual and almost hectic approach to the pleasures of the table, as compared to the more academic detachment of the architect and his pianist-wife.

We ate too much and too heavily and drank fine bottles every day instead of on Sundays, as we hurtled with the passionate, desperate people toward their family ruin and then World War II. They had once been very rich, with a fine cellar, mostly of Burgundian and Alsatian vintages, and by then my husband and I knew more about what and why we were drinking. The good bottles and the delicate fine dishes and all the urgency of disintegration mixed into a strange dream for a time. What is left is sometimes sad in my heart, but always good, sans reproche.

Back again in California, there was the end of Prohibition, a forgotten blight while we'd been away. There was no extra money anywhere, so the new watery beer and the dregs of bootlegged booze were easy to forego. Now and then a few of us would "chip in" for a gallon of young but decent red wine, and eat bread and maybe cheese and talk all night, and plan glowing beautiful exciting futures as the jug emptied. We never felt like clichés-in-Time, which of course we were, politics and poverty and gallantry and all . . .

And since my first years and Father's sure insistence that there could always be good wine if it were looked for, I have found it and not bothered with anything else. By now the skill of growing and making it in California has progressed so far that I feel more secure than ever in my lifelong pursuit. Of course there will be shoddy bottles forever, because of the shoddy men forever born to fill and market them. But they cannot harm me, because I have never stopped learning how to tell the true from the false, with at least six of my five allotted senses. Any good winemaker keeps on learning, too, and this collection of some of the reasons for doing so, and the ways devised to assure that, would give heart to my own first teacher, Rex.

He took a dim view of Brotherly Love, the Immaculate Conception, and Prohibition, according to critics as disparate as my mother and the County Boxing Commission, among others. He smoked cigarettes, mostly hand-rolled with Bull Durham, and pipe-tobacco until he lost his bite with dentures in his late years. He probably downed more than his share of drinkin-likka, as a newspaperman. He should have had a palate like well-tanned buffalo hide. But I never saw him smoke when honest wine was nearby, or falter in his first long silent appraisal of it, whether he was in a rancher's dim barn up in the California foothills, or in a Swiss vintner's cellar, or in a fine restaurant any place.

He was not my only teacher in this "appreciation course" that I shall continue to attend as long as I am con-scient, but certainly he was the shaper, the power behind what I always feel when I know that I am drinking a good wine and that I may soon drink another. Prosit, *to him and all such mentors!*

M.F.K.F
Glen Ellen

HUGH JOHNSON

ESSAY

California Wine:
An International View

OT THE LEAST
SEISMIC EFFECT WAS FELT IN NORTHERN CALIFORNIA
WHEN, ON 16 OCTOBER 1959, AT KING'S COLLEGE, CAM-
BRIDGE, DR. OTTO LOEB BRIEFLY INTRODUCED, WITH HIS
CHARACTERISTIC QUIET BLEND of hesitation and precision, a range of
California wines for the undergraduate members of the University Wine & Food
Society. They were nearly all Cabernets, with some Zinfandels; the labels were
Beaulieu, Inglenook, Louis Martini, Krug, Christian Brothers, and Italian Swiss
Colony. Dr. Loeb, an elderly citizen of London and Trier, was the first foreign
wine merchant to make a discovery that hundreds congratulated themselves on
twenty years later: there are great wines in California.

     I was lucky enough to be in that group of undergraduates. Four years
later, I was able to visit the California wine-country myself. (On an earlier visit,
in 1957, I had unaccountably left the coast unexplored and concentrated on the
Sierras.) I remember vividly how enthralled I was with what I tasted, and how
appalled at the lack of interest and recognition by the public, or facilities for
them to visit the Napa Valley with the slightest degree of comfort. There was
little to choose between the Napa Valley and the Médoc in that respect; the visi-
tor could starve equally well in either.

     Twenty years later, I have the satisfaction of reporting on those re-
mote days like a veteran talking about the Indian wars. Starting in that very year,
and gaining momentum annually ever since, a revolution has changed the world's

way of thinking about California wine, and California's way of thinking about itself. Or rather a renascence. For this is the second time round.

Historians seek the causes of a renascence in the social, cultural, and economic history of its time. They will have a short search for the roots of this one. Given such ideal natural conditions for the vine, a growing, rich, and cosmopolitan population, California's spirit of competition and its urge to excel, it is impossible to imagine the last decade *not* producing what it has, at least in northern California, where the vine was already well established. By the same token, experiments were bound to be made further down the coast and standards raised in the interior valleys. Statistically overwhelming it may have been, but there is nothing surprising in the California wine-boom of the seventies, no qualifying factor that leads one to doubt it will last.

The precise events of the decade, what led up to it, and its significant moments of progress are described elsewhere in this book. In this chapter, I want to register the effect on the rest of the world, on both consumers and producers of wine, of a new front-runner suddenly arriving in their midst. The wine-world is conservative. It bases its notions of quality and even correctness on concepts that have taken centuries to shape. It uses the word "classic" without self-consciousness, giving it a widely understood meaning.

What is that meaning? Does it apply to California wines? Is it begrudged them? What have they done, are they doing, or must they do to win "classic" status? A little history is essential to understand how the "classics" arose—and, most puzzlingly, why they arose where they did. In every case, five elements were essential in conjunction: a tolerable soil, a tolerable climate, a suitable vine, an active local market (or easy transport to one), and the right cellar conditions. Good growing conditions are important, but in the long run, if quality is the aim, not so important as the conditions, natural or artificial, under which the wine is made and matured.

This is the basic reason why northern European wines are historically superior to southern—and, by extension, to those of regions like California with a Mediterranean climate. The weather at harvest time was cooler, the *chais* or cellars cooler, the fermentation cooler, and the storage at a lower and steadier temperature. Cooler vintage weather and slower ripening started the wine with better acid balance; natural atmospheric conditions were ideal for its development.

It is scarcely necessary to list the classics that came about in this way —almost all in the time of the Roman Empire: Bordeaux, an entrepôt with a maritime climate; Saint-Émilion, with its limestone cellars; Burgundy, with one of Europe's main highways as its shop-window, already chilly by harvest-time; the Rhine and Mosel, water-highways with long misty autumns and dank barrel-cellars; Champagne, equally chilly and equipped with huge chalk pits for storage; Piedmont, cold in the fall; the Loire with its caves . . . there are even exceptional cases of excellent cellars in southern countries producing "classic" wines: Rioja and Frascati are two, even if Frascati chose grapes with no inherent balance and stability, so that its wine could not leave its deep cellars without starting to disintegrate. For each of these areas the growers selected grapes whose natural timing of flowering and ripening suited the local conditions—mostly, in fact, fruitful local strains of the woodland vine. Having no means of controlling nature, in other words, they carefully observed it and made the best of what it offered. The results, refined through centuries, have such fully evolved identities that they are now benchmarks no explorer can ignore. They are the classics. They even remain the classics when they are far from being good wine.

The concept of wine quality can also be considered quite separately from membership of the classical elite. A truly vigorous, well-balanced, satisfying, and long-lived wine is often made right outside the classical traditions—and vice versa. Wines we call "great," and unanimously agree in appreciating, are usually those that combine intrinsic quality with a classical idiom.

California is still asking itself whether these two recurrent themes are necessarily complementary, or even necessarily compatible. The question being asked is whether, let us say, California Pinot Noir should be judged by how far it resembles a Côte d'Or wine, or Riesling by how clearly it evokes the Rhine (or the Moselle). The answer is no: it should be judged for its qualities in isolation. But the real-life answer is that comparisons will be made. The problem is that having adopted a "classic" model, it is extraordinarily difficult to set it aside in making judgments.

What happens when established classic and California aspirant are brought face to face in competition? The answer was given dramatically at a famous blind tasting in Paris in 1976. French and Anglo-Saxon tasters alike were taken by surprise. Their training had led them to look for certain "classic" attributes, and to judge a wine, broadly speaking, by how much of the desirable taste and smell in question it offered.

In the Old World it is only in the most successful vintages that these characteristics are found in full concentration. The "claret" we are accustomed to drinking year in year out, for example, is a fairly light, distinctly astringent wine, extremely variable from vintage to vintage. The French tend to drink it brisk and young, appreciating its tannic and acidic "cut." Anglo-Saxons usually prefer to wait until vigor has been replaced by smoothness and bouquet—admittedly running a risk of missing the point where the flavor is at its juiciest.

Faced with very ripe California wines, many of them with higher alcohol levels than their French equivalents, the judges' first thought was that they had French wines of exceptional vintages before them. On the superficial examination of a blind tasting, they matched up closely to their ideal prototypes. I am not saying that they will not do the same in the long run; simply that a single blind tasting cannot provide this information.

I have discussed the matter at length with a number of European friends whose own work in wine is, to say the least, progressive. Piero Antinori, whose influence is changing the face of Chianti, pointed out to me another reason for the striking performance of California wines in such comparisons: "There is an obligatory phase in a market where the consumer is quite new and needs to easily recognize a product. Varietal character is therefore maximized as the distinguishing feature for the public to remember. The more aggressive it is, the greater its initial impact."

Even to experienced French and British palates, it seems, this learning phase is necessary in discovering the real identity and merit of California wines. The trouble, as we all rapidly learn, is that high-impact wines can all too soon pall. Piero Antinori makes another point that I have found worth pondering. "In a short time," he says, "California's winemakers have been able to make some of the best wines in the world and have created a prestigious image, first in California . . . now even in Europe. All of this is the result of great love and enthusiasm united with solid know-how, plenty of money, and a favorable environment—but above all due to the fertile imaginations of some avant-garde producers who have positively influenced the whole field. Their great skill has been in spreading and publicizing some particular technical aspects, definitely important but maybe not determining quality factors, and in making them into the real banner of California enology. The outstanding examples are the temperature-controlled fermentation of white wine and the aging of red and some white wines in small barrels of high-quality oak of various origins. These and other aspects so well publicized have, in my opinion, contributed perhaps more to the prestige and image of their products than to their intrinsic quality."

Modifications in present practice suggest that Antinori's point has already been taken by some winemakers. The day of the "show wine," the big statement in the clearest terms (with or without accompanying maps of subdivisions of the forests of France) is probably coming to an end. The drinker can add an important reason why it should. It concerns the sheer drinkability of show-stopping, high-alcohol, high-extract, usually low-acid wines. I was astonished when I first met what I now call a "one-glass" wine. To one who is accustomed to finish the bottle, each glass leading teasingly to the next, promising more interest and refreshment, I was affronted and disappointed to find that by the end of the first glass, however splendid, I had no desire for another.

Edmond Maudière of Moët et Chandon, who has the privilege of making wine in both Champagne and the Napa Valley, is precise about the "preconceived and false notions" that have led to such disappointments in white wines—above all, the idea that high degrees of alcohol are either desirable or unavoidable. It is, he says, easy to control by picking at the right "*équilibre physiologique.*" Twelve to 12.5 degrees of alcohol is as much as Chardonnay needs for balance and delicacy. To make white wines like red, macerating the skins in the juice and fermenting in oak, is to lose control of their balance and their eventual harmony. Instead, Maudière advocates fermenting in stainless steel or any neutral container, then aging whatever seems the proper proportion of the wine in oak—leaving the final assembling of the wine until tasting has determined precisely how much oak influence gives the best result. (This is, of course, the philosophy behind the *cuvée* of Champagne.)

Maudière's enthusiasm for California's potential is strongly felt, but very specific. He finds the general standard of red wine far above the whites. Like all Frenchmen he attributes at least as much to soil as to climate. The Carneros region can grow extremely fine Pinot Noir of great delicacy, perfect for his *cuvées*, more on account of its poor, hungry soil than its Bay-influenced coolness. He finds excellence in the Chardonnay grown on Mount Veeder and in the thin soils of other Napa hillsides. Monterey and Mendocino, he considers, are both at present underrated for the delicate wines he is looking for.

It is interesting to hear a contrary view to both Antinori and Maudière. Miguel Torres, whose family's work has put Penedés in Catalonia firmly on the fine-wine map, likes heavy strong Chardonnays because they are different, with a distinct image of their own. Rather than wanting to reproduce the harmonies of classic wines, he sees the virtues of inventing new ones. He is not afraid of alcohol, in the right place. Zinfandel he likes best at 14 percent alcohol. On the other hand he cites the advent of "light" wines as proof of the vitality of the industry. As a Spaniard, he would, not surprisingly, like California's winemakers to try Spain's best varieties as an alternative to what risks becoming a narrow range of accepted varieties. The Parellada, which serves him so well for white wine in Penedés, should grow excellently in the North Coast counties. Torres is particularly concerned with costs and prices, reserving his strongest admiration for Gallo, which has shown the way to very drinkable white wines at a lower price than any advanced country can match. It is no coincidence that the Torres company has started production in Chile, which has an ideal environment for the vine. Perhaps it is surprising that California's winemakers have not.

The international consensus seems to be that California has proved herself more conclusively so far with red wines than with white. Fritz Nerath, whose work with the great German Seitz filter company brings him to California at least twice a year, is very specific. Napa Cabernets, he says, have always been outstanding. "There are always people who overdo things," but there is no questioning the stature of the finest California reds.

A German point of view on whites is perhaps likely to be more critical, but Nerath finds fault in particular with many of the cheaper white wines. Poor handling, he says, makes them flat, fruitless and lifeless. He distinguishes between the style of Gallo, whose super-precautions against oxidation before fermentation "result in a slightly reduced or oxygen-starved wine, showing the pre-stages of hydrogen sulfide" (vernacular: rotten eggs), and Guild, whose jug wines are slightly oxidized. Nerath approves wineries (and cites Souverain and Simi) that use great pains (and German techniques) to achieve an ideal content of carbon dioxide at bottling—an effective source of extra liveliness. As for the innovation of Rieslings affected by "noble rot" in the manner of Trockenbeerenauslesen, he freely admits the success of Chateau St. Jean and Phelps has "left the Germans struggling." I asked Fritz Nerath why California Rieslings (not Late Harvest wines) arrive so rapidly at the mature flavor that takes eight or ten years in Germany. He believes low acid levels are the reason, and that harder pruning would help to raise them and give better-balanced longer-lived wines.

It is widely agreed that one towering advantage California has over Europe is its open mind. Rapid adaptability is simply not possible in the classic European regions. Law and custom slow change down to a crawl. To see the speedy unhampered development of new ideas, you must look to such areas as Sicily or the Midi, which have minimal controls.

I do not doubt that the soil—not just the "dirt," but what the French call *terroir*, the land in all its aspects—is next on the agenda for serious study in California. The 100th Anniversary (July 1980) issue of *California Agriculture*, the journal of the University of California Division of Agricultural Sciences, an issue devoted to viticulture and enology, contains no chapter on the land itself and only a single mention of the word *soil* (in relation to pH). If French concern with soil can sometimes seem blinkered, this is surely sand-blind, if not (as Launcelot says of Old Gobbo in the *Merchant of Venice*) high-gravel blind.

Indeed where academics have failed to lead, experienced farmers are now finding their own way. Wines from named vineyards were rare exceptions three years ago. Today they are becoming commonplace. It will, of course, take many years to plot the significance of their *terroir* as against the variety and age of their vines and other factors, but this is certainly the next priority in California's search for its own classics.

H.J.
London

HISTORY: FROM THE MISSIONS TO PROHIBITION

I.1

THE EARLY DAYS IN SOUTHERN CALIFORNIA

by THOMAS PINNEY

WINEGROWING CAME TO CALIFORNIA QUITE INCIDENTALLY, WHEN THE SPANISH AUTHORITIES IN MEXICO DETERMINED TO SECURE THE UNGUARDED COAST of the vast and unsettled territory called Alta California against threats of rival European expansion. Accordingly, in 1769, the traditional arrangement of the Spanish colonial power was set up at what is now San Diego: the trinity of soldier, civilian, and priest, inhabiting presidio, pueblo, and mission. From this growing point at the far southern edge of Alta California, the system spread through the next half century to include civilian towns, army posts, and ranches stretching from San Diego to Sonoma, all linked together by a chain of twenty-one missions. The history of modern California descends directly from this original work of European settlement.

In this system, wine had an essential place on the spiritual side of things, for it was required in the celebration of the mass. It was also, of course, a standard part of the diet to which the Spanish priests had been born. But it was apparently thought at first that the slowly growing chain of small missions could be supplied with wine from Mexico. Not until a decade or more of difficulties and accidents had made it clear that the long supply line to Mexico could not be counted on did the Franciscan fathers make the experiment of growing their own.

Once begun, the spread of vines and wine through the chain of missions was fairly rapid but highly irregular. Roughly speaking, the southern missions were more productive than the northern, and at a few—San Francisco and Santa Cruz, for example—winegrowing did not succeed at all. But there was wine enough to supply the needs of all the missions from those vineyards that did prosper. In the north, the mission vineyards of Santa Clara and San Jose stood out; in the south, those of San Fernando, San Luis Rey, San Diego, and, especially, San Gabriel. Brandy, too, was produced from an early, though undated, point in the development of mission winegrowing. It is likely, in fact, that as much as half or even more of the mission wine was distilled into *aguardiente*, the surest way of preserving the wine amidst difficult conditions in a thinly populated territory without commercial markets. By the early nineteenth century, when the first stray visitors from Europe and the United States to the remote California coast began to report on what they had seen there, the mission vineyards and their wines were singled out for special notice.

Reliable descriptions of the wine made at the missions don't exist. Nor is there any authoritative first-hand information about the methods of grape growing and winemaking, though the labor of both would certainly have been performed by the Indian "neophytes" at the missions. In all probability the mission vines were head-pruned—that is, trained as low, self-supporting bushes requiring no apparatus of posts, wires, or trellises. This was the standard method of vine training for wine grapes in California down to very recent years. Most mission vineyards were probably irrigated. The received account of winemaking (from Bancroft and Haraszthy) says that the grapes were piled on cowhides (wood was scarce) spread upon the ground or supported on posts and were then crushed by the feet of "well-washed Indians"; the juice flowed by some means into leathern bags, from which it was poured into larger vessels to ferment. The residue of skins and seeds was then put into a wooden press—probably a simple beam press—to be squeezed again. This, or something like it, was no doubt the procedure in the earliest days, but the mission priests would probably have acquired a good supply of barrels and other storage vessels from the coastal trade before very many years had passed. A few brickwork cisterns remain at some of the missions; these may have been used for crushing, or fermenting, or storing, or for all three purposes. The missions, dependent as they were on their own resources, very likely produced a number of ingenious adaptations of method and materials in order to make their wine at all, but if so we have no evidence of them. And on the other hand, the general tendency of the Spanish in the New World was strongly conservative; as one of the latest writers on the subject has said, the missions were not interested in developing new technologies but simply took over without modification the traditional agricultural techniques of Spain. As if in proof of this proposition, the only technical handbook we know to have been used by one of the mission fathers is a copy, now preserved at Santa Barbara, of a treatise on general agriculture, including viticulture and winemaking, first published in Spain in 1513.

We do know one thing for certain about mission winemaking: whether the result was wine or brandy, white or red, sweet or dry, fortified or light, it all came from the same grape, now called the Mission. But though this fact is clear, the precise origins of the Mission grape are not. It is undoubtedly a European variety (species *Vitis vinifera*), ultimately of Spanish origin, yet it corresponds to no variety now growing in Spain. In other parts of the New World it is known as the Criolla—Creole, as we would say—and this name perhaps points to its origin. For "Creole" means of European descent born in the colonies and adapted to the new conditions. The Mission/Criolla vine fits this definition, and may be accounted for on the supposition that it is a seedling of some Spanish variety, now unknown and unknowable. The variety has a high claim to our respect, since it was the sole basis of California winemaking from the beginning and for the next fifty years at least. It is well suited to the hot climate of southern California, it yields heavy crops, it makes quite good sweet wines, and it will no doubt continue to be grown in California for many years (there are currently 3,785 acres of Mission grapes in the state's vineyards). After all this has been said, one must add that the Mission is not a distinguished grape, especially for table wine: it is low in acid and lacks distinctive varietal flavor. Even without direct evidence, we are fairly safe in concluding that the dry table wines, both red and white, made by the mission fathers were, at best, rather flat and dull.

The beginning of the end for the missions came in 1833, when the Mexican government issued a decree by which the Franciscans were deprived of all their temporalities in California. The decree did not take effect all at once, and the various missions struggled to protract their lives as long as they could. But their doom was sealed, and by the 1840s only broken vestiges of the old mission life survived. It had never been a very large enterprise, judged by numbers, and winegrowing had never been a very large part of its work. At no time did a trade in wine figure importantly in the economic life of the missions. Such small external trade as they developed was almost entirely in the hides and tallow from the vast mission herds that roamed the hills of southern California. But their winemaking was to have lasting effect, and even when the priests were scattered, the churches crumbling, and the vineyards neglected, the work begun at the missions in growing California wine was being carried forward.

Even before the decree of secularization, individuals outside the missions in California had planted vineyards—one was the original *commandante* of Alta California, Pedro Fages, whose Monterey garden included vines in 1783—and there are other records of such early plantings scattered up and down the state. The shift from domestic gardening to commercial winegrowing in the state first occurred in Los Angeles, in the 1830s. There had been vineyards in Los Angeles from a very early date—the town lay only a few miles from the conspicuously flourishing vineyards of Mission San Gabriel—but when and by whom planted is not now known. In 1818, when the missions were still prospering, it was estimated that 53,000 vines (perhaps about fifty acres) were growing in and around Los Angeles. Twelve years later, the estimate was of 100,000 vines (one must always remember that the "statistics" of early California are more poetic than scientific),★ tended by a scattering of Frenchmen, Yankees, Germans, and others mixed in with the native Mexicans of the pueblo. To this promising scene, around the year 1833, came a Frenchman with the providential name of Jean Louis Vignes, a native of Cadillac in the Bordeaux region; he bought land on the east side of Los Angeles and laid out a vineyard on a site now just across the freeway from Union Station. There he began the successful commercial production of wine and brandy at the El Aliso ranch, as he named it. Two other important firsts are credited to Vignes. In 1840 he made the first recorded export of California wine, sending a shipload from Los Angeles to Santa Barbara and Monterey. And, as early as 1833, it is said, he imported a variety of vines from Europe for trial in his Los Angeles vineyard. Unfortunately, Vignes's experiment with alternatives to the Mission grape does not seem to have had any effect, for the Mission remained unchallenged around Los Angeles for many years to come. Nor do we have any information about the varieties he may have tried. But the episode, if unsatisfactorily vague, is at least worth recording as evidence of the early recognition that something better than the Mission was wanted for the future of California winegrowing.

The example of Vignes's success was quickly followed: a fellow Frenchman, Louis Bauchet; Vignes's nephews, the Sainsevain brothers; the Kentucky trapper William Wolfskill; the Irishman Matthew Keller; the Swiss Victor Hoover; and a number of Mexicans—Tomas Yorba and Ricardo Vejar, to name only two— gave a remarkably international character to the group whose vineyards covered nearly all of what is now downtown Los Angeles. That was also true of the wine-growing on the outlying ranches, whose representative men included the Englishmen William Workman at La Puente and Henry Dalton at Azusa, the Scotsman Hugo Reid at Santa Anita, and the Mexican Tiburcio Tapia at Cucamonga.

In 1847, when, as an incident of the Mexican War, the United States *See* MAP 6 pp. 122–23 took over California, the victors found vine growing and winemaking dotted throughout the Los Angeles basin, at such places as San Bernardino, the Rancho Jurupa (now Riverside), Cucamonga, Azusa, Santa Anita, and Santa Ana, apart from the major concentration in and around the pueblo of Los Angeles itself. There were some scores of growers, and, though figures are lacking, probably some dozens

---

★ Another difficulty arises from the practice of measuring by number of vines planted rather than by acre. In the south the usual measure was 1,000 vines to the acre; in the north it varied, but was typically less, perhaps 650 vines to the acre. One cannot be sure.

of winemakers, headed by Vignes and Wolfskill. Their trade was largely local, but included a traffic with the towns to the north and with the ships that coasted along the California shore. The Gold Rush of 1849 transformed this: the population of California boomed and the scale of trade grew beyond anything imagined in the state's pastoral days. The first to grasp the possibilities and to manage the necessary organization of this new state of things in winegrowing were two German musicians in San Francisco, Charles Kohler, a flute player, and John Frohling, a violinist. Neither had any experience in winemaking or in selling wine, but they understood what was needed to supply the soaring market of San Francisco. With a small capital, they were able to buy a vineyard in Los Angeles in 1854 and to rent a cellar. With Frohling managing the production of wine in Los Angeles and Kohler managing its sale in San Francisco, they soon developed a good reputation and good sales. Their success allowed them to organize a large part of the Los Angeles industry; through contracts with local growers to buy their harvests, and with local wineries to make their wine, the firm was able both to manage the supply in an orderly way and to secure uniformity in the standards of production. Whether in their own vineyards and wineries or those of others, Kohler and Frohling used their own crews, who carried out the whole winemaking process, from picking the grapes to bottling the finished wines, under the direct supervision of Frohling.

Frohling died in 1862, but the firm went on successfully. Just before his death, the partners had taken the next crucial step in the development of the California wine trade by opening an agency in New York City—the beginning of the struggle to secure recognition for the state's wines beyond the remote, and still largely unpopulated, Pacific coast. That struggle would last many years, and be filled with nagging problems of transportation, storage, spoilage, adulteration, and the like. Within a few years, however, Kohler and Frohling were shipping wines in 100,000-gallon quantities to New York. By the middle of the 1870s, Kohler could boast that no sizeable town or city in the United States was without the wines supplied by his firm. By that time, of course, many other California producers, both north and south, were part of the trade, but they were all followers along the path that Kohler and Frohling had opened.

To return to the 1850s, it was clear soon after Kohler and Frohling began their operations that they would need a larger and steadier flow of wine than Los Angeles could currently provide. They solved the problem with the boldness and efficiency that characterized their work by inventing the idea of the Anaheim Colony, directing its organization, and recruiting the Germans who would populate it in order to grow vines for the firm. All this was done in 1857. Capital was raised by selling shares to fifty subscribers, and land purchased along the Santa Ana River, in what is now Orange County, south of Los Angeles. The name Anaheim—home on the Santa Ana—combined the German and Californian themes, and the official name of the company, "The Los Angeles Vineyard Society," expressed its purpose. The property was laid out in twenty-acre parcels, irrigation channels dug, vines set out, and the whole colony screened from the desolate waste surrounding it by a living hedge of willow, sycamore, and alder saplings. When the first shareholders arrived to occupy their properties late in 1859, they moved into an already established farming enterprise and could go to work at once with only a minimum of the homesteading rigors that the ordinary pioneer had to face. In consequence of its careful planning, Anaheim's viticulture flourished: within a few years production reached 300,000 gallons of wine from forty-seven individual winemakers. By the 1880s, just before its sudden demise as a result of the outbreak of a virulent vine disease,* the Anaheim industry produced over a million gallons annually from 10,000 acres of vineyards.

Meanwhile, another important winemaking region in the Los Angeles basin had developed in the San Gabriel valley, at the base of the foothills of the San Gabriel mountains. This was the territory once dominated by the San Gabriel Mission, and its vineyards were literally derived from the stocks of the mission itself. The push that lifted winemaking to a new importance here was given by an early pioneer from Tennessee named Benjamin Wilson, who, after many years of trading in land and cattle around Los Angeles, settled in 1856 at the Lake Vineyard in present-day San Marino and set about improving both his vines and wines. Wilson made trials of new varieties for California and is on record as having produced the first sparkling wine in the state. Like Kohler and Frohling, he set up an agency in San Francisco, and, soon thereafter, one in New York City. From these points, he gradually succeeded in distributing Lake Vineyard wines through a large part of the country.

Wilson's neighbors, among them men of wealth and prominence, also began planting vines, and by the 1870s had made the San Gabriel valley one of the most extensive vineyards of the state. General George Stoneman, governor of California; Lucky Baldwin, the Comstock millionaire;† and Judge Benjamin Eaton were

---

*   Now known as Pierce's disease, and only recently determined to be caused by a bacterium. It is native to the southeastern United States, where the local varieties have some degree of resistance to it.

†   Another of our authors, John Hutchison, has written an amusing anecdote about Baldwin: "Elias (Lucky) Baldwin flung money into his winery with stunning prodigality. Among 7,300 acres of citrus grove, pasture lands, and scores of buildings, he devoted 1,200 acres to grapes and made wine and brandy. The writer Frona Eunice Wait visited Baldwin's place. Her description spouts with admiration and adjectives. 'A second garden of Eden,' she wrote. 'Milton himself could not have done justice to its beauty.' Today it is the site of the Los Angeles County Arboretum and the Santa Anita racetrack. Baldwin's ranch, then encompassing what is now Arcadia, in suburban Los Angeles, had streams, three railroads, tree-lined avenues, three villages, clusters of tenant cottages, and sheep, cattle, and racehorses. 'Here I saw, sampled and surrendered,' wrote the bedazzled Frona somewhat ambiguously." —*Ed. Note*

among the important growers in the valley. Wilson's major rival and near neighbor was L. J. Rose, a German immigrant who acquired the Sunnyslope property just east of Wilson. There he bred racehorses and cultivated vineyards at the same time. Rose ultimately ruined himself, but not before he had made an international name for Sunnyslope wines and Sunnyslope horseflesh. He is remembered on the map still by the town of Rosemead, where he retreated after the collapse of his fortunes.

The headiest days of southern California winegrowing occurred at the end of the 1870s. By that time, the ravages of the phylloxera in Europe had gone so far that growers in California—especially in the south, where Rose, Wilson, and the Anaheim kingpin Benjamin Dreyfus were already operating on what was a large scale for California—saw an opportunity to step in. Rose built a brand new winery in 1879, with a capacity of half a million gallons, to help supply the thirst of Europe. At almost the same time, and in response to the same situation, his neighbor J. De-Barth Shorb, now the heir to Benjamin Wilson at the Lake Vineyard, schemed even more boldly. Partly through English investment, he financed a new operation called the San Gabriel Winery, which was to have a fermenting capacity of a million gallons and a storage capacity of one and a quarter million gallons, all to be supplied by 1,500 acres of surrounding vineyards. It was to be, as Shorb put it simply, "the world's largest winery." This was the high point in the imaginings of southern California winemakers, and the project was never to be realized.

A number of conditions were working together against the future of winegrowing in the Los Angeles region, and their effect grew increasingly evident in the 1880s. First, and perhaps most important, was the failure of southern California growers to produce a good dry table wine; it was not for lack of experiment with different varieties, for they tried everything then established in the state. Los Angeles port, sherry, angelica, and brandy all earned and kept high reputations, but the table wine was not a success—the hot climate, which favored the Mission grape but not the superior table wine varieties, was against it. At the same time, the vineyards of the north, where they *could* make a satisfactory dry wine, were growing in size and reputation: in 1860 Los Angeles made two-thirds of the state's entire production; in 1870 it made a little more than half; by 1890 its share had sunk to less than a tenth of the California total. When competing against the north grew difficult, there were other opportunities for Los Angeles ranchers: oranges, for example, were becoming a glamour crop, secure against competition from the north, and many of the pioneer viticulturists turned orange ranchers instead. Real estate, too, was a live option, as successive land booms swept over the Los Angeles region. Much of Shorb's San Gabriel vineyard, for example, disappeared into the town of Alhambra, which he named and promoted. The most dramatic blow given to Los Angeles winegrowing was the virulent Anaheim disease, which broke out in the vineyards in 1885 and destroyed whatever confidence was left in the future of the region's viticulture. The disease virtually annihilated the Anaheim vines between 1885 and 1887, and though it was nothing like so destructive in the rest of the region, it remained a threat against which growers were helpless.

It would be wrong to say that winegrowing in and around Los Angeles went into a sudden decline. Though the Sunnyslope and San Gabriel wineries, the most ambitious of the region, struggled profitlessly for some years and succumbed before Prohibition, other vineyards and wineries maintained a large production. There was even new development in some areas, notably at Cucamonga at the turn of the century. There Secundo Guasti established the Italian Vineyard Company on the sandy slopes of the district and ultimately extended his vineyards over 5,000 acres—"the largest in the world," they were inevitably called. But the euphoric vision that growers and observers had once had was now gone. In 1876 the judicious and experienced traveller Ludwig Louis Salvator, archduke of Austria, had pronounced Los Angeles "the best grape district in the state" and prophesied that it would "produce more wine no doubt than is now made in the entire state." Ten years later, no one would have said so. Nor would anyone then have joined Shorb in planning the world's largest winery for the slopes of the San Gabriel valley. Despite the fact that Los Angeles has lost its place in the scheme of California winegrowing, we should remember that in the beginning, and for nearly a century following, California wine meant Los Angeles wine.

BIBLIOGRAPHIC NOTE

There is no connected full account of winegrowing at the California missions, so that an outline must be collected from the scattered sources of mission history. Among the special studies, Bowman's "The Vineyards in Provincial California" is outstanding for amount and precision of detail. Edith Buckland Webb's *Indian Life at the Old Missions* contributes a few new items and gives a good idea of the agriculture carried on at the missions. Robert Archibald, in *The Economic Aspects of the California Missions* (Washington, D.C.: Academy of American Franciscan History, 1978), shows that mission winegrowing had little economic importance, contrary to the impression sometimes given. After the mission period and before the annexation of California, the general history of the state, north and south, must be combed, beginning with Hubert Howe Bancroft's pioneering *California Pastoral* (San Francisco: The History Company, 1888). Memoirs such as William Heath Davis's *Sev-*

enty-Five Years in California, edited by Harold A. Small (San Francisco: John Howell Books, 1967), are full of local detail not found elsewhere. For the south of the state, Harris Newmark's *Sixty Years in Southern California* is a primary source; Paul W. Gates, *California Ranchos and Farms, 1846–1862* (Madison: State Historical Society of Wisconsin, 1967), gives much detail on individual vineyards and wineries. Mildred Yorba MacArthur's *Anaheim: "The Mother Colony"* is the most recent account of that enterprise. Of the histories devoted to California winegrowing itself, the two best known are Leggett, "The Early History of Wine Production in California," and Carosso, *The California Wine Industry*. To these may now be added Teiser and Harroun, *Winemaking in California*. Not yet superseded (though not wholly reliable) is the long series of articles published by Irving McKee in various journals between 1946 and 1954 under the auspices of the Wine Institute (see Bibliography).

I.2

ALTA CALIFORNIA'S FIRST VINTAGE

by ROY BRADY

CARELESS WRITERS ARE IN THE HABIT OF SAYING THAT FATHER JUNÍPERO SERRA BROUGHT THE GRAPEVINE WITH HIM WHEN HE arrived in 1769. As spiritual leader of the Gaspar de Portolá expedition that came to plant the first European settlement in California, he needed wine to celebrate the Mass. It's a pretty story, the beloved father carefully tending the vine cuttings through the arduous trek up Baja California and putting them gently in the earth of San Diego with his own hands. The story was pretty enough to cause the California wine industry, or some of its less scholarly sectors at any rate, to observe the bicentennial of California wine prematurely in 1969.

Prettiness apart, the chief defects of the Serra story are the lack of any reason beyond sentiment to believe it and a good deal of reason not to. Moreover, it can now be said with considerable confidence when, where, and by whose hands the vine first reached California and first produced wine there. Serra had a hand in it, but later and less directly.

The Serra story originated with a famous native Californian, General Mariano Guadalupe Vallejo, in 1874 when he was sixty-six. Vallejo said that early Californians, including his own father, who had worked with Serra, had been told by Serra that the latter had brought the grapevine with him in 1769. If vines were brought at all then, it would have been more sensible in every way to send them on one of the ships of the expedition. Moreover, Vallejo's statement was made at a time when the mission period was viewed through a golden haze of nostalgia, and all good things were attributed to Serra. There is no record that Serra himself or any of his contemporaries suggested that he had brought the vine on that first expedition.

Happily, Serra's travel diary for that year has been found. We can trace his slow progress from 15 February, when he left his mission at Loreto far down the east coast of the Baja peninsula, until he reached San Diego four and a half months later, on the first of July. He was fifty-five when he left Loreto with a chronically infected foot and leg, a loaf of bread, a piece of cheese, a broken-down mule, and the serene faith that he would make it through nearly a thousand miles of some of the most inhospitable land on earth. He worked his way slowly up the chain of missions, leaving the northernmost one, Santa Maria, on 11 May. He would have had to gather grape cuttings earlier. In such a warm climate, the vine would break dormancy by the end of February. Cuttings must come from dormant vines and must be kept cool and damp until planted, conditions Serra would have found it virtually impossible to provide. If cuttings dry out or start to grow before planting, the chances of success are almost nil. Serra did not choose the site of the San Diego mission until 16 July, an almost impossibly late date for planting. Even if there were cuttings, the circumstances of the expedition made it unlikely that they would be planted and tended. Portolá had two land parties and three ships. Only Serra's land party fared well. The other lost five members to starvation. The ships were still less fortunate. Contrary winds and currents made it difficult to sail up the coast, and scurvy broke out. The crew of the *San Antonio* was largely incapacitated, and on the *San Carlos* only one sailor and a cook survived to see Serra arrive. The *San José* disappeared without a trace.

To make things worse, Portolá had orders to proceed at once to find the port of Monterey. He believed in obeying orders and took nearly all the able-bodied men on a weary trek up the coast. Indians constantly stole from the sickly little colony left behind and, in the middle of August, decided to wipe it out. The settlers reluctantly used guns for the first time, and the surprise turned the attack after one soldier took a fatal arrow through the throat. Then lack of food threatened to do what the Indians could not. Portolá returned and set 19 March 1770 as the date the settlement would be abandoned if the *San Antonio* did not return from Mexico with supplies. It was sighted the afternoon of the nineteenth. Is it likely that, under such insecure conditions, the Spanish would have given any of their slender energies to the cultivation of a crop that would yield nothing for at least three years?

Nor had they reason to think a local supply of wine to be of immediate importance. Inventories show that the expedition brought ample wine for the Mass. In addition, the port of San Blas had been set up on the west coast of Mexico specifically to supply the missions. Serra lacked both means and incentive for bringing up the vine in 1769.

Now that all known Serra letters have been published, it is apparent that the supply lines to Mexico didn't work very well. Beginning with a letter to Father Verger in August 1772, the lack of wine for the Mass became a recurring theme in his correspondence. As late as 29 October 1783, he complained to Father Juan Sancho that on various occasions they had had to go to the government storehouse for wine. With an unusual touch of asperity, he added, "but we have had to pay like any ordinary soldier—and not a cent reduction allowed us either." In his next reference to wine, on 18 June 1784, also to Father Sancho, Serra mentioned earlier difficulties with the wine supply and then, with a sudden change of theme, made a tantalizing remark, "But God has provided a way out, and now they [the missions] are well looked after in that respect." That was all he said, but he must have meant that California was at last growing its own wine.

To understand what happened, we must go back to 1777, when Serra made his first known effort to get the grapevine. On 1 June he wrote to Antonio María de Bucareli y Ursúa, the viceroy in Mexico City, "Some improvements could easily be introduced from California, . . . for instance fig and pomegranate trees and grapevines." There is no proof that Bucareli responded to the suggestion, but he was notably friendly toward Serra and granted many requests of greater substance. When Serra said "California," he meant Baja, but it is likely that Bucareli found it convenient to send vines from the mainland, since ships were going from there anyhow. In any case, vines were sent by someone, as proven by a letter to Serra from Pablo de Mugártegui, a young friar assigned to Mission San Juan Capistrano. It is dated 15 March 1779, and said, "Snow is plentiful, wherefore, until the severe cold moderates and the floods subside, the vine cuttings which at your request were sent to us from the lower country have been buried." Those cuttings would have produced a small crop in 1781 or, if not then, certainly in 1782.

Father Francisco Palóu, Serra's close friend, said in his biography of Serra that because wild grapevines were abundant around San Juan Capistrano, it was decided to plant some cultivated vines there, and that they had "already produced wine, not only for use at Mass but also for the table." Those must have been Mugártegui's vines.

We know that Palóu wrote his biography quickly in the winter of 1784–85, Serra having died in August of the former year. The 1784 vintage would scarcely have been gathered when he sat down to write. Any wine ready for the table could hardly be a vintage later than 1783. That narrows the first vintage in California to 1781, 1782, or 1783. But Serra wrote to Father Fermín Francisco de Lasuén on 8 December 1781, "I hope . . . that your vines will survive and bear fruit. The lack of wine for the Mass is becoming unbearable." That rules out the first year, since a 1781 wine could have been used by December though still raw.

In a letter written from San Gabriel on 27 October 1783, Serra said, "Many Masses have not been said because of our lack of wine. We have plenty everywhere at present, except at this mission. We met with an accident—when the barrel was being brought here from San Juan Capistrano it fell off the mule, broke into pieces, and all the wine was lost. But the neighboring missions came to the rescue, and will supply the needs in the future." Since the San Blas supply line was not getting more dependable, the new note of confidence must mean that California wine was being made, and perhaps at more than one mission. His letter to Father Sancho the following June (cited above) reinforces that.

What was in that hapless barrel from San Juan Capistrano? It could have been the 1783, but that is doubtful. We don't know when the missions picked their grapes, but it was a California custom throughout the nineteenth century to pick as late as possible, often meaning well into October. In any event, the variety of grape they grew ripens late, and with San Juan Capistrano only a couple of miles from the beach, the climate would be cool, and ripening later still. It is most unlikely that the 1783 vintage could have been fermented and sent to San Gabriel before 27 October. I suggest that the barrel contained the 1782 vintage, California's first wine.

If the wine had been labeled according to modern standards of nomenclature, the label would have read: *Mission San Juan Capistrano* MISSION *1782, estate grown and bottled by Fr. Pablo de Mugártegui and Fr. Gregorio Amurrió.* The second occurrence of the word "Mission" is the modern name of the grape the fathers grew. Though rarely seen today, the name has not passed entirely from California labels. Under the name Mission Del Sol, the Harbor Winery of West Sacramento and Shenandoah Vineyards of Plymouth each make a sweet white wine, doubtless far better than anything the fathers knew.

Exactly how did Father Mugártegui get his vines? It seems that nobody has tried seriously to answer that question. Actually, it is not as difficult as it appears. In early mission days, California was an exceedingly remote, thinly populated area, with tenuous connections to the outer world. Only one or two ships a year came up from Mexico, and few parties chose the arduous land approach. From the time of Sir Francis Drake until the La Pérouse Expedition of 1786, no foreign ships landed in California. The appearance of anybody from outside was an event, and Father Palóu was diligent in recording such events in what became his *Historical Memoirs of New California*.

Closest to solving the problem was Edith Buckland Webb, who devoted the second quarter of this century to a meticulous examination of mission records, but students of California wine history were long unaware of her work. To her I owe discovery of Father Mugártegui's important letter of 1779, which she translated from a transcript of the original in the Museo Nacional, Mexico City. She concluded that the vine arrived in 1779 and let it go at that. Mugártegui's letter implies that the cuttings had been buried just before it was written. I concluded, after reading Webb, as apparently she had, that they had just arrived. The mystery was that supply ships never arrived so early in the year, and cuttings could not have been kept from the previous year.

But there were two other ships that might have served the purpose, the ships of the Arteaga expedition, which sailed very early from San Blas to explore the Canadian coast. They reached a high latitude in the extraordinarily short time of eighty days. It seems just possible by dead reckoning that they could have reached San Diego in time to bring Father Mugártegui's cuttings. Bucareli certainly had the power to use the expedition to carry the vines, though it was a military one. Palóu was aware of the expedition but said nothing of a landing in southern California. Several of the ship's officers kept diaries. Surely one of them would have found a visit to distant California worthy of note. It seemed likely that copies of the diaries would be in the Bancroft Library in Berkeley.★ That proved correct, but my hopes were dashed when they were examined. Some of the officers liked to take latitudes, and they proved the ships to have been several hundred miles south of San Diego the day Father Mugártegui wrote his letter. There was no way for the vines to have arrived in 1779, so it must have been 1778.

There is an entirely plausible explanation for the arrival of the vine in 1778, despite the apparent implication of Father Mugártegui's letter that it arrived the following year. The Capistrano Mission was moved in the summer of 1778. Vines planted in the spring of that year would have been growing during the summer and would not have been transplanted with the mission. They would have waited until they were dormant the following winter. They would have then been dug out of the old site and buried at the new to await planting after the exceptionally cold weather passed.

Two supply ships came up in 1778. The *Santiago* reached San Diego on 15 September, much too late to bring vines, but the *San Antonio* arrived on 16 May

★   I wish to thank Esther Guerrero-Catarrivas of Berkeley for locating the Arteaga diaries and translating the relevant parts of them.

14

after a passage of sixty-nine days. It must have brought the vines, and a new name enters wine history, that of Don José Camacho, commander of the *San Antonio* and bringer of the vine to California.

We have missed the chance to celebrate the bicentennials of the vine and wine in California, but we can still lay down some bicentennial wines of the 1982 vintage. And if a bottle of the 1782 ever turns up, we will know whether California wine lasts as long as they say.

BIBLIOGRAPHIC NOTE

This study began with Edith B. Webb's *Indian Life at the Old Missions* (Los Angeles: Lewis, 1952), in which she came closer to identifying California's first wine than had any other writer. Francisco Palóu's *Historical Memoirs of New California*, 4 vols., translated by Herbert Eugene Bolton (Berkeley: University of California Press, 1926), was essential to the argument for detailed information, including dates, of contacts between Mexico and early California. *Writings of Junípero Serra*, 4 vols., edited by Antonine Tibesar (Washington, D.C.: Academy of American Franciscan History, 1955–66), was equally valuable for its many references to wine or its lack in the first California missions, for including Serra's long lost travel diary of 1769, and for its biography of Serra. Father Maynard J. Geiger's scholarly *The Life and Times of Fray Junípero Serra, O.F.M.*, 2 vols. (Washington, D.C.: Academy of American Franciscan History, 1959), was also helpful, as was his translation of Francisco Palóu's *The Life of Fray Junípero Serra* (Washington, D.C.: Academy of American Franciscan History, 1955). The viticultural argument was based on the classic Winkler et al. *General Viticulture*. Many other works, including those that erroneously date the first California wine back to 1769, also contributed to this study. They caused it to be undertaken.

I.3

THE GOLD RUSH ERA

by THOMAS PINNEY

THE NORTHERN PART OF CALIFORNIA DID NOT WAIT UPON THE GOLD RUSH TO BEGIN WINEGROWING, BUT, LIKE THE SOUTH, INHERITED IT FROM THE MISSIONS; FROM THE ONE AT SONOMA, FOR EXAMPLE, WHOSE very small vineyard was taken over in 1835 by the Mexican official who presided over the secularization, General Mariano Vallejo; or at San Jose, where the mission's success in producing wine and fruit inspired a number of individual growers. The first vines in the Napa Valley, set out by George Yount in 1838, were from cuttings provided by Vallejo's old mission vineyard in Sonoma. Farther to the north, the Danish settler Peter Lassen planted vines around 1846 on his land in what is now Tehama County: according to the traditional story, the cuttings were from the vineyards of the Mission San Gabriel, packed by mule the hundreds of miles to the Sacramento Valley. Other very early names in the winegrowing of the Bay Area include John Wolfskill (brother of William in Los Angeles) in Solano County and, across Suisun Bay on the slopes of Mount Diablo, Dr. William Marsh. A handful of other names might be added to the list of those growing grapes in the region before the Gold Rush, but they would not change the fact that, unlike the growers around Los Angeles, those in the north did not yet make wine in commercial quantities.

The Gold Rush itself, as we have seen, had its immediate effect on the winemaking industry of southern California, since there were not yet any significant producers in the north. The idea of winegrowing did not take long to occur to the gold-seeking newcomers, however. A few vines had been planted by a man named Stevens in 1849 at Coloma, the very spot where the first gold had been found; these, if not the first, must have been among the very earliest grapes planted in the Mother Lode country. Such plantings soon spread up and down the foothills, and by 1856, the earliest year for which there are any figures, about 28,000 vines were distributed through the gold counties of Amador, Calaveras, El Dorado, Nevada, Placer and Tuolumne; two years later the number was 84,000, and by 1860 it was 192,000. This was only a tiny fraction of the state's total, but it was enough at least to make the

symbolic point that another kind of wealth had been recognized among the gold-
fields. The vineyards and wineries of the Mother Lode grew steadily but not spectacularly after their early start; in 1890, for example, the region produced a respectable 600,000 gallons of the state's total yield of 14,626,000.

The most important development in California lay elsewhere, in the
counties to the north and south of San Francisco Bay, but it is good to keep in mind
that even at the very beginning of California's modern economic life, in the Gold
Rush, winegrowing played an unobtrusive but steady part.* One of the oldest wineries in continuous operation in the state, the D'Agostini winery in the Shenandoah
Valley of Amador County, goes back to 1856. Its founder, a Swiss named Adam Uhlinger, came to the valley not as a miner, but expressly to grow vines and make wine,
which suggests that the region already had a promising reputation for quality. In
recent years, the Mother Lode has come into prominence again, with the discovery,
or rediscovery, of its attractively big red wines, some of them the produce of vines
planted in the nineteenth century. Now new plantings and new wineries are re-
affirming the promise it held out to the first prospectors.

The development of winemaking on a significant commercial scale
throughout the north came in the middle of the 1850s; the first fever of the Gold
Rush was over, the population of the state continued to grow, and when men looked
around and asked what they were going to do in California, the possibilities of winegrowing appeared more and more attractive. About this time, the devastation of
some of the European vineyards by the mildew called oïdium seemed to be a providential opportunity for California: the state would become the vineyard of the
world. From this point may be dated the first of several grape-growing booms in the
state: Santa Clara County, for example, had a reported 30,000 vines in 1855; one
year later, that had shot up to 150,000, and by 1857 to 500,000. For the state as a
whole, the increase in plantings was equally dramatic: a reported 1,500,000 vines in
1857 increased to 3,954,000 in 1858—a total more than doubled in the short space
of two years. In 1860 the estimate was of 6 million vines, occupying about 7,000
acres. Even allowing for much fiction in these figures, they indicate that things were
stirring among the vines. The newspapers of the later 1850s make it clear that there
was a new self-consciousness and conviction in the state on the subject of winegrowing; it was to be California's future, and the public prints were filled with notes, reports, and prophecies all dedicated to illustrating the truth of this faith.

Inevitably, much of what was said and done was not very wise or useful.
Unless they had come from a background of European winemaking (fortunately,
many did), the California pioneers could know nothing of the problems of viticul-

* James Marshall, the actual finder of gold in California, had a vineyard in Coloma; after some
earlier experiments at Coloma, John Sutter, the owner of the land where the discovery was made,
became a vine grower and winemaker at his Rhine Farm on the Feather River.

ture and winemaking. Nor did they have any immediate help to turn to. There was no manual of the elements of viticulture or winemaking based on California conditions; there was no careful identification of varieties, let alone any organized knowledge of their qualities based on actual trial; there was no understanding of the adjustments in Old World methods that needed to be made to suit California. The only winemaking tradition in the state was that of the missions, limited as that was to the makeshift simplicities of the frontier. In these circumstances, Californians consulted the authorities of the eastern United States and of Europe. The advice of horticulturists in Boston, Philadelphia, and Long Island, where the leading nurseries then were, and of winemakers in Cincinnati, the home of the most flourishing industry, was extensively relied on—at least in print—even though such advice could have no reference to California's conditions, and might be more harmful than an open-minded ignorance. What actually went on in vineyard and cellar was perhaps not much affected by this. But it is clear that the times were an equal mixture of enthusiasm and uncertainty, and that the industry was anxiously looking for a guide to set it on the right path. As the committee on wines at the California state fair put it in 1860, after reporting on an unsatisfactory lot of ill-made wines, "Whoever will enlighten [California winegrowers] on the most approved modes of culture, and, above all, the scientific and practical treatment of the grape juice in the making of wine will be a great public benefactor."

A start in the search for enlightenment had been made in 1854 with the founding of the State Agricultural Society, which made winegrowing one of its main interests and did what it could to meet the problems of the infant industry. The society sent visiting committees through the state to report on what growers and winemakers were doing; it printed information in its *Transactions* (with a subsidy from public funds); it sponsored competitions at the state fair; and it commissioned a treatise on viticulture and winemaking from the enterprising leader of Sonoma winegrowing, Colonel Agoston Haraszthy. This "Report on Grapes and Wines of California," published in the society's *Transactions* for 1858, does not seem to be much known now, having been obscured perhaps by Haraszthy's later and better publicized *Grape Culture, Wines, and Wine-Making* (1862). Yet it deserves special notice, for it was the earliest attempt to write a guide to California winegrowing based on California experience and was widely distributed through the state. The modest little "Report," then, began that flow of technical and scientific information for which the California wine industry has since become so notable a source.

Some of the best-known names in California winegrowing down to Prohibition were established in the 1850s. A few, but very few, survived the wreck of Prohibition and continue today in one form or another. To make a rapid survey, starting in Sonoma County and moving clockwise round the Bay, there was first of all Agoston Haraszthy's Buena Vista vineyard and winery, just east of the town of

Sonoma, where Haraszthy had settled in 1856 and where he competed with General Vallejo for the winemaking honors of the region. At Santa Rosa, Isaac DeTurk, who became king of the large-volume producers of Sonoma County, began his operations in 1858. The Sonoma Valley was notable for a large number of German growers and winemakers, among whom Jacob Gundlach and Emil Dresel were eminent. Two large ranchers in the Sonoma Valley, the Scotsman William Hood and the Pennsylvanian William Hill, also became substantial winemakers in the 1850s. In Napa County, Charles Krug planted his first vines in 1858 and made wine from other men's grapes in that year, but though there were a few other growers and winemakers in the county then, Napa did not begin to flourish for another decade. Sonoma, thanks largely to Haraszthy, took a long lead on the other northern counties, and was the first to compete seriously with Los Angeles for the leadership in production. Indeed, down to the 1870s, the three *appellations* of Los Angeles, Anaheim, and Sonoma pretty well divided the kingdom of California wine among them.

In Yolo County, the beginnings of the Orleans Hill Vineyard had been made by 1859; this later came into the hands of Arpad Haraszthy, son of Agoston, and was one of the prominent labels in nineteenth-century California. The El Piñal vineyard and winery near Stockton, begun by the West brothers in 1852, was for many years the dominant establishment in San Joaquin County. The Livermore district in Alameda County, later to be an important source of white wine production, was not developed as a winegrowing area until the 1880s, but there was a substantial planting going back to the early fifties at Mission San Jose; it was eventually taken over by Senator Leland Stanford and is now perpetuated in the Weibel Winery. Santa Clara County, as we have seen, attracted Frenchmen, among them the Pellier brothers, from whose establishment the Mirassou Winery descends, and Charles LeFranc, claimed by the Almadén Winery as its ancestor.

The successful spread of viticulture around San Francisco Bay was partly owing to the fact that San Francisco was the main market; but, as mentioned earlier, it was partly an expression of the region's climatic advantage over southern California for purposes of winegrowing, especially for dry table wines. The region is by no means climatically uniform—there is a sharp difference between the temperatures in the Carneros region at one end of the Napa Valley and in Calistoga at the other, as anyone who has driven between them on a July day will know—but compared to the south, the extremes of temperature are less marked, the winter rainfall rather greater, and the ameliorating effect of the Bay quite distinct. The northern grower thus had conditions favorable to the production of a well-balanced dry table wine that his southern rival did not. The fact became clear at once upon the introduction of varieties other than the Mission—the Zinfandel grape, for example, which gave an agreeable wine in Sonoma but which, though it did better than the Mission, always disappointed when grown at Los Angeles. By the end of the decade, the ring of counties around the Bay had all been explored and tested for vine growing; so had the Sierra foothills and the Sacramento Valley in between, where fairly large plantings had been made in Sacramento, Sutter, and Tehama counties. Only the great Central Valley and the Salinas Valley, among today's important winegrowing regions, were untried by this point—though of course these are very large omissions.

As California's winegrowing rapidly changed from a series of individual trials to an important economic activity, it began to receive some official recognition. The first positive notice came in 1859, when, in order to encourage this promising infant, the legislature decreed that new vine plantings be free from taxation until they were four years old; growers thus would not have to pay taxes on their investment until they had a crop to sell. The next official move was made in 1861, when, at the urging of the State Agricultural Society, the legislature passed a resolution appointing a "commission upon the ways and means best adapted to promote the improvement and growth of the grape-vine in California." Three commissioners were appointed, one to report on California, one on South America, and one on Europe. Colonel Haraszthy was appointed to the last of these commissionerships, and it was in that capacity that he went to Europe on the journey that has seemed so momentous in the history of California winegrowing and that will be examined later in these pages.

At this point, one may pause to survey the state of winegrowing as it was in 1860, only about eighty years after the first European vine had been brought to the new territory, forty years since Mexican independence had made it possible for other nationalities to live in California, thirteen years after the U.S. takeover, and eleven since the advent of the Gold Rush. The most obvious fact is that the vine had been established as a permanent part of California agriculture, spread as it was throughout the state and flourishing as it did nowhere else in the United States. The question was not whether anything would come of viticulture but only how important a share it would have of the state's future. We see now that the confident hopes of that time, despite all sorts of unforeseeable vicissitudes and obstacles, have been more than realized.

Still, we ought to appreciate the courage of that confidence in the early days. The general ignorance of California conditions and the absence of any reliable help have already been mentioned; there were no experts, only hopeful enthusiasts. And, apart from the problems of producing the wine in the first place, the early growers did not know what market they were producing for. They did not even have a reliable supply of bottles in which to put their wines until the founding of the Pacific Glass Works in 1862 began to settle that problem. Yet more troublesome, in the longer run, was the question of transport: California lay 3,000 miles from the Atlantic coast, where the markets, the publicity, the sources of decisive opinion, all lay.

How was that remote but essential world to be reached? Assurances of a transcontinental railway were beginning to be made, but who would hazard his time, labor, and money on a mere assurance? Many growers did, or at least they went ahead anyway, and the fact that their confidence was rewarded should not confuse our perception that they took a large chance. Besides all this, the industry, as an industry, was still entirely unorganized, and had not yet begun to achieve any recognition outside the boundaries of the state or any control within it. Standards of production, of description, of marketing, did not exist, and would all have to be invented through painful experience. Still, a start, and much more than a start, had been made. In 1860, one observer might have stressed how much had been accomplished; another, how much remained to be done. Both would have been right.

BIBLIOGRAPHIC NOTE

The *Transactions* of the California State Agricultural Society, published by the state at Sacramento and beginning with the volume for 1854, contain much original detail: accounts of visits to individual properties, letters and articles on winegrowing, and reports of exhibitions and judgings. Haraszthy's historic report appears in the volume for 1858. The most convenient summary of the statistics of early wine production in the state is found in the California State Board of Agriculture *Report* of 1911, part 5 (Sacramento, 1912); this gives imperfect statistics from 1850 until 1891, when the reports become both more accurate and fuller. Peninou and Greenleaf, *A Directory of California Wine Growers and Wine Makers in 1860*, touches on most of the early history in northern California. Based on MS census records, it is a highly valuable outline of winegrowing in the first years after statehood. The histories by Leggett, Carosso, and Teiser and Harroun should also be consulted, as should Sullivan's *Like Modern Edens*.

I.4

Note: The Contributions of the Chinese *by* JACK CHEN

"WHEN YOU DRINK, REMEMBER THE WELL DIGGER," advises an old Chinese saying. The Chinese farmers who came to the Napa and Sonoma valleys in the early 1860s would be happy to have that as their epitaph. They would have been astounded and delighted that the pioneering work they did in those lovely valleys has grown into the flourishing, statewide, multimillion-dollar enterprise of the 1980s. They cleared and terraced the land, laid out the vineyards, cultivated, pruned and tended the vines, harvested the grapes, blended and tasted the wines, and later even made wine themselves.

They were there soon after Agoston Haraszthy himself. When Haraszthy undertook to get the wine industry going and arrived back in California with 195,000 selected vines from Europe, he faced the task of quickly getting them set in the soil. But where would he find the labor? California's population in those days was 380,000, and there should have been a ready pool of labor for such work. But this was a peculiar place and time. Gold mining was still the main drive in the state and the men brought in by the Gold Rush were not the kind who would willingly engage in the hard labor of laying out vineyards. For the most part, the men who came to California from the eastern states, Europe, and Latin America came in a spirit of adventure and venture with one aim in mind—to pick up the "rocks," make their fortunes and get back home as soon as possible. And they could do this only by mining precious metals or taking advantage of the golden opportunities in boomtime San Francisco and the other towns serving the Gold Rush. A surprising number of them were professionals—lawyers, doctors, and preachers; not laborers, but gentlemen who had, or could raise, the considerable sum it took to get them through the 180-day trek across the continental plains, mountains, and deserts or the long journeys across the Panama Isthmus and around the Cape. These were followed by a dubious element of speculators and greedy toughs. These men did not come to Wild West California to farm. They were not potential vineyard workers and had no desire to be. In a labor-short state, they demanded a minimum wage of thirty dollars a month, with board, for vineyard work they did not want anyway— two or three times the eastern states' wage rate. With such men, Haraszthy would have gone bankrupt even before he got the vines into the soil. In this crisis, he found the only alternative: he contacted the Chinese labor contractor Ho Po. The word went out and in short order Haraszthy had a labor force of several hundred Chinese farmers, skilled in all the varied types of farm work and building he needed.

Chinese immigrants had come to the West Coast in ones and twos in 1848. They came in larger numbers to join the Gold Rush in 1849. But these were a different sort of Forty-Niner. Apart from a few merchants, they were mostly working men and farmers from South China's Guangdong Province, men with families back home, whose hopes, compared with those of the white immigrants, were modest indeed. It was natural and man-made disasters at home—drought, flood, famine, or war—that had driven them to seek their fortunes in America. The few hundred dollars they regarded as a "fortune" might be lost by a miner in a single minute's gambling in San Francisco. The great majority of them had their wives or families waiting for them in China, and they were willing to do any work that promised to better their condition in a reasonable time. For most of them, the going eastern rate for the job, the eight dollars a month with board that Haraszthy was willing to pay, seemed to be a good wage, and they accepted it with alacrity. With his vines and his work force, Haraszthy was in business. From 1871 on, his hardworking, conscientious Chinese workers cleared and prepared the land on his Sonoma Valley Buena Vista estate, planted his vines and tended them. They built him two large wineries of yellow gray sandstone and in 1863 dug tunnels for aging his wine, 12½ feet high and 170 feet back into the solid limestone of the south branch of the Arroyo Seco Canyon. When the main work was done, he kept on a hundred Chinese permanently. It was not long before other winegrowers followed his example.

Chinese vineyard workers were in Napa and Sonoma for many years from the 1860s to 1890s, and much of their handiwork can still be seen there. Digging out the scrub and tenacious oaks, they cleared the fields and protected them with piled stone fences. They built miles of stone walls, still standing solid, green with moss and lichen, along the Silverado Trail. They built many wineries, including the Greystone, then the largest winery of dressed stone in the world. Reinforced by builders of the spectacular tunnels on the Central Pacific's transcontinental railroad, Chinese who were experienced with explosives, they carved out wine storage tunnels in the walls of the valleys: the Schramsberg cellars, cut in the late 1860s and 1870s,* and the Cresta Blanca and Beringer tunnels in 1876 and 1880. They cut three cellars totaling a fifth of a mile in Livermore in 1884. North of Calistoga, in 1888, they dug 5,000 square feet of tunnels for Jacob Grimm; their pick marks are still clearly visible. Three shafts go back 120 feet into the hillside. A round room connecting the tunneling has an intricate beehive ceiling laid in brick. In back of the

---

*   Jones, *Vines in the Sun.*

central tunnel, a natural spring maintains the proper humidity. Storybook Mountain Vineyards operates a winery there today. All survived the quake of 1906.★

The historian William Heintz of Glen Ellen estimates that in the 1880s Chinese made up from 80 to 85 percent of the vineyard workers of California. The state then had 100,000 acres planted to vines. By 1890, Napa Valley had 166 wineries, and the state was producing $1,000,000 worth of wine. At one time, from the 1870s to 1890s, Chinese were also doing practically all the work of raisin making. They were in demand as workers because they were diligent and nimble-fingered and, farmers from childhood, were good at stoop labor. They did not incapacitate themselves with heavy drinking. They loved the vines. When heavy rains hit the valleys in 1887, turning fields and roads into quagmires impassable to vehicles, they brought the harvest out by hand.

A number of them went in for making wine themselves. Young Moon of Glen Ellen, and later Santa Rosa, was a winemaker and distiller of brandy at the turn of the century. As a young man, he had worked at the old Chauvet winery and distillery in Glen Ellen. Recognized as an experienced distiller and blender, he became cellar boss for Chauvet. The Buena Vista Winery has photographs of Chinese doing the most varied work, from applying fertilizer to blending. They grafted vines and cleaned the vats and fields after the phylloxera infestation in 1870. The Chinese Cultural Center in San Francisco has a winepress used by Chinese winemakers "in the old days." Chinese familiarity with the vine in California should not be surprising. Chang Chien, the Chinese explorer of Central Asia under the Han dynasty, introduced the grape from the "Western Regions" to China in 125 B.C., and ever since then China has cultivated the grape and other vines.

By the time the Chinese immigrants ended their work in the vineyards, a good foundation had been laid for California to become chief winemaker for the United States and to challenge the leading winemakers of the world. Charlotte T. Miller has written a graceful tribute to them. "Without the Chinese who worked so diligently . . . there would not be the great wineries, beautiful cellars . . . and green fields which make the Napa valley one of the most inviting places in the world in which to live."†

Few realize that part of the golf links at a country club near St. Helena was once a China Camp. Several hundred Chinese vineyard workers lived there in tents and makeshift barracks, from which they went out at dawn on contracts negotiated by Ho Po and others to work in the wineries. Only the spirits of these men linger here today among the tall trees that dot a meticulously kept lawn. Only a few Chinese families, such as that of the late Shuk Chan of Napa, once connected with the wine industry as labor contractors, now remain in the valleys.

★ Heintz, "Role of Chinese Labor."
† Jones, *Vines in the Sun*.

24

The gold and silver lodes petered out or became uneconomical to mine. The railways the Chinese had helped to build brought in a new type of settler attracted to the growing agricultural possibilities of California. An economic crisis hit the state in the mid-1870s, with resulting unemployment. An agitation began against the Chinese immigrants. They were accused of "stealing jobs." In 1882, the Chinese Exclusion Act was passed by Congress, banning further Chinese immigration, and by the 1890s this was taking effect. Veteran immigrants were dying out or, disheartened, were packing up and returning to China. The agitation spread to the vineyards. A punitive tax of $2.50 a month was levied on the Chinese workers there. Labor leaders forced a number of winemakers to put a "Made with White Labor" label on their bottles. Racist legislation and threats of direct action followed. The Chinese understood very well what impended when the Santa Rosa *Daily Democrat* editorialized in early 1886: "We all want to get rid of the Chinamen. They can be starved out by non-patronage." Within weeks, all but 100 of the 600 Chinese in Sonoma County had fled. That was bitter fruit indeed in the California wine country. But when you ask the old timers now about Napa and Sonoma Chinese, they and their descendants are spoken of with unstinting respect and affection as fine workers, good men. The valleys remember them: the Chinese of St. Helena, of Rutherford, Napa, Calistoga, of Glen Ellen, of Chico. . . .

I.5
THOSE
WHO WORKED the LAND

by SUE EILEEN HAYES

IN HIS *NOTES ON VIRGINIA* THOMAS JEFFERSON, PATRIOT AND PHYSIOCRAT, WROTE, "THOSE WHO LABOR IN THE EARTH ARE THE CHOSEN PEOPLE OF GOD, IF HE EVER HAD A chosen people, whose breasts he has made His peculiar deposit for substantial and genuine virtue."* Although Jefferson celebrated the value to the national life of the

---

* Adrienne Koch and William Peden, eds., *The Life and Selected Writings of Thomas Jefferson* (New York: Modern Library, 1944), p. 280.

yeoman famer working his own land, his own agrarian experience as a gentleman farmer more closely resembled that of California's agricultural entrepreneurs than it did the family farmers he eulogized. Beginning during the era of the missions, most California agricultural production required more labor than the landowners, whether religious orders or private citizens, could provide. As a result, extensive agriculture became heavily dependent on seasonal farm workers, a system that has persisted through the secularization of the mission lands, the Gold Rush, and the bonanza farming and "busts" of the nineteenth century to the present. Unlike the eastern or midwestern family farm, where supplemental labor tended to be provided by a few hired hands who were typically employed year-round, had close contact with the farm family, and were frequently aspiring to farm ownership themselves, many California farmers employed large numbers of workers intermittently, typically for short-term cultivation or harvest activities.

Obtaining an adequate supply of agricultural labor has been a recurring concern of California farmers. The missions lost neophytes to disease and desertion. The presidios fared even less well, although, or possibly because, their discipline was more strict. During the Gold Rush and the succeeding three decades, Indian labor, either voluntary or coerced, met the needs of some farmers. In the 1850s, black slave labor was advocated by some enthusiasts of large-scale farming until the prevailing antislavery climate of the state cooled their ardor. Chinese workers were widely employed between 1850 and 1890 in fruit, vegetable, and wheat farming, in the wine industry and in conversion of the San Joaquin Delta tule marshes to farmlands. In retrospect, the social and economic position of the Chinese farm workers in California was, considering the wages, working conditions, and racial hostility they encountered, not much better than slavery. A spokesman for California farm employers appeared to acknowledge this when he wrote in 1854 that Chinese farmworkers should "be to California what the African has been to the South."★

Chinese agricultural workers were not driven from California's fields by the urban workers who so vociferously supported the Chinese Exclusion Act in 1882, or by an influx of domestic farm workers. Rather, it appears that they gradually moved into more desirable nonfarm jobs, and during the following decade, in a generally depressed agricultural economy, their departure had little effect. By the turn of the century, as the economy began to revive, agricultural producers turned to two other ethnic groups, the Japanese and the Hindustani. In 1907, Japanese immigration was virtually halted by the "Gentleman's Agreement" between the United States and Japan restricting passports to nonlaborers or those with families

★ *California Farmer*, 25 May 1854, quoted in Cletus E. Daniel, *Bitter Harvest* (Ithaca, N.Y.: Cornell University Press, 1981), p. 27.

or property already established in America. But in spite of it, Japanese workers remained dominant in many fruit and vegetable crops, as well as grapes and sugar beets, until about 1915. One characteristic of Japanese agricultural workers that led initially to their enthusiastic acceptance and later to their rejection by employers was a willingness to work as tightly organized groups. It was a common practice for Japanese contractors to underbid competitors from other ethnic groups for jobs, which made them very attractive to potential employers; this aggressiveness became much less attractive when the Japanese "bosses" cooperated among themselves in setting prices, blacklisting "bad" employers, and organizing harvest-time "quickie" strikes.

Between 1920 and 1929, Filipino immigrants, many of whom had previously worked in Hawaii, entered the California agricultural labor force. Lettuce harvest work in the Salinas area before World War II and asparagus cutting in the Sacramento–San Joaquin Delta until the mid-1960s were almost Filipino monopolies. As with the Chinese and Japanese, the rapidly growing presence of an ambitious, diligent ethnic minority group aroused public hostility, including armed attacks on Filipinos. Although the number of Filipinos in the agricultural labor force decreased substantially during the Depression years, particularly after 1934, when thousands of Filipinos accepted free transportation back to the Philippines, many others remained as skilled lettuce and table-grape harvesters.

It has been estimated that well over one million Mexicans entered the United States between 1900 and 1940, with the bulk of the migration occurring before 1930. Many of these immigrants, as well as large numbers of temporary workers before and during World War I, entered the California agricultural labor force. A major factor in early Mexican immigration was the civil war that, beginning in 1911, left rural Mexico in turmoil for a decade or more. Despite the repatriation of Mexican nationals during the Depression, which resulted in the return to Mexico of at least 100,000 people, Mexican workers gradually came to dominate the seasonal agricultural labor force. This trend was reinforced by the "bracero" program, which between 1942 and 1967 regulated the recruitment and employment of temporary Mexican agricultural workers in the United States.

The exodus of ex-farmers and farm workers from Texas, Arkansas, Missouri, and Oklahoma, generally lumped together by Californians as "Okies," began in the 1920s as farm ownership declined, soil fertility decreased, and agricultural prices fell. Their numbers grew, and their presence was increasingly commented upon as the Depression deepened. Although the Okies were a substantial percentage of the California farm labor force by the late 1930s, they were not evenly represented among all crop activities. They were most prominent in the cotton industry, not unusual since many had had experience raising cotton in their home states. They also worked in fruit crops. (World War II attracted many of these workers to migrate to urban areas to obtain employment in war industries or into oil field employment in the southern San Joaquin Valley and other parts of the state.)

At the termination of the "bracero" labor program in 1964, many California agricultural employers feared crippling labor shortages, contending that domestic labor supplies were inadequate and the available workers would not be skillful or motivated enough to replace the braceros. The anticipated labor crisis did not, in most cases, develop. While supplemental bracero labor was authorized in a few cases until the end of 1967, most employers discovered that enough workers were available to meet their needs. Some of these workers had been present all the time—native-born workers discouraged from employment by low wages and the competition of braceros. Others were ex-braceros who had legally migrated as a result of relationships established during their employment. Still other workers had migrated illegally to California, responding to the push of low income and high unemployment in Mexico and the pull of potentially better opportunities in the United States.

Which of this multitude of groups labored in the vineyards of the Golden State? Accounts of the employment of Indian labor in the missions provide fine detail with regard to grain production, livestock raising and gardening, but are less illuminating about the role of Indians in wine grape cultivation or wine production. The vineyard employment of Indian workers, who are known to have been part of the labor force in other crops in the same area, has not been researched. One might, for example, speculate about Chief Olas, near Nicolaus, whose obituary in 1865 described him as "the proprietor of a small vineyard and orchard which he cultivated with industry and skill."*

Japanese workers were extensively employed in the grape industry in the San Joaquin Valley; their presence was noted, unhappily, in 1901, when they were key participants in a strike for higher harvest wages. Ten years later the U.S. Immigration Commission, in a report on immigrant labor in agriculture, mentioned the presence in the grape industry of "Japanese, the East Indians, Mexicans, American Indians, German-Russians and Italians," as well as "the comparatively few Americans and North Europeans and the Armenians taking employment as pickers."† Filipino workers entered the industry after 1920, along with increasing numbers of Mexicans, who replaced workers of other nationalities as they moved to farm

---

* *Marysville Appeal*, 18 November 1865, quoted in Sherburne F. Cook, *The Conflict Between the California Indian and White Civilization* (Berkeley and Los Angeles: University of California Press, 1976), p. 322, n. 115.

† United States Commission of Immigration, *Immigrants in Industry: Agriculture* (Washington, D.C., 1911), p. 585.

ownership or nonfarm employment. Okies never participated extensively in the grape industry, preferring to concentrate in more familiar areas, such as tree fruits and cotton.

There has been little change in the composition of the labor force in the vineyards since the repeal of Prohibition. The Filipino members were frequently single men, many of whom specialized in harvesting table grapes. As they aged and moved out of agricultural employment, they were replaced by a new generation of immigrants from Mexico. Today almost all pruning, cultivating, and harvest work in the wine industry is performed by workers of Mexican descent or nationality.

It is abundantly clear that without the contribution of the hundreds and thousands of workers who labored anonymously in the vineyards throughout its history, there could be no California wine industry. Those who labor in the earth may not receive the recognition accorded to the entrepreneurs who employ them or to the innovators who have led the industry to its present prominence, but their role is indeed one of substantial and genuine virtue.

BIBLIOGRAPHIC NOTE

Among the sources used in preparing this essay were the following: Harry E. Cross and James A. Sandos, *Across the Border* (Berkeley: Institute of Governmental Studies, 1981); Lloyd H. Fisher, *The Harvest Labor Market in California* (Cambridge, Mass.: Harvard University Press, 1953); Ernest Galarza, *Merchants of Labor* (Charlotte, N.C.: McNally and Loftin, 1964); Stuart Jamieson, *Labor Unions in American Agriculture*, U.S. Department of Labor, Bureau of Labor Statistics Bulletin 836 (Washington, D.C.: Government Printing Office, 1945); William Metzler, *Farm Workers in a Specialized Seasonal Crop Area*, University of California, Giannini Foundation of Agricultural Economics Research Report 289 (Berkeley: Giannini Foundation of Agricultural Economics, 1966); Harry Schwartz, *Seasonal Farm Labor in the United States* (New York: Columbia University Press, 1945); Walter J. Stein, *California and the Dust Bowl Migration* (Westport, Conn.: Greenwood, 1973); Paul S. Taylor, "Foundations of California Rural Society," *California Historical Society Quarterly* 23 (September 1945).

I.6

NORTHERN CALIFORNIA FROM HARASZTHY TO THE BEGINNINGS OF PROHIBITION

by JOHN N. HUTCHISON

THE DISCOVERY THAT CALIFORNIA HAS THE EARTH'S BEST RANGE OF CLIMATES FOR GRAPES COINCIDED WITH THE SUD-DEN EMERGENCE OF A THIRSTY MARKET: the boisterous, open-handed new Californians of the Gold Rush era were drinkers. Their wealth went readily for whatever creature comforts or extravagances would bring some relief from the mud streets, gunslinger law, and bad whiskey that made the frontier so uncomfortable. San Franciscans sent their laundry to Hawaii or China on sailing ships. They imported opera stars from Peru and pianos from Vienna. They brought in ice from Alaska to chill Champagne shipped from Reims. And there were even a few serious commercial winemakers before 1850. But the last half of the nineteenth century was the formative period for the industry that has made California one of the great wine regions of the world.

If one person can be singled out as having touched off the phenomenon, it is Agoston Haraszthy de Mokesa, an imaginative Balkan immigrant who was for many years called the Father of California Wine. Although revisionist history has questioned his reputation, a careful search has found no other figure so able to excite his contemporaries to plunge into winemaking in the early years of statehood.

Haraszthy arrived in California with the Gold Rush tide. He was at-tracted not by the mines, but by the business prospects in southern California. A man so energetic that in a sense he finally overran his own destiny, he engaged in enough occupations in his fifty-seven years to supply both the governmental and commercial needs of an entire town. In those in which he failed or lost interest, he seemed not to be more than briefly dismayed. By the time he began to exert a major influence on the California wine industry, he had already shaken off a long series of reverses, moving on to each new venture with scarcely a pause.

Haraszthy was born a Hungarian in 1812 in what is now part of Yugoslavia. He was an aristocrat with connections in the court of the Austro-Hungarian Empire. By the time he was twenty-eight, he had already demonstrated his talent and versatility; he was an officer in the imperial bodyguard, a prosperous *vigneron* and silkworm grower, a public official, a member of the Hungarian parliament, and the husband of a Polish noblewoman, who had borne him three sons.

Haraszthy apparently came to the United States in 1840 as a political fugitive after he had aided in the escape of a Hungarian separatist jailed by the imperial government. An atmosphere of legend had already begun to rise about him, probably a product of his flamboyant and innovative spirit, but he may have encouraged it; he seems to have had a Barnumesque knack for promoting himself and his enterprises. He settled first in Wisconsin, where he founded a town briefly called Haraszthy. He allowed himself to be called a count and a colonel, titles that historians have challenged as questionable, if not spurious. With an English partner, he established a steamboat line, a sawmill, a gristmill, and a brickyard. In 1842 he returned to Hungary and brought back his wife, their children, and his parents.

In Wisconsin he resumed his enterprising life, dealing in grain and livestock, opening a second general store, and engaging in politics. He wrote a book about the United States that was published in Hungary and attracted immigrants to America. He is credited with first introducing sheep and hops to Wisconsin.

Descriptions of Haraszthy in Wisconsin as a dashing, black-bearded man who hunted on horseback, wearing a red sash over a bright green shirt and riding through briar patches with zesty abandon, suggest that he would have been attracted to pioneer California in any event, but the sensational news of the discovery of gold probably triggered his decision to go there. He did not, however, succumb to the popular fever and rush to the diggings; he headed for southern California. In the summer of 1849, the restless Hungarian gave a partner power of attorney over his Wisconsin interests. With his whole family (except his mother, who had died), he joined a wagon train leaving St. Joseph, Missouri. There were by this time three more children—daughters, including one in arms—in addition to his sons, Agoston's fifty-nine-year-old father, known in Wisconsin as "the general," and, with the general, a new wife.

The Haraszthy entourage, an unlikely cast in a real-life melodrama, survived the awful hardships of some 2,000 miles of oxcart travel and arrived in San Diego late in the year, intact except for the eldest son, Gaza. He was only fifteen, but he dropped out in New Mexico to join a troop of U.S. Army dragoons. The partner back in Wisconsin, cheerfully accepting a rumor that the entire party had perished on the journey, wasted no time in confirming the hearsay. He sold Haraszthy's property and skipped with the money. Haraszthy, on arrival in San Diego, was virtually bankrupt.

It was not the first time that the Hungarian entrepreneur had been down to a shoestring, and it would not be the last. Such reverses scarcely slowed him. By planting time in 1850, he was farming 160 acres of fruit and vegetables, and soon thereafter he and partners were founding Middletown—today part of San Diego, which still has a Haraszthy Street where Agoston put it. He owned a livery stable, a butcher shop, and an omnibus company. He became the first sheriff of San Diego County, and his father was a judge and a councilman. As Lieutenant Haraszthy of the volunteer militia, this immigrant led in the capture of three outlaws, took them into custody as Sheriff Haraszthy, lodged them in the jail built by Contractor Haraszthy, and presided over their trial in his capacity as Judge Haraszthy. Soon, however, he resigned all these local civic duties and got himself elected to the first state legislature. There he persuaded it to enact a law that enabled him to collect some money owed him by San Diego for building the jail, which meanwhile had toppled down because of shoddy construction. He served only one term in the California assembly, and never went back to San Diego.★

Early in 1852, Haraszthy bought more than 200 acres in what is now the heart of San Francisco. It must have been an unusually sunny spring; the curious configuration of the city's coastal hills, the cold and warm sea currents, and the air temperature off the coast produce cold fogs of such density that *Vitis vinifera* does not thrive there, although it prospers mightily if planted a few miles farther inland. But Haraszthy planted grapes there. He put other vineyards in San Mateo County to the south, virtually astride the San Andreas earthquake fault and also lacking in adequate sunshine.

Meanwhile, he was building a house, plunging into San Francisco life, shipping table grapes from southern California to the San Francisco market, growing strawberries, raising cattle and grain, and refining ore from the gold and silver mines. He soon replaced his father as smelter for the U.S. mint. Between 1853 and 1857, he acquired and developed land to which the title was disputed, and that litigation, as well as his conduct of the mint, entangled him in serious troubles. Suspecting that the smelting process was wasting substantial amounts of gold, which escaped up the flues, he resigned his appointment, having pledged his properties to cover the losses if he were held responsible. He was, in fact, indicted for embezzlement and his property confiscated, but, after three years of sensational controversy and publicity, was exonerated and his property restored.

★ See also Paul Fredericksen, "The Authentic Haraszthy Story," *Wines & Vines* (1947), a research study for the Wine Advisory Board that describes Haraszthy's talent for pervading the life of his community.

Haraszthy's career was several times blemished by misfortunes that may have been ethically tainted but seem only products of his reckless activism. From each setback he emerged quickly with new ventures, and so it was that he left the inhospitable climate for his vines and the tribulations of bureaucracy and turned his forceful spirit to the county where he put his lasting mark on the viticulture of California. In 1856 or 1857 (the date is disputed), Haraszthy took up residence near the town of Sonoma, where he bought 560 acres of gentle slopes. Sixteen acres were already planted with grapes and there were the remnants of a winery. Haraszthy threw himself into his new project. By 1864 he had acquired 6,000 acres of land, planted 400 of them in grapes, built an ostentatious, elaborately landscaped Pompeian villa, and carved deep tunnels into the hillside behind his new stone winery. His estate he named Buena Vista. Parts of the old cellars are today a showpiece for a winery preserving the name.

While Haraszthy strove over his own acquisitions, he simultaneously promoted winegrowing with the fervor of an evangelist. With contagious verve, he persuaded friends and investors to enter viticulture, and many of them became important in the trade. In his first year at Buena Vista, he is said to have imported 165 varieties of grapes. He wrote a treatise for the State Agricultural Society, sold thousands of cuttings and rooted vines, and won first prize for his vineyard at the state fair. Perhaps his greatest influence was as a publicist. In less than two years, he changed the shape and direction of California winemaking and moved its center of gravity to northern California from Los Angeles County, where it had its commercial beginnings. Many others were major contributors to the booming new industry; some had been serious practitioners and experimental planters before he was. But the astonishing Hungarian, with his enthusiasm, his driving energy, and his instinct for promotion, had with his own hands and wit done more by 1860 than any other individual to point the world of wine toward California. He was to achieve much more before an accident far from his adopted land snuffed out his life.

The 1860s came on with a feverish expansion of vineyards in California. It was powered by the rising market for table grapes early in the decade, and by tub-thumping campaigns by land agents to attract Americans westward. A state bureau reported in 1862 that California was home to 10.5 million vines—more than eight times the 1856 number. Wine grapes and wineries had spread through the foothill counties, into the Central Valley, and around San Francisco Bay. In that decade, too, transcontinental rail transportation at last truly made California part of the United States of America, with immensely improved access to markets in the East.

Haraszthy was the most active single influence in the California wine industry in the 1860s. In a speech at the Sonoma County Fair in the first year of the decade, he called for the establishment of a state agricultural school. In 1868, the charter of the University of California at Berkeley authorized a college of agriculture on that campus; but it was not until 1906 that the Davis campus added the University Farm to its agricultural facilities, which were eventually to include the world-famous Department of Viticulture and Enology.

Haraszthy was an irrepressible innovator. Some credit him with the first experiments with redwood to replace oak cooperage. (It is still used, albeit in decreasing amounts, not for adding flavor, as does oak, but for maturing wine without adding extracts to it.) At a time when the state officially repressed Asians, he employed Chinese workmen and fought against a legislative effort to impose a discriminatory tax upon them, although his efforts may have been motivated by purely financial interests.

In 1861 Haraszthy was appointed by the governor, under instruction of the legislature, to explore and report on winemaking in Europe. With his customary zeal, he ranged through France, Germany, Switzerland, Italy, and Spain. He interviewed wine people, tramped through vineyards and wineries, read and gathered literature, took bundles of notes, and bought thousands of grapevines. A linguist, speaking almost every language he encountered, he translated easily from publications and conversations, writing tirelessly while he traveled. On his return to California, he produced a thorough report for the legislature and almost simultaneously finished an ambitious book on grape culture and winemaking, published in 1862.

Haraszthy had paid all the expenses of his trip, on which he was accompanied in Europe by his son Arpad, then a student in France. He had also paid for about 100,000 vines of 300 tagged varieties that he had shipped home.* It was his misunderstanding that the state would reimburse him and administer the distribution of the specimens to growers throughout the state. He accordingly submitted a bill for $12,000, scarcely a third of the nursery value of the plant collection alone, he estimated.

---

* Thomas Pinney, author of several previous essays in this book, has given this additional perspective on replacing the Mission grape in California: "Haraszthy is now especially remembered as the man who brought new grape varieties to California. In this matter, however, he has unjustly received far more credit than he deserves. The need for better varieties in place of the Mission grape was recognized very early and very widely; as has been noted already, Jean Louis Vignes made some effort to do something about it in Los Angeles in the 1830s. Kohler and Frohling, too, brought new varieties to Los Angeles. When winegrowing began to develop into a serious trade in northern California, growers were quick to see what Vignes had seen earlier—that they would have to have more, and better, grape varieties than the Mission. Like Vignes, too, some of the most important of these pioneers were Frenchmen, mostly clustered in Santa Clara County. Pierre Pellier is credited with introducing the Grey Riesling, French Colombard, and Folle Blanche to California sometime before 1855 (the date is disputed). They were planted in his brother's nursery and vineyard near San Jose. Also at San Jose, Louis Prevost had some sixty different varieties planted around 1854; his neighbor and fellow Frenchman Antoine Delmas imported 10,000 cuttings from France in 1854 and was

He never got a cent. Most of the vines were wasted, their identification lost. Pleading poverty and repudiating the agreement that Haraszthy had thought was firm, the legislature turned down his request. Politics was in part responsible; by 1862, the colonel was on the wrong side of a controversy over the Civil War. As he had so often done before, however, Haraszthy shook off the disappointment at once. A week after the state senate rebuffed him (and in the same room in which they had done so), he was elected to the presidency of the State Agricultural Society. Within weeks, he was embroiled with the lawmakers again on the proposal to tax Chinese. He was also stirring other pots: proposing that California grow almonds, prunes, and cotton (all have since become major crops in the state), fighting an effort to impose a new federal tax on wine, and planning a huge increase in his vineyard acreage.

Haraszthy was already burdened with high-interest mortgages on the 400 acres of grapes, the house, and the winery at Buena Vista. But he boldly committed himself to a program meant to grow in ten years to 6,000 acres of vines. In March 1863, he and nine silent backers, led by the banker William C. Ralston, founded the Buena Vista Vinicultural Society. It was a device to dodge a law forbidding a corporation to own more than 1,440 acres of farmland. Agoston and his son Arpad, educated in France in engineering and Champagne making, took on the formidable task of producing 2,600,000 gallons of wine annually by 1873. Champagne was to be a major product.

Long before the ten-year goal was near, the "society" signaled failure. Arpad quit in 1864, and his father left in 1866, squeezed out by the investors. Life turned sour; he was injured in a distillery fire, and some investments failed. Agoston Haraszthy de Mokesa, the bold and brilliant cynosure of California viticulture, was through with wine. He went to Nicaragua, and there, amid a new set of enterprises,

awarded a special premium by the State Agricultural Society in 1855 for the best and largest collection of varieties. By 1858 Delmas had 350,000 vines of 105 different varieties. Many other names, by no means all those of Frenchmen, might be added to this list. The German Jacob Knauth imported Riesling vines in 1853 that later became the nucleus of the famous Orleans Hill Vineyard in Yolo County; another German, Frank Stock, brought the Riesling, Sylvaner, and Traminer to San Jose in 1858. American pioneers such as Bernard Fox near San Jose, the brothers West in San Joaquin County, and A. P. Smith of Sacramento all made extensive importations of new varieties, cultivated them commercially, and offered them for sale. Smith, for example, had more than a hundred varieties of vinifera for sale by 1859, among them the Black St. Peters, which, there is reason to think, may have been a variant name for the Zinfandel. By the end of the 1850s, to put it no earlier than that, California was well supplied with a wide selection of grape varieties from all the proven regions of European viticulture. The work of matching variety with locality had still to be done, of course—it is only just begun today—but at least we need not suppose that growers were without any options until Haraszthy at a stroke delivered them from their dependence on the Mission." —*Ed. Note*

he drowned in 1869 in a flooding stream. Legend followed him all the way; a story went around, never substantiated, that he had been eaten by alligators.

The generally promising economics of the wine trade in the 1860s brought some profound changes. They attracted large numbers of serious, conscientious growers and vintners, and they also brought in some scamps and inept tyros. Charles Krug in Napa County and General Mariano Vallejo, who preceded Haraszthy in Sonoma, were respected growers who planted substantial vineyards to imported varieties superior to the still-popular Mission. Vallejo had been the Mexican governor of Alta (Upper) California until he was deposed by filibusterers from the United States in 1846. He owned a huge land grant, and, suspicious of the active Russian colony on the Sonoma coast, strategically placed relatives on other vast tracts in the county. A skilled and enthusiastic horticulturist, Vallejo imported rare fruit trees, experimented with grape varieties, and made commercial wine and brandy. He became a close friend of Haraszthy's. His daughters Natalia and Jovita married Haraszthy's sons Attila and Arpad in a double ceremony at the general's home in Sonoma. George Yount, a contemporary of Vallejo's, pioneered vineyards in Napa County. In 1860, Charles Krug from Germany, who had had his training at Buena Vista and had made wine for others in Napa since 1858, founded his winery at St. Helena and subsequently became a pillar of the state viticultural board.

　　Less successful was Sam Brannan, an apostate Mormon and unprincipled plunger. He had been active in San Francisco politics and commerce in the 1850s, founded the town of Calistoga at the end of that decade, and, along with other enterprises, established vineyards and a winery. He was no expert on the subject, but he planted in what has become some of the most valuable wine land in America. His whole Calistoga project, including a distillery, racetrack, and spas, failed. He died broke.

　　It was not altogether unusual that a man whose fame rested on different foundations was caught up in the enthusiasm for winemaking. Such personalities as Leland Stanford, William Randolph Hearst, and John A. Sutter shared the same interest. Sutter, at whose El Dorado County mill gold was discovered in 1848, grew grapes and made wine as early as 1841. Some of the wine, it is said, may have been made from wild grapes; it is hardly credible, however, that a drinkable beverage could come of *Vitis californica*. In 1849, Sutter established a vineyard in the neighboring county of Yuba. This man, whose career soared like the rocket and came down like the stick, died poor and seems not to have contributed lasting benefits to viticulture, but he illustrates the eagerness with which so many striving newcomers seized on the wine business as a road to fortune. There were two Yuba county growers who did do well. A. P. Smith is reported to have planted a hundred grape varieties there, and Jacob Knauth, another Yuba grower, won an award in 1861 for wine made from "foreign" grapes.

By 1870, Sacramento County was planted with almost two million vines. In Stanislaus County, there was only one winery in this period, but it was a big one for those days. It was called Red Mountain. Adam Uhlinger, a Swiss, was among pioneers who settled what they named Shenandoah Valley, now in Amador County. In 1856 he founded a winery, bought from him in 1911 and until recently operated by the D'Agostinis. There are still occasional nineteenth-century Mission and Zinfandel vines producing in the county, where the industry, smothered by Prohibition, has returned to acclaim in recent years. Alameda County, at the southeast corner of San Francisco Bay, had numerous wineries in the 1850s and 1860s, some with names as attractive as those that come today from high-priced agency brainstorming. Linda Vista, Los Amigos, and Willow Glen were among them. Robert Livermore, an early Alameda County landowner, gave his name to a valley that has ever since provided leadership in the development of distinguished California wines, with Wente and Concannon among those of renown.

Viticulture and winemaking were firmly established as leading enterprises in the state by the 1860s. There was some trade with foreign countries during the period. The files of the *California Farmer* contain references to export of California wine to Australia, British Columbia, China, Hawaii, Mexico, and Peru. "Port" from Mission grapes, made in Los Angeles, was enjoyed in Canada, Denmark, England, and Germany. The rise of a real wine trade beyond the state's boundaries came just as the industry began to suffer from fraud, however. Americans were developing an appetite for wine faster than they were learning to tell the good from the bad. In the early 1870s, the demand for wine and the eagerness of Californians to appease it encouraged unscrupulous people to adulterate wine, misrepresent its origins, and even to make it without any grapes at all. Even if Americans had not been able to devise such deceptions themselves, they could easily have found instruction in Europe. Haraszthy, traveling there in 1861, passed through Cette (now Sète) in southern France, notorious, he wrote, as "the great manufacturing place of spurious wines . . . sold to all parts of the world."

Even California's honest wine was often inferior by modern standards, or by the better European gauges of the day. The Mission grape made poor wine at best, but whatever the grape, California's fertility and overabundant sun often developed high sugar and low acids, or the grapes were overcropped or were left too long on the vines. Such wines tend to lack appetizing character. The flat, but alcoholic, flavor of these and the outright faking of others began to erode the reputation of California wine. Fraud was common in the 1870s. T. Hart Hyatt, in his handbook on grape culture, complained about the "bogus, doctored adulterations which are so often met with in the wine markets, especially in the Eastern States." He quoted from the report of a committee of the St. Louis Horticultural Society on five wines it examined, all "purporting to be from Lake Vineyard, Los Angeles, California." They were labeled Hock, Mound Vineyard, Port, Sherry, and Angelica. Said the committee, the wines were very sweet, very alcoholic, and "smelt marvelously like brandy." They removed the labels and invited some of the best wine judges in the city to taste. The consensus was that all the wines were doctored. There was some speculation that they were not even wines.

Frona Eunice Wait, whose *Wines and Vines of California* (1889) is an important, although flawed, record of the times, claimed that "certain French firms export to American purchasers red wines that were made in California and shipped to France for purposes of adulteration or at least of deception." She reported that "there is at least one large house here" (she was referring to a California establishment) that "has shipped 6,000 cases of claret to New York during the year just passed, in French boxes, nailed with French nails, in French straw, either labeled St. Julien or other Bordeaux imitations. And these wines thus shipped are not of so high a quality as those sent out genuinely, but the demand of the former exceeds the latter, and better prices are obtained. The firm has 50,000 bottles of California claret now on hand, with bottles, labels and corks." Mrs. Wait's writing is often turbid, but her point here is crystal-clear: both the French and the California wine merchants were cheating. She usually distinguished between winegrowers and wine imitators, but she noted that they were sometimes the same person, and she had welcome words for the Pure Wine Law passed by the legislature. It forbade the sale of wine not from the pure juice of grapes and prohibited the use of aniline dyes and "chemical antiseptics." The law also decreed that California wine must be labeled as such. Wait quoted the Berkeley professor E. W. Hilgard on what tests could be made to detect the addition of coloring to wine, called the greatest temptation to adulteration. Her book lavishes more encomiums than criticisms on winemakers and wineries, however, and she did not document her charges of fraud with any names.

Fraud also hit the California industry in an ironic turnabout. In 1872, Arpad Haraszthy wrote of the shipment to the United States of beverages he claimed were European in origin though falsely labeled as Californian:

The reputation of California wines in Eastern States is at this moment undergoing one of the severest trials that can be put upon the product of any country: that of palming off upon the confiding public spurious, inferior and barefaced imitations of the same, which never saw the soil of our state, nor resemble wines in any particular. This unscrupulous traffic is carried on openly throughout the Eastern States, and millions of gallons of these compounds over and above the actual product of this are probably sold. It is of the greatest importance to our winemakers to ascertain by what means this evil can be stopped, else it will soon become difficult to retain the fair reputation we have already gained.

The basis for the fake wines was usually cider, he said, flavored and colored with various chemicals and given whatever labels were currently popular, including "California White Wine." He also condemned the European export to the United States of "compound liquids sent to us, literally, as ballast for ships, and called claret." Such abuses were occurring at the very time when individual growers were finding it difficult to sell their grapes. The problem brought some growers together. The Los Angeles Winegrowers Association, organized in the late 1860s, bought and operated a winery, and there were similar but smaller groups of growers in other counties.

Planting continued, however, in Sonoma, Contra Costa, Santa Clara, Alameda, San Joaquin, and other counties. In Napa, where the foundation was laid in the 1860s and 1870s for the high reputation the county enjoys today, landowners were putting in vines at a fast pace. Charles Krug was extending: in 1876 he made nearly 300,000 gallons of wine and 17,000 gallons of brandy. Jacob Schram was expanding Schramsberg. W. C. Watson started Inglenook in 1872 and four years later had seventy acres of vines. He sold out to the Finnish sea captain Gustave Niebaum in 1879. The Beringer brothers, Gottlieb Groezinger, and a long list of wine family names now forgotten were carpeting their valley with vineyards. Napa had become the rival that was to surpass all other counties in the reputation of its wines.

But in 1873, while the California industry was still expanding with high hopes, almost the whole world was sinking into economic depression that produced widespread panics, collapses, and ruin. It was three years before the slump hit California agriculture. When it finally came, in 1876, the bottom fell out of the barrel. The calamity was short-lived but severe. Grapes sold for less than the cost of picking them, and wine went for ten cents a gallon. Growers and farmers whose resources could not tide them over abandoned or ripped out their vines. Two out of three wineries went under, but hard as it was for those who failed, the crash had a healthy effect on wine quality. It shook out a great many bad grape varieties and some bad winemakers, and by 1880, the 45 California wineries that survived (there were 139 in 1870) were prospering again. There was record production in 1880—10.2 million gallons. It coincided with a streak of bad weather in Europe that, with the phylloxera that had ravaged Europe for the past decade, produced a worldwide wine shortage. California benefited temporarily.

In its stage as a sucking, louselike aphid, phylloxera withered the vines. In a few years, this stealthy, incredibly destructive pest had completely ruined France's most important industry and had spread through Europe to Russia, parts of Greece, Algeria, South Africa, and parts of Australia. California had it, too; the northern parts, and to a lesser extent the warmer regions, were swept by it. The story of phylloxera is one of the most curious in the relationship of entomology to economics. The louse was identified in southern France and England at a time when botanists and their wealthy patrons eagerly collected plant specimens from foreign lands without adequate attention to the pests or diseases they might also be introducing to new environments. The first discovery of phylloxera was probably at Kew Gardens, the great arboretum near London, and there it was surmised that the insect originated in the United States. It had lived for unnumbered millennia on the roots of native grapevines, for so long that the host grape was relatively immune to it. Found widely from the eastern seaboard to the midwestern United States, the louse was apparently not native beyond the Rocky Mountains. It may have been brought to California on infested cuttings or rootstocks from Europe, or maybe on Concord vines from an eastern state. Some historians suspect that it could have arrived on varieties that Haraszthy imported from Europe; in California, the pest was first scientifically identified in his own Sonoma County. The disastrous ravages of the insect abroad are vividly described by Philip M. Wagner:

The social consequences were appalling. Wine growing was wiped out in one region after another, as the winegrowers stood by helplessly. (Some of the regions have never resumed production.) No means of subduing the insect could be found—and none has yet been found. The destruction of vineyards took away the livelihood of hundreds of thousands, reducing large areas to poverty. It inspired wholesale migrations: as from the Bordeaux district over the Pyrenees into northern Spain, where the Rioja people were taught to make red wine Bordeaux fashion; and from the Rhone Valley and other parts of the Midi to Algeria in search of land that phylloxera *had not reached. . . . The story of the full impact of this insect invasion on the course of Western history is still to be written.**

Some have called the destruction wreaked on France by the pest a greater catastrophe than the nation's defeat by the Prussians in 1870. California growers were slow to recognize the incursions of phylloxera. Even after they knew they had it in the vines, many of them tried to conceal the infestation; mentioning it was taboo, like admitting to venereal disease. "First it mystified, then it was dismissed as a passing blight, then it was fought with oratory and indignation, and finally it aroused something approaching panic."† (A. P. Haynes noted that French peasants in the Champagne district were even more stubborn than Californians about admitting its presence on their vines; regiments from the French army had to reinforce the government's quarantine measures to control the insect.) Perhaps because the winged form is not usual in California, it spread more slowly than it had raced through Europe, but by 1890 the dread aphid had spread through most of California's vineyard districts. Some areas kept free of it, however, and some are still free.

* Wagner, *Grapes into Wine*, pp. 28–29.
† Ibid.

French growers tried primitive soil sterilants of the day, including highly toxic mercury compounds. They and the Californians both attempted to drown the insects by flooding the vineyards. Almost nothing practical worked, until finally they came around to an obvious solution: if native American vines were resistant to phylloxera, which does its worst damage by attacking the roots, why not graft *Vitis vinifera* scions to rootstocks of their American cousins? It is the portion above the stump, or rootstock, of a grafted grapevine that determines its character and that of its fruit. After years of experiment, most of the world's *Vitis vinifera* scions are now grown on a hybrid of a native American grape species called *Vitis rupestris* crossed with a *vinifera* variety, Aramon. Californians adopted the practice after Frenchmen had blazed the trail. A.P. Haynes, in a report in 1893 from the University of California, credited the French with providing most of the research and reporting on phylloxera.

Phylloxera, Pierce's (Anaheim) disease, and other grape ailments, and the need for better methods of grape cultivation, brought enlightened California growers to see the need for more science. Two outstanding horticulturists of the day were fortunately dedicated to the improvement of the state's wines and vines—Eugene Woldemar Hilgard and George Husmann, a scientific winegrower in Missouri and preeminent authority on resistant rootstocks who in 1866 published a book titled *The Native Grape and the Manufacture of American Wines*. Missouri had surpassed Ohio to become the second most important grape-growing state (after New York), but pests and low prices were ruining the trade. Impressed by California during a trip there, Husmann left behind him his professorship in horticulture at the University of Missouri and took up winegrowing in the Napa Valley. Husmann's predictions of a fabulous future for the grape ("America will be, from the Atlantic to the Pacific, one happy and smiling Wineland") were naively overblown, but his horticultural knowledge was important to the young industry.

The true father of California wine science, Hilgard came to the state in 1875, after some experience with vineyards in Illinois, Mississippi, and Michigan. He joined the faculty of the University of California and was dean of its college of agriculture while it was still on the Berkeley campus. Almost his first report was on phylloxera. He planted a vineyard and maintained a wine cellar at the university; started in 1880, this was the beginning of the University of California's work in viticulture and enology. Pursued at the Davis campus after 1908, it has brought worldwide acclaim and leadership in those sciences. "U.C. Davis" is a shorthand designation understood by professionals in all the wine languages on earth.

When many Californians were harvesting grapes with insufficient regard for their sugar-acid balance, and were making wine with slipshod methods and losing large amounts to spoilage, Hilgard was preaching earlier harvesting, avoidance of overcropping, sanitary winemaking, and low-temperature fermentation. He wanted lighter, cleaner, tastier wines. To that end, he studied the performance of each grape variety in relation to the climate in which it was grown, and carefully recorded the performance of each variety in the formation of wine from the moment the grapes were crushed. Hilgard derided the "pernicious axiom once promulgated to the public that 'any fool can make wine.' " "It is high time," he wrote in a report to the president of the university after the vintage of 1895, "that the haphazard methods even yet commonly pursued in this state should be discarded . . . so that hereafter California wines may appear on the world's market under their own labels, instead of being, as has heretofore been too largely the case, disguised under foreign ones of good quality, while the poorer qualities were sure to be placed on the market with the true statement of their California origin."★ It would be a long time after Hilgard's death before the California industry gave his advice full acceptance, and it is probable that Hilgard would have been most discouraged had he known that almost a century later, floods of California wine would yet be labeled "Chablis," "Burgundy," and "Rhine," not to speak of other borrowed appellations.

Philip Wagner remarks that to read Hilgard's reports on his exhaustive and innumerable experiments "is to behold a powerful and original mind at work and to realize how much a region, a people and an industry can be indebted to a single man."† Hilgard was not only a voice of science; he was a voice of conscience in an industry often damaged by unscrupulous winemakers and dishonest merchants. In the main, however, growers, makers, and merchants wanted to improve wine quality and repute. Among them were the organizers of the California Board of State Viticultural Commissioners, led by a man with whom Hilgard was often in dispute, but who was also a stalwart in the effort to advance the standing of California wine. He was Charles A. Wetmore.

The state legislature supplied funds and authority to establish the board in 1880—the same year in which it financed enological and viticultural research at the university. The board was active for fourteen years, during which it conducted an educational program, sponsored industry meetings, published numerous studies and statistics, and established quarantines to thwart phylloxera. Wetmore, a San Francisco newspaper writer interested in wine, was made executive officer of the board, which he had been instrumental in founding. He then became a winemaker, planting a large vineyard in the Livermore Valley. He called it Cresta Blanca, and his wines took gold medals in Paris in 1889. After many permutations of ownership,

★   E. W. Hilgard, *The Composition and Classification of Grapes, Musts, and Wines* (Sacramento: Superintendent of State Printing, 1896), p. 3.
†   Wagner, *Grapes into Wine*, p. 56.

and no longer made under the chalky hillside that gave it its name, Cresta Blanca makes wines today in Mendocino County.

"He lacked the fire of Haraszthy," writes A. J. Winkler of Wetmore, "but his enthusiasm was so infectious that another boom in planting resulted (1880–1886)."[*] Wetmore, like Haraszthy and Hilgard, wrote voluminously. He and the professor, as well as the institutions each represented, were often in conflict. The board was commercially oriented and "practical." Its nine members included seven growers or makers chosen from as many agricultural districts and two chosen at large; Arpad Haraszthy was the first president and served for eight years. The board and the college, in spite of their testy relations, both moved the quality, reputation, and presumably, the profit of California winemaking forward with giant steps. The board was abolished in 1895, leaving the university as the only official body concerned with the welfare of the industry. It was not until after Prohibition that an industrywide effort, in the shape of the Wine Advisory Board and the Wine Institute, was organized to promote California wine and defend its interests.

Arpad Haraszthy, whose older brothers Gaza and Attila were also *vignerons*, was important in the California wine trade. He lobbied in Washington, D.C., on behalf of the brandy makers, he campaigned for phylloxera control, and he was a steadfast proponent of better grapes and better wines. Like Wetmore, he served on the state board and quarreled with Hilgard. In partnership with Henry Epstein, he made and marketed champagne, and he ran an unsuccessful vineyard in Yolo County. He wrote tirelessly on viticulture and wine. His dedication shows in some articles he wrote for the *Overland Monthly* in 1871 and 1872. They were republished in 1978 by the Book Club of California, introduced with a short biography by Ruth Teiser and Catherine Harroun, who quote Wetmore on his friend and colleague "whose constant and unwavering hopefulness have given us all strength." Wetmore went on to describe Haraszthy's "unspotted integrity, his cheerful candor, his constant breathing of aspirations for ideals of perfection." Arpad died in 1900. Neither his private nor his business life had been a full success, but he was a genuine contributor to the industry he had served for nearly half a century.

Wetmore had numerous winegrowing neighbors of importance. Carl Heinrich Wente, new from Germany, moved to the valley in 1883 from an apprenticeship with Charles Krug in Napa County. That same year, Irish-born James Concannon, on the advice of the archbishop of San Francisco, bought a farm just across the road from Wente on which to produce altar wines, which were in short supply in the great cluster of Catholic parishes around San Francisco Bay. Olivina, the estate of the Twenty Mule Team borax tycoon Julius Paul Smith, had its mansion and winery on 1,900 acres. Ernest Wente, the son of the Livermore Valley pioneer and

[*]   Winkler et al., *General Viticulture*, p. 6.

the grandfather of those who operate Wente Bros. today, described Olivina's splendor in reminiscences written not long before he died in 1981 at the age of ninety-one. Also among Ernest Wente's boyhood memories was the handsome Chateau Bellevue established by Alexander Duval with money from a fortune made in building South American railroads. Wente also recalled a period in the early 1900s when wine sold for six or seven cents a gallon and grapes for six dollars a ton in the year of surplus.

Sonoma, which in the late 1870s became the largest wine-producing county, moving well ahead of Los Angeles, strengthened that dominance in the 1880s in spite of the ravaging phylloxera. Captain J. H. Drummond had an important property north of Sonoma called Dunfillan Vineyard. The Kunde family still grows fine grapes where Charles Kunde founded Wildwood. At least one woman was a Sonoma County winegrower of note—Mrs. Kate F. Warfield at Agua Caliente, just outside the town of Sonoma. She entered wines in the St. Louis Exposition of 1884 and took first prize for Riesling. Isaac DeTurk, a member of the state viticultural board who began planting in 1863, had a winery and vineyards at Santa Rosa. Grapes were also grown westward around the settlements of Fulton, Trenton, Forrestville, and Occidental. Northward they spread up the Russian River Valley through Windsor, Healdsburg, Geyserville, and Cloverdale. Deep in the redwood and fir forests where the river cuts through the last hills before the sea, three brothers named Korbel, from what is now Czechoslovakia, were sawmillers. When they ran out of trees in 1886, they planted vines among the massive stumps and built the brick building that is now the core of the large winery where the present owners, the Hecks, specialize in sparkling wine. In 1889 Sonoma County made five million gallons of wine.

Italian Swiss is still vigorously alive on the spot where it began, an innovative venture in an industry marked by remarkable departures. Andrea Sbarbaro was a self-made San Francisco banker who formed a commune south of Cloverdale in 1880. He organized a hundred Swiss and Italian immigrants, each to be sustained and paid while developing a vineyard community and eventually to acquire clear ownership of a vineyard property. The experiment failed as a social venture, however, and the colony became a private operation. After a poor start, it evolved into a giant complex of wineries and vineyards, for some years the largest in the nation.

Sbarbaro and his winemaker Pietro Rossi were not the first Italian names to appear in California wine annals, but they were in the vanguard of a wave of their countrymen who over the next three decades wielded considerable power in the industry. Although German winegrowers were far more numerous than Italians in the nineteenth century, grandsons and great-grandsons of these newcomers from Tuscany, Emilia-Romagna, Sicily, and other wine districts of Italy spread through the wine business of the state. Their names would cover pages, but just to mention those of Petri, Guasti, Sebastiani, Martini, Franzia, and the spectacularly successful Gallo family is enough to illuminate the immensity of the Italian contributions. It rose with the tide of immigration from southern Europe, which brought with it the use of wine as a staple as common as bread. It encouraged the production of coarse, but wholesome, low-priced wines, and it went a long way toward establishing wine in California, if not in most of the nation, as a family beverage, not just an occasional festive treat. Many of the pre-1900 Italians settled in Sonoma County, growing vines on the hillsides, which were less vulnerable to frost than the bottomlands. Overhead sprinkling for frost protection had not been developed, and, besides, to the frugal immigrants, level bottomlands were usually the place to grow grain. Most of these farmers made wines to sell in bulk. It is only in recent decades that Sonoma County has emerged to compete seriously with Napa as a "premium" district, although it is demonstrably equal to the challenge in soil and climate.

Two U.S. senators were substantial investors in Sonoma County winemaking late in the century. George Hearst, whose money came from mining and went in part to set up his son William Randolph in the newspaper business, had a large vineyard and winery near the town of Sonoma; and James G. Fair, who divided his energies among politics, the development of the railroad, and the planning of San Francisco's resplendent Fairmont hotel, owned a large winery and extensive vineyards at Lakeville, near the brackish slough now called the Petaluma River.

Another U.S. senator was the winegrowing champion of those days, however. Leland Stanford, whose achievements included the amassing of a railroad fortune, the governorship of California, and the founding of a great university, was impressed by the success of his brother Josiah, with whom he owned a vineyard and winery at Warm Springs in Alameda County. Leland turned the enterprise over to Josiah and shifted his dreams and his attention to Tehama, an upland county at the northern end of the Central Valley, far beyond the wine districts encircling San Francisco Bay. There Stanford bought 9,000 acres of an old Mexican grant given originally to Peter Lassen, a remarkable Scandinavian who planted a small vineyard at Viña about the middle of the century with Mission grapes he is said to have brought there on horseback from southern California. Lassen's memory is alive today because a dormant California volcano named for him obligingly erupted in 1914, sixty-one years after his death.

Stanford bought the property from Henry Gerke, a German immigrant who had planted seventy-five acres of grapes on it. Gerke, when the purchase was made in 1881, had a small winery. Stanford's project soon dwarfed it. He toured Europe, selecting grapevines and recruiting winemakers. In five years, he had what has been described by Irving McKee and others as the largest vineyard in the world.

With 2.6 million vines on 3,575 acres, it was still being expanded. Hubert H. Bancroft describes the immense undertaking. It had two acres of cellars, 350 employees, and more than 800 casks of 1,600- and 2,000-gallon capacity. Stanford might have profited by studying the Tehama climate more thoroughly before he plunged. It is quite cold in winter and in the summer often blazes with temperatures over 100° Fahrenheit. Unsuited to good table wines, the Stanford grapes were mainly diverted to brandy production, and, early in the new century, the mammoth venture came to an end. Stanford, who died in 1893, had by then enlarged his total holdings in Tehama and neighboring Butte County to 55,000 acres.

From Sacramento southward, the vine fared better. The Central Valley had numerous winegrowers in the 1880s. In San Joaquin County, where the first commercial *vigneron* was George West, who planted in 1852, there were 4,000 acres by 1888. West developed a very large brandy business before he died in 1889. El Piñal, the winery he left, grew until in 1920 it stored fifteen million gallons. In Fresno County, Francis T. Eisen was the wine pioneer. Starting in 1873, he was making 250,000 gallons a year by 1885, and his success drew a number of others into winegrowing, although his greatest fame came from his book on raisins. The Mattei Vineyard was one of the newcomers, finally increasing to 1,200 acres. Robert Barton, an English mining engineer working in San Francisco, started a Fresno winery in 1881 and sold it in 1888 for a million dollars. His profit was said to be 145 percent.

By the 1880s, with wine pumping out of scores of California wineries, San Francisco had become an important center for wine merchants. There are few cities in the world with temperatures as suitable to wine storage. The normal low in January is 48° Fahrenheit. The normal high is 64° in September. Millions of gallons rested in the cool vaults and cellars there. Mrs. Wait described one belonging to C. Schilling & Company, which was under construction in 1889, designed to hold 1.5 million gallons. There were many others: Kohler & Frohling, the pioneers; Le Normand Brothers; Gundlach & Co.; Sherwood & Sherwood; Goldberg, Bowen & Co.; and perhaps fifty more. San Francisco also had a large cooperage establishment, where the proprietor, David Woener, employed 100 workmen making barrels and casks from Arkansas and Indiana white oak.

The industry lurched through the century's last decade, riding from shortage to surplus and battered by calamities. Overproduction in some districts, phylloxera and Pierce's disease in others, and prices that fell as low as ten cents a gallon drove many growers to the wall. Annual production had risen from fifteen million gallons in 1887 to twenty million in 1891, and then it fell back again as bankrupt farmers ripped out their vines and a hard frost damaged the vineyards that remained. The wild careening of wine economics from boom to bust has been one of the industry's familiar characteristics since its early commercial days. Determined to protect themselves from such instability, seven big wine dealers organized the California Wine Association in 1892. It grew so large and influential that it and a contemporary organization, the California Wine Makers' Corporation, representing the wineries, virtually dominated the trade for years thereafter. For a period of time the CWMA contracted to supply five million gallons annually to the CWA, which also acquired dozens of wineries and had the financial stamina to survive the loss of fifteen million gallons of wine in the 1906 San Francisco earthquake and subsequent fire. Leon Adams, in his classic and definitive book, describes the audacious Englishman Percy T. Morgan, who conceived the CWA and, after the fire, went on to build Winehaven, the largest winery in the world at the time. At its own pier on the Bay at Richmond, it loaded cargoes of wine sold abroad under the "Calwa" and "Big Tree" brands. In England, the trademark of a California redwood was familiar enough then to be etched into wineglasses used in the bar trade.

Not even the massive power of the CWA and the Wine Makers' Corporation could cope with the spastic production problems of the industry. In 1897 there was an immense harvest, flooding the market with thirty-four million gallons. The next year, it was down again, to nineteen million. Such fluctuations brought price wars between the giants and grief to smaller operators. As the twentieth century arrived, wine still often sold in bulk for fifteen and twenty cents a gallon. Lush yields came again in 1901 and 1902, glutting the market and panicking some of the small producers. Then there was a short crop in 1903. There was little advertising; most wineries sold in bulk for bottling under the few familiar wine merchants' labels. The acceptance of California wine outside the state was still limited, and there was no significant campaign to compete for the attention of the average American consumer, who was likely to favor beer, hard liquor, or no alcoholic beverage at all. Given these inhibiting elements, the progress made by California's wine industry was impressive not for its merchandising, but for the awkward vigor with which it had established itself in only half a century, from a standing start. By 1904 it was capitalized at an estimated $80 million (a giant sum then) and employed 60,000 people.

In the half century since Haraszthy's Buena Vista venture, a long procession of enthusiastic, conscientious growers and vintners had poured their energies and their ambitions into a remarkable endeavor—to make California, within their lifetimes, a wine region that would challenge the products of a thousand years of European experience and glamour. Among them were some rascals, slipshod greenhorns, and untalented managers, but on balance the California wine community was typified, as it is today, by its devoted application to making each vintage better than the last best one.

In the scant two decades remaining before Prohibition blighted it, the industry attracted some new and influential people and technology, and its marketing expertise improved to some extent, but the hustle, the spectacular successes, and the dismal reverses with which it had rolled and pitched between 1850 and 1900 were absent. The University of California became an acknowledged authority. Frederic Bioletti, a distinguished enologist at the university, succeeded Hilgard and surrounded himself with men of the quality of William Vere Cruess, food scientist and yeast expert of world renown. Names that were to endure emerged in the industry. There was Louis M. Martini, who made his first wine in 1907 in San Francisco, twenty-six years before he was to open the winery in the Napa Valley that is now so well known. There was Samuele Sebastiani, eight years out of Tuscany in 1904 when he bought an old winery in Sonoma that has evolved into the giant now owned by his descendants. At Rutherford, in the Napa Valley, Georges de Latour started a small winery in about 1900 that he called Beaulieu and that achieved the prestigious standing it still enjoys.

Wine prices were fairly stable through 1910. There was a glut of grapes in 1911 that shook the market, but by 1913 they were selling well again, and they did so until Prohibition. There were 144 million vines in California in 1910; by 1920, under Prohibition, there were 155 million, of which a large percentage were table grapes and grapes sold for home winemaking. Fairly early in the twentieth century, winegrowers were becoming sensitive to the shadow of Prohibition. It had had a faint beginning in the United States almost as far back as the start of wine commerce in California. Maine, the first state to do so, outlawed alcoholic beverages in 1851. By 1855 there were thirteen such states. In 1869 the Prohibition Party was founded, dedicated to achieving national legislation. Kansas put Prohibition into its constitution in 1880, the decade in which the maniacal Carry Nation began her fearsome assaults on the Demon Rum. In 1907 Georgia touched off a new wave of antisaloon fever when it outlawed liquor, and hundreds of counties and local jurisdictions, mostly rural, were added to those that had already exercised "local option." In 1914 the Hobson Resolution for a constitutional amendment establishing Prohibition was narrowly adopted by the U.S. House of Representatives. California had produced fifty million gallons of wine in 1912. In the year 1919, when the outlawing of alcoholic beverages finally became national under the Wartime Prohibition Act, the state's output was down to twenty-seven million gallons, in great part because growers saw a dark future. The small cloud that had appeared so long before over Maine had now spread across the nation, and an industry that had been proud and prosperous was condemned as the nefarious instrument of the Devil.

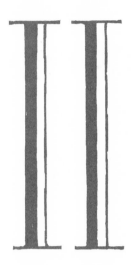

II

HISTORY: FROM PROHIBITION TO THE PRESENT DAY

1 & 2. RUTH TEISER AND CATHERINE HARROUN

II.1

The VOLSTEAD ACT, REBIRTH, AND BOOM

by RUTH TEISER AND CATHERINE HARROUN

WINEMAKING IN THE UNITED STATES INCREASED DURING PROHIBITION. MOST OF THE WINE CAME, AS BEFORE, FROM CALIFORNIA GRAPES. Now, however, only a small portion came from California's professional winemakers. More than 90 percent came from home winemakers and illicit entrepreneurs; the line that divided the two categories was often obscure. The situation came about quite unexpectedly through what initially seemed a minor provision in the congressional act implementing the Eighteenth Amendment. The Prohibition laws applying to wine, indeed to all so-called intoxicating beverages, were complex and frequently changing. At their base lay the constitutional amendment simply stating that "the manufacture, sale, or transportation of intoxicating liquors within, the importation thereof into, or the exportation thereof from the United States and all territory subject to the jurisdiction thereof for beverage purposes is hereby prohibited." The definition of "intoxicating liquors," the exceptions, and the mechanism for enforcement were left to be spelled out by the National Prohibition Act. It was known as the Volstead Act after its sponsoring congressman from Yellow Medicine County, Minnesota, Andrew J. Volstead, although the lawyer Wayne B. Wheeler, general counsel for the Anti-Saloon League, claimed authorship. But neither of them could have anticipated the consequences of 33 of the act's more than 10,000 words. They were put in as a concession to the traditional rights of American farmers to make hard cider and other beverages from home-grown fruit. The passage read: "The penalties provided in this Act against the manufacture of liquor without a permit shall not apply to a person for manufacturing nonintoxicating cider and fruit juices exclusively for use in his home, but such cider and fruit juices shall not be sold or delivered except to persons having permits to manufacture vinegar." Curiously, the term "nonintoxicating" in relation to these homemade beverages was never defined. The Volstead Act clearly stated that intoxicating beverages were those containing one half of one percent or more of alcohol by volume, but this definition was never applied to homemade wine and other fruit drinks.

The permits referred to in the act were for the exceptions to the flat prohibition stated in the Eighteenth Amendment. They were principally permits to make vinegar, wine for sacramental uses, wine and spirits for medicinal uses, wine for flavorings in nonbeverage products, and industrial alcohol. The act seemed to exclude the home winemakers from the necessity of holding permits. However, through another curious inconsistency in the web of laws and regulations promulgated by the enforcement agencies and courts, they were technically required to have them. Permits were issued to male heads of households and allowed them to make up to 200 gallons a year for home use. In one of the many futile attempts to strengthen administration of the Prohibition laws, these home permits were temporarily cancelled in 1925. A total of 45,000 had been issued in California alone, but no one knew what relationship the number of permits bore to the actual number of home winemakers, bona fide or simulated. And there was never any real attempt made to regulate homemade wine, its alcoholic content or its manufacture. As President Hoover's hand-picked Wickersham Commission concluded in 1931 concerning home winemaking, "it appears to be the policy of the government not to interfere with it." Thus, principally because of this anomaly, total wine production in the United States averaged at least 76.5 million gallons a year during Prohibition, compared to little more than 50 million in the single biggest pre-Prohibition year. The population of the country was growing, but per capita wine consumption outpaced it. Americans had consumed an average of 0.47 of a gallon of domestic wine apiece in the half century before Prohibition; 0.53 in the decade preceding it. They averaged 0.64 of a gallon, according to the most conservative estimates, in the years between 1919 and Repeal.*

PROHIBITION BEGINS

Prohibition began on 1 July 1919, and lasted until 5 December 1933. The first six months, plus a few days, were under the War Prohibition Act, passed in November

* Figures compiled from U.S. Tariff Commission, *Report 134*, 2d ser. (1939), table 180, p. 392, and data tabulated by Charles H. West and Gerald G. Pearce, Federal Land Bank, Berkeley, California, 1934 (mimeographed sheet headed "Federal Land Bank at Berkeley," Wine Institute), and compared with various other statistical compilations.

1918 to conserve manpower and prevent foodstuffs from being turned into alcoholic beverages. Its opponents tried to prevent its enforcement, pointing out that the war was over. Its proponents pointed out that the treaty had not been signed, and they prevailed. In San Francisco a loudly lamenting procession of saloon keepers, restaurant owners, and their customers escorted a hearse bearing the remains of John Barleycorn down Market Street. In Los Angeles an equally noisy crowd held a wake at the once elegant Baker Block, more recently the center of the city's bohemia. The next day nobody could legally buy a drink of anything stronger than 2.75 percent beer. Its status was being tested in the courts, and the attorney general announced that everything else was illegal. However, Congress was still struggling to define what everything else was and how the law against it would be enforced. Not until late October was the act passed that provided enforcement for both wartime Prohibition and the Eighteenth Amendment.

Having cleared the House and the Senate, the act was sent to President Woodrow Wilson. The expectation was that the president, who had been ill since September, would allow it to pass by default. He did no such thing. He vetoed it on the grounds that wartime conditions no longer prevailed and the act should be rewritten to remove the part referring to them. For a moment, the "wet" forces were pleased, anticipating a presidential order ending wartime Prohibition and at least a reprieve until the Eighteenth Amendment went into effect the next January. Their pleasure was brief, however, for the House overrode the veto within two hours of receiving it, the Senate the day after. The Volstead Act went into effect immediately on 28 October 1919. Even 2.75 percent beer was gone so far as the law was concerned.

Observance of the law during the next two and a half months was uncertain, however, and on 16 January 1920, John Barleycorn had to be buried all over again—not this time with as much vehemence or naïveté, though, for apparently many had found that "dry" was not an absolute term. Los Angeles had made attempts at enforcement, but San Francisco had apparently decided to relax until the Eighteenth Amendment took over. The *Chronicle* of 16 January carried an announcement by the Techau Tavern that that night was the last when "wines and liquors" could be served publicly. In the city's "Little Italy," diners tried to drink up all the red wine on hand. They could not, however. There was no end to the supply; San Francisco's Italian restaurants managed to provide their diners with "dago red" all through Prohibition. Much of it was made in their own basements or those of quasi home winemakers nearby.

The half year between the two farewells was of importance to commercial winemakers, for although they could not sell their wine in the United States after 1 July, they could sell it abroad until the end of the year, and many did. The California Wine Association sold more than a million dollars' worth of Italian

Swiss Colony's famous Golden State Champagne in the Orient. But it also sent three ships full of still wines to Europe, found no buyers there, dumped some in Germany, lost some more when one of the ships ran aground, and finally managed to recover a small part of the expense of the venture by selling for medicinal purposes what it brought back.

Attempts to get rid of the Prohibition amendment or modify its regulations and enforcement practices never ceased. In June 1920, the United States Supreme Court handed down the first major blow to those who could not believe that so unnatural a law was permanent. The Ohio legislature had ratified it on 7 January 1919. Many Ohioans and others across the nation thought that the amendment had been put over by the nation's Temperance-minded women while the soldiers were still overseas, and they wanted to put ratification to state referendums so that now all the people could decide the issue. The Supreme Court ruled that neither that amendment nor the Nineteenth, giving women the franchise, was subject to submission to popular vote.

But if big battles were lost, smaller skirmishes were sometimes won. The year after that defeat, the wets succeeded in getting an act through Congress that made it illegal for a Prohibition enforcement officer to search a private dwelling without a warrant, a great source of relief to home winemakers and especially to the ever-growing number of basement "illicit winemakers," as they were called in the statistical tables. The same act carried benefits for bonded commercial winemakers as well. The Volstead Act had provided that a doctor could write prescriptions for up to a pint of liquor each ten days if he believed it would afford relief to the patient from "some known ailment." Now a sufferer from a known ailment could get a quart. The provision was also good news for druggists, for pharmacies were the major legal retail sellers of alcoholic beverages. They also sold (and sometimes concocted themselves) the therapeutic tonics that the law allowed. These were usually sweet wines laced with minerals and beef extract so that they could qualify as being "unfit for use for beverage purposes." Nevertheless, they were sometimes sold in delicatessens as well, and Mabel Walker Willebrandt (of whom more later) wrote that friends had told her they were "palatable and exhilarating." The best known of them was Paul Garrett's Cucamonga-made Virginia Dare Wine Tonic.

Therapy for the body and soul was important to legitimate winemakers, for the principal legal uses for their wines were medicinal and sacramental. There was especially sharp competition for the church market. After all, even at the industry's lowest ebb well over 100 bonded wineries were operating in California. At the beginning of Prohibition, there were just over 700, but the number declined steadily. By mid-1924 there were 642. In 1926 the number dropped below 500, in 1928 below 400, and in 1932 below 200. Just before Repeal, when California's wine industry was undergoing upheavals of trial-and-error attempts to adapt to a future it could not entirely predict and when some wineries were giving up their bonds in the face of the uncertainty, the number may have fallen briefly to 130, but the lowest figure given in the existing records of the Department of Internal Revenue is 140 as of the end of 1932.*

The list of wineries that held bonds changed from year to year, and not all made wine or even blended it every year. But the industry remained active. The amount of wine made under bond did not decrease in proportion to the decrease in the number of wineries. It fluctuated much as it had done in the years before Prohibition. The 1921 crush, for instance, produced five and a half million gallons, while the next year's totaled more than thirteen million. Not surprisingly, considering the nation's general economy that year, the 1929 crush fell to just over two and a half million gallons. But the annual average from the 1919 crushing season through that of 1931, just before production surged in anticipation of Repeal, was nearly eight million gallons—about 90 percent of all wine made commercially in the United States.

The government gave permits to bonded wineries to make wine and tried to keep track of every gallon, but it did not dictate what kinds of wine should be made, or how much. Controlling those factors were demand and the Prohibition authorities' permission to sell. It took the California Wine Association a 1928 court decision to get permission to dispose of a stock of pre-Prohibition champagne for sacramental use. (A rabbi had made application for some of it, which was initially denied.)† Paul Masson was permitted to sell for medicinal purposes the champagne for which he had long been famous. But in order to explain to the authorities why so much was lost during manufacture, he had to give them a short treatise on champagne making, especially the practice of removing corks for the *dosage* and the frequent breaking of bottles under pressure from their contents.‡

For a few years in the early 1920s, wines were removed from bonded wineries for medicinal and sacramental purposes at the rate of more than four million gallons a year, most of them made in California. Then sacramental wines, which had been accounting for well over two million, suddenly dropped to under a million and stayed there until Repeal. The reason, as given in fine print in the 1926 annual report of the commissioner of internal revenue, was one of the myriad direc-

---

* Much of the data on bonded wineries in the Prohibition period is drawn from U.S. Commissioner of Internal Revenue, *Reports* (1919–26), and *Statistics Concerning Intoxicating Liquors* (1926–33). The lowest figure cited for the number of bonded wineries is from the *San Francisco Examiner*, 11 May 1933, p. 17.

† *San Francisco Chronicle*, 17 May 1928, p. 5, and 20 May 1928, p. 10.

‡ Paul Masson Champagne Company file, U.S. Department of Internal Revenue wineries records, 1920–ca. 1953 (uncatalogued collection, Department of Special Collections, Shields Library, University of California, Davis).

tives relating to Prohibition. The commissioner's Decision No. 3779 reduced the amount of sacramental wine allowed to individuals for use in their homes by half, from two gallons to one per adult per year and from ten gallons to five per family per year. These individuals and families were leaders and members of so-called "non-hierarchal" religions. The decision was clearly an effort to reduce the gallonage being used or sold illegally. It may be assumed to have done so, although there are still people alive today who recall buying wine, even after 1926, from self-styled clergymen who did not appear particularly holy. The Volstead Act denied the sale of wines "for sacramental purposes or like religious rites" to anyone but "a rabbi, minister of the gospel, priest, or an officer duly authorized for the purpose by any church or congregation." In response, certain new sects, sects with certain new religious rites, were established.

Neither the spirit nor the letter of Prohibition ever prevailed. As the attorney general's chief prosecutor of Prohibition violations wrote, with a virtuoso's use of the negative, "No one who is intellectually honest will deny that there has not yet been effective, nation-wide enforcement." The quotation is from the first chapter of *The Inside of Prohibition*, a book the prosecutor Mabel Walker Willebrandt wrote just after she resigned and just before the 1928 presidential election. In it she pointed out many of the problems of Prohibition enforcement: "leaks" through imports across the seashores and borders and through the widespread clandestine manufacture of beer and spirits; inconsistencies in enforcement and in prosecution of offenders; political preferment rather than competence and honesty as criteria for employment in enforcement agencies; inconsistencies in the laws, local, state, and federal; and, of course, organized crime in bootlegging. Among her suggestions for cures were restructure of the enforcement agencies, more rigid enforcement and prosecution, more frequent carrying of cases to the Supreme Court, and the election of Herbert Clark Hoover.

As soon as President Hoover took office, he made a strong attempt to tighten up enforcement of the Prohibition laws, and he appointed a committee to look into enforcement problems and make recommendations.* This was the Wickersham Commission, named for its chairman, Congressman George W. Wickersham. Its findings supported Mrs. Willebrandt's observations in general, and were somewhat more specific, but, as Wickersham complained, it was difficult to secure accurate data. There were a few telling statistics, however: when the enforcement agencies were reorganized and Bureau of Prohibition employees put under the Civil Service in 1927, 59 percent of them failed the examination, although everyone who wanted was given a second try. And, up to 1930, more than a thousand Prohibition enforcement agents had been dismissed for "bribery, extortion,

---

*   *San Francisco Chronicle*, 9 March 1929, p. 1, and 30 March 1929, p. 13.

theft, violation of the National Prohibition Act, falsification of records, conspiracy, forgery, perjury and other causes." The report added that the number represented only those cases "actually discovered and admitted or proved to such an extent as to justify dismissal. What proportion of the total they really represent it is impossible to say."*

While the bonded winemakers had to compete fiercely in a buyer's market, California's vineyardists found to their astonishment that they had a seller's market beginning in 1919.† In June of that year, just before wartime Prohibition took effect, when some growers had already pulled out vines and planted fruit trees and others had left their vines unpruned, easterners of a type never before seen in California suddenly appeared in the vineyards. They were fast-talking fellows who offered higher prices for grapes of all kinds than the growers had ever received before. The pre-Prohibition price for the best red wine grapes had averaged $25 a ton in the best years. Now offers started at $30 and soared occasionally by the end of the season to $70. When the dust settled on that year's harvest, the average paid for wine grapes was totted up at $50 a ton. The next year, the average rose to $75, and in 1921 it hit the Prohibition period high of $82. Prices for raisin and table grapes also rose; home winemakers and illicit winemakers made little distinction among the three types, and about nine-tenths of all California's Prohibition period grapes and one-tenth of its raisins as well were estimated by the agricultural economists of the time to be going into the production of wine. Most years, wine grapes sold for higher prices than table or raisin grapes, but the prices of all rose and fell together.

Carl Wente, who was managing Bank of America branches in the San Joaquin Valley during those years, described the eastern grape buyers as a shady lot. He did not know if they were representing others or were simply free-lance brokers. They were buying for shipment to eastern winemakers, and he did know that they ran up the price of grapes to such heights that it caused disastrous land speculation. Vineyardists would take advance payments on the year's vintage and buy more land. People who knew nothing of grape growing would pull together what capital

---

* U.S. National Commission on Law Observance and Enforcement, *Report on the Enforcement of the Prohibition Laws of the United States* (Washington, D.C.: Government Printing Office, 1931), known as the Wickersham Report.
† Principal sources for the following material on grape and land prices and vineyard acreage are California Department of Agriculture Crop and Livestock Reporting Service, reports 1924–82; typescript of draft of report by Edward E. Wahrenbrock for the Wickersham Commission (1931), with notes and corrections by Sherwood W. Shear (private collection); Bureau of Agricultural Economics, U.S. Department of Agriculture, "The Economic Outlook for Grapes," *California Grower*, February 1930, p. 24; Sherwood W. Shear, "Looking Ahead at the California Grape Industry," *California Grower*, March 1932, p. 5; Carl Wente, "Economics of Grape Growing in California, 1918–1942," remarks at Livermore Wine Week dinner 24 October 1962, typescript in Bank of America archives; and Stoll, *Grape Districts of California*, p. 48.

they could and then, like the vineyardists, ask the banks and insurance companies for loans. San Joaquin Valley vineyard land went from $100 an acre to $500, and by 1923 some was selling for $1,000 an acre. Then the price of grapes collapsed and land values followed closely. Both had soared too high, and there were other factors, notably the vineyardists' longstanding practice of planting heavily in good years, with the result that when the new vines came into bearing the market was oversupplied. California's grape-bearing acreage had increased from 300,000 acres in 1919 to 400,000 in 1923, and it would reach a Prohibition high of more than 650,000 in 1928, creating an even bigger glut than that of 1923. Eighteen thousand acres of grapes went unharvested that year. Between the two troughs, prices rose somewhat, but then in 1929 they dived to an average of $25 a ton, the sum that had delighted pre-Prohibition growers.

A case in point is the Alicante Bouschet, notable for its thick skin, which makes it a good shipping grape, and for the generous amount of red pigment in both its skin and pulp.* It was particularly beloved of the Italian home winemakers because it made a robust-looking wine similar to many of the red wines of southern Italy. It was also beloved of bootlegging winemakers. In 1928 one buyer at the Pennsylvania Railroad yards serving the New York area took 225 carloads of Alicantes in a single auction transaction. "The only inference is that these grapes went to someone who is manufacturing wine in vast quantities," noted *Business Week*. What the magazine might have added is that enormous quantities of wine could be made from that many carloads of Alicantes, for after the grapes had been pressed initially, sugar and water could be added to the mass and more pigmented liquid would result from subsequent pressings. In *Wine: An Introduction*, Amerine and Singleton report that "some eastern winemakers were able to make as much as 600 and even 700 gallons of 'wine' from a ton of grapes by this method," although the average for winemaking using ordinary methods was 150 to 160 gallons per ton. At the rate of 700 gallons to the ton, the unnamed buyer of the 225 carloads would have made more than two million gallons—2,170,350 to be precise. The Alicante Bouschet had not been highly prized or widely planted before Prohibition, when most of the state's grapes went to its own wineries. When the preponderance of the market shifted to the central and eastern United States, however, the Alicante Bouschet quickly became the "big name" grape because of its unique characteristics, and prices for it rose faster than for any other variety. It even rode out the glut of 1923. It sold for

---

*   Principal sources for information on the Alicante Bouschet are "Jolly Wine Grapes Roll Eastward to Market," *Business Week*, 7 September 1929, pp. 39–40; Frederic T. Bioletti, "The Alicante Bouschet," *California Grower*, January 1932, pp. 8–9; E. W. Stilwell, "Spectacular Performance of the Alicante Since 1919," *California Grower*, January 1932, p. 5; and Sherwood W. Shear, "Looking Ahead at the California Grape Industry," *California Grower*, p. 5.

$100 to $120 a ton in both 1923 and 1924, rising at the end of the latter vintage to $185 a ton, a price rarely achieved again until the late 1960s and then only for varieties of the highest prestige.

Year by year, new Alicante Bouschet acreage, planted in response to its popularity, came into bearing, so by 1929 the price had fallen to almost the same level as other red wine grapes. In 1932 Sherwood W. Shear, of the Giannini Foundation, who devoted much of his distinguished career to analyzing the economics of grapes and wine, warned California vineyardists that the outlook for the Alicante Bouschet was unfavorable and production should be reduced. For once the growers seem to have heeded advice. Perhaps they also reacted to the California post-Prohibition winemakers' lack of enthusiasm for the variety, which was based at least in part upon the university specialists' low opinion of it. Whatever the reason, plantings fell from a Prohibition high of more than 38,000 acres to under 5,000 in 1980.

Although bigger and undoubtedly more competitive than most, the Pennsylvania Railroad auction mentioned in *Business Week* was typical of many across the country. Most of the grapes shipped from California were either sold or consigned to brokers to be auctioned. "What Wall Street is to the investment world, the Pennsylvania yard is to the grape business," *Business Week* explained, noting that the Pennsylvania Railroad had superseded the Erie Railroad, which had previously hauled in most of the grapes for the New York area, by building this yard especially for auctioning fruit. It was given over to California grapes from September through November.

It is a vast field of parallel tracks on which loaded cars are parked. Between them run narrow platforms. Each car is opened and samples of the grapes placed outside for inspection. Buyers are given long programs listing the cars to be offered on each day. They look at the grapes, make notes on their lists and later bid for what they want in the auction room. . . . So rapid is the bidding that half a million dollars worth of grapes have been sold in an afternoon. To protect the bidders and the cashiers against bandits, no money changes hands at the auction.

Bootleggers never buy themselves. They commission speculators to bid in the grapes they want. At the yard a carload is the smallest sale that is made. . . . The ordinary speculator buys two or three cars and has them shipped to a siding in his own neighborhood. There he sends word around and families gather for the year's supply of wine [grapes]. To cart away their purchases they come with toy wagons, wheelbarrows and even baby buggies. Perambulators became so numerous at the Manhattan Produce Yard that the railroad was forced to rule them off the grounds. . . . Grapes that cost $2.50 a lug retail for $3.50 and $4. . . . A single lug represents, with the addition of sugar and water, two to two-and-a-half gallons of home-made wine.★

★ "Jolly Wine Grapes Roll Eastward to Market," *Business Week*, pp. 39–40.

That would have made the home winemakers at least as efficient as the commercial wineries. The agricultural economists did not believe they were, but perhaps the economists reckoned without the formidable properties of the Alicante Bouschet, which accounted for a large proportion of the grapes shipped to the New York area.

For those winemakers who preferred to shop still closer to home, peddlers took the grapes to the streets with the heaviest populations of Italian, Jewish, Hungarian, Polish, and other immigrants. For these were the people in New York and elsewhere in the United States who drank wine with their meals by custom, and many had made their own in their homelands.* One of the most pointedly chauvinistic attempts at legislation during the 1920s was a bill passed by the House requiring deportation of aliens who violated the Volstead Act. The Senate ignored it.

Chicago was the second largest market for California grapes, a much smaller market than New York, but important. We have a description of the system by which vineyardists sold there direct to jobbers, in contrast to the auction system. It comes from a man who as a youth grew grapes in California and sold them in Chicago at the railroad yards team track at Twenty-First and Archer streets. Here grapes from all over California were sent in refrigerated cars, iced. The owners who handled their own sales would travel by passenger train and meet their cars, the jobbers who were their customers, and the jobbers' customers, who were brought along to choose their grapes, at the team track. The cars were opened, the grapes inspected, the choices made, and then the grower and the jobber would bargain. Prices were fluid and bargaining continued until a mutually agreeable, or at least bearable, settlement was reached. Finally the jobbers' customers would cart off their purchases, as few as 20 or as many as 200 lugs, to make their wine. Those grape growers willing to undertake selling direct to jobbers were undoubtedly better rewarded than those who consigned their grapes to commission merchants. And the team track was an excellent business training ground for many a vineyardist who went on to success in the wine industry after Prohibition.

Chicago was, of course, the center of Prohibition period gangsterism. The Capone mob was more interested in hard liquor than wine, however. Only rarely did its long arm reach out to touch the California wine industry. One Central Valley winemaker was said to have been scared out of his winery by threats from Capone, but the story has not been substantiated. Others were asked to sell wine to gang representatives, and undoubtedly some did. Toward the end of Prohibition, Capone was widely reported to have threatened representatives of a California company with death if it shipped grape concentrate for home winemaking to Chicago without "making a deal."

* Constantine Panunzio, "The Foreign Born and Prohibition," *Annals of the American Academy of Political and Social Science*, September 1932, pp. 147–54.

Shippers of grapes to New York and Chicago were said to have been the victims of extortionists who routinely demanded tribute for allowing cars to be unloaded, or unreasonably high fees for handling the unloading. The racketeering that affected wine itself was, however, usually local and took the form of individuals or small organizations paying officials to look the other way, lose papers, drop charges or drop evidence-laden bottles, and make token raids.

But both petty racketeering and gangsterism were inadvertently fostered by the many Americans who were generally law-abiding but chose not to abide by the Prohibition laws. To a large proportion of the population, Prohibition was a joke, and cops-and-robbers attempts to control proscribed beverages were entertainment. The newspapers were full of cartoons making fun of Prohibitionists and often of Mrs. Willebrandt. People read headlines such as these from San Francisco newspapers with amusement:

CLARET TANKS FOUND IN AUTO

CONFISCATED WINE DESTROYED AT PACIFIC AND BATTERY

BOOKSHOP BOOTLEGGING

BAY STREET UNDERGROUND WINERY RAIDED

W.C.T.U. VS. CALIFORNIA TONICS

WINE SHAMPOO BANNED

CERCLE L'UNION RAIDED*

HORSE WILL HAVE TO WRITE OR LOSE HIS QUART OF FIZZ†

San Francisco was also a major market for California grapes, fifth or sixth in the nation, while Los Angeles bought fewer grapes than typical cities of the Midwest whence most of its inhabitants had come. San Francisco took more of the better varieties of wine grapes than the out-of-state markets. It took fewer of the tough-skinned "shipping grapes" that would not deteriorate on the long haul across the continent: Alicante Bouschet, Mission, Zinfandel, Carignane, Grenache, Grand Noir, Mataro, Petite Sirah, and Petit Bouschet. Many of these were being phased out in the pre-Prohibition efforts to improve the quality of California wines, but eastern winemakers, who were likely to mix them with such table grapes as Tokay, Malaga, Muscat, Almeria, and Emperor, made few distinctions. As viticulturist

---

*   The Cercle de l'Union was, and still is, a club of French-Americans, who by preference drink wine with their meals. Most private clubs evaded the Prohibition laws with few problems.

†   This, at the beginning of Prohibition, related to a show horse who could not fill out the forms requesting that he be allowed to continue his custom of drinking a small bucket of champagne before entering the Santa Barbara show ring. It was the kind of report that appeared again and again in the newspapers throughout Prohibition.

A. J. Winkler noted, "They thought anything wrapped up in a grape skin would make wine."*

San Francisco, however, was choosier and could afford to be. The railroad haul to the city was usually short enough not to damage delicate varieties, and some of the grapes were brought in by motor truck from coastal valley vineyards that had kept on growing fine wine varieties. If the weather was warm, these grapes sometimes started fermenting en route, giving the home winemakers who purchased them a head start. *The California Grower* described the scene at arrival in the city of "juice grapes," which was the euphemism used during Prohibition to describe wine grapes as distinct from table and raisin grapes.

> *One of the interesting sights of San Francisco during the vintage season is the grape market on the Drumm Street tracks just off Broadway. Each day during September and October from 30 to 40 cars, all practically [sic] juice grapes, are opened and hundreds of purchasers are on hand to inspect the offerings and buy the grapes they need for the manufacture of their year's supply of "non-intoxicating" fruit juices. During the height of the season, on Saturday afternoons and Sundays, the tracks are crowded with Italians from the near-by Telegraph Hill and North Beach districts and the handlers of grapes do a thriving business.†*

Edmund A. Rossi of the Italian Swiss Colony family, who was a partner in Asti Grape Products Company during Prohibition, recalled in a 1969 interview that his firm had regularly shipped not only its own produce but grapes bought from its northern Sonoma County neighbors to San Francisco. Its customers were French, Germans, and others, as well as Italians. If the buyers desired, the firm would crush the grapes for them at the old Italian Swiss winery near the grape market, then deliver the juice in barrels to their homes ready for fermenting. There were even independent service men who would follow up a couple of months later to handle the bottling. Asti Grape Products also made "Moonmist" grape juice and concentrate, named after the nearby Valley of the Moon. There were several similar firms specializing in nonalcoholic grape products, and nearly all of the bonded wineries produced them too, in an effort to make ends meet. Most were used for home winemaking, and it seemed for a time as if one of them would be the salvation of California's grape-based industries.

The salvation movement was led by a man who even now remains a controversial figure. He was Donald D. Conn, a railroad traffic specialist, who

---

* Albert J. Winkler, "Viticultural Research at U.C. Davis, 1921–1971," interview by the Regional Oral History Office, Bancroft Library, University of California, Berkeley in 1973, p. 14.
† "The San Francisco Grape Market," *California Grower*, December 1930, p. 24. Other sources of material on shipping include "Seven Cities Take Half Our Grape Shipments," *California Grower*, April 1930, p. 10; Stoll, *Grape Districts of California*, pp. 46–47.

before settling in the state had won the gratitude of the California grape industry by unsnarling a tie-up that had caused a severe shortage of refrigerated rail cars. The grape market never regained the ebullience it had experienced in the first years of Prohibition. Vineyardists' profits were predictably low, sometimes zero, always uncertain. In 1926 Donald Conn came riding out of the Midwest ready to change all that. He was a big, self-assured man. Those who recalled him with admiration said he could have become governor of California, maybe even president of the United States. Those who remembered him with disapproval said he was a promoter, given to stating as facts things that were only hopes, and that he cared more for personal power than for the California grape industry. Even his detractors, however, considered him a vigorous, skillful leader of the California Vineyardists Association, the organization that he initiated and managed for five years.★ Whether or not he led it to oblivion remains a moot question.

THE SEARCH FOR STABLE GRAPE MARKETS

The California Vineyardists Association was organized late in 1926, and in June 1927 Donald D. Conn was named its managing director. Recruiting members, he held a big mass meeting of grape growers in Fresno six days after he took office, and a month later he had signed up 7,500 vineyardists. By 1932 there were 12,000. The aim of the association was industry stabilization, primarily through orderly marketing and shipping, and also through increasing the demand for grape products. Just before taking over as general manager, Conn related later, he went to Washington and had a four-hour conference with officials of the attorney general's office "particularly about the right to make and market concentrates." Grape juice concentrates were simply reduced grape juices, easy to make in a winery. It was also easy to ship, warehouse, and make wine out of them. The potential customers for concentrates were all the legally sanctioned home winemakers across the nation. A number of grape products companies and wineries had been making them, but no mass market had been developed.

Conn now proposed to cultivate one. He envisioned buying up California's surplus grapes and making them into concentrates, thus stabilizing the

★   Much of the information on the California Vineyardists Association, Fruit Industries, Ltd., and the career of Donald D. Conn is from Donald D. Conn, *The California Vineyard Industry Five Year Report* (San Francisco: California Vineyardists Association, 1932); Regional Oral History Office interviews (see Bibliographic Note); many newspaper articles, chief among them those in the *San Francisco Examiner* and *San Francisco Chronicle*, 26–28 April 1932; and the minute books of the board of directors of Fruit Industries, Ltd. (in private collection).

entire grape market and bringing economic health to the whole industry. It would be unfair to charge him with ignoring other grape and grape product markets meanwhile, however, for he was active in fresh fruit and raisin marketing organizations. But increasingly his attention focused on grape juice concentrates. Two months before the 1928 presidential election, he called upon Herbert Clark Hoover, then secretary of commerce, and discussed his concentrates plan for relieving the grape surplus in Hoover's home state. Conn alleged that the soon-to-be president approved it, saying, "I think it will be the salvation of the grape industry. But first make sure that it is legal." Mabel Walker Willebrandt, then assistant attorney general in charge of Prohibition enforcement, also approved it and helped work out the details with him, said Conn.

Hoover having been elected, Conn went frequently to Washington to do "legislative work" on the Federal Farm Relief bill, and, at the end of 1929, he took a group of representatives of the California Vineyardists Association to the Department of Justice to discuss the legality of concentrates for home winemaking. Hopes of federal loans for grape purchases on the one hand and assurance of noncriminal status on the other then led him to instigate the formation of another organization made up of a group of leading, mostly old-time, California wineries that would make the concentrates. This was Fruit Industries. Its initial meeting was held in San Francisco in January 1929. In March it signed an agreement with the California Vineyardists Association to buy grapes from its vineyardists to produce concentrates. It was given assurances from Donald D. Conn that the Federal Farm Board would make liberal loans for such a purpose. The next year, the California Vineyardists Association assumed the responsibility of managing Fruit Industries. Donald D. Conn, as might be anticipated, thus became manager of both organizations.

Meanwhile, just before the 1929 vintage season, when the Fruit Industries winemakers were to start producing concentrates in quantity, another move was made to protect the legality of marketing them. "Pursuant to the request of the California Vineyardists Association, who are desirous of knowing the attitude of the Bureau of Prohibition toward certain phases of their business," the commissioner of Prohibition prepared Circular Letter No. 488. Dated Washington, D.C., 6 August 1929, it was issued in mimeographed multiples addressed "To Prohibition Administrators, Special Agents, and Others Concerned." The letter summarized the portion of the Volstead Act relating to what it termed "the unrestricted manufacture of non-intoxicating cider and fruit juices" and noted that "the shipment of juice grapes, grape juice and concentrates by carload lots, or otherwise, for resale, for that purpose, is entirely within the law." It instructed the authorities not to interfere with such shipments or "such manufacture and use in the home" unless there should be clear evidence of unlawful sale.

The letter must have brought tears of joy to the eyes of the old-time winemakers, who were having a thin time of it and were hoping to increase their profits by making concentrates. Not only was the venture in effect authorized by the Bureau of Prohibition, but the insertion of the word "unrestricted," which did not appear in the Volstead Act, meant that the 200-gallon limit would not apply. With the kind of benevolent paternalism Conn hoped the government would maintain, James M. Doran, the commissioner who had signed the letter, stated, "We want to protect the grape industry."

Vine-Glo was chosen as the name for Fruit Industries' concentrates, advertised as "the pure juice of California wine-grapes, for home use only." It came in eight varieties: Port, Virginia Dare, Muscatel, Tokay, Sauterne, Riesling, Claret, and Burgundy. A customer could fill out and mail in a coupon in a Vine-Glo ad, or place an order through a pharmacy or other store displaying the Vine-Glo emblem. However he ordered it, a five or ten gallon keg of juice for making his chosen wine would be delivered to his home and fermentation started by the Fruit Industries service man. In sixty days, the man would return to bottle the wine, take the keg away, and start another batch if it was wanted. The five-gallon keg sold for $14.75, the ten-gallon size for $25.40, and there was no charge for the bottling or the bottles.★

The stock market crash of October 1929 may have helped Vine-Glo sales, for according to some economists hard times stimulated home winemakers' bootlegging. The sale of concentrates apparently contributed in part to the decline in fresh grape tonnage shipped from 1929 on. More stimulus for Vine-Glo sales probably came from the publicity engendered by an incident late in 1930, just as the product's promotion program was getting underway. Early in November, Fruit Industries announced that, having established distribution facilities in Milwaukee, it would begin selling in Chicago in mid-December. Almost immediately following the announcement, on 14 November 1930, a front-page headline in the *San Francisco Chronicle* informed readers: AL CAPONE ORDERS BAN IN CHICAGO ON GRAPE PRODUCTS. An Associated Press article with a 13 November Fresno dateline began: "The Fresno Bee said today orders had gone out from the headquarters of Al (Scarface) Capone . . . that grape concentrates, new product of the Fruit Industries, Ltd., of California, could not be sold in Chicago and death would be the price of disobedience."

Reporters looked up Donald D. Conn. He confirmed that he had received death threats in anonymous letters, and he declared that Fruit Industries was "not interested" in dealing with racketeers and would not consider paying pro-

★ Advertisement in *California Grower*, February 1931, pp. 17–18; Vine-Glo advertising pamphlet, "This Tells the Story" (private collection).

tection money if approached. He pointed out that Fruit Industries was a respectable organization and that it "secures its financing from the Government and commercial sources." The government had, in fact, given it a loan of a million dollars and would give it three times that.

The Capone story lingered in the newspapers for several weeks. One article reported that Mabel Walker Willebrandt had asked the federal authorities for protection from the Capone mob. Conn denied it, but he did mention that Mrs. Willebrandt, who had resigned the year before from her job as assistant attorney general in charge of prosecuting Prohibition cases, was now chief counsel for Fruit Industries, Ltd. The revelation added much to the pleasure of those who found everything about Prohibition curious, inconsistent, and amusing. Mrs. Willebrandt, after a dignified interval, gave an interview about the sound legal status of grape concentrates. The next month a vigorous campaign for Vine-Glo was launched in California with the slogan, "Let's all help to popularize Vine-Glo and bring prosperity to the grape industry of California." In spite of the dismal state of the economy in general, the campaign seemed to be working.

Then the axe fell. In October a case involving the little-known Ukiah Grape Products Company was decided by a federal court judge in Kansas City. He ruled that anyone having any part in growing, producing, handling, or selling any product he knew was intended for making any beverage containing more than one half of one percent alcohol was guilty of violating the Volstead Act. That knocked out not only Vine-Glo but also the wine bricks that were being marketed. "Solidified merriment," the bricks were called. They were made by mixing concentrate with pomace, and dried. Although most carried instructions not to mix them with water and yeast or the mixture would ferment, they, like Vine-Glo and other concentrates and juices intended for the home winemaking market, were forthwith banned by the Prohibition authorities. The court decision even cast doubt on the shipping of "juice grapes," although that had no practical effect. What did happen, however, was that Donald Conn's great salvation scheme was wrecked.

The next spring, that of 1932, Conn's five-year contract with the California Vineyardists Association came to an end and was not renewed, although he was kept on for a year with nominal status. He ended his five years with a blast, however, in the form of a report that summarized all that the organization had done to stabilize all the grape and grape products markets, and charged the government with playing politics with the industry. The report was released to the newspapers and later, after carefully conferring with Mrs. Willebrandt on the advisability of the wording, Conn accused the government authorities of "betrayal." In long press interviews, he recapitulated all the Washington clearances he had garnered, cited the approval given by Hoover, and then noted that the California Vineyardists Association had decided to shift its loyalties. While it had previously stood firmly on the side of the government authorities in upholding Prohibition, it now aggressively advocated legalization of "naturally fermented" beverages.

Arpaxat Setrakian, the combative San Joaquin Valley grape grower, charged that "out of a clear sky Donald Conn has turned soaking wet." Others had too by then, however. Although officially it favored Prohibition, the Wickersham report swayed many. Released in January 1931, it pointed out faults in the laws and enforcement practices, but managed to straddle most issues in its conclusions. George W. Wickersham himself indicated that he did not favor repeal, but suggested putting it to a vote of Congress and the states in order to create "intelligent discussion of the question." For this he was labelled "moist," and Congressman Emanuel Celler called the work itself the "Wicked-and-Sham Report." But President Hoover, rising above all that, preferred in his message to Congress on the subject to see the report as indicating continued improvement in enforcement of the laws. He rejected its rather vague suggestions for revision of those laws and reaffirmed his conviction that he and all government executives should "enforce the law with all the means at our disposal without equivocation or reservation." It was a point of view that did not win him enough votes in November 1932 to keep him in office.

Meanwhile Fruit Industries, some of whose members thought that Conn, not the government, had been the betrayer, went back to promoting the products that they had been making before the Vine-Glo balloon was sent up: medicinal and sacramental wines, grape syrup, "cooking wines," wine sauces and flavorings, wine tonics, wine jelly. And it kept its collective eye focused on the future, when Prohibition might be expected to end. When Repeal came, Fruit Industries, Ltd., emerged as the nation's largest winemaking organization.

Roosevelt's overwhelming victory left little doubt that Prohibition was doomed. The election was held on 1 November 1932. On the same day, California voters elected an overwhelmingly wet legislature and a wet governor, and repealed the state's prohibition law. Two days later, it was announced that the Grape Growers League of California had been formed in San Francisco. The following week California state police officers were told to stop chasing Prohibition lawbreakers, and San Francisco's chief of police ordered his force to refrain from arresting bootleggers. Then Los Angeles repealed its city dry law. The next month, Congress met and proposed what a year later became the Twenty-First Amendment, repealing the Eighteenth. At that same session of Congress, representatives of the Grape Growers League turned up in Washington at a House committee hearing, to join big beer interests in arguing for legalization of 3.2 percent beverages.*

* House of Representatives, 72d Cong., 2d sess., *Modification of the Volstead Act: Hearings Before the Committee on Ways and Means* (Washington, D.C.: Government Printing Office, 1932).

The league was organized by men who were primarily winemakers, but clearly it was not yet prudent to include "wine" in an organization name. Sophus A. Federspiel, a longtime wine man, was president; he was now a partner with Horace O. Lanza in the Colonial Grape Products Company, a major Prohibition period wine producer. Edmund A. Rossi was first vice-president. He and his twin brother had only recently got back the right to use the name of Italian Swiss Colony, the company with which their family had long been affiliated, and they were anticipating switching the winery's production back from "grape products" to wines. Second vice-president was Georges de Latour, owner of Beaulieu winery, which continued operating throughout Prohibition, producing (with the help of the Wente family winery) the state's most prestigious sacramental wines. Treasurer was Louis M. Martini, who had started making wine in 1906 and was now making it at L. M. Martini Grape Products in the San Joaquin Valley. Secretary was Harry A. Caddow, who had been one of Donald D. Conn's staff members. The board of directors included Lee Jones and E. M. Sheehan, who would be leaders in the newly re-emerging industry.

Edmund Rossi, W. L. St. Amant of Beaulieu, and H. O. Lanza testified at the House committee hearing that large quantities of homemade and illicitly made wine were going untaxed, and they joined the brewery representatives in urging that these beverages be made legal so that they could bring in much needed tax revenue. They were astonished when, in March, 3.2 percent beer but not wine became legal. Finally, in May, they were given permission to make 3.2 percent wine, and they did, although it was never a howling success. Perhaps the best remembered was made by Italian Swiss Colony; it was 12 percent or 14 percent wine diluted with water, sweetened, and carbonated. The same month, a double boon of even greater benefit was bestowed upon the winemakers, however, by a notable relaxation of the limitations on medicinal wines. Beginning 15 May, doctors could prescribe unlimited amounts of anything containing up to 14 percent alcohol. A San Francisco druggist immediately announced that he would sell table wine on prescription at $9 for a case of twelve fifths. That was calculated to be about half the price charged by the city's "bootleg night clubs."

Even more liberal was the ruling that people who lacked "some known ailment" for which doctors would prescribe wine could now buy certain wine tonics containing up to 22 percent alcohol that had small amounts of minerals and vitamins added to them, but not enough to render them unpalatable. One could not ask for, or refer to, the tonics as "wine," however. They had to be named by formula number. Formula No. 6, for instance, was sherry; Formula No. 4, port. They sold for $1 a pint and $1.50 a quart, and there was no limit to how much anyone could buy. Fruit Industries was reported to be selling the tonics in bulk to a New York firm that was bottling them and distributing them across the country.

In response to these expanded markets, California's bonded wineries expanded their production, tripling it from the 1931 vintage season to that of 1932, and then doubling that the next year in anticipation of Repeal. In October 1933, the Wine Producers Association, which had succeeded the discreetly named Grape Growers League, sent out a wire service newspaper release that began: "Wine crushing in California is in full swing but with a cheerful atmosphere distinctly at variance with the crushing of recent years. Imminent prospect of Prohibition repeal has brought a new verve to the harvesting of the grape, a new zest to pickers, and a new twang to the manufacturing processes." The name printed on the release letterhead was Harry A. Caddow, secretary, but the author was clearly Leon D. Adams, an enthusiastic young newspaperman and generator of ideas, who had taken up the cause of wine as the world's civilized beverage and who would have a hand in the organizations that led the California wine industry back to respectability and success.

REPEAL AND RECONSTRUCTION

As one state after another ratified the Twenty-First Amendment, the government authorities also acted in anticipation of Repeal, allowing new wineries to secure bonds and start producing for the future. On 5 December 1933, the date Franklin Delano Roosevelt proclaimed Repeal, there were 380 California wineries in operation, more than half as many as there had been before the noble experiment began, and more than twice as many as there had been in the spring of 1933. Most of the new bond holders were men who had old wineries that had long been out of operation. Now they started checking their casks for leakage (finding a great deal) and wine-souring microorganisms (finding a great many) and trying to tighten up, clean up, and buy more cooperage.

Cooperage was in very short supply. Many old casks had been knocked down and shipped all over the country and the world to be used as water tanks. Others had simply mouldered away. There was a shortage of oak, but redwood was in good supply. There are still in use today big redwood tanks built just after Repeal, although the wood of that great California tree, which had earlier allowed the state to build the world's biggest tanks and affected its winemaking profoundly, is no longer held in as high esteem as formerly.

Coopers sprang to. The California Barrel Company was the largest, and it was headed by a man who became one of the leaders of the revival of the state's wine industry. He was Frederick J. Koster, a San Francisco boy in the old pattern who, after completing two and a half years at Boys' High School, got a job at a lumber company to help support his family. His progress from clerk to industrialist was rapid, his enthusiasm for public service unbounded, his devotion to the California wine industry demonstrated in the most practical ways. As head of the highly respectable California State Chamber of Commerce, he called a meeting of wine industry men at the fashionable Del Monte Hotel in Monterey to plan for the industry's future. An aura of illegality and bootlegging still clung to winemakers. Such a meeting supporting their respectability, even prestige, was important not only to the way they thought of themselves but to the way the business community (mainly the banks) and the public saw them. It was a psychological and financial boost that the wine men needed badly. More practically, Koster's company supplied cooperage to wineries on extremely liberal terms to their underfinanced owners. Many a bond application listed the California Barrel Company as a creditor. So far as is known, no cooperage was ever repossessed.

The industry needed such help, for the Depression was still on. Not only was there a shortage of capital, but a large part of the population was short of cash for buying either food or wine. Many winemakers were short of cash themselves, so that was no surprise. There were, however, two surprises, both unpleasant, lying in wait for them. It turned out that the home winemakers and the illicit winemakers had no intention of giving up their pursuits just because Prohibition was off. Home winemaking remained legal, as it has to this day, but the selling of homemade wine and wine made beyond bonded premises was, and remains, illegal. However, the customers were loyal. The illegal winesellers did not pay taxes, and their costs were usually far less than those of bonded wineries, so their product was a bargain. That is, it was a bargain if you liked the way it tasted, and its customers had got used to it and did like it. In all truth, much of the legally made wine put on the market in the first rush of Repeal was pretty poor stuff, for the industry that had been in chains for more than a decade had lost many of its best grapes and its best men, and its technology was out of date.

The second unpleasant surprise was that the public's taste had changed. At least more of those who bought commercially made wines now preferred sweet wines, wines with higher residual sugar and alcohol content than table wines. The winemakers were astounded, for in the first decades of this century, when they had last operated relatively freely, they had sold nearly two gallons of dry wine to every gallon of sweet. Now the ratio was one of dry to four of sweet. The lack of availability of sound data noted in the Wickersham report had apparently left them unaware that sweet wines had been creeping up on table wines even before 1919. Nor were they entirely aware that the proportion of production of sweet wines in Prohibition period bonded wineries had increased since 1921 so that finally they were making three quarters of a gallon of sweet wine to every gallon of dry.

Then suddenly in 1932, anticipating the return to the good old days, the production of dry wine made in the bonded wineries jumped to more than four times their sweet wine, and not until 1934 did the winemakers respond to the public's curious switch in tastes by increasing their sweet wine production above their dry wine. A case in point is the Petri family, which had gone out of the wine business just before Prohibition and come back into it just before Repeal. Petri made its first post-Prohibition wines in three wineries in northern California dry wine–producing valleys, then found that in order to meet its customers' demands it had to buy sweet wine from L. M. Martini Grape Products to tide it over until it could buy a winery in the Central Valley and start making its own sweet wines.

And there were other problems. A major one was the law that allowed each state to dictate its own regulations for wines sold within its borders: the kinds of wines, the labels they carried, even the kinds of containers they could be put into. The regulations differed so widely and were in some cases so complex that it was almost impossible for individual winemakers to comprehend them and to comply. Still another problem was quality. It was quickly realized that if some wineries put poor wine on the market, discredit was reflected on all.

It was also realized that the small Wine Producers Association could not cope with all these difficulties. Its leaders were among the most effective advocates of a new, larger and stronger organization. So on the morning of 20 October 1934, a group of wine men met at the Clift Hotel in San Francisco for an all-day discussion of "Outstanding Problems Programmed for Consideration and Action." The advance announcement, which apparently served as an invitation, contained an agenda established by a ten-man committee that had met six days earlier. The announcement did not suggest a name for the organization that was proposed, but apparently not only a name but articles of incorporation, a constitution, and by-laws were brought to the Clift meeting. The name was the Wine Institute.

According to existing records, representatives of fifty-three wineries turned up; twenty-four signed up. Perhaps the rest were not authorized to commit their wineries or were uncertain about the advisability of paying the required dues in those Depression days. Among the men who did sign up their wineries immediately were Edmund A. Rossi and Horace O. Lanza, leaders in the earlier organization who would be leaders in the new. If you talked with old-timers three decades later, almost all claimed to have been founding members, for by then it was an organization with which they were proud to be affiliated. Chosen to head the Wine Institute was A. R. Morrow, perhaps the most highly respected wine man in the state. He had been manager of the California Wine Association before Prohibition and later took it into Fruit Industries.

Considerable recruiting was necessary to bring the institute to sufficient size to be representative of the industry. A. P. Giannini, whose interest in his state's agricultural industries was evidenced by his personal establishment of the Giannini Foundation of Agricultural Economics, and by his Bank of America's financing of the majority of California wineries, helped the recruiting. Harry A. Caddow, manager, filling the same position he had held in the Wine Producers Association, and Leon D. Adams worked hard getting members.

Nevertheless, at first there was not always enough income from membership dues to cover the rent and payroll. Adams recalled that on one occasion Caddow went to Lee Jones of Shewan-Jones while he himself went to Edmund Rossi of Italian Swiss Colony and got them to pay their dues in advance in order to carry the organization over. By the time the first annual meeting was held in August 1935, however, 188 wineries had joined and they represented 80 percent of the state's wine production. One of the first actions they took was in the interest of quality. They worked with the California Department of Public Health to establish quality standards and forbid certain practices, among them the one so dear to the hearts of home winemakers, adding sugar to the must.

In 1938, four years after the Wine Institute was organized, another organization was formed that represented all the winemakers and sponsored many of the Wine Institute's programs. The Wine Advisory Board, a marketing order group under the California State Department of Agriculture, was voted into existence by the majority of the state's wine men. A mandatory organization, it required all wineries to pay into a state fund a small sum for every gallon of wine they sold. A national advertising campaign got underway immediately and was reflected in increased wine sales. Some of the Wine Advisory Board funds went into promotion of a kind that simply informed people about the use of wine. Many small publications on wine and food were distributed. Particularly effective was a wine study correspondence course Leon Adams wrote. One received a booklet and a quiz on its contents. When the quiz was returned, one was sent the second booklet and another quiz, then the third, then the fourth. Finally one received a certificate with a gold seal. It looked something like a college diploma and climaxed one's acquisition of both the basic facts about California wines and a little of their romance. A few still have these certificates hanging on their walls.

Another project sponsored by the Wine Advisory Board, one of the last before it went out of existence in 1975, was an interview series undertaken by the Regional Oral History Office of the University of California. The interviews of wine industry men whose memories reached back through Prohibition to the beginning of this century make up twenty-one volumes of recollections and form an irreplaceable historical record. Wine Advisory Board and Wine Institute funds also went for innovative scientific research. Most of this work too was carried out by the University of California, and the results have brought lasting benefit to the state's grape growers and winemakers. The university has been a leader in the advance of the state's viticulture and enology since Professor Eugene Woldemar Hilgard arrived on the Berkeley campus in 1874. Hilgard spearheaded the university's battle against the devastating phylloxera and the fight for better grape varieties and better winemaking practices. He also campaigned for state funds to start instruction in viticulture and enology. The present Department of Viticulture and Enology, which in the late 1930s began its gradual move from Berkeley to the Davis campus, traces its history back to 1880, the year the state granted those funds to Hilgard. When it celebrated its centennial in 1980 with a symposium on grapes and wine, the department could look back with satisfaction upon having furnished the state and the world with many a California-educated expert. By then it had become a center for advanced research and education that drew students from all over the United States and many foreign countries.

The department could also look back with satisfaction upon its part in reviving the California wine industry after Prohibition. Wine studies had, of course, been dropped for those thirteen and a half years, but a few men who had been active in 1919 returned in 1933. The literature available on winemaking had almost disappeared. Frederic T. Bioletti, who had been hired by Hilgard, wrote papers that told novice winemakers and rusty winemakers what to do step by step. He edited others' papers as well, and he guided another man whose career had begun before Prohibition and who led the university's post-Prohibition program of teaching winemaking both on the campus and in the field. This was William Vere Cruess, a farm boy from central California who had been a brilliant student at Berkeley and now tirelessly gave short courses, and spoken and written advice, to a new generation of wine men. Cruess also led his younger staff members out to the wineries to educate them in what was being done and to suggest to the winemakers what might be done better.

Bioletti also brought to the university young viticulturists who were to influence the industry profoundly. Harold P. Olmo, a geneticist, developed remarkable new hybrids by combining established varieties. Resulting from his work there are nearly two dozen hybrids that have added to the state's ability to make a wide variety of wines of proven quality and put good grapes on the nation's tables. All this was done by years of steady-handed cross-pollinization in the vineyards. Future creators of new hybrids may well use instead genetic engineering in the laboratories.

A. J. Winkler, who came to be the nation's leading viticulturist, was another of the men brought to the university by Bioletti. He worked with Maynard A. Amerine, a brilliant student who went directly on to the staff as an enologist. Amerine came to be the university's authoritative voice on both grapes and wine, writing and speaking as tirelessly as Cruess, and undertaking with Winkler research on grapes that has significantly improved the state's vineyards. Studying grape varieties in relation to wine quality on the one hand, and in relation to weather conditions that affect their growth on the other, the two men developed the Region I to V system that has guided California wine grape growers in the choice of what varieties to plant and where best to plant them, continuing an effort that had begun in the nineteenth century. Their work has been refined but never supplanted. It has been a major factor in the coming of age of California wines.

The journey from Prohibition to maturity was, however, a difficult one for most wineries. Many more started it than completed it. There were 804 bonded wineries in the state in 1934, an all-time high. A decade later there were only 465. The Roma Wine Company was the great success story that emerged from Prohibition.* In 1923 J. B. Cella, who had for many years been selling wine in New York, some of it made in California by the Petri family, bought the Roma Wine Company near Lodi. It was a winery of no great distinction, but it was located in a fertile vineyard area. Cella must have been surer than most in 1923 that Prohibition would not last, for, leaving his brother Lorenzo in New York to run their sales organization, he came to California to build up the insignificant Roma. During Prohibition, under his guidance, it made medicinal and sacramental wines and all the other grape products he could think of, and he added a new building full of equipment that was advanced for that period. Much of it was improvised and ingenious, for there was little to be had ready-made. Thus in the autumn of 1933, on the eve of Repeal, Roma could boast of being the largest winery in the United States and the most advanced as well, although some gave Lee Jones's nearby Shewan-Jones winery the latter distinction.

Roma had been a member of the California Vineyardists Association, but J. B. Cella had not been a leader in it, and he did not take his company into Fruit Industries. Roma remained independent. Although its sales lagged behind those of Fruit Industries, its wines carrying the Roma label became more successful on the market than any of those bearing Fruit Industries' numerous labels. One reason for its overall success was that it was bottling most of its wines rather than selling them in bulk, and was promoting its name aggressively. It knew the uses of publicity, and when in 1935 Roma bought the newly built Santa Lucia Winery in Fresno, it added a bottling line there—as automatic a bottling line as existed in that day, when hand filling and labeling predominated—and sent out the word that now its Fresno winery was the biggest and best in the nation and in the world.

Nothing seemed too small or too large for Roma to use in promoting its wines. In 1937 it backed a Fresno venture called the world's first Wineteria, a self-service store modeled upon the self-service "groceterias." It hired the tallest man in the world as its traveling representative. And it gained nationwide attention and loyalty with its weekly live radio broadcasts from the 1939–40 Golden Gate Interna-

---

*   Principal sources for material on the Roma Wine Company are a Roma publication, *The Roma Romancer* (October 1934); "The Story of Roma Wines of California," *Wine Review*, July 1940, reprinted by the Roma Wine Company; information supplied to the writers by J. B. Cella II; and sales statistics published in the *Pacific Coast Review*, 1933–37.

tional Exposition. There Art Linkletter interviewed visitors, and their voices were carried to their home towns across the country.

So successful did Roma become that at the beginning of World War II, when national whiskey companies went shopping for California wineries to tide them over wartime production restrictions, Schenley Distillers made the Cellas an offer too good to refuse. And, although Schenley declared its intention to expand and improve the enterprise, it did so for only a few years. Gradually Roma faded from the consciousness of the public that had once known it so well.

The Petri Wine Company, born again in 1933, was a different kind of success story. It flourished well enough under second-generation Angelo Petri, but after 1934, when his son Louis came into the firm, it took off and became for a time the nation's major wine producer. Energetic, innovative, ambitious Louis A. Petri saw to it that the Petri name too was impressed upon the public. A singing radio commercial ending "Pet-Pet-PeTRI WINE" imprinted itself indelibly upon the memory of many a listener. A cleverly designed little bottle full of Petri wine but carrying the label of a major chain store brought in welcome profits. Even cleverer was Louis Petri's wine ship, devised because, as Petri later explained, "The railroads really were making life miserable for all of us," meaning all California winemakers. He bought half of a wrecked World War II T-2 tanker, had it rebuilt, and fitted it out with tanks to hold four million gallons of wine. Railroad rates for Petri and his fellow winemakers dropped suddenly as soon as the tanker went into service.

Louis Petri's business tactics were also unusual. He added four wine companies to the family holdings, the big Mission Bell of K. Arakelian and the venerable Italian Swiss Colony among them. Then he turned the whole group into a family-owned cooperative, United Vintners, which he sold to a vineyardists' cooperative he had organized, Allied Grape Growers. Finally he helped negotiate the sale of Allied Grape Growers (which by then included the Cella family vineyards, which they had held out of the Roma sale, and Inglenook, the old-line Napa Valley wine estate) to Heublein, Inc. Until 1983, when Heublein, by then a subsidiary of R. J. Reynolds Industries, sold its major wineries back to Allied Grape Growers, it was the second largest California wine producer, but less than half as big as Gallo, which has been the leader since 1968.

The Gallo brothers' rise was slower than either the Cellas' or the Petris', but their enterprise was longer-lived. In the late 1920s, while they were still high school students in Modesto, Ernest and Julio Gallo grew grapes and sold them to home winemakers. Not until the last autumn of Prohibition did they go into the wine business, with one of the permits issued in advance of Repeal. That year, in a simple wooden building by the railroad tracks in Modesto, they made a modest amount of wine and sold it all in bulk to New York customers whom Ernest Gallo himself called on. They were, as they still are, inclined to do things themselves, plough their profits back into their business, plan carefully, and grow prudently. By 1936 they had built a small winery of their own on Dry Creek, where their present huge headquarters winery now stands, and in that year they made more than a million gallons of wine. Four years later, they started bottling their wines under their own label, promoting it with care, and, even more important, developing a merchandising system with a corps of Gallo-employed sales and service men who kept a sharp eye on the bottles in retail stores so that they were stored, displayed, and rotated properly. Ernest presided over sales and promotion, Julio over grape selection and production, as they still do today. They both also continue tasting their wines every day they are at the Dry Creek complex, which includes their offices, the company's superbly equipped laboratories, storage tanks, blending and bottling facilities, and a bottle manufacturing plant, which, as soon as it went into operation in 1958, brought down bottle prices for all California winemakers.

Still family-owned and operated, this remarkably self-sufficient organization has become the nation's, probably the world's, largest wine producer, and the American wine industry's pace-setter. Its notable contribution to the American winedrinking public is to have made available to people all across the country wine that, bottle after bottle, is of dependable quality. Innovative in developing new types of wine (fruit-flavored "pop" wines, for instance), the Gallo organization has, at the same time, continually improved its standard *vins ordinaires* and traditional sparkling wine, and responding to America's increasingly sophisticated taste, added premium varietal wines as well.*

Cooperatives assumed an important place in California's wine industry in the post-Prohibition years. A cluster of grower-owned wineries, fostered by the New Deal's program of aiding agriculture, sprang up around Lodi.† Others were scattered throughout the state. By 1951, when Fruit Industries took over the name of the pre-Prohibition California Wine Association, most of its old-line members had been replaced by cooperatives. The same period saw the beginning of unionization of a substantial number of winery workers. In 1937 a small AFL local was organized in the San Joaquin Valley, its task made easier by the employers' fear of Harry Bridges's domination of the rival Warehousemen's Union. In 1940 it merged with the newly created AFL Distillery, Rectifying and Wine Workers Local 45, later the

---

*   Information on the Gallo winery's history and activities is principally from articles in magazines of general circulation and newspapers, and from Charles M. Crawford, vice-president, E. & J. Gallo Winery.

†   *Wines & Vines*, September 1937, passim; *Lodi News-Sentinel*, 17 September 1938, p. 1.

Winery, Distillers and Allied Workers Union Local 45, which came to hold contracts with the producers of the largest part of the state's gallonage.*

The wineries that survived through the 1930s did not have an easy time of it, for wine prices were low and distribution chaotic, and production in most years seriously exceeded demand. In the same kind of effort that the California Vineyardists Association had made to stabilize the market by putting part of the state's grapes into a product other than wine, a plan was created in time for the 1938 vintage. This time the product was brandy. The plan was known as the prorate, and it was funded by the federal Reconstruction Finance Corporation and private banks. The Bank of America, which had had a hand in working out the idea, ended by contributing more than 80 percent of the private financing, although it had expected to contribute only half.

With these funds, 45 percent of that year's potential wine was distilled into beverage brandy and high-proof fortifying brandy and placed in long-term storage. Some 10,000 growers and 250 wineries participated. It was a most complex undertaking. It took a tremendous amount of organizing, and then cooperage and storage facilities had to be found, and all the brandy that went into the pool had to be certified as to quality. Maynard A. Amerine, who was a university representative on the committee named to taste all the samples, recalled that the tasting was done in San Francisco: the brandy makers would bring their samples in, wait anxiously for them to be certified, and then rush the certificates back to their banks in time to get their loans so that they could pay their field men the next day.

The prorate was fairly effective in the short run and very effective in the long run. The brandy, taken out of storage in 1942 and 1943 during the World War II shortage of spirits, found a ready market. Those who had waited so anxiously for their certificates now found that their almost forgotten equities in the pool brought them welcome returns. More than that, the prorate in effect initiated California's postwar success with beverage brandy. California wine had, of course, been distilled into brandy since the late eighteenth century, and in the late nineteenth such men as Stanford, Naglee, and Baldwin had made famous brandies. Even during Prohibition fortifying brandy and a small amount of beverage brandy had been made, but the tradition had almost been lost. A. R. Morrow, who had presided over the California Wine Association's production before Prohibition, believed that brandy had to be 100 proof and unblended. Men like Otto Meyer, whose family had made brandy in Germany and France for several generations, and Alfred

---

* Data on labor are principally from Stanley M. Bennett, "Collective Bargaining in the Wine Industry of the Central San Joaquin Valley: 1937–1953," M.A. thesis, Fresno State College, 1953; Ron Taylor, "Trampling Out the Vintage," *Coast*, Fall 1973; David Drum, "Return to Delano," *California Grape Grower*, December 1980; and articles in magazines of general circulation.

Fromm brought to California the European tradition of blended brandy of lower proof as a more pleasant drink, and they guided California brandy on its path to its present success. The Christian Brothers became the pioneer and remained the state's leading brandy maker, accounting for about 30 percent of the state's annual nineteen million gallons until 1982, when it was overtaken by Gallo.

The prorate, which was the taking-off point for this success story, was not continued in 1939 for a number of reasons. One was the protests of fine wine grape growers in the northern valleys, whose crops had almost always been more resistant to economic woe than the average. But so well had the plan worked in the eyes of the Bank of America and some winemakers that a new organization was put together by the bank and some nineteen wineries in the hope of continuing to stabilize the market. It was a nonprofit corporation called Central California Wineries, Inc., and it made contracts with other wineries so that it effectively controlled a large part of California's wine production. In 1940 it bought two large wineries, the one in Kingsburg that L. M. Martini Grape Products had occupied and the big Greystone cellar at St. Helena, in the Napa Valley. It was on its way to becoming a dominant organization in the old California Wine Association pattern when the government threatened it with violation of the antitrust laws. An indictment was drawn up naming the Bank of America, Central California Wineries, and almost every important winery in the state, charging them with entering into a "conspiracy to raise, fix, control and stabilize" prices.

Protests were made in Washington by Californians, and the attorney general shortly thereafter issued a memorandum stating that if there had been infractions of the law they were undoubtedly committed unwittingly, and suggesting that the proposed indictment be dropped. It was, but not without a public accusation on the part of the grand jury foreman, Dean David E. Snodgrass of Hastings College of the Law, that the attorney general had obstructed justice and should resign. Nevertheless, though the Californians were not indicted, Central California Wineries soon ceased to exist, selling its properties to Schenley Distillers, which had the year before bought the long-established Cresta Blanca. With the addition of Roma and the two C.C.W. wineries in 1942, Schenley suddenly became California's biggest winemaker. That same year, National Distillers bought Italian Swiss Colony, becoming the state's third largest, after Fruit Industries, which fell into second place. Also in 1942, Seagrams bought control of Paul Masson from Martin Ray, who had bought it from Masson himself, and the next year Hiram Walker Distillers bought three wineries in San Benito and Sonoma counties. This was the first significant infusion of outside money into the California wine industry, and it occurred because the distilling companies were so restricted by World War II regulations that buying into the California wine industry looked like an easy way to diversify with an allied product.

Though allied, it was dissimilar, as California's wine men had been protesting for decades whenever lawmaking bodies tried to lump wine in with whiskey and gin. By dominating an industry they did not understand, the largest distillers almost wrecked it, bidding up grape prices to unwarranted levels and costing themselves millions of dollars as well. In 1950 Schenley started withdrawing from the field, in 1953 National Distillers sold its California properties, and in 1953 Hiram Walker withdrew. Only Seagrams stayed, remaining loyal to the Paul Masson winery. It had been an exciting series of business maneuvers, yet in the long run they seem to have done no harm. In fact, either because of them or in spite of them, or possibly some of both, sales of California wines in the 1940s were well above those of the previous decade. "Tie-in" sales requiring the buyer of spirits to buy wine also, illegal though they were, may have been a factor in the increase. They probably put wines in the homes of some Americans for the first time.

THE WINE REVOLUTION

In 1946 California wine sales finally broke over the hundred million gallon level. After a slump the next year, they jumped that barrier again in 1948, then rose gradually all through the 1950s and 1960s to go well above two hundred million gallons in 1971. While that extra hundred million took twenty-three years to add, the next hundred million took only eight, for in 1979 sales reached 314,000,000 and in 1981 a total of 358,000,000 gallons.★ There in numbers is the story of the "wine revolution" in America. (The term was first used by Leon D. Adams.) Increased interest in dry table wines was part of the wine revolution. After having continued to lag well behind sweet wines since Prohibition, they started creeping up on them in the late 1950s. Finally, in 1967, California sold more dry wine than sweet, and in 1980 was selling five and a half bottles of dry wine to every one of sweet (dessert and appetizer) wine. Another significant change was the shift from red wines to white. Never before 1976 had California sold more white than red wine. By 1981 white exceeded red by more than three bottles to one, and in response many vineyardists had increased their plantings of white wine grapes.

Why these changes have occurred is the subject of endless speculation. One factor is quite certainly fashion, and another is quite certainly improved technology. Given the technology applied by most California wineries before the Second World War, it was easier to make sweet wine than dry, and easier to make red wine than white. Increased cross-fertilization with European enology and advances pi-

★   Statistical data on the California wine industry since Prohibition are from economic research reports of the Wine Institute and annual statistical issues of *Wines & Vines*.

oneered by both commercial wineries in California and the university have made posssible the technological revolution that all who speculate upon the matter agree is the major factor in the wine revolution.

As California wine has become increasingly popular among people who like to speculate about it, read about it, write about it, and above all drink it, there have been increases in the number of wineries and in the areas growing wine grapes. The number of bonded wineries dropped in the early 1960s to a post-Prohibition low of just over 200. Then it started increasing year by year, so that by the end of 1983 there were nearly 650. The state's large wineries had grown significantly, but not many new big ones had been established. What had happened was that small wineries had proliferated.

Ever since the nineteenth century, the idea of owning a vineyard and making wine had been the romantic goal of many Californians who had little knowledge of the viticulture, the technology, or the economics of such a venture. Most were well enough financed wine lovers who thought that connoisseurship equated with success. For some it did then, and has in recent years, when combined with self-education, educated employees, business acumen, more capital than they had anticipated, and patience. One can speculate that these factors applied to the wine-growing ventures of such prestigious small wineries as Trefethen and Chappellet in the Napa Valley, Jekel in the Salinas Valley, and San Pasqual near San Diego. These ventures all fit into the category that veteran wine industry observer Louis R. Gomberg has characterized as "the wave of the future." As he has pointed out, they have brought into the wine industry men from the fields of "medicine, law, physics, engineering, business, industry, commerce," and, he might have added, the world of entertainment, most carrying with them a commitment to quality that has enhanced the international reputation of California wines.

It was not these small handcraft wineries but the big ones that felt the impact of the agricultural labor movement that began in the mid-1960s. California's field workers had been attempting to better their situation since the Depression. The upsurge of efforts by vineyard workers three decades later was carried forward mainly by two groups, one predominately Filipino, the other predominately Mexican, banding together uneasily in a sometimes bloody strike and a spectacular march that won them contracts with large southern San Joaquin Valley growers of both table and wine grapes. Led by Cesar Chavez, these United Farm Workers carried boycotts all the way to the consumers, and waged a long jurisdictional battle with the Teamsters union until 1978, when the Teamsters withdrew from the fray.

The field workers' battles took place almost entirely in the large valleys. In the smaller valleys, many growers banded together successfully to arrange not only equitable wage agreements but health and retirement plans equal to those of the unions.

The 1960s also saw the beginning of a second wave of out-of-state capital coming into the California wine industry. At first it was mainly from North American firms. National Distillers returned to the state in 1967 when it bought Almadén. In 1969 Heublein bought United Vintners and Beaulieu. In 1971 Seagrams bought additional interest in Paul Masson, so that it then owned it 100 percent. Most spectacular, however, was the arrival in 1977 of Coca-Cola of Atlanta. It bought the small Napa Valley winery Sterling, and the middle-sized Monterey Vineyard of the Salinas Valley, to which it added an eleven-million-gallon facility in a determined effort to challenge the supremacy of Gallo, United Vintners, and Almadén, with its Taylor California Cellars wines. Then suddenly in 1983 a major part of the California wine industry changed ownership. Shortly after Heublein sold its big wineries back to Allied Grape Growers, Joseph E. Seagram & Sons bought Coca-Cola's wineries. Adding them to its Paul Masson Vineyards, it displaced United Vintners as the state's second largest wine-producing organization.

Overlapping that infusion was another from European wine companies, which were adding to their Continental properties ventures in this new land that they would hardly have considered favoring with notice two decades earlier. Now they were impressed by the excellent record that California wines had been racking up in the marketplace and in international tastings. Société Moët-Hennessey bought land in an established viticultural area near Yountville, planted fine grape varieties, built a winery, and in 1977 started producing a sparkling wine that has been favorably compared to its famed Moët et Chandon Champagne. Another Champagne house, Piper-Heidsieck, joined Sonoma Vineyards to make Piper-Sonoma sparkling wine. Baron Philippe de Rothschild joined Robert Mondavi in a venture to produce Bordeaux-style Cabernet Sauvignon in the Napa Valley. The German brandy and wine house of A. Racke bought the venerable Buena Vista near Sonoma, which journalist Frank Bartholomew had reestablished as a pioneer "boutique" winery in the early 1940s. Other Europeans and even the big Japanese company Suntory joined the California wine industry. They were pushed by international economic factors, but they were also pulled by the same promise that California winegrowers had seen in their state since before the Gold Rush.

Under the dual pressures of success on the one hand and urbanization of agricultural land on the other, the search for new places to grow grapes that had begun tentatively after World War II now intensified. Places where vineyards had been planted but long forgotten were investigated and added to the state's ever growing wine grape acreage. Temecula, for instance, in a southern California semidesert area, was supplied with water and is now a thriving grape-growing area. The Salinas Valley, home to lettuce but considered inhospitable to vines, became a leading viticultural area after Edmund Mirassou of fast-urbanizing northern Santa Clara County led a group of winegrowers including Paul Masson and Wente Bros. into planting there. Corporate investors, who came into the grape-growing business in the 1960s because agricultural land then offered worthwhile tax savings, have been particularly important in the development of vineyards in Monterey County and elsewhere in California. The Paso Robles area, the Santa Maria area, the Santa Ynez Valley, and many others have been added to the state's winegrowing regions. And meanwhile more land for grape growing has been found in the established areas: Napa County wine grape vineyard acreage increased from 15,000 acres in 1971 to 27,000 in 1981, Sonoma County's went from 11,000 to nearly 29,000, Fresno County's from 20,000 to 37,000. The state's total acreage in wine grapes nearly doubled in that decade, and its percentage of fine varieties increased in response to wine drinkers' more discriminating tastes.

BIBLIOGRAPHIC NOTE

In addition to the sources cited in the footnotes, this chapter is based on many articles in the grape and wine trade press, newspapers, and publications of general circulation, and upon ephemeral material in numerous private and public collections. Much has been taken from the series of interviews with California wine industry men conducted by the Regional Oral History Office of the Bancroft Library, University of California, Berkeley, between 1969 and 1974. The principal interviews drawn upon are those with Leon D. Adams, Maynard A. Amerine, Harry Baccigaluppi, Burke H. Critchfield, William V. Cruess, Andrew G. Frericks, Maynard A. Joslyn, Louis M. Martini, Otto E. Meyer, Harold P. Olmo, Louis A. Petri, Edmund A. Rossi, Ernest A. Wente, and Albert J. Winkler. We have also drawn upon information supplied informally by wine men and women we have talked with over the years, and upon the excellent technical and semitechnical books published in recent decades.

II.2

Note: Home Winemaking

by RUTH TEISER AND CATHERINE HARROUN

HOME WINEMAKING IS LEGAL IN THE UNITED STATES but with certain restrictions. Under present federal law, any adult may make wine for personal or family use in the home. An adult is defined as a person over eighteen years of age or over the minimum age at which his state or local government makes it legal for him to purchase wine. A winemaker with two or more adults in his household may make a maximum of 200 gallons of wine each calendar year. If there is only one adult in the household, the maximum is 100 gallons. The wine thus made is for "personal or family" use, according to the law, which does not, however, define "family." Serving homemade wine to guests in the home is not mentioned, but the law specifically prohibits selling it. There is no tax on homemade wine, and the winemaker need not register with any federal agency, although some state or local governments may have special requirements.

Before 1978, when Congress passed the law that now obtains, only a head of family was allowed to make wine at home. A head of family was defined as someone who "exercises family control or responsibility over one or more individuals closely connected with him by blood relationship or relationship by marriage, or by adoption, and who are living with him in one household." Bachelors and married men living apart from their families were specifically excluded. Although gender was not mentioned, the home winemaker was assumed to be male. Before he began making wine, this head of household had to fill out a form and file it with a federal agency. The earlier law reflected traditional concepts of the American family, and its longevity reflected the federal government's resistance to change. The new law reflects recent American demographic changes.

The home winemaking law of 1978 was enacted at the behest of Senator Alan Cranston of California, who noted in a letter to his colleagues that approximately 20,000 applications a year were being filed with the Bureau of Alcohol, Tobacco and Firearms, which "dutifully receives, files, and maintains these registration forms but does nothing else with them. . . . No one at BATF can ever recall any enforcement activity involving a home wine making registration form. No one has been prosecuted for failing to register."

Most American home winemakers are people who like to do things for themselves, people who like to find out how things are done by doing them, or people who like to experiment in the hope of making what they consider the best possible wine. Supplies, equipment, and advice for such amateurs are available in many communities from firms that cater to small winemakers. From them one can usually order fresh grapes (although some people go out and buy or even pick them themselves), frozen grapes, and concentrates. The latter two allow winemaking in any season. Books, classes, and competitions are also available. Of the many manuals, those most often recommended are *Guidelines to Practical Winemaking* by Julius H. Fessler (published by the author, Box 5276, Elmwood Station, Berkeley, California 94705) and *Grapes into Wine* by Philip M. Wagner (Alfred A. Knopf); both are frequently revised.

At various places throughout the state, the University of California Extension offers courses of immediate or peripheral interest to home winemakers. So do a number of California state universities and community colleges. For serious home winemakers, there are competitive tastings, some privately organized, some held at the California State Fair and county fairs. A number of serious home winemakers in California have advanced from amateur to professional status, successfully establishing regular bonded wineries of their own.

VITIS SILVESTRIS

nigra

VITIS SILVESTRIS *nigra*

Vitus silvestris, *the indigenous wild form of the grape species, as evidenced in paleobotanical research, is of ancient origin, long predating the ice ages. Once abundant in the European population of* Vitis s., *it has largely disappeared from existence (Map I, pp. 90–91). Compare* Vitis silvestris alba, *page 121.*

SOURCE FOR DRAWING: Zdenko and Greta Turković, *Ampelografski Atlas* (Zagreb: 1952–63). Illustration redrawn, slightly reduced (4 ½ %).

1984

illus.p84

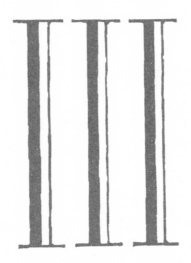

GEOGRAPHY, CLIMATE, & VINTAGES

1. MAYNARD A. AMERINE & PHILIP M. WAGNER

2. BOB THOMPSON

*

III.1

THE VINE
AND ITS ENVIRONMENTS

by MAYNARD A. AMERINE and PHILIP M. WAGNER

BEFORE THERE CAN BE ANY WINE, THERE MUST BE SUITABLE GRAPES. BEFORE THERE CAN BE SUITABLE GRAPES, THERE MUST BE A CLIMATE they will find congenial. California illustrates these statements. There exist thirty-odd species of grapes (the genus *Vitis*), most of them unsuitable for wine. California's indigenous species of grapevine, *Vitis californica* and *Vitis girdiana*, are among those that are worthless for winemaking. Not until the mission fathers brought in the grape they had used for wine in Baja California (a variety of obscure origin but clearly belonging to the European species *Vitis vinifera*) was any wine made in California proper. Even then, congenial though conditions were, nearly two centuries had to pass before the most suitable grape varieties, all of this same species, were fitted to the climatic conditions of various parts of the state.

This chapter is given over to the basic climatic and geographical requirements for winegrowing, with special reference to the characteristics that distinguish the general climate and geography of California from those of the rest of the continent and to the real and important differences among the numerous viticultural districts within the state. Before getting into all that, it may be helpful to devote some pages to the grapevine itself: the history of the genus, the places where it is at home, the things that have happened to it in the course of its evolution, and the differences between the wild vines and those that are cultivated. Climate and geography are the leading factors in all of these.

THE ORIGIN OF *VITIS*

The thirty-odd species of *Vitis* are widely spread throughout the northern hemisphere, and the northern hemisphere only. As a wild plant form, *Vitis* originated there; and through all the convulsions of geological history, with their associated climatic changes, no representative of the genus ever managed to break the hemispheric barrier, or, if it did, to survive. The irony is that some of the best viticultural climates in the world are in the southern hemisphere, specifically in Chile, Argentina, Australia, and South Africa. Like California they had no suitable grapes until these were brought in from the winegrowing centers of Europe.

As for its beginnings, we know no more about the grapevine than we do about the beginnings of mankind. The first evidence is from the tertiary period, dating back over a million years, and it consists of the imprints of grapelike leaves in fossil digs, and of fossilized seeds from the same period. Of these clues, the leaf imprints are least trustworthy because they could as easily be the precursors of the maple, the plane tree, or various other deciduous woody plant forms. But the fossil seeds are unmistakably those of grapes. There is another confirmation in the fossil remains of what for the paleobotanist is unmistakably the pollen of grapes.

Besides demonstrating the great age of the genus *Vitis*, the evidence of the seeds illuminates a contemporary riddle. In spite of their many differences, all of the thirty-odd species of *Vitis*—except two—carry the same number of chromosomes and crossbreed spontaneously. The other two species are *Vitis rotundifolia*, the muscadine grapes of our southeastern states, of which the Scuppernong is best known, and some near relatives found in subtropical Central America and other parts of the Caribbean area. Recently they have been successfully crossbred with *Vitis vinifera*, but genetically and morphologically, they are far removed from all the other grapevine species.

This division of *Vitis* into two orders corresponds with two easily distinguished types among those fossil seeds. One type shows distinct radial wrinkles, or ribs, on its hard surface, as do seeds of contemporary muscadine grapes; the other is smooth, lacks such wrinkles, and has a pronounced "beak,"* as is generally the case today with the seeds of all grape species but the muscadines. The genetic barrier between the muscadines and all the others, plus the evidence of those seeds from the tertiary, suggests an evolutionary breakaway of great age, and perhaps a much later evolution, under very different conditions, of the primal smooth-seeded grapevine into the numerous interfertile, and hence genetically closely related, species. The course of this latter evolution, leading to the many grape species of today, is far from worked out. But the general outline is fairly clear. In the late tertiary period, the climate of that part of the globe with which the earliest evidence of the grapevine is associated was very different from today's: warm and humid, with lush vegetation. Grapevines were a part of this flora well into what we call the high latitudes.

---

* A. M. Negrul, "Arkheologicheskie nakhodki semian vinograd" [Archeological finds of grape seeds], *Sovetskaya Arkheologiya*, 1960, no. 1: 111–19.

All that changed with the onset of the Ice Age, with its ponderous ebb and flow of the ice cap—the cycles lasting approximately 100,000 years each. As the glacial ice cap advanced, it was preceded by a drastic change of climate: forests and lush vegetation disappeared and were succeeded by treeless tundra or steppe, cold and dry and windy, in which the grapevine could no more survive than trees. Hence a retreat and broad dispersal into widely separated survival areas or shelters farther south on the Eurasian and American continental masses. Needless to say, these served as refuges for much else in the way of flora and fauna. In each of them, the familiar process of natural selection responded in ways appropriate to the diverse conditions. As part of the process, the many species of *Vitis* came into being, to this day remaining genetically close enough to be interfertile and to share a good many visible characteristics, but astonishingly different in other ways: nature of fruit, length of the growing season they require, hardiness, adaptability to varying types of soil and degrees of humidity, resistance to fungous diseases and animal parasites if they are present—sometimes a resistance that lingers on millennia after the parasite or disease that prompted it has disappeared—or lack of resistance if they are not. Map 1 shows the approximate size of these refuges. Those of southeastern North America and eastern Asia were especially fecund in species. The complexities of the large group of East Asian species, and for that matter of the American species, whose habitats are located all across the continent east of the Rockies, and from southern Canada to the Caribbean, are still only partly understood. A mystery that has so far eluded explanation is the existence of so few species on the west side of each of the great continental masses, in contrast to the wealth of species on the eastern sides. The species unique to the westward side of North America, *Vitis californica* and *Vitis girdiana*, have already been mentioned. Whether western Europe had ever been the habitat of more than one species was long a matter of dispute, prompted by the substantial differences among the innumerable varieties actually in cultivation—for example, between those of the Mediterranean basin and those of the cold-temperate north. It is now generally agreed that botanically these are variants of the same all-embracing species, *Vitis vinifera*.

See Map 1 pp. 90–91

A matter of nomenclature should be cleared up at this point to avoid future confusion. In discussions of this, the most important of all grape species, three different terms are commonly used: *Vitis vinifera*, the all-embracing name; *Vitis silvestris*, applied to the indigenous wild forms of the species; and *Vitis sativa*, often applied to the cultivated varieties of the species.

The once abundant European population of *Vitis silvestris* has now largely disappeared. It is commonly thought to have been victim of the same, or similar, diseases imported from America (phylloxera, oïdium, downy mildew, and black rot) that all but wiped out the vineyards of Europe in the nineteenth century. But because it is an arboreous plant and those parasites are not especially fond of forest conditions, it has not been entirely wiped out. Land clearance and over-zeal-ous forest management may well have been worse destroyers. In any case, enough individual vines of the wild species survive, especially in the remoter and less popu-lated areas, such as the central Balkans and the southwestern Pyrenean area of France, to indicate the extent of the species's domain. This stretched from as far north, in warmer times, as Scandinavia and Scotland to the Caucasus on the east and the Atlas mountains of North Africa. And there is plenty of evidence of the way in-dividuals of the species evolved into large climatic or geographic subgroups without separating themselves in the botanical sense from the species. The northern limit of the species in Europe today runs in an approximately west-east line, a line made jagged by regional and local climatic influences large and small, from a point on the Atlantic coast of Brittany to the Elbe, and from there roughly southeast through Austria, Hungary, Romania, and southern Russia to the western shore of the Caspian sea.

So far, this account has been limited to the wild vine, and man has had no place in it. It is time to introduce him. Whether any part of a plant—fruit, seed, leaf, stalk—is of interest or value to man is beside the point in natural selection. But in neolithic times the fruit of *Vitis silvestris*, though small-berried, tart, short on sugar, and inclined to be bitter, was sufficiently attractive to be gathered in season, much as huckleberries, blackberries, and other wild fruits and nuts are still gath-ered today, to be eaten fresh or, in some cases, stored.

The wild vine is a dioecious plant, meaning that the population is divided between male vines and female vines, nature's way of promoting variation and adaptability. The seedling offspring of the female vine was winnowed out by the prevailing conditions and only the fittest survived. In this way, the vine changed with circumstances, the main one being climate. *Vitis silvestris* in the Pyrenean area is not like that of northeastern France and the Rhine valley. *Vitis silvestris* from the Black Sea country is different in yet other ways, without actually departing the spe-cies. And, finally, at the far eastern perimeter of the species area, there evolved, over great stretches of time, forms so different it seems hardly possible that they could be embraced in the same species, though botanically they are. This was the Caucasus refuge region of glacial times, lying south and west of the Caspian sea and protected from the north by the Caucasus range. Mount Ararat dominates the landscape.

As *Vitis silvestris* responded to this climate, so different from that of maritime western Europe, there were striking morphological changes, such as the texture and pattern of foliage and the large compound clusters of fruit. The berries were larger, sweeter, blander, frequently oval or greatly elongated, and white as often as black. Most important, the normal division of wild vines into male and female was complicated by the presence of hermaphrodite vines. That is to say, the

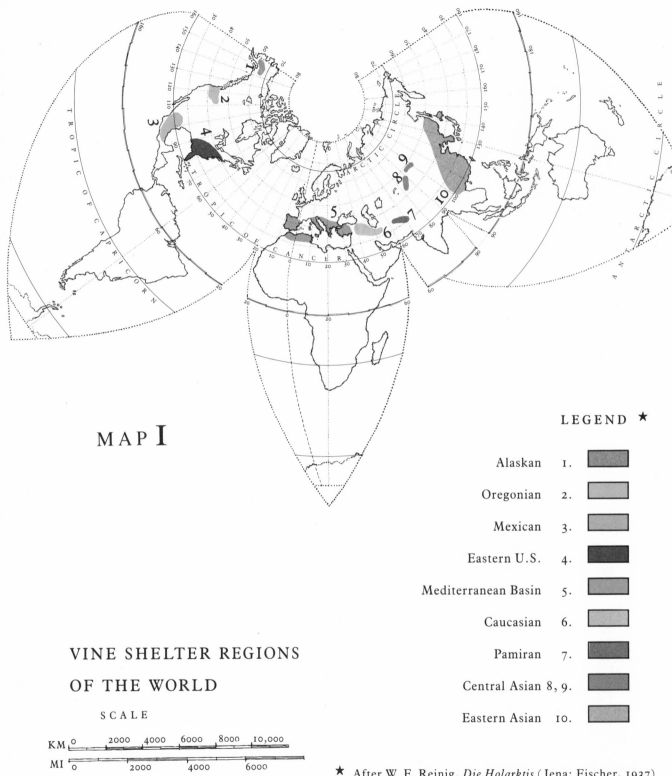

MAP **I**

LEGEND ★

Alaskan	1.	
Oregonian	2.	
Mexican	3.	
Eastern U.S.	4.	
Mediterranean Basin	5.	
Caucasian	6.	
Pamiran	7.	
Central Asian	8, 9.	
Eastern Asian	10.	

VINE SHELTER REGIONS

OF THE WORLD

SCALE

KM 0   2000   4000   6000   8000   10,000

MI 0   2000   4000   6000

RF 1:200,000,000

★ After W. F. Reinig, *Die Holarktis* (Jena: Fischer, 1937)
See bibliographic note, page 120.

MAP **I**

DISTRIBUTION OF VINE SHELTERS
AFTER THE GLACIAL PERIODS

IN NORTH AMERICA, EUROPE, AFRICA, AND ASIA

The grapevine grows in the temperate zones, requiring a long, warm, frost-free period for development and unable to survive temperatures lower than −20° C (−4° F) during dormancy. Historically, before the glacial periods, the vine was widely distributed throughout the Northern Hemisphere, much of which once had such a climate. During the successive ice ages, however, when climatic conditions changed, the vines perished in those areas covered by the ice cap and survived only in ten refuges spared by the ebb and flow of the glaciers. Not only did the vine persist in these refuges, but also different species—sometimes more than one—survived in each shelter area. Following the last ice age and the eventual birth of viticulture in the Middle East, the vine began its slow westward immigration. The consistency of legend and history and the science of paleobotany suggest that the grapevine has been among the most widely used and highly celebrated plants to flourish after the ice ages.

✱

The genus Vitus *predominates in the Northern Hemisphere and probably originated in the Middle East. Although several related genera are found in the Southern Hemisphere, none of these are of importance as food.*

MAP I, opposite page, conformal and near equal-area projection redrawn after Bartholomew.

flowers of these vines had functioning pistils, or ovaries, but the pistils were surrounded by stamens holding functional pollen. Unlike the usually dioecious vines of *Vitis silvestris*, these were therefore capable of self-pollination, a characteristic of utmost importance to man, since it assured regularity and abundance of yield and consistency in the character of the fruit.

Also, if propagated vegetatively (that is, by encouraging cuttings to root rather than by sowing seeds), a vine selected for one or more special characteristics, such as appearance and flavor of fruit, could be multiplied indefinitely. Such a vine and those thus multiplied from it would be what today we call a *variety*, a *cultivar* (horrid word!), or a *clone*. The isolation, multiplication, and planting of such desirable individual vines was the beginning of viticulture. Even so, a powerful motive was needed for the switch from the random harvesting of wild grapes: the grape—a seasonal plant, irregular in quantity and quality, and also in competition with numerous other fruits—had not been more than an incidental food source. That powerful motive made its appearance, apparently in this same sub-Caucasian region. It was the discovery, symbolized by the legend of Noah, that crushed ripe grapes in some sort of waterproof container made a natural beverage that was pleasant, that could temporarily banish dull care and sorrow, that was nourishing, and that could be stored. In this way, grapes became a year-round article of consumption, containing, as we now know, practically everything in the list of minimum daily requirements commonly printed on packages of breakfast food. But if wine were to become part of daily fare, there would clearly have to be a more abundant and reliable supply than the random harvest of wild grapes. Suitable individual vines would have to be multiplied, planted, and tended. So it was that *Vitis sativa* and its principal product found a place in the primitive agriculture that had begun to replace nomadism. On this, the remarkable consistency of legend and history in this part of the world supports the findings of ampelographers and archaeologists.

Following the birth of viticulture in the Middle East, the slow invasion westward began, all of it since the retreat of the last ice cap and most of it within the past several millennia. It was a forked migration that found congenial climates for the vine along both paths. One led south through Palestine, where *Vitis silvestris* had never penetrated; from there it found its way into Egypt and on westward, eventually meeting and mingling with its cousins in the Atlas mountains and leaping the straits of Gibraltar into the Iberian peninsula to meet others. The other path of this viticultural migration out of the Caucasus led due west, skirting north of the Mediterranean, penetrating the Greek peninsula and the lands lying about the western side of the Black Sea, and continuing on westward.

These regions were already well populated by wild vines. As we have seen, the mutability of the species *Vitis silvestris* in the presence of climatic variations had had the effect of producing locally adapted subgroups within it. A. M.

Negrul, the Russian ampelographer, reduced all these differing clusters of wild *silvestris* population to three basic groups, or *proles* as he called them, a classification now quite generally accepted. He called these *orientalis* for the Caucasian group; *pontica* for those growing about the Black Sea; and *occidentalis* for those of the Danube watershed, the Balkans, Italy, the Iberian peninsula, and western Europe generally. What happened, as viticulture spread west along with human conquest and migration, was a constant intermingling of the invading *orientalis* with the native representatives of *silvestris*, which is to say, those of the *pontica* and *occidentalis proles*. In these matings, the native vines had their local adaptation to offer, the *orientalis* greater productivity, in most cases improved fruit quality, and, most importantly, the gene responsible for hermaphroditism, which is the generally distinctive trait of the cultivated grape. The genetic remoteness of the parents promoted hybrid vigor as well.

Out of this process of intermingling and selection emerged the mixture of varieties, or *encépagement*, of the Mediterranean basin. There are innumerable differences of detail. But because the climate with its hot, dry summers, mild, wet winters, and relentless sunshine during the growing season is much the same from end to end, and because crossbreeding is spontaneous, the grapes and the wine they yield have a family resemblance. Though a few wines stand out, there isn't a great deal to choose or distinguish among well-made red wines from any part of the Mediterranean basin, whether they be from the east coast of Spain, the lower Rhone valley, Algeria, or the Dalmatian coast of Yugoslavia. Where the sharp qualitative distinctions begin to emerge among European wines is again mainly a matter of climate and geography. It relates to the contrasts between the two-season climate of the Mediterranean basin and the very different four-season temperate climate (in all its variations) that lies to the north of it. The contrasts simply can't be missed, whether one first encounters them as a tourist, a botanist, a meteorologist, a student of human social institutions, or an ampelographer.

In the wild, as noted already, the grapevines of temperate western Europe constitute a group quite different from those farther east and south. Not only that, they formed lesser groups corresponding to lesser climatic differences. Those of mild and humid Atlantic France, for example, differ from those in northeastern France and the adjacent regions of Germany, where maritime influences give way to continental ones. Then at some point hermaphroditism made its appearance among the occidental subgroups. Just how, is a matter of conjecture. In some places, it may have appeared spontaneously, by mutation. There was the Danubian route from the east, bypassing the Mediterranean basin entirely and leading deep into central Europe almost to the Rhine. And, of course, pre-Roman and then Roman colonization of Gaul and the Iberian peninsula automatically included the introduction of the cultivated Mediterranean varieties. We know that they were

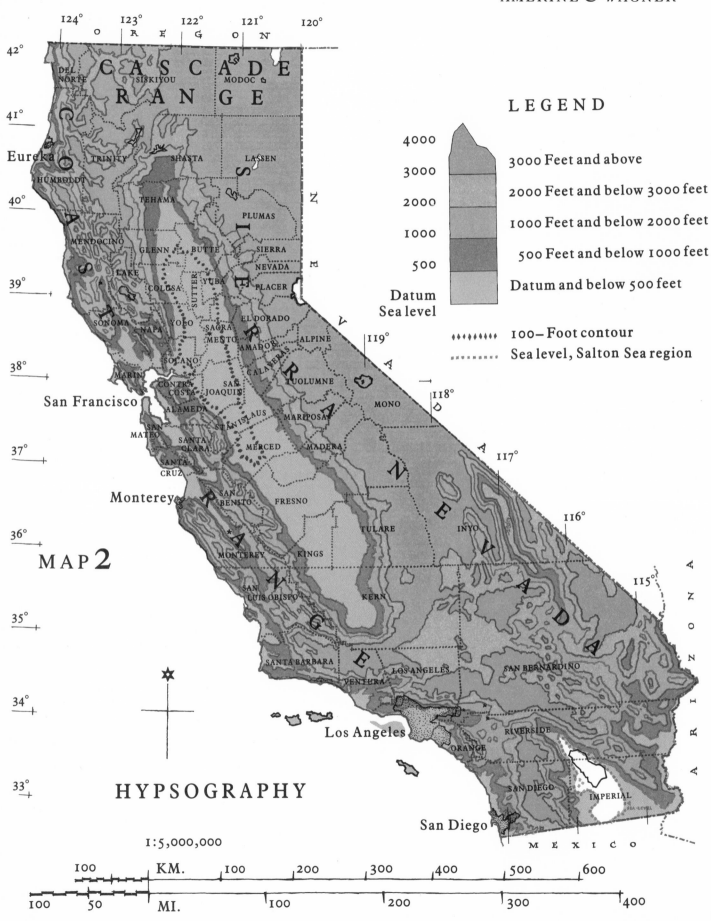

LEGEND

4000
3000
2000
1000
500
Datum
Sea level

3000 Feet and above

2000 Feet and below 3000 feet

1000 Feet and below 2000 feet

500 Feet and below 1000 feet

Datum and below 500 feet

✦✦✦✦✦ 100—Foot contour

.... Sea level, Salton Sea region

MAP 2

HYPSOGRAPHY

1:5,000,000

Place names

O R E G O N

124° 123° 122° 121° 120°

42°
41°
40°
39°
38°
37°
36°
35°
34°
33°

CASCADE RANGE

DEL NORTE
SISKIYOU
MODOC

Eureka

COAST

TRINITY
SHASTA
LASSEN

HUMBOLDT

TEHAMA

PLUMAS

MENDOCINO
GLENN
BUTTE
SIERRA

LAKE
COLUSA
YUBA
NEVADA

SONOMA
SUTTER
PLACER

NAPA
YOLO
SAGRA-
MENTO
EL DORADO
ALPINE

SOLANO
AMADOR
CALAVERAS

MARIN

CONTRA
COSTA
SAN
JOAQUIN
TUOLUMNE
MONO

San Francisco

ALAMEDA

SAN
MATEO
STANISLAUS
MARIPOSA
MADERA

SANTA
CLARA
MERCED

SANTA
CRUZ

Monterey

SAN
BENITO
FRESNO

MONTEREY
KINGS
TULARE
INYO

SAN
LUIS OBISPO
KERN

SANTA BARBARA

VENTURA
LOS ANGELES
SAN BERNARDINO

Los Angeles

ORANGE
RIVERSIDE

SAN DIEGO
IMPERIAL

San Diego

M E X I C O

SIERRA

NEVADA

RANGE

A R I Z O N A

I D A H O

119° 118° 117° 116° 115°

Scale bars

100   KM.   100   200   300   400   500   600

100   50   MI.   100   200   300   400

MAP **2**

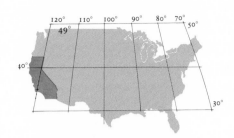

CLIMATE AND HYPSOGRAPHY
OF CALIFORNIA

Lying between the 33° and 42° latitudes north, California would be expected to possess a temperate climate; yet it has many climates, from tropical to near-arctic. One reason for this remarkable range is the physical geography, or elevation, of the state—an important factor modifying climate. Much of California is mountainous, and, owing to frosts and sometimes to lack of soil, grapes can seldom be grown above about 1,000 meters.

The Pacific Ocean also affects climate, and it limits the growth of grapes along the California shoreline from Monterey north by lowering temperatures in the coastal region. Most of the state's grapes are grown in the great Central Valley, with its single access to the cool sea breezes through the Carquinez Straits. The northern and southern extremes of this valley are its warmest. Other valleys—those of the Russian River, the Napa River, and the Salinas River—drain into the San Francisco Bay or the Pacific Ocean. In each case the climate nearest the mouth of the river is the coolest.

Other factors may modify the climate within these drainage basins. Vineyards facing west receive the afternoon sun and ripen their fruit earlier than those facing east. Strong afternoon winds may break off growing shoots in some areas.

carried well up the Rhone valley and over into what is now the Bordeaux district, and indeed that some went as far north as the Rhine and Moselle valleys. Though for climatic reasons most of these did not succeed, the Mediterranean immigrants clearly survived long enough to crossbreed with the surrounding wild vines, with highly beneficial results. From then on it became another chapter in the same old story of human selection from among the wild vines, their introduction into culture, and further crossbreeding.

This process took place much later than the introduction of viticulture from the east into the Mediterranean basin. Much of it has occurred since the beginning of the Christian era. On the whole, the cultivated varieties that emerged in these temperate areas north of the Mediterranean basin and today yield the superior and highly individual wines of western Europe—such grapes as the Pinots and Chardonnays, the Rieslings, the Traminers, the Sauvignons, the Cabernets and the Malbec tribe—are much closer to their wild ancestors than are the Mediterranean varieties. This can be demonstrated etymologically: *Sauvignon* is only a variant of *sauvage*, or wild; *Sémillon* means *sémis*, seedling. In some cases a familiar cultivated variety of temperate Europe is not even one generation removed from the wild. Plant some seeds of the *Petit Verdot* grape, much used in the Médoc, and what you get are a lot of seedlings barely distinguishable from the parent. This could not happen in the case of a highly evolved and crisscrossed Mediterranean variety. Seedlings derived from it would be a mixed lot, many of them throwbacks to its complex ancestry.

It is a matter of frequent observation that fruits (not only grapes) which have been crossed and recrossed, while improved in one particular or another, such as shipping quality or the ability to withstand cold storage, are likely to lose much of their individual personality. It is a parallel observation that fruits not far removed from their wild forbears are likely to be the ones of greatest individuality in aroma and flavor, as well as in other characteristics. Compare wild blueberries and *fraises de bois* with their supermarket counterparts. Among wine grapes, it is curious that the ones we call "noble" because of the individuality of aroma and flavor they impart to their wines are in many cases semi-wildlings originating in climatic zones where hazards abound and the growing season is an obstacle race from start to finish.

CLIMATE

The climate at any given place on the earth's surface is influenced by a multitude of factors: pressure and winds, altitude, ocean circulation, solar radiation and its absorption (that is, temperature), cloudiness, precipitation (rain, snow, and hail), and so on. The temperature in European vineyards has changed in the modern period. K. Müller reports that warm years exceeded cool 280 to 135 between A.D. 864 and 1552. From 1553 to 1947, cool years exceeded warm 225 to 169.* The vintage in Europe may vary from early September in warm years to late October in cool years. Prior to the development of the thermometer in the eighteenth century, vintage dates gleaned from church artifacts provided historians with their most sensitive record of variations in growing seasons and hence of the state of the food supply.†

No viticultural subject has generated such diverse opinions as the relation of the vine to its environment and to the composition and quality of the resulting musts and wines. The vine grows in a restricted zone from 0.5 to 5 or more meters below the surface and from 1 to 4 or more meters above. Beneath the surface, the structure, texture, composition, moisture content, and temperature of the soil are important parameters. Above the soil, the minimum and maximum temperature, day length, night and day temperatures, hours of sunshine, velocity of wind, humidity, and so on, are all factors in vine growth. To complicate the problem, different varieties and rootstocks are more or less tolerant to variation from the climatic norms, for the reason indicated above. Furthermore, each year the vine passes through its dormant and vegetative periods. At each stage, it is more or less sensitive to deficiencies or excesses of nutrients, moisture, and, particularly, temperature.

In normal grape ripening in temperate regions, the fruit of most cultivated varieties will reach a sugar content of about 20 percent. In the coolest areas, it will not attain this much sugar and will thus produce insufficient alcohol for a balanced table wine. It is possible to add sugar, a common practice in Germany and the eastern United States. Even with the addition of sugar, however, there may be excess total acidity in the unripe grapes. Various procedures are then necessary to remove the excess acidity in order to make a palatable wine. In the hottest areas, the imbalance may be just the opposite: too much sugar and too little acidity.

The interrelation of climate, geography, and the variety of grape determines the potential for fruit and wine quality. Man, of course, can influence it by pruning, training, irrigation, fertilization, cultivation, time of harvest, sugaring, control of fermentation, and aging. These factors vary from year to year, from region to region, and from variety to variety. But most enologists agree that climate has the greatest influence on wine quality. Solar radiation and the direction of exposure are important climatic components of wine quality. In cool years and regions, the

* K. Müller, "Weinjahre und Klimaschwankungen der letzten 1000 Jahr," *Der Weinbau.* Wissen. Beihefte 1 (1947): 83–103, 123–41.
† See E. L. Ladurie, *Times of Feast, Times of Famine: A History of Climate since the Year 1000*, trans. B. Bray (New York: Doubleday, 1970).

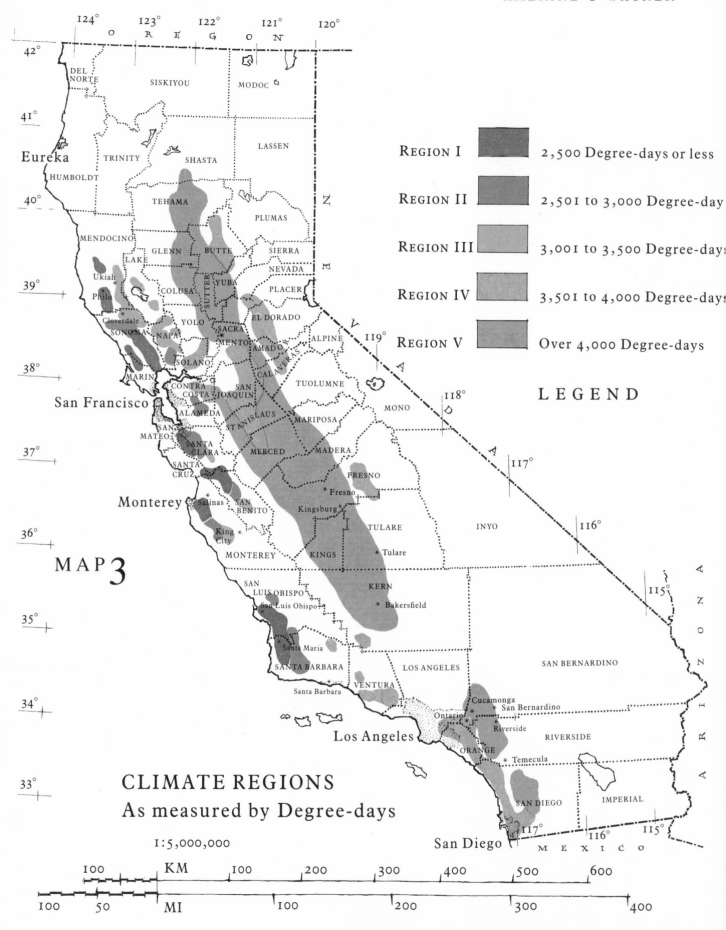

AMERINE & WAGNER

LEGEND

REGION I — 2,500 Degree-days or less
REGION II — 2,501 to 3,000 Degree-day
REGION III — 3,001 to 3,500 Degree-day
REGION IV — 3,501 to 4,000 Degree-day
REGION V — Over 4,000 Degree-days

MAP 3

CLIMATE REGIONS
As measured by Degree-days

1:5,000,000

100   KM   100   200   300   400   500   600

100   50   MI   100   200   300   400

MAP 3

CLIMATE REGIONS OF CALIFORNIA
AS MEASURED BY DEGREE-DAYS

The state's earliest commercial grape growers noted that during September and October grapes became far riper in California than in most European countries, an observation first documented in the 1880s by Eugene W. Hilgard of the California Agricultural Experiment Station. By the turn of the century, Hilgard's successor, Frederic T. Bioletti, was able to differentiate between the grape-growing areas of the interior valley and the coastal regions.

Vine growth starts at about 10° C (50° F). For the vine to flower, the average daily temperature must reach 17° to 20° C (63° to 68° F). In the 1920s, A. J. Winkler instituted state-wide studies using temperature summation—the total of average daily temperatures above 10° C during the growing season—as a factor influencing the composition of grapes at maturity. In the region of the least temperature summation, grapes ripened later and at a given sugar content had less acidity and color and a higher pH than in warmer regions. Winkler and M. A. Amerine later classified the grape-growing regions of California into five climate zones defined according to their heat summation, Region I being the coolest and Region V the warmest. The irregular shapes in five different colors represent the approximate configurations of the various climate zones; they include brush, hilly woodlands, pasture or non-vinous crops as well as grapes. That is, areas shown in color are not proportional to the actual acreage of grapes under cultivation.

radiation supply of the vineyard and the date of fruit set are especially critical. In the years of highest quality, the amount of radiation during ripening is more important to wine quality earlier rather than later in the season. It is also a matter of common observation that during the growing season climatic influences are more critical (and limiting) in areas of low temperatures than in warmer areas.

TEMPERATURE

Vine growth normally starts at about 10° C (50° F), though the temperature at which growth starts varies somewhat from one variety to another and from one year to another. In effect, temperature below 10° C (50° F) has little effect; it is temperatures above this that control the vegetative and fruiting habits of the vine.

Climate not only determines the date of the start of growth but also that of flowering. Average daily temperatures of 17°–20° C (63°–68° F) are necessary for flowering to occur. Again there are significant variations among varieties, regions, and years in the date and average temperature for the start of flowering.

The totaling of average daily temperatures above 10° C (50° F) over the whole of the growing season is called temperature summation. Each degree above 10° C is called a day-degree. For example, the average temperature on a given day in June might be 20° C (68° F). The accumulation of heat for that day is therefore 20 minus 10 or ten day-degrees in degrees Celsius, or 68 minus 50 or eighteen day-degrees in degrees Fahrenheit.★

Early in the viticultural history of California, it was observed that the climate was warmer than that of northern European winegrowing countries. The temperature summation data of A. J. Winkler show this clearly.† For instance, no California area had as low a heat summation as the German areas for which reports were obtained. Winkler's landmark paper gave mean monthly temperatures and heat accumulation above 10° C over the growing season for fifty-one grape-growing regions of the world. Temperature is the climatic factor of predominant importance to wine quality in California. The effects of other factors, such as rainfall, fog, humidity, and duration of sunshine are much more limited than that of heat.‡ Table 1

★ The concept is not a new one. E. Guyot and C. Godet, "Le climat et la vigne," *Landw. Jahrb. Schweiz.* 49 (1935): 17–20, gives reports on temperature summation for France and Switzerland from 1899; there is a good historical survey of papers on the subject going back to 1872 in P. Viala and P. Vermorel, *Traité générale de viticulture*, vol. 1 (Paris: Masson et cie., 1909).
† A. J. Winkler, "Temperature and Varietal Interrelations in Central-Western Europe and Algeria," *Wines & Vines* 17, no. 2 (1936): 4–5.
‡ A. J. Winkler, J. A. Cook, W. M. Kliewer, and L. A. Lider, *General Viticulture*, 2d ed. (Berkeley and Los Angeles: University of California Press, 1974). For recent temperature summations for many regions, including California, see D. Jackson and D. Schuster, *Grape-Growing and Winemaking* (Orinda, Calif.: Altarinda Books, 1981).

lists recent temperature summations during the growing season for major grape-growing districts of the world.

See TABLE 1
pp. 112–13

It has been shown that, for the same variety, the total acidity and amount of color in the skins was higher in the coolest regions of California than in the warmest regions. It has also been reported that the pH was lower and the time of harvest later at the same sugar content in the cool as compared with the warm regions. ★

On the basis of these observations, M. A. Amerine and A. J. Winkler classified California vineyards into five climatic regions. In Region I, the heat summation during the growing season was less than 1,389 degree-days calculated in degrees Celsius (2,500 in °F); in Region II, 1,390–1,667 (2,501–3,000 in °F); in Region III, 1,668–1,844 (3,001–3,500 in °F); in Region IV, 1,845–2,222 (3,501–4,000 in °F); and in Region V, 2,233 (4,001 in °F) or more.†

These climatic regions are shown in Maps 3 and 4. Region I includes the cooler parts of Mendocino, Sonoma, Lake, Napa, Alameda, Santa Clara, Santa Cruz, San Benito, and Monterey counties; Region II the warmer areas in the same counties, as well as San Luis Obispo and Santa Barbara counties; Region III the warmest areas in the same counties. Region IV is primarily the area from Merced through Yolo County in the Central Valley, as well as areas in San Bernardino and San Diego counties. Region V includes the northern and southern counties of the Central Valley, as well as the desert grape-growing areas of Riverside and Imperial counties. Amerine says:

See MAP 3
pp. 98–99
& MAP 4
pp. 102–3

The climatic conditions of the present regions merge from one into the other so the boundaries are not definite. Neither are the conditions uniform within a given region. Thus, these divisions should be considered as gross demarcations. It is to be hoped that refinements will be developed so as to delimit subregions within the present regions, thereby ensuring the greatest potential for quality when the most favorable climatic subregion for a given variety is planted to that variety. . . . Decades of careful observation will be required.

He adds, "I think we'll turn out to have no fewer than ten and possibly even fifteen climate zones in California."‡

A study in Baden found that the greater the daily heat summation above a temperature of only 5° C (41° F) and the more the hours of sunshine between

★   A. J. Winkler and M. A. Amerine, "Color in California Wines. II. Preliminary Comparisons of Certain Factors Influencing Color," *Food Res.* 3 (1938): 439–47; and Winkler et al., *General Viticulture*, 2d ed.

†   M. A. Amerine and A. J. Winkler, "Composition and Quality of Musts and Wines of California Grapes," *Hilgardia* 15 (1944): 493–675.

‡   M. A. Amerine, *The University of California and the State's Wine Industry* (Berkeley: Regional Oral History Office, Bancroft Library, 1972).

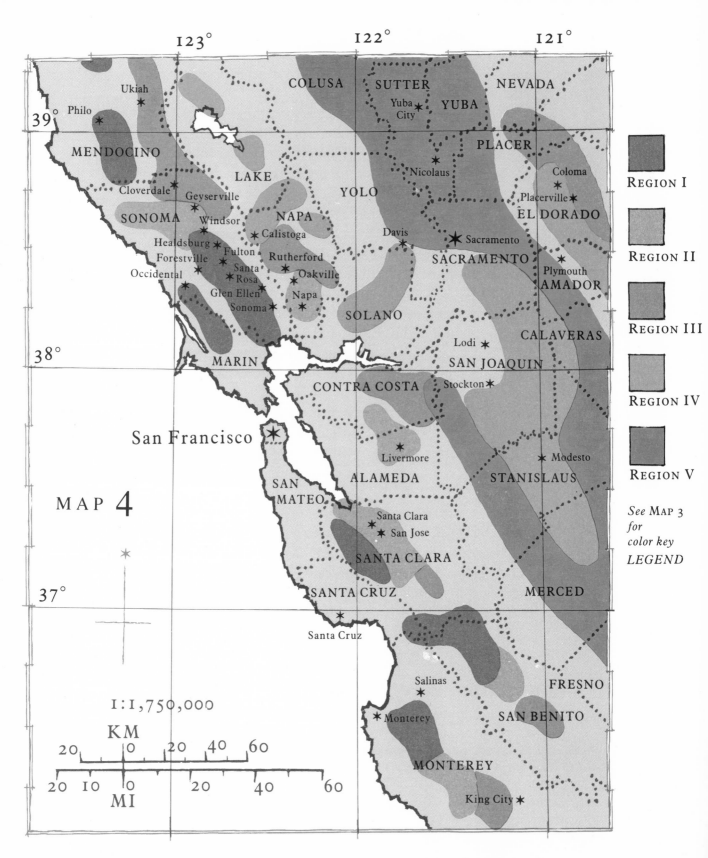

CLIMATE REGIONS: As measured by Degree-days

Detail: San Francisco Bay region

MAP **4**

1:25,000,000

CLIMATE REGIONS IN CALIFORNIA
AS MEASURED BY DEGREE-DAYS

DETAIL: SAN FRANCISCO BAY REGION

Most enologists agree that of the many influences on the quality of wine, climate is one of the most important. The grape-growing regions near San Francisco demonstrate how significantly access to ocean breezes affects the climate of California valleys, causing dramatic differences in temperature even within short distances.

In the Russian River Valley, the grape-growing areas nearest the Pacific Ocean are in Region I. Further up the valley, the zones change successively to Regions II and III and, near Ukiah, to Region IV. In the Napa Valley, the Carneros area nearest the San Francisco Bay is in Region I; from Oakville through St. Helena, Region II conditions prevail; and, finally, near Calistoga, a mere forty miles from the Carneros region, the climate zone is Region III. The Salinas Valley also illustrates these abrupt changes in climatic regions: near Salinas, Region I conditions exist; further south the conditions are those of Regions II and III; and past King City the climate is of Region IV. (The colored areas showing the climate zones are not proportional to the actual acreage planted to grapes.)

blooming and harvest, the higher the must sugar and the better the quality of the wines.★ The daily heat summation above 5° C (41° F) between budding-out and harvest gave nearly as good a correlation with quality as the seasonal heat summation. The total seasonal heat requirement for crop maturation also differed among varieties: Traminer, Sylvaner, and White Riesling required the most degree days, Müller-Thurgau the least, and Chasselas Doré (Gutedel), Ruländer (Pinot Gris), and Pinot Noir (Spätburgunder) were intermediate. Similar results can be expected in other regions with these and other varieties.

There is also a high degree of correlation between the seasonal temperature summation and both the mean temperature of the warmest month and the average temperature during the ripening period.† The degree of this correlation varies from region to region. Orffer suggests that under South African conditions using heat summation as a measure of grape maturity and quality does not apply too well where time of ripening and wine quality are concerned.‡ Why this should be, we do not know.

Not only is temperature summation important, but warm days and cool nights at the same heat summation have a favorable effect on the color of the berries. On the other hand, low night temperatures have been indicted for the excessive herbaceous aroma in the wine from varieties such as Cabernet Sauvignon and Sauvignon Blanc grown in such cool regions as the Loire Valley in France and the Salinas Valley in California.

Among the temperature data faithfully recorded—absolute monthly minimum, daily maximum, and daily minimum temperatures—only temperature summation during the growing period is highly significant to wine quality. Most viticulturists strongly recommend that the heat summation of new viticultural regions (preferably ten-year averages) be carefully determined before vines are planted.

SPECIFIC CLIMATIC AND GEOGRAPHIC EFFECTS

The climatic influence, as suggested, is likely to be more critical when grapes are grown in a region where climate is limiting—that is, in very cool regions. For the northern European vineyards, temperature is the limiting factor,§ so limiting on

★   H. Trenkle, "Die Vermendung phänologisch-klimatologischer Beobachtungen bei der Gütebervertung von Weinbergslagen," *Wein-Wissen.* 37 (1982): 327–38.
†   A. J. G. Pirie, "Comparison of the Climates of Selected Australian, French and Californian Wine Producing Regions," *Australian Grape Grower Winemaker*, no. 72 (1978): 73–74, 76, 78.
‡   C. J. Orffer, "The Effect of Time of Ripening on the Quality of the Wine in the South Western Cape," *Inter. Symp. Qual. Vint.*, Cape Town, 1977, pp. 291–99.
§   D. Pospišilová, "Ökologisch bedingt Veränderlichkeit der Weinrebsorten," *Wein-Wissen.* 33 (1978/79): 266–76; 34: 1–8, 143–50.

some occasions as to compel abandonment of viticulture, as it did with the onset of the mini–Ice Age about a thousand years ago. William the Conqueror's Domesday Book of 1085 lists thirty-eight vineyards in England, some as large as ten acres, and five that lasted for more than a century. Temperatures recently recorded in these locations were insufficient for viticulture.★ In marginal regions, early ripening varieties are more likely to produce satisfactorily and to survive as vines than late ripening varieties. Varietal differences in resistance to low winter temperatures are often linked with the length of growing season their crop may require. A. M. Negrul's classification of *Vitis* into subgroups or *proles* takes different ripening conditions into account.† The varying responses of different varieties to heat are especially apparent in a cool climate. Early-ripening varieties are not at their best in a long-season climate.

Do grafted vines differ from own-rooted vines in heat requirements? Some say yes for grape cluster weight and size but no for berry number, weight, and size. Berry number, weight, and size do vary with climatic conditions, as do leaf size and shoot length. Seed weight varies with local environmental conditions, but seed number and size are genetic factors less influenced by climate. This is the reason many ampelographers depend on seed size and shape in classifying closely related varieties of grapes.

REGIONAL EFFECTS

In the warmer districts, grapes at the same degree of sugar have less total acid and a higher pH. They also ripen earlier and have less color than grapes grown in cooler conditions. Note especially the very low color of grapes grown in Region V compared to Regions I and II. Some varieties, notably Grenache, can only be used for producing a rosé wine when grown in the warmer regions but will have sufficient pigment to produce a red wine in the cooler regions. It has also been observed in California that high temperatures late in the season result in particularly low-acid and high-pH musts. The warmer regions, IV and V, are more than 50 percent warmer (based on heat summation above 10° C [50° F]) during the growing season than the cooler regions, I and II. The level of total acidity changes at varying rates for different varieties and in different climatic regions. It is noteworthy that the total acidity of the musts of grapes grown in Region I is 50 percent or more higher than that in Region IV or V.‡

★   H. H. Lamb, *The Changing Climate* (London: Methuen, 1966).
†   A. M. Negrul, "On the Origin and Breeding of Grapes on a Genetic Basis," in *N. I. Vavilov and Agricultural Science* (Moscow: "Kolos" Press, 1969).
‡   M. A. Amerine and M. A. Joslyn, *Table Wines: The Technology of Their Production*, 2d ed. (Berkeley and Los Angeles: University of California Press, 1970).

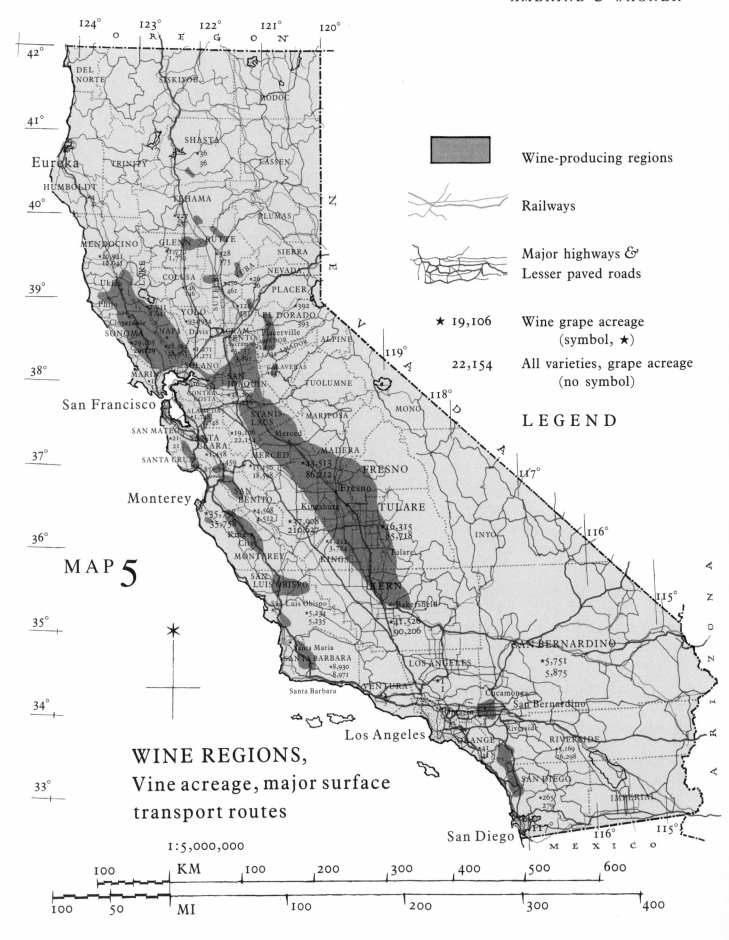

124° 123° 122° 121° 120°

OREGON

42°

41°

40°

39°

38°

37°

36°

35°

34°

33°

NEVADA

119°

118°

117°

116°

115°

ARIZONA

DEL NORTE

SISKIYOU

MODOC

Eureka

SHASTA

LASSEN

HUMBOLDT

TRINITY

★4

TEHAMA

PLUMAS

★227
287

MENDOCINO

GLENN

BUTTE

SIERRA

★10,941
10,941

★3,570
1,775

★828
775

Ukiah

COLUSA

YUBA

NEVADA

★26
76

Philo
★2,941
2,941

★146
116

★450
461

PLACER

LAKE

SUTTER

★128
131

★392

Cloverdale

YOLO

EL DORADO

★934/914

SONOMA

NAPA

Davis

SACRAM-
ENTO

Placerville

393

ALPINE

★29,105
29,129

★28,361
28,363

★1,271
1,271

Sucram to

AMADOR

★1,030

★36
36

SOLANO

MARIN

CONTRA
COSTA

★38,200
38,220

SAN
JOAQUIN

AMADOR

3,891

CALAVERAS

TUOLUMNE

MARIPOSA

MONO

San Francisco

ALAMEDA

★1,718
1,748

SAN MATEO

★21
21

SANTA
CLARA

★19,106
22,154

Merced

STANIS
LAUS

MADERA

SANTA CRUZ

★1,458
1,459

★87

MERCED

★43,513
86,212

FRESNO

Monterey

★35,758
35,758

SAN
BENITO

★15,456
18,598

★4,568
4,512

Fresno

Kingsburg

★37,908
210,627

TULARE

King
City

MONTEREY

★1,212
3,724

KINGS

★16,315
85,718

INYO

Tulare

SAN
LUIS OBISPO

KERN

Bakersfield

San Luis Obispo

★5,234
5,235

★41,526
90,206

SAN BERNARDINO

Santa Maria

★5,751
5,875

SANTA BARBARA

★8,930
8,971

LOS ANGELES

Cucamonga

San Bernardino

Santa Barbara

VENTURA

★1
1

Ontario

Riverside

RIVERSIDE

Los Angeles

ORANGE

★41

★3,169
16,298

San Diego

SAN DIEGO

IMPERIAL

★265
279

117°

116°

115°

MEXICO

MAP 5

WINE REGIONS,
Vine acreage, major surface
transport routes

1:5,000,000

100   KM   100   200   300   400   500   600

100   50   MI   100   200   300   400

LEGEND

�	Wine-producing regions
～	Railways
～	Major highways & Lesser paved roads
★ 19,106	Wine grape acreage (symbol, ★)
22,154	All varieties, grape acreage (no symbol)

MAP 5

1:90,000,000

WINE REGIONS OF CALIFORNIA, VINE ACREAGES BY COUNTY, & THE NETWORK OF SURFACE TRANSPORT

Since its early history, when Los Angeles was the state's wine-growing center and San Francisco its commercial outlet, the wine industry of California has depended for its development on satisfactory means of transport. The rivers and ports, roads and railroads of the state have all served to get California grapes to the wineries and wines to the markets. The major rivers, the Sacramento and the San Joaquin, and their tributaries drain the Central Valley; there is a workable network of numerous smaller rivers from the coast ranges to the Pacific Ocean. Liners call at the major ports of Stockton, Oakland, San Francisco, and Wilmington. In modern times, a significant amount of wine shipping depends on vast fleets of trucks—many wineries, individually or in groups, run their own trucking businesses—and on railroads. Rail spurs go directly to the loading docks of a large number of wineries.

Besides major cities, the map identifies places of historical or current relevance to the California wine industry.

The vine acreage by county shown on this map has been taken from the California Grape Acreage Report *prepared by the California Crop and Livestock Reporting Service in May 1983. These statistics show that 363,496 acres have been devoted to growing wine grapes, over 49 percent of the total 738,549 acres devoted to grape growing in California.*

FRUITFULNESS

It is well known that the number of fruitful flowers (primordia) that develop in the bud the previous growing season is influenced by environmental conditions. More flower primordia are formed at 35° C (95° F) than at 20° C (68° F). In contrast, vegetative growth falls off at higher temperatures. Grape varieties differ in their performance at low temperatures: White Riesling is reasonably fruitful after three months at 20° C (68° F), whereas Muscat of Alexandria and Thompson Seedless produce few fruitful buds at the same temperature.

Light is necessary for the initiation of the flower primordia in the bud during the period of normal development, late spring to early summer. Shading experiments reduce the number of flower buds initiated. Again varieties differ: White Riesling and Muscat of Alexandria are unfruitful at low intensities of light and fruitful at moderate intensities; Syrah (Shiraz) is only fruitful when light intensities are high. Length of day per se does not seem to have much effect on fruitfulness although the increased quantity of light on long days does promote it. Some studies suggest that a subtle factor such as the rate of change of the length of day may regulate fruit bud initiation.* No good data seem to be available on the effect of water deficiency on fruitfulness. If there is one, in most cases it may be to reduce fruit bud initiation. Excess moisture may have a similar effect.

FLOWERING

Cool and humid conditions during blooming may result in unsatisfactory fruit set. Viticulturists distinguish a condition where few berries are formed (called *coulure* in France). Likewise, berries may be formed but develop only into small green fruit (called *millerandage* in France). In both cases, there is a loss in crop. In the second, the musts will be abnormally high in acid if the green berries are crushed, with a serious reduction in the quality of the resulting wine.

SECONDARY EFFECTS OF CLIMATE

FROSTS

In one region of Michigan, spring frosts caused substantial crop reduction in eleven of the twenty-one years from 1957 to 1977.† The actual danger point varies considerably with species and variety; dew point and surface moisture; pre-freeze environmental conditions; stage of bud development; and the various

---

* M. S. Buttrose, "Climatic Factors and Fruitfulness in Grapevines," *Hort. Abst.* 44 (1974): 319–26.
† D. E. Johnson and G. S. Howell, "Factors Influencing Critical Temperatures for Spring Freeze Damage to Developing Primary Shoots on Concord Grapevines," *Am. J. Enol. Vitic.* 32 (1981): 144–49.

factors influencing ice formation (nucleation), such as duration of exposure, exposure temperature, and supercooling; and ice formation due to the presence of bacteria and the ability of ice to seal the tissue. For Concord grapes $-5.7°$ C ($19.8°$ F) to $-3.1°$ C ($26.4°$ F) is the danger level for wet buds.

When ambient temperatures fall below about $-2°$ C ($28.4°$ F), growing shoots are partially or completely killed. Also, much depends on the timing of the frost. Most grape buds contain secondary and tertiary flower primordia as well as the primary one. If a secondary shoot has not already started growth from the bud, it may develop and replace the killed primary shoot and, in some cases, produce some fruit. However, only certain varieties have sufficiently fruitful secondaries for this. The ability to produce a second crop, as frost insurance, is a trait sought after in breeding new grape varieties.

In a few areas, early fall frosts endanger the vine and its fruit. They may cause premature defoliation and prevent proper ripening of both fruit and wood. In some areas (the Yakima Valley of Washington, for example), an early fall freeze may kill vigorously growing young vines. As a countermeasure, withholding irrigation water in the late summer encourages early dormancy and, since dormant vines are more resistant to low temperature, the hope is that this may reduce the damage from early fall frosts.

Many viticultural areas are occasionally subject to damage from frosts during blooming. Areas near lakes and rivers are less frosty. The immense Central Valley of California seldom suffers from frosts. In contrast, the coastal valleys, particularly the vineyards on the valley floors (compared to those on the upper slopes) may suffer serious frost damage from time to time. Since the vineyards in these areas produce fruit with a high monetary value, it is worthwhile to provide some form of frost protection.

Where irrigation water is available, flooding the vineyard may help maintain the temperature above the danger point. Burning oil in smudge pots has been widely used to raise vineyard temperature. The practice is of doubtful value since the particulate matter of smudge smoke is no barrier to heat radiation. The smudge pots are placed on the side of the vineyard from which the prevailing wind blows. Environmentalists object to the method because the black smoke contaminates the air.

Valley vineyards particularly suffer because of temperature inversion: the coldest air collects in the vineyards on the valley floor as warm air radiates upward. By use of windmills, it is possible to mix the warmer air from ten to twenty meters above the ground with the cold surface air and thus sometimes keep the temperature of the vineyard above the danger point. Public weather warnings are provided by radio, so the windmills need only operate when dangerously low temperatures are forecast. Windmills are expensive, as is their operation, and they are useless except when the temperature differential is marginal. But if one saves 50 percent of the crop (say two to three tons per acre) and grapes are worth $500 per ton, the saving is obviously worth the cost. Unfortunately windmills are noisy, and neighbors may (and do) complain. Some vineyards, particularly in Germany and California, have sprinkler systems, which are turned on before the temperature drops to freezing. At 0° C, the water freezes on the growing shoots and forms a protective layer that is effective even if the ambient temperature drops to −2° C or lower.

Some protection against frosts comes from delaying pruning as late as possible (about one week) before vine growth starts. The delay in bud burst (*débourrement*) reduces the risk of frost damage to the new growth. However, a vineyardist with fifty or more acres cannot afford to delay pruning too long if he is to finish the whole vineyard before shoot growth starts. A common practice is to do rough pruning first and come back for final pruning as late as possible. When fall frosts occur with the fruit still on the vine, the resulting wines may have a "frost" aroma. This peculiar odor has been blamed on a higher phenol content.★ Frosts that occur before the vine goes dormant also cause the leaves to drop, which stops photosynthetic activity and prevents normal ripening. In some cases, as with very young vines, they may kill the most tender growth.

WINTER KILLING

In California's vineyard regions, as in the Mediterranean basin, winter killing of vines is not a problem. The same cannot be said of classical winegrowing areas in parts of the temperate zone such as central and eastern Europe or, for that matter, Germany, parts of France, and much of the eastern United States. When mean winter temperatures fall below −3.6° C (25° F), there is danger of killing the dormant tissues of *Vitis vinifera* vines. Depending on the severity of the low temperature, this may mean killing of buds, partial or complete killing back of dormant canes, damage to the trunk by splitting (which opens the way to subsequent infection), killing to the ground (which raises a special problem because renewal shoots from the ground level will be of the rootstock rather than of the scion variety in the case of grafted vines), or, finally, complete destruction of the vine, roots and all. This is more likely to occur when dormancy has been disturbed by a mild spell followed by a deep freeze. As insurance against these annual hazards, it is customary in central Europe and Russia to bend down and bury all, or most of, the dormant canes of the vine. An alternative is to develop multiple trunks in the hope that at least one will survive. Yet another is to bury a single sucker cane, originating at, or close to,

★   K. Wucherpfennig and G. Bretthauer, "Zur Verarbeitung von 'Frosttrauben' zu Wein unter besonderer Berücksichtigung der fluchtigen aromastoffe," *Wein-Wissen.* 223 (1968): 174–85.

ground level. This can then be lifted to form a new trunk in case of need, or otherwise pruned off in the spring. In North America east of the Rockies, the hazard of winter damage is compounded by the usual extremes of a continental climate plus the broad sweep of exposure to frigid Arctic air masses when they move south and southeast, which occurs frequently. Barriers of elevation between the Rio Grande and the North Pole that might divert such air flow are negligible. For the vinifera species, this is alien land. It is what accounts for the development by natural selection of much hardier species in North America, such as *Vitis riparia*, *Vitis labrusca*, *Vitis rupestris*, *Vitis lincecumii*, *Vitis berlandieri*, and so on. By themselves they are valueless for wine, but they have great worth as rootstocks and as breeding material for new and hardier varieties.

HAIL

Hail is rare in California and only a few cases of serious damage are known. For example, Mendocino County had appreciable hail damage in 1982. In Switzerland and parts of France (particularly Beaujolais and Sauternes), hail has on occasion caused severe, but localized, damage. If it occurs early in the season, damage to fruit usually heals over. If it occurs during ripening, the result can be ruinous. If hail breaks off the growing shoots and their clusters, as it sometimes does, the crop for the current year is lost. The need to retrain the vine not only involves a reduction of the following year's crop but also may require substantial labor.

WIND

Cold air streams are an important climatic factor delaying ripening grapes grown in cold conditions. At higher elevations above the valley floor, where cold air streams mainly occur, must acidity is higher than at lower elevations. Everybody familiar with central California's heat knows the favorable effect of cool afternoon winds in reducing the temperature (and, of course, producing a lower average daily temperature). When the vine's shoots are one to two meters long, very high winds may break them off, resulting in significant loss in crop. Where such winds occur, the canes have to be especially firmly tied up. In areas of daily high wind (as in the Salinas Valley of California) photosynthetic activity is reduced because of stomatal closure.* This, of course, slows down ripening and delays the date of harvest, sometimes disastrously.

RAINFALL AND HUMIDITY

In regions with summer-fall rainfall, which is to say in four-season climates (France, Germany, Hungary, the United States east of the Rockies),

---

* B. M. Freeman, W. M. Kliewer, and P. Stern, "Influence of Windbreaks and Climatic Region on Diurnal Fluctuation of Leaf Water Potential, Stomatal Conductance, and Leaf Temperature of Grapevines," *Amer. J. Enol. Vitic.* 33 (1982): 233–36.

TABLE **I**

SEASONAL HEAT SUMMATIONS

FOR MAJOR GRAPE-GROWING DISTRICTS OF THE WORLD

HEAT UNITS IN GROWING SEASON

	In Degree-Days CELSIUS *10° base*	In Degree-Days FAHRENHEIT *50° base*
FRANCE		
Chablis	950	1,710
Loire	950–1,100	1,710–1,980
Champagne	1,050	1,890
Beaujolais	1,150	2,070
Côte d'Or	1,180	2,120
Alsace	1,230	2,210
Médoc	1,350–1,400	2,430–2,520
Hermitage	1,450	2,610
GERMANY		
Mosel-Saar-Ruwer	950–1,150	1,710–2,070
Baden	1,050	1,890
Rheinhessen	1,050–1,100	1,890–2,070
Rheingau	1,050–1,200	1,890–2,160
Rheinpfalz	1,200–1,250	2,160–2,250
CALIFORNIA		
Monterey	1,200–1,300	2,160–2,340
Santa Clara	1,250–1,300	2,250–2,340
Livermore Valley	1,250–1,400	2,250–2,520
Napa	1,300–1,450	2,340–2,610
Sonoma	1,200*–2,000†	2,160*–3,600†

In Sonoma.

†*In the upper Russian River Valley.*

TABLE I *concluded*

HEAT UNITS IN GROWING SEASON

	In Degree-Days CELSIUS 10°*base*	In Degree-Days FAHRENHEIT 50° *base*
CHILE		
Maipo Valley	1,350–1,400	2,430–2,520
SOUTH AFRICA		
Tulbagh	1,150–1,250	2,070–2,200
Stellenbosch	1,300–1,400	2,340–2,520
Paarl	1,400–1,450	2,520–2,610
NEW ZEALAND		
Canterbury	900–1,100	1,620–1,980
Gisborne	1,250–1,300	2,250–2,340
Auckland	1,300–1,350	2,340–2,430
AUSTRALIA		
Coonawarra	1,150–1,250	2,070–2,250
McLaren Vale	1,300–1,400	2,340–2,520

SOURCE: Jackson and Schuster, *Grape-Growing and Winemaking.*

NOTE: *Grapes normally start growth when the average daily temperature reaches 50°F (10°C). The summation of the average daily temperature above 50°F is the effective temperature influencing vine growth and the composition of the fruit. The heat summation for the growing season (about April 1 to October) is called the degree-days. Obviously, the higher the heat summation, the warmer the climate. To calculate the degree-days, subtract 50 (for Fahrenheit) or 10 (for Celsius) from the average daily temperature for each day of the growing season and summate. Cool regions have a heat summation of 1,700 to 2,000 degree-days (using °Fahrenheit) or 950 to 1,200 (using °Celsius). Very warm regions have heat summations as high as 5,000 degree-days (using °Fahrenheit).*

another variable is introduced. It is obvious that sunlight is restricted on cloudy days (less heat summation). Other factors being equal, this results in lower sugars and pH and higher total acidities in the musts. On the other hand, it seems to improve pigmentation. In regions such as these, the rainfall during the growing season can vary widely. East of the Mississippi the vintage coincides with the tropical hurricane season. Ten or more centimeters (4 inches or more) have been known to fall the day before picking was planned to begin. There are also exceptional conditions in normally rainless regions. In the North Coast area of California as much as 5 cm (2 inches) in July and 20 cm (8 inches) in early October have fallen. In 1982 from 2.5 to 7.5 cm (1 to 3 inches) were recorded in the grape-growing areas before 8 October. July rainfall has little impact on the quality of the crop, but October rainfall can be very harmful: lower sugars (not only from water in the cluster but also from that imbibed into the fruit), delayed maturing (lack of heat), delay in harvesting (during the rain and after it because water standing in the vineyard makes the use of trucks or tractors difficult or impossible). The growth of mold and rot increases and quality is reduced. Although at the present time the problem of early and excessive growth of the parasitic mold *Botrytis cinerea* is arguably the major viticultural problem of Europe, under the dry climatic conditions of California it is seldom a major consideration, except in the coastal areas. However, even in California, growth of botrytis at bloom-time has caused some dropping of flowers. Modern fungicides have helped prevent the worst ravages but have not eliminated botrytis as a major viticultural problem in the cool, wet years.

California's relative freedom from rainfall and excessive humidity during the growing season is the reverse of the situation in most of the United States east of the Great Plains. This, together with the problem of freeze damage, which has already been discussed, has frustrated repeated efforts to grow the *Vitis vinifera* grapes of Europe that go back to the earliest colonial years. There has lately been a renewal of efforts to adapt vinifera to these inhospitable regions of high summer-fall precipitation and humidity and extremes of temperature. It may still turn out that there are limited areas in the eastern United States where vinifera will survive and produce with sufficient regularity—helped, of course, by the new fungicides, insecticides, nematocides, other soil fumigants, and herbicides. The existence of such miniclimates is not yet fully demonstrated, though there have been limited successes here and there. If such miniclimates do eventually prove out, it would not be stretching things too far to compare them with the refuges that brought *Vitis* through the Ice Age. The difficulties created by abundant rainfall and humidity in the growing season, together with winter damage, also motivate contemporary efforts in Germany and other European winegrowing countries, as well as in the United States, to improve the disease resistance and winter hardiness of vinifera by hybridization and clonal selection.

Returning to the specific problem of botrytis, if the high humidity occurs after the fruit starts to ripen, its effects can be beneficial. For botrytis to get well started, the relative humidity must be above about 93 percent for twenty-four hours. This allows the fungus to infect the fruit uniformly. The growth of the fungus loosens the skin and, if warm, dry conditions follow, the berries shrivel and high-sugar musts result. This phenomenon is called *pourriture noble* in France, noble rot in English. The sweet table wines of Germany and the Loire and the Sauternes of France are the result of this symbiosis of climate and mold. In some years recently in California, especially in the Salinas Valley, a number of such sweet table wines, called "Late Harvest," have been produced.

CLOUDINESS

Cloud, fog, haze, and smog during daylight hours reduce solar radiation and result in lower temperatures and reduced daily heat summation. Whether this has a favorable or unfavorable effect on must and wine quality depends on whether it is a warm or cool region or season—that is, on whether there has been too much or too little heat summation for normal ripening.

MICROFLORA

It is obvious that rainfall may wash off yeasts, bacteria, and other microorganisms. With moist, warm conditions, undesirable microflora may develop. According to a recent study, the yeast population on the grapes at harvest in a cool season was much lower than normal. Lactic acid bacteria were absent, and few acetic acid bacteria were found. However, grapes attacked by *Botrytis cinerea* had much more mold.*

Variation in the distribution of yeasts and other microorganisms has been reported from many areas. One study notes that wild types of yeasts (*Kloeckera* sp.) are dominant in warm, dry years, whereas *Hanseniaspora* sp. yeasts are prevalent in cool, humid years. We believe these variations in the microflora do not have a major effect on wine quality. They may, however, have minor effects, which may influence nuances of flavor. Unfortunately, no data are available for California.

EXCESSIVE HEAT

Temporary excessively hot conditions early in the season may be harmful to the vine and hence to the fruit. During ripening, such conditions may have disastrous effects. The maximum temperature the vine can withstand without harmful effect is about 40° C (104° F), but this differs somewhat with the variety, the duration of the high temperature, the moisture in the soil, and other factors. Shriveling and, eventually, raisining occur if the high temperature continues.

---

*   S. Lafon-Lafourcade and A. Joyeux, "Les bactéries acétiques du vin," *Bull. Office Intern. Vigne Vin* 54 (1981): 803–29.

CALIFORNIA'S CLIMATE

See MAP 2
pp. 94–95
& MAP 5
pp. 106–7

Few areas of its size have so many climatic regions as California, ranging from very hot deserts to permanently snow-covered mountains. The grape-growing regions have a primarily Mediterranean type of climate. The Pacific Ocean and the partial barrier of the Coast Range, with advantageously placed gaps running through it on the west, and the towering Sierra Nevada to the east have profound effects on the climate of the grape-growing regions in between.

Along the coast itself, the climate is so cool that grape growing is out of the question, generally speaking. The absence of vines on that unforgettable drive down U.S. Highway 1—from Eureka in the north through San Francisco and along the peninsula to Santa Cruz—is enough to confirm this. Along the northern half of that windswept, fog-bound coast one might as well be in the Scottish Hebrides, which are known to be inhospitable to grapevines.

The keys to most of viticultural California—the distribution of the principal regions and their differences—are those gaps through the coastal ranges. Through them the rivers of the interior find their way to the ocean and the tempering effect of the cool maritime climate finds its way inward to make viticulture possible. Take the Russian River as an example. The Sonoma Valley is its watershed. The river flows southward behind the first coastal mountains, then turns abruptly west and reaches the ocean through a gap some fifty miles north of San Francisco. At the mouth of the river, the temperature summation does not even qualify it for Region I. About fifteen miles inland, where the summation is that of Region I, excellent wines are made; a further twenty miles up the river, where it comes down from the north, it is Region II; and at Ukiah, sixty miles from the Pacific Ocean, the tempering influence of the ocean has spent itself, resulting in the hot-country viticulture of Region IV, at least on the valley floor. Some culs-de-sac in the Coast Range have cooler temperatures.

The Napa Valley is an even more dramatic illustration of this interplay of maritime and interior climates. This picture-book valley is well defined on each side by mountains, the much loftier Mount St. Helena closing it in at the top, and an arm of San Francisco Bay at the bottom. By contrast, the Sonoma Valley is too large and spread out to be easily summed up. The Napa Valley is drained by the Napa River, which empties into the Bay. The Carneros district, nearest the Bay, is in Region I. Oakville, twenty miles up-valley, is in Region II. Calistoga, thirty miles from the Bay at the northern end, has Region III conditions.

The great valleys of the Sacramento and San Joaquin rivers, together composing the vast Central Valley, illustrate the influence of the Pacific winds in yet another way. The prevailing afternoon wind comes in from the San Francisco Bay through the Carquinez Strait and over the lower coastal mountains. The Lodi-Stockton-Modesto area, including the delta formed by the junction of the Sacramento River draining the northern Sierra Nevada, and the San Joaquin River drain-

116

ing the southern, receives the cool maritime breeze first and consequently has the lowest heat summation (Regions III–IV). The northern and southern extremes of this huge heat-collecting basin (Redding at the northern end and Bakersfield at the southern) get much less of the cooling breeze and have much higher heat summation (Region V). A fourth such gap through the Coast Range is provided where the Salinas River, flowing north along the eastern side of these mountains, finally empties into Monterey Bay. Here again we have that familiar sequence of heat summations: the coolest part lying immediately in from Monterey Bay and the summation of heat increasing as one travels south up the valley.

The Sierra Nevada slopes from 1,000 meters up have a short growing season and are subject to late spring and early fall frosts; permanent viticulture is not possible. Finally, the deserts are too dry and hot for table wine grapes, though where irrigation is possible, as in the Coachella and Imperial valleys, they are often used for growing early-ripening table grapes.

SEASONAL CONDITIONS

After Repeal the California wine industry advertised "every year a vintage year in California." If this means that grapes reach maturity every year, it is nearly always true. There have been cool years in the coolest areas when grapes did not ripen sufficiently for table wines. It is now recognized that there are significant differences in the composition and quality of wines produced from a single vineyard and grape variety from one year to the next. The best illustration comes from a detailed report on the 1935 and 1936 seasons. In 1935 St. Helena (Region II) had 1,265 (2,276 in °F) degree-days, while in 1936 it had 1,480 (2,664 in °F). Statewide, grapes ripened nine days earlier in 1936, had a 0.9° higher sugar, 0.11 percent less acid, and about 15 percent less color. There was also an *apparently* greater yield of alcohol from the same measured must-sugar content because of the shriveling, even raisining, of the berries in 1936. The juice of the freshly crushed grapes used for measuring the must-sugar content came from the more swollen, less ripe berries. During fermentation the sugar from the shriveled and raisined fruit dissolved and fermented, which gave the apparently higher yield of alcohol (based on original must-sugar). With some varieties, Zinfandel for example, this occurs in many years. Differences in the amino acid content of grapes are known to occur in warm and cool years, but it is not known whether amino acid content is related to wine quality.

GRAPE DISEASES

The relation of grape diseases to climate and geography is a complicated one. It is well known that some rots and molds develop better in grapes at high temperatures than at low ones and vice versa. Cold, wet vineyard conditions, for example, favor the development of collar rot. In areas with winter freezing, where the trunks or arms of the vine may crack, black knot or crown gall can be serious. Summer bunch rot, rhizopus rot, and black-mold rot are problems in California, primarily in the warm San Joaquin Valley. Blue-mold rot, on the other hand, grows well under cool, humid conditions. Downy mildew, anthracnose, and black rot, serious problems in the eastern United States and Europe, are not known in California. Powdery mildew, which cool weather favors, is the most troublesome fungous disease of grapes in California.

GEOGRAPHIC AND SOIL CONDITIONS

Over and above climatic variables, there may be specific geographical conditions that influence grape maturity and wine quality. Soil temperature varies with solar radiation, moisture content, and soil structure and content. This inevitably influences vine growth, including the time of budding out. Excessive dryness in the soil is unfavorable to the maturity of wine grapes and the quality of the wines produced. Even in a cool, but dry, year, soils may have too low a moisture content—for example, 1974 in Germany.[*] Soils that retain adequate moisture generally produce better wines. Excessive soil water results in reduced sugar and higher fixed acids, but the climatic conditions need to be taken into account. Excessive soil moisture is less likely to have deleterious effects on grape and wine quality if not prolonged. In the case of poorly drained soils with an impermeable subsurface layer (at 0.5 to 1 meter in parts of California), excess soil moisture is surely undesirable. Gypsum and cover crops have improved the water permeability of such soils. Grapes in hot, dry regions, of course, require very large amounts of water, and irrigation is necessary. Its influence on grape composition and wine quality has been vociferously debated. European enologists often claim irrigation harms wine quality, forgetting that most of their vineyards receive summer and fall rainfall. Too much or too little water is doubtless harmful. Most viticulturists recommend irrigation only when there is a shortage of soil moisture and when, as in many areas of California, the necessary rainfall cannot be expected.

In valley-floor vineyards, excess water storage capacity can have an influence on must and wine composition. In hillside vineyards, elevation and water supply, which is sometimes deficient, as well as heat radiation are factors. The color and texture of soil surely have an influence on vine growth, probably mainly a temperature effect. In such marginal climatic areas as Germany, seemingly minor influences such as altitude, slope, and orientation may have a decisive effect on must and wine quality. Vine row direction to secure maximum radiation can be important.

Many popular commentators and almost all vineyard owners attribute some magical property to vineyard soils. As indicated in the preceding sections, there are differences between regions and localized areas (exposure, valley floor versus hillsides, and so forth). Some of these differences are due to variations in temperature, some perhaps also to moisture (and thus related to soil temperature),

[*]   D. Hoppmann and K. Schaller, "Der Einfluss verschiedener Standortfaktoren auf Qualität und Quantität der Reben," parts 1 and 2, *Wein-Wissen.* 35 (1980): 299–319, 371–77.

soil microorganisms, and vineyard and enological practices. How many of the differences are due purely to soil factors has not, to our satisfaction, been scientifically determined. Skeptics have observed that many a vineyard in Europe that is noted for the quality of its wine embraces more than one soil type. In Europe, but not to our knowledge in the United States, the humus content of the soil is reported to influence grape maturity favorably.

GRAPE DISEASES RELATED TO GEOGRAPHY

Nitrogen deficiency and excess both exist in local areas in California. The former results in weak growth and lower production, the latter in excessive growth and reduced crop. Application of nitrogen is useful in local areas but should be controlled by analysis of the vine tissues. A number of vineyards in California suffer from excess salinity, others from excess alkali. Vines in such areas are usually small and produce poor crops. In both cases, it is necessary to remove the excess, usually by drainage and leaching and, in the case of alkali, by applying gypsum, lime, or sulfur. Potassium deficiency is another condition that has been reported in grapes in California. Fading of leaf color and marginal leaf burning, weak growth, and uneven ripening are some of the symptoms. Very sandy soils that have been scraped in land-leveling operations are prone to this deficiency. Zinc deficiency has also been found in grapes in a number of local areas in California, and boron is a problem to growers when it is excessive or deficient. The latter may derive from the soil or from irrigation water with a high boron content. Only a few cases of magnesium deficiency have been reported. Iron deficiency, common in calcareous soils in other parts of the world, is rare in California.

OTHER SOIL PROBLEMS

In many areas of California, soil nematodes are a threat to establishing and maintaining a vineyard. To reduce and possibly eliminate them, soil fumigation, usually with methyl bromide, has been used. Many vineyardists prefer to remove the nematode-infested vines and allow the soil to lie fallow for one or two years before fumigating. Phylloxera-infested vineyards also exist in many areas of California (Sonoma, Napa, and elsewhere). In these areas, vines on phylloxera-resistant rootstocks are planted. Phylloxera can be eliminated by use of carbon bisulfide, but it is too expensive for large areas.

Soil compaction from the use of heavy tractors and harvesters may be a problem in some areas. An impervious subsoil layer (hardpan) occurs in some San Joaquin vineyards, which can be broken up by subsoiling (deep cultivation) with special equipment. Finally, weeds in the vineyard need to be controlled, if for no other reason than their use of moisture and soil nutrients. Moreover, a few species of weeds have undesirable flavors if any of the vegetative parts get into the harvested fruit. Frequent cultivation and herbicides are used to control weeds, but care is needed not to use herbicides that will interfere with fermentation or the wine's flavor.

BIBLIOGRAPHIC NOTE

In addition to the works cited in the footnotes and Bibliography, this study has drawn on the following materials: N. J. Becker, "Vergleich verschiedener Methoden zur Beurteilung kleinklimatischer Warmeuntershiede an Rebstandorten," *Wein-Wissen.* 24 (1972): 105–12; D. Boubals, "Pour la nouvelle émigration viticole; comment aborder la création de nouveaux vignobles hors d'Europe," *Progr. Agric. Vitic.* 99 (1982): 253–57; C. E. P. Brooks, *Climate Through the Ages*, 2d ed. (New York: Dover, 1949); C. Flanzy and C. Poux, "Note sur la teneur en acides aminés du moût de raisin et du vin en fonction des conditions de l'année (maturation et fermentation)," *Ann. Technol. Agr.* 14 (1965): 87–91; A. G. Freitas and A. Machado Gracio, "Caractéristiques bioclimatiques des cépages et vignobles," *Bull. Office Inter. Vigne Vin* 44 (487) (1971): 796–826; M. Geiger, "Der Einfluss von Kaltluftströmen auf den Ertrag von Reben," *Wein-Wissen.* 30 (1975): 129–43; J.-P. Le-Grand, "L'expression de la vigne au travers du climat depuis le moyen âge," *Rev. Franç. Œnol.* 16 (75) (1979): 23–50; L. Levadoux, "La sélection et l'hybridation chez la vigne," *Annales École Nationale d'Agriculture* 28 (1950): 165–358. L. Levadoux, "Les populations sauvages et cultivées de *Vitis vinifera L.*," *Annales Amel. Plantes* 1 (1956): 59–113; L. Müller, "Rapport entre la qualité du vin produit, le cépage et l'environnement," *Bull. Office Intern. Vigne Vin* 55 (1982): 97–107; A. M. Negrul, *Voprosy proiskhozhdeniia i selektsii vinograda na geneticheskoi osnove* [Problems of grape origin and selection according to genetic principles], in *N. I. Vavilov i sel'skokhoziaistvennaia nauka* [N. I. Vavilov and agricultural science], ed. D. D. Breshnev et al. (Moscow: Kolo, 1969), pp. 323–39; A. Poulard and M. Lecocq, "Écologie et biogéographie des levures apiculées dans les vignobles français," *Rev. Franç. Œnol.* 17 (82) (1981): 31–35; J. A. Prescott, "The Climatology of the Vine (*Vitis vinifera L.*). The Cool Limits of Cultivation," *Trans. Roy. Soc. South Australia* 89 (1965): 5–23, and "A Comparison of France and Australia on the Basis of the Temperature of the Warmest Month," *Trans. Roy. Soc. South Australia* 93 (1969): 7–15; R. A. Preston-Whyte, "Climatic Classification of South Africa: A Multivariate Approach," *S.A. Geogr. J.* 56 (1974): 79–86; W. F. Reinig, *Die Holarktis: Ein Beitrag zur diluvialen und alluvialen Geschichte der zirkumpolaren Faunen-und-Florengebiete* (Jena: Fischer, 1937); M. Rives, "Les origines de la vigne," *Recherche.* 6 (53) (1975): 120–29, and "Centre d'origine et diversification specifique dans le genre *Vitis*," *Eucarpia* (1962): 197–201; B. Safran and N. Hochberg, "Caractéristiques bioclimatiques des cépages et des vignobles," *Bull. Office Intern. Vigne Vin* 45 (1972): 581–94; A. Vereš, "Caractéristiques bioclimatiques des cépages et des vignobles," *Bull. Office Intern. Vigne Vin* 45 (1972): 570–80.

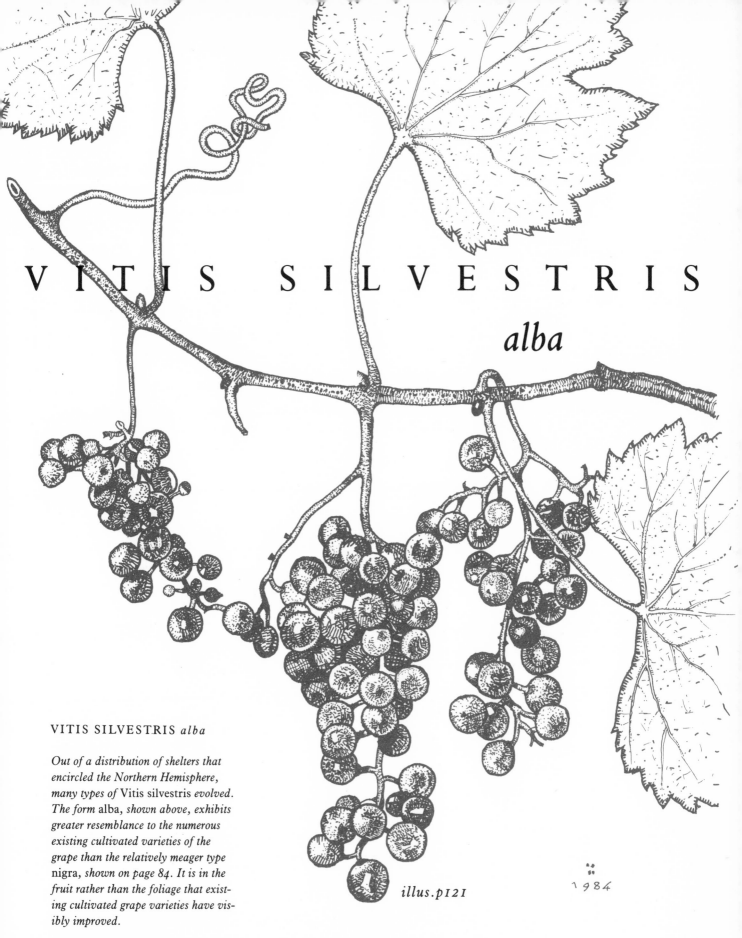

VITIS SILVESTRIS

alba

VITIS SILVESTRIS *alba*

Out of a distribution of shelters that encircled the Northern Hemisphere, many types of Vitis silvestris *evolved. The form* alba, *shown above, exhibits greater resemblance to the numerous existing cultivated varieties of the grape than the relatively meager type* nigra, *shown on page 84. It is in the fruit rather than the foliage that existing cultivated grape varieties have visibly improved.*

SOURCE FOR DRAWING:
Zdenko and Greta Turković, *Ampelografski Atlas* [Ampelographic Atlas] (Zagreb: Poljoprivredni nakladni Zavod, 1952–63).

illus.p121

1984

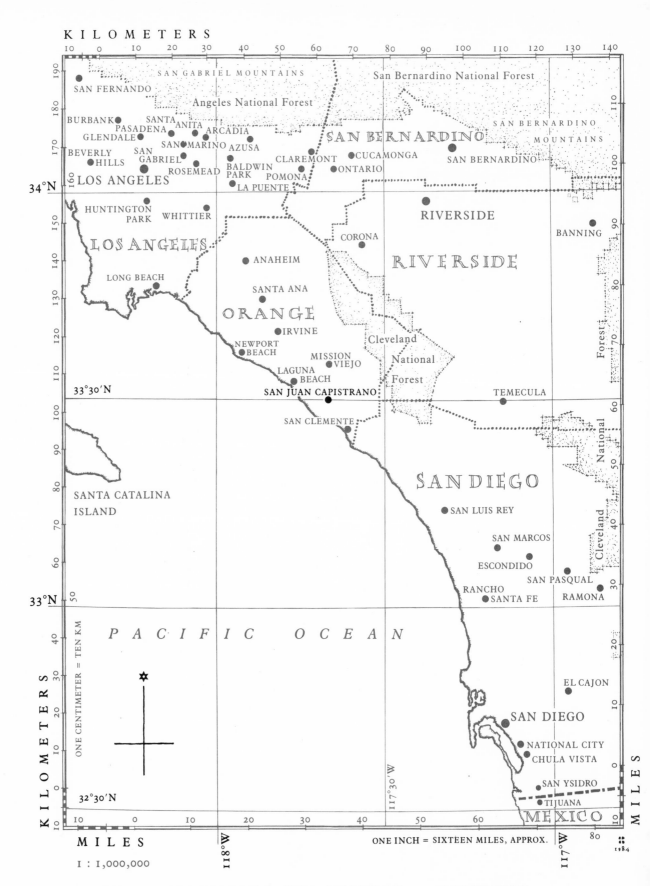

SAN GABRIEL MOUNTAINS   San Bernardino National Forest

Angeles National Forest

SAN FERNANDO

BURBANK   SANTA   ANITA

PASADENA   ARCADIA   SAN BERNARDINO

GLENDALE   SAN MARINO   AZUSA   MOUNTAINS

BEVERLY   SAN   CLAREMONT   CUCAMONGA

HILLS   GABRIEL   SAN BERNARDINO

ROSEMEAD   BALDWIN   POMONA   ONTARIO

LOS ANGELES   PARK

LA PUENTE

34°N

HUNTINGTON   RIVERSIDE

PARK   WHITTIER   BANNING

LOS ANGELES   CORONA

ANAHEIM   RIVERSIDE

LONG BEACH

SANTA ANA

ORANGE

IRVINE

NEWPORT   Cleveland

BEACH   MISSION   National

LAGUNA   VIEJO

BEACH   Forest

SAN JUAN CAPISTRANO   TEMECULA

33°30′N

SAN CLEMENTE

SAN DIEGO

SANTA CATALINA   SAN LUIS REY

ISLAND

SAN MARCOS

ESCONDIDO

RANCHO   SAN PASQUAL

SANTA FE   RAMONA

33°N

PACIFIC   OCEAN

EL CAJON

SAN DIEGO

NATIONAL CITY

CHULA VISTA

SAN YSIDRO

32°30′N   TIJUANA

MEXICO

KILOMETERS   ONE CENTIMETER = TEN KM

MILES

1 : 1,000,000

SOUTHERN CALIFORNIA: LOS ANGELES TO SAN DIEGO

MAP **6**

1:25,000,000

SOUTHERN CALIFORNIA: REGION OF THE FIRST VINE PLANTING & WINEMAKING IN CALIFORNIA

Winegrowing began in California at San Juan Capistrano; afterwards it moved slowly north and south along the coast in the isolated missions of the Franciscans. The two missions nearest the pueblo of Los Angeles, San Gabriel to the east and San Fernando to the north, were particularly successful at winemaking. When the missions were abandoned, what they had started was continued in and around Los Angeles, and for many years to come California wine meant Los Angeles wine. Anaheim, to the south of the city, and Cucamonga, to the east, also developed as centers of considerable wine production, and as settlement was slowly established on the vast ranchos of the region, there was hardly any community, from Santa Barbara to San Diego, that did not make at least a modest beginning in commercial winemaking.

The Anaheim disease that struck in the mid-1880s, the development of profitable new crops, especially oranges, and the real estate boom set off by the coming of the railways all combined to turn the Los Angeles region away from winegrowing at the same time that the industry was expanding in the north. By the end of the 1880s the vineyards of the south, though still considerable, had dwindled to satellite status.

After the repeal of Prohibition there were enough hardy roots still alive to begin sprouting again: wineries reopened in Los Angeles and in every direction around it. But most of these secured only a local trade, and before long they disappeared under the unchecked growth of the metropolitan city. Recent development in the south has been far removed from the city, at Temecula in Riverside County, and around Escondido, in San Diego County.

THOMAS PINNEY

123

III.2

The

VINTAGES of CALIFORNIA

by BOB THOMPSON

YEARS AGO THE CALIFORNIA WINE INDUSTRY DEVISED A SLOGAN TO THE EFFECT THAT "EVERY YEAR IS A VINTAGE YEAR." IT HAS BEEN PILLORIED ever since because certain sorts of generalities are not acceptable to the winedrinking public. I began harboring unkind thoughts of my own about this sweeping claim when the Louis M. Martini Pinot Noir 1958 did not turn out at all like its silky forerunner from 1957. However, in spite of reservations, which should be real, there is a sort of truth about the claim that haunts anyone who tries to write a vintage chart for California.

"Every Year is a Vintage Year" had its genesis in a climate that ripens grapes for winemaking far more reliably than that in any part of Europe, even such sheltered districts as Italy's Piedmont, or France's Rhone. Any French winemaker would be astonished to learn that Californians routinely expect the average potential alcohol of all grapes of any red variety to be 12 percent or more. Only once in the past decade, and only in one district, has any variety failed to come up to that level, even though that span of time encompasses two years of drought and two of relentless autumn rains, two seasons of uncommon cool and two of withering heat.* In other words, Every Year, etc. The industry puts another, less deliberate stamp on the idea by pricing wines without reference to quality in a vintage. A handful of small producers do price by vintage, but most valuations rise or fall with the national economy, even among the smallest cellars. Still, in none of this is there any implication that every year is a carbon copy of the one that went before. For all of the subtle reasons outlined in the previous essay, the wines of each new vintage differ from their forerunners, often dramatically. For all who missed the 1957 and 1958 Pinot Noirs, almost any two consecutive years of any ageworthy variety will teach the practical lesson just as well.

* The exception was 173 acres of Cabernet Sauvignon in Alameda–Santa Clara counties in 1976, as recorded in the California Department of Agriculture's annual *Final Grape Crush Report*, 1976–81, and in the Federal-State Market News Service and California Crop and Livestock Reporting Service's annual *California Grapes, Raisins, and Wine*, 1972–75.

124

California has another vintage-affecting departure from Europe, one that evolves from its relationship of topography to oceanic weather. To recall the basics to mind: Europe has no mountain range adjacent to and paralleling its coast; California has the Coast Range. Without coastal mountains, western Europe has remarkably consistent bands of climate, and thus plant life, extending west to east, with the coolest band in the north and the hottest in the south. With coastal mountains, California has no such bands at all. Temperatures grow erratically hotter in the Coast Range for more than 100 miles to the north of San Francisco because the mountains grow higher and steeper in that direction, with only a few narrow gaps allowing cool maritime air to penetrate inland. Contrarily, temperatures grow sporadically cooler to the south because the Coast Range is generally lower in that direction, and has a number of major gaps in it as well. An added layer of complexity is the winter rainfall pattern, heavy north of San Francisco, light south of the city. Neither temperature nor rainfall hews to county lines, but shifts markedly over much smaller patches of ground.

In Europe, a region and a grape variety are substantially synonymous. If the season is good, it is good for everybody, or almost everybody, within a region. In California, the erratic climate patterns have led to interplantings unthinkable in Europe. Almost every coastal county has flourishing vines of White Riesling (Moselle and Rheingau), Chardonnay (Burgundy and Champagne), and Sauvignon Blanc (Bordeaux and Loire). It has them not only within itself, but sometimes within single parcels of land, and it has parallels in black grapes. The season that favors one variety in a single vineyard may not favor the others, but may favor two different varieties in vineyards only a few miles apart. Every Year, etc. In short, the difficulties in ranking California vintages stem from the fact that its problems are not at all those of Europe, which invented the practice of vintage-dating wines and perfected the scheme of assigning years to positions at varying distances from the ideal, basing judgments on the success or failure of whole regions to ripen their grapes.

Still, climate and geography give drafters of California vintage charts their most reliable current material. In an era of explosive growth, the wineries themselves are far harder to think about. By any reasonable standard, a majority of wineries in a district—better yet, a climate region—make a vintage what it is. If more than half do well, it is a good vintage. If more than half produce unattractive wines, it is not. Well and good if all of the wineries have established a continuity of style, using a more or less specific source of grapes. But where is the yardstick when half of the wineries are making their first or second tour around the track, and many of the rest are shifting from one source of grapes to another year by year?

Through the early 1960s, only the Napa Valley among California districts had enough veteran winemakers to give a clear image of a vintage, and then only in Cabernet Sauvignon, Pinot Noir, and White Riesling. It did not have enough winemakers to cloud the issue. It did not have enough other grape varieties to add to the burden. André Tchelistcheff at Beaulieu Vineyard, George Deuer at Inglenook, the family Mondavi at Charles Krug, and Louis Martini at his winery could, and did, define vintages in the Napa Valley, and, by extension, the rest of California. Fred McCrea added some grace notes on Riesling from Stony Hill, as did Lee Stewart at Souverain. Stewart, and Jack and Mary Taylor at Mayacamas, did the same for Cabernet Sauvignon. None of these three could change the basic picture painted by the big four. Although a handful of knowledgeable collectors paid close heed to vintage variations during this veritable paradise for form players, nearly all published reports ignored the slim but solid evidence. Now Napa has fully 100 wineries contending for a right to contribute to any definition of a year not only in Cabernet Sauvignon, Pinot Noir, and White Riesling, but also in Chardonnay, Chenin Blanc, Sauvignon Blanc, Gewürztraminer, and Merlot. Until the late 1960s, Sonoma County had virtually no one making vintage-dated wine on a steady basis. Until then vines hardly existed in Monterey, San Luis Obispo, and Santa Barbara counties. Now Sonoma produces almost as many vintage-dated wines as Napa, and the Central Coast is not too far behind. Even the San Joaquin Valley yields a few.

With the flood of new wines has come a flood of published and broadcast opinion on the quality of California vintages, much of it contradictory, some of it formed in short memories and narrow exposure, nearly all of it based on the nervous frets of growers with grapes on the vine rather than on the taste of developing wines in bottle. The overwrought alarms of television news about harvest season rains in 1982 make an almost perfect case in point. They have left the vintage to begin life with an unearned handicap. The probability is that many other recent judgments were made on grapes rather than wine. On the other side of the coin, more than enough pronouncements on vintages have blamed nature for the shortcomings of inexperienced winemakers.

In some calmer era, astute observers will select a roster of reliable performers in each variety and each district, and monitor their results more thoroughly than those of the mass of wineries, just as the Bordelais measure their vintage by the classed growths and not the coops. This implies longer rosters of veteran winemakers drawing their grapes, if not from estates, then at least from the same vineyards year after year. It also implies critics following the evolution of selected wines over long periods rather than just the year of their release. Even after these conditions are met, sage buyers will remember that any general ranking of a vintage will overlook the bad wines of good years and the good wines of bad years. Meanwhile, no one is ready to put up with Every Year, etc.

What is there to know about vintages past? A vintage is only one of four things if I read the Europeans right:

POOR
(unbalanced, disagreeable wines)
CHARMING
(wines likely to be at their most pleasing early in their careers)
SERVICEABLE
(sound, steady wines but not exciting)
FINE
(complex, balanced wines promising long life)

"Fine" can have subtle shadings leading through excellent to outstanding, or whatever ultimate compliment one thinks to bestow. Even with this simple framework, however, agreement is rare among collectors about where each vintage ought to rank. Too much depends on which wines one had when, where, and with whom. The following is, therefore, no more than one handicapper's view of what collectors have to look back upon.

1960
Crops of average size yielded good wine across the board. Napa Valley Cabernet Sauvignons remain appreciable.

1961
Spring frosts cut crops by half and more all around the North Coast. Intensely concentrated Cabernet Sauvignons from Napa retained youthful qualities two decades later. A scattering of Cabernets from other districts also remain good to drink, though less powerful.

1962
October rains weakened all of the late varieties, especially even tough-skinned Cabernet Sauvignon. Poor, except that a handful of Cabernets harvested before the deluge were, and are, fine.

1963
For the first time, Napa had enough Chardonnays to take a measure. They were splendid early and stayed that way for at least a decade. The Cabernet vintage went unsung, even was cursed, but has aged very well indeed.

1964
Chardonnays were not quite the equals of 1963, more serviceable than fine. Napa Cabernet Sauvignons from an extremely short crop were beautifully balanced, and continue to age well. More than fine, outstanding. The sparse sampling of Zinfandels from Sonoma County was uniformly rich and balanced.

1965

Chardonnays from Napa equalled the 1963s for early complexity and balance, and have aged longer. Outstanding. Pinot Noirs from cool areas in Napa and Sonoma reached a rare peak. Cabernet Sauvignons ran in the pack, epitomizing the idea of a serviceable vintage.

1966

All of the Napa and Sonoma wines from a warm vintage were big, sturdy, and rather plain. The stars of the season were Livermore Sauvignon Blancs, splendid early and still in perfect form as late as 1981, when my patience ran out and I drank the last ones I had.

1967

October rains plagued the San Francisco Giants in the World Series, and weakened all of the late varieties after September rains weakened the early ones. Poor, except. A few Cabernet Sauvignons escaped, and remain fine as taunts to generalizers.

1968

This vintage yielded the finest Napa and Sonoma Chardonnays of the decade, wines that remained superb accompaniments to food in 1982. It also yielded truly memorable White Rieslings in Napa, the first vintage in which there were enough vintage-dated ones to allow many comparisons. Pinot Noirs performed very well early, but were not long-lived, perfect examples of a charming vintage. Cabernet Sauvignons also peaked early, but have held surprisingly well into the 1980s. Charming edging toward fine? Sonoma Zinfandels hit a remarkable peak early, and held it for a long time.

1969

A year good for White Riesling, and serviceable for all else except Napa Cabernet Sauvignon, which remains outstanding after beginning with little or no fanfare.

1970

A much-touted vintage, it turned out serviceable for Chardonnay, and fine for Cabernet Sauvignon from north of San Francisco, but as a group the latter never has quite lived up to the first hopes . . . or to the 1969s.

1971

This may be the exceptional vintage that proves not every year can be a vintage year even by the easy definition of Every Year, etc. Poor all around.

1972

Another season of World Series rains soaked the Oakland Athletics and washed out much, but not all, of a most promising Cabernet Sauvignon crop. Nothing else stood out as extraordinary, although a few fine White Rieslings and Pinot Noirs surfaced.

1973

The year was superior for the early ripening Chardonnay and the late ripening Cabernet Sauvignon, although the latter went to market unheralded and still is in the process of awakening doubters. The unusual aspect of the season was a widespread occurrence of *Botrytis cinerea*, which yielded California's first real vintage of late harvest white wines, especially White Rieslings. Incidentally, most of the vineyards affected by the Noble Mold were comparatively new ones in Monterey, Napa, and Sonoma counties.

1974

For vineyardists, the season was perfection. Steady weather led to steady ripening. Every variety performed well everywhere. Zinfandel from Sonoma could hardly be improved. The Cabernet Sauvignons from north of San Francisco were showy wines coming out of the fermentors, and have been much praised ever since. In the long run, they may be overshadowed by the 1973s, but only after a hard fight.

1975

Opposite to 1974, this was a troubled growing season, but one that yielded complex, balanced wines, especially in Chardonnay and Cabernet Sauvignon. Many of the latter are far more subtle than either the 1973s or 1974s, though perhaps fated for shorter lives. If so, an excellent example of charming. This also was the first season in which there were enough Gewürztraminers to compare, and the process could not have been more rewarding. Several from Sonoma and Napa continued in perfect condition in 1982.

1976

The first year of a drought produced thick, intensely flavored wines in which balance was difficult to achieve. Many are excessively alcoholic, so suited to people with palates toughened by late harvest Zinfandels. Few wines of any type appeared truly ageworthy in the early going, but some Cabernet Sauvignons seemed in 1982 to be settling into unexpectedly long stride.

1977

The second year of the drought brought much better balanced wines, revealing in the process how much effect informed growers can have on reluctant nature. White Riesling was ofttimes excellent. Sauvignon Blanc had one of its best years. Cabernet Sauvignons have begun to look promising as long agers of attractive complexity and balance—that is, fine.

1978

As in 1974, many wines were showy early. However, many Chardonnays from north of San Francisco have weakened already. The Cabernet Sauvignon had early charms, and may have more stuffings. Zinfandels harvested for balance rather than strength come close to equaling the 1974s and 1968s. This was another banner year for botrytised White Riesling.

1979

One of the most enigmatic vintages of recent times for most of the ageworthy types. Chardonnays from north of San Francisco gave little early pleasure, but may have the balance to age well. For the first time there were enough from south of San Francisco to generalize about, and they had enormous charm in youth, but no track record on which to base a guess about how well they will last. Pinot Noirs had a charming year everywhere. As for Cabernet Sauvignons, a majority show the promise of being fine.

1980

Chardonnays from north of San Francisco had an early elegance and balance, but many showed early signs of short life. Those from south of San Francisco looked much like their predecessors. Sauvignon Blancs from all quarters seemed poised to age well for two or three years at least. Many Gewürztraminers show a promise unequalled since 1975. Mixed emotions surrounded the reds as they were going to bottle.

1981

For whites, a direct reversal of the form of 1980. Several bellwether Chardonnays appeared ready to enjoy long, distinguished lives, while their counterpart Sauvignon Blancs showed signs of maturing early. Both are appealing. No reds are ready to be judged.

1982

Late spring rains and early autumn rains crowded growers at both ends of a cool season. However, the only thing that should be dismissed from this vintage now is the howl of disaster sent up by unknowing reporters. A huge tonnage of fine fruit went to the cellars, though a substantial tonnage of rain-damaged fruit was left on the vines.

IV

CULTIVATING THE VINE
IN CALIFORNIA

1. AMAND N. KASIMATIS

2. ZELMA LONG

3. CAROLE P. MEREDITH

IV.1

GRAPE VARIETIES

by AMAND N. KASIMATIS

TO KNOW HOW IMPORTANT GRAPE VARIETIES ARE TO THE CHARACTER OF WINE, WELL-VERSED DRINKERS NEED THINK OF ONLY TWO EXAMPLES: Gewürztraminer and Cabernet Sauvignon. Understanding is not much more difficult for newcomers to wine who have pondered over the differences between Golden Delicious and Granny Smith in selecting the variety of a backyard apple tree. With grapes as with all plants, the term *variety* distinguishes differences among the members of a species. Granted, comparing a glass of Gewürztraminer wine with one of Cabernet Sauvignon would suggest that varietal differences are not subtle at all. However, mighty differences of color and flavor come from minute origins. Gewürztraminer owes much of its pungent spiciness to a compound called linalool, which it shares with its near relatives, the Muscats. The herbaceous taste of Cabernet Sauvignon appears to stem from another compound, known as 2-methoxy-3-isobutylpyrazine, also the source of flavor in bell peppers. The amounts of each are a few molecules per bottle.

As much as these aromatic compounds matter to wine drinkers, they are among the lesser distinctions separating Gewürztraminer and Cabernet Sauvignon as vineyardists see them. Pest resistance, growth habit, ability to bear, and ripening times are of vital economic importance, and stem from other, equally minute chemical and genetic variables in the vines. Altogether, there are so many such differences that researchers recognize more than five thousand varieties in the species *Vitis vinifera*. And yet the range of their differences is so narrow that, looking at vines of any member of the species, one cannot doubt the family resemblances between it and the rest.

132

For practical purposes, California wines are made entirely from *Vitis vinifera*, the European wine grape. As noted in the preceding chapter, grape species native to California are useless for winemaking, and species native to other parts of North America do not grow as well in the state as does vinifera. A classification of California grapes into raisin, table, and wine varieties has led some to assume that some important commercial varieties in the state are not vinifera, or that their use is restricted, but the division is not botanical at all; neither is it legally restrictive. It is simply economic.★ Although the California grape industry was founded on the Mission variety and was dominated by it for a century, the need for different varieties more suitable for winemaking became apparent almost at the outset. The importing of cuttings from Europe began with Jean Louis Vignes during the late 1830s. It reached its peak between 1858 and 1880, when something on the order of three hundred varieties were being grown in the state, most in small trial blocks, but many in commercial acreages. Importing still continues on a limited scale, though some varieties new in recent years have come from breeding programs in California.

The winnowing process has been relatively swift, leaving contemporary California growers with no more than a hundred varieties. Only sixty are planted in significant amounts. Of these, fourteen dominate acreage totals. The primary names are familiar from their appearances on the labels of varietal wines. Although California's climate often is characterized as Mediterranean, a striking majority of successful wine varieties have their origins in northern rather than southern and eastern Europe. Of the important sixty, France contributed about half, notably including Cabernet Sauvignon, Chardonnay, Chenin Blanc, Pinot Noir, and Sauvignon Blanc. Germany added (White) Riesling. Italy accounts for several varieties, most importantly Barbera, and, although there is some difference of opinion and no proven scientific verification as yet, in my opinion also Zinfandel (known as Primitivo). Spain's contributions include Grenache, Carignane, and Palomino. California grows seven varieties developed here from parentage divided about equally between northern and Mediterranean Europe. In terms of total acreage planted, the proportion of French grapes is about the same as their varietal dominance for the state at large, but almost complete in the coastal counties. The 1981 statewide acreage for

★ *Vitis vinifera*, Thompson Seedless, for example, is classified as a raisin grape. The most extensively planted variety in the state with 270,500 acres in 1981, it was used as follows in that season: 1,020,000 tons dried for raisins, 452,666 tons crushed for wine, 203,000 tons consumed fresh (i.e., as table grapes), and 42,000 tons canned. Of 405,000 tons of table grapes produced in California in 1981, 44 percent went to wineries for winemaking. In contrast, 96 percent of the 1,785,000 tons of wine grapes went directly to California wineries; the remainder were shipped fresh to other states and Canada for winemaking purposes.

wine varieties is 42 percent of French origin, compared with 12 percent for Californian varieties, 10 for Italian, and 10 for Spanish.*

Reliable vineyard statistics date only from 1919, and highly detailed
ones only from 1972, yet enough old records survive to show why some varieties
have prospered while others failed, and to substantiate the fact that climate is not
alone in producing failures, but that the trend toward varietal wines has caused the
decline or outright disappearance of some useful blending grapes. Many characteri-
zations by E. W. Hilgard and his University of California associates do not sound
too far off the mark today.† By 1895 they recognized White (Johannisberg) Riesling
as significantly superior to any of five other varieties they categorized as Rhenish.
Cabernet Sauvignon was a clear favorite among varieties described as "Bordeaux, or
Claret-Type." The researchers were dubious about the future of all Burgundian
black grapes. Their notes also show substantial awareness of where many varieties
should be planted for optimum results. In descriptions of White (Johannisberg)
Riesling, they point to cooler climates as most favorable to success, specifying the
Santa Cruz Mountains as an exemplary location. Recommendations on Cabernet
Sauvignon are less specific of location, but again suggest cooler rather than warmer
regions. Carignane was seen as a useful variety for such warm coastal regions as the
upper Russian River Valley and for the interior valleys as well.

Much as Hilgard and his colleagues recognized superiority on the part
of some varieties, their evaluations were aimed at wines made by blending. Seldom
did they suggest varietal wines. For example, the notes on Cabernet Sauvignon suggest its discouraging harshness could be tempered best by a 50:50 blend with Beclan. A variety called Gamay Teinturier also drew favorable notice for its ability to
soften Cabernet Sauvignon, one of a number of grapes favored not for its completeness, but for its qualities as a component in blends. On the other hand, the researchers rejected Petit Verdot, Malbec, and Merlot for California, as having most of the
same faults as Cabernet Sauvignon but not all of its virtues.

Of course some of the early conclusions have been revised in the face of
greater experience. Beclan has faded nearly to extinction, while Merlot has come
into some favor. Some varieties of promise have disappeared with hardly a trace. To
give but one example of the latter, Hilgard's report was most hopeful about a German red, Affenthaler, as an alternative to Cabernet Sauvignon for clarets. By 1944
official enthusiasm had waned, although some interest remained.‡ By 1963 the variety was no longer included in University of California publications on grapes for

* California Crop and Livestock Reporting Service, *California Grape Acreage, 1981* (Sacramento, 1982).
† Hilgard, *Report of the Viticultural Work During the Seasons 1887–93.*
‡ Amerine and Winkler, "Composition and Quality of Musts and Wines of California Grapes."

winemaking.* Gone with it are scores of other intriguing names, such as Aspiran Blanc, Bakator, Bermestia Rossa, and Mantuo de Pilas. Still, Affenthaler and a few other varieties aside, the early reports remain far more impressive for the accuracy of their judgment than for their errors. Indeed, the more recent studies by university researchers have added very few imported varieties to the roster tested by Hilgard. Rather, they have concentrated on a steadily dwindling number of outstanding successes, the majority of them balanced enough within themselves to do well in making varietal wines.

If early grower surveys are any indication, practical vineyard managers were far less rigorous about varietal identities than were university researchers. An 1890 census of growers lists 540 in Napa County.† More than 65 percent of them are shown as growing "Riesling," a name that almost certainly encompassed substantial acreages of Sylvaner, Walschriesling, and others clustered by Hilgard as "Rhenish." In the absence of varietal wines, there was little reason for growers or winemakers in Napa or elsewhere to think much about fine points of varietal identity. The principal upshot of their viticultural carelessness during and after importation of cuttings was confusion for later workers. Colombard became West's White Prolific for a time. One strain of Pinot Noir was identified as Gamay Beaujolais by university workers, an error only recently defined. A few of the broken threads never have been pieced back together. Some varieties never have been properly identified during their long careers in California and their origins still are being studied. Only recently has an apparent similarity been noted between Zinfandel and the Primitivo, grown in Apuglia, Italy. Growers meanwhile have become learned not only about varieties, but about clones, which are shadings among a single variety.

The one-time prevalence of Riesling in Napa also suggests another great change in the regional composition of California vineyards. At the turn of the century, the valley was something of a bastion of German-descended vintners. Zinfandel was planted more frequently than Riesling, and in much larger acreages, but only a dozen Napa growers identified themselves as sources of Cabernet Sauvignon or other traditional Bordeaux varieties. One listed Pinot Noir and none listed Chardonnay. Santa Clara and the Livermore Valley were, in contrast, largely French as wine districts. In Livermore, 22 of 160 growers had plantings of Cabernet Sauvignon, another 17 had Sauvignon Blanc, and 14 were growing Pinot Noir. Only a handful of Santa Clara growers specified varieties planted.

*   Amerine and Winkler, *California Wine Grapes.*
†   Board of State Viticultural Commissioners of California, *Directory of the Grape Growers, Winemakers, and Distillers of California* (Sacramento, 1891).

After Prohibition had wrought its damage on the quality of California's vineyards, a new and more detailed academic research program accompanied, and frequently led, a revolution not in varieties planted, but in where and to what extent well-recognized ones were replanted. The two main features were a slimmed-down roster and a far greater homogeneity of plantings among the districts. Working as Hilgard's successor, F. T. Bioletti had divided the state's winegrowing regions into cooler coastal and warmer interior valleys before Prohibition. Beginning in 1935, A. J. Winkler and Maynard Amerine amplified the work of their predecessors in a number of important ways. The most visibly effective of these was their system of temperature measurement (heat summation), which divided California into its now familiar five climate regions (see preceding chapter), and recommended specific grape varieties for planting in each.* In broad, the planting recommendations put French and German varieties on the coast, Iberian and Italian ones in the interior. Without the advantage of any legal underpinnings, their system began to steer new plantings between 1944 and the early 1960s. It became an important force in directing which varieties were planted where between 1968 and 1974, the period of the great surge of vineyard development that still governs what kinds and qualities of grapes are available to the state's winemakers.

Growers, for their part, became more and more conscious first of variety, then of clone. Market successes of some varietal wines and failures of others worked sometimes with, sometimes against, improved understanding of viticulture in establishing the present proportions and placements of varieties in California vineyards. Concurrent with the Amerine-Winkler studies, another researcher at the University of California, Dr. Harold P. Olmo, was breeding new varieties in an attempt to solve the lack of table wine varieties suitably adapted to the warm interior regions. Out of a laborious, painstaking process that Olmo began in the middle 1930s have come eleven new wine varieties, nine for table wines, two for port-types. Ruby Cabernet and Emerald Riesling were the first two releases, both in 1948, both adapted to the San Joaquin Valley. Ten years later came Calzin for red wines and Flora and Helena for white wines, plus Rubired and Royalty, two red varieties for port-types. In 1973 Olmo released Carnelian, and in 1975 Centurion, both red varieties suited to table wine production in the San Joaquin Valley. Also in 1975 came Carmine, a red closely related to Merlot.

Crossbreeding, in effect, attempts to expand nature's work by combining traits of varieties of distant origin. Europe's climates, as diverse as but not identical with those of California, yielded most of the three-score varieties California inherited after centuries of careful selection. Controlled cross-pollination yielded Olmo's varieties at a much faster pace, though speed is relative indeed. The

---

*   Amerine and Winkler, *Grape Varieties for Wine Production.*

average elapsed time from first cross-pollination to commercial release of a new variety was fifteen years. Olmo's eleven varieties are the end-products of more than 225,000 separate attempts. The meticulous work included selecting parent plants, hand pollinating, and growing the resulting seedlings to maturity. Then came fermenting and testing a wine from each vine. Most of the first-trial fermentations took place in standard wine bottles, of which hundreds filled Olmo's laboratories at Davis each harvest season. Those that showed any promise led to later, larger test lots of as much as five gallons. The genuinely promising nascent varieties were cultivated in large enough numbers for trials in several locations in the state, and in test lots of almost commercial size. In many cases, commercial wineries participated in growing varieties of high promise and making wine from them. While rates of survival are minuscule in such work, Olmo's successes have greatly altered vineyards in the San Joaquin Valley. Ruby Cabernet, after thirty-four years, is grown on 14,500 acres there, more than any traditional European red varieties except Barbera and Carignane. The newer Carnelian is planted on 1,825 acres. Centurion is approaching 1,000. The dessert wine grape Rubired is grown on 9,700 acres. Emerald Riesling's acreage is 3,070.*

IV.2

The SCIENCE OF GROWING GRAPES

by ZELMA LONG

THE ESSENCE OF CALIFORNIA WINE DEVELOPMENT IN THE LAST TWENTY YEARS HAS BEEN ITS GROWTH AND CHANGE FROM DESSERT TO TABLE WINE PRODUCTION. The face of California vineyards has changed radically. Traditional grape growing areas have expanded their plantings and new areas have emerged. Viticulture, the science of grape growing, has developed new methods of planting, pruning, trellising, and harvesting, and better ways to protect grapes from insects and disease. As more acres of classic European fine wine grapes are planted, there is increasing attention to growing grapes in the manner that most enhances the quality of the wine they make.

* *California Grape Acreage, 1981.*

WHAT MAKES GOOD-QUALITY WINE GRAPES?

This is a topic to develop heated discussion among any group of winegrowers! The best test of the quality of a wine grape is whether it makes a fine wine, one of aroma, intense flavor, distinction, balance, and the quality called "finesse" (refinement). Several factors contribute to grape quality. One is variety: Cabernet Sauvignon or Sauvignon Blanc, for example, have more character, flavor, and potential for improvement during aging than Carignane or Grey Riesling. A second is climate: cool weather, just warm enough for the grapes to mature, tends to intensify varietal character and, in red grapes, their color. Another variant is soil: that which provides adequate, rather than excessive, moisture and nutrients seems to produce better wine grapes. Crop level is important: too small a crop can throw the vine into an imbalance of leafy vegetative growth that will shade the fruit and lessen its flavor, while too much can prevent the grapes from maturing properly, also reducing the intensity of their flavor. Vineyard spacing also matters: vine spacing, trellising, and exposure to afternoon sun can affect the composition of grapes, and, consequently, that of the wine they go into. Vine material is also a concern: different rootstock varieties are available, and each wine grape variety selected to graft onto the rootstock may include significant variations, called clones. The interrelationship of rootstock, varietal clone, and a particular site can affect grape and therefore wine composition—its chemistry, aromas, and flavors. Finally, there is vineyard care: decisions on pruning, irrigation, and protection of the vines from insects and disease affect vine vigor. Extremes, either too much or too little vigor, may impair grape quality. An important factor for crop level and quality is that each vine in the vineyard be productive. For example, a vineyard producing four tons an acre will likely produce better quality fruit if each vine bears a moderate crop, rather than having some of its vines weak or diseased, bearing no crop, while others are heavily loaded with grapes.

VIRUS DISEASE–FREE GRAPE STOCK

Because grapevines are propagated or reproduced from their green tissue rather than from seed, they have, over hundreds of years of propagation, accumulated virus diseases. Usually not transmitted through seeds, these diseases are carried on and on in the wood. Known viral diseases in California vines include leafroll, fanleaf, yellow speckle, and asteroid mosaic. Leafroll is the most widespread virus in California, and the cause of the beautiful red fall vineyard colors so beloved by tourists in the wine country. However, the effect of virus disease is often to weaken the vine, to lower its capacity to produce, and to reduce the ability of the fruit to mature. In the 1950s, the U.S. Department of Agriculture and the California Department of Food and Agriculture started the Grapevine Certification and Registration Program. Its goal was to provide growers with stock free of such virus diseases as leafroll and fanleaf virus. The University of California at Davis's departments of plant pathology and of viticulture and enology developed techniques both for selecting virus disease–free stock, a process called "indexing," and for producing stock free of virus disease using heat therapy and indexing combined. The Foundation Seed and Plant Material Service managed a "mother block" of virus disease–free grape varieties, which they distributed to registered growers.* In turn, growers developed "registered blocks" of vineyards, inspected annually by the California Department of Food and Agriculture, selling the stock to viticulturists all over the state.

Indexing, the initial technique for selection of disease-free stock, was accomplished by grafting buds of candidates for certification onto "indicator" grapevines—varieties especially sensitive to a virus, which would show its presence quickly, so that technicians could determine which vines were likely to be free of virus disease. (There is a distinction between "virus-free" stock and "virus disease–free" stock: the former implies total absence of the virus organism, the latter, the absence of any overt expression, or symptom, although the plant might possibly still harbor latent viruses.) Researchers in the late 1960s, unable to find disease-free stock of some wine grape varieties, developed a method of heat therapy to kill virus in diseased stock. The buds of candidates for certification were grafted onto disease-free rootstock and grown in controlled conditions at 38° C (100° F) for approximately sixty

---

*   *Registered Virus Disease–Free Grape Varieties (April 1980) Rootstocks*: Couderc 1202, Couderc 1613, Couderc 1616, Couderc 3309, Dog Ridge, Foex 33 EM (33 E.M.), Freedom, Ganzin 1 (AxR #1), Harmony, Kober 5BB (5BB), LN33, Millardet & de Grasset 41B (41B), Oppenheim 4 (SO4), Richter 99 (99R), Richter 110 (110), Saint George, Salt Creek, Teleki 5A, *Vitis rupestris* Constantia. *Wine Varieties*: Aleatico, Alicante Bouschet, Alicante Provencial, Aligoté, Alvarelhão, Aramon, Baco Blanc (22A), Barbera, Burger, Cabernet Franc, Cabernet Sauvignon, Calzin, Carignane, Charbono, Chardonnay, Chasselas Doré, Chenin Blanc, Clairette Blanche, Cortese, Early Burgundy, Emerald Riesling, Feher Szagos, Fernão Pires, Flora, Folle Blanche, French Colombard, Fresia, Furmint, Gamay, Gewürztraminer, Grand Noir, Green Hungarian, Green Veltliner, Grenache, Grey Riesling, Grignolino, Grillo, Helena, Inzolia, Lagrein, Malbec, Malvasia Bianca, Mataro, Melon, Merlot, Meunier, Mission, Montua de Pilas, Muller-Thurgau, Muscadelle du Bordelais, Muscat Blanc, Muscat Ottonel, Muscat Saint-Vallier, Nebbiolo, Nebbiolo Fino, Orange Muscat, Palomino, Pedro Ximenes, Petite Bouschet, Petite Sirah, Peverella, Pinot Blanc, Pinot Noir, Pinot Noir (B.G.), Pinot Saint-George, Primitivo di Gioa, Red Veltliner, Refosco, Rkatsiteli, Royalty, Rubired, Ruby Cabernet, Saint Émilion, Salvador, Sangiovese, Sauvignon Blanc, Sauvignon Vert, Scarlet, Seibel 5279 (Aurora), Seibel 9110 (Verdelet), Seibel 10868, Seibel 13053 (Cascade), Sémillion, Shiraz, Souzão, Sylvaner, Syrah, Tannat, Teroldico, Tinta Madeira, Tinta Cão, Touriga, Traminer, Trousseau (Bastardo), Valdepeñas, Verdal, Walschriesling, White Riesling, Zinfandel.
Source: Foundation Seed and Plant Material Service, University of California at Davis.

days. Vines propagated from these buds were put through the indexing program. If it showed them free of virus disease, they were released for further propagation. This "heat-treated" stock—both rootstock and scion wood—has provided healthier, more productive vines, and is in wide use in California.

There has been some controversy among winemakers about the effect of heat treatment on the composition of the grapes and on wine quality. Experimental comparisons of clones of Pinot Noir are going on at Carneros Creek Winery. Comparisons of Cabernet Sauvignons are being conducted at the Oakville Experiment Station under Dr. Cornelius Ough, and at Beaulieu Vineyards under Dr. Austin Goheen. In all of these, wine will be made from the different clones and evaluated for its quality. Meanwhile, the issue remains unresolved. Winemakers who feel that virus has an important role in quality consider it one of the natural stresses that make the vines "struggle," producing fine wine. Probably more common in California is the feeling that a healthy vine, because it can consistently bring grapes to maturity, has a better chance to produce good quality year after year. Certainly, vineyard cultural practices must be tied to the health of the vine. If a grower is dealing with a virused vine, he must use every ounce of care and knowledge to produce a good crop and ripen it. But the same techniques applied to healthy vines may cause them to be understressed and overproductive, giving fruit of only average quality.

CLONAL SELECTION AND NEW VARIETIES

What is a grape "clone"? Strictly speaking, a clone is the propagation of a group of plants from a single known source. However, most people think of a clone as a vine viticulturally or enologically "different," and in this sense "clonal selection" might be a better term. At the Foundation Seed and Plant Material Service, clones refer to plants from different sources, or, for example, from different periods of heat treatment of a single source. The clones produced are not guaranteed to be viticulturally or enologically different. Dr. Harold Olmo has worked on the clonal selection of Cabernet and Chardonnay, with most striking results in Chardonnay. In the early 1960s, Chardonnay was a shy-bearing grape, difficult to manage and to grow, and not recommended by Davis for planting. Selection of healthy, productive clones has changed average Chardonnay production from two tons per acre to current yields of four to five, the basis for a major market expansion of good quality grapes. Olmo has also developed numerous new wine and table grape varieties. Most of the wine grapes were designed to improve quality in the warmer regions of California. The most widely planted are Ruby Cabernet, a cross between Cabernet Sauvignon and Carignane (14,500 acres), Rubired, developed for its high amount of red color (9,700 acres), and Emerald Riesling (3,100 acres).

ROOTSTOCK AND GRAFTING

Phylloxera is the small aphid native to the eastern United States that destroys the roots of the traditional European wine grape, *Vitis vinifera*. Protection against it is achieved by grafting the European vines onto the roots of native American vines impervious to phylloxera. The grafted wood used to produce the grapes is termed a scion or "budwood"; the phylloxera-resistant roots are called "rootstock." In California all areas that originally had vineyards hurt by the phylloxera epidemic of 1860 to 1900 must continue to use native American rootstock. Currently this includes about 25 percent of the state's acreage: the majority of vineyards on the North Coast and a small percentage of the Central Valley. Vineyards in new grape-growing areas such as Monterey and the Central Coast are on "own roots," that is, they do not use different rootstock.* Viticulturists acknowledge that different types of rootstock with the same scion create vines that vary in vegetativeness, vigor, and productivity. In the early 1970s, the University of California at Davis developed and recommended two basic rootstocks: St. George, for unirrigated, shallow soils; and AxR— the best all-around rootstock for California coastal counties—for deeper, more fertile soils. Other rootstocks, such as SO4 and 99R, have been used experimentally.

Fifteen years ago, most vineyards were field-grafted, i.e., the bud was grafted onto a field-grown rootstock in August or September by skilled "budders." With the explosion of planting in the 1970s, a gradual transition took place from field-budding to bench-grafting. This technique, used successfully in Europe for years, produces large quantities more easily and requires less specialized skill than field-budding. Originally, bench-grafted plants were grafted in January, grown in the greenhouse, and planted in June. Although this technique can be successful, the vines are delicate for the first six to eight weeks, needing a great deal of attention and considerable water until they are established. Now it is more common to move the grafts from the greenhouse to a field nursery, where they grow from June until dormancy. They consequently produce hardier vines when they are removed and planted in the vineyard as dormant stock the following year.

MIST PROPAGATION

From 1970 to 1980, California plantings of wine grapes expanded from 157,000 acres to 337,000 acres; 130,000 of these were planted in 1972–74 alone. The tech-

---

*　In the fall of 1983, a wingless, slow-moving variety of phylloxera emerged in two adjacent vineyards east of Gonzales in Monterey County, infecting ten acres of Johannisberg Riesling and Sylvaner. The growers in the area feel that they will be able to contain the pest: it has been identified speedily and they have the resources of modern technology and a program for the substitution of resistant rootstock in annual replacement programs. —*Ed. Note*

nique called mist propagation made this rapid expansion possible. Before 1970, the normal, time-consuming method of propagation was to select dormant wood at pruning, root it in the field through the next year, and dig it up the following winter for sale and planting. Mist propagation, a standard nursery technique with other plants, involves taking a two-bud section and a leaf from a green shoot, putting it in a light, porous planting mix under temperature-controlled conditions, and misting it to maintain 100 percent humidity. The cuttings root, and are soon transferred from flats to pots, where they are ready to plant in about two months' time. This technique produces three to four generations of plants each year and expands the planting season. Mist-propagated plants particularly spurred the growth of vineyards on "own root" in such new areas as Santa Maria and Monterey and Kern counties.

UNDERSTANDING THE GRAPEVINE

The phytotron, an exotic piece of equipment installed in 1965 at the University of California at Davis, has increased our understanding of grapevine physiology. A small building constructed on a railroad track, it has a 1,000,000-to-1 ratio of gears and an electric eye. Its orientation follows the sun through the day to obtain maximum sunlight and light intensity. Inside, vines grow with rates and cycles of change in nutrition, soil water, humidity, and air temperature under close control. Light intensity, constantly monitored, can be changed with screening and filtering. In this environment, Dr. Mark Kliewer can change one climate factor at a time and learn its effect on the grapevine. Work both in the phytotron and in the vineyard has shown the importance of sunlight to bud fruitfulness: exposure of leaves and buds to sunlight is the *single most important factor* that influences grape production. Understanding this has led to increased emphasis during pruning on leaving "sun canes" (grape shoots growing in the sun) rather than "shade canes." The type of trellis used and the direction of the vine row also affect how much light a vine receives.

Leaf stomates are small pores on the underside of leaves through which carbon dioxide is assimilated from the air and water is transpired. If stomates are closed, there is less loss of water, less exchange of carbon dioxide, and less photosynthesis. Defining the conditions that affect the opening and closing of stomates has helped us understand how the vine is working. For instance, higher wind conditions close vine stomates, which explains why in the windy areas of Monterey, under otherwise good light, temperature, and water conditions, the grapes are slower to ripen. Vine studies have also shown that an amino acid, arginine, plays an important role in nitrogen nutrition. Stored nitrogen becomes available to the vines at bud break as arginine, which is depleted as the vine grows. An arginine test on canes can

142

be done routinely to track the vine's nitrogen level. Since it is highest through winter storage, a check in January or February can determine nitrogen fertilizer needs for the spring. Another test for fertilizer needs or nutritional problems is petiole analysis. The petiole, the stem on the leaf, collected during bloom, is analyzed for nitrogen, phosphorus, potassium, and boron content. Three areas that need more investigation are water physiology, the regulation of hormone growth, and the effects of stress. Too much water, too little water, or improper timing of water application can adversely affect the quality of the grape and the crop level. We desperately need better knowledge of when the vine really needs water; how these needs affect grape composition, and therefore the wine; and how best to measure the amount of water available to the vine. Vine hormones (vine growth regulators) are as important to plant life as our hormones are to us. They affect growth, fruit set, ripening, color increase, and "hardening" (dormancy) of the canes. Understanding the action, interaction, and release-timing of hormones may ultimately allow the viticulturist to control some of the vine's activity to benefit quality and crop. Vine stress conditions—the lack or excess of heat, light, moisture, and nutrients—affect the quality and quantity of the fruit. It appears that stress is neither all good nor all bad; better understanding will allow the viticulturist to manipulate and control it advantageously.

VINE TRELLISING AND SPACING

In the early 1960s, grape vines were on vertical trellises of two to three wires, 36 to 42 inches high. In time, there was a movement to more elaborate trellising, such as cross arm ("T") trellises, that was more compatible with machine harvesting as well as increasing exposure of the leaves to the sun. These trellises had at least two important effects: the increased light raised the crop level by increasing fruitfulness of the buds and also produced more shoots and leaves, which in turn produced more sugars and nutrients for the grapes, maintaining the quality of the enlarged crop. Recent Australian research has confirmed that the newer trellis systems, which allow better light penetration into the vine, improve wine quality by affecting pH, phenolics, aroma, and flavor. In some areas, however, where deep soils and good water access produce vigorous growth, vines on more elaborate trellises grow too much leaf canopy. This shades the fruit excessively, affecting its composition, reducing the air circulation through the vine, increasing the susceptibility of the fruit to mildew and botrytis, and reducing the production and quality of fruit.

Several new directions for trellising are emerging. In large San Joaquin Valley vineyards, for example, there is a movement to a simple, one- or two-wire vertical trellis, 4½ to 5 feet off the ground, which has the advantages of better light exposure, adaptability to machine pruning, and improved air circulation to reduce the growth of botrytis and mildew. In the coastal counties, which have a continuing need to improve their grape quality, more thought is given to matching a specific trellis system to a given site: to the soil, its depth, its richness, its water retention, and to the vigor of the grape variety grown on it. The emphasis is on minimizing excessive shading of the canes, leaves, and grapes, and on obtaining the maximum light and air circulation through the vine, while at the same time protecting the grapes from sunburn.

In addition to trellising, vine spacing will affect exposure of leaves and grapes to light. Spacing, the distance between the vines in a row and between the vine rows, will affect crop yield per acre and ease of cultivation. Professor A. J. Winkler established the classic California vine spacing of eight feet between vines, twelve feet between rows (8 × 12 gives 454 vines per acre). His work was done on unirrigated land at Napa Valley's Oakville Experiment Station. With time, spacing has been adapted to differing conditions of soil, moisture, and varietal vigor. Where vineyards have less vigorous vines or sparser soil and the vines grow less dense canopies, spacing is often six by ten feet (726 vines per acre). Recent studies by Keith Bowers, A. Kasimatis, Lloyd Lider, and Mark Kliewer of the University of California at Davis at a test plot in the Oakville Experiment Station indicate a 9 percent increase in yield when spacing was changed from eight feet by twelve feet (454 vines per acre) to eight feet by nine feet (605 vines per acre). Spacing decisions also may take into consideration a traditional European point of view: vine spacing that produces a higher proportion of vine wood to crop (achieved with more individual vines per acre) produces more flavorful grapes for winemaking. In the Central Valley, viticulturists are also exploring closer spacing. Less vigorous varieties such as Flora and Gewürztraminer produce more when planted closer together. With more vigorous varieties such as French Colombard, however, ten feet between rows instead of twelve can create a "jungle" through which it is impossible to move farm equipment. A practical problem for the vineyardist who grows several varieties on soils needing different spacing is to be able to adapt equipment to, or to have different equipment for, the varying widths between the rows.

PRUNING

See FIGURES 1–3 pp. 146–47

In California the three most common types of pruning are head-trained vines with spurs (short two-bud branches to provide the fruitful buds); head-trained vines with canes (longer eight- to sixteen-bud branches); and cordon-trained vines with spurs (permanent vines along the trellis wire). The first, usually called "head training," is an older method done without the need for trellis wires. Many twenty- to twenty-five-year-old California vineyards are trained this way. The second type, commonly called "cane pruning," was developed by Professor Winkler. When small-clustered

144

varieties such as Chardonnay, Cabernet Sauvignon, and White Riesling became more widely planted, cane pruning provided more buds on the vine (two to four eight- to sixteen-bud canes plus four two-bud spurs), increasing the number of small clusters so that the vine could bear a moderate crop. This type of pruning requires the most time and skill. If a pruner mistakenly chooses a "shade cane"— one that has grown all its life in the shade, so that its buds are less fruitful—the vine may bear less fruit than it should. The third system, the cordon, has been used for varieties such as Chenin Blanc for years. The major current change in pruning is a strong movement from traditional cane-pruning to cordon-pruning: it takes less time and less skill, and it spreads the fruit out along the vine wires, providing more light, better air circulation, and better access for the application of chemicals to control mold and mildew. The cordon system, unlike the cane system, is adaptable for machine pruning and harvesting. Originating in Australia, machine pruning began in California in 1978–79. Because it is now often used to pre-prune—chopping off the excess cane growth prior to hand pruning—some viticulturists feel that it may become a way of life in large Central Valley vineyards.

IRRIGATION AND GRAPE QUALITY

Is irrigation harmful to wine quality? Too little water causes excess stress on the vine, which may result in shriveled, raisiny, immature, or dehydrated grapes. Dehydration sometimes masquerades as ripeness, for it causes sugar and acid to increase, normally a good sign. Once it starts, however, it is unlikely that there will be the development of the aroma and flavor compounds that make the grape tasty and good for wine. Conversely, too much water, either from excessive irrigation or a high, constant water table, may cause a vine to produce a crop with diminished aroma and flavor because it is too large to mature. Irrigation is not harmful to and, in fact, may improve wine quality if properly applied to a vineyard needing water. The measurement and control of water application is an emerging science in the grape industry. The old way was to dig a hole and look at the dirt. Often water used to be applied to vineyards on a formula schedule. Now viticulturists are paying closer attention to the specific needs of the vine, watching it for such signs of water stress as a lessening of growth, shorter spaces between the nodes at the growing end of the cane, or darkening of the new leaves. They also use tensiometers and neutron probes, both of which give an indication of water in the soil. The neutron probe, which does its readings in a vertical aluminum pipe buried in the area being monitored, senses soil moisture at different levels. Among other tools in the developmental stage are the autopyrometer, the infrared thermometer, and the use of prediction modeling. The first measures the amount of moisture in the leaf. The infrared thermometer senses the leaf temperature; if it rises quickly, more water is needed.

FIGURE **1**, FIGURE **2**, FIGURE **3**

VINE TRAINING AND PRUNING

Figure 1★

HEAD-TRAINED VINE WITH SPUR PRUNING

The viticultural practice of pruning grapevines dates from earliest times. Cutting away spent vegetation from the dormant plant after the fall frosts have killed the leaves directs energy into the following year's growth and influences the quality and size of the crop. Head pruning, the oldest of the three principal methods used in California, retains spurs—-year-old segments of vine that bear the next year's fruit.

★Figures 1, 2, 3, redrawn by E.B. from Division of Agricultural Sciences, *Grape Pest Management* ed. William Moller, Publication No. 4105 (1981; rpt. Berkeley: Division of Agricultural Sciences, University of California, May 1982), p. 38.

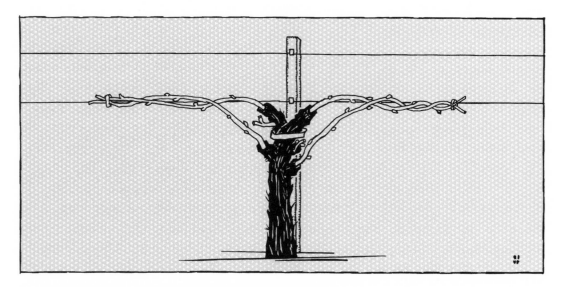

HEAD-TRAINED VINE WITH CANE PRUNING

A widely used method, cane pruning retains mature canes—those stems or shoots that have become woody—that grow into the following season's bearing branches. Although cane pruning yields a larger number of grape bunches than head pruning, it requires greater time and skill. Trellising is often used to support the canes.

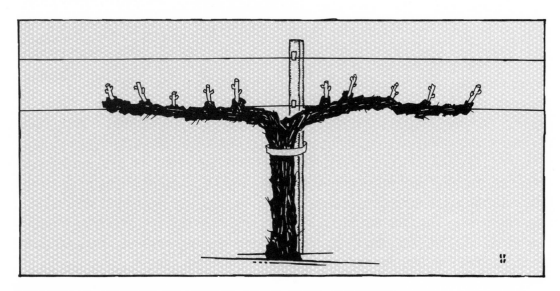

BILATERAL CORDON TRAINING WITH SPUR PRUNING

The distinguishing feature of cordon training is the greatly elongated trunk, extending in two horizontal arms (cordons) aligned with each other and growing in opposite directions. Over the greater part of its length the cordon bears short spurs that rise only from its upper side. The spur pruning it uses requires less skill than cane pruning, and the cordon permits better control of pests and light and can be adapted to pruning and harvesting machines.

Prediction modeling is a mathematical method that takes into account such data as the percentages of canopy, wind, and light, and uses them to predict water needs.

There have been two traditional irrigation practices: furrow irrigation in flat land where good water is available, and overhead sprinklers. In 1970, a new system, drip irrigation, came into use. Israel pioneered its application as a way of distributing a limited water supply; flooding and overhead sprinklers use far more water. Drip irrigation employs plastic lines strung along each vine row with one or two drippers or emitters at each plant, moistening the soil only around the roots of the vine. The water can also carry nutrients to the vine if desired. Drip irrigation has made vineyard development possible in areas that were formerly "too dry" to develop—that is, where there was not enough water for overhead irrigation. Irrigation is becoming a major vineyard expense. The cost of the energy needed to pump and distribute water has in some cases begun to exceed the cost of labor! Some vineyardists are trying new low pressure sprinkler nozzles (30–60 pounds per square inch), which require less horsepower. Irrigation management is of increasing concern to the grower as its relationship to grape quality and to farming costs becomes more apparent. There is a trend toward winter and spring water applications where rainfall is deficient, applying water up to or through July to maintain good vine growth, then slowly cutting back to stress the vines toward maturing flavorful grapes rather than producing more leaves and canes.

VINEYARD PESTS AND DISEASE

In terms of cost of damage and control, powdery mildew has been the most prevalent vineyard problem, causing the most harm to the most acres. Its effect on quality is a major concern to growers and winemakers alike. Mildew appears on the surface of canes, leaves, and grapes as a creamy white powder and stops their growth. Judicious use of elemental sulfur in the vineyard has been the traditional means of control, but this must be done with care; an excess of sulfur dust on the grapes coming into the winery can cause a rotten egg smell (hydrogen sulfide) in the fermenting wine. In 1982 Bayleton, a chemical used in Europe, was approved for use to fight mildew. It is a limited systemic that works most effectively to prevent the development of mildew rather than to kill off what already exists. As long as it is applied and allowed to dry, it does not have to be reapplied after rain or irrigation. Three or four applications during the season are considered sufficient, in contrast to five to eleven applications of sulfur.

Bunch rot and botrytis are problems for grape growers and winemakers alike. Of the fifty-two different fungi that have been isolated from rotting grapes, botrytis is the most prevalent. In coastal areas nearly all fruit rot is caused by this fungus, while in the Central Valley other organisms are frequently found as well. Botrytis often attacks during mild weather following rains. The berries turn a purplish color and begin to shrivel, the sugar concentration increases, and a grayish mold grows on the berries. In certain situations a botrytis attack on Sauvignon Blanc, White Riesling, Sémillon, or Gewürztraminer produces very sweet grapes, resulting in a wine of a luscious, apricot-honey character. However, botrytis also destroys color in red grapes and produces an oxidizing enzyme very difficult to control in the winery. During the 1970s, a systemic chemical called Benlate came into increasing use for control of botrytis. The fungus now seems to have developed some resistance, however, and its use appears to be lessening.

Not all vine diseases have been identified. In the 1970s a mysterious "vine dying condition" puzzled growers. In 1978, William Moller of the University of California at Davis identified the fungus Eutypha as a cause. Its spores land on pruning wounds in the winter and cause the vine to die. Recommendations for its control include cutting out the infected area of the vine during the summer; avoiding early fall pruning, since initial rains carry large spore loads; and protecting pruning wounds, if possible painting them with a fungicide. Pierce's (formerly Anaheim) disease is another vine killer, not widespread in California but a substantial problem in the North Coast region. Research in the 1970s led to a better understanding of it. The cause has been shown to be a bacterium spread by insects such as the sharpshooter leafhopper, and a number of herbaceous weeds have been identified as hosts in addition to the susceptible grape varieties. Of the latter, Chardonnay is most at risk, Chenin Blanc among the least. While no fully effective control is known, it is recommended that herbaceous weeds that are known hosts be removed and that planting of susceptible varieties be avoided in areas abounding in such weeds (for example, the Napa River area of the Napa Valley).

VINEYARDS AND INTEGRATED PEST MANAGEMENT (IPM)

Simply put, integrated pest management is the use of more than one strategy for control of a vineyard problem, looking at the whole picture, a holistic approach. The opposite to IPM is "one problem, one reaction." For example, botrytis in vineyards can be thought of as controllable by a fungicide spray. The IPM approach, however, would in addition include control of vegetative growth, trellising to promote air circulation, controlling tightness of clusters, and developing better ways to distribute the fungicide onto the vine. The move toward IPM has occurred through an increased understanding of the vine, the vineyard, and the surrounding environment as a whole system, not just as individual parts, and through an increased knowledge of the effect of one action on other systems. For instance, a vineyard usually has several kinds of mites. Some harm vine leaves; some help by preying on other harmful insects. Sulfur, applied for mildew control, kills mites; Bayleton, applied for the same reason, does not. Consistent use of one or the other will cause a change in the vineyard mite system, and so may have effects on the vines beyond mildew control. Other reasons for interest in IPM are the increasing cost of chemical application, continued concern to use no more chemicals than needed to maintain control of disease, and the tendency of vine diseases and pests to develop resistance to a chemical with its repeated use.

T-BUDDING

One of the most difficult decisions a vineyard owner makes is what variety to plant. Since vines take three years to produce the first crop and five to seven to produce a full, mature crop, he is forced to forecast market needs that many years ahead, an extremely difficult task, compounded by the need to match the variety properly with soil and climate. For those needing to change varieties to better meet the demands of market or of microclimate, T-budding, with its relative ease of application and short "down time" on the crop, has been a blessing.

It was applied in 1978 by Curtis Alley, a viticulturist of the University Extension, University of California at Davis, working with industry vineyard managers. In T-budding the upper part of a mature vine is cut off and a new varietal bud placed in a "T"-shaped slit in the bark. Budded in early to mid-summer, by harvest the graft has developed into a green shoot of the new variety. Depending on its vigor, the new vine may produce one-third to one-half of a normal crop the next year, and be back to a full crop in two to three years.

"VEGETATIVE" CHARACTER AND OTHER SPECIAL PROBLEMS

When thousands of acres of new vineyards were planted in Monterey County, a strong, intense "bell pepper" or "asparagus" character was noticed in certain varieties, such as Cabernet Sauvignon and Sauvignon Blanc. It appeared to be a basic component of varietal character, extremely strong and aromatic at low concentrations, and very difficult to remove or "blend out" with other wines. Chemically, it is believed to be 2-methoxy-3-isobutylpyrazine. Its appearance in intensely aromatic concentrations is associated with grape-growing areas of cooler climates, fertile soil, excess irrigation, and vigorous vegetative vine growth. Several approaches have been taken to prevent development of this vegetative character. Cabernet Sauvignon planted in cool, fertile areas has been converted to white varieties. There has been some success with stressing the vine, irrigating and fertilizing less, creating water stress as vines approach maturity.

The Monterey-Salinas valley area has two viticultural characteristics that require special attention, wind and lack of rain. Because of the windy days, irrigation is often done at night, when it is calmer, and trellises are usually vertical (T-trellises can produce a "kite" effect). Because of the possibility of wind damage, more shoots are left when training the vines, and shoots have to be carefully "positioned" on the vine. Rainfall in the area is between seven and ten inches annually, basically a desert amount, so that close water management is necessary. Fortunately, good control is possible since the grower is not faced with high water tables or excessive water that is difficult to drain away.

NEW DIRECTIONS

A major change in California viticulture has been the appearance of machine harvesting. The development of harvesting machines has combined university engineering with private, individual, and business development. In the 1960s, the first grape harvesters were designed for eastern trellising systems. Late in the decade came the first of the two major types of machine harvesters, the "rod shaker," variously also called a "beater," "slapper," or "foliage shaker." Using a set of long, flexible fiberglass rods, it hits canes and fruit, knocking the grapes off and into a collection system. It also tends to knock off leaves, and is more effective at removing fruit from canes and cordons than from the center of the vine. From 1976 to 1980, machines were developed on the "rail shaker" principle. These have two metal rails horizontal to the ground and aligned in the direction of the vine row. Positioned on each side of the vine, they move side to side as a pair, striking slightly below the head of the vine. Although they do not knock off leaves as easily and are very effective in removing grapes from the center of the vine, they are less effective in removing grapes from the ends of the canes or cordon arms.

Machine harvesters have obvious economic advantages. Increased labor costs and the farming of single vineyards of thousands of acres make it desirable to bring in more grapes cheaper and faster. There are some advantages with respect to wine quality as well. Machines can harvest at night, bringing in cooler grapes; and their speed makes it possible to bring in a large number of grapes at the peak of maturity. In many vineyards, machine harvesting has been coupled with field crushing. Because machine-harvested grapes are often juicy and partially crushed, the process is completed in a portable crusher in the field rather than in the winery. Machine harvesting suits some varieties better than others. Poor candidates have too much vegetative growth, are too difficult to knock from the cluster, or are too thin-skinned and juice too easily. Chardonnay, Chenin Blanc, French Colombard, and Cabernet Sauvignon can be harvested by machine with medium ease, while Muscat Blanc (Canelli), Sémillon, Grenache, and Zinfandel are more difficult. Machine harvesting has other disadvantages too: there is potential for including the immature berries of a second crop; a tendency for leaves to get into the mix; and an increased possibility of oxidation and phenolic extraction in the crushed grapes. If the grapes break up too much while being removed, they can leave their juice on the leaves and vine. Lost juice can be costly; the yield in tons decreases with increased juicing. Because of juice loss, at least one major Central Valley grower has moved from machine to hand picking. The extent of machine harvesting is not precisely known. Estimates put it at 10 percent of the grapes in the North Coast area and 25 percent in the Central Valley. Certainly there is still room for improvement in machine design. It is likely that the long-term trend, especially in the Central Valley, will be toward more mechanical harvesting. In 1978 machine pruning, developed in Australia, came into use experimentally in some San Joaquin Valley vineyards. The machine uses saws or cutter bars to make horizontal and vertical cuts on the vine. Machine pruning tends to leave more fruiting wood. The vines look different—machine pruning creates a "hedgehog" effect rather than the neat, trim look produced by hand pruning. Initial observations are that crop level of a vineyard increases slightly with machine pruning. Machine pruning is also being used as a pre-pruning aid, to cut the major part of the vine brush before hand pruners move in for final wood selection. The extent of use of machine pruning is not known, but estimates put it at 5 percent of the vineyards in the Central Valley.

In the area of soil management, increasing attention has been given to deep ripping, breaking up the soil to a depth of three feet prior to planting so as to eliminate compacted layers. Weed control has changed from solely physical measures (cultivation) to some use of strip spraying under the vines. A variation is to strip spray under the vine and mow the weeds between the rows. On the positive side, this technique allows a grower to get into his vineyard earlier in the spring. However, perennial weeds may compete with the vine for water. Roundup, a product available only in the last several years, is the first chemical to succeed in killing such obnoxious weeds as morning glory and Bermuda grass. Its application must be done early in the growing season under the best of quiet air conditions, because contact with the vine may kill it. The recent use of sprinkler systems for frost protection has been described in chapter 3.

The close tie-in of vineyard and winery is traditional in Europe, where grapes are not bought and sold but made into wine by vineyard owners. However, in California, vineyards and wineries are often not linked and, moreover, are frequently competitive. Even viticultural research has often not been connected to wine quality. But now this is changing: more vineyard research follows through to the wine; more wineries own their vineyards. Enologists, because of their desire to improve wine quality, are moving more and more into the vineyards, searching for ways to improve the grape before it reaches the winery. Their assumption is that whatever affects the composition of the grape—its color, pH, acidity, flavor, size— potentially affects the wine's style and quality. The author believes that this tie-in will be a major factor in the improvement of the quality of California wines in the next fifteen years.

BIBLIOGRAPHIC NOTE

Some specific sources for this chapter were Flaherty et al., *Grape Pest Management*; Weaver, *Grape Growing*; Winkler et al., *General Viticulture*.

IV.3

GENETIC ENGINEERING

by CAROLE P. MEREDITH

GENETIC ENGINEERING HAS BEEN MAKING HEADLINES BOTH IN THIS COUNTRY AND ABROAD AND RESEARCH ACTIVITY IN THIS AREA IS MUSHROOMING IN university laboratories and in many newly formed private companies. We read about the expectations for dramatically improving staple crops like corn or soybeans, but what about grapes? Grapes are also a major crop, actually the world's largest temperate fruit crop. Are these new techniques applicable to grapes? And if they are, what can they offer to grape growers and winemakers?

The answer to the first question depends upon one's definition of genetic engineering. At one extreme, we can call what plant breeders have been doing for decades genetic engineering, for they have been deliberately manipulating genetic traits. Or we might restrict our definition to "gene splicing"—the introduction of a foreign gene via recombinant DNA methods. Between these two poles lies a range of other genetic techniques. For the purposes of this discussion, "genetic engineering" will refer to a number of newly emerging cellular and molecular techniques with which plants can be genetically changed. Unlike conventional plant breeding, these techniques do not involve crossing one plant with another via pollination but instead utilize plant cells that are grown in culture, much as yeast or other micro-organisms are grown.

If a piece of plant tissue (e.g., a piece of leaf or a section of stem) is provided with nutrient medium and the right conditions, the cells within that piece of tissue will not only stay alive and healthy, but will grow and divide. The cultured cells will continue to grow and divide as long as fresh nutrients are regularly supplied, and they can be maintained in culture indefinitely. Grapevine cells can be readily cultured in this manner and grow and divide vigorously. Under certain special conditions, cultured cells of some plant species can be regenerated into whole plants. This process is almost routine with a plant like tobacco, the model system for plant cell culture, but is much more difficult for most other plants. With grapes, while plants can now be regenerated in certain limited circumstances, they cannot yet be routinely obtained from established cell cultures. Because plant regeneration will be an essential component of genetic engineering in grapevines, quite a bit of research activity is currently being aimed at improving this process. Progress in this area is steady and encouraging and plant regeneration from cultured grape cells will one day certainly be routine.

The capacity of a cultured cell to produce an entire plant makes possible a "plant-cell-plant" cycle, in which genetic manipulations can be performed at the cellular level, with cultured cells, and the genetically altered cells can then be returned to the whole plant state via regeneration. Of the several kinds of genetic manipulation possible with cultured plant cells, two have particular significance: gene transfer and mutant selection. Gene transfer involves the introduction of a foreign gene into a plant cell by means of recombinant DNA or similar techniques. This kind of genetic modification has only recently been convincingly demonstrated for plants, and only with model species such as tobacco. Even though it can now be accomplished in a model system, it will be many more years before we can even consider using this approach with grapes. The relative ease with which plants such as tobacco can be manipulated is the result of many years of work by dozens of researchers all around the world concentrating their efforts toward one goal. Grapes, like many other important crops, have not yet received this kind of attention. While there is no reason to think that gene transfer will not eventually be possible with grape cells, many details must first be sorted out in model systems before the technology can be applied to grapes.

At the present time, mutant selection represents a much more feasible approach to genetic engineering of grapes. This approach is based on the fact that mutation is a natural, albeit rare, event by which genes change. A plant cell culture represents a very large population of cells—a small flask may easily contain 100 million—and a few of these will carry mutant genes. (The number of mutants may be increased by treating the cells with a mutagen, but this is usually unnecessary.) We are not interested in just any cell with a mutant gene, however. The mutation must be in a gene that will affect the plant characteristic we seek to modify, and must affect it in the right way. It becomes essential, then, to have some means of finding this extremely rare mutant individual among the millions of other cells. A selection strategy must be devised that will permit only unusual cells with the sought-after characteristic to grow. As these rare cells grow and divide, they form small colonies, which can be isolated. Plants can then be regenerated from these colonies and evaluated for their expression of the new characteristic.

What are the prospects for mutant selection in grapes? Many characteristics of a grapevine are not currently amenable to this kind of modification. For example, this approach could not yet be used to produce a grapevine with specifically modified flavor components, as our current state of knowledge is insufficient for identifying a mutant cell that would produce such a plant. (Such knowledge will require substantial basic research in the area of grapevine biochemistry.) The characteristics we choose to modify in the near future must be fundamental ones that affect individual cells. Fortunately, there is no dearth of grapevine problems that meet this requirement. Two areas in particular are environmental stress and biological stress, two major limitations to grapevine productivity.

Environmental stress encompasses all those aspects of the plant's environment present in other than optimal states: very low or very high temperatures, too much or too little water, and excesses or deficiencies of nutrient elements all constitute such stresses. With respect to grapes, the environmental stresses economically important in California include salinity, boron toxicity, drought, zinc deficiency, boron deficiency, and temperature extremes. Varieties with increased tolerance to certain of these stresses would be of value in affected areas. If vineyard acreage continues to expand as expected, more and more marginal sites will have to be considered, as the best sites are already taken. For example, we will have a growing need for varieties that can tolerate saline soils. Salinity stress can be imposed on cultured cells and inhibits their growth much as entire grapevines are inhibited in salt-affected areas. The salinity stress constitutes a selection mechanism whereby mutant cells whose salt tolerance is improved can be identified and isolated. There is still a great deal to be learned about the influence of salinity on grapes, but when this phenomenon is better understood it will become possible to utilize mutant selection techniques to produce improved varieties that can better withstand its toxic effects.

Biological stresses encompass all those organisms that parasitize, feed on, compete with, or otherwise reduce the productivity of a crop. This category includes viral, bacterial, and fungal diseases, nematodes, insects, and weeds. While there are countless biological stresses affecting grapes, one of them, Pierce's disease, which significantly reduces grapevine productivity in parts of California and is widespread in the southeastern United States, is of particular interest. The bacterium that causes the disease is thought to produce a toxin that may be responsible for the disease symptoms. Since cultured grape cells are sensitive to the toxin, it is possible that the toxin could be used as a selection agent by which to identify mutant cells that are toxin-resistant.

Two critically important features should be noted. First, gene transfer and mutant selection differ only at the earliest stages. Whether one is concerned with identifying a rare mutant cell or finding a cell that has received just the right piece of foreign DNA, a selection screen must be conceived in order to isolate these cells. Plants must be regenerated and carefully characterized to insure that the new trait is both stable and agriculturally valuable. In practical terms, this means that the work undertaken over the next few years with regard to mutant selection will be directly applicable to gene transfer when this technology becomes more fully developed. So while valuable agricultural improvements may be achieved using the technology that is currently available, research in this area is, at the same time, providing the basis for an even more sophisticated technology.

The second important feature to be noted is that, unlike conventional grape breeding, the newer approaches will allow us to engineer single changes into existing varieties without changing anything else. If one starts with cells from Chardonnay, for example, and selects a mutant or introduces a foreign gene, the net result is still essentially Chardonnay. Conventional grape breeding, on the other hand, produces completely new varieties, which must be extensively evaluated over long periods of time before anyone is willing to risk planting them. They are often slow to be accepted by wineries and consumers because they do not carry well-established varietal names. As varieties produced by cellular and molecular genetic techniques may differ from the parent variety by no more than a single gene, they will still be essentially the same variety, distinguished merely by different clone numbers. Not only will prolonged evaluation be unnecessary, but the new material should be readily acceptable to wineries and consumers.

The outlook for genetic engineering with grapes is promising. Results may not come as fast as with some staple food crops, such as corn or soybeans, simply because of the large number of researchers worldwide who concentrate on those crops, but progress will be steady. Genetic engineering cannot be expected to produce miracles, but there is good reason to expect that it will eventually result in improved grape varieties that bear high quality fruit on land once considered unsuitable for vineyards and with less need for expensive, energy-intensive defensive measures against environmental and biological stresses. When these limitations are overcome, our diverse grape varieties can fully express their potential for productivity, varietal character, and wine quality.

WINEMAKING STYLES AND TECHNIQUES

V. 1

A WINEMAKING PRIMER

by BOB THOMPSON

IN PRIMITIVE OUTLINE, MAKING WINE IS ONE OF THE SIMPLEST PROCESSES MAN USES TO PRODUCE A FOOD.

Newly picked ripe grapes are brought in and crushed or pressed to free the juice for fermentation, a natural interaction of grape sugars and yeasts that will take place spontaneously in almost any kind of vessel.

At or near the end of red wine fermentation, new wine is drawn off its skins and seeds. What does not flow freely is separated by pressing. (The major procedural difference between red and white winemaking is that all juice for white winemaking is separated from the grape skins and solids by draining and pressing before fermentation begins, rather than when it is complete.)

The new wine is then stored in barrels to soften and clarify.

When clear, it is bottled and the process is complete.

In old wineries, familiar equipment does familiar work. Even in wineries that look as if they had just been designed by NASA engineers, the basic, unchanging steps are clear to see. In no few cellars the progression is straight: grapes arrive at one end of the building and bottled wine leaves at the other. However the winery is laid out, the first stop for arriving grapes is the destemmer-crusher, a two-part machine that separates grapes from their stems, then breaks the berry skins. Mechanically harvested grapes may bypass the crusher in favor of another machine, the dejuicing screen. Once in a while someone will use a press to crush the fruit. Near at hand are the fermenting tanks. A few open-topped wood or concrete tanks remain in service in some of California's venerable cellars, but most fermentors now are of stainless steel with jackets of circulating coolant. Another alternative for some white wine fermentations is the barrel. Within easy reach of the fermentors are the presses. Most wineries have separate ones for reds and whites. Some use two different types. The purpose, always, is to squeeze as much as wisdom allows out of a ton of grapes. Also close to the fermenting tanks is at least one machine used to clarify must (a trade term for unfermented or fermenting juice) and raw new wine. Commonest of these swift mechanical aids to gravity is the filter, but centrifuges are catching up in numbers.

This much of a winery is at the hurried end of the business. Grapes have a season. Once it arrives, time is of the essence until the fruit has been crushed, the wine fermented, then racked clean, which is to say partially clarified and moved into a clean storage tank. Beyond this point, time marches slower, sometimes moves hardly at all. The slow department in a winery is the aging cellar. In wineries of size, it likely will hold a mixture of stainless steel, large tanks of redwood, oak, or both, and oak barrels. Small wineries may lack one or another of these types of cooperage, depending on the types of wine being made. As a rule of thumb, the less done to a wine between crushing and first racking, the longer it will stay in the aging cellar, but it takes a large thumb to encompass the rule, let alone the variations. Beyond the aging cellar comes a bottling line, which can be very rustic for dry reds but, for sweet whites of low alcohol, must be a technological whiz of a machine in an antiseptic environment. Finally comes the bottle-aging cellar. The financially secure may hold on to treasures until they have come to perfection, but the realities of business require most vintners to send their wines out to the world after a short rest cure from the shocks of bottling.

Although the primitive recipe that begins this section is enough to allow anyone to make something that could be defined as wine, it carries no guarantees. Bare potability depends on a number of necessary refinements using some of the equipment described here. Real quality demands subtle exercise of a long series of choices not answerable by a mere yes or no, but options ranged along finely calibrated scales extending from none to a lot . . . of materials measured in parts per million, of processes measured by microns, above all of time measured in all the spots on both clock and calendar. At what degree of ripeness to pick the grapes? What is to be the rate of fermentation? When to separate reddening juice from skins and seeds? How much fining, and with what? How much residual sugar? How much filtering? How long in barrel, if a barrel there is to be? From which species of oak, grown in which forest, should it come, and how should it be coopered? The sum of a winemaker's decisions produces a wine of welcome nuances and individuality, or a featureless blob, or, rarely, an outright failure. If there is more than one wine to be made, the options amplify in proportion. What can be outlined as a foolproof process is in practice almost infinitely complex. The essay that follows is a fine winemaker's account of some of these complexities.

V.2

THE VINIFICATION OF FINE WINE

by WALTER SCHUG

WINE IN AMERICA, AND ESPECIALLY IN CALIFORNIA, STARTED OUT AS AN ETHNIC AND ECCLESIASTICAL PRODUCT. IMMIGRATING SPANIARDS, GERMANS, ITALIANS, FRENCH, and others produced it for themselves and their countrymen. It was a part of daily life, little fussed over. The ravages of the root louse phylloxera and Pierce's (Anaheim) Disease, World War I, Prohibition (1919–33), and the Depression, followed by World War II, left the United States with little more than the idea that wine was a cheap source of intoxication, however. Consumer and producer must share the blame for wine's downfall—they simply failed to inspire one another any longer! Contrary to popular belief, grape growing and winemaking never ceased, but too often lost were intent, art, skill, and the concept of quality. Starting after World War II, much of the credit for rebuilding the necessary technology and cadre of skilled winemakers goes to the University of California. Even after years of teaching and coaching, the emphasis in much of the California wine industry was not on the fascinating metamorphosis of aging wine, but on the efficient conversion of x pounds of grape sugar into so many gallons of alcoholic products. Finally, in the 1960s, professionals and enthusiastic enophiles began to experiment with renewed vigor, rapidly raising enological and viticultural standards in all areas. They tried everything. Their trials and questioning were met with both success and failure. Over-oaking and pushing processes and maturity to the limits produced many unharmonious wines. But these trials also established the parameters of quality.

THE BASICS OF WINEMAKING

California winemakers, faced with hundreds of grape varieties, can't be provincial about wine styles or techniques. Applied to the same basic winemaking process, the winemaker's skill makes the differences in style and complexity and produces the nuances and individuality of a wine. White wines, in particular, offer an enormous range of opportunities in fermentation temperatures, oak aging (or its avoidance), and—perhaps most important to drinkers—the final sugar-acid balance. In comparison, the range of options open to a red winemaker is narrow. The range of sweetness levels is much more prescribed. With rare exceptions, some wood aging is requisite. Coaxing distinctions from grape variety into wine is, thus, a most subtle game for winemakers to play.

HARVEST AND CRUSH

A winemaker's responsibilities start in the vineyard, making sure that the fruit reaches optimum maturity. Maturity is determined first by visual inspection (appearance of grapes and vines, color and taste of the berries), then by a thorough laboratory analysis of a sample from the field. It is tested for (a) sugar content (expressed in degrees Brix or Balling, a measure of soluble solids, mostly sugar of the grape juice); (b) titratable acidity (total acid in must or wine, expressed as grams of tartartic acid per 100 milliliters; tartaric, malic, lactic, and citric are the major acids found in grapes); and (c) pH—the amount of acid (measured as hydrogen ions, H +) active in wine. Typically, fruity white wines such as White (Johannisberg) Riesling and Chenin Blanc are harvested at 19 to 22° Brix. Fuller ones are ideal at 22 to 23.5° Brix, as are most reds. Total acids at harvest should range from 1 percent in the less ripe varieties to about 0.6 percent in typical reds. The pH should ideally fall at the lower end of a 3 to 3.5 range.

All of the above criteria of ripeness may go out the window when white grapes are attacked by *Botrytis cinerea*, better known as Noble Mold (in French *pourriture noble*, in German *Edelfäule*). It is responsible for the great Sauternes of France, the Trockenbeerenauslesen of Germany, and the "Selected Late Harvests" of California. Botrytis penetrates the berry skin to extract nutrients. Water evaporates through the damaged skin, increasing sugar, acid, and other components of the juice, allowing, with luck, a nectarlike wine. Brix readings may reach from 30 to 45°, in rare cases to as high as 60°. Total acids usually exceed 1 percent by a slight amount. White Riesling and Sémillon are particularly susceptible varieties. Chardonnay and Gewürztraminer also can be infected with glorious results.

In all winemaking, berries are harvested by hand as whole clusters, while machines generally pick individual berries, leaving most of the stems hanging on the vines. By either method, grapes should be picked during the cooler portions of the day. Once the fruit is picked, processing should begin as rapidly as possible. Crushed berries are subject to potential oxidation and phenolic extraction, which can cause unwanted changes in pH (higher), color (browning), and flavor (bitterness), especially during warmer temperatures. Hand-harvested fruit goes into a destemmer-crusher. Rotating paddles inside a perforated drum separate berries from stems. The berries fall through the perforations onto rubber-coated rollers, which break the skins but leave the seeds intact to prevent bitterness, and then are pumped into the cellars. The paddles push the larger, lighter stems out of an open end of the drum, from where they are usually composted and returned to the vineyard. Machine-harvested fruit does not require the drum-and-paddle part of the mechanism, but can be dumped directly onto rollers for crushing. A small amount of sulfur dioxide (SO_2) is added to newly crushed berries as an antioxidant and inhibitor of undesirable enzymes, wild yeasts, and bacteria. The condition of the fruit and the plans for processing determine the amount needed, generally 50 to 75 milligrams per liter (mg/l).

Juice drained off crushed grapes is called free-run. It is not necessary in the production of quality wine to separate it from press juice—which is juice extracted from grape solids by pressing. White wine pressing must be done with care, however, if press juice is to be included with free-run without prior treatment to remove astringency. Of the several types of presses, I particularly favor one called the pneumatic membrane tank press because it yields a high volume of juice with a low proportion of solids (about 2 to 3 percent). Solids, mostly grape pulp and seeds, increase bitterness or astringency in juice and wine. (It is partly to gain astringency that red wines are not pressed until at, or near, the end of fermentation, but what is desirable in reds is not wanted at all in whites.) The amount of bitterness and astringency depends not only on the type of press, but also the length and severity of pressing, and the condition of the fruit. Directly after pressing, and before fermentation, solids in white wines should be reduced to between 1.5 and 2 percent. Any lower percentage could adversely affect ultimate wine quality by stripping the juice of nutrients needed by the yeast cells to produce an efficient fermentation. I favor the centrifuge as a fast, effective tool for achieving a proper level of solids. The traditional way is by settling the juice for up to twenty-four hours, then decanting the clear product from the sediment, usually by pumping, sometimes by gravity flow. Juice clarification also lowers the level of elemental sulfur, a residue from dusting vines against mildew, which in turn reduces the potential for forming hydrogen sulfide (H_2S), the odor of which is described as similar to rotten eggs. Juice yield varies by grape variety and maturity of the fruit.*

In California acidulation of juice with tartaric acid may be necessary for both white and red wines, especially if pH is 3.5 and above. This lowers pH, causes unstable potassium bitartrates (crystals sometimes found in bottled wines) to drop out, and makes juice and wine bacteriologically much more stable, since organisms that cause spoilage thrive on high pH wines. Tartaric acid, which is also naturally

---

* The approximate composition of White Riesling at 20° Brix is: juice, 76.6 percent; pomace, 19.2 percent; stems, 2.1 percent; lees, 2.1 percent.

found in grapes and wine, is used for larger additions since the flavor of citric, fumaric, or malic acid is too obvious and foreign to wine. Citric and malic acid also are subject to reduction by bacteria while tartaric is not.

It is possible to make a white wine, termed a Blanc de Noir, from most red grape varieties by using techniques for white winemaking. There must be an immediate separation of the juice from the skins. The longer the skin contact and the greater the pressure during separation, the more color pigments will be extracted from the skins.

FERMENTATION

Fermentation makes the wine in more ways than one. The conversion of sugar to alcohol by yeast meets the basic definition of "making" wine. More than that, a clean, steady fermentation makes a wine easy to age; an erratic one means trouble and extra work for as long as the wine is in the cellar. Microscopically small yeast cells are naturally present in the soil and on the fruit, and eventually can cause any juice to ferment. To aid the start of fermentation and to control the type and number of yeast cells present, wineries usually choose to inoculate the must (juice from crushed grapes) with cultures of dry or liquid starter. Many wineries practice cross-yeasting from tanks already inoculated and at peak fermentation.

Yeast converts grape sugar into alcohol (ethanol) with varying degrees of efficiency (the conversion rate is approximately $^\circ$Brix $\times$ 0.56 = percentage of alcohol). Many individual yeast strains have been isolated to perform specific kinds of fermentations. To retain varietal distinctiveness, the winery may want slow, fast, or cold fermentors, or ones capable of reaching high levels of alcohol or achieving certain flavor characteristics. Not all fermentations are allowed to "go dry"—that is, to ferment all available sugar. Unfermented grape sugar still present in wine is referred to as residual sugar. Fermentation produces large amounts of carbon dioxide (CO_2) and generates energy in the form of heat.* Accumulation of CO_2, which is heavier than air, can be very dangerous for the winemakers if cellars are not well ventilated. During violent, uncontrolled fermentations, some alcohol and some components of aroma are lost to the atmosphere. Excessive temperatures can bring fermentation to a premature halt (stuck fermentation, which is extremely difficult to restart and bring to completion).

Fermentation temperatures for fresh and fruity wines such as White Riesling and Gewürztraminer range from 8° to 12° C (46–54° F). Generally they are controlled by thermostats linked to cooling jackets in, or on, the fermentor. To finish these or similarly styled wines with some residual sugar, the thermostat is low-

---

$\star$ Depending on the $^\circ$Brix, 19°–21.5° in white wines with the exception of Chardonnay, one liter of grape juice will produce 18–23 Kcal (kilocalories), or 750–1,000 kJ (kilojoules) on average.

ered toward the end. Once the fermentation is throttled, the new wine is clarified by centrifuging or filtering with diatomaceous earth (fossilized marine algae). This is followed by an adjustment of free SO_2 (up to 30 mg/l), which will hold the wine at its desired residual sugar level for further processing. Chardonnay, and by some wine-makers Sauvignon Blanc, is generally fermented to a fatter and softer complexity. The grapes having been harvested at higher Brix and the must left in longer skin contact, fermentation temperatures are generally higher, at 15° to 20° C (55° to 60° F), and often are encouraged to warm just slightly at the end to make sure all sugar ferments. I like to employ a mid-fermentation racking—the transfer of wine from one tank to another by pumping—which allows the winemaker to coast through the last grams of sugar conversion without worrying about development of H_2S or other off-flavors from the breakdown of spent yeast cells. Mid-fermentation racking of high Brix wines such as Chardonnay introduces oxygen and revitalizes the yeast population so the wine can reach total dryness, even at 14 percent alcohol and higher.

Ideally, white wine fermentations in tanks proceed at a rate of about 1° Brix a day, finishing in somewhere between fifteen and twenty-five days. Some white wines, especially Chardonnay but also Sauvignon Blanc, may be fermented wholly or partly in barrels. Winemakers begin with a higher solids content (usually 2 to 3 percent), which contributes to the complexity of the finished wines. Yeast strains are usually Montrachet and Champagne. Fermentation temperatures range between 15° and 20° C (59° and 68° F), the juice having been chilled beforehand to slow the fermentation rate. Barrels are filled no more than three-quarters full to prevent foaming over. This technique, with oak and oxygen present as catalysts, results in less fruity wines than tank fermentation, and they are richer and heavier in body. It also increases the chance of fermentations going wrong. To minimize such troubles, each barrel must be monitored closely and filled immediately upon completion of active fermentation.

Red wine fermentations proceed quite differently from white fermentations. For fine red wines, skins and solids must be kept with the juice to extract color and tannins. This raises some extra questions of temperature control and sanitation. Old-fashioned, small, open-top fermentors are somewhat self-regulating in temperature and provide predictable results, but sanitary conditions are difficult to maintain. In consequence, a great majority of all California red wines ferment in sanitary, closed stainless steel tanks with cooling jackets. These jackets hold the circulating must between 22° and 28° C (72° and 82° F). Because forming CO_2 attaches itself to the skins, they float to the surface and form a dense cap in which temperatures can rise as much as 10° C (50° F) higher. The cap must be cooled to remove impacted heat and prevent bacterial spoilage, and broken up to improve color extraction. The most commonly used method of control is pumping juice from the bottom of the tank over the top of the solid cap for approximately fifteen minutes two or three times a day. Exact frequency depends somewhat on the rate of fermentation. The latest generation of fermentors breaks up the cap automatically with a series of large paddles turning at one and a half revolutions per minute, or by the whole tank rotating on a horizontal axis. Runaway fermentations, caused by the explosive development of yeast cells, are hard to bring under control. Usually it is a matter of bringing an overheated fermentation down to a lower temperature quickly. If temperature shock is too great, a fermentation can stick, leaving an undesirably high level of sugar.

Most red wines benefit from pressing when residual sugar has declined to 4–8° Brix after a fermentation time of four to six days at ideal temperatures. For quality wines, the press wine should be reincluded with the free-run if pressing has been gentle. Air pressure presses provide maximum control. Many winemakers continue to favor basket presses with sensitive automatic controls. Some use continuous screw presses for their efficiency of operation, although these are most difficult to manage, generating excessive harshness and solids when overused. Such harsh press wines must be overtreated to make them usable.

Malolactic fermentation is a secondary fermentation that sometimes occurs spontaneously, in which bacteria convert malic to lactic acid. The resulting flavor components add desirable nuances to some wines, but not to all. Many wineries now inoculate all red and some white wine musts with a culture of *Leuconostoc oenos* (also ML 34 or PSU-1) to start malolactic fermentation. Temperatures and nutrient levels are much more favorable for this during alcoholic fermentation than after, but it can, and often does, take place afterward. Red wines racked off the skins to large stainless steel or oak tanks to finish primary fermentation usually complete malolactic fermentation as well if temperatures do not drop below 15° C (59° F). In any case, it is preferable to complete malolactic fermentation before moving the wine into barrels for aging. Much work needs to be done in this field, especially since many high pH wines (3.5 and over) become "headache wines" because they develop diacetyl, acetoin, and histamine as by-products of a bacterium called *Pediococcus cerevisiae*.

AGING

If fermentation is more or less analogous to the birth of a wine, aging can be likened to its formal education. The process begins with a series of abrupt treatments that clarify and stabilize the new wine, then settle into a more patient pattern of allowing flavors to evolve. Patterns for whites and reds differ somewhat, mostly as a matter of time. A wine fermented totally dry need only be racked off sediment in its fermentor before cellar work begins. As previously noted, wines with residual sugar are centrifuged or filtered to arrest fermentation, and have a small addition of SO$_2$. The combination of treatments removes yeasts and their nutrients from the wine so fermentation cannot begin again. First and subsequent rackings—transfers of wine from one vessel to another, clean one—leave behind solids that otherwise would make the bottled product cloudy or subject to spoilage. A wide range of fining agents are available to speed clarification. Some of the commonest are gelatin, egg white, and a variety of fine clays, especially bentonite. They can be used singly or in combination, depending upon which solids the winemaker seeks to remove from his wine. Proteins exist naturally in wine, and can cause a haze, especially if the wine is subjected to high temperatures. Fining with bentonite removes proteins (through electrostatic attraction). The process is sometimes called heat stabilization. Another stabilizing process demanded by the average customer is the removal of bitartrates. Most newly fermented wines are supersaturated with this harmless compound, which looks like ground glass, but in no other way resembles it. Lowering the temperature of the wine to $-4°$ C ($25°$ F) for several days usually crystallizes enough bitartrates onto the bottom of the tank to keep them from showing up in the bottle. From time to time, wineries sell crystallized bitartrates for processing into the familiar cream of tartar.

All stabilizing treatments are best performed on young wines, before valuable aging bouquets begin to form. The bouquets of age can be diminished or lost by excessive handling of a finished wine. Red wines are generally more stable than white and require a minimum of treatment. Most of them clarify without fining agents after malolactic fermentation has been completed, and can be racked to barrels directly or after a coarse filtration with diatomaceous earth. Some of the light, intensely fruity wines such as White (Johannisberg) Riesling, Chenin Blanc, and Gewürztraminer may go directly from stainless steel fermenting tanks to stainless steel storage tank, and then to bottle without ever seeing oak or other wood cooperage. Certainly the goal in making these wines is to avoid any suggestion of oak flavors, even when they spend a brief time in well-seasoned wood as a means of softening and maturing them. For wines with more bouquet, the need for small barrel aging varies greatly with the grape variety and the desired style. Constant monitoring is advisable to achieve harmonious wines not overpowered by oak, one of the few sources of flavors in wine that can be controlled completely by the winemaker. Sauvignon Blanc, for example, seems to respond beautifully to subtle aging in 2,000- to 3,000- liter German oak casks for up to six months. When it is fermented dry at 12.5 to 13.5 percent alcohol, a softening of the wine can be expected without the degree of oxidation and wood extraction probable with a 220-liter French barrel. Chardonnay, on the other hand, seems to have flavors that fit hand in glove with those won through aging in barrels rather than casks. Pinot Noir is the most delicate among red wines and can be ready for bottling after only six months in oak. Slow aging in the protective custody of the bottle provides much greater benefits than more time in oak. Cabernet Sauvignon, especially in its full-bodied form, usually requires up to two years in small French or American oak barrels, and Zinfandel and Syrah between twelve and eighteen months.

The most intense oak flavors leach out in one or two uses of a barrel, but differing styles and varieties permit barrels to be handed down to lighter wines, lengthening their useful life, and shaving the interiors also refreshes them. Wineries consider not only the amount of time wine spends in oak, but the geographical source of the wood that goes into barrels and the coopering techniques used in making them (see Timothy Mondavi's essay "Barrels in Modern Winemaking" in this book). Ours and many others use barrels of Limousin oak for Chardonnay and Pinot Noir; Nevers oak for Cabernet Sauvignon. Other forests in France also lend their names to barrels made from wood grown in them. Forests in Germany and Yugoslavia, too, grow oak suited to aging wine, though most of their wood is used for tanks or casks rather than barrels. Some wineries choose American oak for tanks, barrels, or both. Larger oak casks or tanks are ideal holding vessels after barrel-aging and prior to bottling. The minute variations in aging character of each barrel can be evened out, and red wines can settle out following a light fining with egg whites that smoothes astringency or bitterness. These larger vessels are finding increasing recognition for producing harmonious, complex wines between the extremes of stainless steel tanks and new oak barrels.

Blending of varieties and vineyards is another source of complexity in wine. New regulations effective in 1983 raised the minimum required varietal content from 51 to 75 percent. Most red and white premium wines have close to 100 percent varietal content, but it should be understood that a high varietal content is not an automatic guarantee of quality, and that judicious blending will improve many pure varietal wines. Traditionally compatible blends include Merlot and/or Cabernet Franc with Cabernet Sauvignon, and Sémillon with Sauvignon Blanc. A large number of California wineries including ours use as much as 15 percent of Merlot in Cabernet Sauvignon, and 5 to 10 percent of Sémillon in Sauvignon Blanc. Many winemakers feel that they can make a better balanced wine by combining the fruit from several vineyards. Others bottle and label some, or all, of their vineyards separately. I feel that vineyard designations should be reserved for wines of outstanding character.

FINISHING AND BOTTLING

A few subtleties separate white wine and red wine finishing and bottling techniques. For whites, sophisticated producers may use the ancient and gentle isinglass (a proteinaceous material obtained from the flotation bladder of the sturgeon) for fining after aging and prior to bottling. Isinglass fining leaves the wine clean to the taste and sparkling clear without stripping it of its newly developed, desirable esters. The counterpart fining of reds is best done with egg white, as described in the section on aging. At Joseph Phelps Vineyards, we generally bottle Gewürztraminer and White Riesling during February and March, Sauvignon Blanc in June or July, and Chardonnay in August following harvest. Several other wineries bottle whites somewhat later. Red wines are bottled after oak aging, as described on page 190. To guarantee stability in the bottle, all white wines are adjusted to 35 parts per million of free SO_2. Its proper use preserves fruitiness and varietal aroma and inhibits browning from enzymatic oxidation. Red wines require less (30 ppm). Among white wines, only those with residual sugar need sterile (membrane) filtration. Reds that have not undergone malolactic fermentation may also require a membrane filtration. Light red, nouveau-style wines and rosés are commonly among this group.

During bottling, flushing bottles with an inert gas such as nitrogen or CO_2 reduces the chances of excessive oxidation in the bottle. The industry generally relies on the factory sterility of new glass, so that removing lint by vacuum or rinsing is the only precaution taken. Bottling can be done manually, with semi-automatic equipment, or with high-speed automatic lines that will fill several hundred bottles a minute. The important consideration is minimizing aeration and turbulence to prevent oxidation and loss of bouquet. High-quality bottling lines use sanitary stainless steel for all parts that come in contact with the wine, and are capable of purging air from the bottles before filling and again just before the cork is pressed in. All well-made wines improve considerably during the first six months after bottling. Most reds improve for at least a year. Some are enhanced by even more time. Cabernet Sauvignon is a particular example. For economic reasons, some Cabernet Sauvignons and other long-aging wines are released to market long before they reach their optimum quality, with the expectation that they will be cellared by knowledgeable customers.

BIBLIOGRAPHIC NOTE

Among the materials used in preparing this essay were Amerine et al., *The Technology of Winemaking*; Amerine, *Wine Production Technology in the United States*, in which two articles, Long's "White Table Wine Production in California's North Coast Region" and Martini's "Red Wine Production in the Coastal Counties of California, 1960–1980," are of particular relevance; and Troost, *Technologie des Weines*. Also useful are the acreage and crop reports compiled and published annually by the California Crop and Livestock Reporting Service in Sacramento.

V.3
Note: Bottles

by DAN BERGER

BEFORE ABOUT 1800, GLASS BOTTLES WERE produced largely by hand, making them so expensive as wine containers that only such great wines as First Growth clarets—the Château Lafites and Latours—went into them. Otherwise most of the good clarets that were sold in London, then the major market for Bordeaux wines, were shipped in cask, a good portion of them for restaurant use.

Even when molded glass bottles became popular, wine was still shipped in large containers; indeed, London imported quantities of Bordeaux in cask as late as the 1960s. Before the wide use of bottles, buyers brought their own containers to be filled by the wine merchant. Similarly in the United States, in the days before (and occasionally after) Prohibition, it was common for the buyer to fill his own jug at the local purveyor's. The quality of the wine varied with the maker and the casks bore their names. Honest wine merchants earned their reputations on the assurance that the wine in the casks was genuine as marked.

Although there was a loss in aesthetics, molded bottles revolutionized the sale of wine, making it possible to offer higher quality to a wider audience. Since most red wines improve with time in a closed, neutral container, the possibility of bottle-aging after purchase also meant a general improvement in quality.

As bottles became almost commonplace, so did the need for standardized shapes at lower costs. Particular shapes and colors, associated with different places of origin, incidentally gave consumers more confidence in their purchases. A straight-sided, steep-shouldered bottle became the familiar container for the red and white wines of Bordeaux; a fatter, gradually sloped bottle was used for Burgundy, often for the wines of the Loire and, in a much exaggerated form, for Champagne; the tall and thin *flûte* and the similar hock, or Rhine, bottle stored the wines of Alsace and Germany; the squat *Bocksbeutel*, the wines of Franconia and Chile; and a more or less Bordeaux-shaped bottle served for Chianti, although some, usually of lesser quality, came in plump, raffia-covered *fiaschi*. There are also occasional proprietary bottles for those willing to pay. Christian Brothers' molds had Gothic-like arches into which the labels fit; Hanzell has had its insignia impressed into the shoulder of the bottle. In 1983 Chateau Bouchaine in the Napa Valley created a unique Burgundy-like design for its exclusive use.

Americans, who have casually adopted the place names of Europe for their wines (*chablis* to denote any white wine, *burgundy* to indicate any red, and so forth), have also taken over the shapes, but not the standard designations, of European bottles. More than a few Cabernet Sauvignons, the grape of Bordeaux, have been bottled without a qualm in Burgundian-shaped bottles, and the same shape has been used with abandon for Riesling, a wine type of Germany. There has been a change in the past few years, however, toward standardized bottles for fine American wines. Most Cabernets, for instance, are now put up in the traditional dark green Bordeaux-shaped bottle, often one with a push-up bottom. Called the punt or kick, the indentation in the bottom may be there to help hold the bottle on the bottle-making form during production or to collect the sediment that forms as the wine ages. Some think it is meant to aid in dispensing the wine with the greatest panache: thumb in the punt while holding the rest of the bottle cradled by the other four fingers.

The color of the glass is important if the wine is intended to age for a long time, since it can filter out harmful light rays that might alter the quality adversely. There is evidence that the darker the color, the more efficient it is for the purpose. But the choice of color is also very much a matter of tradition. Bordeaux green, as some manufacturers call that darker shade, is used for Cabernet Sauvignon, Merlot, Zinfandel, and claret; emerald green and Georgia green for Pinot Noir, Chenin Blanc, and French Colombard; and amber or, colloquially, beer-bottle brown, for certain styles of Riesling. Traditionally in Europe, brown hock bottles are used for Rhine wines, green or greenish blue for Mosel.

Although various shades of green have been used for Chardonnay in California, many winemakers in the mid-1970s realized that the appearance of fine-quality Chardonnay was distorted by too dark a color. Some began buying Chardonnay bottles from France, where the shape is slightly fatter around the upper middle and the color a more compatible dead-leaf green. Although it is now the choice of many Chardonnay producers, dead-leaf, a dirty green with hints of brown noticeable in sunlight, is generally unavailable from American glassmakers. Owens-Illinois, Inc., this country's largest manufacturer of glass bottles, does not make it because, relative to their total production, the demand is too low. Some wine producers such as Chateau St. Jean, who use the Burgundy shape and color almost exclusively, have gone to Dome Glass of Canada or to glassmakers in New Zealand.

In 1979, Owens-Illinois created, and in 1980 began to market, a bottle halfway between a hock and a burgundy style. Called the composite, the universal, or the California bottle, it is about an inch shorter than the thirteen-inch hock bottle. Because the slightly squashed hybrid resembles a hock more than a Burgundy bottle, it looks acceptable when filled with white wine, but the unaccustomed shape is somewhat unnerving when filled with red.

The thirty-two different shapes and colors of wine bottles that Owens-Illinois makes are just a small part of the giant glassmaker's total production. Because it is inefficient to change over a production line for a small run of bottles made to a special set of specifications, there are limits and restrictions on how much of what the firm will produce. To avoid the problems that an unpredictable supply of bottles imposes, two of the largest winemakers in California, E. & J. Gallo and Heublein Wines (formerly United Vintners), have for several years made their own. Gallo's bottle-making facility at Modesto runs twenty-four hours a day year-round, producing enough bottles to fill some forty-five million cases a year. Heublein's Madera Glass has not only made bottles for all of its brands, but in 1982 began seeking outside buyers, entering into direct competition with Owens-Illinois. Some of Madera Glass's products are even wooing some California wineries away from imported glass, since Madera is capable of making some of the specialized shapes.

Confident that its California bottle will make a broad impact in the market, Owens-Illinois is counting on the universality of a standard size, which will make cases easier to stack and will fit better in most refrigerators, where the hock bottle often stands too tall. For the manufacturer, the bottle may be cheaper to produce because the bottle-making line never has to be stopped and changed over. Collector's items they may not be, but today's bottles have the advantage of costing only about twenty-five cents each. Furthermore, modern glassmaking methods have made them much more serviceable, stronger, lighter in weight, and more consistent at the neck for a tighter seal.

Until the law changed on 1 January 1979, the sixteen permitted sizes of bottles in the United States were based on English measures. The most widely used, the fifth—four-fifths of a quart—contained 25.6 ounces. Since the regulations applied only to U.S. containers, Europeans and others outside their legal purview could, and did, ship in bottled wines in any size they chose. The most common, the 750-milliliter bottle, containing 25.4 ounces, was also indiscriminately, and confusingly, called a fifth.

Now it is mandatory for all wines imported through U.S. customs or bottled in the United States to come in sizes based on liter measures. The current legal sizes are 50, 100, 187, 375, and 750 milliliters; 1, 1.5, and 3 liters; and, for large quantities, 4- to 18-liter containers if they are filled and labeled in even amounts—that is, 4, 5, 6, and so on, but not 6.5 liters. The bottle for sale on an airline is the 100-milliliter size.

V.4

Note: Corks

by DAN BERGER

THE GRAPE AND CLONE MAY BE SELECTED CAREFULLY FOR THE SOIL AND CLIMATE, the growing conditions may be perfect, the wine-maker precise and inventive, and the aging ideal, but the result may wind up undrinkable if the cork is spoiled.

A wine is only as good as its cork, so the saying goes, and though this is a bit of a generalization, it is true that a poorly fitting cork or one that is moldy or creased can cause enormous problems for even the best of wines. Yet before the middle of the eighteenth century, cork was not used to stopper bottled wine. Oil-soaked rags, softwood pegs, or wax were the common methods of sealing. Tradition says that the monk Dom Perignon discovered that cork worked better.

Today we know that the cork is a marvelous invention. If chosen carefully, it may touch a wine for years without imparting any off odors; it is impermeable; it compresses for ease of getting into and out of the bottle; and it doesn't change greatly when it gets a bit moist. It will, however, dry out when exposed to air, which is why bottles of wine made to be aged are laid on their sides—so that the liquid in the bottle touches the cork and keeps it moist and expanded against the sides of the neck of the bottle.

Almost all of the cork used to stopper wine bottles comes from Portugal; a small amount comes from Spain. Cork oak trees have been experimentally planted in various parts of the United States, most recently by Doug Meador, owner of Ventana Vineyards in Monterey County. But in the past the climate has proved detrimental to quality cork, and most experiments have been disappointing. Planted as a sapling, the cork oak, *Quercus suber*, takes forty years before fine cork can be obtained from its bark. After a harvest, it is best to wait between ten and thirteen years before the next good crop of cork. The fact that each tree will bear a usable amount of cork for more than four centuries is of little immediate benefit.

In the summer when the sap is high, the bark is stripped from the cork tree, soaked in very hot water, then air-dried for several months. During that time, experts smell each piece to make certain it has not contracted a fungus, which would make it worthless for wine bottles. Such spoiled pieces of cork are not wasted; they can be used to make bulletin boards or other products that will not come into contact with food or wine. On occasion some tainted cork does slip by and is made into corks for wine. When that happens, the producer should detect the spoilage and discard the entire lot. Occasionally winemakers have been offered "great deals" on cork, unwittingly bought the tainted supply, and wound up taking a huge loss when they found it imparted a "corked" odor to their wine. It is an aroma easy for the wine to pick up and the consumer to recognize. The smell is musty and "dirty." Such an odor, detected at a restaurant, should prompt rejection of the bottle.

After the cork has been properly air-dried, "baskets" of cork are formed. The appropriate grade of cork goes into each basket, starting with the highest quality, listed as "superior" or some similar term, followed by first quality, second quality, and so on. (Each cork firm has its own designation of quality levels.) Rarely does a producer of quality wine in the United States, France, Germany, or Italy use anything below fifth quality, and most producers use only first. The lowest levels usually wind up in the wine bottles of Eastern European countries.

A small amount of cork is set aside by each producer for making champagne corks, and much of that is graded again. Today, almost no champagne corks are solid cork from one end to the other. The price makes that financially impossible. Almost all are "agglomerated": chopped up pieces of cork glued together, to the ends of which are glued slices or rounds of the finest quality cork. These are made by cutting the best quality cork into strips, then die cutting them into rondelles, which represent only 10 percent of the entire champagne cork. The second layer of rondelles, usually second-quality cork, is glued onto the agglomerated end.

Champagne corks are originally straight, not mushroom-shaped as they appear after they are removed from the bottle. To get the cork into the bottle, it is necessary to squash it down in a machine, then force it through the narrow neck. The metal cap placed atop the cork prevents the wire net that is added later from tearing it. The net is secured by winding it around the flange on the bottle neck.

Getting a cork inside the bottle is not easy without the proper equipment. Hand-corking devices used to be relatively simple contraptions. The cork was placed in a handlike holder and squeezed a bit, and the holder was then placed on top of the bottle. Finally, a hand-operated plunger jammed the cork into the bottle. Often a bottle or two would break and the corker could get a little liquid refreshment if he was careful about the glass. Today, automatic corking machines can seal hundreds of bottles in a minute.

To make corking a bit easier, many American firms ask that their corks be "chamfered"—that is, beveled on the ends. This not only makes them a bit easier to get into the bottle, but easier to get out, especially if the opener is using a two-pronged "Ah-So" cork puller. However, chamfered corks are disappearing as modern corking equipment becomes more sophisticated.

The length of a cork is chosen for the type of wine being bottled. If it is intended to be consumed within a year or two, the shortest cork is satisfactory. Most 1.5-inch corks (about the smallest found in American wine bottles) would be satisfactory, for example, for Chenin Blanc or Riesling made dry. However, ageworthy wines need better protection than a 1.5-inch cork would provide. So many producers offer a 2.25-inch cork, which is normally also of higher quality than a shorter one. The longer corks offer an extra degree of protection against deterioration from constant contact with alcohol on one side and from possible rot in a damp, dank cellar on the other.

Even with long corks, many châteaux in Bordeaux and houses in Burgundy recork their wines every twenty-five years or so to lessen the possibility of deterioration. Recorking is a tricky process and should ideally be done by an expert. Since the wine is delicate and in an old bottle, it may easily be ruined by oxidation if the recorker is not careful. The bottle must be carefully stood upright and the cork very carefully withdrawn. Then any ullage (head space) created by evaporation is filled with more of the same wine from another bottle, and a new, clean cork inserted. Finally, a new lead capsule goes on the recorked bottle.

It is agreed that recorking is a good idea for old bottles whose corks may have deteriorated enough to endanger the contents. What, however, is to be done with a wine so old and rare that only three bottles exist? Does the château sacrifice one of the three as "topping wine" and wind up with only two? No one is saying much about it, but it has been alleged that some châteaux may use new wine to top up old wines when recorking.

Young wines intended to be consumed early need no special protection. Many Germans and other producers of such youthful wines are now using agglomerated corks made of pieces chopped and glued together, which offer good protection for short periods of time. A screw cap offers just as good protection, of course, but no fine wine producer can afford to tinker with his image by using one. (Still, some are trying. Alcoa's subsidiary Closure Systems International has for many years taken out advertisements in major wine journals showing an obviously expensive "chateau-bottled" wine in a bottle with a threaded neck. The text says, "Our roll-on closure offers more than convenience. It protects your wine from leakage, evaporation and intrusion with an airtight seal.")

The same sort of reasoning—loss of image—has kept many wineries from using the new plastic corks. Made of an inert material that will not impart any negative qualities to the wine, these are manufactured under various names such as Cellucork. They are totally impermeable, colored to look like cork, have a bit of resilience, and offer good protection. Plastic versions of cork are not as resilient as real cork, however, and a few have been known to crease in corking machines, creating a dangerous situation as far as air reaching the wine is concerned.

Corks stay put in the neck of a bottle by friction and because they are compressed when injected into it. But, as a wine ages, eventually the cork becomes used to its shape and loses its resilience. It can then become loose in the neck and react to fluctuating temperatures. When the temperature of the wine in a bottle goes up, the liquid expands, pushing on the cork; if the cork is so inclined, it will move out of the bottle. In either direction, a cork pushed a bit too much begins to lose its sealing capabilities and may begin to leak.

A cork that has remained in the bottle too long also has a tendency to soak up the liquid, and that eventually may cause leakage. Such bottles are called "weepers." The liquid lost is replaced by air, which means that oxidation is to be expected in weepers. If you should find a bottle in a wine shop that has leaked considerably, you will be right to suspect a certain amount of oxidation in the wine.

The ancient tendency to refill prestigious bottles with lesser wine has led to the custom in restaurants of presenting the wine sealed and of allowing the customer to examine the cork, which not only gives a hint of the condition of the wine but also of its authenticity. Brands on corks are common for fine wines, indicating not only the house name but often the vintage. Branded corks sometimes become collector's items; a fine dinner at an exciting restaurant is often noted on the side of the cork.

V.5
ENOLOGICAL AND TECHNOLOGICAL DEVELOPMENTS

by ZELMA LONG

IT IS IMPORTANT THAT CONSUMERS, TASTING, READING, LISTENING, AND LEARNING ABOUT WINE, DISTINGUISH CAREFULLY BETWEEN QUALITY AND STYLE. Quality ranges from a good basic wine to one of nuances and complexity. In its simplest form wine can be a pleasant, undistinctive drink with no offensive characteristics such as excessive acid or tannin or unpleasant aromas. A wine one step up on the quality scale meets this description but has more aroma, flavor, and varietal distinctiveness. At the peak of quality is the rarer wine of intense aromas and flavors, complexity, harmony, balance, and finesse. Any wine grapes that are sound and reasonably mature can, under good conditions of quality control, be made into good basic wine. Grapes of distinctive character such as Chardonnay, Zinfandel, White Riesling, and Cabernet Sauvignon, matured in climates that produce varietal intensity, will produce wines of distinction. Great wines are a product of great varieties—Cabernet Sauvignon, Pinot Noir, Chardonnay, White Riesling, Sauvignon Blanc—grown in exceptionally appropriate locations in exceptional vintage years, and made by winemakers who recognize, sustain, and enhance the potential of the fruit.

In contrast with quality, style is the unique set of characteristics a winemaker can elicit from a wine by varying winemaking techniques. Style in wines is like style in the world of high fashion, where very different and beautiful garments can come from the same fine cloth. A high level of quality may be sustained in a variety of different styles. For example, Californians have produced three styles of fine quality Chardonnay: a rich, oaky, barrel-fermented style; a more delicate, fruitier style; and a fine sparkling wine. A winemaker's style comes from a unique set of decisions among thousands of variations in the winemaking process: choice of fruit, harvesting, crushing, fermentation, clarification, aging, and bottling. In recent years there have been two stylistic trends: for the less expensive wines produced in larger volume, to ensure a character and flavor that are consistent from year to year; and for more expensive wines produced in lower volume, to enhance and promote intriguing differences.

Despite all the advances in technology that will be described here, the ability of the winemaker to elicit the best from the grape is still an art based on intuitive judgment. The timing of the harvest is the first critical decision for the winemaker, who is much concerned about the condition and composition of the grapes being harvested. To make good wine, the grapes must be sound: free of excess mold, botrytis, and raisining. They must also be mature: fully developed in the compounds that give wine its appealing aromas and flavors. In the past twenty years, many changes, such as in field sampling and the assessment of the grapes' maturity, have improved the quality of the harvest. To decide if a vineyard is ready to harvest, a good, representative "sample," or cross section, of grapes must be taken to check for maturity. Enologists at the University of California at Davis have studied different methods of sampling, and their observations and recommendations provide the basis for improved sampling techniques now widely used throughout California. When you pick a growing apple to eat, it may be "green" (underripe), mushy and flavorless (overripe), or delicious (a perfect texture and flavor). Grapes also have this peak of ripeness, and the best wine is made when they are at their maximum flavor. Judging their maturity is a combination of science and intuition. The change in Brix (percentage of sugar) very roughly parallels the increase in color and flavor, so it is closely monitored. Total acidity and pH (see below), of great relevance to the flavor and balance of the wine, are measured as the grapes ripen. Programs are beginning for the routine assessment of grape juice aroma and for measurement of changes in color and in malic acid. To make the critical decision of when to pick, the winemaker combines these quantifiable differences with tasting the grape, feeling its changes in firmness, and looking at the vine and its degree of stress.

Winery standards for grape condition at delivery have increased and are often incorporated into grape purchase contracts. MOG (material other than grapes, such as leaves) is usually limited to a maximum of 3 percent. Defects such as rot (mold) or raisining may cause a winery to refuse delivery. Contrary to practices fifteen years ago, most wineries now insist that grapes be picked the same day they are to be delivered for crushing. Other items of increasing concern are the amount of second crop (the less ripe fruit on the vine), and the temperature of the fruit (it should not be too hot) at delivery. In the 1970s, grape payment systems based on Brix (and, to a lesser extent, acidity) became more widely used. Bonuses of up to 55 percent above the basic price per ton encouraged growers to leave their grapes on the vines until they were ripe (sometimes risking poor weather conditions) instead of picking them early and green. In the coastal areas, many wineries also pay substantially higher base prices to growers who have developed a reputation for consistently fine grapes, providing them with added impetus to give close attention to the timing of the harvest and the condition of the fruit. The most important factor in the improved quality of grapes has been the closer interaction of grapegrower, winemaker, and winery owner. In earlier years, the grapegrowers' focus, as also that of the University of California Extension Service, was to produce healthy vines, a good crop load, and sound, disease-free grapes. Now the focus has moved toward locating and managing the vines to produce an adequate crop of *flavorful* grapes.

Weather conditions at harvest are on the average less severe in California than in Europe, but the fact that the harvest decision is ultimately always a critical one shows that conditions *do* vary and do provide difficulties in getting the optimum quality grape into the winery. For instance, in the North Coast area, 1972 suffered bad harvest rains. Many grapes were difficult to get out of the muddy fields and many never fully ripened. The 1976 drought caused dehydration of some grapes so that they did not mature properly. A September rain in 1978 created ideal conditions for the excessive development of botrytis not only in White Riesling but in normally less susceptible varieties such as Sauvignon Blanc, Chenin Blanc, and Chardonnay. In 1979, October rains brought mold and rot to Cabernet Sauvignon and left several thousand tons in the North Coast unharvestable. A heat wave in early October 1980 caused the percentage of sugar in Cabernet Sauvignon grapes to climb so fast that some grapes had to be harvested at higher than desirable levels. In fact, few years have had perfect weather conditions from July to October, the period of grape ripening.

CHANGES IN WHITE WINEMAKING

After a tour of a modern California winery, visitors often ask: "How was the wine made before—how is it different now?" California white wines have improved dramatically in the last twenty years, not only because better white wine grapes are being grown, but because there have been a large number of changes in the winemaking process. The resultant wines are of better color, of more intensely fruity and varietal aromas, and of fresher flavor, and they lack the defects that more frequently occurred under the less controlled circumstances before the 1960s.

The first important step in the improvement of California white winemaking was controlled, consistent use of sulfur dioxide (SO_2) to prevent wine oxidation and preserve fruity aromas. Prior to 1970, levels of 100–125 mg/l (milligrams per liter) were used when the grapes were crushed, more if the grapes were in poor condition. After the white wines were made, levels of 30–35 mg/l of free, or "active," sulfur dioxide maintained the wine quality. Recently, California winemakers have been lowering the amounts of sulfur dioxide during crushing, if the grapes have come in in good condition. North Coast wineries have been using 30–50 mg/l total sulfur dioxide, and Central Valley producers are using 50–100 mg/l.

SKIN CONTACT AND JUICE REMOVAL PRIOR TO PRESSING

Skin contact is a system developed in the 1970s for holding the crushed white grapes and their juice in mutual contact for two to thirty-six hours before pressing. It changes the aromas and flavors of the wine, and it increases the speed of the pressing operation by allowing juice to be drained off before the grapes go to the press. Research indicates that prolonging contact at warmer temperatures increases phenolic (tannin) extraction, and therefore color and body, while cooler contact increases fruity aromas with slower phenolic extraction. The rate of extraction triples for every 10° C (50° F) rise in must temperature. Prolonged extraction at high temperatures risks excess bitterness and overextraction in the wine. Must chillers, also used widely in Australia, enable winemakers to cool down to 13–15.5° C (55–60° F) grapes that have been harvested warm (24–32° C; 75–90° F) immediately after crushing, thus enabling close control of extraction during the skin contact period.

Systems for removal of white juice prior to pressing are of two kinds: stationary batch systems and continuous systems. Stationary systems provide both juice separation and skin contact. Usually horizontal or vertical tanks with internal screens and some version of a sloped bottom, they are suspended above the presses. Sometimes they have refrigeration jacketing. They enable winemakers to use the skin contact process, to drain off the juice into a holding tank, and to move the skins by gravity or conveyor into the press. Often the juice drained directly from the de-juicers is so low in solids that it needs no further clarification. Continuous systems such as drag screen dejuicers or screw conveyors over screens have been designed primarily to make pressing more efficient and are routinely used in large Central Valley wineries; they reduce must volume going into the press by draining off up to 75 percent of the juice. Alternatively, in a more European style, the grapes may go directly from the crusher into the press. This method fell out of favor in the seventies because it was slow and produced wines that were too delicate. Now, however, with more winemakers and consumers favoring more delicate wines, there is some renewed interest in "direct to press" handling of grapes.

PRESSING

Concerns in pressing have been quality of juice, total yield per ton, and speed (tons per hour). With improved presses, juice yield has moved to an average of 170–80 gallons per ton of good quality juice, compared to a yield of 155–60 gallons per ton using older basket presses. In the late sixties and early seventies, press juice was considered to be of lesser quality than free-run, the juice drained before pressure is applied. But the combination of better presses, better monitoring, and more skillful handling has raised the quality of press juice. Now enologists generally regard well-made press juice as richer in body and varietal aroma than free-run, with which it is now frequently blended before, or during, fermentation.

Four types of presses have been used in the wine industry: vertical basket presses (the old-fashioned wood presses); horizontal metal presses; pneumatic, air-operated bag presses; and continuous presses. Major considerations in press design have been speed, juice quality (measured by the percentage of suspended solids and the amount of phenolic material), yield of juice per ton of grapes, and cost. For speed, continuous presses, which allow constant feeding of grapes and removal of juice, have been the most popular and widely used in California's larger wineries. Because they operate at high pressures and produce higher average solids, they require careful operation and close monitoring to maintain high juice quality. Major quality improvements in Central Valley winemaking have been realized by improvements in continuous presses. Ten or twelve years ago, continuous screw press designs caused much grinding of the pulp all along the barrel of the press, creating bitter astringent juice. Newer continuous "bi-valve" presses have short screw sections and regions of high pressure that reduce the grinding. The horizontal basket press has been the workhorse of the smaller and medium-sized wineries, producing good yield of quality juice at a reasonable speed and cost. In design, these are the major successors to the old-fashioned basket press. Pneumatic presses using air pressure in rubber bags have been very effective in giving good yield of high-quality juice with low solids and phenolics. A new design, generally called a tank-press, extracts normal yields of juice at very low pressures and is becoming very popular with coastal wineries.

JUICE CLARIFICATION

Natural juice clarification is accomplished by settling. Small California wineries were settling white juice in the forties, but not until the seventies, with the advent of the centrifuge as a solids removal aid, was white juice throughout California routinely clarified before fermentation. Additional methods of clarification are juice filtration and the use of pectic enzymes to aid natural clarification. Each method may affect juice composition and the speed of solids removal. The trend in the seventies was toward the increased use of centrifuges. In the early eighties, in the coastal counties, there is movement back to natural settling.

Centrifuges hasten the process of removing solids by spinning the juice at high speed. They have several advantages: the reduction in the number of stainless tanks that may be tied up for from twenty-four to forty-eight hours while the juice is settling (freeing them for fermentation, reducing tank capital costs); the quick removal of juice solids that may be difficult to settle naturally or be in poor condition owing to bad weather; the ability to control the amount of solids left in the juice for fermentation. Their disadvantage is their ability to strip the wines of complexity if not used with care. Decanters and lees filters (plate and frame filters run with filter cloths at high pressure) are also used in California for immediate clarifications of juice solids from settled juice. Since the amount of solids in settled juice is only 25 to 40 percent, immediate filtration recovers juice in condition for use with premium wines at substantial savings to the wineries.

FERMENTATION

Temperature control of fermentation, barrel fermentation, preservation of residual sugar from fermentation, and experimentation with different yeasts are major developments in white winemaking. (For a discussion of barrel fermentation, see Walter Schug, "The Vinification of Fine Wine.") Research has shown fermentation temperatures to affect both the formation and the retention of wine esters. Advocated as long ago as 1911 by R. Jordan, the idea that cool (10–15° C; 50–59° F) fermentation produces wines of greater fruitiness finally became established in the forties. By 1947 André Tchelistcheff at Beaulieu and Robert and Peter Mondavi at Krug were using stainless steel coils inside wood fermentors to control fermentation temperature. Since that time, the increased use of stainless steel double-wall tanks with refrigerant in the jackets and the increased sophistication of their control systems have enabled us to produce wines with fresh, clean, intense, varietal fruit. Stainless steel tanks have many advantages over wooden ones. They are more easily cleaned; they can be used for both red and white wine; they do not require burning of sulfur to keep them in good condition when empty; and cooling systems can be built into their walls. Stainless steel tanks can also be manufactured in larger sizes and are cheaper on a per gallon basis than wood tanks.

The first refrigeration equipment was external to the fermentors—coils or pipes, blanketed by cool water, through which the wine flowed. Tanks with cooling jackets built into the walls offer some major advantages. The wine can be chilled without the extra pumping needed for external chillers, reducing both labor costs and excessive handling of the wine. Refrigeration in the wall of the fermentor can respond instantly to temperature changes, holding temperature in a very narrow band, while the traditional external chillers required substantial cooling down by a range of 4° to 7° C before letting temperatures rise again, creating a roller coaster temperature instead of a consistent one. Additionally, refrigerated fermentors can be cooled simultaneously; an external chiller can handle only one tank at a time. However, cooling jackets are not effective on very large fermentors; external heat exchange units must be used.

An important partner to the refrigeration system is the temperature control system. At first, tank refrigeration was controlled manually by hand valves.

Soon simple temperature sensors and controllers regulated the flow of refrigerant to the tank; and now larger wineries have central banks, some computer-operated, that allow readout and control of all fermentors in a winery. These controllers can be hooked into computers that collect fermentation temperature information for each fermentor. The result is closer, centralized control, less labor, and more information about the fermentations.

Residual Sugar in Wines

Traditionally in California, concentrate (concentrated grape juice at 60 percent sugar) was used to sweeten a fermented dry white wine to produce, for instance, a sweet Chenin Blanc. In the 1970s, two other sweetening techniques emerged: use of a sweet reserve and stopping fermentation. Use of a sweet reserve, or slightly fermented grape juice, was a German technique for fermenting white wine dry and sweetening it with a prescribed amount of sweet juice. This allowed precise control of the level of sugar in the wine. Problems in holding the sweet reserve in good condition with refrigeration encouraged interest in a third method, stopping fermentation. Refrigerated tanks and wine chillers allow winemakers to stop fermentation at a desired sugar by chilling the wine, then removing the yeast by centrifuging, filtration, or natural settling. Currently most smaller coastal wineries producing sweet wines use refrigeration and subsequent clarification to stop fermentation at a desired level of sugar.

Yeast

Europeans still widely use natural yeast fermentations, but, for the most part, California vineyards have not built up a good, reliable natural wine yeast population on their grapes. "Wild fermentations" (from natural yeasts) often produce unpleasant aromas or "stuck" (unfinished) fermentations. Many years ago, Professor William Cruess of the University of California at Berkeley began the collection of pure wine yeast cultures for starting fermentations. In the 1960s, at the Davis campus, the Montrachet strain of yeast was most commonly used in winemaking (later in a dried form). In the 1970s, winemakers began to explore other kinds of yeast, looking for differences in aromas produced, rate of fermentation, foaminess, reliability in finishing fermentations, behavior under different temperature conditions, absence of unpleasant aromas, and absence of volatile acidity ("vinegariness").* Wineries have thus not only increased the range of yeast they have to choose from, but have developed better methods for growing yeast starters. Some

---

* Some of the yeasts available and used to some degree in the industry are: Assmanshausen (UCD 679); Burgundy (UCD 51); Champagne (UCD 595); Champagne (UCD 505); Epernay (Rankine 729; UCD 585); French White (Pasteur Institute); French Red (Pasteur Institute); Montrachet (UCD 522); Steinberg (UCD 529); Prise de Mousse (UCD 594); Epernay 2 (Geisenheim Institute); Steinberg (Danish Fermentation Industry 228); Fermivin; Vi-a-dry K-1; Vi-a-dry Wädenswill; Champagne Epernay (UCD 590); Geisenheim 1949 (UCD 591).

add dried yeast directly to fermentors, but others add it to a small quantity of juice, let it grow one or two days to a high population, then add this starter (called a "hot" starter) to the juice to get a more energetic start of fermentation. Where yeast strains are not available in dried form, techniques are used to propagate the liquid starters up from so small an amount as a cup to hundreds or thousands of gallons. More and more, wineries are monitoring the number of yeast cells in their starters and in the juice after inoculation, to be sure that the fermentations will start properly.

MEANING AND IMPORTANCE OF pH

pH is a measure of the number of charged hydrogen atoms (called ions) in a wine. These ions come mainly from the natural malic and tartaric acids in the grape juice. By nature these acids give up or release (dissociate) some of their hydrogen atoms when they are in juice or wine. The numbers used to express pH (in wine, it usually ranges from 3 to 4) are a shorthand for the number of free hydrogen ions. As the pH number goes from 3 to 4, the actual number of hydrogen ions goes down. In other words, our numerical expression for pH is inversely proportional to the actual number of hydrogen ions. Acid and pH are related because the grape acids are the source of the hydrogen ions. The amount and kind of grape acid affects the potential number of hydrogen ions that are available, and a high acidity is often, but not always, associated with a low pH (many hydrogen ions). These free hydrogen ions, although few in number, have a powerful effect on the wine, affecting its color, flavor, stability and resistance to bacterial growth. California winemakers have in recent years come to appreciate the significance of pH and to pay attention to viticultural practices and harvest timing that affect it. In winemaking, ion exchange for tartrate stability reduces pH; the addition of acid, especially of tartaric acid, can reduce pH; and malolactic fermentation, by changing from the stronger malic to the weaker lactic acid, can increase pH.

See TABLE 2
p. 184

STABILIZATION

Excessively warm or cool temperatures may cause deposits or the appearance of haze in bottled wine. Excessive heat may precipitate protein, causing a cloudy or milky material to form; excessive cold crystallizes potassium bitartrate—cream of tartar—the familiar layer of crystals that many consumers have seen on the cork of a bottle of refrigerated wine. Since 1960, however, extensive research at the University of California at Davis into the chemical nature of wine protein and bitartrate has increased our ability to reduce the occurrence of these precipitates. Bentonite, a clay in powdered form, has been used extensively to remove excess protein. Changes in practice have involved timing of bentonite addition (before, during, or after fermentation) and use of different methods to test wines for their bentonite needs. The removal of excess cream of tartar has traditionally been by chilling the wine to $-4°$ C ($25°$ F). The chilling creates a "supersaturation"

TABLE **2**

WHY IS pH IMPORTANT IN WINEMAKING?

CRITERION	Low pH (3.4–3.5)	High pH (3.6–4.0)
BACTERIAL GROWTH	*less growth*	*more growth*
WINE OXIDATION	*less oxidation*	*more oxidation*
WINE COLOR		
kind of color	*red*	*red with bluish-purple overtones*
amount of visible color	*more color*	*less color*
SO$_2$ ACTIVITY	*more activity*	*less activity*
FLAVOR	*more crisp, tart*	*less crisp, tart*
AROMA (varies with type of varietal wine)	*in Cabernet: "berry/fruity"*	*in Cabernet: "chocolaty"*
STABILITY		
protein stability	*more stable*	*less stable*
tartrate stability	*more stable*	*less stable*

in the wine of the potassium bitartrate, which hastens its crystallization and subsequent precipitation. In recent years, tiny cream of tartrate crystals are added during the chilling. The crystals act as nuclei or foci for the crystallization, making the chilling process more effective. German research and development of equipment have resulted in some practices that hasten bitartrate removal: heavy doses of bitartrate crystals for seeding, quick chilling for short periods of time, and filtration to remove all bitartrate crystals formed. Another method is the ion exchange process, which removes the potassium ions (from the potassium bitartrate) in exchange for hydrogen ions. Large California wineries are beginning to adopt this process. A beneficial side effect, one that improves general quality, is the reduction of pH due to the increase in the number of hydrogen ions. A number of California wineries still open the winery doors in winter and let the cold air chill the wine. This less technical approach does not yield consistent results, but seems suitable for wines with lower bitartrate content, especially for wineries whose more knowledgeable customers are unconcerned with the appearance of tartrate crystals in their wines.

MALOLACTIC FERMENTATION

Malolactic fermentation is the conversion by malolactic bacteria of wine's malic acid to a weaker acid, lactic acid. Beneficial effects are reduction in the sensory tartness of the wine and addition of aromatic constituents, by-products of the bacterial activity, which add complexity of aroma. Malolactic fermentation may also diminish varietal fruitiness and intensity. For the most part, California white wines do not undergo malolactic fermentation: winemaking practices that employ moderate levels of sulfur dioxide, substantial acid levels in the juice, cool fermentation, and immediate clarification after fermentation create conditions unfavorable to the growth of malolactic bacteria. Also, the generally fresh and fruity white wine styles of California are better maintained in the absence of malolactic fermentation.

However, coastal region winemakers, intrigued with the traditional occurrence of malolactic fermentation in French white Burgundies, have been experimenting with malolactic fermentation in Chardonnays. Those who use it, so far only a small number, feel that it adds to the depth and complexity of the wine and moderates the strong, fruity varietal character. It has not been simple to put Chardonnays through a malolactic fermentation and end up with a fine wine. Special conditions must prevail: the juice must be of good quality; there must be moderate pH; there must be moderate, but not high, malic acid, lest the wine lose too much acid and become "flabby" after the fermentation is complete; and there must be moderate to high tartaric acid. The juice must be low in sulfur dioxide and the malolactic bacteria should be added during fermentation for best results. The alcoholic fermentation is done at warmer temperatures (16–18° C; 61–64° F) since the bacteria are sensitive to cooler temperatures.

BARREL-AGING

Changes in selection and use of barrels for both red and white wine aging may be the single most dramatic and influential factor affecting the quality and style of California wines in the last twenty years. Because of the cost both of barrels and of the labor to handle wine in barrels, barrel-aging has been confined to the more expensive varietal wines and is just now beginning to be used on generic wines. According to André Tchelistcheff, Beaulieu used French oak barrels in the 1920s, when the de Latours brought them from France for their Cabernet aging program. In 1939, Beaulieu built a barrel storage area for French and American oak barrels. Tchelistcheff also recalls tasting in 1939 a fine 1937 Wente Chardonnay that had been aged in European puncheons. Robert Mondavi continued to explore the use of barrels for aging red and white wines, first at Charles Krug, and later at the Robert Mondavi Winery (see the essay by Timothy Mondavi below). Barrel-aging of white wines, primarily Chardonnay, began to expand dramatically in the 1970s. Soon Sauvignon Blanc, and to a minor extent Chenin Blanc, began to see some barrel-aging. The trend has been to use French oak for Chardonnay, both for barrel fermentation and aging. Both French and American oak have been used with good success for Sauvignon Blanc.

Many facets of barrel-aging affect the wine quality and style, and winemakers have dealt with such questions as how long the wine should be kept in barrels; whether to use new or old barrels, and in what proportion; what kind of French oak to use (Limousin or Nevers); how to prepare the barrel for use; and how "clean" (free of yeast sediment) the wine should be when it goes in. Wine that is held too long in barrels or in contact with too high a proportion of new oak produces exaggerated, oaky wines. The effect of the new oak is moderated by reducing the percentage of new barrels used for any one wine. With few exceptions, most oak-aged Chardonnays see no more than 25 percent new oak, and stay in barrels from four to eight months. Moderation of the effect of new oak is also achieved by using barrel fermentation. Wines fermented in new oak do not smell or taste as "oaky" as those fermented in tanks, then stored in new oak, even if the length of stay in the barrels is the same. Winemakers speculate that the yeast (protein) in fermentation has a "fining" effect on the barrel tannins.

Twelve years ago, it was considered important that wine going into barrels for aging be clarified by filtration or centrifuging. More recently, some winemakers have observed the traditional Burgundian procedures of leaving the wine on the yeast sediment for six to eight months after completion of the fermentation. Better selection of yeast and better juice clarification have eliminated off aromas such as hydrogen sulfide, the rotten egg smell, once associated with prolonged contact with yeast lees. Experimentation has led some enologists to feel that with prolonged contact the yeast moderates the astringency of the extracted wood tannins and gives additional complexity to the wine aromas. This technique is used in only a small percentage of California white winemaking.

As Californians purchased more barrels for wine aging, more French coopers exported to the United States, and California winemakers observed style or taste differences among wines produced in barrels from different coopers. These taste differences are thought to be related to the different heating techniques (various combinations of steam, hot water, or fire heat) French coopers use to bend and set their barrel staves. Trials continue by California winemakers to use these differences in defining their own wine styles.

YEAST-FREE FILTRATION

A major improvement in white wine quality came with an industry-based winemaking improvement, filtration of sweet wine to remove yeast before bottling. Left in bottled sweet white wine, yeast may reactivate and begin fermentation, creating a fizzy, cloudy wine. Older methods of prevention such as pasteurization just prior to bottling killed the yeast but reduced the fresh fruitiness of the wine, while the addition of yeast-inhibiting chemicals affected the wine's aroma and flavor. Two types of filtration were developed for yeast removal: depth or pad filters that would hold back all yeast in the wine as it passed through them; and delicate membrane filters with openings, or pores, smaller than yeast. The filters and their housings are carefully cleaned, usually with heat, to be sure that they are free of yeast when the wine is passed through them. As the wine filters through, all the yeast is removed, and the wine can be bottled without fear of refermentation. This technique maintains the fresh, fruity, attractive qualities of white wines and is responsible in part for the general quality improvement of sweet white wines.

CHANGES IN RED WINEMAKING

The major changes that have come about in making red wine in California reflect the changes in the red varietals grown, the improved attention to proper harvest time, the more controlled use of extraction techniques during fermentation, and the refinements of barrel-aging. Although some fine California Cabernet Sauvignon wines were made in the early 1900s and in the 1930s to 1960s, the recent worldwide attention to California red wines is an appreciation of our ability to achieve consistency of quality at all levels of winemaking from inexpensive to expensive.

CRUSHING

The process of removing the stems and crushing the grapes seems on the surface to be merely mechanical and, for the most part, has been carried out for years in the same manner all over the state. The Garolla-type crusher, a rotating perforated basket with internal paddles, crushes and destems the grapes. The addition of rollers and variable-speed drives allows better control of handling different grape varieties. Recently, attention has focused on two variations, the use of stems in some red wine fermentations, and the use of whole (uncrushed) grapes. Pinot Noir fermentations in Burgundy use stems routinely to give tannin and complexity. Coastal winemakers in California, eager to produce Pinot Noir wines of the quality of great French red Burgundies, have been experimenting with stems with mixed results. Some feel that stems add tannin, backbone, and peppery character; some feel that they add astringency and green character. Stems in small amounts have also been tried in Cabernet Sauvignon fermentations. Whole red grapes are sometimes used in Burgundy to slow the rate of fermentation. A few coastal winemakers are experimenting with this technique, but it has not yet been widely adopted for Pinot Noir.

FERMENTATION

Management of the extraction of color, tannins, and flavors from the skins of the grapes during fermentation has a dramatic effect on the finished wine. To generalize, less extraction results in a fruitier wine of lighter color and body, drinkable sooner; more extraction results in a darker, richer, more complex wine requiring longer aging to achieve its peak. Extraction is enhanced by higher fermentation temperatures, by longer contact between the skins and wine, by more mixing of the skins and wine together, and by the presence of alcohol. The way these techniques are combined depends on the style of wine the enologist wishes to achieve. Fermentation of sugar to alcohol produces heat as a byproduct. If not removed, the buildup can kill the yeast after it reaches 32–38° C (90–100° F), causing a "stuck" fermentation. Traditionally, fermenting in small containers of two- to three-ton capacity, combined with frequent mixing and reasonably cool cellar temperatures (13–18° C; 55–65° F), naturally cooled the fermentation. With the advent of stainless steel double-wall tanks with refrigerant in the jackets and "fine-tuned" temperature management using automatic temperature controllers, makers of red wine have moved from temperatures of 21–24° C (70–75° F), still used for lighter or fruitier wine styles, to 26–32° C (79–90° F), now used for richer styles intended for barrel- and bottle-aging.

The traditional mixing technique to keep the fermenting wine and floating skins in contact has been to pump over: pumping the red wine from the bottom of the fermentor over the top of the cap to wet and break up the skins. Variations include using a sprinkler for automatic or semi-automatic pump-over; using different lengths and timings for the pump-over; punching down, the traditional European method of pushing the cap physically from the top into the wine; and keeping the cap submerged by installing a device in the fermentor that prevents the skins from floating to the top. Also, in recent years, automatic rotating fermentors

have achieved extremely effective and more easily controllable extraction by mixing. Work done at the University of California at Davis and at individual wineries
indicates that these variations in mixing techniques do indeed affect the composition and style of the wine. Undoubtedly, the pump-over remains the most common
mixing technique employed in red wine fermentations in California today, but the
trend is to refine it to produce a style unique to each winemaker.

At 21–24° C (70–75° F) red wine fermentations are usually complete—
free of sugar—in one week. Many California red wine fermentations finish on the
skins, but enologists wanting lighter styles may press the grapes and remove the
wine from the skins before the fermentation is over. A development in the last ten
years, especially for achieving richer, longer-aging red wines, is extended skin contact. Modeled after traditional *Grand Cru* Bordeaux red winemaking, where some
châteaux may leave the skins, seeds, and wine in contact for three to four weeks, this
process lengthens the period for extraction of color and tannin components from
the skins to the wine. University research has not yet assessed the changes during
this period, but many winemakers are using the technique for reserve or special
lots, feeling that longer contact enhances the chance for extra varietal flavor, richness, and body.

Carbonic maceration and thermovinification are special red fermentation techniques that are used to a limited degree. Both originated in Europe. Carbonic maceration, whole grape fermentation, is used in Beaujolais to produce fresh,
fruity, low tannin red wine. In the same way, some California Gamay Beaujolais
grapes are dumped whole, without crushing or stemming, into a fermentor. Yeast
may or may not be added, and intracellular (internal) fermentation takes place until the grapes break down. The resulting wine can be deliciously fresh and fruity,
but is usually not for long aging. Several small wineries produce distinctive wines
using carbonic maceration. Thermovinification, developed in France and Germany, involves crushing and immediate heating of the must to high temperature
(69–71° C; 156–60° F), which extracts color from the skins to the juice. It is kept
hot for half an hour, then cooled and pressed to separate the skins from the juice.
The fermentation of the juice then takes place separately from the skins, as in a
white wine fermentation. Thermovinification produces a softer, less tannic red
wine, different in character from wine made by traditional red fermenting methods. Used only experimentally in California, it is not, to the author's knowledge,
a standard process at any winery.

MALOLACTIC FERMENTATION

John L. Ingraham and Ralph E. Kunkee, of the University of California
at Davis, and André Tchelistcheff, of Beaulieu, were among the enologists working
in the late 1950s and 1960s to identify and understand malolactic fermentation, to

develop pure strains of bacteria, and to introduce to the industry the idea of inoculation. During this time *Leuconostos oenos* (known industrywide as ML34) was isolated from a Napa Valley winery and selected for development. Bacterial inoculation of the wine after the alcoholic fermentation is over has now become a common practice with California red wines. In the 1970s, Napa Valley winemakers began to inoculate for malolactic fermentation *during* the alcoholic fermentation, which provides better conditions for the bacteria (more heat, less initial alcohol, more nutrients) although there is some competition between yeast and bacteria. Some winemakers are experimenting with different bacteria looking for strains that will dependably cause completed malolactic fermentations under more difficult conditions (cooler temperatures, higher acidities, and lower pHs) and favorably affect wine aroma.

BARREL-AGING

California winemakers have given a great deal of attention to barrel-aging. It is used primarily with Cabernet Sauvignon, Pinot Noir, and Zinfandel from cooler regions. American oak is favored for Zinfandel, while the majority of the more expensive Cabernet Sauvignons age in French oak. There is wide agreement, supported by Vernon Singleton's research at Davis, that French and American wood give different extractives and different flavor effects. The differences between them are less pronounced as the barrels grow older and may be less pronounced when stave-aging and coopering techniques are nearly the same. American oak continues to be used for less expensive red wines because of its lower initial cost.

In highly flavored, intensely varietal Cabernet Sauvignons, as much as 100 percent new oak may be used for aging the wine, but this is the exception. Depending on the wine style, 5–25 percent new oak may be used each year. The length of time a red wine spends in barrels depends on the wine's structure and style, the effect the winemaker desires, and the age of the barrels it is in. Wines that are lighter in color or body or are meant to be fruitier may be kept in barrels only six months, while heavier Cabernets may be kept in barrels for eighteen, twenty, and occasionally twenty-four months. Wines often stay in new barrels for a shorter period of time to reduce the risk of excess oakiness. The wine that evaporates during barrel-aging is replaced by weekly topping, opening the barrel and filling it up. In the seventies, rolling became more common—filling the barrel, rolling it until the bung was a quarter turn down and always submerged in the wine, and not refilling for four to six months. This method is now considered to be less oxidative, while the weekly topping tends to hasten the maturation of the wine. Both techniques are widely used.

ROSÉ WINES

Rosé, or pink, wines form a major part of California's wine production, close to 25 percent of all California wine sold in the United States in 1980. There are two wine-making techniques. The simpler is a blending of red and white wines; the more complex involves the contact of skins and juice of the crushed red grapes, until the desired pink color has been extracted from the skins into the juice. The juice is then drained from the skins, and has the subsequent cool fermentation and handling typical of a white wine. Improvements in rosé winemaking have come with increased use of the second technique, which produces a delightfully fresh, fruity wine. Some made from a single grape, such as Grenache, Gamay, Zinfandel, or Cabernet Sauvignon, can have true varietal distinction.

OTHER WINEMAKING CONSIDERATIONS—RED AND WHITE

OXIDATION

In general, oxygen is regarded as harmful to white wines if introduced in large quantities. It can reduce or eliminate varietal character and cause browning of the wine. Some California winemakers have used the most extreme oxygen protection, blanketing white wines with nitrogen or carbon dioxide at every step of the winemaking process. Most winemakers protect white wines from oxidation by maintaining proper levels of sulfur dioxide (an antioxidant); by keeping tanks and barrels full so that they will not be exposed to air during storage or, if they are not full, replacing any air in the headspace of the tank with nitrogen or carbon dioxide; and by maintaining pumps, filters and bottling equipment properly so that as wine is moved from place to place, it will not pick up air from faulty equipment. Routine monitoring of wine movements assures minimal oxidation.

If air is introduced slowly in very moderate quantities, as in barrel aging, it may be considered favorable for the development of mature, complex aromas and flavors. There has also been a trend toward regarding moderate oxidation in the fresh juice as a benefit. It causes the browning and precipitation of oxygen-sensitive pigments that might otherwise brown later in the wine, and it aids the start of fermentation. For this and other reasons, the concentration of sulfur dioxide used as a juice antioxidant has diminished over the past fifteen years from an average of 125 parts per million to 50 (and as low as 30).

Red wines are less sensitive to the ill effects of oxygen, although in extreme doses browning, loss of fruit, and development of aldehydes (sherry bouquet) can occur. Over the last twenty years, trends in handling red wine have gone from aerative handling, with less attention to air protection, to more extreme concern with air protection, to the current more careful matching of aerative/nonaerative techniques to the wine composition and style. Red wines of more delicate, aromatic, fruity character, lighter in tannin, are now more protected from air. Heavy-colored, intensely flavored, more tannic wines need the positive effects of oxygen to soften and create complex flavors. Slow uptake of oxygen during aging in barrels causes polymerization of the smaller, more astringent phenolic tannins to larger, softer ones that usually precipitate.

FINING

Casein (milk protein) and egg white are traditional California fining agents. While frozen egg white is often used when fining large quantities of wine, fresh egg white has come into favor in smaller wineries in the last few years. PVPP (polyvinylpolypyrrolidone), a modern synthetic agent with a proteinlike structure, is used selectively to remove browning-sensitive phenolic compounds in white wine. Gelatin, a traditional fining compound, still finds wide use, while isinglass, used in several countries for many years, came into limited use in California in the 1970s as a superior clarifying agent for white wines.

THE WINERY LABORATORY

Technical advances in analysis and quality control are due in part to the increasing number of university-trained enologists operating winery laboratories. Currently, most of them routinely monitor alcohol, total and volatile acidity, free and total sulfur dioxide, residual sugar, protein and tartrate stability, phenolics, and pH. Other important techniques in use in winery laboratories in recent years include enzymatic analysis of malic acid and glucose-fructose; measurement of carbon dioxide with a Van Slyke apparatus or by titration; dichromate procedure for accurate alcohol measurement; distillation process for accurate measure of free and total sulfur dioxide in red wine; and, in research laboratories, use of high performance liquid chromatography to measure organic acids, sugar, amino acids, and alcohols. Wineries have become more sophisticated microbiologically. Good laboratories maintain a "library" of yeast and malolactic cultures, which they propagate up each year for harvest fermentations. They also are able to identify problem yeast and bacteria if they occur in wines. A very important laboratory function is to do "trial" finings, blendings, and additions. Before a process is applied to a wine in the cellar (for example, egg-white fining to remove excess tannins), it is done on different levels on a small scale in the laboratory. Sensory evaluation, tasting, is used to decide the appropriate amount, and then the work proceeds in the cellar.

WINETASTING

Tasting is the heart of winemaking. Wine quality is known by its aroma, flavor, and balance, and is not yet subject to complete chemical analysis. Though winetasting programs vary from winery to winery, wines are usually tasted daily during fermentation when they are changing quickly, then less frequently during the aging process when they are changing more slowly. Tasting is used to estimate a wine's quality level (is this a regular or reserve wine?); to decide on acid or fining additions; to monitor the aging process of the wine; to be sure the wine is in good condition; and to decide blends of vineyards or varieties. In short, the tasting of wine provides the basic game plan for the winemaking process.

COMMERCIAL WINERY LABORATORIES

A fairly recent development has been the proliferation of winery laboratories and winery consultants, especially in the coastal areas. These businesses, similar to French commercial laboratories, provide technical winemaking and quality control services to wineries so small that they cannot afford full-time enologists. The laboratories also maintain and sell yeast and malolactic cultures, and can provide sophisticated and special analytical capabilities that even larger wineries may not have.

DEVELOPMENTS IN WINEMAKING IN THE CENTRAL VALLEY

Of 237,000 acres of wine grapes in California in 1980, 196,000 were in the San Joaquin, Stanislaus, Merced, Madera, Fresno, Tulare, and Kern counties of California's Central Valley. In terms of the volume of wine produced, this area is California's most important, and provides the basic wines for the industry: the generics, the jug wines, the table wines, and the less expensive wines of good quality that have been most Americans' introduction to winedrinking.

The Central Valley has certain special viticultural characteristics. Most important are its warm temperatures. Daytime highs can get into the 100s. As you move south, nighttime temperatures also get warmer, moving up into the 80s in the Bakersfield area. Central Valley soils are fertile and crop yields are high, from seven to fourteen tons per acre depending on the grape variety. Water quality varies; there tends to be more salinity on the west side of the valley. Higher temperatures seem to increase the average pH of the grapes grown. Thompson Seedless, Chenin Blanc, and French Colombard are the white grapes grown most successfully; Barbera, Ruby Cabernet, and Grenache (for rosé) are the best reds.

The grapes seem to mature at lower sugars than do coastal grapes. At 18–19° Brix for whites, the grapes have a good acid–pH balance and sufficient flavor for harvest. In the past ten years, grape growers and winemakers have moved toward lowering their Brix at harvest from an average of 21° to 19° for whites, from 23° to 19° for rosé, and from 23° to 22° for reds. They have also focused more on pH as a key to harvest, trying to bring in white grapes at 3.1 to 3.4 pH and reds at 3.3 to 3.6 pH. Because of the volume of grapes and winery size, the scale of winemaking in the Central Valley is in a different world from that of the coastal counties. Wines are fermented in large quantities in 100,000- to 700,000-gallon containers. There are no batch processes, such as for pressing; processing is designed to be continuous.

In the past twenty years, major changes have occurred to improve Central Valley wines. Equipment made of brass and mild steel, a source of wine stability problems, has been supplanted by stainless steel. Increased use of refrigeration to control fermentation temperatures has brought a major improvement in quality. Because of the warm daytime temperatures, grapes being crushed are often at 38° C (100° F). Ten to fifteen years ago, they would have been slightly chilled, then allowed to ferment at temperatures as high as 32° C (90° F). Now juice is routinely chilled to 15.5° C (60° F) and fermented cool. Since the large fermentors are outside, they must be well insulated to prevent the daytime temperatures from heating up the fermentations. Another major improvement in quality has been the installation of centrifuges in the 1970s to clarify white juice before fermenting it. The use of sulfur dioxide has decreased with better clarification and cooler fermentation. Because of somewhat higher pHs and warmer temperatures, Central Valley winemakers work to protect the wine from oxidation. They use nitrogen during wine storage and transfer to exclude air pickup, and maintain proper levels of sulfur dioxide in the wine to provide additional protection. With few exceptions, barrel-aging is not used in Central Valley winemaking. It is too expensive, and unsuited for the volumes of wine being handled.

LOW ALCOHOL WINES

Recently, a new group of wines has emerged, called light, soft, or low alcohol. They are produced by harvesting the grapes at low sugar (15–17° Brix) and fermenting out to 8 to 10 percent alcohol; or by harvesting at higher Brix and using a combination of heat (about 43° C; 109° F) and vacuum distillation to reduce alcohol to as low as 7 percent; or by using some combination of the two. The resulting wines are more delicate in body and character than more traditional styles.

JUICE PRESERVATION FOR PROLONGED FERMENTATION

Australian winemakers have developed juice-holding techniques that allow them to ferment wines continuously the year around, much as beers are brewed. The basic system for white juice involves pressing the grapes, clarifying the juice to reduce grape solids, then adding sulfur dioxide (1,200 ppm). A few winemakers use filtration and refrigeration to hold the juice, but less refrigeration is needed with high sulfur levels. When the winemaker wants to ferment the juice, it is put through a heat and vacuum distillation that volatilizes and draws off the sulfur (down to 100–150 ppm). When yeast and yeast nutrients are added, fermentation takes place. California winemakers have journeyed to Australia to observe these techniques, and have applied them most effectively to inexpensive white wines, which are often at their best when fresh, just after fermentation.

V.6

Note: The Earliest Barrels

by WALTER HORN AND ERNEST BORN

THE PRACTICE OF STORING AND MOVING WINE in wooden casks made its appearance in Europe in the first century B.C. in the territories of the Celts and of the Illyrians. Pliny the Elder (A.D. 23/24–79) states that "in the neighborhood of the Alps people put [wine] into wooden casks and closed these round with hoops." In his intriguing *Dionysos*, Edward Hyams ascribes this invention to the Allobroges, a Celtic tribe that lived in and around the valley of the Isère, one of the principal alpine tributaries of the Rhone, the region where wine was first grown north of Italy. Hyams names Pliny the Elder as the source for his contention "that the practice of storing and moving wine in wooden casks was of Allobrogian origin." This may be straining the available evidence, but Hyams is surely on solid ground when pointing out that the custom of storing and moving wine in barrels had a prelude in the Near East, recorded by Herodotus (ca. 484–425 B.C.), who says that trade in wine was carried on in palmwood casks floated down the Euphrates River from Armenia on circular boats made of skin. Strabo (64/63 B.C.–A.D. 21 at least) informs us that "wooden casks larger than houses" (πίθοι ξύλινοι μείζους οἴκων) were used to store wine in Cisalpine Gaul, and that the Illyrians brought their wine from Aquileia at the head of the Adriatic to various markets in wooden casks in exchange for slaves, cattle, and hides.

    The Romans, who, like the Greeks and Egyptians, stored and carried their wine in earthenware amphorae, were startled by this ingenious innovation. Hyams believes that this invention of storing wine in huge containers formed by a multitude of separate pieces was dependent on the more temperate climate prevalent in the lower Alps, where barrels could more easily be kept in good condition than in the hot, dry climate of the Mediterranean countries. The wooden barrel was capable of storing wine in larger quantities and at considerably lower cost than the more breakable and considerably smaller amphora (the equivalent of 25.5 liters). Its

Adapted from an illustrated and historically documented chapter on the origins and medieval history of the wooden barrel in Walter Horn and Ernest Born, *The Plan of St. Gall*, 3 vols. (Berkeley and Los Angeles: University of California Press, 1979), 1:293–305.

primary contribution to Western life appears, however, to have lain not so much in this as in the fact that it enabled man to develop superior vintages by offering more favorable conditions for the aging of wines. Edward Hyams regards this as the great difference between the wines of antiquity (made from sweet grapes and stored in heavily pitched containers offering poor conditions for maturing) and the wine of modern times (made from smaller and more acid grapes and susceptible to oxygenation by air filtering through the pores of the wood).

When faced with the problem of storing wine in bulk, the ancients did so by putting it into large earthenware vessels (πίθοι, *dolia*) covered by a convex lid (*operculum*) sealed to the body of the vessel by a heavy layer of pitch. These vessels were buried to the rim in a deep layer of sand. Some of the larger *dolia* were so high that a fully grown man could stand erect inside without being visible. These large earthenware containers must have been extremely expensive, since their manufacture was dependent on firing ovens of unusual dimensions; and transporting them, even over small distances, posed delicate problems, in view both of their weight and of their susceptibility to breakage. It is also quite obvious that there was a non-transgressible upper limit to the size of an earthenware container that had to be fired in a single piece.

The barrel was free of any such limitations. Since it was composed of numerous long, narrow staves (*laminae, tabulae*) forced into position by iron hoops (*circuli*), its volume could be extended to previously unfeasible proportions, as witnessed by the casks "as large as houses" that Strabo saw in Cisalpine Gaul and the monster cask in Heidelberg Castle, which has a storage capacity of 49,000 gallons—232 times the volume, for example, of the large *dolium* of the Maison Carrée in Nîmes. The transport of such large containers posed no problem whatsoever, since they were assembled on the spot. Smaller barrels could even be rolled on the ground. Since they were set up above ground, the contents of these containers were more easily tapped than those of the buried *dolia*, and the process did not require that the container itself be opened, another advantage in aging wine.

The oldest extant wooden barrel, to the best of our knowledge, is a cask lifted, together with numerous other Roman objects, from a pond outside the city of Mainz in Germany. Some eighty other such barrels, many quite well preserved, dating from the first to the third century A.D., have so far been identified in various spots along the Danube, Rhine, Thames, and the Firth of Forth. Although the Mainz barrel was originally filled with fillets of fish, normally barrels served as casks for transporting wine, after which they were almost invariably reused as well linings.

The earliest pictorial representations of wine barrels are found on Trajan's Column (A.D. 113), where Roman soldiers are shown loading wine barrels onto a Danube boat at a fort in what is now northern Yugoslavia, and in a number of Gallo-Roman stone reliefs showing barrels being moved on boats or on wagons. One of the latter, a Roman stone relief now in the Musée Saint-Didier at Langres, fills the entire length of a four-wheeled wagon, and to judge by the size of the mules by which the cart is drawn and the height of the body of its driver, it must have had a length of roughly seven feet. The earliest reliable medieval representations of stave-built wooden barrels appear in the famous plan of St. Gall, a master plan for a Benedictine monastery drawn up during the first quarter of the ninth century. The cellar (*cellarium*) that forms an integral part of the monks' cloister delineated on this plan contains five large and nine small barrels. The large barrels (*maiores tunnae*) are fifteen feet long and have a central diameter of ten feet. The small barrels (*minores*) are ten feet long with a maximum diameter of five feet. Neither the larger nor the smaller ones could possibly have been dragged through the narrow doors of the cellar, which are no more than three feet wide. They must have been assembled inside. The staves of the small barrels take a turn toward the concave as they reach the end of the cask. This same form appears again in the famous Bayeux Tapestry (1073–83) in a scene that shows William's army setting out to conquer England in 1066, and carrying on carts a provision of wine and weapons. The inscription, executed in a kind of embroidery, leaves no doubt about the nature of the load:

ET HIC TRAHUNT CARRUM CUM VINO ET ARMIS.

AND HERE THEY PULL A CART WITH WINE AND WITH ARMS.

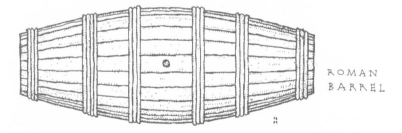

ROMAN
BARREL

THE TYPICAL ROMAN BARREL *was more slender (ratio, average diameter to length, ca. 1:3) than the barrel familiar to us today and often seen in California wineries (proportion ca. 1:1.4)—a type that, compared to the Roman example, seems short and dumpy. The Roman barrel adapted with ease to the problems of handling and maneuvering by men and to the simple means of lifting and transport available to those men at that period. The shortness of today's barrel is closely related to the widespread use of sophisticated lift trucks typically operated by one person with no more effort than that required to drive a small motor vehicle. The slender Roman shape required less precision and skill to fabricate than does the shorter, modern type. By medieval times cooperage techniques had greatly advanced, as can be seen on the Plan of St. Gall parchment manuscript (ca. 820 A.D.).*

E.B.

V.7

Note: Barrels in Modern Winemaking *by* TIMOTHY J. MONDAVI

TODAY BARRELS ARE USED IN THE WINERY alongside wooden and concrete tanks. Barrels ensure "breakdown" cooperage—they can be kept full, preventing oxidation. Concrete tanks, if untreated, have the disadvantage of being subject to spalling, or pitting of the interior surface, which allows the wine to extract calcium. For this reason, the latter are now usually lined with glass or tile, or wooden tanks are used in their stead. In concept, a traditional wooden tank is quite similar to half a barrel. Both taper toward one end and have a bilge, or slight inward curve to the taper. European tank makers still use fire to set the slight curve to their staves, just as barrel makers do in setting the curve of a barrel. The essential difference between tanks and barrels is size. A single 3,000-gallon tank stave weighs about as much as an empty 60-gallon barrel. This creates significant differences in wood selection and construction techniques. The long staves of a tank cannot be split like those of a barrel but must be sawn to the correct curvature. Wood must be taken from exceptionally tall oaks, free of knots and straight grained. There are three variables to be considered: diameter of the tank, width of stave, and height of stave. A template is made for each stave width for milling so that the base of the tank will be broader than the top and the tank will have the correct taper. These differences led to European coopers and tank makers originally forming separate guilds. In France today, while there is no longer the formal organizational distinction between coopers and tank makers, each craft has its distinct set of skills, which must be learned separately. The development of glass and glass bottles changed the need to market wine in barrels, essentially eliminating the requirement that barrels be transportable. However, some use of casks for transportation has continued, and even today Austria sells much of its wine from wood containers in taverns called *Weinstuben*.

One of the most significant advances in terms of wine containers was the development of stainless steel. Modern wineries use it extensively because it is inert, neither absorbing from the wine nor giving off character to it; it is totally impermeable to oxygen and does not allow evaporation; it is readily cleaned and can be sterilized; and it is possible to control the temperature. It is also currently less expensive than any of the other containers. A 200,000-gallon stainless steel fermentation tank without jacket, but with foundation, costs roughly 65 cents per gallon; a 12,000-gallon tank, about $1.50 per gallon. A 60-gallon French oak barrel (225 liters) costs about $5.00 per gallon, American oak roughly $2.30 per gallon (both costs include support systems, the pallets on which the barrels rest). Compounding that with operating costs, including the manpower required to manage hundreds of little barrels in comparison with one large tank, the expenses are quite high. Additionally, there are relatively higher costs for the evaporation of wine in barrels (roughly a 5 percent loss per year) as compared with wine in tanks. Replacement cost is also a factor. Barrels have variable lives, all of which are shorter than stainless steel: one stainless unit as opposed to thirty-five staves, two heads, and a number of hoops to hold them all together.

Given all the costs and, perhaps most important, the potential microbiological problems associated with a container that cannot be sterilized, why are barrels used so extensively and why do they remain so important to so many winemakers? In essence the answer is the contribution of the wood to the styles of wine and to the flavors that help us differentiate among wines. The evaporation of water and alcohol through the staves of a barrel concentrates the wine. The processes of filling, topping, and emptying incorporate air into the wine. And the wine absorbs extractives from the oak surface.

Evaporation occurs because the barrel is somewhat like a semi-permeable membrane, allowing water and alcohol to diffuse through the wood. The remaining wine becomes slightly more concentrated in flavor and character. Evaporation increases with higher temperatures and lower humidity. The cellar's humidity has a significant impact on the relative rates at which alcohol and water are lost. At roughly 60 to 65 percent relative humidity, both are lost at approximately the same rate. If the storage area is more humid, alcohol is lost more rapidly than water and the alcoholic percentage of the wine tends to decrease. However, if the humidity is less than 60 to 65 percent, the percentage of alcohol in the wine increases.

Since the barrel is a semi-permeable membrane, it allows water and alcohol to escape, but it does not allow appreciable air to get in. (Water and alcohol are relatively small molecules, air or oxygen in air much larger.) This is demonstrated during the aging cycle when a partial vacuum develops in the headspace within a barrel. Air is a vital part of barrel-aging and in controlled, realistic amounts can augment and improve the character of the wine. It is not introduced into the wine through the pores of the wood, but enters during filling, when there is turbulence; during topping to eliminate the ullage that develops through evaporation; during racking; and also during emptying of the barrel. Even in barrel-aging, it is possible to keep oxygen pickup to an absolute minimum by making the barrel inert prior to filling, by minimizing topping, by the use of great care in the topping process, and by treating the succeeding tank with carbon dioxide or nitrogen to make it inert prior to emptying the barrel. Air improves wine in a number of ways. It "softens" the tannin. (Actually, it hastens oxidation and changes in the tannin that result in a softer taste.) It modifies the color of a red wine from a bright purple or a dark, dark red (as in a very young wine) to a tawnier, more developed color. And, if not carried too far, it tends to enhance the bouquet of the wine as well.

Because oak meets the requirements of porosity, strength, and flavor, it is the wood of choice. The porosity and strength of oak are functions of physical makeup. As the tree grows, it sets up growth rings, adding to its girth each year. The sapwood, or conductive portion of the tree, is the cambium layer and new wood just under the bark. As additional rings grow, the older ones, or heartwood, become the structural support of the tree, while the new outer sapwood carries on the conductive functions. The structural aspects, in part, develop through the plugging of the old conductive vessels of the tree with foamlike intrusions, called tyloses, which harden and add strength as the sapwood becomes heartwood. The tyloses form in sufficient numbers to fill the conductive vessels completely and to block effectively the penetration of liquid through them, one reason that only heartwood is used for staves. The number of tyloses produced varies by the type of oak and is a consideration in choosing wood for coopering.

Heartwood is the only wood for tight cooperage. The rays of the heartwood radiate from the pith to the bark, giving additional support both to the tree and to the barrel made from it. Further, the rays make it that much more difficult for the wine to penetrate through the width of the stave of the barrel. Nor can the wine penetrate lengthwise through the stave, because the tyloses have filled the pores of the former conductive tissue. The relative proportion of springwood and summerwood has an impact on the wood itself and is affected by climate. The warmer the climate, the faster the tree grows; the cooler the climate, the slower. Slower-growing trees tend to have more extract and higher densities in the heartwood. The chemical makeup of that tissue is cellulose and hemicellulose for structural support, but more important from a winemaking standpoint are the aromatic compounds (lignins) and wood tannins (phenolic compounds) that are extracted into the wine. Tannin contributes to the wine's longevity and adds to its structure and feel, but the lignin contributes the vanillin, syringaldehyde, and other compounds responsible for the aromatic development of the wine during barrel-aging. The species of oak also affects the relative amounts of extract, phenolics, and aromatic characters that wine picks up. American oak, predominantly *Quercus alba*, tends to have a higher bouquet and stronger oak aroma (lactone). However, European oak, principally *Quercus robur* and *Quercus sessilis*, has more extractable solids and more phenolics.

Since most California wineries produce more than one variety of wine, it has become a high priority to make each wine true to style. Aspects of winemaking often regarded as "traditional" in Europe are becoming very important to California winemakers: harvesting the grapes at the optimum maturity for best varietal character; selecting the proper length of skin contact and temperature of fermentations; and selecting the type of oak and the length of aging in barrels. An openness among winemakers that promotes the free flow of information has helped to produce considerable advances in these areas in a short time.

Barrel-aging is only a small part of winemaking. There are, however, many other variables in the use of barrels that we have found contribute significantly to a wine's style. Barrels, therefore, have come to be one of the major interests at Robert Mondavi. Our earliest experiments concerned different species of oak, primarily *Quercus alba* from the United States and *Quercus sessilis* (or *petraea*) and *Quercus robur* (or *pedunculata*) from Europe. We also did research on the differences between oak from different regions, especially from the French forests of Nevers and Limousin. In the mid-1970s, our experimentation brought us to question the impact of coopering techniques on the characteristics contributed by the barrel to the wine, including evaluation of air-dried versus kiln-dried oak; the duration of air-drying of the staves; steam and fire versus fire-only for bending the staves in forming the barrel; the level of toasting on the inner surface of the barrel staves; and the importance of the thickness of the stave (the thinner-staved château-style barrel versus the thicker-staved transport-style barrel). In addition, we have studied barrel fermentation in various oaks coopered by a selection of companies in France. We taste constantly throughout the wine's development during each experiment with the goal of matching the varietal character of the wine with the character imparted by the barrel.

Based on our research, we now choose French oak almost exclusively for barrel-aging our varietal wines. In most cases, we prefer the character contributed by oak from the Nevers forest, although for Pinot Noir and Chardonnay we prefer Limousin oak. In regard to coopering techniques, our experiments with using steam and fire for bending the barrel staves were an attempt to eliminate the interior blistering caused by using only fire. Since it creates crevices in which bacteria might become trapped, blistering made thorough cleaning of barrels more difficult. However, after extensive evaluation of wines aged in barrels coopered by both steam and fire, we felt that the steam leached too much character from the wood. As a result, we returned to the use of traditional fire-only coopering techniques. We have also found that air-drying the staves prior to coopering—giving extended exposure to the elements—tends to remove the harsher wood characteristics and tannins, leaving the more subtle oak character we prefer for our wines. We are currently evaluating wines aging in new French oak barrels made of wood air-dried for two, three, or four years.

We have extended the concept of air-drying and French coopering methods to our research on American oak. American barrels are usually made from kiln-dried oak that has been sawn, rather than split, and bent with steam only. In 1977 we had 160 air-dried American oak barrels coopered in Europe by traditional French methods. The wine aged in them showed that the coopering techniques did have considerable influence on the contribution of oak character, though differences in oak types (*Quercus alba* versus *Quercus robur*) were still apparent. Air-drying tended to reduce the green sharpness in bouquet and the "rough mouth" feel characteristic of American oak. The use of flame for setting the staves seemed to soften the tannins and give a heightened aroma as well as additional complexity from the slightly toasty character.

Our research on toasting levels began when we noted that our shipments of barrels from France were not uniform in the degree of toasting on the inside stave surfaces. (Toasting is caramelization of the wood rather than charring, in which the wood actually catches fire, as in an American oak Bourbon barrel.) To determine the effect this had on our wines, we began in 1978 to specify the level of toasting—light, medium, or heavy—on each barrel made for us by French coopers. By following many experimental wines through their development, we have found that toasting has a significant influence on the style of wine. A normal to heavily toasted barrel can contribute a subtle "toasty" character to both the nose and flavor, providing an additional dimension of complexity. Results of our tastings show that the varietal and vintage characteristics of a wine determine the desirable amount of toasting just as they determine the amount of new oak and length of aging. Pinot Noir and Chardonnay, the traditional grapes of Burgundy, tend to benefit from a higher level of toasting on the staves, while Cabernet Sauvignon and Fumé Blanc (dry Sauvignon Blanc) do better with lighter toasting.

In summary, we have found that the species of oak tends to be the most important influence on the style of a wine, closely followed by the method of coopering, and finally, within a given species, the place of origin of the oak. However, our research on coopering techniques and oak types must be constantly reevaluated with the characteristics of each vintage. Wine is not made by formula, but by following preferences of taste and flavor.

VI

SOME REFLECTIONS ON THE WINES

1. GERALD ASHER

2. FORREST R. TANCER 3. PAUL DRAPER

4. THE EDITORS 5. ELEANOR McCREA

6. JEAN R. WENTE 7. THE EDITORS 8. JACK L. DAVIES

9. DARRELL F. CORTI 10. DORIS MUSCATINE

11. THOMAS D. TERRY, S.J.

*

VI.1
CABERNET SAUVIGNON

by GERALD ASHER

CABERNET SAUVIGNON WAS INTRODUCED TO CALIFORNIA IN OR BEFORE THE 1880s WITH OTHER VARIETIES FROM SOUTH-WESTERN FRANCE, INCLUDING THOSE traditionally associated with Cabernet Sauvignon in the vineyards of Bordeaux and some, such as Tannat, used for less opulent wines grown in the Béarnais region closer to the Pyrenees. As in France, these varieties were seen as means to an end—the production of claretlike red wine—not as ends in themselves. No more than in France did California growers at that time seem to be seeking to make a "Cabernet Sauvignon," and, with rare exceptions, it was only after Prohibition, when attempts were made to break with European place names applied generically to California wines, that Cabernet Sauvignon became the name of a *wine* as well as of a grape variety, thereby confounding end and means in a way that is still not resolved. Most of us can only guess at the style and quality of those pre-Prohibition wines made from Cabernet Sauvignon grown in California, though a half bottle of the 1936 vintage from E. H. Rixford's legendary La Questa vineyard at Woodside, tasted recently, gave me some idea of how they might have been. La Questa's reputation ("the most expensive Cabernet listed . . . on most . . . California wine lists of the early 1900s," according to Frank Schoonmaker in *American Wines*), was based on "red Bordeaux varieties planted," says Charles L. Sullivan in *Like Modern Edens*, "in the precise proportion as they were then grown at Château Margaux."

A half bottle almost fifty years old cannot be relied on, and when I broke the blob of wax that sealed the cork and poured wine directly, without decanting, I was expecting little more than a ghostly curiosity. To my surprise, the wine was deep red, almost opaque, merely tinged with terra cotta at the glass edge; there was that immediate and extraordinary bouquet with hints of chocolate, charcoal, and cassis we associate with distinguished classed growths of the Médoc; on the palate the wine was lively, intense, impeccably balanced. It was, in fact, among the best wines of Cabernet Sauvignon genre that I have tasted.

A more recent, and therefore more practically influential, legacy of California Cabernet Sauvignon has been handed down by Louis M. Martini, Charles Krug, Inglenook, and Beaulieu Vineyard, Napa wineries that alone from the end of Prohibition until the renaissance of the sixties and seventies ensured a continuum of fine winemaking in the state. During that time, they invested their skill and greatest effort in Cabernet Sauvignon wines. Remarkably, we can still see, within the scope of the disparate styles they chose, the seeds of all options available to winemakers today. They composed a theme that has since been taken up in ever widening fugue and variation. At Charles Krug, for example, Cabernet Sauvignon was unblended, and aged in well-seasoned vats and barrels; at Inglenook proportions of Cabernet Franc and, in later years, Merlot were introduced in quantities carefully judged to give subtlety without changing the essential character of Cabernet Sauvignon—a character further protected by aging in neutral German oak ovals; considerable varietal and geographic blending at Louis M. Martini, on the other hand, produced agreeable wines ready to be drunk early and with less regard for varietal purity; and at Beaulieu, of course, young American oak was used to dramatic effect on intense, unblended Cabernet Sauvignon to create the Private Reserve of Georges de Latour.

The contrasts in these familiar styles were etched in my memory at a dinner in the fall of 1979 when the 1951 Cabernet Sauvignons of Beaulieu Vineyard and Louis M. Martini were served with a 1956 Charles Krug and a 1941 Inglenook. The wines were presented to us in receding order of vintage—first the Charles Krug, with fruit so persistent and finish so soft that the wine left a sweet impression against which the Louis Martini seemed at first to be austere. It was certainly less direct than the others, but eventually revealed a youthful, berrylike bouquet that softened the wine and flattered the palate. The Beaulieu Vineyard Private Reserve that followed, richly preserving all those characteristics associated with Rutherford, with Cabernet Sauvignon, and with American oak that André Tchelistcheff combined into one of the most particular and consistent wines made anywhere, brought us more bluntly to the essence of Cabernet Sauvignon; and that was carried on by the Inglenook 1941, an immense, muscular wine, dark almost to the point of blackness, yet with bouquet unexpectedly fresh and elegant. Despite its size, there was no burn of excessive alcohol, no distortion of flavor or character: it had the perfect balance then characteristic of this estate.

These extraordinary wines of the forties and fifties, with an occasional glimpse or guess at pre-Prohibition production, remind us that Cabernet Sauvignon has a history in the state, and is certainly not a product of the recent wine revival. They provide a perspective in which we can better judge the potential and what seems to be the natural style of Cabernet Sauvignon in California. True, preoccupation with the grape is fostered by its associations with the great classed growths of Bordeaux (though none uses it to the exclusion of all others), a challenge as compelling to any winemaker as the Matterhorn is to a mountain climber, but that would soon be over if the wines to which Cabernet Sauvignon contributes did not so frequently touch our highest expectations of red wine.

In his *Bordeaux Antique*, R. Etienne suggests that evidence enough exists to show that today's Cabernet Sauvignon grape descends from Biturica, which in turn descended from Balisca, brought to Bordeaux in antiquity from the eastern shore of the Adriatic, where modern Albania now is. Pliny the Elder was familiar with Biturica in the first century and wrote (I quote and translate loosely) that "it flowers well, is resistant to wind and rain, and does rather better in cool than in warm regions," all of which makes sense to us today. Columella (according to René Pijassou of the University of Bordeaux: I have searched for the exact quote without success) confirmed Pliny's observation that Biturica stood up well to rain, and added another attribute familiar to us—it gave wine that kept well and improved with age.

Cabernet Sauvignon vines grow not exuberantly, but vigorously, and, when properly cultivated, yield sparingly. Their buds open late, an advantage in areas prone to spring frost, as are both the Médoc and the floor of Napa Valley. The dark green leaves are indented deeply in a way that causes the lobes to overlap slightly, a varietal characteristic. Its fruit is most appreciated by winemakers for reliable acidity and for the intensity of color and flavor inherent in the tough, resistant skin. Bunches are small and irregularly shaped, but the berries are perfectly spherical, black, and tightly packed together. They have a high proportion of seed and little juice.

Cabernet Sauvignon grapes give a wine that is distinctive, and most who have tasted it would recognize it again even when blended with other grape varieties. The characteristic smell and flavor bring forth references to violets, black currants, eucalyptus, tar, and, in older wines, chocolate and charcoal. In California, vocabulary has recently been extended to include vegetables of various kinds, perhaps through a misconception of the French tasting word *végétal*, which means "vegetable" only in the sense that we distinguish plant life from animal and mineral. It should not be surprising to find echoes of fruits and flowers in Cabernet Sauvignon, however: all wines share at least traces of most of the acids, alcohols, and esters occurring in everything from pineapple to roses. It is Cabernet Sauvignon's richness in this respect that makes the variety such an important component of a great wine.

But Bordeaux has always been more concerned with terrain, with the "best sections" of a vineyard and what to plant there than with grape varieties as such and where to plant them. The great growths of Bordeaux, and therefore Bordeaux wine as we know it today, evolved from the discovery that a knoll of sand and gravel at Haut-Brion, though barely different from land that surrounded it, nevertheless produced wine of greater distinction. John Locke, the philosopher, went there in 1677 to see for himself, and described in his journal "a little rise of ground, lieing open most to the west. It is noe thing but pure white sand, mixd with a little gravel," he continued. "One would imagin it scarce fit to beare any thing. . . . This, however, they say, & that men of skill and credit, that the wine in the very next vineyard, though in all things seeming equall to me, is not soe good." Arnaud de Pontac, the owner of Haut-Brion at that time, was a man of influence and wealth, able to ensure exposure of his wine to those best able to appreciate and recommend it. The style of winemaking in Bordeaux changed to accommodate this newly understood potential as much as to adjust to new market needs, and claret was transformed from the uneven beverage it had been since the Middle Ages to what the London Gazette, in the early eighteenth century, referred to repeatedly, and with determined fascination, as New French Claret. But "if the *régisseurs* gave great importance to the role of the soil," says René Pijassou, in his 1980 treatise *Le Médoc*, "they gave no recognition to the virtues of grape variety as a factor of quality." In the carefully detailed working instructions left by Berlon, Château Margaux's great *régisseur* at the time of transformation, there was no indication at all of which grape varieties were to be used. At that time, white grapes were freely mixed with black in the château's vineyard (the white vines of Château Latour were grafted to black only in 1813), and Merlot was still unknown in the vineyards of the Médoc.

The emergence of Cabernet Sauvignon as the preferred grape of Bordeaux, after 1815, was probably due more to the properties of the vine than to the quality and style of the wine produced from it. Writing in 1850, Edouard Lawton, the well-known Bordeaux broker of the period, said that Cabernet Sauvignon (then referred to as Carmenet Sauvignon) had been planted in the vineyards extensively during the preceding twenty-five years because the variety budded late, a protection from spring frosts, and was resistant to flower-drop in wet and cold seasons. As late as the 1830s, Château Latour continued to experiment with all manner of grapes, including Syrah from the Rhone, and only in 1849 was there a policy established that, since terrain was of prime importance, selection of grape varieties was to be made in accordance with soil compatibility. Most Bordeaux châteaux today still use grape varieties in proportions dictated by the soil composition of their vineyards. Rarely do they plant varieties specifically with a predetermined style in mind, disregarding soil. It is in this sense, above all, that the soils of a Bordeaux château dictate the recognizable style of its wine. Bordeaux still thinks vineyard first and vine variety second. Though by 1970 Cabernet Sauvignon dominated the Médoc through the style it imposes, it represented only 48.6 percent of the vines planted there, and an even smaller proportion of the vines of Saint-Émilion and Pomerol.

In California, on the other hand, emphasis on winemaking rather than on grape growing has allowed, indeed encouraged, more play to a winemaker's expression of the character inherent in specific grape varieties, than to the style and quality dictated by a particular vineyard site. It is a difference of attitude accentuated by giving grape and wine the same name in California, creating an assumption, at least, that one should faithfully reflect the other. For some varieties, particularly most whites, depending on fruit aromas and flavor for their character and style, that might be justified. But Cabernet Sauvignon develops through the transformations of age, acquiring grace and subtlety, flavor and bouquet not present in its early youth. We value mature Cabernet Sauvignon wines because they *are* so much more than the fermented juice of a particular grape.

Yet even in those instances where much is made of origin—Martha's Vineyard in the Napa Valley, for example—its importance seems to lie in the extent to which it brings out the character of Cabernet Sauvignon planted there. Few California winemakers would be comfortable expressing the style of a particular vineyard, using without concern whatever grape variety or varieties seemed most apt to the location. Most, consciously or not, seek out growers whose vineyards give the greatest opportunity to express best the variety of special interest to them. This is notably true of Cabernet Sauvignon. Joe Heitz, a distinguished proponent of vineyard identification, says, nevertheless, that he "tries to make a first-rate California Cabernet Sauvignon, one that reflects the character of the vineyard." He does not say that he "tries to make a first-rate Martha's Vineyard, one that reflects the character of Cabernet Sauvignon." He thinks Cabernet Sauvignon, makes his wine from Cabernet Sauvignon alone, and is impatient with those who prefer to blend. "They look to France," he says, "when our soils and our climate are different." In one respect, at least, Michael Rowan of Jordan Vineyard in Alexander Valley agrees. "Vineyards in Bordeaux are traditionally on meager soils. Producing fine wine from richer California vineyards is a new art. We cannot rely on the experience of Bordeaux. The expression of Cabernet Sauvignon is changed here, and we learn as we go." Ric Forman, previously with Sterling Vineyards, also accepts that California's climate, in particular, brings out greater richness, but complains that it has been too often presented in a heavy-handed way, just for effect. "It is an added quality that we should use," he says, "but not to the extent of wrecking the inherent finesse of Cabernet Sauvignon. Bigger is not better."

The "heavy hand" originated in a system by which growers were paid for grape sugar rather than grapes. In 1975, for example, when a cool, slow ripening season delayed sugar formation, there were stories of growers who cut the canes to allow dehydration to concentrate low sugar in the grapes. Today, wineries often agree in advance to pay the price for 24° Brix grapes, marginally high for elegance, if they can retain the right, should they prefer, to have the grapes picked at a lower sugar concentration for the same price. In the early seventies, a "heavy hand" also reflected the eagerness of a new generation of winemakers to explore the extent to which they could push the varietal's intensity. A key sentence in the edition of Amerine and Joslyn's *Table Wines* then in use as a standard text at the University of California may have spurred them on. "The most common defect of California wines," ran its message, "is their lack of distinctive aroma or bouquet rather than the presence of any specific disease or defect." Whether or not that was true of wines of the Central Valley, the mass-production area closest to the Davis campus, it probably was never intended to refer to the limited production of coastal Cabernet Sauvignon wines.

"It was a time," says Warren Winiarski of Stag's Leap Wine Cellars, referring to the early seventies, "when California winemakers were asking what Cabernet Sauvignon grapes *could* give, as opposed to what they *should* give." Massive, often charmless wines found ready acceptance among those who, often new to wine, allowed themselves to be impressed by scale before they had learned to recognise standards of balance, subtlety, and just plain drinkability. Dense, oversized wines matched the abundant enthusiasm typical of the newly converted. But such wines crushed any balanced, restrained wine tasted alongside them, so that the rosettes, medals, and endless accolades bestowed on them by county fairs, newsletters, and tasting groups further encouraged excess. The public, lacking guidance, accepted the rosettes and medals as recommendations, and were disappointed to find so many of them attached to wines that were unacceptably harsh and coarsely flavored. It was no consolation to be told that the wines would "live" forever.

Fortunately, the tradition preserved by Martini, Krug, Inglenook, and Beaulieu Vineyard, now strengthened and extended by others, continued, without fanfare, to provide balanced wines that perceptibly evolved from, and maintained, earlier styles. The point at which balance was again recognized as the key quality of a California Cabernet Sauvignon, as it is of any wine, was marked by the 1976 tasting in Paris at which Winiarski's Stag's Leap Wine Cellars' 1973 Cabernet Sauvignon was acknowledged the peer of any in the world. Stag's Leap had had some recognition in California, too, but the benchmark there at the time was still set by intense, exceedingly tannic wines that overwhelmed Stag's Leap in any direct comparison. European tasters had few preconceived ideas of how California wines were supposed to taste, and even fewer of the criteria by which they were being judged so articulately in California. Winiarski claims that he did not aim at any particular style for his 1973, but admits, at least, on reflection, to having sought moderation in all decisions along the way. Balance and moderation are now his consciously defined goals, increasingly shared by most other winemakers in California, however diverse the paths they use to arrive at them.

Balance in wine starts in balanced grapes, and Louis P. Martini says "perfect grapes grown in a perfect spot, would need little help. But not much in this world," he is quick to add, "is perfect." Martini blends to achieve the particular balance he prefers in his wines, bringing Cabernet Sauvignon grapes from his old vines in the Mayacamas mountains between Napa and Sonoma to add strength and a certain soft richness to the flowery, more pointedly acid, fruit of equally mature Cabernet Sauvignon vines grown in the cool Carneros region close to the Bay. He uses Merlot, too, to round out his blends, but only enough to arrive at the balance he seeks. Though it is an article of faith with him that no wine need be undrinkable when young in order to age, a Cabernet Sauvignon, he believes, is better for having all the Cabernet Sauvignon that balance and harmony will allow.

To Joe Heitz, "all the Cabernet Sauvignon" means *only* Cabernet Sauvignon. He feels that in the otherwise imperfect world lamented by Louis Martini, his own perfect grapes are indeed grown in perfect spots. "Blending," he says, "is all right for those who have to buy up lots here and there of what they can find. But the best wines are vineyard wines made from grapes where everything necessary is there within the fruit." André Tchelistcheff would once have agreed with him. Unblended and clearly defined Cabernet Sauvignon from designated vineyards was, and is, what Beaulieu Vineyards' Georges de Latour Private Reserve is all about. But though Tchelistcheff feels that a classic like the Georges de Latour Private Reserve must meticulously maintain its consistency of style, he now believes that softer, less assertive, more complex and more pleasing wines can be made from California Cabernet Sauvignon by blending, especially with 10 to 15 percent Merlot.

It is a philosophy widely shared in California; indeed, those using 100 percent Cabernet Sauvignon for production of fine wines seem to be in the minority. But with less than 2,600 acres of Merlot vines bearing in 1980, compared with over 22,000 acres of Cabernet Sauvignon, it is clear that California is far from the proportions of Merlot and Cabernet Sauvignon often common in Bordeaux. Freemark Abbey adds 12–15 percent Merlot to the Cabernet Sauvignon of its Bosché Vineyard wines. Charles Carpy, claiming that it enriches and rounds out the Cabernet Sauvignon, says "it also adds a hair of color," acknowledging that in California, at least, Merlot is often more deeply colored, stronger in alcohol, and richer in texture than is Cabernet Sauvignon. That is exactly what Michael Rowan likes about Merlot: "its concentrated, almost candy-like, fruit." "It is a flavor," he says, "that gets under the Cabernet Sauvignon and seems to push it forward, making it both more vibrant and more accessible." He uses roughly 10 percent Merlot in all his blends.

The strength and richness of California Merlot is a problem to Cathy Corison of Chappellet. She seeks a lean style for her Cabernet Sauvignon, picking carefully to keep grape sugar under control so that no Chappellet Cabernet Sauvignon need ever exceed 12.5 percent alcohol. "Merlot," she explains, "is sometimes bigger than Cabernet, and I trial-blend to check proportions to suit each vintage." But despite the problems, she would not want to work without the extra dimension of flavor and texture that Merlot brings.

In Monterey County, Bill Jekel, of Jekel Vineyard, uses no Merlot at all. He would, he says, if he felt his wines needed some softening influence, but learning to adapt to conditions in Monterey County—"so different from Napa and Sonoma"—he has also learned how to draw the best from the grapes of his Cabernet Sauvignon vines. A number of new factors came together in Monterey: ungrafted new clones of heat-treated Cabernet Sauvignon were set in a cool climate with low rainfall on soils that varied from sand and gravel to hard adobe clay. Greater control of water through irrigation was both a blessing and a disaster until the growers had learned how to handle it. On their own roots, Cabernet Sauvignon vines in Monterey were vigorous, but those who tended them, often new to viticulture, did not understand that the vines needed to be stressed at certain critical periods. Some say that improvement in Monterey Cabernet Sauvignon is due to maturing of the vines over the past decade, but Jekel disagrees. "We have learned how to handle the vines," he explains, "how to adapt our winemaking to the grapes produced here." He refers to better water control, fermentation techniques that drive off excessive aromatics, and aging procedures that bring out a distinctive style for Monterey Cabernet Sauvignon. "I don't see why Monterey Cabernet Sauvignon must taste like a Napa wine. All that is important is that it should be enjoyable. Local identity is part of the pleasure of wine."

Accepting such differences has not been easy in California. At recent public hearings that preceded labeling regulation changes for California (and all other U.S.) wines, one wine enthusiast, a lawyer, argued that he liked best Beaulieu Vineyard Private Reserve and fell into the common error of assuming that what he preferred must be, in some way, intrinsically superior. When he found that the wine was made from 100 percent Cabernet Sauvignon, he decided to campaign in favor of 100 percent Cabernet Sauvignon for *all* California Cabernet Sauvignon wines so that they could *all* taste like the Private Reserve. He was insensitive to the many variants possible and permissible in California Cabernet Sauvignon, and expected them all to conform to some predetermined type. As Peter Quimme (John Frederick Walker and Elin McCoy) said in *American Wines*, no one should "hold a wine's own unique character against it as if it were a defect."

The unique character of a California Cabernet Sauvignon, whatever it owes to the region where the grapes were grown and the proportion of other varieties introduced, is also based on the wood in which it is barrel-aged. The neutral German oak ovals brought to Inglenook by its founder, Finnish sea captain Gustave Ferdinand Niebaum, continued in use throughout the years from 1939 to 1964 when his widow's grandnephew, John Daniel, was in charge. Bordeaux wines, too, had been aged in Baltic oak until the early nineteenth century. Perhaps it was the British naval blockade of the Napoleonic era that first forced Bordeaux growers to use wood from nearby Limousin forests. Whatever the cause, the effect was to add a further strand to the flavor of a fine Bordeaux wine. In California, French oak was first used consistently, as everyone knows, at Hanzell Vineyard in the 1950s. Until then, redwood vats and American oak barrels had been the standard aging vessels. Both Louis Martini and Charles Krug had used well-seasoned barrels to avoid oak flavor, whereas Beaulieu Vineyard had deliberately included a proportion of new oak for the Private Reserve. "I liked the vanilla aroma of American oak," says André Tchelistcheff. "It brought a richer and distinctive style to the Georges de Latour." Beaulieu Vineyard Private Reserve still spends two years in American oak before bottling. Paul Draper of Ridge also uses American oak to enrich his Monte Bello Cabernet Sauvignons, and at Jordan Vineyard, too, American oak plays an important stylistic role. After normal fermentation in stainless steel, the Cabernet Sauvignon is racked into large American oak vats for malolactic fermentation before transfer to small French oak barrels and American oak barrels for aging. Michael Rowan finds the character that each wood gives complements the other, and each brings out a different strain of fruit and flavor in Cabernet Sauvignon. Ric Forman and Robert Mondavi use French oak alone, and both study carefully the type and condition of the wood they use. Mondavi tries to ensure that his top reserve wines go into new wood, as do the Bordeaux first growths. "I find it gives backbone and vitality to the wine," he claims, and uses it for the same reason that he prefers Cabernet Franc to Merlot in his blends (though he uses both). "Working with the French," he says, "has taught me that elegance and vigor can go together. I have learned what can be done to sculpt a wine and give it structure."

The different uses of woods, the what, how much, and if-at-all of blending, the choice of yeast and control of fermentation itself, the varied microclimates and terrains of California—all play their part in determining the style of an individual wine. It is easy to generalize and claim that California Cabernet Sauvignon is richer than its Bordeaux counterpart, and then be silenced by a comparison of Clos du Val's classically reserved style with the exuberance of La Mission Haut-Brion. It is easy to suggest that California Cabernet Sauvignon is "forward" and less durable than Bordeaux and then remember the Rixford La Questa 1936. It is easy to imagine that California Cabernet Sauvignon (as if there were only one) cannot match the variety of Bordeaux. Easy, that is, until we try to imagine what that one wine would be.

*

VI.2

PINOT NOIR

by FORREST R. TANCER

WHICH GRAPE VARIETY MAKES THE GREATEST RED WINES OF THE WORLD—CABERNET SAUVIGNON OR PINOT NOIR? AMONG WINE LOVERS THIS IS A NEVER-ENDING argument, to which there is no simple answer. At its height Cabernet Sauvignon, from both Bordeaux and California, has been called the wine of kings; but so have truly fine Pinot Noirs. Of all the great wines made of the vinifera varieties, certainly Pinot Noir is the shyest. The grape variety grows in France, Germany, Austria, South Africa, Italy, South America, Australia, and, of course, in the United States, where it was first planted in California and, more recently, in Washington, Oregon, and the Finger Lakes area of New York. But only in a few small areas of the world, most particularly Burgundy, has it given continuing notice of its real quality. Even there, winemakers are pleased with one good year in three.

Why do so many of the world's talented winemakers wrestle with a wine that so often results in failure, a wine of which so few can be proud? They roll up their sleeves because of Pinot Noir's potential for greatness. Perhaps the country that has struggled the most energetically to make a superior Pinot Noir has been the United States; more specifically, California and the Pacific Northwest within the past ten to fifteen years. At best, today, we can say that we have produced some very good ones, in a few cases wines with an inkling of true greatness.

There are many, particularly those whose model is Burgundian, who believe that California can never produce a great Pinot Noir. I resolutely disagree. Not all wines from Burgundy are superior, and not all California Pinot Noirs are bad. The truth lies somewhere in between. Burgundy, an area that lies south of Paris on a latitude similar to that of Washington state, produces wines typically noted for their elegance, finesse, and true varietal character. Fine Burgundies are voluptuous, harmonious, complex wines that gracefully combine an intensity of flavor, a delicacy of flowers and fruits in their scent, and a rich, meaty texture. There are overtones of silk and velvet, sometimes hints of peppermint or fleeting aftertastes of raisin. The wines linger long on the palate. However, for years Californians have felt that Pinot Noirs should be dark, robust wines in the same style as some California Cabernets or Zinfandels, but Pinot Noirs, in spite of their richness, are not wines of tremendous color or tannin. Their style is in their complexity, their subtlety and shading, strengths that we are striving hard to bring out in California.

The noble ones—Chambertin, Corton, La Tâche, Romanée-Conti—have been analyzed for decades for that magical factor in the Côte d'Or that makes them so remarkable: the soil, the slope of the land, the average daytime or nighttime temperature, viticultural practices such as cropping, or techniques of winemaking such as adding sugar to increase the alcohol and intensity. Of course, it is probably all of these. Pinot Noir is the predominant grape in both Burgundy and Champagne wines. Since the soil in which it grows is infused with limestone, some observers give that factor heavy weight. Many vintners have observed and been influenced by such French criteria as the size of the crop (yields in the best of the Burgundian vineyards in the best of years are extremely low, equivalent to 1 to 2.5 tons to the acre) and type of soil, alkalinity seeming to intensify varietal character. Americans have also observed that French exposures are southern, the climate cool, the growing season long; that frost is often a springtime problem; and that evening temperatures are chilly, daytime temperatures relatively moderate.

In contrast, California has hundreds of individual microclimates, diverse interactions of soil, climate, and the lay of the land, which directly influence the tone and nature of the wines (see chapter 3). To complicate matters, the vineyards have been planted to a variety of different clones, each producing wines of a distinct nature. In the early days of making Pinot Noir in California, when the emphasis was on rich and red, the wines lost some of their expected complexity. Blended with other wines, Pinot Noir gained more intense color and tannin, but its delicate raspberry and violet components did not lend to marrying with brasher varieties. Although blending has been forsaken by most winemakers, its early use confused the American consumer who, having become accustomed to the bigger, meatier, less intricate versions, does not know the identity of true California Pinot Noir. Those few who blend today, usually with Petite Sirah or Gamay (a practice with historical precedents in Burgundian winemaking traditions), try to obtain a style typical of a light Rhone, which assures a greater longevity.

Like most vinifera varieties, Pinot Noir can be grown in a broad range of climates—from very cool to very warm. Unlike Chardonnay or Cabernet Sauvignon, however, it makes extremely good wines only in cool climatic areas, a qualification underscored by both the French and American experiences. During the onrush of planting in California in the early 1970s, little heed was taken to planting Pinot Noir in individual cooler microclimates appropriate to its culture. There were, of course, exceptions, but for the most part Pinot Noir was planted next to Chardonnay, Chardonnay next to Cabernet Sauvignon, and Cabernet Sauvignon next to White Riesling. Since Pinot Noir did not turn out to be nearly as adaptable as its neighbors, it was the few vintners who sought out areas that reminded them of Burgundy's soil and climate who made the strongest beginning in producing an exceptional California Pinot Noir.

For all California winemakers, however, it has been a Sisyphean struggle. The noted viticulturist and enologist André Tchelistcheff, winemaker at Beaulieu Vineyards from the 1930s to the early 1970s, believes California has the variety and the climate. Until recently, however, it has not planted Pinot Noir vineyards on the tough, gravelly, marginal soils that give French wines their outstanding character. Tchelistcheff thinks great Pinot Noirs made before these newer regions came into production were made accidentally. In his own winemaking experience (he made extremely fine Pinot Noir all those years at Beaulieu), he felt he made great ones on only three occasions, 1946, 1947, and 1968, and then only because of an accident of nature such as humidity, seasonal tonnage, or late maturity.

If soils constitute one of the controversies that surround Pinot Noir, clonal selection is another. There are as many opinions as there are clones—hundreds of them in America, all originally cuttings from Burgundian vineyards. While many agree with the late Martin Ray (who made some noteworthy wines from them in California) that we need the original Burgundian clones, others feel that clonal variation and mutation are so great that, assuming the clone *is* Pinot Noir, whichever clone one has makes less difference in the wine than the differences caused by temperature, climate, and viticultural practices. The University of California at Davis has spent considerable effort isolating disease-resistant clones to impart specific Pinot Noir qualities. (Perhaps a clean, well-maintained vine might be a more critical factor.) However, climate can produce different results from the same clone. A cool year in Forestville may produce wines with good, intense color and high varietal aroma. A short, hot growing season in the same vineyard, no matter what precautions are taken to maintain the same crop level, and so on, may produce Pinot Noir lighter in color, perhaps no less varietal but certainly less intense in character.

Another viticultural controversy is at what level of maturity Pinot Noir should be picked. The old style of red winemaking in California always led to picking grapes at full maturity to produce wines at their richest and most opulent. Acidity and pH were not primary concerns. Now, particularly with Pinot Noir, we find that acidity and pH are far more important than sugar content in creating varietal intensity and richness.

In the Yarra Valley of Australia, the optimum sugar level is 21° Brix; in Burgundy, where it is the legal practice to add sugar, somewhere in the 21° to 22° range. In California, we have customarily been picking at 24° or 25 ° (but each area has a different level of maturity). We are now finding that somewhat lower sugar, higher acids, and lower pHs produce wines of greater aging potential and relatively more delicacy, avoiding the ripe fruit which gives a raisiny, heavy, plummy · character.

Since its introduction in 1885 at the California Agricultural Experiment Station, Pinot Noir has received only lukewarm recommendation for planting in the state. It now grows on some 9,000 acres. A moderately vigorous grape, it is but a modest producer, yielding from one to five tons per acre. Since lower tonnages produce wines of greater intensity, it is not surprising that some of the most successful California bottlings have come from vineyards yielding under two tons an acre. The vines are usually cane- or cordon-pruned, and the variety is relatively early maturing. Sparse foliage is an aid to harvesting, and the fruit cuts easily by hand or machine. The small cluster is very prone to sunburn and raisining if not properly cared for viticulturally. Recent innovations of T-trellising and cane management have lessened the problems of sunburn in the cooler coastal areas of California (see chapter 4). Among its predators, the leaf roll virus tends to reduce the growth of the vine and the color of the fruit, especially in older vineyards, making it essential to plant disease-free stock. It is subject to infection by *Botrytis cinerea* in wet years of warm spring weather, and, in the Napa Valley, to Pierce's (formerly Anaheim) disease, transmitted by the blue-green sharpshooter leafhopper. Because it leafs early, it is also prone to frost damage in the spring.

Pinot Noir is grown throughout California. In Mendocino County, in the north, there are approximately 400 acres planted, the bulk in and around Ukiah, where there are deep alluvial soils. The climate varies dramatically, from cool in the Anderson Valley and the Navarro area to warm around Ukiah. Many pleasant wines have been produced, but few of real significance. Toward the coast, the Anderson Valley, a cool apple-growing area much like Sebastopol in Sonoma County, has perhaps the greatest potential with its strong maritime influence and long, cool growing season. The interesting wines from Fretter Wine Cellars and Navarro Winery, both in the Navarro area, are medium-bodied, made in a direct style, with intense fruit.

During the onrush of planting in the 1970s, a great deal of Pinot Noir was planted in Sonoma County, reaching a peak of nearly 3,000 acres. Since 1978, however, many of those vines have been removed or budded over to white varieties more suitable to the climate. Like Napa and Mendocino counties, Sonoma County is extremely varied in its climatic conditions. To the north, Cloverdale and Healdsburg are basically too hot for growing Pinot Noir. To the south and east, where the Alexander Valley has proved to be fine for growing all of the other major *vinifera* varieties, Pinot Noir has not done exceedingly well. One notable exception is the wine from Alexander Valley Vineyards, where they pay extreme care to viticultural particulars and grow their low-cropped vineyard on a very steep, west-facing slope. Their medium- to full-bodied wines show good color and a typical rich, violetlike character. The fruit component and good acidity of the Pinot Noir from both Sonoma and Mendocino counties, especially from Alexander Valley, make them useful in the production of sparkling wines in an area not ideally suited for premium red Pinot Noir table wine.

Among the areas that show tremendous promise is the lower Russian River appellation area including the Green Valley appellation. The climate is directly influenced by the maritime intrusion. A break in the western hills called the Petaluma Gap allows ocean breezes and fogs to roll across the region. It is almost always windy, and fogs often do not burn off during the summer until after 11:00 A.M. The terrain is hilly, with marginal soils, which are rocky in many cases, but acidic rather than limestonelike or alkaline. During the growing season, cool temperatures dominate. The area is also blessed with the cool nighttime temperatures I feel are essential to color and varietal development. The growing season is longer than in other growing regions in the county. If the Alexander Valley growers are harvesting grapes at optimum sugars in the first week in September, the lower Russian River grapes are not ready until early October. While the area is not extensively planted with Pinot Noir, most of the small wineries do produce it, and the promise it shows will probably lead to an expansion.

Joseph Swan has been making Pinot Noir of intense texture and a very Burgundian style in the Forestville area for many years. The wines from De Loach, Bynum, Dehlinger, Domaine Laurier, and Iron Horse, to mention a few, are less coarse and with more delicate, pronounced fruit than those of other areas of Sonoma County. Although the styles for the most part are lighter and the color medium, the 1979 De Loach is extremely dark in color, very assertive and fruity; and the Dehlinger is lighter in color but with the same fruit intensity. Hanzell, a winery founded by James D. Zellerbach of San Francisco at the end of World War II, still produces Pinot Noirs matured in small oak barrels. During its early days, aided by unseasonably cool weather, it turned out the county's first big Burgundian style wines. Located near the town of Sonoma, the vineyard is generally warmer than the lower Russian River Valley, more like Alexander Valley, its grapes producing a tremendous intensity of spicy fruit. The assertive wines usually show the effects of the warmer climate, richer, hotter, less subtle than their western counterparts.

The Carneros area, further south, is divided between Sonoma and Napa counties, with the bulk of the grapes planted in Napa. It is an area of cool maritime influence bordering directly on the Bay, with salt water intrusion very close to the vineyards. The fog and the continual breezes that blow across this rolling, hilly land are very similar to the cool conditions in the Forestville and Sebastopol areas. Temperature is moderate throughout the long growing season, the nights cool. The soils are relatively acid and claylike, in many cases of a coarse, rocky texture. From that area, Acacia, Carneros Creek, and Z-D have produced examples of full-bodied, ample California Pinot Noir. Buena Vista, which has gone through revitalization and has now several hundred acres in the Carneros district, and La Crema Vinera in Petaluma, which buys its grapes from the Carneros region, have also started to make some creditable Pinot Noirs, for the most part relatively delicate, not too over-powering, with good fruit and acidity and moderate pHs. Madonna Vineyard produces lush wines; St. Clair Vineyard ones that have a more austere style. At Carneros Creek, although they think the climate and growing conditions important, they feel that clonal selection is the key to high quality. At Acacia, the winemaker has chosen particular vineyards where he feels he can get characteristic flavors.

The Napa Valley was widely replanted to vinifera during the early periods of premium winemaking after Prohibition. The southern end of the valley holds the most promise as a Pinot Noir growing region, together with a few micro-climates in the northern half. Many of the Pinot Noir vineyards from the center of the valley and north have been changed over to Cabernet Sauvignon, Zinfandel, Chardonnay, or Sauvignon Blanc, varieties that do better there. With the arrival of Domaine Chandon and Schramsberg, a large amount of Napa Valley Pinot Noir has gone into the production of sparkling wine, a good utilization in that area. Napa Valley is more prone than some areas to climatic variations from year to year. A long, extremely cool growing season, as in 1980, has the potential of producing some lovely, intense Pinot Noirs in the California style. But warm or hot growing seasons have tended to produce many wines that are relatively lacklustre, innocuous, and uninteresting.

Phelps, Raymond, Burgess, Stonegate, and Trefethen make Pinot Noirs heftier in style than those of the Carneros region. Stylistically, the desired principle for the central Napa Valley is the more intense California style, higher in alcohol and more aggressive than wines from the southern end of the valley. Some interesting exceptions exist in hillside plantings such as Smith-Madrone Vineyards. Although located in a warm area, it produces supple wines of lovely fruit and intensity without being overly alcoholic. Smith-Madrone's small vineyard gets no sun in the afternoon, and is consequently cooler than its valley floor neighbors. Robert Mondavi, who has done considerable experimentation with clones as well as vinification techniques, has been producing some good Pinot Noirs from the valley floor. His wines are extremely fruity, youthful, and aromatic, with some complexity of oak.

In the Santa Cruz Mountains, to the south of San Francisco, are among the oldest winegrowing areas in California to plant Pinot Noir. The relatively high-lying area (about 2,000 feet above sea level) has under 100 hilly acres of the grape. Although there is a substantial variety of styles, the wines are usually intense because of the low yield per acre. Such wineries as David Bruce, Martin Ray, and new-comers such as Santa Cruz Mountains, Mount Eden, and Congress Springs have been striving for a softer, fatter Burgundian style. Further to the south, the great Monterey area, planted in the early and mid-1970s, is a new home for all varieties, many of which have done extremely well. Pinot Noir, unfortunately, has not been one of the latter. Although the climate seems to be perfect—a long, cool growing season with substantial maritime influence—the soils are often rich and deep and the vines do not struggle on the valley floor.

To the east, the chalky limestone hills of the Pinnacles have produced some of the best Pinot Noirs of California. Because of the mediocre soils, the cropping is low. Although the area is warm, the weather is moderated by the coastal influence of the Monterey area. The harmonious, earthy wines have rich extract, good color, and great finesse—probably the most Burgundian in California. Chalone has produced consistently excellent Pinot Noirs since the 1960s from this area, as has Calera, whose vineyard produces less than two tons to the acre. Calera feels that the soil is the critical factor.

Santa Ynez Valley, the Santa Barbara region, and the San Luis Obispo area further to the south make up a newer winegrowing district, varying dramatically in its microclimates. Some extremely cool sections, particularly in the San Luis Obispo–Paso Robles area, receive a very large maritime influence. Here marginal soils with chalky limestone qualities have the potential of producing some fine Pinot Noirs. André Tchelistcheff feels that this area has a bright future. It is so young viticulturally, however, that it is still too early to know what its specific winemaking style will be. Beyond these areas, the grape is grown in southern California, the Central Valley, and the Delta, but none of these locations produces a Pinot Noir of great consequence.

The winemaking techniques for Pinot Noir are different from those for Cabernet Sauvignon. Being a relatively light variety in fruit tannin, Pinot Noir often benefits by the addition of stems to the tank after crushing, which produces more tannic astringency. Winemakers such as Joseph Swan return 50 to 70 percent of the stems to the must. Francis Mahoney, at Carneros Creek, sometimes adds 50 to 60 percent, but has put in as much as 100 percent. Over the years, I have added 25 percent, Michael Richmond from Acacia only 10 percent, Josh Jensen of Calera about 70 percent. Each winemaker chooses the percentage that best suits the style dictated by his grapes. Stems also make Pinot Noir more colorfast. Often criticized in America for being a light-toned red wine, Pinot Noir is not, in fact, a dark wine in Burgundy. Typically, it tends to be light, reddish, often with brown edges, none of which is necessarily negative for Pinot Noir wherever it is made. Color is not the watchword as it is with Cabernet, Zinfandel, or Petite Sirah. The complexity of Pinot Noirs is in their aromas, flavors, and in their long silky texture. A number of winemakers, myself included, are incorporating stems with increasing frequency, along with whole uncrushed berries as in a carbonic maceration fermentation. This serves two purposes: the stems get into the wine and the whole berries slow down the fermentation. In my experience, once the berries are pressed, this method gives higher fruit extraction to the wines.

Winemaking practices of the 1960s and 1970s called for fermentation of red wines at relatively cool temperatures—in the 70° to 75° F (21°–24° C) range. In an attempt to get greater extraction, temperatures have gradually risen. In order to get maximum body and richness, it is now strongly felt that one needs to ferment Pinot Noir at between 80° and 90° F (26.7°–32.2° C). This, of course, has a tendency to make the fermentation relatively short, one reason I like to use whole berries to prolong its length. In Burgundy, where the wines are customarily fermented at relatively high temperatures for short periods of time (sugar additions are usually made when the wine is almost dry to prolong the fermentation), they are often left on the pomace in the tank for as long as two weeks after fermentation has ceased. Some winemakers in California also follow this procedure, called "vatting," which extracts all there is to be extraced from the skins into the wines.

There are many winemakers who believe that Pinot Noir needs to be fermented in open-top tanks or in small fermentors, so that there is the maximum amount of contact when the wines are pumped over or punched down (to incorporate the pomace that has separated out during fermentation into the juice). There is disagreement over whether the wines should be pumped over mechanically from the bottom to the top or punched down manually with a stick or paddle. Many winemakers feel that pumping over is far too severe a process for Pinot Noir, and that it needs to be dealt with so delicately that only the very gentle action of punching down is correct. Another variable, the number of times the wine is pumped over or punched down each day, ranges from one to ten, depending on the finished style the winemaker prefers.

While this is not the place for a detailed discussion of the process of chapitalization as practiced in all the winemaking regions of France, California winemakers are particularly interested in the effects of the addition of sugar to fermenting Pinot Noir musts. They wonder if perhaps sugar is the magic ingredient that gives the roundness in the mouth, the seductive depths of flavors of a great Burgundy. Sugar is a flavor enhancer in cooking, but in wine? If we were allowed to add sugar, could we pick at lower sugars, higher acids and thus keep the pH under control? Would we gain greater extraction?

It should be kept in mind that chapitalization serves several purposes. It ups alcohol levels: because of the coolness of the climate, Burgundian Pinot Noir, at full maturity, does not achieve the sugar levels easily obtained in California (where grapes can be "ripe" without being completely physiologically "mature"). In Burgundy, too, the must is placed in open-topped fermentors and an average of 1° of alcohol is lost during the fermentation. Sugar adds volume as well; both higher alcohol and more volume returns more money. Each Burgundian has his theory about how and when to add the sugar and of what type it should be—cane or natural grape sugar produced especially for the purpose. But then it is also said that the greatest of all Burgundies are made with no, or very little, chapitalization. We need detailed studies to answer these questions.

One of the critical elements in creating the long, silky texture and the faint hint of cheese often associated with the flavor of Pinot Noir is the induction of a malolactic fermentation. There are winemakers who believe in inducing this during the primary fermentation, while others feel that it is important to wait until it is completed. The type of yeast used is also of critical importance. In France, the wild yeast found on the grapes and in the winery begins the primary fermentation. In the cellars of Burgundy, it is almost certain that the same wild yeast is reproduced from year to year. In the cleaner, more sterile atmosphere of a California winery, that is not necessarily the case. There have been experiences, in fact, where wild yeast has led to off odors or incomplete primary fermentation. In California, therefore, the practice has generally been to use commercially available yeast (Champagne strain, Montrachet, or UCD 51, for example). There are winemakers now, however, such as those from Calera, who strongly believe that wild yeast is of critical importance in getting a specific zonal flavor.

All Pinot Noirs need some oak aging. In general, because it tends to be too assertive and to clash with the fruit tones, American oak has not been suitable. There are many California producers, however, who like the woody extract that distinguishes wines that have been aging for a substantial period of time in new oak barrels. The incorporation of that much oak makes their wines more astringent and full-bodied. (There are now winemakers experimenting with stirring or mixing the wine and its lees periodically during the aging in barrels. They hope this process will give the wine greater flavor development.) Louis P. Martini, on the other hand, carrying on the style established by his father, obtains consistently elegant, grapey wines by aging in massive oak casks of considerable vintage. They impart no overtones of the wood, but provide a change of air that subtly complements but does not overwhelm the essential fruit. The Pinot Noirs of 1957 and 1965 are fine examples. Along with Joseph Swan and Michael Richmond, I believe that oak should be a subtle accompaniment, one that does not intrude into the Pinot Noir character. In great Burgundies, oak is an underpinning and cannot substitute for a lack of body in the wine.

After the wines are removed from the barrels, there is another controversial decision: should they be filtered, fined, or bottled in a relatively unfined and unfiltered state? Many winemakers feel that because of its complex subtleties, Pinot Noir should have only very minimal rackings while aging, and be bottled at the finish with whatever resulting clarity has been obtained. Others feel that because Pinot Noir tends to be somewhat high in pH after the secondary fermentation, it needs to be filtered and clarified to avoid any potential bacteriological spoilage. Burgundies, including Pinot Noir, typically throw sediment including color pigments because the variety is not particularly colorfast. In Burgundy, the rule has been not to filter and to fine lightly, usually with egg white, which is also commonly used in California. I believe that Pinot Noir needs to be filtered and should be clear and brilliant in color when it is put into the bottle. A style of Pinot Noir that emphasizes more of the fruit and the intricacy of the wine need not be lost if the filtration is properly done.

Once the wine is in the bottle, how long will it take for it to reach its peak? What is its aging potential? Are Pinot Noirs meant to be drunk young or to be aged? I believe that, unlike Cabernet Sauvignons, Pinot Noirs are not particularly long-lived wines. There are Burgundies from the 1930s that are still drinkable, and indeed wonderful, but in my opinion they are the exception. At that time, it was common in Burgundy not only to chapitalize with sugar, as they still do, but also to add brandy in order to give the wine more staying power, not practices we pursue in California. Most winemakers feel that Pinot Noir will benefit from some age, although the fruit and promise of its youth often make it attractive to drink young. On the basis of its balance of fruit and acidity, it will age well and develop in the bottle. Tannin, although a factor, is a less predominant influence than in Cabernet Sauvignon, and the reason that the acid level of the grapes is critical during the harvest.

In California, we have been making Pinot Noir for a very short time—not more than 30 years of serious experience with the variety. In Burgundy, winemakers have the cumulative experience of 500 years of growing grapes on the same piece of dirt, of changing clones, of perfecting techniques, and even they are still experimenting, searching for the perfect wine. In California, we are at the beginning of an effort that promises fine Pinot Noir; eventually our experiments with soils, climate, clones, levels of cropping, and viticultural care will come together in grapes that will produce a distinctive style of wine that can reproduce itself from one year to the next. That is what makes a tradition.

There will probably never be many great California Pinot Noirs. There are never many great Pinot Noirs in Burgundy. But in California Pinot Noir has been badly maligned. Some of the negative feeling is justified: in tasting hundreds, one is struck by the sameness; many of them are just . . . boring. Perhaps Cabernet Sauvignon and Chardonnay were easier grapes to develop here. Their styles are more straightforward and understandable. Potentially, Pinot Noir is a wonderfully rich, full-bodied yet graceful red wine, most agreeable to serve on a variety of occasions, but especially versatile at the dinner table. It has an affinity for cheese, is particularly appropriate with red meats, and powerful enough to complement game. In California we expect wines of uniformity; Pinot Noir gives us many styles, which have to be judged individually. Until it receives support and due recognition, much less will be made in California. Even now some wineries of great repute are abandoning it because they want to concentrate on wines in which there is more immediate interest.

On one thing there is consensus: California will ultimately be successful with Pinot Noir. Talk to any winemaker and you will find Pinot Noir is his most difficult child. To many parents, the most difficult child is also the most challenging. And the most challenging child is often the most rewarding.

BIBLIOGRAPHIC NOTE

A very good introduction to the personality of Burgundy and its individual properties is *The Wines and Vineyards of France* by Alexis Lichine. Bern C. Ramey's *The Great Wine Grapes and the Wines They Make* also has a good, brief description of Pinot Noir from a California viewpoint.

VI.3

ZINFANDEL

by PAUL DRAPER

THE NOBLE LINES OF CALIFORNIA'S CABERNET SAUVIGNON, CHARDONNAY, AND PINOT NOIR STEM FROM THEIR ARISTO-CRATIC FOREBEARS in Europe. Scions easily adapted to the benign climate of the Golden State (La California—the imaginary earthly paradise of the sixteenth-century novelist Rodríguez de Montalvo) and two of the three have clearly proven themselves worthy of their birthright. Like any other children of famous parents, they seem destined always to be compared with their European progenitors.

Enter Zinfandel, the Horatio Alger of varietals, the "True American." Born of peasant stock somewhere in Europe, Zinfandel did not make its name and fortune in its native land. It did not come to the attention of its monarchs nor was it tutored and polished by the English wine trade until worthy of knighthood. Not until it was planted on the hillsides of California's cool Coastal Range did it find its ideal soils and climate. By the 1880s, it was recognized in California as the commercially viable variety of choice for making the best dry red wines. The orphan had found a home where, properly handled, it could produce wine of such quality that it might someday stand beside the noblest varieties of the world.

THE ZINFANDEL MYSTERY

Zinfandel has long been referred to as the "mystery grape," and at least one of its leading students, Dr. Harold P. Olmo of the University of California at Davis, thinks it might be best if we continue to consider it a mystery until all the research is done. He may be reacting to the various theories of the last few years, often mentioned in the press, for which no historical or scientific sources are quoted. For simplicity, the mystery of Zinfandel might be divided in three parts:

1. *Where precisely did it originate?*

2. *How and when did it reach the East Coast of the United States?*

3. *How and when did it reach California and achieve broad distribution?*

ORIGINS

Dr. Austin Goheen of the University of California at Davis made the chance discovery of a look-alike grape in southeastern Italy that led to research at Davis. A paper by W. H. Wolfe and Harold Olmo, read at the June 1977 American Society of Enologists conference, found the two to be identical ("Application of Isozyme 'Finger Printing' to Specific Problems of Varietal Identification: Comparison of . . . Zinfandel and Primitivo di Gioia"). No historical research has yet been published as to when Primitivo was first recorded in Italy. Statements have been made in the press that it was not found there until late in the nineteenth century, after phylloxera had destroyed many of the vineyards of Europe, when hybrids and foreign varieties were being imported to test their resistance to the root louse. These reports quote no research to substantiate the statements. Olmo has mentioned that growers in Italy have occasionally referred to Primitivo as a foreign variety in discussing it with viticultural researchers. The mystery of origin clearly remains unsolved. The most detailed recent historical studies of Zinfandel's arrival on the East Coast and in California have been done by historian Charles L. Sullivan. What follows on these subjects is a summary of the data he has published.

ARRIVAL ON THE EAST COAST

The 1830 catalogue of the established and reputable nursery of William Prince of Long Island listed the major wine grapes of Europe and included a "Black Zinfardel, of Hungary." In 1834 Samuel J. Perkins of Boston exhibited a "Zinfindal" and a grape of the same name won a prize in 1839 in the collection of Otis Johnson of Lynn, Massachusetts. J. Fiske Allen, the leading New England authority on grape culture in the 1840s and 1850s, described "Zinfindal" in his *Practical Treatise . . . on the Grape Vine* in 1848; his description is very close to what we know as Zinfandel today.

Allen's description of another variety, Black St. Peter's, is virtually identical to that of the "Zinfindal." In a footnote, Charles Sullivan mentions an English report of 1857 that describes a particular Black St. Peter's variety as a vine raised from seed in 1775 by a certain Daniel West in St. Pancras (London), and notes that it became popular in England. In 1789 a William Speechley in London lists a St. Peter's grape whose description is quite similar to our notion of Zinfandel.

Maynard A. Amerine, who has done viticultural and enological history, noted in a letter to *Wines & Vines* in March 1982 that the forty-second edition of the Prince catalogue included "Zinfardel (erroneously Zinfindal), medium, round, black, with a thick bloom, large double-shouldered cluster, requires to hang long after coloring to perfect its maturity. Introduced by the late George Gibbs of Long Island, from Germany." The fascinating last sentence reportedly did not appear in earlier or subsequent catalogues. Despite the similarities in historical descriptions, however, we cannot assume that "Zinfardel," "Zinfindal," and Black St. Peter's were the same grape, let alone that they were identical to our Zinfandel. The potential for future historical and viticultural research is intriguing.

ARRIVAL AND DISTRIBUTION IN CALIFORNIA

In New England the established nurserymen had developed what could be referred to as the standard New England collection of grape varieties, which they consistently offered in their catalogues. Some of those included, principally table grapes, could serve for winemaking as well. The list typically might have offered names like Black Hamburg, Muscat of Alexandria, Golden Chasselas, Black St. Peter's, White Malvasia, Syrian, and occasionally "Zinfindal." In the 1850s, a number of people in California interested in the possibilities for viticulture and horticulture brought in collections of cuttings from the East Coast. Several men entered the results of their efforts with them in exhibitions of their day and provided us with some historical data.

Two of the most often noted were Captain Frederick W. Macondray, the first president of the California Agricultural Society, who brought in vinifera grapes from New England on one of his sailing vessels, and J. W. Osborne, the owner of Oak Knoll farm north of the city of Napa. In 1857 both men entered exhibitions of vinifera grapes at the Mechanics' Institute Fair in San Francisco with standard New England collections that included "Zinfindal." In 1859 Osborne sold two wagonloads of cuttings from Macondray to a Sonoma vineyardist, William Boggs. The cuttings were again a standard collection and included "Zinfindal." Boggs showed the variety to General Mariano Vallejo's winemaker, Dr. Victor Faure, who asked for cuttings; in 1862 he reportedly produced a small amount of wine from the first crop off the vines and thought it a good "claret."

During this same period, Antoine Delmas, a member of the large colony of French growers in Santa Clara County, was cultivating and selling vinifera cuttings, among which were the Zinfandel look-alike from New England called Black St. Peter's and many varieties he imported from France, such as Cabrunet, Medoc, and Black Meunier. Delmas stated that he provided the Black St. Peter's to General Vallejo. Boggs did note that Vallejo had some vinifera vines that resembled Zinfandel, called Black St. Peter's, which could have been the vines sold to him by Delmas. In 1858 Delmas made a red wine that was judged best at the 1859 California State Fair. The young "claret" had been made from foreign grapes that "had been selected more as table fruit than for wine making." Supposedly this was the Black St. Peter's version of the Zinfandel.

The variety was widely known to nurserymen and growers in the Sacramento area at an early date. A. P. Smith had exhibited it at the State Fair in 1858 and the official records spelled it "Zeinfindal." He is reported to have gotten it as early as 1855 from the New Englander Wilson G. Flint. James Nickerson, another established Sacramento nurseryman, exhibited Black "Zinfandal" at the Fair in 1859, as did Smith, and by 1860 Smith was reportedly making good "claret" from his vines. By 1861, growers James Marshall of Grass Valley and Charles Covillaud of Marysville had written in approval of the variety. In the same year, Colonel James Warren found Zinfandel at Covillaud's ranch and praised this "rare variety," which he thought came from the Rhine Valley of Europe. By 1865 Benjamin Bugbey of Natoma Vineyard had selected Zinfandel as one of the five best for the future of California winemaking. Four years later, Nevada City winemaker F. Seibert won one of the first awards given for pure Zinfandel and George West of Stockton produced the first successful white Zinfandel. Back in Napa Valley, Jacob Schram praised the "Zenfenthal" as perhaps the best grape available for red wine. By the time of the vast grape plantings of the 1880s, Zinfandel was at the top of the list of the most suitable red varieties.

In spite of the fact that he has often been credited with bringing Zinfandel to California, the name of Agoston Haraszthy has not been mentioned here as a part of its history. There is no evidence from the period that he had any role in its introduction or dissemination. Haraszthy was a prolific writer and the greatest publicist for California wine that the industry has ever had, yet in all his writings, including his many reports published in the *Alta California* and the *California Farmer*, he never mentioned Zinfandel, let alone any role he had in its history, and he is not reported to have been a modest man. It appears that his son, Arpad Haraszthy, writing thirty-two years after the key event he describes, claimed accomplishments for his father for which there is no evidence. At the time of which he was writing, Arpad was a boy of eleven who had been sent off with his mother and sisters to live in New Jersey and receive a proper education. He returned once for two months in 1857 before leaving for Paris to study civil engineering. Instead he learned winemaking, with special emphasis on sparkling wines, and returned in 1862 to take over production at his father's winery. In 1886, seventeen years after his father's death, he wrote a four-page statement claiming that Agoston had imported the Zinfandel to his Crystal Springs nursery, just south of San Francisco, in 1854. Two years later, he changed his story and claimed that his father had imported Zinfandel direct from Hungary while in San Diego in 1852. No documentary proof can be found for these claims other than Arpad's statements, which were heatedly disputed when they were published.

One of the most detailed rebuttals came from nurseryman William Boggs in a letter to the *St. Helena Star* dated 8 June 1885. Boggs had been one of two directors, and Agoston Haraszthy president, of the Sonoma Horticultural Society, for which Boggs in 1859 had purchased the Zinfandel cuttings mentioned earlier (important as there were virtually no vinifera vines in Sonoma County except the Mission variety), but Agoston never claimed any connection with the purchase or dissemination of these Zinfandel vines. Arpad repeated his claims again and again, however, until a myth grew that still influences journalists today.

If Zinfandel's origin and travels to the New World remain mysteries, its arrival in California and its distribution there seem on the way to clarification. Wines bearing the varietal Zinfandel label appeared at least as early as 1883. George Husmann, in *Grape Culture and Wine Making in California*, states that Zinfandel is "one of the most valuable grapes for red wine in good locations, and properly handled. I have yet to see the red wine of any variety, which I prefer to the best samples of Zinfandel produced in this state."

The relative quality of these early wines can probably best be attested by the enthusiastic acceptance of the variety. In addition, it is difficult to believe that some of the exceptional Zinfandels produced just after Prohibition were the first efforts of the winemakers who made them. I had the opportunity eight or ten years ago to assess the quality of a group of Zinfandels from the 1930s with several knowledgeable tasters. The standouts were the 1937 Larkmead from Napa County and the 1939 Fountain Grove from Sonoma. Both were in perfect condition, but their quite astounding freshness, especially that of the Larkmead, would probably argue that a fair percentage of Petite Sirah was included in these Zinfandel clarets. On another occasion, again with a group of seasoned tasters, a Bordeaux wine merchant and I were treated to a blind tasting of the 1935 Simi Zinfandel and the 1924 Château Margaux. Both were in perfect condition and there were no signs that either was beginning to fade. It was agreed that one of the wines was an old Médoc, but the group was evenly split on which one. The Simi had developed into a lovely old claret with a great deal of staying power. I have not been fortunate enough to find Zinfandel vintages of this quality from the forties or fifties, but I did again from the late sixties and early seventies. These latter wines from several small producers presaged the explosion of the quality wines of the last few years.

ZINFANDEL AND WHERE IT IS GROWN

Just what does this mysterious world traveler look like, and where is it planted? The Zinfandel grape is of medium size; round, black, thin-skinned; it grows in medium-sized, winged, tightly packed clusters. While Cabernet is cane- or cordon-pruned on trellis, Zinfandel is head-pruned with no trellis. Zinfandel ripens unevenly and sets a fairly large second crop that typically ripens two weeks after the first. It is difficult, therefore, to judge ripeness accurately, but any experienced grower soon learns his vineyard and knows when to pick to achieve a particular sugar level. It is planted extensively from the coolest to the warmest regions. In my experience, Zinfandel consistently produces the best quality wines when grown in Regions II and III. In the warm Regions IV and V, it tends to overproduce (up to twelve or even fifteen tons per acre) and can lack color and character. In addition, some of the thin-skinned, oversize berries can burst within the cluster during final ripening, leading to bunch rot.

In the very cool Region I, the warmer years may produce great wine; however, the cool years do not always provide enough heat for ripening before the early rains. When moisture from heavy fog or rain is trapped in the tightly packed clusters, it can cause bunch rot. Hillside vineyards seem to provide the best consistent quality, as the poorer soils and lack of excessive ground water tend to produce a smaller crop that ripens every year. In cool years, these vineyards, with their good drainage and higher elevations, have the additional advantage of drying out quickly after a light rain, with less chance of damage to the crop.

As a winemaker, I have produced my most outstanding Zinfandels from cool areas and when the vineyard yield has been in the 1.5 to 3.5 tons per acre range. If the average yields from a complete acre of fully mature vines in the cooler Coast Range were, for example, approximately 3.5 tons, I would expect three times that yield and a significant difference in quality from similar vines in the richer, irrigated soils of the San Joaquin Valley. For a hundred years, Zinfandel has been one of the most extensively planted red wine varieties in California. Olmo and Amerine, writing in *Wines & Vines* in August 1938, mention that "by 1884 approximately two fifths of the state's acreage was Zinfandel." Only in the last fourteen years or so has Cabernet Sauvignon achieved significant acreage. In 1936, shortly after Repeal,

228

Zinfandel led the red wine varieties with 53,343 acres, while Cabernet was so insignificant as not to have a separate listing. One crucial aspect of this long history of extensive planting has, however, put Zinfandel at a distinct disadvantage in today's more sophisticated and quality-conscious market. The recent dramatic increase in Cabernet planting that accounts for most of that variety today has been in the cool regions. In 1981 there were still 10,589 acres of Zinfandel in San Joaquin County in Regions IV and V, but only 652 acres of Cabernet, while in Napa County, in Regions I, II, and III, there were 1,948 acres of Zinfandel but now 5,002 acres of Cabernet as well. Both grapes produce their best quality in the cooler regions, yet there are large quantities of Zinfandel available from the warm areas that have hitherto gone into generic wines and not been identified by variety. The danger is clearly present, however, that the reputation of Zinfandel could suffer if lower quality wines should appear under the varietal label in any quantity. The average Cabernet on the market may be of better quality than the average Zinfandel for no other reason than that a far greater proportion of it is planted in cooler areas. In the late nineteenth century George Husmann, in *American Grape Growing and Wine Making*, recognized the problem when he stated that "a Zinfindel claret from locations best adapted to it, carefully made, is good enough for anyone. Unfortunately, there is much made not up to these standards."

THE MANY STYLES OF ZINFANDEL

Zinfandel has often been praised for its versatility. It is made with varying degrees of success in many styles, which for the sake of discussion I have designated White; Rosé; Nouveau; Early Maturing (Beaujolais-style); Late Maturing (claret-style); Late Picked (dry); Late Harvest (sweet); and Port.

White Zinfandel is popular as a "picnic" wine and is typically made with some residual sugar. If a good deal of fruit is retained, it can be more elegant when fairly dry. For the whitest wine with the least tint of red color, the juice is best drawn off at the crusher or crushing hopper. If drawn off at the press, there seems to be more color. It is then cooled and usually either centrifuged or fined to reduce solids. A yeast culture is added, often the Montrachet strain to accentuate fruitiness. Once fermentation is begun, the juice is typically held at 10° to 13 °C (50° to 55 °F), which lengthens fermentation time to approximately three or four weeks. It is racked off or centrifuged off the lees, and sulfur is added. Malolactic fermentation is not considered desirable. Aging is often in large tanks, either stainless steel or, if possible, oak, to aid clarification and add complexity. After three or four months in the tank, it is fined, chilled to eliminate the possibility of later precipitation of tartrate crystals, then filtered and bottled. It is best when served cold.

Zinfandel Rosé may be simply a white with too much color, or the full pressings of the unfermented skins, or the free-run taken off the skins early in a red wine fermentation. A malolactic fermentation would be undesirable, as it could reduce the acidity and crispness of the wine.

Zinfandel Nouveau—that is, Zinfandel fermented under carbonic maceration, where fermentation reportedly takes place partly inside the unbroken berries—is perhaps a more interesting light style than rosé. A modified tank with a large top door that permits direct dumping of a whole gondola or other picking container of uncrushed grapes seems best. The stems are, by necessity, included. The weight on the berries in the bottom will break perhaps 20 percent, but augering in a hopper or pumping from a crusher will certainly break a great many more. A relatively small amount of juice obtained by pressing unfermented Zinfandel grapes can be pumped into the tank to fill the space between the unbroken berries and to begin fermentation. The term carbonic maceration refers to the fact that when the grapes are not crushed and are not subsequently aerated by punching down or pumping over, they ferment under anaerobic conditions surrounded by carbon dioxide. Reportedly a fermentation takes place in the cells, an anaerobic cellular process that forms alcohol, produces carbon dioxide, kills the cells, and releases color. The special yeasty odors produced by this method may be due not so much to this anaerobic fermentation as to the fact that the slow gentle nature of the intracellular process retains volatile fermentation products that would be normally lost in a more rapid, active fermentation and through aeration in pumping over. This method extracts less tannin and seems to produce lower levels of tartaric acid, so the wine tends to be quite soft and usually undergoes the malolactic fermentation.

As the wine is typically on the market by Thanksgiving in this country, it must be rid of any off odors very quickly, so the cleaner Champagne yeast strain might be preferred to the Montrachet for fermentation. The tank can be pumped over gently each day without aeration; otherwise it is closed, with a pressure relief valve in place. Often the juice is allowed to ferment at warm temperatures and the free-run reaches 0° Brix in five to eight days. As many as 70 percent of the grapes may still be unbroken, though the juice inside them ferments part way to dryness by this stage. In pumping the stems and whole berries to the press, almost all are broken and when the press juice is combined with the free-run, the sugar might typically be in the 5° to 7° Brix range. As fermentation odors must be minimized, immediately upon a reading of dryness, the wine is vigorously racked—that is, splashed as it is pumped from one tank to another—and then cooled down. It may be vigorously racked five more times in the following thirty days. Because tartrate stability—the tendency for tartrate crystals to precipitate later in the bottle—can be a very real problem, it is then fined and chilled further. Once fermentation odors have passed off, it is filtered, bottled, and sent to the market. It is meant to be drunk within a year and seems at its best drunk cool but not chilled. This method provides a particular quality of fresh, yeasty fruit that is very appealing to some, but because I must live with those yeasty odors during crush each year as a winemaker, my personal preference lies elsewhere.

The two most difficult styles to distinguish, let alone name, are the two that encompass most of the red table wine marketed as Zinfandel. The first could be called the Early Maturing style, and it is this style that has often provided the California equivalent of a Beaujolais. When marketed, it is ready to drink, shows fresh, often intense, fruit, and is generally at its best within three or four years of release. It may hold for many more years, but it is questionable whether or not it develops quality, and it does lose freshness. Since the 1940s, this style has become the "traditional" California Zinfandel. Because of the large number of Zinfandel makers and their individual methods, it is difficult to describe a typical approach, but if one could, it might be something like this: The grapes are thoroughly crushed and destemmed, the fermentors pumped over vigorously and often to aid maceration. The fermentation on the skins is relatively brief, perhaps three to four days on the average, and six at the most, with the wine drawn off the skins well before dryness. Through care in picking or by blending, the alcohol is held under 14 percent and is typically 12 to 13 percent. The wine is then rough-filtered or centrifuged and transferred to large tanks, usually redwood, but occasionally oak or stainless steel. Aging in small cooperage is generally too costly and the components of the oak thus contributed could be atypical for the style. A malolactic fermentation is considered undesirable by most because it lessens the intensity of the fresh fruit and reduces the total acidity, but several of the larger, traditional producers get a natural malolactic fermentation in virtually all their red wines. The length of aging varies, but two or three years in large tanks might be the norm. A successful example of this style is a lovely, soft wine with the fresh berry fruit of the Zinfandel.

The second major table wine style can be called Late Maturing, or claret-style, Zinfandel. It is the approach that I most often attempt as a winemaker, so I hope I will be forgiven if my enthusiasm colors my description. Claret is the word the English use to describe Bordeaux red wine. I use it here to describe any variety when it is made as though it were a fine Cabernet Sauvignon. The long vatting and the small cooperage aging are expensive relative to other available techniques, so it is only worthwhile to make this style if the grapes are of the highest quality and the finished wine can bring a good price in the marketplace. In my experience, grapes grown in the cooler regions and not overcropped are the best suited. They should be picked when fully mature but not overripe. Fully crushed and destemmed and pumped over daily, the must ferments to dryness in eight to ten days. All of the high-quality press juice is combined with the free run because it adds complexity and richness. A malolactic fermentation is desirable and, for the small wineries at least, is a component that particularly distinguishes this approach from the preceding one. The wine is rough-filtered, settled, and then racked to small oak cooperage for aging for a year to a year and a half, depending on the body and the fruit. It is typically rough if drunk young and will improve considerably with two to three years of bottle age. The best examples continue to develop with six to ten years, but there have undoubtedly been wines made in this style that have not lived up to expectations. Zinfandel is less tannic than Cabernet and may well need a small percentage of Petite Sirah to give it the backbone for long aging. Due to the increased extraction, the malolactic fermentation, and aging in small oak barrels, the wine is usually fuller in body than the preceding style and more intense and complex in character.

Dry Late Picked Zinfandel is not unfamiliar to me as a winemaker. These Late Picked wines are over 14 percent in alcohol and sometimes as high as 17.5 percent. They can be handled in either of the two preceding styles. The intensity of the fruit is usually great, but can suffer if the jam, plum, or raisin quality of overripeness is too dominant. The wines range from complex, but rather heavy, table wines to huge, dark, tannic wines with no perceptible saving grace. My experience is that these wines are best drunk after a year or two in bottle; only a very few improve with extended aging. If they are held, they often retain the alcohol and tannin, but little of the richness and intense fruit, of youth. I find the heavier versions of this style difficult to match with food in all but unusual circumstances. There is a dedicated, if very limited, market for them, but they should be clearly labeled to warn off the average consumer in search of table wine. The description of sweet Late Harvest Zinfandel parallels the dry almost word for word, but with the addition of 0.5 to 14 percent residual sugar. Heavy and noticeably sweet, these wines are even more difficult to match with food. Several makers produce a successful Zinfandel Port using techniques covered in the essay on dessert wines below (pp. 280–93). The market for quality California port is quite limited.

THE DRAWBACKS OF VERSATILITY

As a winemaker, I believe it is harder to make good Zinfandel than good Cabernet, especially if, as is often the case, the grapes come from a less suitable region. As the U.S. market becomes more knowledgeable, producers are now finding that low quality Zinfandel simply will not sell. Unfortunately, in the meantime, it has done no favors for the name of Zinfandel. In my opinion, serious producers enhance their own reputations and, in the long run, their financial return when lesser wines are sold in generic blends rather than under the varietal label.

The much touted versatility of Zinfandel has had the great disadvantage of confusing the consumer rather than attracting him. For several hundred years,

Cabernet Sauvignon has been made in Bordeaux, and its presently recognized style developed there over the past hundred. This style sets a standard that also seems to limit the range of variation and experimentation with the varietal in California. I feel that this limitation has been a positive influence for quality. The far steadier California climate has permitted winemakers to get the grapes fully ripe virtually every year. (My only objection is that it has also allowed them to get the grapes over-ripe, which has meant a bigger but less elegant style.)

In contrast, Zinfandel has neither suffered from nor been blessed by such limitations, which has meant in its case that less discipline has been practiced in the vineyard and in the winery. If the grapes, for example, have ripened more quickly than expected, the winemaker has been able to turn out a Late Picked or a Late Harvest wine, or one blended down below 14 percent alcohol but retaining heavy overripe characteristics, an approach not accepted for Cabernet. Since the principal use of wine is as a complement to food, and the overripe wines are rarely a good match for the typical dinner, they contribute little to Zinfandel's general popularity.

The broad spectrum of Zinfandel styles might be more acceptable if a nomenclature were developed and each style clearly labeled. With the wine available in quantity in the national market, the producers are now selling not just to a small, highly informed group, but to a broader public who want a quality table wine, not a wine that is overly tannic, highly alcoholic, or noticeably sweet. When the average consumer picks out a Zinfandel unassisted, he may expect a soft, light wine and get a heavy, overripe one, or expect a complex claret and take home a simple picnic wine. The flood of very different Zinfandels, many from small producers in the process of establishing their names, has coincided with the entry into the market of a flood of new consumers. But the problem is not limited to the novice. The absence of a clear classification of styles on labels has meant that even the knowledgeable consumer, faced with so many, has little or no idea what Zinfandel to buy to meet his taste. Even the retailer, if consulted, cannot help him unless he has conscientiously tasted all of his wines, a task that, due to the sheer number of brands, is becoming more and more difficult. I would predict that anyone interested in successfully marketing Zinfandel will find in the near future that the use of prominent indications of style on the label will be a virtual necessity. Going a step further, I would advise a Zinfandel producer establishing himself in the marketplace to clearly identify his name with one particular style.

For all the difficulties that have, and continue to, beset its path, the orphan Zinfandel has now joined the nobility. Its richness of flavor, its complexity, and its potential for elegance have assured it a major place among the fine varietals of California.

BIBLIOGRAPHIC NOTE

Essential background for this essay was provided by the work of historian Charles Sullivan on Zinfandel and on Agoston Haraszthy. See Charles L. Sullivan, "Zinfandel: A True Vinifera," *Vinifera Wine Growers Journal*, Summer 1982, 71–86, and "A Man Named Agoston Haraszthy," *Vintage Magazine*, February 1980 (part 1), 13–19; March 1980 (part 2), 23–25; and April 1980 (part 3), 11–17. See, too, Sheldon Wasserman, "The Great American Zin" (unpublished manuscript). In addition to these sources, I am indebted to Leon Adams, Maynard Amerine, and Harold Olmo.

VI.4

OTHER RED WINES

by THE EDITORS

ALEATICO

RARELY FOUND AS A BOTTLED WINE from California, Aleatico bears the strong stamp of its family, the Muscats. Originally from Tuscany, the reddish brown to orange wine is made here in much the same sweet, *vino santo* style. Only two wineries in this country have sold varietal Aleatico in recent times. California has but 173 acres of the grape. In spite of its distinctiveness, the variety has not found favor because of its poor vigor and productivity (an average of 6.2 tons per acre at Davis), and its tendency toward a high pH in the must. Still, it is recommended to wineries with a desire to capitalize on its subtle but distinctive flavors.

ALICANTE BOUSCHET

Alicante Bouschet had its greatest days in California during Prohibition, when its tough skin made it ideal for shipping to home winemakers. Part of their fondness was owing to its red juice, which allowed them to make as much as 700 gallons to the ton by adding water and sugar! Since Repeal, the grape and its wines have ebbed to a position more in keeping with its overall quality. Acreage has declined from 28,000 in 1940 to less than 5,000 in 1980. Amerine and Winkler (1944) found wines from Alicante Bouschet grapes to be of ordinary quality. Some critics called its flavor coarse, others said common. Wines of Alicante Bouschet were not helped by the variety's tendency to overcrop, which leads to low sugar musts. The University of California at Davis has no flavor association for Alicante Bouschet, but one wine industry official always was able to spot it because the aroma reminded him of the smell of the isinglass curtains once used in automobiles.

Alicante Bouschet's primary use is for blends. Only four wineries in this country still produce the varietal wine. One of them has managed to make a wine that surpasses the general critical view. The variety originated in France as an 1865 cross between Grenache and a still earlier hybrid, Petite Bouschet. The vine produces well, yielding a highly colored must. Unfortunately, the color is not stable. A second problem is acidity, too high in cool regions, too low in warm ones. The University of California researchers do not recommend it for planting.

BARBERA

The focus of Barbera production in contemporary California is in the San Joaquin Valley, where the variety's natural high acidity yields pleasant wines offered both as varietals and in blends, all balanced for early consumption. A handful of producers in the coast counties strive for long-lived wines, some more closely echoing those from its native Piedmont in northern Italy. Of the state's 18,000 acres, all but a handful are in the Central Valley. Fresno County, for example, has 5,100 acres. In contrast, Sonoma has 48, Mendocino 21, and Napa 12. While San Joaquin Valley Barberas are properly valued for their early, easy drinkability, those from the North Bay counties have earned the most consistent critical praise.

The finest Barberas are tart, fruity wines with good red color. Their high acidity makes them proper candidates for malolactic fermentations, though they are difficult to control in this process. Some high-acid Barberas, especially ones with a blended proportion of Petite Sirah, have been uncommonly long lived. Although some Barberas have considerable style, barrel aging has played almost no part in it, perhaps because the wine is not well recognized by consumers and thus cannot command a profitable price. On at least two occasions, small wineries have made varietal Blanc de Noirs from Barbera. A few wineries have made wines from grapes harvested late. Thirty-two U.S. wineries now sell the wine as a varietal.

While not a vigorous grower, Barbera will consistently yield more than eight tons per acre in the San Joaquin Valley, and about four in coastal conditions. The variety especially recommends itself to California because of its acidity. Tannin is moderate, but sufficient, when coupled with acidity, to require long aging of wines from vineyards in Regions III and IV. The variety is difficult to ripen in Region II, and even in cool Region III. In Region V, it may not have enough acidity at ripeness for balanced wines. One of its most attractive aspects for growers is the ease with which it may be harvested either by hand or machine.

CARIGNANE (ALSO CARIGNAN)

This is a very old variety, originally from Spain. It has been grown in the Midi of France for many centuries, but dates only from the Prohibition era in California, when it became popular because it shipped well to home winemakers across the continent.

Although wines from grapes grown in Regions IV and V retain moderate acidity and fine color, they have few distinguishing aromas or flavors. Those from cooler areas are not vastly different, though some critics sometimes think well of them. Those earning the greatest praise have come from the warmer parts of Region III, especially northern Sonoma and Mendocino counties. The best Carignanes may have a faint kinship of flavor to Cabernet Sauvignon, but are much commoner.

Thirteen U.S. wineries are now selling varietal Carignanes. However, nearly all wine from the variety serves in blends for burgundy, claret, and other non-varietal types. In this role, its popularity is gaining. Plantings have decreased from slightly more than 31,000 acres in 1940 to nearly 21,000 in 1980. The great majority of this total is in the San Joaquin Valley.

Vigor and productivity recommend Carignane to the grower. The variety averages 8 to 10 tons in the San Joaquin Valley, as much as 6 in coastal counties. Upright growth makes it easy to train. Its greatest drawbacks are a susceptibility to mildew in cool regions and bunch rot in warm ones. In warm years, a tendency to low acidity in overcropped vineyards can lead to stuck fermentations.

CHARBONO

Charbono has been grown in California since the 1880s or earlier. In spite of the long history, plantings always have been limited, especially since Prohibition. At present there are fewer than 100 acres in California, and only seven wineries produce or sell a Charbono wine in this country.

Warm climate Charbonos suffer a flatness from low acidity. From grapes in cool regions, the wine is richly colored and well balanced, and at the very least has agreeable flavors. One is tempted to say it does not have a pronounced aroma, and that it acquires only modest bouquet in the course of aging well, but something about it has inspired a Charbono Society, the only grape variety to have its own fan club in this country to this point. The club, it might be added, celebrates the wine at black tie dinners.

The variety ripens rather late, especially in Region I, the only climate that sustains good acidity. In compensation, it resists mildew and other moisture damage. It is a weak grower, except in fertile soil, producing only moderate crops. In spite of the occasional high quality of this variety's wines, University of California researchers do not recommend it.

GAMAY (NAPA GAMAY) AND GAMAY BEAUJOLAIS

Although from different varieties of grapes, the generally light red wines called Gamay and Gamay Beaujolais are almost as close as fraternal twins in character. Most of the time, they are made in a fresh, fruity style, soft, agreeable, immediately accessible, sometimes with a touch of residual sugar to underscore the fruit. In this vein, both varieties lend themselves to wines in the early-maturing *nouveau* tradition of Beaujolais. A number of California wineries use the French technique of carbonic maceration to make such wines. At the other extreme, a small but not insignificant number of winemakers attempt through longer wood aging and other special care to make a California equivalent of a Beaujolais-Villages. The goal is easier set than gained. The most reliable charm of either variety is an unexpected intensity of fruit flavor that can be most welcome when found in a moderately priced, straightforward wine.

There is not enough space here to explain fully the California saga of naming and misnaming Gamay and Gamay Beaujolais vines and wines. Gamay Beaujolais is now taken to be a clone of Pinot Noir, and legally can bear either name. Although the family resemblance is evident, its lighter wines seldom achieve the richness and finesse of more favored clones of Pinot Noir. Like Pinot Noir, it performs best in cooler regions. Of the 3,750 acres planted in California, nearly all are in the coastal counties, and about equally divided among Mendocino, Monterey, Napa, San Benito, Santa Barbara, and Sonoma counties.

The other Gamay—some think it is the true Gamay, others think it is the grape known in France as Valdiguié—is, to make matters worse, known in California as both Gamay and Napa Gamay. Wine from the grape has been bottled under both names and as Gamay Beaujolais, the latter with reference to the wine's style rather than its grape. Whatever its true identity, the grape is the later ripening and more productive variety of the two, but one with thin-skinned, easily damaged berries. It prospers in a wider range of climates than the grape called Gamay Beaujolais, yielding balanced, attractive wines in Regions I to III. Plantings cover 4,400 acres, 1,100 of that total in Napa, the majority of the remainder in other coastal counties.

GRENACHE

Grenache is a northern Spanish variety known there as Garnacho. It acquired the name Grenache in France, where it is widely grown in the Rhone Valley. The grape only occasionally is used to make red wine in California, being reserved principally for rosés and tawny ports.

Red wines from Grenache grapes grown in the cooler regions of California retain enough acidity and color to be pleasant, if not distinguished. In warmer areas, color dwindles to orange, and acidity is too low to make an appealing red. It is from these districts that most varietal rosés come. A general difficulty for Grenache wines is that they tend to oxidize during aging. Some also develop a bitter taste for reasons that are not clear.

Seventeen U.S. wineries currently sell Grenache either as a red or a rosé. More than 13,000 of 17,000 acres are in the San Joaquin Valley. Production of the variety in coastal conditions averages slightly more than six tons. In the interior valleys, it can be expected to yield more than eight, to a maximum of eleven. Bearing can be erratic. Wines are well balanced only from Regions I through III. Those from Regions IV and V are too low in acidity, too high in pH. University researchers recommend Grenache to growers, but to wineries only for rosé wines from cool regions, and for dessert wines from warm ones.

GRIGNOLINO

Because of differing clones, the red wines of this variety show tints from orange rose to light red in color. The paler clones also are used to make a distinctive rosé by one, sometimes two of four wineries selling the varietal. The wines also have varying degrees of acidity depending on where grown. At their best, they are fruity, with a distinctive flavor. Grignolino originated in northern Italy, where it is much favored for yielding tart, tannic wines needing considerable age. Clonal variation in California is so great as to make the variety difficult to describe. There are only 58 acres planted, 40 of them in Santa Clara County, the remaining 18 in Napa. It is even possible that more than one variety currently is identified as Grignolino. What is most commonly understood as Grignolino yields grapes of light color and sometimes high tannin. Fruit matures well, except that it does not withstand early rains. The variety is moderately productive.

MERLOT (SOMETIMES MERLOT NOIR)

One of the chief varieties of Bordeaux, Merlot was known in California no later than 1895, but very lightly regarded then. After disappearing during Prohibition, it remained in eclipse until a small awakening of interest in the mid-1960s, then caught hold quickly, and was much planted during the boom of the early 1970s. The first post-Prohibition varietal Merlot wines came from the vintages of 1968–69, when a handful were produced in the North Bay counties. At present, eighty U.S. wineries sell Merlot. Acreage increased from virtually none before 1960 to more than 2,200 in 1980.

Good Merlot grapes from cool regions produce well-colored wines of pleasing color and flavors unmistakably akin to those of Cabernet Sauvignon. The valuable difference is that tannins are less forceful, allowing wines to mature earlier, and to be enjoyable even before reaching peak form. In California, Merlot is questionable only for producing wines of somewhat low acidity in Region III and warmer.

The variety made its comeback largely because winemakers, seeking a softening blend grape for Cabernet Sauvignon, looked to Bordeaux and saw its use there. Much of California's annual crop still goes to that end, but now, in a neat reverse, many producers of varietal Merlot are blending in small percentages of Cabernet Sauvignon to stiffen wines that are too soft by themselves. Aging in new oak

238

is a common technique. The usual choice is European wood, but a few producers use American oak barrels. Many of the most praised Merlot wines have come from Napa and Sonoma counties, which shared many of the earlier plantings and still have the largest acreages. Of the total state acreage, Napa has 650 acres, Sonoma 520. Next is Monterey with 360.

PETITE SIRAH AND SYRAH

These and related varieties constitute an ampelographical tangle that still has not been completely unravelled. What is widely grown in California is called Petite Sirah, or even Petite Syrah. It is probably not the same variety as that grown as Syrah in Hermitage on the Rhone, as Shiraz in Australia, or, on very limited acreage, as Syrah in California. Differences in the vineyard can be seen readily, but differences in the wine—if any—are only beginning to be discovered, because Syrah has been available only since the vintage of 1974. Although Petite Sirah grapes have a long history in California, the varietal wine has been generally available only since the mid-1960s. (Louis M. Martini and Larkmead for a time offered a varietal Duriff during the 1940s. It probably was from what we know as Petite Sirah.)

Petite Sirahs are richly colored to outright inky wines, and characteristically tannic. Some find their aroma of black pepper highly distinctive. Others see the wine as less distinctly aromatic. In either case, Petite Sirahs are slow to age, which, one suspects, has slowed their acceptance. A few stylish producers have used new oak to add complexity to their wines, but slow sales make this costly technique difficult to support. There are now more than sixty U.S. wineries selling Petite Sirahs, a roster that has lost several members in recent years.

Syrah, at its peak form in Hermitage and Australia, has an aroma described as smoky, the bouquet scented, almost floral, and easily recognizable. Two wineries make Syrah in California, one from a Hermitage strain, the other from an Australian one. Both must yet establish a track record. Acreage statistics distinguish between Petite Sirah and Syrah. Total acreage of the former is 8,500, less than in 1940 and earlier, when Petite Sirah was a popular shipping variety for home winemaking. Acreage of Syrah remains slightly less than 100. Much of the annual tonnage of Petite Sirah goes as blending wine into burgundy and other nonvarietals.

Petite Sirah yields well (more than five tons in coastal vineyards, almost eight in the interior valleys), producing tannic wines of excellent color. The variety is subject to rain damage in cool districts and sunburn in warm ones. Healthy fruit is easy to handle at the winery. Syrah, in comparison, bears less well (slightly more than three tons in the same vineyard that yields more than five of Petite Sirah), but is more resistant to both mold and sunburn. It is like Petite Sirah in having tannins that require long aging of its wines.

Ruby Cabernet

The first red wine from grapes deliberately bred in California to meet regional climate requirements, Ruby Cabernet at its best is an unmistakable relative of its famous parent, Cabernet Sauvignon. It also is unmistakably not Cabernet Sauvignon, but a simpler, commoner wine in flavor and texture, traits probably owed to its other forebear, Carignane. Well-made Ruby Cabernets from warm growing conditions remain, nonetheless, a milestone for winemakers in the interior valleys to remember in making any red. The wines have distinctive flavors, good balance, and an unsuspected ability to age. Several made in the late 1960s and early 1970s remain sound, vital wines in 1983, although they have not improved enough to merit systematic cellaring by connoisseurs. Currently, a majority of Ruby Cabernets are styled for early consumption by minimizing tannins, using little or no oak for aging, and perhaps leaving just enough residual sugar to point up their fruit flavors. From time to time, one is made more in the traditional vein of claret from Cabernet Sauvignon. In all, Ruby Cabernet is made by nineteen wineries in this country.

A high producer (eight tons in the interior valleys, more than five in warmer parts of the coastal districts), Ruby Cabernet yields well-balanced musts from Regions IV and V, where the great majority of its 14,500 acres are planted. Its principal drawbacks are a tendency to excess tannins in cool years or cool regions and sometimes to an excessive malolactic fermentation, which some wineries, therefore, choose to prevent entirely.

Generic and Semi-Generic Red Wines

U.S. law provides for the production and sale of nonvarietal wines called red (generic), and burgundy, claret, and chianti (semi-generic). The borrowed place names reflect the origins of California's pioneers, but do not guarantee close matches with the originals. Indeed it is difficult to describe them, because each winery makes such wines to its own style. California burgundies seldom contain much Pinot Noir, and clarets little Cabernet Sauvignon, except when overplanting produces excesses of the fine varietals. (And then the Cabernet Sauvignon is more likely to end up as burgundy than claret.) The law makes no requirement as to grape varieties used in any of them.

With or without fine grapes, these are wines generally meant to be bought and drunk much in the way Europeans drink their ordinary wines. No small proportion goes to market in large containers—jugs until marketing departments added decanters and magnums to the bottling possibilities. (A few varietal producers still put outstanding wines in magnums for extra-long aging, but they now must explain what once was understood as a gesture to unusual quality.) Wine-in-a-box is another choice of outsized container. Cans have again made an appearance as a small convenience container, several earlier trials having failed. It should be noted that California's everyday red wines have earned much higher reputations than their

European counterparts. Bottling at the winery and brand identity play an important role in keeping California standards high.

ROSÉ

Rosé, or pink, wines can be produced from almost any well-colored red wine grape by allowing only a brief period of skin contact, usually six to twenty-four hours. Varieties with less color may remain on the skins for a longer time. This results in less varietal aroma than a red wine from the same grape. Rosés also are made by blending red and white wines. The quality of a rosé will depend on the grapes used and the producer's skill. Most California and imported rosés are styled on the sweet side (1 to 3 percent residual sugar). Our own predilection is for the drier style, whether produced by blending or as varietals from Cabernet Sauvignon, Pinot Noir, Gamay, or Zinfandel, but, except occasionally, not from Grenache. The tendency is to make these drier wines low in alcohol (less than 11 percent) and high in acidity, to be served young and slightly chilled. This diminishes their varietal character, but they can be very pleasant drinking.

VI.5

CHARDONNAY

by ELEANOR McCREA

TO A LOVER OF CHARDONNAY WINES, THE GRAPE VARIETY ANNOUNCES ITSELF AS UNMISTAKABLY AS THE THEME OF BEETHOVEN'S FIFTH Symphony. No other white grape has a more complex aroma. No other white wine has a more welcome caress as it lingers on the palate. The varietal aromas of the grape have been described variously as like green apple, lemon, or citrus, all indicating a fruity flavor and high acid. From extremely ripe fruit come also the descriptions figlike, pineapple, ripe apples, melon, and honey. From the oak of the aging process come the adjectives earthy, toasty, vanilla, caramel, and buttery. Mix them all together and add a distinctive stony edge, known in France as *pierre à fusil*, or gunflint, and you come close to putting on paper a taste and bouquet that can only be hinted at without a bottle in hand. The emphasis will vary from vineyard to vineyard and winemaker to winemaker, and the year of the harvest makes an enormous difference in the balance of the wines, but always from ripe fruit will come the distinctly Chardonnay flavor.

Given a sound wine and a good cork, it surely seems wicked to open a bottle of Chardonnay before it has had several years of bottle age. Here is a wine, more like a red wine than a simple white, that achieves a development in the bottle almost impossible to describe to those who have not experienced it. Almost all the harsh or astringent qualities disappear, and in their stead the wine becomes almost oily in texture and has a long, lingering finish most peculiarly satisfying to those who love it. The innocent, fragrant aroma of the grapes takes on a deeply mature bouquet, full of the nuances of the wood in which the wine has rested. The color becomes more golden, and the whole bottle becomes one of the more satisfying experiences for a wine lover.

As an example, I cannot remember a vertical tasting of Stony Hill Chardonnays where the younger wines have been selected over the older ones, even though to a knowledgeable palate a young one has greater promise. In the past year or two, the 1973 and 1974 vintages have been competing with each other for notice, while their sibling of 1978, which has even more promise, tended to lag behind until the magic of the bottle came to its aid, as it did only in the last few months of 1982.

The most distinguished of the Chardonnay wines, it should be noted, are almost invariably 100 percent of the variety, since even the most minute quantity of any other blending grape immediately diminishes the characteristic aroma and flavor. If fine Chardonnay is as unmistakable as Beethoven, still there are many variations on the theme. Given that the wine is soundly made, the variables are great, and many of them lead naturally to experimentation by an adventurous vintner. Every step from vine training through bottling opens avenues that lead to individual styles in a wine that responds gracefully to many approaches.

Not in California, as in France, is the day of the vintage announced to the whole village by the mayor. Here, the individual winemaker, after many days of judging his grapes with a careful eye and tongue, not to mention his saccharometer, will finally choose the day when, he believes, the grapes have reached the right balance of sugar and acid to make the wine in his own style. Should he want his wine to be very light, he will pick at 22 to 22.5° Brix, but if he desires a richer, longer lasting, headier wine, he will wait a few more days for 23.5 to 24° Brix. At the same time, he must be measuring the amount of acid in his grapes, lest it disappear on him, as it unfortunately tends to do in the hot Septembers of a California harvest. The balance between the sugar and acid is the beginning of the style of the wine, and the date of the harvest is thus crucial.

Picking the small, intertwined clusters by hand with knife or shears can be a slow process, and recently mechanical picking has been used where possible in large, flat vineyards. Machine harvesting tends to be most successful where field crushing, with its accompanying blanket of carbon dioxide, can be used, since Chardonnay is notably prone to oxidation.

The next great variable the winemaker is faced with is the amount of pressure to be exerted on the grapes in the press. Should he use largely free-run juice, get the absolute maximum he can wring from his grapes, or something in between? Only trial and error will tell him, but too little pressure will give him a thin wine, and too much may make it stodgy or bitter.

Next he must choose his yeast for the fermentation, having destroyed any wild yeast by adding sulfur dioxide to the grapes in the press. (Variations again: there are several vintners now experimenting with using no sulfur dioxide and allowing the must to oxidize in the settling tank, believing that the oxidized elements will drop out with the yeast and thus produce a wine less likely to oxidize in the bottle.) The most frequently used yeasts in California are Montrachet and Champagne, but there are others. Again, only trial and error will give each winemaker the correct answer for his particular grapes.

Much experimentation is going on with the process of fermentation. Shall it be in stainless steel with a refrigerated jacket to keep the fermentation cold and thus preserve the maximum of young fruit quality? Or shall it be in oak cooperage of one size or another, which may keep the fermentation going more smoothly and completely and also add some complexity to the wine? There is something to be said for each method, or a combination of oak and stainless steel, but Chardonnay does have an unfortunate propensity for a "stuck" fermentation, and the warmth of the oak tank or barrel fermentation helps prevent this. I remember querying two different, prestigious winemakers in Burgundy on this subject in 1958 and receiving two totally different answers to my question of how each got his wine to ferment out. One said that he wished he always could; and the other replied that it was easy, just to heat it up. Remembering this later, we once applied an electric blanket to one reluctant cask, and it worked! The University of California at Davis is in the process of researching the problem as a result of the difficulties so many vintners had with stuck fermentations after the hot harvest of 1981, and perhaps they will come up with a better answer.

As the fermentation subsides, the particles of solids suspended in the juice tend to drop out and the wine clears, but to make sure of getting rid of any off flavors and the occasional still active yeast cell, most vintners resort to some more complete method of clarification. The more old-fashioned use a diatomaceous earth, such as bentonite, or egg white, which carry down the small particles in much the way coffee grounds are cleared from a campfire coffee pot. The more modern equipment is a centrifuge, which can be brutal, but when used with care does a beautiful job. In the Burgundy district of France, where the acid balance of the wine tends to be much higher than in California, it is a common practice to induce a malolactic fermentation before bottling, thus reducing the malic acid in the wine. There are some California vintners experimenting with this method also, but unless the acid on picking has been very high it does tend to produce a wine of somewhat bland flavor, less appley and fragrant.

When the fermentation is complete, choices abound again. When the wine is racked off the lees, shall it go into small oak barrels, into oak or stainless steel tanks, or into oak casks of more neutral size than the fifty to sixty gallon barrels presently so much used? It is easy to overwhelm the beautiful fruit of the wine with wood flavors, but a bit of oak does indeed bring out the character of the wine. Here the skill of the winemaker and his devotion to his task are surely paramount, for it is a matter of constant vigilance to observe what is happening to his wine and to take steps to achieve the desired result.

Much discussion and experimentation is taking place over which varieties of oak should be used, and what size—always remembering that the smaller the container, the greater the exposure of wine to the surface of the barrel. French barrels of fifty to sixty gallons are the most frequently used, with woods identified as Limousin, Nevers, and Allier being the most popular. Each has a subtly different flavor, each is preferred by some winemakers over the others. Some wineries opt instead for Yugoslav or American oak. Oak flavors diminish with each succeeding use, but it is a fortunate winery indeed that can afford the present price of nearly $300 a French barrel for annual replacement. Perhaps this is one of the reasons for the less predominantly oaky flavor of Chardonnays from many of the newer California wineries—their barrels are simply aging. At Stony Hill, we buy a few new barrels every year, keep the old ones, and move the wine around from one to another as taste indicates. It is a wonderful game requiring infinite patience and a lot of work. (For more on barrels, see chapter 5.) Nor must the winemaker ever neglect to keep his barrels topped up, that is, full to the brim, lest oxygen invade the barrel. Haraszthy, in *Wine-Making in California* (1862), quotes a German winemaker as saying, "You should sooner forget to kiss your wife on returning home than to leave a vacancy in your barrel."

When the wine has reached the complexity and maturity the winemaker is seeking from the barrel, it is time for bottling. Usually, the wineries of California seem to bottle their Chardonnays in the August following harvest. The wine is filtered into the blending tank and proceeds from there to the bottle, every care being given to prevent any oxidation or contamination. Though many Chardonnays are released the autumn after bottling, it is surely preferable if possible to give them a year in the bottle before they go to market, and a few more years in private cellars before they are opened.

Since Chardonnay has been from time immemorial the great white grape variety of the Burgundy district of France, it is surprising how short its history is as a major factor in the California wine scene. While there were undoubtedly a few acres here and there before Prohibition, including a small planting of twenty acres at Wente Brothers in Livermore, the records are scant. It is pleasant to surmise that some of the fame of the early California chablis might have come from the fact that it was enhanced by small amounts of Chardonnay. After Prohibition, various lovers of French Burgundies, eager to improve the body of their wines, began to plant experimental plots of Chardonnay, most of them obtaining their budwood from the Wentes or from the University of California, but even as late as 1948 the university was advising prospective growers that Chardonnay was difficult to grow and not to be depended on as to set.

Prior to 1959, there appear to have been as few as two hundred acres planted in all of the state, even though Amerine and Winkler had reported in 1944 that the quality was uniformly high in cool regions and often exceptional even in warmer ones. Being extremely shybearing, particularly in mountain vineyards, where the yield may be as low as one to two tons per acre, and the frequent victim of various vineyard pests, it apparently did not appeal to the early growers. But with the improvement of rootstock and the perfection of selected budwood, the yield has increased, and present plantings are reported to be close to twenty thousand acres. By way of comparison, France had thirty thousand acres in 1971, half of that total in Champagne.

The men who pioneered the post-Prohibition planting of Chardonnay in California, such as Herman Wente in Livermore, William Silvear at Chalone, Louis P. Martini at Monte Rosso, and Fred McCrea at Stony Hill, all sought land rich in chalky soils similar to the land of the Côte d'Or in Burgundy. The earlier California plantings were pretty well concentrated around San Francisco Bay and northward into Napa and Sonoma counties. Now many acres are growing successfully to the south in the cooler sections of Monterey, San Benito, and Santa Barbara counties. There never will be complete agreement on the right exposure to be sought, but cool nights and plenty of hours of sun are essential to achieve a true ripening, which would lead one to prefer mountain tops where possible. With the limitation in irrigation almost always present on a mountain vineyard, the yield is small, seldom more than two or three tons to the acre, but as many a grower found during the recent drought years, the flavor of the grapes seems to be more intense.

From all of this, it would now appear that Chardonnay is a more vigorous and reliable grower than originally thought, particularly when planted on one of the newer rootstocks, such as Ganzin #1 or AxR #1. It thrives on a great variety of soils, producing maximum tonnage in the heavier valley soils. Because of its lush growth, it should be cane-pruned, preferably on wire. Apparently temperature has more to do with its quality than soil, the cooler regions I and II of the University of California classification system producing wines of better balance and more luscious flavor.

During the years 1975 to 1981, the acreage more than tripled, from 4,900 to 13,670, with an additional 6,096 acres planted but not bearing at the vintage of 1982. The laws of supply and demand will almost surely begin to take their toll in lower returns to growers. It will be interesting to see whether the better-known regions of the North Coast, which now average $1,190 a ton, will maintain their differential from the Santa Barbara–San Luis Obispo–Monterey–San Benito area, now averaging $925.

Beginning in January 1983, the regulations of the Bureau of Alcohol, Tobacco and Firearms require that any wine labeled as a varietal must contain a minimum 75 percent of that variety, a jump of 24 percent from the previous minimum requirement. This in itself may absorb a proportion of the new bounty, but it is to be hoped that some small percentage will be added to the generic white wines of larger bottlers and thus raise the inherent quality of their product. If the price should go down, as it is almost bound to do, there will also be less temptation to blend in less expensive grapes even for the 25 percent allowed by law. In any case, there should always be available to the interested connoisseur an almost infinite set of variations on Beethoven's theme, surely enough to suit any palate.

VI.6

SAUVIGNON BLANC

by JEAN R. WENTE

CALIFORNIA SAUVIGNON BLANC IS ALWAYS BEING DISCOVERED, A FORLORN LUXURY PERMITTED BY THE GRAPE'S HUNDRED YEARS OF HISTORY IN THE state and dictated by the uncompromising character of its wines. Unlike the majority of varieties in California, Sauvignon Blanc has a clear past. One of the earliest and certainly the dominant importation of cuttings came from Château d'Yquem in 1878. These cuttings came as a combined effort of pioneer Livermore Valley growers Louis Mel and Charles Wetmore. Mel had family connections with the Marquis de Lur Saluces, proprietor of the renowned château. When Wetmore traveled in Europe to collect data on grape varieties and winemaking techniques, Mel provided him a letter of introduction to the château. With it Wetmore obtained from Yquem cuttings of Sauvignon Blanc, Sémillon, and Muscadelle du Bordelais, the three classic varieties of Sauternes.

Mel planted a share of the cuttings in his El Mocho vineyard. The rest went to Wetmore's vineyards at nearby Cresta Blanca. The latter plantings disappeared years ago. However, those at El Mocho continued to produce into the early 1960s, first for Mel, then for Wente Bros. after our family bought the vineyard in 1939. More important to other vineyard districts in California and the rest of the country, El Mocho vines have yielded all of the cuttings of two of the varieties, Sauvignon Blanc and Sémillon, for Wente Bros. nursery stocks, as well as for its own vineyards. One descendant is the University of California at Davis's heat-treated clone No. 1 of Sauvignon Blanc. Nursery records at Wente show other direct descendants of El Mocho vines in nineteen of the twenty-nine California counties reporting plantings of Sauvignon Blanc, and in several other states.*

Whatever the ancestral source of a vineyard, expert tasters have no trouble identifying California Sauvignon Blancs by their distinctive flavors. The University of California's associative descriptions of these flavors are basic and reliable: "Fruity, green olive, faintly herbaceous."† Popular writers have added dozens of poetic elaborations to the basic theme. Some of the more arresting ones say the wine suggests burnt almonds, peaches, peaches touched by gardenias, apricot pits, dried orange peels, green tomatoes. Other writers have called the wines appealingly grassy, fresh with hints of cucumbers and tangerines, dusty dry, flinty, and austere with wet sand aroma. Privately, Ernest Wente always referred to a good Sauvignon Blanc as having the flavor of fresh, ripe figs, while Herman Wente was reminded of a good cigar butt!

These pronounced qualities have produced trepidation in academic observers of Sauvignon Blanc wines. Maynard Amerine and A. J. Winker noted in the 1940s that wine from the variety would not be popular with consumers because of its strong flavors.‡ They recommended blending with less forceful varieties as the best means of making Sauvignon Blanc acceptable to a general audience and have echoed that judgment at regular intervals ever since. Now and again a group of consumers will bear out these fears, but they almost always turn out to be inexperienced winedrinkers. My own, long-held theory is that Sauvignon Blanc appeals only to people who are sure of their ability to detect nuances in wine. For them, the very

---

*   Alameda, Amador, Kern, Los Angeles, Mendocino, Monterey, Napa, Nevada, Riverside, San Benito, San Diego, San Joaquin, San Luis Obispo, Santa Barbara, Santa Clara, Sonoma, Sutter, Tulare, and Yolo counties. The states are Washington, Oregon, Texas, New Mexico, Ohio, Maryland, and the Carolinas. El Mocho descendants are also planted in British Columbia, Canada, and Mexico.

†   M. A. Amerine and V. L. Singleton, *Wine: An Introduction for Americans* (Berkeley and Los Angeles: University of California Press, 1966), p. 36.

‡   M. A. Amerine and A. J. Winkler, "Composition and Quality of Musts and Wines of California Grapes," *Hilgardia* 15 (February 1944): 547.

different complexities of this wine become a true pleasure. The difficulty seems to be that potential Sauvignon Blanc drinkers have not been left in peace long enough to make the discovery in their full numbers.

The pre-Prohibition history of Sauvignon Blanc as a grape (though not as a wine) was virtually confined to the Livermore Valley, in the hills east of San Francisco Bay. That it should have arrived so early in an area so perfectly suited to all of the subtleties of its character was an extremely happy accident, but one that did not go unrecognized. A double gold medal winner at the Paris Exposition of 1889 came from Charles Wetmore's Cresta Blanca vineyards, the first definite recognition of Livermore's suitability for the variety. Livermore Sauvignon Blanc wines were faring just as well at home. At the Panama-Pacific International Exposition in San Francisco in 1915, wines under the labels of Beaulieu Vineyard, A. Finke's Widow, Gundlach-Bundschu, and Napa Sonoma Wine Company all won gold medals. All had been made by C. H. Wente from Sauvignon Blanc grown in his own vineyards and sold in bulk.

Whatever gains Sauvignon Blanc had made to this point were lost between 1919 and 1933, the duration of national Prohibition. In the early years after Repeal, Livermore resumed its virtual monopoly on Sauvignon Blanc, and quickly rebuilt its reputation as a growing region for the variety. A Wente Bros. Sauvignon Blanc won the Grand Prix at the 1937 Paris International Exposition. At the 1939 Golden Gate International Exposition, Wente Bros. won the Grand Prize for white wines with a varietally labeled Sauvignon Blanc, one of the earliest bottlings to bear the grape's name. Perhaps the greatest tribute to California Sauvignon Blanc of that era came in the form not of a medal, but of a compliment. When the owner of Château d'Yquem—the son of the man who had sent cuttings to California—visited Livermore, he sampled seven consecutive vintages of Wente Bros. Sauvignon Blanc, then wrote in the guest book, "I am glad to find my children doing so well in California." These successes did not cause the variety to become widely planted in any great hurry. The spread of Sauvignon Blanc into other districts proceeded slowly over the next two decades.

Still, and oddly, considering its reputation as a variety too flavorful for public favor, by the beginning of the contemporary California wine boom in the early 1960s, it had the largest planting of any variety used to make varietal white wine. Its total acreage in 1961 was 1,962. In contrast, Chardonnay plantings were so few and small that the classic Burgundian variety did not receive a separate entry in that year's annual state crop report. Ten years later, Sauvignon Blanc plantings had declined slightly to 1,594 acres, while Chardonnay had increased to 3,057. By 1981 Chardonnay accounted for 19,700 acres, Sauvignon Blanc for 9,588. The recent blossoming of Sauvignon Blanc reflects the probability that the cadre of experienced American wine drinkers finally has respectable numbers.

This time the popularity is based on a wide range of styles from many districts, ranging from Mendocino on the north coast all the way to Temecula in the south, and inland into the Sierra foothills. Another immeasurable, but undeniably important, factor in Sauvignon Blanc's growing acceptance is the widespread use of Fumé Blanc as a synonym on labels. Why Sauvignon Blanc suffered under its own name is a mystery, but suffer it did. Louis P. Martini recalls bottling exactly the same wine under the names Sauvignon Blanc and Sauterne, and selling a good deal more of the latter. Credit for adopting Fumé Blanc as an alternative name goes to Robert Mondavi, who introduced it in the late 1960s, when there was a serious oversupply of the variety. It succeeded so quickly that by 1980 Alexis Bespaloff reported in *New York Magazine* that half the wines in a large tasting were named Fumé Blanc.

The three basic styles of Sauvignon Blanc in California echo somewhat those of four French wines, Sancerre and Pouilly-Fumé from the Loire River Valley, and Graves and Sauternes from Bordeaux. Sancerre and Pouilly-sur-Loire are adjacent communes. Both yield fresh, crisp, fruity wines. Sancerre, in particular, is meant for early drinking, but neither it nor Pouilly-Fumé is expected to be aged in bottle. Both are made 100 percent from a variety identified sometimes as Blanc Fumé, sometimes as Sauvignon Blanc. Graves produces full-bodied, smooth-textured wines with flavors the French describe as earthy or flinty. Almost always, dry Graves have a generous proportion of Sémillon blended with the Sauvignon Blanc, but still are considered in France as being 100 percent of Sauvignon. Fine Graves are among the most predictably ageworthy of dry whites. Sauternes are the luscious, sweet, honeyed wines picked late, after *Botrytis cinerea*—the Noble Mold—has concentrated the grape juices. The Sauternes district adjoins Graves, but is set leagues apart from it by climate conditions favoring botrytis. Here Sémillon is the majority partner in a blend with Sauvignon. Fine Sauternes are almost ageless.

In echoing the range of French styles, California has neither a strict geographic basis nor a consistent set of names. Many of the wines labeled as Fumé Blanc come closer to Graves than Pouilly, while many of those called Sauvignon Blanc approach the light freshness of a Sancerre. As contrasted to France, where there usually are heavy summer rains and the potential for rain and/or hail and/or frost during the autumn, California summers and autumns are dry enough in many districts to require irrigation to bring crops to maturity. Whether a vineyard is irrigated or dry-farmed, the combination of long growing seasons and appropriate cultural practices permits warmer districts a range of styles from light and dry to full and sweet. Where a winemaker wishes to use 100 percent Sauvignon Blanc from a cooler growing area, the light, fresh style may be the only option. It might be noted that cooler growing areas tend to intensify the varietal characteristics of

Sauvignon Blanc to the point where blending may not only expand the options, but, thinking of Amerine and Winkler's remarks, may be necessary.

To achieve the light, fresh style requires picking the grapes early, when they are at 20 to 21° Brix, giving alcohols of 11 to 12 percent and total acidity of about 0.7 to 0.8 grams per 100 ml calculated as tartaric. Fermenting and aging the wine is designed to retain a maximum of fruit flavors. Usually this means fermenting temperatures of 10.2–12.5° C (50–55° F), then little or no aging in wood. Wines of this style go to bottle soon after the vintage, frequently as early as March or April. Fuller, richer wines closer in character to Graves need riper grapes and more time in both cellar and bottle. Harvesting for these usually occurs at sugar levels of 22 to 24° Brix, resulting in alcohols of 12 to 13.5 percent. With the higher sugars goes a slightly lower acid level, usually 0.55 to 0.65 grams per 100 ml titrated as tartaric. To achieve this character requires Sauvignon Blanc grown in a moderately warm region.

In pursing a richer wine, the variations are almost as numerous as winemakers. To increase extract, the juice may spend a day in contact with the skins before fermentation begins. Fermentation temperatures often are warmer than 12.5° C (55° F). Indeed there has been a recent return in several wineries to the old practice of barrel fermentation. The effort is to achieve distinct wood overtones in the finished wine. (Barrel fermentation gives more even temperatures than fermenting in unjacketed tanks, minimizing the risk of stuck fermentation— see chapter 5.) In most cases the winemaker does not ferment in barrels from the beginning, but only after the must has fermented to about 6 percent residual sugar in a temperature-controlled tank. Barrel fermentations are not only warm, but yield a small amount of tannin to the wine. Some wines made this way are 100 percent of Sauvignon Blanc, but many have a blended proportion for balance and complexity. Usually it is the classic companion, Sémillon, but other varieties may fit. Chenin Blanc, Pinot Blanc, and French Colombard all have been used in California. Whether wines in this style ferment in barrels or in temperature-controlled stainless steel, most of them spend enough time in oak cooperage to pick up a definite overtone from the wood. At present the majority of oak-aged Sauvignon Blancs and Fumé Blancs are aged in European oak, usually French, sometimes Yugoslavian. In earlier eras, the main choice was American oak, which still finds use. On my palate, the moment any oak becomes detectable it becomes a detraction. However, one of the pleasures of wine is the sheer range of choice. The dimension of wood in Sauvignon Blanc (or any wine) is a conscious decision for the winemaker. Wines of this rich character are seldom bottled in fewer than eight months. Many wait for a year to fifteen months. The well-balanced ones profit from as many as three or four years of bottle-aging, and may stay in peak condition for ten years and more. A number of older vintages grown in Livermore have aged this long with ease. As this heavier style becomes more complex, diehard Sauvignon Blanc drinkers love it more, but its general popularity seems to diminish.

Last are the sweet styles. Sugar at harvest for these wines ranges from 28 to 32 ° Brix. Alcohols are usually about 13 percent, leaving residual sugars of 4 to 10 percent. As in Sauternes, Sémillon almost inevitably is a distinctive partner in a blend with Sauvignon Blanc. Although Sauternes provided the original inspiration, few of these wines have been affected by *Botrytis cinerea* in California until recent years. Livermore, which historically produced most sweet Sauvignon Blancs, does not lend itself to the growth of the Noble Mold. Neither, apparently, did old plantings in Napa and other regions where sweet Sauvignon Blancs have been made without botrytis during the past four decades.★ Such wines could be very good given enough time to develop distinct bottle bouquet. However, they were never more than modestly successful in the marketplace, and have fallen even farther out of favor since botrytised Rieslings have become a steady part of California winemaking. New plantings have begun to change the face of sweet Sauvignon Blanc. Monterey County has repeatedly produced botrytised Sauvignon Blanc in recent years. In 1982 the Napa Valley yielded several. From time to time, someone produces one by inducing botrytis on harvested grapes in a controlled environment. Although the jury still is out, these may challenge botrytised White (Johannisberg) Rieslings more successfully than nonbotrytised sweet Sauvignon Blancs were able to do during the 1970s.

For the Sauvignon Blanc grape, climate Regions II and III would seem to be the most ideal. As examples, the midsection of the Napa Valley is Region II and Livermore is Region III. However, Sauvignon Blanc is grown in almost all the grape-growing regions of California. In the Livermore Valley, average annual rainfall is twelve to fourteen inches. Vineyards in general and Sauvignon Blanc in particular require upwards of twenty-four inches of rainfall per year to bring an average crop of three and a half to four and a half tons per acre to maturity. This means irrigation in many of California's coastal districts and nearly all of its inland ones. In the coolest districts, irrigation must be stopped early enough in the season to stress the vines as grapes ripen. Otherwise, an excessive herbaceous flavor results.

Soil, climate, age of the vineyard and the condition of individual vines determine the overall approach to pruning Sauvignon Blanc. In the Wente Bros. vineyards in the Livermore Valley, the practice is to cordon-prune the vine, leaving

★ As a group, these came to be known as "Chateau" Sauvignon Blancs from the habit of several producers of labeling the wine with that word to indicate sweetness. Examples with long histories include Chateau Beaulieu, Chateau Concannon, and Chateau Wente. In 1961 Cresta Blanca made the still-remembered Premier Sémillon, the first sweet wine from an induced-botrytised Sémillon grape.

six two-bud spurs. This method fairly well assures a crop of approximately four tons per acre. In cooler areas such as Monterey County, pruning becomes important for sun exposure and air movement through the vines to aid in ripening the fruit. Amador County has the opposite problem, with sunburn being a factor; pruning techniques can help.

The Sauvignon Blanc cluster is small, conical in shape, and tightly packed with medium-sized berries that have heavy bloom. (Bloom is the waxy coating that gives the ripening fruit a grayish, smoky appearance, the reason, perhaps, for its name of Blanc Fumé—Smoky White— in France's Loire River Valley.) When the grapes are fully ripe, the color softens to a pale green to light yellow. Sauvignon Blanc's habit of ripening at mid-season offers winemakers flexibility of style extending all the way to late harvest without undue risk from early rains or autumn frosts. Sauvignon Blanc is a light producer when young, but as a mature vine is noted for its vigorous growth. In some regions it will bear as much as six tons per acre unless controlled by pruning. The variety is subject to shatter— failure of improperly pollinated or unpollinated flowers to set fruit—because of heat. Undercropped young vines also are subject to this difficulty.

VI.7

OTHER WHITE WINES

by THE EDITORS

BURGER

BURGER'S ORIGINS ARE UNKNOWN, PROBABLY FOR LACK OF interest. Most valued and most used in California as a neutrally flavored base for inexpensive sparkling wines, or as a blending element in table wines, it does make a rare appearance in a varietal wine. In the early 1980s, there was but one, a sweet wine from thoroughly ripened grapes. The principal plantings of Burger's modest 188 acres are in the San Joaquin Valley and southern California. The vines will bear immense crops on fertile soils, good ones wherever vines will grow. The vines themselves are hardy, but the thin-skinned berries are very susceptible to damage from picking and early rains. The University of California once gave limited recommendation to the variety, but no longer does.

CHENIN BLANC (PINEAU DE LA LOIRE, ONCE WHITE PINOT)

Increasingly winemakers in California are treating Chenin Blanc the way chefs treat chicken, as a sort of tabula rasa. Where chefs cover chicken with distinctive sauces to vent their need for self-expression, winemakers capitalize on the bland charms of Chenin Blanc by electing for any amount of residual sugar that suits them and aging the wine in any container from neutral steel to flavorful new oak.

Chenin Blanc began to flower in California late in the 1950s, after Robert Mondavi introduced the name at Charles Krug, and after cold fermentation and improved filtration techniques made wines with residual sugar less easy prey to delayed fermentation or other spoilage in the bottle. Before those transforming events, dry wine from the grape had enjoyed a meager popularity, usually under the incorrect name of White Pinot. The rarely used alternative name of Pineau de la Loire probably explains the source of the erroneous one, which seems to have disappeared from labels since the late 1960s. In the early 1980s, by far the majority of Chenin Blancs go to bottle with perceptible residual sugar, usually in the range 0.8 to 2.5 percent, and no hint of oak flavors. Most of these wines spend little time in wood. When they do, the cooperage is large, well-seasoned, or both. Some spend none, fermenting and aging only in stainless steel. The sweet, fruity approach is as well suited to California Chenin Blancs as it is to Vouvrays, the principal among several French ancestors from the Loire River Valley. At the other extreme, Chenin Blanc is fermented dry, wholly or partly in European oak barrels, then aged for a short time in the same, or similar, wood. Wine buffs call the style, with only faint derision, "poor man's Chardonnay." The approach is pursued by a tiny number of small producers in the coastal counties. Between these two poles come bottlings with every subtle shading of sweetness and oak aging. Although a few labels note proportion of residual sugar, many ignore the range of possibilities altogether, no doubt to the occasional confusion of buyers who get one style when expecting another. Nearly all producers of Chenin Blancs recommend that the wine be drunk in youth while its fruit flavors are at a peak.

The Napa Valley pioneered Chenin Blanc and popularized it. The district remains a prime source of prized examples, but with increasing competition from other regions, including Sonoma, Mendocino, Monterey, and San Luis Obispo counties, and that part of Yolo and San Joaquin counties called the Delta. The San Joaquin Valley produces huge volumes of varietal Chenin Blanc of a quality that has done much to help California's reputation as a source of appetizing, inexpensive wines. Plantings have increased markedly, from 8,700 acres in 1971 to 37,500 in 1981, making it the second most planted variety in the state after Thompson Seedless. In the interior, Kern County alone has 4,100 acres. Six other counties in the San Joaquin Valley have 1,400 to 2,700 acres each. Among the coastal counties, Napa and Monterey have the largest acreages, 1,700 and 2,300, respectively. Its yield in the San Joaquin Valley reliably ranges between eight and eleven tons when trained to avoid overcropping. In coastal conditions, tonnage is five to eight. The plant can be depressingly vigorous to pickers, who have difficulty harvesting fruit from its thick tangle of canes. Chenin Blanc is a mid-season ripener. The vines are generally healthy, but thin skins leave the berries subject to botrytis and less welcome molds.

EMERALD RIESLING

The earliest, and to date most successful, of the white varieties developed by Dr. H. P. Olmo at the University of California, Emerald Riesling is widely planted as a vine, but only modestly available as a varietal wine. Olmo's goal was to develop a grape that would yield wines similar to White Rieslings from vineyards in warmer districts than the latter will tolerate. Unlike the similarly motivated Flora (see below), it performs quite well in its assigned role, producing well-balanced wines in Regions III and IV. While critics have not found Emerald Riesling's flavors as complex or charming as those of White Riesling, they have admired them. Well-regarded examples have come from the warmer southern end of the Salinas Valley in Monterey County, from the Lodi area, and from Madera in the central San Joaquin Valley. Alas, the varietal wine has not succeeded in the marketplace as well as it has with critics. It is less visible now than it was in the late 1960s. Acreage devoted to Emerald Riesling was only 3,100 in 1981, surprising in view of the variety's ability to give high yields and good acidity, equaling French Colombard. It can be harvested more readily than the latter. In interior vineyards, twelve tons per acre of properly mature fruit is not uncommon. The vine's only serious weakness in warmer regions, where nearly all of it is planted, is susceptibility to bunch rot. Extra care must be taken in the winery to avoid oxidation.

FLORA

Bred by Olmo to permit Gewürztraminer-like wines from warm growing areas, Flora has not succeeded at that, performing more reliably in the same climates as its parents, Gewürztraminer and Sémillon. Released in 1959, it is not widely planted. However, at least two wineries in Napa and Mendocino regularly produce small amounts of off-dry varietal wine from it. Though it is less fragrant than wines from the parent, the kinship to Gewürztraminer is distinct. The variety's lack of acceptance is probably owing to the lack of striking advantages over the better established Gewürztraminer. It yields slightly better, with slightly higher acidities, but has not the same distinctiveness of varietal character. There are only 370 acres, almost two-thirds of that rather misplaced in Kern County.

FOLLE BLANCHE

The grape variety earned its curious name, which means "Crazy White," in the Charentes district of France, where it once was an important contributor to

Cognac. In California it produces an unusually tart wine of neutral to delicate flavor. A small proportion from Sonoma and Napa goes to make California's lone varietal Folle Blanche. Nearly all of the rest of a small supply goes into cuvées for sparkling wine. Total acreage in 1981 was 280, with 100 of that in San Benito County, 65 in Monterey, and 55 in Napa.

FRENCH COLOMBARD

Although Colombard has been one of California's most important grape varieties since pre-Prohibition times, the varietal wine from it has prospered only since the late 1960s. There is room to suspect that the wine had to await the coming of temperature-controlled fermentation before it could blossom. Unbridled examples have powerfully perfumey, almost resinous aromas. Cold fermentation seems to render the perfume more delicate. A great majority of available bottlings balance the grape's natural high acidity with a slight residual sweetness. Wines in this style are bottled soon after fermentation ends and hurried to market in the fresh bloom of their youth. A few are made dry but otherwise in much the same vein. A tiny minority of wineries produces the wine through barrel-fermentation, barrel-aging, or both. Wines made in the tart-sweet style from grapes grown in the warmer parts of Sonoma and Mendocino counties have won the type its greatest praise, but many from the San Joaquin Valley do well in comparative tastings. In addition to its role in varietal wines, the grape appears often in generic blends and in sparkling wines.

Like Folle Blanche, French Colombard came to California from the Charentes district of France, where it is important in Cognac. The variety's identity was lost before Prohibition, causing it to be identified for a time as West's White Prolific after the man who first imported it. After Prohibition nearly exterminated plantings in California, the variety became known briefly as Winkler, after A. J. Winkler, professor of viticulture at the University of California. Winkler helped provide the correct identity. Renaming Colombard as White Prolific was not all wrong. The vine is vigorous and a heavy producer. Its long-term average in tests in the interior was seven tons per acre, but fourteen was not a rarity. In coastal conditions, it reliably produces five to six tons per acre. Against the virtues of high production and good acidity, growers must balance the defects of difficulty of picking and a tendency to produce too high alcohols. With the latter comes an intense varietal aroma some find disagreeable.

GEWÜRZTRAMINER

Gewürztraminer enjoyed a little boomlet between 1975 and 1979, poor thing. The wine had been around, but largely ignored, at least since the early 1950s. Louis M. Martini had a near monopoly on the market until the late 1960s. A few adventurous producers joined in just in time to make several splendid dry to off-dry ones, especially from the two end vintages of the boomlet era. In addition, the grape proved then to lend itself to newly discovered Late Harvest styles. The result was much too much Gewürztraminer. More than forty new wineries rallied to the banner. By 1981 Sonoma County alone had more acreage planted to the variety than the whole state had had in 1971. Prices to growers dropped in 1981 and plummeted in 1982. As early as 1981, growers started budding over to other varieties.

The primary difficulty for Gewürztraminer is that it is a self-limiting wine. An intense varietal character has much in common with some of the Muscats owing to a shared aromatic compound called linalool, the source of flowery to spicy perfumes separating both types from most of the rest of the wines in the world. Gewürztraminers also share with Muscats a faint to distinct bitterness in the finish. The two qualities join to make two small glasses of Gewürztraminer richly satisfying, perfect for the hors d'oeuvres hour, but hard for wine salesmen and restaurateurs to understand. Because one bottle can go such a long way, too few are opened in the first place. That the name is hard to pronounce properly does not improve the situation.

Beyond these limitations in the marketplace, the grape is hard to grow, and the wine hard to make. Winemakers say that Gewürztraminer has no character at all until fully ripe, and that it makes flabby wines if overripe. Growers believe, with apparent cause, that the two events are mere hours apart. Once crushed, the red-skinned grapes tend to impart (usually) unwanted pink color to the wine. Characteristic low acidity leaves it prone to oxidation unless well handled. Not least, the wine can be harsh from alcohol and its innate bitterness. One can only hope the pendulum does not swing too far away from the optimism of the late 1970s, for skillfully made Gewürztraminer ranks among the most attractive of California white wines, and fills a gastronomic need few others can.

A very few California producers make the wine dry, as their Alsatian counterparts commonly do. This style favors genuine spiciness of flavor, of the sort that will stand up to sausages, *choucroute garnie*, Hunan cookery, and other seasoned fare. The approach increases the risk of harsh finish and varietal bitterness. However, most winemakers working with the dry style seek a well-modulated bitterness as part of a balanced whole. Risk run and victory won, dry Gewürztraminer becomes an intriguing and durable wine. Several from favorable vintages have reached peak development only after four or five years. Such wines are fermented cool to cold. Many spend time in large, well-seasoned wood to soften them rather than to impart any wood flavors. Bottle-aging finishes this softening process.

By far the majority of contemporary producers make their Gewürztraminers with perceptible sweetness, usually with residual sugars in the range 1 to 2.4 percent. In this style, fermentation is almost certainly cold, between 45 and 55° F (7 and 13° C) and aging takes place primarily or entirely in stainless steel. This approach sustains the more perfumey, less spicy qualities of Gewürztraminer's varietal character. Some tasters have likened the resulting flavors to lichee, others to cold creams. Whatever the specific flavor association, these wines naturally fall into place as sippers with light hors d'oeuvres rather than foods of hearty flavor. Most producers recommend drinking them soon after bottling to capitalize on the fresh qualities of their youth.

A tiny proportion of Gewürztraminer becomes Late Harvest wine, in styles equivalent to a range encompassing Spätlese, Auslese, and Beerenauslese. Although the tough-skinned grape does not yield easily to *Botrytis cinerea*, California's long, rainless harvest seasons occasionally allow this to happen. Because the grape has so powerful a character, the resulting wine ofttimes is more varietally identifiable than counterparts made from White Riesling. The best of them are superb nectars, capable of making an optimist out of almost anyone.

For almost all of these styles, vineyards in Sonoma County have dominated critical favor to a remarkable degree, perhaps because Sonoma has the longest history as well as a substantial proportion of the plantings. However, in recent years, wines of challenging quality have come from Mendocino County (especially Anderson Valley), the Napa Valley, Monterey, and, more latterly still, San Luis Obispo and Santa Barbara counties. Total acreage in 1981 was 4,700, but sure to decline before its large proportion of young vines could bear full crops. Principal plantings are in Sonoma (1,275 acres), Santa Barbara (1,200), Monterey (1,000), and Napa (525).

GREEN HUNGARIAN

A variety of uncertain ancestry, Green Hungarian makes an indistinctly flavored wine almost always styled for immediate consumption. On average, the varietal appears under seven labels. Most bottlings of Green Hungarian in recent years have been dry to slightly off-dry, but two of the principal producers make a frankly sweet wine of it. Few consumer publications have taken notice of the varietal wine in recent years, although several of the sweeter bottlings have won awards as high as Silver at the Los Angeles County Fair since 1980, and the wine has a loyal following.

Most of the state's 400 acres of Green Hungarian are in four counties, Kern, Mendocino, Napa, and Sonoma. Although not recommended by the University of California, the vine is favored by growers because it is a prolific producer and virtually trouble free.

GREY RIESLING

Grey Riesling has been described as the surprisingly bright child of a witless parent. No Riesling at all, it has evolved during decades in California, some say from the Trousseau, others from the Chauché Gris, both of France. Neither variety is highly regarded there, nor is Grey Riesling much admired at the University of California. Still, the wine is distinctly popular. Nearly all of the wineries making Grey Riesling ferment the wine cold in stainless steel, and bottle it soon after fermentation is complete. Usually made off-dry in tribute to its supposed Germanic qualities, Grey Riesling is pleasantly fruity to faintly spicy, and has enough balance to benefit from a year or so in bottle. The pink-skinned grapes will impart a faint rosy blush to wines unless care is taken to avoid this. A majority of bottlings come from wineries in Napa, Alameda, and Mendocino although the largest acreage of Grey Riesling is in Monterey County. The state total in 1981 was 2,437. Monterey had 700 acres, Alameda 450, Napa 300. Grey Riesling is not recommended for planting by the University of California because its wines are soft and undistinguished compared with other varieties. However, the vine is recognized as a vigorous grower yielding average crops of well-balanced wines in cooler regions.

MALVASIA BIANCA

One of the Muscats, Malvasia usually is made as a fortified sweet wine to allow a characteristic harsh quality time to mellow. However, a few wineries make Malvasia Bianca as a light Muscat after the fashion of Muscat Blancs.

MUSCADELLE DU BORDELAIS (ALSO SAUVIGNON VERT)

An integral, though small, component of both Sauternes and Dry Graves, Muscadelle has long been in California, though seldom as a varietal wine, and then sometimes under the alternate name of Sauvignon Vert. The vine is troublesome to grow and the wine is held to be less attractive than that from Muscat Blanc. This reputation and a minuscule acreage aside, three wineries have offered varietal Muscadelle on occasion in recent years, and a fourth produces Sauvignon Vert regularly. Acreage is not reported as Muscadelle. As Sauvignon Vert, the variety had 500 acres in the state in 1981. Sonoma had 200 acres, Napa 100. In both counties, the vine goes back to the pre-Prohibition era.

MUSCAT BLANC (ALSO MUSCAT CANELLI, MOSCATO CANELLI, MUSCAT DE FRONTIGNAN)

Few varieties give wine drinkers such a ready opportunity to test varietal character as the Muscats. Their strong family flavor can be found in fresh grapes at the market as well as in bottles of varietal wines. Among all the light Muscats, the most refined flavors are found in those made of Muscat Blanc. Cold fermentation and aging in stainless steel enhance the richly perfumed aromas of this variety. The wine almost always is made off-dry to outright sweet, primarily to suit the perfumes but partly to mask a characteristic slight bitterness. Muscat Blanc by any of its names begs for early drinking while a maximum freshness remains in its fruit flavors. There are 1,400 acres planted to the variety in the state, a small total divided in bits and pieces among sixteen counties, most of them coastal. However, the largest acreage, 343, is in Tulare County.

PINOT BLANC

A secondary variety to Chardonnay in Burgundy, Pinot Blanc has an equally dim role in California. Its less specific varietal character and higher total acidity make it a useful grape for making fine sparkling wines, probably the dominant use. Unusually high levels of tannins in the skins combine—curiously—with a tendency of the must to darken with oxidation. Nonetheless, a few table wine producers take pains with Pinot Blanc. The finest of the resulting wines, the majority from Napa, some from Sonoma and Monterey, have competed favorably with well-regarded Chardonnays. Most of these Pinot Blancs bear the marks of barrel fermentation, aging in new European oak barrels, or both, a style that enhances the similarity to Chardonnay. In the early 1980s, there appears to be a slight trend toward more, rather than fewer, Pinot Blancs in this style. Pinot Blanc also is made as a straightforward, light, dry white without discernible oak aging. Total acreage of this comparatively low-yielding variety in California in 1981 was 2,000. Monterey County dominated plantings with 1,100 acres. Next in line was Napa County with 221.

RKATSITELI

A grape widely grown in Georgian Russia, Rkatsiteli was brought to this state because of its ability to yield high-acid wines in relatively warm growing conditions. It has been the subject of an on-going experiment by the Concannon Vineyard in Livermore Valley since the 1960s. Theirs has remained the only vineyard and only varietal wine, and it is being phased out.

SAINT-ÉMILION (UGNI BLANC, TREBBIANO)

One winery, Brookside in Cucamonga, in southern California, regularly produces a varietal wine from Saint-Émilion, a variety of little fame in California or elsewhere. The majority of its 1981 acreage of 1,300 was in three counties, Kern, Stanislaus, and Tulare, all in the San Joaquin Valley. Lack of acidity, even in cool regions, and neutral flavors have caused the University of California not to recommend it.

SÉMILLON (CHEVRIER)

Somehow, Sémillon from California has not been able to capture the public fancy in spite of its admirers among winemakers and University of California faculty at Davis. In France the grape is not expected to stand alone in wine, but goes into blends with the similar Sauvignon Blanc in both dry Graves and Sauternes. In Bordeaux and in California, Sémillon tends to have more lush fruit flavors than Sauvignon Blanc, which is often described as herbaceous rather than fruity. Used alone in California, Sémillon can feel dull on the palate and be a bit too lush in flavor to suit many critical palates. However, at its best it can produce memorably rich, satisfying wines. In recent years, several have come from vines in the Santa Cruz Mountains south of San Francisco. The variety also has yielded excellent wines in Livermore, Napa, and Sonoma, the most praised of these being light and refreshing

259

in style. Monterey begins to be heard from. Unfortunately, some of the most-praised producers have stopped bottling Sémillon for lack of interest in the marketplace. Since 1980 the variety's alternate name, Chevrier, has come into use, probably in the hope that lightning will strike as it did earlier for Sauvignon Blanc and Fumé Blanc.

A majority of Sémillons from all parts of California are made dry or just off-dry, and given no more than modest time in oak before bottling. With the recent upsurge of interest in botrytised wines in California, the thin-skinned Sémillon has been a natural point of focus because of its role as the heavily botrytised partner of Sauvignon Blanc in Sauternes. To this point, the best-known examples have been made from grapes on which the beneficial mold was induced, rather than natural. Total 1981 acreage in California was 2,900. Monterey had the largest plantings, 625 acres. Alameda, Sonoma, and Napa each had about 200. The ability of the variety to produce fair yields of fairly well-balanced wines in moderately warm growing regions has caused it to be planted in several San Joaquin Valley counties, especially Kern, Stanislaus, and Tulare, each with more than 300 acres. In these regions, it is better suited to slightly sweet than dry wines because of its characteristic, though slight, lack of acidity.

SYLVANER (FRANKEN RIESLING)

One of the secondary grapes to White Riesling in Germany, Sylvaner has suffered declining popularity in recent years, but seems far from extinguished. Its gentle wines are surviving nicely not only under the basic names, but under several geographic guises such as Monterey Riesling, Sonoma Riesling, and others. By whatever name, nearly all are fermented cold in stainless steel, left with a bit of residual sugar, bottled quickly, and sold for early use in informal settings. Sylvaner had only 1,400 acres in the state in 1981, about half of that in Monterey County. The rest was spread rather evenly among other coastal counties. Owing to its susceptibility to bunch rot, it performs well only in relatively cool conditions where early rains are not a problem. In Region III and warmer areas, it suffers from low acidity and high pH.

WHITE RIESLING (JOHANNISBERG RIESLING)

Of all the wines that have profited from improved equipment and technique in California wineries, White Riesling has to rank first. Not so many years ago, a typical one was heavy, coarse, and dry, closer kin to Soave than to Schloss Johannisberg. Now California wines from the greatest grape of German origin are redolent of a whole galaxy of appetizing perfumes from delicately floral to richly apricotlike, depending on ripeness at harvest and residual sugar.

But a funny thing happened to White Riesling on its way to the pantheon. The evolution toward a Germanic range of styles left nomenclature far behind developments. It could, and did, happen that one 1977 bottling went to mar-

ket with 6 percent residual sugar and a standard label while another had but 2.6 percent residual sugar and was identified as Late Harvest. With and without special
identification, White Rieslings range all the way from bone dry to 25 percent residual sugar. The public, presumably bewildered, has turned away from a wine at its
finest hour. In the midst of the white wine boom, wineries are dropping the varietal
from their lists, and growers are rooting the grape out of their vineyards. Alack!
Youthful White Riesling from California's coastal counties is one of the world's
finest companions to sweet-meated Dungeness crab, steamed cockles, mussels,
sand dabs, and scores of other fish and shellfish.

It may be fate. White Riesling has had name troubles from its
beginnings in California. What we now call White Riesling came to California
before Prohibition in company with, or not long after, Sylvaner and several other
German varieties. It appears that the whole lot were given the name Riesling by
early winemakers, although White Riesling's separate identity was recognized by
university researchers. After Prohibition and after varietal labeling made it important to distinguish between varieties, producers of true Riesling settled on Johannisberg as a specific (and salable) qualifier, leaving Riesling as a catchall for wines of
Sylvaner or blends of miscellaneous Germanic varieties. Since the early 1970s, a
few prestigious producers have changed their labels from Johannisberg Riesling to
White Riesling as a gesture toward ampelographic accuracy and American independence, but the process goes slowly if at all. Indeed, one winery that used to
call the wine White Riesling changed to Johannisberg as soon as new, German
owners took over.

Whatever might be in a name, the new era of White Riesling dawned
with the vintage of 1968, when Lee Stewart produced one with many of the charms
of a good German wine at his old Souverain Cellars in the Napa Valley. It had the
haunting floral scents and berry-tart juiciness that had been missing earlier in California. Stewart picked a bit earlier than his neighbors, fermented cool, and retained
a shade less than 1 percent residual sugar in the finished wine, which he bottled soon
after the harvest. Though oak flavors were no part of the design, the wine did spend
time in large oak casks to soften it. Such is still the outline of the most foodworthy
of California White Rieslings.

The next chapter came in 1972 and 1973, when Wente Bros. and
Freemark Abbey produced markedly botrytised wines from White Riesling.
Concentrated in flavor, and with residual sugar levels equaling German Auslesen
and Beerenauslesen respectively, these wines made deep impressions on critics and
other winemakers alike. Critical clamor combined with technical challenge to pull
most of the major producers into the hunt. By 1978 at least four wineries had
reached and surpassed the maximum sugar levels of Trockenbeerenauslesen. No
fewer than a dozen regularly produced wines with botrytis-aided sweetness equiva-

lent to Auslesen and Beerenauslesen. The numbers hold good in the early 1980s in years favoring the growth of botrytis during the harvest season.

Impressive as this chase was, and is, the degree to which it removed the focus from foodworthy wine to sideshow spectacular sealed not White Riesling's doom, but its decline. Many producers who could not find botrytised grapes settled for overripe ones, resulting in a good many wines of high alcohols and residual sugars between 2.5 and 4 percent—a balance suited neither to dinner nor dessert. If we hear the drinking public correctly, it is these in particular that have caused casual wine buyers to look elsewhere. Meanwhile, the wine has become too good to be ignored for much longer. As the experimental era ends and mature styles develop, a helpful nomenclature for labels is sure to follow. With that a broad audience should join us diehards who have remained loyal.

Much-praised White Rieslings in the foodworthy style come from a remarkable range of districts, including the Anderson valley in Mendocino County, parts of the Sonoma and Alexander valleys in Sonoma County, the hills of the Napa Valley (and a few scattered spots on the valley floor), the midsection of the Salinas Valley in Monterey County, and both the Santa Maria and Santa Ynez valleys in Santa Barbara County. For the most part, these vineyards slope, often from relatively lofty beginnings. Botrytised grapes for concentratedly sweet wines come, contrarily, mostly from bottom lands along streams, where morning fogs can linger. The most consistent areas are near the Salinas River in Monterey County. Patches along the Russian River in Sonoma County are almost as regular. Less predictable, but excellent sources are low-lying vineyards along the Napa River in the Napa Valley, the Russian River in Mendocino County, and the Santa Maria drainage in Santa Barbara County. A moderate producer subject to sunburn and oxidation, and with at least a mild bent toward low acidity in all but the coolest locations, the variety was planted to 11,100 acres in California in 1981. The four main counties were Monterey (3,500 acres), Santa Barbara (2,500), Sonoma (1,500), and Napa (1,400). In spite of the variety's troubles in the marketplace and in the vineyard, its proponents are certain to keep it a considerable factor while it regains its equilibrium.

GENERIC AND SEMI-GENERIC WHITE WINES

In California, white wines other than varietals go to market under a broad spectrum of names that, in general, do modest service in clarifying character. In recent years, there has arisen a trend among smaller producers to offer blended wines under simple names such as White Table Wine. For the most part, these are efforts to escape accusations of stealing European names. Most such wines are dry, or at least dry enough to go well with meals. Some have distinct character, having been blended from press wines, surpluses, or marginally satisfactory lots from fine grape varieties. A majority are plainer results of blending such wines with commoner ones.

The historically dominant habit is to name blended wines after European models. The commonest semi-generic name at present is chablis, which promises, and often delivers, a wine dry enough to accompany food. Increasingly in recent years the bald term has been modified—Emerald Chablis, Gold Chablis, etc.—for purely commercial purposes. Next most popular of these names is rhine and commercial variants such as Rhineskeller, Rhinegarten, and the like. These quite reliably deliver the sort of bland sweetness associated with such commercial German wines as Liebfraumilch and Moselblümchen. White wines with Italianate names also tend to be perceptibly sweet, but rather heavier in character than ones called by Germanic names. White chianti, vino bianco, vino da pranza, and similar names all are in the market, usually from volume producers and at low prices. No regulations limit the grape varieties that may be used in these wines, or the characteristics imparted by residual sugar or other winemaking techniques. Because of this, no form obtains, but this does not keep some of the wines from being better than average, even measured against varietal bottlings of comparable technical qualities.

BLANC DE NOIRS

Blanc de Noirs (literally "white of blacks") are a relatively recent development in California. If generic and semi-generic whites are difficult to describe for lack of form, these are close to impossible. The tradition of such wines in Europe calls for them to be dry, and only faintly tinted with the hues called partridge-eye and salmon pink. These pale colors are achieved by separating juice from skins quickly, usually with little or no pressing. This aside, they are made exactly as white wines are. In California, for lack of tradition and legal definition, wines called Blanc de Noir range from water white to pinks deeper than typical rosés. They also range from dry to distinctly sweet. Some ferment cold in stainless steel and go to bottle as soon as possible after the harvest. Others age for as much as a year in oak barrels. A handful even ferment in wood. Some Blanc de Noirs are blended generics, but the majority are varietal. Every major black grape has been used in varietal bottlings. Pinot Noir appears to dominate, but Cabernet Sauvignon, Merlot, Zinfandel, and Gamay all come into frequent play, and there have been at least two Blanc de Noirs from Barbera. Names vary by proprietary whim: Blanc de Pinot Noir, Pinot Noir Blanc, White Zinfandel, Zinfandel Blanc.

VI.8

SPARKLING WINES

by JACK L. DAVIES

WHEN FRANCE'S COMMISSIONER OF AGRICULTURE, M. HENRI GROSJEAN, VISITED CALIFORNIA IN JANUARY 1893, A LOCAL NEWSPAPER QUOTED HIM as saying, "The champagne manufactured here, I must admit, I have found very fair." He also said, "I think that there is a possibility of the exportation of California champagne to France, but it will be under very trying circumstances."

Grosjean's observations were accurate in all respects, and accurate prophecy as well. During the past century, California has become one of the major sparkling-wine producing regions of the world. Two years before Grosjean's visit, production of sparkling wine in California was estimated at 20,000 cases. By 1973 total production in the state was about 6,650,000 cases. The 1973 figure compared with approximately 21,500,000 cases in France, 8,900,000 in the Soviet Union, 5,500,000 in Italy, and 2,000,000 in West Germany.* Since 1973, California production has reached 10,000,000 cases, still without penetrating the French market.

California sparkling-wine making reflects vast change over the years, in both technology and marketing. Substantial change still is taking place, but at least four eras of history can be defined. Experimentation, substantial risk taking, some terrible failures, and, finally, emerging success and recognition marked the pioneer period from the 1850s through the 1880s. Pre-Prohibition, the period from the 1890s to 1919, was an era of decline in effort, investment, and progress. Post-Repeal, from 1933 to 1946, brought a struggle to reestablish earlier beginnings and to explore new techniques. Since the end of World War II, a virtual explosion of development in California sparkling-wine making has taken place. Huge investment, new technology, vigorous marketing approaches, and a renaissance in traditional winemaking methods have brought these wines to their present state of high development, and left the industry poised to take still greater strides.

See DIAGRAM I
p. 267

Nicholas Longworth made the first sparkling wines in the United States in Ohio in 1842. His first effort was accidental. Later he refined the process on the

---

* Office International de la Vigne et du Vin, *Mémento de l'O.I.V—Édition 1975* (no. 536); Wine Institute bulletins.

basis of the French *méthode champenoise* and, using the native Catawba grape, produced what he called "Sparkling Catawba." The first to succeed in California was a Tennessean, Benjamin Davis Wilson, after whom Mount Wilson is named. In 1855, at his vineyard near San Gabriel, he produced champagne that gained immediate recognition throughout the state. Although the *Alta California* reported in March 1855 that "Mr. Wilson's experiment of making a first quality champagne wine promises to be entirely successful and we believe the time is not far distant when California will be an exporter of wine," Don Benito Wilson did not stay with it.

Shortly afterward, Jean Louis and Pierre Sainsevain launched a more substantial venture. Leaving Louis to manage their "El Aliso" vineyards, Pierre traveled to France to acquire equipment and know-how for champagne production. He returned in 1857, to San Francisco rather than to the southern California vineyards, to establish a new firm. There was considerable excitement. Enraptured, the San Francisco French language newspaper *Echo du Pacifique* wrote, "It is his [Sainsevain's] intention to found in San Francisco an establishment for the manufacture of California champagne wine. For this purpose he has brought with him the materials necessary for the accomplishment of his object, and a man competent and capable of organizing the new enterprise, which is beyond doubt destined to have a fair future."

Pierre Sainsevain and his competent and capable French Champagne maker, Pierre Debanne, set to work immediately near San Jose, laying down 50,000 bottles in 1857. They later marketed the wine as "Sparkling California" at twelve dollars a dozen, according to a visiting committee of the State Agricultural Society. In a letter to Arpad Haraszthy, Pierre wrote that with his second vintage in 1858 he had increased production to 150,000 bottles.

Other winemakers were eager to take up the challenge. General Mariano Vallejo, with the aid of a French Champagne maker, also entered the field. The *Alta California* of 25 April 1862 reported: "General Vallejo has bottled a champagne, from the vintage of 1859 which, for body and flavor, will compare favorably with the imported brands." But, like Wilson and Sainsevain, Vallejo soon dropped out.

These early beginnings were difficult. The only technique was the *méthode champenoise*, mechanically primitive in comparison with later developments, and so, necessarily, artful. The method requires a second fermentation, clarification, and marketing of the wine all in the same bottle. Evolved more than 300 years ago in the Champagne region of France, it begins with selection of wines prepared especially for the purpose. The winemaker adds sugar and a special yeast to wine in a bottle and seals it. After completion of the secondary sugar fermentation in the bottle, it is held for an extended period, usually between twenty-four and thirty-six months but sometimes longer, to achieve the desired maturation and complexity through contact with the yeast sediment. After aging, and through the use

See FIGURE 4
pp. 268–69

of riddling—frequent shaking over a period of time—the yeast sediment is collected in the mouth of each bottle, frozen, and removed. This step, called the disgorgement, involves removing a temporary bottle closure and allowing the internal gas pressure to blow out the sediment. A clear bottle of sparkling wine remains. Before the bottle is recorked, a *dosage*, or syrup, usually wine and sugar, sometimes with brandy, is added to replace the wine lost during disgorgement and to set the final level of sweetness in the champagne.

In early California, the selection of grape varieties for champagne making was not well understood, so even technically competent results were often discouraging. And technical competence was not a given. Bottles, imported from France at substantial cost, often blew up because of inadequate control of the bottle fermentation. In addition to any troubles the Californians caused themselves, there was substantial competition from French Champagne, which was popular and highly regarded, and from Longworth's Ohio "Sparkling Catawba" and "Sparkling Isabella."

Wine pioneer Agoston Haraszthy and his son Arpad made a more determined next effort. To prepare for their venture, Arpad went to work and study in the Champagne house of de Venoge at Épernay in 1860. On his return to California, he took charge of all winemaking at the Buena Vista Vinicultural Society in Sonoma, and started production of bottle-fermented champagne.

The first small trials were satisfactory but, with the decision to increase the volume of production, significant trouble emerged. Reports of the U.S. Department of Agriculture tell a familiar story of the time: In 1863, 9,000 bottles were a total failure; in 1864, of 72,000 bottles about 550 dozen (6,600) were sold and the remainder rejected; in 1865, of 42,000 bottles 50 percent were failures. The failures were attributed to characteristics of the Mission grape for which Arpad's training in France had not prepared him. The record, however, again seems to indicate a more general lack of understanding of the technical requirements for bottling the basic wine.

The experience profoundly affected all concerned with the Buena Vista undertaking. Agoston personally absorbed the losses. Arpad, unable to maintain support of the society's directors, left in 1864. However, efforts to produce champagne continued. Agoston took a progressive step in employing Pierre Debanne, Pierre Sainsevain's former Champagne master. In 1866 Debanne produced 40,000 good bottles, advancing to 90,000 the following year. Agoston reported to the board of directors, "We can congratulate ourselves that we have succeeded at last, thoroughly, in the manufacturing of Champagne." Financial differences remained, however. In 1866, discouraged at the lack of agreement with his directors, Agoston himself left.

DIAGRAM I

SOURCE: Wine Institute, San Francisco

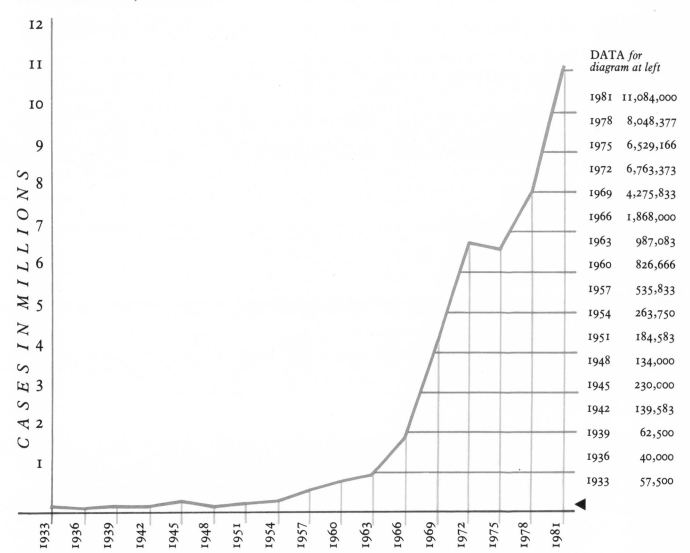

DATA *for diagram at left*	
1981	11,084,000
1978	8,048,377
1975	6,529,166
1972	6,763,373
1969	4,275,833
1966	1,868,000
1963	987,083
1960	826,666
1957	535,833
1954	263,750
1951	184,583
1948	134,000
1945	230,000
1942	139,583
1939	62,500
1936	40,000
1933	57,500

PRODUCTION, SPARKLING WINE IN CALIFORNIA SINCE REPEAL, 1933

Repeal brought an initially slow-paced revival of sparkling-wine production. However, as the worst long-term effects of Prohibition and the interruptions of World War II were overcome, the industry was ready for a remarkable growth.

Beginning in the early 1960s, powerful marketing forces made their impact: increased overall interest in wine, broader supermarket distribution, the new product stimulus of "cold duck," and, significantly, the entry of the E. & J. Gallo winery into sparkling wine production and sales.

FIGURE **4**

THE MÉTHODE CHAMPENOISE

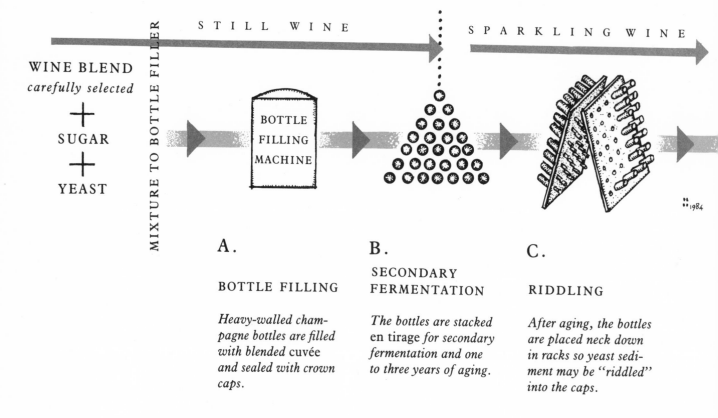

A.

BOTTLE FILLING

Heavy-walled champagne bottles are filled with blended cuvée and sealed with crown caps.

B.

SECONDARY FERMENTATION

The bottles are stacked en tirage for secondary fermentation and one to three years of aging.

C.

RIDDLING

After aging, the bottles are placed neck down in racks so yeast sediment may be "riddled" into the caps.

Arpad, meanwhile, had become a wine merchant in San Francisco, representing the Buena Vista Vinicultural Society as sole agent. This arrangement continued until 1867 when, with new financial backing, he gave up the Buena Vista agency to commence his own production of champagne.

The golden days of the pioneer period were approaching. In his *Across the Continent—1865*, Samuel Bowles wrote, "Champagne is mother's milk, indeed, to all these people; they start the day with a 'champagne cocktail' and go to bed with a full bottle of it under their ribs." According to *Hunt's Merchants Magazine*, production at Buena Vista reached 120,000 bottles in 1868. Priced at twelve to fifteen dollars a dozen, they sold just below French Champagnes.

Arpad Haraszthy, with the support of his new partners, abandoned the Mission grape to experiment with other varieties: Riesling, Burger, Muscatel, and Zinfandel. Of several *cuvées* he developed, "Dry Eclipse" became nationally famous

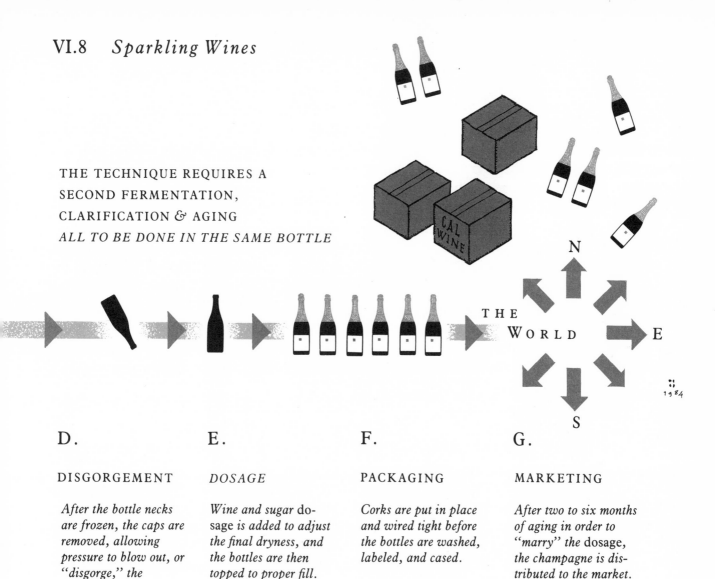

THE TECHNIQUE REQUIRES A
SECOND FERMENTATION,
CLARIFICATION & AGING
ALL TO BE DONE IN THE SAME BOTTLE

D.

DISGORGEMENT

*After the bottle necks
are frozen, the caps are
removed, allowing
pressure to blow out, or
"disgorge," the
sediment.*

E.

DOSAGE

*Wine and sugar do-
sage is added to adjust
the final dryness, and
the bottles are then
topped to proper fill.*

F.

PACKAGING

*Corks are put in place
and wired tight before
the bottles are washed,
labeled, and cased.*

G.

MARKETING

*After two to six months
of aging in order to
"marry" the dosage,
the champagne is dis-
tributed to the market.*

and a substantial commercial success. In 1880 a local newspaper reported:
"Haraszthy champagnes have obtained a fixed standing in those [European]
countries." By 1883 Arpad had thousands of bottles of "Eclipse" in "vaults under
the city" at 530 Washington Street in San Francisco. A convention of the Knights
Templar in that year was so taken with "Eclipse," it was reported, that they totally
depleted the stocks in the city and left piles of orders for wine to follow when they
departed for home. In that same year, the *Chicago Tribune* reported that California
was producing 18,000 cases of champagne a year compared with 5,000 to 6,000 ten
years earlier. W. H. Murray, in *The Builders of a Great City*, cited California production in 1891 at 20,000 cases.

Other pioneers had begun to enter the field, among them the first
whose labels would endure to the present: Almadén in 1876, Korbel in 1883, and
Paul Masson in 1884, all seeking to perfect the *méthode champenoise* in the United

States. Others came along who were destined to failure. Most were conventional, but we can only guess at the method employed by Adolph Reiklen, who in 1889 set up the American Champagne Co. in San Francisco, stating that his "Reiklen Process" was so advanced that it was conducted "in a secret room; where no one might be admitted."

Competitions, an early feature of industry development, took place both in the United States and in Europe. California sparkling wines fared well on both continents. The Columbian Exposition of 1893 in Chicago included a competition in which both Haraszthy and H. Le Franc of Almadén entered prize-winning bottle-fermented champagnes. The San Francisco "Mid-Winter Fair" in 1893–94 had numerous entries in the sparkling-wine category, including those of Haraszthy and Paul Masson, a sparkling Muscat from Italian Swiss Colony, and a carbonated wine by Antonio Domenici. From 1875 to 1889, Haraszthy won fifteen awards, including three in foreign competitions.

During the late 1800s, general wine industry problems affected makers of sparkling and table wines alike. George Husmann wrote, in words prophetic of events almost a hundred years later, that the making of white wine from red grapes "is often advisable, and especially now, when white wines sell so much more rapidly, and at higher prices than reds!" No one apparently picked up the clue that red grapes, even then, provided the basic wine for most French Champagnes. Husmann, a most prolific observer of his day, tells us that by 1888 wines were being carbonated as well as produced by the *méthode champenoise*. Carbonated versions sold at ten dollars a case and "natural" sparkling wines such as "Eclipse" at sixteen dollars. By then, California wine was also being shipped to New York for carbonation and bottling.

Increased quality among the early producers, the arrival of new ones, and widening recognition in the market marked the end of the century. By then there were perhaps a dozen well-established firms producing quality *méthode champenoise* wines marketed nationally and, to some extent, exported. But, from 1895 onward, the first waves of Prohibition being felt in state after state heralded the end of success. In a sort of last hurrah, Italian Swiss Colony imported yet one more French Champagne master in 1909. Two years later, one of the resulting wines won a Grand Prix at an international competition in Turin, Italy. In 1919 the Volstead Act brought champagne making to an end. Provisions of the law did, however, permit very limited, regulated production. Paul Masson and a few others continued to produce a small amount throughout the long, dry years.

As with table wine, Repeal in 1933 found California sparkling-wine producers ill equipped to meet renewed demand. Appropriate vineyards, skilled personnel, and adequate facilities were lacking. From Repeal until the end of World

War II, progress and development took two main courses. First there was a revival of some pre-Prohibition firms using the *méthode champenoise*: Almadén, Korbel, Italian Swiss Colony, and Paul Masson. (Haraszthy's firm and his renowned "Eclipse" did not reappear.) The second effort involved employment of a new technology, the Charmat, or bulk, process developed in France by Eugene Charmat in about 1907. In this process, blends of new wine are assembled in specially designed steel tanks with a capacity of 2,000 to 30,000 gallons, capable of withstanding pressures of around 150 pounds per square inch. Precise amounts of sugar and active yeast culture are added, causing the so-called "second fermentation" of sugar to take place in the tank, as opposed to the traditional bottle fermentation. The by-product carbon dioxide dissolves in the wine, leaving it effervescent. The now sparkling wine is filtered from the tanks into bottles, in place of riddling and disgorgement, and is ready for market.

See FIGURE 5
pp. 272–73

The Charmat process can create an appealing, sound, and relatively inexpensive sparkling wine through use of controlled technology. Extended aging is not normal, nor is the use of the highest-priced grape varieties. During the years of Prohibition, Chateau Gai in Canada had begun producing Charmat sparkling wines. When the U.S. wine market began to revive after Repeal, Chateau Gai moved across the border and set up a new Charmat facility in New York State. The first California producer of Charmat sparkling wines appears to have been the Padre Vineyards Company in southern California in 1935, closely followed by the Roma Wine Company of Fresno. Use of the new method expanded steadily thereafter, especially among new producers.

Serious effort to regulate wine labeling also followed Repeal. Regulations adopted then, reflecting recommendations by the Association of Western Wine Producers, remain the basis for sparkling wine labeling today. First, the association distinguished carbonated from sparkling wines, holding that "wines that are carbonated, that is, wines to which carbon dioxide has been added, should be so labeled." Second, it recognized that the word *champagne* merited definition. If it was not produced in France, then the label had to be "qualified by the name of the state or country where the wine is produced." In addition, *champagne* was to be "construed to mean a sparkling wine in which the after part of the fermentation is completed in the bottle." Clearly, use of the Charmat process was not contemplated by this definition. Later, Charmat-process sparkling wines were permitted to be called *champagne* so long as the words *bulk process* appeared prominently on the label. The most immediate and apparent effect of these regulations was that production of carbonated wine did not revive in California, and it has been seen only rarely since. Degrees of final sweetness never became a subject of regulation, but common

FIGURE 5

THE CHARMAT PROCESS, BULK TECHNIQUE

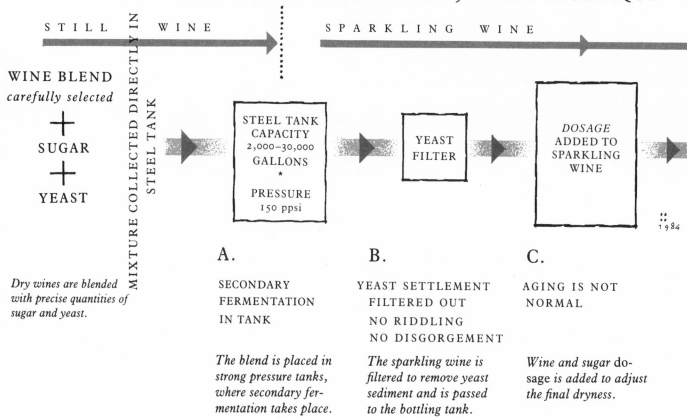

STILL WINE   SPARKLING WINE

WINE BLEND
carefully selected

+

SUGAR

+

YEAST

MIXTURE COLLECTED DIRECTLY IN STEEL TANK

STEEL TANK
CAPACITY
2,000–30,000
GALLONS
★
PRESSURE
150 ppsi

YEAST
FILTER

DOSAGE
ADDED TO
SPARKLING
WINE

Dry wines are blended with precise quantities of sugar and yeast.

A.

SECONDARY
FERMENTATION
IN TANK

The blend is placed in strong pressure tanks, where secondary fermentation takes place.

B.

YEAST SETTLEMENT
FILTERED OUT
NO RIDDLING
NO DISGORGEMENT

The sparkling wine is filtered to remove yeast sediment and is passed to the bottling tank.

C.

AGING IS NOT
NORMAL

Wine and sugar dosage is added to adjust the final dryness.

usage in California followed worldwide practices. Sparkling wine labeled *Brut* contains 0.5 to 1.5 percent residual sugar; *Extra Dry* 1.5 to 2.5 percent; *Demi-Sec* 2.5 to 4.0 percent, and *Sec*, 3.5 percent or more.

The immediate post-Repeal era had seen a struggle to start again and to reestablish a position versus French Champagne, which had flowed illegally into this country throughout Prohibition. Total California production remained at a virtual plateau from 1933 (57,500 cases) through 1939 (62,500 cases). Then the World War II years brought increased demand for champagnes at the same time that supplies from France were largely cut off. A few new producers appeared, notably Weibel (1938) and Mirassou (1945), both using the *méthode champenoise*. By 1945 sparkling wine output in California had reached 230,000 cases. It almost doubled, to 410,000 cases, in 1946 when America celebrated the war's end. Postwar availability of French Champagne brought California producers down from that peak, but

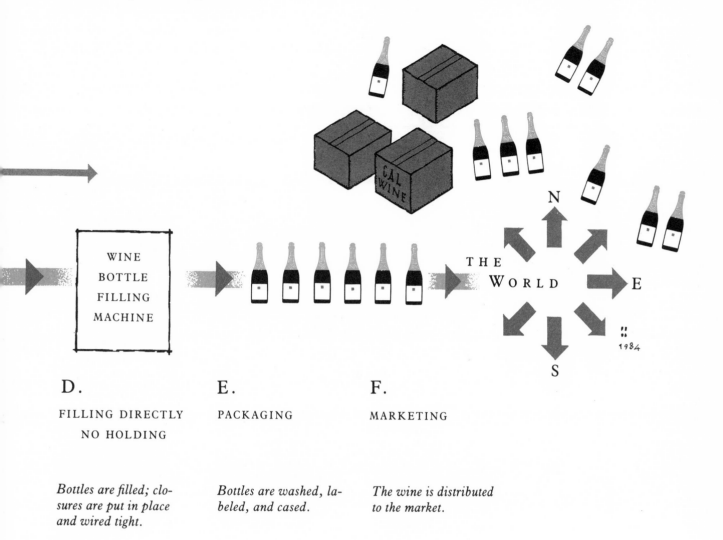

D.

FILLING DIRECTLY
NO HOLDING

Bottles are filled; closures are put in place and wired tight.

E.

PACKAGING

Bottles are washed, labeled, and cased.

F.

MARKETING

The wine is distributed to the market.

left them at levels of demand respectably above prewar ones. California production increased modestly from 1947 (174,000 cases) through 1953 (205,000 cases).

But the basis for a massive revival of California sparkling-wine making was beginning to come together. Prohibition losses of personnel and vineyards had been replaced. Fundamental work at the University of California at Davis was beginning to be understood and recommendations adopted. Americans overseas in the military service had drunk wine for the first time, liked it, and come home as potential consumers. Then, as demand increased, there were several remarkable developments in California sparkling-wine production. The most effective of them was the technical perfecting of the transfer method. For years producers had been seeking to combine the benefits of bottle fermentation with more cost-effective means of processing. In the late 1940s, Philo Biane, the California Wine Association, and Frank Pilone at Padre Vineyards Company had tried transfer

See FIGURE 6
pp. 274–75

FIGURE **6**

THE TRANSFER PROCESS

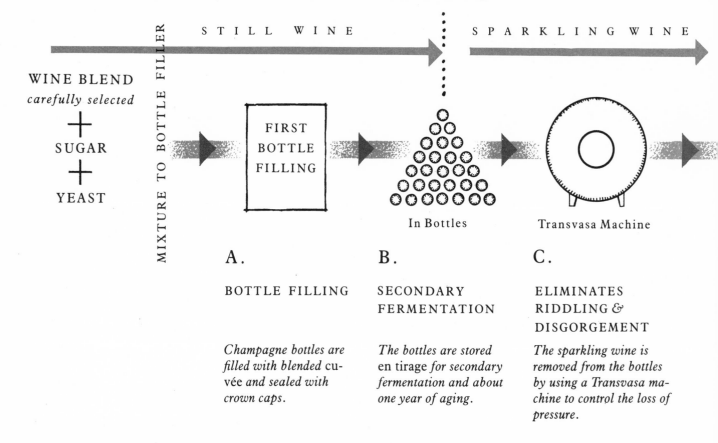

STILL WINE   SPARKLING WINE

WINE BLEND
carefully selected

+

SUGAR

+

YEAST

MIXTURE TO BOTTLE FILLER

FIRST
BOTTLE
FILLING

In Bottles

Transvasa Machine

A.

BOTTLE FILLING

*Champagne bottles are
filled with blended cu-
vée and sealed with
crown caps.*

B.

SECONDARY
FERMENTATION

*The bottles are stored
en tirage for secondary
fermentation and about
one year of aging.*

C.

ELIMINATES
RIDDLING &
DISGORGEMENT

*The sparkling wine is
removed from the bottles
by using a Transvasa ma-
chine to control the loss of
pressure.*

methods of their own design, but it remained for the method to be perfected in Germany during the 1950s, especially with equipment produced by Winterwerb, Streng, MBH, at Mannheim.

The heart of the transfer method is the so-called Transvasa machine, which permits the contents of a bottle to be emptied, filtered to remove the yeast sediment, and rebottled in a second bottle with only a minor loss of carbon dioxide from the wine. Just as in the *méthode champenoise*, new wine is bottled with an addition of sugar and yeast, then stored on its side while the "second fermentation" takes place. The Transvasa eliminates riddling and disgorgement, and also does away with bottle variation. But it is possible to age the wines in the bottle with the yeast sediment for longer periods than is practical in the Charmat tank, inducing somewhat greater complexity and somewhat finer effervescence. The process is also more costly than Charmat, so wine blends must be selected that will benefit from

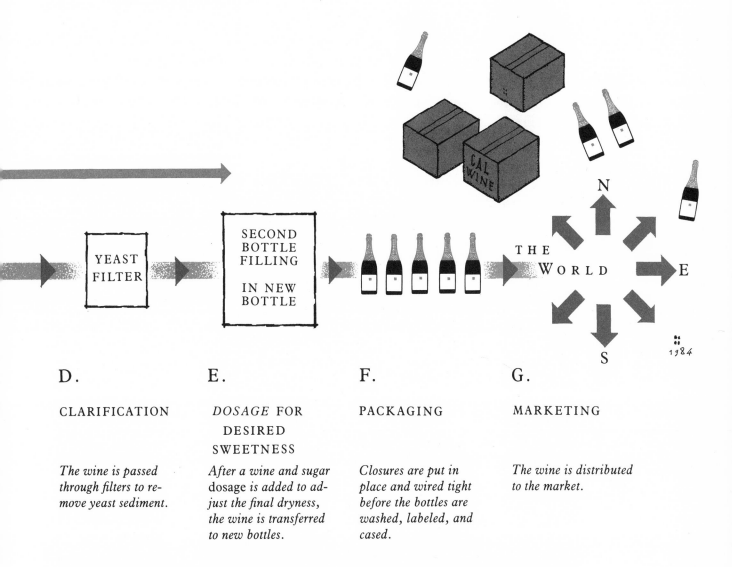

D.

CLARIFICATION

The wine is passed through filters to remove yeast sediment.

E.

DOSAGE FOR DESIRED SWEETNESS

After a wine and sugar dosage *is added to adjust the final dryness, the wine is transferred to new bottles.*

F.

PACKAGING

Closures are put in place and wired tight before the bottles are washed, labeled, and cased.

G.

MARKETING

The wine is distributed to the market.

the increased maturity and justify the greater investment. In practice, this usually means using grape varieties with more character than those used for typical Charmat wines.

Paul Masson changed from *méthode champenoise* to the newly developed technology in 1959, concurrently with construction of spectacular champagne cellars at Saratoga in Santa Clara County. Almadén and Weibel shifted to transfer production in the early 1960s. These three have continued to dominate transfer-process production since then.

But the postwar era was not dominated by changes in sparkling-wine equipment alone. Important contributions were coming from other directions as well: the vineyard, the making of the base wines, and marketing. Choice of grapes received greater attention as the University of California urged more careful matching ⌐f soils, climate, and variety. Researchers tried Sauvignon Vert and Green Hungarian, for example, to add more flavor or acidity to the base wine blends. Every new trial was not a success, but willingness to experiment persisted. An important advance came through broader use of refrigeration to control fermentation of the base wines, leading to fresher, cleaner, crisper sparkling wine.

New producers, beginning to appear with regularity, were choosing from among the methods of production those best suited to their grape resources and marketing objectives. In 1945 Christian Brothers began production under the Charmat process, becoming one of the most important makers in the state. Also in the 1940s, Hanns Kornell arrived from Germany and found work at Fountain Grove in Sonoma, where *méthode champenoise* production had been started in 1939. In 1952 he struck out on his own, forming the Hanns Kornell Champagne Cellars and becoming one of the most respected producers of *méthode champenoise* wines over the following decades. Beaulieu Vineyard began intermittent production of *méthode champenoise* wines that same year. And, finally, in 1965, E. & J. Gallo of Modesto began producing Eden Rock champagne by the Charmat method, going on to become one of the largest producers of sparkling wine in the world within twenty years.

Beginning in the 1960s, Almadén and Paul Masson had both recognized the importance of a broader opportunity for the distribution of sparkling wine in the burgeoning supermarkets of America. Almadén had particular success in building popular recognition for its Blanc de Blancs label. But Gallo's entry marked the most dramatic change in sparkling-wine sales. In its first year of marketing, 1966, Gallo shipped approximately 75,000 cases of sparkling wine out of a total California production of some 1,870,000 cases. Just five years later, the state's production had risen to about 7,800,000 cases, of which Gallo shipped more than 3,200,000!

Newcomers Kornell and Beaulieu Vineyard notwithstanding, *méthode champenoise* production had declined slowly throughout the postwar era. Of the pre-Prohibition producers, only Korbel continued to employ the traditional method. But a renaissance was in the making. Martin Ray, who had owned the Paul Masson Winery for a period in the early 1940s, began production at Saratoga of small quantities of well-aged *méthode champenoise* wines made with Pinot Noir and Chardonnay, the traditional grape varieties of the Champagne district of France. Ray's Madame Pinot champagne made from Pinot Noir in 1949 and his Champagne de Chardonnay in 1952 were forerunners of the next wave of change.

In 1965 my wife Jamie and I (we had been shareholders in Martin Ray's Mt. Eden venture) purchased the defunct Schramsberg Vineyards in Napa Valley and reactivated the estate with the sole purpose of producing *méthode champenoise* wines using Pinot Noir, Chardonnay, and Pinot Blanc. The successes at Martin Ray and Schramsberg seemed to validate the use of traditional Champagne district grape varieties in California. A renewal of *méthode champenoise* production followed, propelled by several merging forces: Americans had begun to discover wine, as the skilled efforts of Gallo and others steadily broadened the market. The cocktail hour had begun to offer champagne as well as white table wines. And a national revival of interest in cooking focused more emphasis on food and wine, including sparkling wines.

On this scene emerged a new, foreign player. Moët et Chandon, France's largest Champagne producer, established Domaine Chandon in the Napa Valley, dedicating it to quality *méthode champenoise* production. Respecting its French origins, the company labeled its products "sparkling wines" rather than "champagne." From 5,000 cases put down in 1973, production jumped to more than 400,000 cases in 1981. The company now grows more than 700 acres of varietal grapes in several locations.

With Chandon's coming, a pivotal question arose: would this new, very substantial effort divide the market with established brands, or would it help broaden consumption of premium champagne? Chandon clearly boosted the market. Total shipments of California sparkling wine continued to grow as Chandon's own sales rose from 5,000 to more than 150,000 cases between 1976 and 1981.

An unprecedented number of others have joined the *méthode champenoise* revival. In 1979 the owners of Chateau St. Jean, a prestigious Sonoma table-wine maker, announced that they were establishing a separate facility dedicated to bottle-fermented champagne making. At almost the same time, Piper-Heidsieck became the second French entry, announcing formation of a joint venture with Sonoma Vineyards to produce a Piper-Sonoma *cuvée*.

Other, more recent *méthode champenoise* producers include S. Anderson, Culbertson, Geyser Peak, Iron Horse, Tijsselling, Scharffenberger, Ventana, and Wente. Foreign investment has continued. The French Champagne houses of Roederer and Deutz have purchased land in Mendocino and San Luis Obispo counties, respectively. The leading Spanish sparkling-wine producers, Codorniu and Freixenet, both have announced plans to begin California production. In 1982 the trade journal *Wines & Vines* listed thirty-four producers of sparkling wines in California. Of these, fifteen were believed to use the *méthode champenoise*.

The *méthode champenoise* revival focused great attention on the notion of "style" in the composition of a sparkling wine. The winemaker sees "style" as variations between light versus full-bodied, fresh or mature, fruity or austere, complex or simple wines. He influences these effects through the blends of grape varieties, through timing of the harvest, control of fermentation, use of oak containers, formulas of *dosage*, selection of yeast cultures, and much more. It is the epitome of art in winemaking, and bottle-fermented wines tend to show the greatest range of such individualism.

TABLE 3

SPARKLING WINES

ESTIMATED SHIPMENT FIGURES

TECHNIQUE	VOLUME IN CASES		GROWTH FACTOR*
	1965	1981	
Charmat method	865,000	8,224,000	9.5 times
Transfer method	380,000	1,000,000	2.6 times
Méthode champenoise	55,000	765,000	13.9 times
	*	*	*
Totals	1,300,000	9,989,000	7.7 times

Dramatic growth in sparkling wine shipments was highlighted from the mid-1960s onward by a renaissance in méthode champenoise. *For the first time, European winemakers undertook direct investment in California facilities, and by 1982 California* méthode champenoise *production for the first time exceeded imports of French Champagne to the United States.*

* Quotient of the volume in 1982 divided by the volume in 1965.

New technology continues to contribute to change. By 1970 Korbel had patents on a means of automatic riddling. For at least two decades, French, Spanish, and Australian technicians have been developing other devices for reducing the amount of labor needed for hand-riddling bottles. The French Champagne industry has finally approved such devices, and their application is now widespread there and increasing in California.

Change was apparent in the transfer and Charmat segments of the industry as well. New *cuvées* were introduced by Almadén, Cresta Blanca, Paul Masson, and Weibel. Taylor California Cellars became an important new Charmat producer in 1982. Flavored sparkling wines received new attention, including an almond-flavored *cuvée* produced by Franzia.

Although production of carbonated wines has virtually ceased, there was one interesting effort at their revival during the 1960s. Justin Miller, an English-born, California-trained food technician, had developed and patented a means of infusing carbon dioxide into individual bottles rather than into tanks. Dedicated to achieving change in U.S. labeling regulations, he argued that the distinction between carbonated and sparkling wines was largely semantic and that the labeling regulation was unjustified. He poured enormous energy and capital into legal efforts to effect change, without success. Some vintners employed the "Miller Way" process briefly, but it did not become a permanent part of the technological repertoire.

Another method of achieving a degree of sparkle in wines requires stopping the original fermentation of grape juice before it is completed, and filtering the wines out of the original fermentation tank while they are still saturated with carbon dioxide. This process, common in the production of Italian Asti Spumante, always produces a perceptibly sweet finished product. In California only a very few specialty producers use it, the popular Louis M. Martini Moscato Amabile being a leading example.

The impact of events since 1960 has been profound. Precise figures are not available, but informed analysis indicates the magnitude of change with the estimated shipment figures shown in the accompanying table.*

In 1883, having just visited Arpad Haraszthy's San Francisco cellars, David Nesfield wrote in *The Vine Land of the West*, "Let us hope, however, that the day of small beginnings is at an end, and that another decade, as it undoubtedly will, may see California wines prized all over the world for their purity and rising continually in popular estimation in proportion as their virtues become known."

The small beginnings have clearly ended.

---

* Wine Institute bulletins; Louis Gomberg, *The Gomberg Reports*; author.

BIBLIOGRAPHIC NOTE

The principal earlier survey of sparkling wine development in the United States is found in Paul Fredericksen's "One Hundred Years of American Champagne," *Wine Review* 15 (June 1947): 22, 24; (July 1947): 14, 16. References are also found in Leon D. Adams, *The Wines of America*, especially with regard to early beginnings in Ohio. William P. Heintz's "The Woes of Early Champagne Making," *Wines & Vines* 60 (June 1979): 93–94, is also of interest. Important technical papers, among them "A Review of the Transfer System of Champagne Production," have been presented by Leo A. Berti.

VI.9

DESSERT WINES

by DARRELL F. CORTI

DESSERT WINES ARE NOT MUCH IN FAVOR WITH AMERICAN WINE DRINKERS RIGHT NOW. THIS WAS NOT ALWAYS SO. LESS THAN A GENERATION AGO, dessert wines, or, rather, sweet or dry wines made by fortification, accounted for the largest amount of wine shipped from California. Fortification in this sense means the addition of grape spirits to stop fermentation, leaving the wine more or less sweet or dry. Since the time when crystal decanters filled with port, sherry, or Madeira on the dining-room sideboard were the symbol of hospitality, these wines have come to be abused, maligned, and unpopular. The reasons why are numerous, but let's take a stroll through the world of California dessert wine and see.

The notion of dessert wine in California is a difficult one. Does it refer to wine drunk with dessert or used as dessert? Until recently, naturally sweet, low alcohol wines were not generally produced in California. The use of *Botrytis cinerea*–infected grapes, which produce this wine in Sauternes and in the German wine-growing areas, was not popular. When Californians spoke of dessert wines, they meant fortified wines bearing names like port, sherry, or muscatel. At the repeal of Prohibition, table wines, with under 14 percent alcohol, were in little demand. Fortified wines, sherry, sold well. Leon Adams states that, "Before Prohibition table wines outsold dessert wine by 3 to 1. In 1935 wineries shipped three gallons of dessert wine to one gallon of table wine." * At that time, dessert wines were classified as "fortified" wines, having been strengthened or "fortified" with brandy up to 20–22 percent alcohol. The reason for their market dominance was easy to understand. They were cheap sources of alcohol. In our discussion of "dessert" wines, there is no good and proper descriptive term. "Fortified" is now rejected by the federal government as misleading; "dessert" is the common term, but fails to connote anything about the dry, high alcohol wines used as aperitifs. The concept found in the wineproducing countries of the Mediterranean basin of "generous" wines (*vinos generosos* in Spain; *vinhos generosos* in Portugal) or "liqueur" wines (*vins de liqueur* in France and *vini liquorosi* in Italy) doesn't exist in California. Since there is no good descriptive name, regretfully, this class of wine as a whole tends to suffer.

George Husmann, an early winegrower, writing in 1888, classed these sweet wines, but not the dry ones, as "cordials rather than wine." They were not considered by this author to be wine—that is, "pure, fermented juice of grapes." Here we have an instance of a bias against them as being unnatural. In a strict sense they are not *natural*, found in nature; but the examples often cited by historians of the best ancient Greek and Roman wines were probably of the "natural" high alcohol, sweet type. Pramnian, Caecuban, and Chian were probably wines produced from high sugar, raisined grapes. They were stable due either to high alcohol produced from high sugar grapes or, in cases of lower alcohol, to high residual sugar owing to the yeast's inability to convert all the natural sugar to alcohol. In any event, deterioration, as Husmann concludes, was "probably kept under [control rather] than precluded."† These wines were paragons. Special drinking vessels were created for them. They were rare and expensive and aged well. They were luxuries for that era.

When wine was first brought to California, long before it was made or grown there, it was probably sweet and higher in alcohol than current table wine. Transport from Mexico in cask or skins was difficult. Wine had to withstand great trials. Since precise ideas of fermentation are only 120 or so years old, much, if not all, of that wine would have been unpalatable to modern taste. Wine was the common beverage in those times, and its earliest use confirms just that. However, there were two tables, one of them the altar. Altar wine, used for the celebration of the Eucharist by the Spanish missionaries, would have had to have been a natural high sugar/high alcohol wine that would be possible to keep free from "corruption"— that is, from becoming acetic. High sugar wines or those fortified with either alcohol or concentrated must were probably the types brought by these early settlers. Since canon law prohibits the use of wine that is becoming vinegary, and since grapes were

---

* Adams, *Wines of America*, p. 29.
† Husmann, *Grape Culture and Wine Making in California*, p. 295.

not planted immediately upon the Spaniards' arrival in Alta California, the problem of finding wine for Mass was grave. Wine was to remain for a while, at least, a necessarily imported item. A lack of altar wine was a frequent complaint from Father Junípero Serra. In fact, the first mention of vine cuttings postdates the establishment of a number of missions. The eventual production of brandy in crude stills could make a potable, useful beverage out of wine that was usually undrinkable and allow for the production of stable altar wine.

In the wilds of California, strongly flavored wines, crudely made, yet sweet, were probably most welcome. Brandy definitely was. In fact, taste in those days probably preferred a heavy, sweet, slightly sour wine to a watery, decidedly vinegary one. Sweet, "dessert" type wines were likely the first of California's production; what we now call table wine would have been more difficult to produce. Angelica, the sweet wine that the mission period gave birth to, is probably also California's most original one. The missions produced angelica by merely fortifying fresh grape juice and more or less letting it age. Early writers were more impressed with mission brandy than with mission wine. However, with the dissolution of the mission system, the coming of statehood in 1850, and the commercial production of California wine, the production of imitative types of fortified wines began.

By the 1850s California wine lists offered wine types like port and sherry. In fact, since fortified wines require aging to develop high quality, they generally sold for more money than table wines. William Wolfskill, a Los Angeles producer, sent a gift of wine to President Buchanan between 1856 and 1859. It consisted of one case each of "fine old [*sic*] California port," a case of red wine (unnamed), one of white (also unnamed), and some angelica. Reported in the *Los Angeles Star*, there is a description of the angelica, called a unique California wine, as "a most palatable and agreeable drink, but woe to him who drinks too deeply."

The Sainsevain Brothers, pioneer wine merchants in San Francisco, in an advertisement about 1857, list only the following wine: California white wine, red wine, but (note) California brandy, angelica, and port. Luxury-type fortified wine had recognition and primacy of place if nothing else by being called by a specific name rather than by an anonymous color. The imitative nature of this fortified wine production had several causes, perhaps the foremost of which was the winemaker's desire to have a complete line of wines: table and fortified. This notion remains a difficult one to eradicate in the California wine industry.

In a study of the formative years of that industry, Vincent Carosso comments that in the 1860s and 1870s "White wines, champagne and sweet wines were the most important types commercially. Common red wine . . . still lagged behind the other varieties." [*] At this time also there was a decided division in where

★ Carosso, *California Wine Industry*, p. 87.

certain wines would be produced. Fortified wines require fairly high temperatures to increase the sugar content in the grapes in order to produce a sweet flavored wine. The warm areas of the state, the Central Valley and the Los Angeles area, especially Cucamonga, began to be recognized as areas specialized in the production of these wines. In Fresno, an enterprising grape grower, Francis T. Eisen, started planting in 1875 and by ten years later was specialized in brandy and fortified wine production.

Taxation was to play an important part in the production of fortified wine. A ninety cent tax on the brandy used to fortify wines was deemed "exorbitant" in 1889 due to the oversupply of brandy and the taxing of the spirits before and after production. At this time, much as in a number of other wineproducing countries, spirits other than those made from grapes could be used for fortifying. The passage in 1890 of the "Sweet Wine Bill" guaranteed that grape brandy would not be taxed before being used as a fortifying agent; only the resulting wine would be. One can readily see the benefit: it insured the exclusive use of grape brandy, as opposed to corn or other grain spirits.

By 1886, J. Gundlach & Co., wine merchants in San Francisco, wrote, "The production of sweet wines has been considerably restricted; prevailing prices appear to offer little inducement for this branch of our industry." Table wines had risen to the forefront. Quality fortified wines had begun to lose ground. Husmann remarked, "I do not think that California will ever be willing to wait 10 years before they can thus ripen and sell their wines and go into the tedious process of establishing them." ★

By the turn of the century, imported port, sherry, Madeira and such were available to such an extent that California wine of the same name found a market based on price, if not on quality. On the morning of 16 January 1920, however, when Prohibition was enforceable nationwide, port, sherry, and Madeira decanters disappeared from many sideboards. By the end of Prohibition, there was little aged wine available in California. The only wineries with stock were those that had made altar or medicinal wines. U.S. consumption of wine shipped from California in 1940, according to Leon Adams, "was eight-tenths of a gallon per capita, compared to a mere half gallon in the highest pre-Prohibition year . . . more than ⅔ of the total consumed. Almost all of the increase was of the port-sherry-muscatel group. . . . If this country would ever consume as much table wine as dessert wine, . . . it would represent the millennium."† A populace inured for thirteen years to bad

---

★   Husmann, *Grape Culture and Wine Making in California*, p. 308.
†   Adams, *Wines of America*, p. 33.

distilled spirits looked on dessert wine as a cheap source of alcohol. Adams describes the scene:

The misuse of dessert wine by the "winos" endangered the legal and social status of wine following Repeal. What made it worse was the word "fortified," invented by the British to describe sweet wines preserved by the 200-year-old process of adding brandy to arrest fermentation. Unfortunately, the American wine regulations in 1936 had copied those of England, and included this frightening nine-letter word as the legal designation for dessert wines. As a result, "fortified" wine began to be blamed for the miseries of the depraved alcoholics who drank it because it was cheap. Many people, to avoid associating themselves with "winos," even banned the 20 percent wines from their homes. Soon laws to tax "fortified" wine out of existence or to prohibit its sale entirely were proposed in several state legislatures. The legislators had no objection to port, sherry, tokay, or muscatel, overlooking the fact that they contained brandy, but they imagined that any wine called "fortified" must pack some mysterious power. In 1938, the vintners decided to get rid of the word, and they persuaded the Government to ban it from all labels and advertisements. But the thought of dessert wine as "fortified" stuck in the public mind. In 1951, Treasury officials recommended to the House Ways and Means Committee that the Federal tax rates on wines be tripled on the ground that such wine was competing unfairly with high-taxed whiskey. A bill containing the new rates was promptly voted by the Committee. It was a body blow to the wine industry. At stake were the keys to its very existence: the historic tax advantage of wine over liquor and beer, the classification of wine as an article of food, and the treatment of winegrowing as an agricultural pursuit separate from the distilling and brewing industries. Alarm spread through the vineyard areas, and growers from all of the grape states besieged Washington with protests. Amendments to the tax bill in the Senate Finance Committee provided for smaller increases, resulting in the present rates of 17 cents per gallon on table wines and 67 cents on dessert wines. But to get the last mention of "fortified" erased from Federal regulations required an act of Congress, the wine law of 1954. ★

The marketing of fortified dessert wines has been chancy for a number of years. Sales figures for 1982 show a decrease of some 6.2 percent. To be a producer of fortified dessert wine at this point would be a bit unnerving. Fortified wine types now produced in California as semi-generics are port, sherry, madeira, malaga, and tokay. Of these, the most important is sherry. Less than twenty years ago, Maynard Amerine remarked in his *Technology of Winemaking,* "Sherry is the most important California wine type. Production in 1955 was about 30 million gallons." † This is

---

★   Ibid., p. 34.
†   M. A. Amerine et al., *The Technology of Winemaking*, 2d ed., p. 391.

astounding given today's market for dessert wines. But what kind of sherry was this? What form and quality does California sherry have?

First, most California sherry is produced in a manner completely different from that of its Spanish prototype. At its earliest, sherry in California was a more or less fortified white wine that was allowed to age in cask and acquire a more or less oxidized flavor and color. It was named after the wine it most closely resembled. Husmann observed that white wine was fortified with alcohol to 18–23 percent, the blend then stored in cask in a heated room at 140°–150° F for three to four months, acquiring an aged taste and flavor. This room was called an oven. In *Winemaking in California*, Ruth Teiser and Catherine Harroun note that in 1878 George Crane, a Napa Valley physician, bankrolled a Portuguese immigrant, John Ramos, who built a 26,000-gallon heater, bought wine from Crane and, using the Madeiran method, produced what the authors call California's first "baked" sherry.

In 1888, the use of a particular yeast to produce the characteristic Spanish sherry flavor was not recommended by Husmann: "Many varieties acquire sherry flavor just by aging. Mr. Dresel's Mission, 20 years old had marked sherry flavor [which I] . . . would prefer to artificial sherry." ★ This comment is quite interesting, since the production of sherry in Spain is accomplished through the use of a yeast population growing on the surface of wine, which produces the particular aroma and flavor of what is called "*flor*" sherry. To my mind, this is sherry properly spoken of. The California method of fortifying and aging, either with heat or without, is more appropriate to madeira than to sherry. This does not mean that no Spanish wine is produced this way. Of the two types of sherry produced in Spain, Finos have *flor* and Olorosos do not. California baked sherry, with sufficient age, does take on the perfumey grapey aroma of some styles of Oloroso. In fact, I have shown this type to Spanish experts who have commented very favorably on the wine's quality. I have seen examples of California *flor* sherry that it would be difficult to say were not Spanish. A private solera produced and maintained in his home cellar by Professor A. Dinsmore Webb of Davis produces wine difficult not to classify as a Spanish original. In the 1930s Professor William Cruess from Berkeley brought sherry *flor* yeast to California. Originally called *Saccharomyces beticus* from the Roman name for southern Spain, *Baetica*, this yeast has now been reclassified as *Saccharomyces fermentati*. The classical method of producing *flor* sherry is to keep casks of 14 to 15.5 percent fortified white Palomino wine three-quarters full, allowing the aerobic *flor* to grow on its surface. Once the yeast has completed its cycle, it falls to the bottom of the cask and another generation of yeast begins to grow. The resulting mass produces what is called the "mother," and the slow decomposition of the dead yeast cells contributes to the wine's flavor. The production of acetaldehyde is char-

★   Husmann, *Grape Culture and Wine Making in California*, p. 324.

acteristic of this type of sherry, with its yeasty aroma rather like freshly baked bread crust. If the wine is not systematically refreshed, the *flor* stops growing due to the concentration of alcohol through evaporation. This type of wine is generally called Fino, Flor Fino, or Pale Cocktail Sherry.

In 1951, the "submerged" *flor* process, a technique developed in Australia and Canada, was brought to California. It uses a closed container in which *flor* yeast and oxygen are introduced in the base wine, called sherry material or "shermat." The yeast rapidly produces the required amount of aldehyde aroma—the characteristic perfume—but not the concomitant depth of flavor. Submerged *flor* wines are usually aged in small casks to develop flavor or blended with baked wines to give those the aroma of *flor*.

Depending on the length of time a wine is baked, a process usually accomplished in large cement tanks lined on the inside with heating coils, or in pressurized stainless steel tanks, the wine can have a more or less oxidized flavor. When sufficiently matured in wood, this oxidized flavor becomes round and harmonious. It is this wine that probably epitomizes California sherry. As in Spain, these basic wines are generally dry, without residual sugar. To produce a medium, sweet, or cream sherry, specially prepared blending wines are used. In California they run from heavily baked concentrated must to very old in-cask wines with a lot of aged character. A simple grape concentrate, freshly made, gives a sweet, almost syrupy, flavor, but because it usually also results in a cloudy wine, it is seldom used anymore. While it is possible to age a sweet sherry in cask, it is sometimes more advantageous to place the cask in the sun, as they do at the Sebastiani winery in Sonoma. Generally, the finest sweet types are produced by the judicious blending of a number of different elements and styles of wine. Sherries therefore depend very much on man's intervention. The finest result from using the best quality base material and blending with great care.

Certain wines bear the label Solera Sherry. A solera is nothing more than a moderately complicated system of fractional blending designed to keep a mass of wine at a constant age and quality. Done properly, the blend can be maintained with minimal variation. If forced, or "milked," the result is merely a product with the name but little aged quality. The process, which dates from Napoleonic times in Spain, involves the interblending of younger to older wine in consecutive steps, the youngest introduced into the next older, and so on (never the youngest to the oldest).

Currently, the production of surface *flor* in California is minimal. At one time a Ripon-based winery produced a great deal for Paul Masson. I have seen it recently only in the dessert wine aging cellars of Brookside Winery in Cucamonga, where it is started every year and a solera is not maintained. Thirty years ago, there were surface *flor* sherries produced in a number of wineries. One of the most interesting was at Beaulieu Vineyard. When bottled, it had had seventeen generations of yeast on it. A bottle drunk recently showed great character on the nose and the typical shortness or flatness on the palate from having been bottle aged. This style of wine would prefer the expansiveness of a cask to the confines of a bottle.

The production of submerged *flor* is now centered in Delano in the Central Valley at Sierra Wine Company. They supply most, if not all, of the submerged *flor* wines required for blending. A particularly interesting bottling there bears the name of the production vice-president, Phillip Posson. Perhaps the most notable sherry solera in California is that of Louis Martini Winery where the base wine, composed of both *flor* and baked elements, goes back to about 1929.

A notable baked sherry is that of East-Side Winery of Lodi. Their cocktail sherry is famous in the dry sherry class. Christian Brothers, to celebrate the centennial of the winery's foundation, has produced a very lovely medium wine, Private Reserve Sherry. It seems that wine like this can only be produced once in a hundred years! Some of the bulk young baked wines with *flor* added for fragrancy are interesting aperitifs. The sweeter styles generally suffer from hasty production methods or careless blending.

With the production in California of large quantities of brandy, the fortification of red wine was possible, and the production of port began. Fortification to produce high alcohol was one of the ways to achieve stability. A method called syrup fermentation was also used, and we have knowledge that more than one producer made wines using it: Henry Crabb, an early Napa Valley vineyardist, added grape syrup—boiled-down must—to his fermenting wine to produce port. In 1872 George West of Stockton entered three of his ports in an exhibition, the 1871 vintage made with boiled-down juice.

Using the syrup method, one could, at that time, avoid the brandy tax and produce a high alcohol sweet wine less expensively. When the syrup or grape concentrate was added slowly to the fermentation, the yeast simply used up the sugar, creating more alcohol, until the level rose to a point where fermentation stopped. There are some curious facts about port unique to California. Until recently, to make port a government official had to be present, and was responsible for checking on all of the fortifying spirits used in arresting fermentation. But fermentations are strange happenings, and sometimes fortification was best done at 2:00 A.M., when the official was not present. When that happened, and the wine was too dry by the time the official arrived in the morning, the winemaker would have to make another wine to blend with it, stopping the fermentation sooner to compensate for the lack of sugar in the first one. A winery no longer has to work under these constraints. It may be one reason that there has been an increase in small specialists making California port.

Like sherry, port figures in the lists of early producers. Unlike that from Portugal, these wines, and most still produced in California, are anonymous fortified red wine, more or less sweet, more or less colored. In the past, with high quality wines, there was more emphasis placed on cask-aging than on the production of "vintage" types. "Vintage" wine is very dark colored, very fruity, full-bodied, bottled young—usually before its third year—and aged in bottle. This is not the only type of port, but happens to be the most prestigious. Cask-aged wines, "wood port," requiring a lengthy tie-up of capital and of stocks, are less in favor currently. In California, I feel, they may be the better wines. The oldest California port that I have tasted was undated and put up in a whiskey bottle. It had a crude label saying "California Port" and bearing the state's Great Seal. It was obviously of the syruped type of fermentation and while a pleasant, interesting drink of great richness and aroma, not anything like port. It resembled an Italian Passito wine made from semi-dried grapes or Vin Santo with a distinct raisiny tone.

In California there are currently two kinds of port production: those that use traditional varieties and those that don't. Since according to Ernest Cockburn, late head of the great English port firm of Cockburn, Smithes, "the first duty of port is to be red," in California a number of varieties are used to produce a dark colored wine, at times with little thought as to what it tastes like. In California, with some producers, it is almost as if "the wines are dark, strong, and sweet, let's call the product port." Cask-aging here produces a distinctly finer product. In fact, at times well-aged California tawny port more closely resembles its Portuguese prototype than any other wine of the class. In this regard there is a lovely Tinta Madeira wine, a varietal tawny, produced by East-Side Winery in Lodi that exemplifies all the best characteristics of this style. The other type produced in California, partially cask-aged, partially bottle-aged, is an interesting beverage showing softness and fruit, sometimes at the expense of character. California producers generally do not turn out distinct types, although they market the wines as such. The majority of tawny wines for sale in California are not tawny reddish yellow in color, but full red. Most ruby ports are not ruby in color, but either too dark or too light. In fact, this name is not much used today, the term "port" being a catchall. Some vintage wines show vintage character, dark color, fruit, and tannin, but most bear a date because the wine was made during that vintage. They are, in effect, "late bottled vintage" wine. In fact, it seems that sometimes there is more thought given to another label on the merchant's shelf than to a product that exemplifies the name on the label.

Since 1948, in the Central Valley at Madera, the Ficklin family have been specialist producers of California port. Their wine—sold as Tinta Port and made from grapes bearing the names of classic Portuguese varieties such as Tinta Madeira, Tinta Cão, and Alvarelhão—has been recognized as the classic California wine. At one time, they produced an amount of dated wine, bottled generally after three years in wood, then further bottled-aged. At times it was also produced as a wine from a single grape variety. Now they make Tinta Port on a modified solera scale, bottling after some five or six years in wood, and blended with most, if not all, of the preceding years kept in the master blend.

Americans have increased their consumption of Portuguese Vintage Port, and four small California producers started specifically to make this style. The oldest, J. W. Morris, currently being reorganized, is followed in succession by Andrew Quady, James Prager, and Russell Woodbury. All generally use varieties from climates cooler than the Central Valley, varieties generally used for table wine: Zinfandel from Amador County or Sonoma, Petite Sirah, Pinot Noir, and Cabernet Sauvignon. Some of these vintage wines may make the grade; others may not. The makers have, I think, been spurred on by the possibilities shown in the apparent quality of the young wines. But vintage port is not for the fainthearted or the easily discouraged. It takes a great deal of time to come around and man is so impatient!

The worst thing to come out of port production has been that at times it has become a dumping ground for winemaking mistakes. A stuck fermentation in a red wine, one that wouldn't ferment to dryness, has sometimes been "salvaged" by dumping in fortifying spirit and calling the result "port"—or, worse yet, a varietal "vintage port." Brandy will fix a number of ills and since the base product would have been portlike, given its natural course, who cares about the result of fortification? Although it is true that some wines can be salvaged this way, there is no reason why the wine type ought not to be made correctly in the first place.

If port is already a maligned wine type, the most maligned is white port. Generally produced in unspeakable fashion from whatever white grapes or decolorized must is around, it is mostly used as a blending wine for cheap jug table wines or sold as a source of alcohol for "winos." A few of the California wine types, like tokay, could not exist without it in the blend. At its best, white port can be a lovely, soft, aromatic wine; at its worst, a pale, water-white, nasty concoction reeking of alcohol.

Amerine has stated that sherry was the most important wine type at one time. Perhaps the most denigrated was, and is, muscatel, or (as it was—perhaps still is—called) "old muskrat" or "muscadoodle." The stigma attached to muscatel is incredible, and unbelievable damage seems to have been done to it. Its type is probably the easiest to identify and the least sought after at present. Examples such as the well-matured Portuguese Sétubal, the fragrant French Muscats Beaumes-de-Venise and Frontignan, and the ruby-colored Australian Brown Muscat have a special status in the international wine pantheon. California could produce a good quantity of very fine Muscat-based fortified wine, but it doesn't. In fact, the ones that exist number only about half a dozen: Novitiate of Los Gatos's Black Muscat, from the black-skinned Muscat Hamburg variety, and their Muscat Frontignan; Beaulieu Vineyard's Muscat de Frontignan from the Napa Valley; Weibel's Black Muscat; Quady's Essencia from Orange Muscat. Concannon in the Livermore Valley has stopped producing its Muscat Frontignan, but Beringer bottles a related variety, Malvasia Bianca. The sale for these wines seems at best stagnant. If produced in small enough quantity, like Quady's Essencia, the wine sells, but probably due more to a perverse customer attitude toward small production wines than to a fondness for Muscat. Low alcohol table wine styles, such as Moscato or Muscat Amabile, seem to do much better. Perhaps the basic trouble started with the terrible defamation of the wine when, at Repeal, California shipped millions of gallons of poor quality, alcoholic muscatel. It may take another generation or two to see again the virtue of this lovely wine.

With the exception of those mentioned and perhaps a very few others, Muscat-based wines are poor products in California. In the ten years that this writer has sat on the dessert wine panel of the Los Angeles County Fair, it has been the exception to find a lovely Muscat wine; in fact, one is stunned by the lack of Muscat character found in what is sold as this type. It is as if the particular aroma, the musky scent, had to be exorcised. This was not always so.

Tasting recently some half-bottles from the early 1940s, sold in screwcapped bottles for the cheap alcohol market, I was struck by the intensity of Muscat flavor and aroma and the aged finesse the wine showed. It was style as is not seen even in the very important bottlings of today. Granted that a great amount of Muscat of Alexandria, the most important grape of the Muscat family in California, one with an almost cinnamonlike perfume, goes into light table wine today, still a renaissance of this wine is in order.

At one time, Concannon made an amount of Muscat Frontignan (also called Muscat Canelli or Muscat Blanc à petits grains) using a brandy distilled from the same wine for fortification. The intensity of perfume was splendidly overpowering. The wine was costly to make and has been discontinued. Production of the best wines requires mainly that the highly scented Muscat varieties be fully ripe when harvested. In fact, a slight raisiny effect sometimes enhances the Muscat tone. Careful fermentation to the point of fortification with good clean spirit, then careful aging, seem all that this rather generous wine requires. Since it is made so seldom, perhaps it is that carefulness that is the stumbling block!

Three California dessert wines are like actors in search of a play. They really don't fit in. California madeira, marsala, and, by extension, malaga and tokay have little to say to their European counterparts. While still classed as a semi-generic, malaga really doesn't exist. A small amount was once produced, but there has not been any on the market for at least thirty years. According to the late George West, who made wine in the last century, California malaga was the result of luck! He took common red wine that had been fermented on its skins ten days, did not add spirit, and found that a malaga-like change took place with five years aging. It seems unlikely that this would have produced the thick, heavy wine found on the Mediterranean coast of Spain.

Marsala, like madeira and tokay, is a blended wine. The true marsala varieties, Catarratto and Grillo, are grown in the Central Valley, but rarely if ever find their way into the California wine. Marsala is a baked wine base flavored and sweetened with caramelized must or concentrate to reach the desired sweetness and character. As it is made in California, it is solely a recipe ingredient, or finds use as the basis for flavored styles having coffee, almond, or egg yolks as the dominant flavor. This type is easy to imitate and its lower price over the cost of the real thing would seem to be its sole virtue. But I have tasted some very old samples from Franzia in Ripon and Gibson in Elk Grove that were aromatic, soft, interesting wines, rather like old blending sherry.

California madeira owes its existence to the semi-generic name. We do not grow much of the madeira varietals in California and, as noted, our production of baked sherry is in fact more like that of madeira. The use of heated rooms—now large sealed vats—to bake the unfortified wine is the same process for making Madeira as on the island of the same name. The difference in California is that we do not use the classical varieties, our base wines do not have the same composition, and we have lower acidities, both volatile and tartaric. True Madeira has a tang the California version lacks. What is curious is that California opted from the beginning for the name *sherry* for this oxidized type and never used *madeira* to any extent. Was it because the island's production had been virtually obliterated by oïdium (1852) and phylloxera (1870) and the wine had nearly disappeared from the market by the turn of the century? Or was it because of the greater availability of sherry? San Francisco wine merchant price lists of the time quote their highest prices for old, true Madeira.

The legendary Hungarian wine Tokaji from the northeastern part of that country bears no relation to what California calls tokay. The California table grape variety Flame Tokay, or Tokay, has nothing in common with Tokaji, except perhaps a vague color resemblance. In any case, California wineries rarely make tokay from Tokay grapes and never from the main Hungarian variety, Furmint. Again, the imitative name seems to derive from the great esteem in which this legendary wine was held. As a name, *tokay* has been in California for a long time. Wineries produced and merchants listed it in the 1860s. Perhaps Tokaji was different then and the California version closer to the fact than now. Tokaji comes from botrytised grapes. When the marketing question arises, the temptation to cash in on a famous name at a lower price is understandable. California tokay is produced by blending angelica, white port, and sherry or red port for sweetness, body, and color. Again, well-aged, it is an interesting liqueur-type wine, but rarely met with. Perhaps it could be called an original California type, but unfortunately its quality production is negligible to nonexistent.

The most original California wine is angelica. This wine, or rather this grape product called wine, dates from the earliest mission period. It was nothing more than unfermented grape juice run off into casks containing spirit. The spirit brought in alcohol to prevent spoilage and the grape sugar gave sweetness and flavor. The product stabilized and, being naturally sweet, needed only aging to become palatable. This traditional method is an old one that produces such varying products as the Ratafia of Champagne and the Pineau of Cognac. Italy, Spain, Greece, and Cyprus make similar wines. The earliest California production was from the then ubiquitous Mission grape, a variety sometimes still used to make this wine. No longer can angelica be made for unblended drinking in the traditional way, since the government stipulates that only fermenting grape juice can be fortified. Fermentation would have to produce a small amount of alcohol, technically 0.5 to 1 percent, and then the wine could be fortified. One of the oldest directions for making this wine, again from Husmann, states:

Angelica or Sweet Muscatell [sic]. *This is generally made from Muscat of Alexandria, by letting the grapes get very ripe, then crushing and pressing them, and as soon as this is done, add about a quart of grape brandy of the usual strength to each gallon of must, also stirring in about a gallon of fresh lime to each 100 gallons of must. This suppresses fermentation, and clarifies the wine within two days. As soon as it is clear, it is drawn off into casks, which are filled; and only need ageing* [sic] *to make it more palatible* [sic].*

Another set of directions by Théophile Vaché of Cucamonga suggests that an amount of must from Burger (a white variety) should be blended with Mission juice to correct the latter's deficient acidity. Fortification then takes place. Aging is obligatory.

Curiously, some winemakers still make Mission-based angelicas. East-Side Winery produces Mission Antigua, a dark-colored, rich wine, aged in casks in a very warm atmosphere. It has more in common with dark blending sherry than with angelica. Brookside has stocks of a similar wine. J. W. Morris, under reorganization as this book goes to press, has been producing angelica from Sierra Foothill Mission grapes. The wine is called Sierra Sabrosa. Heitz Cellars produced a "Cellar Treasure" angelica from Black Monukka, a dark-skinned table variety. Harbor Winery produces the most unusual angelica, not in a fortified style but in one using

* Ibid., p. 306.

a syrup fermentation. Harbor adds fresh grape concentrate slowly during the fermentation of the free-run juice of late harvested Mission grapes from very old Amador County vines. When the high alcohol produced slows down the fermentation, more concentrate is added to raise the sugar level to the desired point and to arrest fermentation. The acidity of the must is adjusted prior to fermentation and once the wine is racked, it is left to mature in cask. This is the only wine made commercially in this old fashion in California. Its name is Mission del Sol. Several other producers have started copying this production with varying success. As is known from the production of angelica, aging is what gives this wine quality and character. Although it definitely has to have something other than age going for it, it is the wine type that best responds to aging. The redoubtable Schoonmaker and Marvel write that, "It is said that Angelica takes its name from Los Angeles. Better products have taken their names from smaller towns." ★ *Sic transit gloria mundi!*

Domaine Chandon, the Napa Valley sparkling wine producer, makes an important angelica-type wine called Panache. Produced from the red-colored juice of pressed Pinot Noir, it is fortified, then aged for a brief period in cask. While sweet, it has the high acidity of the early picked sparkling wine stock it is made from and is sold not as a dessert wine but as an aperitif. As a matter of fact, here is a dessert wine used as an aperitif that brings us right back to where we started: with an amorphous class of aperitif/dessert/sweet/dry fortified wines.

Some of the finest examples of old California wine that I have tasted have been very old angelicas. Silky, harmonious, and elegant, they have been paragons of liqueur wines. Novitiate has produced an admirable bottling, vintage 1973, released late in 1982. A few bottles laid down for further aging (but they are hard to come by) would repay the effort.

Throughout wine history, sweet, fortified, or high alcohol wines have been considered special. They have not been everyday wines, but luxury wines, wines for special occasions, wines for ceremonies. For the time being, they are in eclipse. It is to be hoped not for long. As Fernand Braudel observes, "Every luxury dates and goes out of fashion. But luxury is reborn from its own ashes and from its very defeats." †

★   Schoonmaker and Marvel, *American Wines*, p. 211.
†   Braudel, *Civilization and Capitalism, 15th–18th Century*, vol. 1, *The Structures of Everyday Life: The Limits of the Possible* (New York: Harper & Row, 1981), p. 186.

VI.10

FRUIT, BERRY, & OTHER WINES

by DORIS MUSCATINE

ALTHOUGH TO MOST PEOPLE WINE MEANS A BEVERAGE MADE FROM GRAPES, THERE ARE MANY POSSIBLE ALTERNATIVES. STRAWBERRIES, RASPBERRIES, elderberries, blackberries, ollalieberries, boysenberries, gooseberries, pomegranates, apples, apricots, peaches, plums, cherries, pears, pineapples, kiwis, currants, dried fruits, rhubarb, oranges, grapefruit, dandelions, roots, flowers, and honey have all, after proper processing, ended up in a wine bottle.

By federal law, "wine" by itself means grape wine. Any other type, such as blackberry wine or plum wine, must specify the fruit from which it is made on its label. Further, non-grape wines must come entirely from one designated fruit. Using another fruit, such as pineapple, to flavor a grape-wine base is illegal. Fortifying specified fruits with a high proof brandy is within the regulations.

Some wines have the word "pure" or "natural" on their labels, but the legal definitions of these terms are complicated and often more confusing than helpful to the consumer. For this reason, the Bureau of Alcohol, Tobacco, and Firearms is currently considering whether to continue their use.

Bottlings with a proprietary name like Thunderbird and Ripple, however, are called special natural formula wines. Their recipes, which may include added natural (but not synthesized) flavorings, must be registered with the bureau, but their label does not have to reveal the contents to the buyer. Thunderbird, a grape-base wine, tastes like citrus. Ripple, made from pears, tastes more like strawberries. Spañada, a low-alcohol type of sangria, and Tyrolia, a sweet white made in Rhine style, are currently the best sellers in the category sometimes referred to as "pop" wines. This group represents between 6 and 7 percent of the total U.S. market, a decline from their share of 10 percent a few years ago.

Most of the American non-grape home winemakers and some commercial producers are in areas where wine grapes do not prosper. Non-grape wines appeal widely to buyers and makers whose heritage may have introduced them to the fruit and berry wines of Scandinavia, the British Isles, and other parts of Europe. They are particularly popular in the Pacific Northwest; in California three major wineries make them.

The process for making wine from fruit, berries, and other natural bases differs somewhat from that used for grapes. Because their natural sugars are generally much lower than those of grapes, and their acidities much greater, it is permissible to add sugar and water to obtain a proper balance. The sugar increases the alcohol content, the water dilutes the acidity. This process is known as amelioration.

Crushing or releasing the juice also requires different procedures from normal winemaking. Fruits with pits need only a very light maceration and the juice a much shorter time in contact with the solids. The juice from fleshy fruits such as apples is pressed out and separated immediately from the pulp. Berries and dandelions release their juice in heated water, rhubarb pulp in cold. A mixture of honey and hot water is the base for the pre-biblical drink mead. Kiwi wine tends to age too fast if the juice and pulp stay too long in contact, so it is best to strain the clear juice from the crush as soon as possible, according to Tom Kelly of Gibson winery, which introduced the variety in 1978.

The addition of wine yeasts and yeast nutrients helps the fermentation; sulfur dioxide aids in preventing the brown discoloration that attacks fruit juices. Most of these wines taste better if not fermented completely dry and, being less stable than grape wines, often require the addition of pectic enzymes, pasteurization, and clarification. They are best drunk within a few months of bottling, while they still retain a fresh and fruity character. After a year or so, they tend to lose their verve and clarity of color.

For the winemaker, grape and several other fruit juices now come in bottles and cans and as concentrates, which gives them, as it does honey, the advantage of year-round availability. For commercial wineries, fruits come frozen in 55-gallon containers. Thawing, not usually a benefit for food products, breaks down the pulp of fruit and releases the juices, eliminating the need for crushing.

The major California producers of fruit and berry wines are Bargetto in Soquel, Gibson in Elk Grove, and San Antonio in Los Angeles. E. & J. Gallo produces substantial amounts of half a dozen fruit wines under the Boone's Farm label.

In addition to its production of varietal grape table wines, the family-run Bargetto Winery releases about 6,000 cases annually of strawberry, pomegranate, plum, apricot, ollalieberry, boysenberry, and raspberry wine. The biggest sellers are apricot and ollalieberry. Most of the fruit comes from local sources—Santa Cruz, Watsonville, and Hollister—but the pomegranates are from the San Joaquin Valley. Sometimes Bargetto also imports strawberries and boysenberries from the Northwest. The winery ferments almost dry, then adds sugar up to the equivalent of the natural fruit. Bargetto wines are distributed throughout California and in seven western states.

More widely known for its generic table wines, port, sherry, muscatel, and vermouth, Gibson is also a major producer of sweet fruit and berry wines and mead. Gibson's 75,000 cases a year of pure fruit and berry wines include bottlings of raspberries, blackberries, loganberries, strawberries, currants, cherries, kiwis, honey, and Concord grapes. The winery also makes Farley's Hard Cider, an unfortified apple wine.

KOSHER WINES

The Manischewitz and Mogen-David style of sweet wines from Concord grapes is that associated most frequently with kosher winemaking. However, "kosher" essentially denotes a sacramental condition. In ancient times, Jewish religious observances often involved the pouring of libations on the temple altar. Idolatrous ceremonies such as the Dionysian rites used wines in similar fashion. Most probably to insure that the wines used sacramentally were employed only for that purpose, the Jews developed a body of protective laws against spiritual contamination. The strict observance of these rules and their official certification, rather than a style of winemaking, produce a wine that is kosher according to Jewish law.

All of the operations, from grape harvesting through final bottling, must be rabbinically supervised to insure that there is no contamination from ritually prohibited substances. All of the equipment used must also be "kashered," that is, either brand new or ritually sterilized and retained solely for the purpose of making kosher wine. And the people involved in making the wine must themselves be observant of the Jewish tradition.

In 1979, Hagafen Cellars of Napa, under the supervision of the Orthodox Rabbinical Council of San Francisco, began production of premium dry table wines certified as kosher. The grapes for the first release of 300 cases, a 1980 Johannisberg Riesling with 2 percent residual sugar, came from Rene di Rosa's Winery Lake Vineyard in Napa's cool Carneros Creek district. The White House served it at a state dinner honoring Prime Minister Menachem Begin of Israel. The winery has since added to its list a Chardonnay from Winery Lake and a Cabernet Sauvignon, blended with a small amount of Merlot, from Yountville. Hagafen wines are available in California and from major outlets in Massachusetts, New York, New Jersey, Illinois, Minnesota, Rhode Island, and Washington, D.C.

VI.11

Note: Altar Wines

by THOMAS D. TERRY, S.J.

WINE AS A SOURCE OF STRENGTH AND JOY AND INTOXICATION HAS BEEN USED IN RELIGIOUS CEREMONIES FOR THOUSANDS OF YEARS. The cult of Dionysus, or Bacchus, the god of wine, was very popular among the Greeks and Romans. In early Judaism wine was poured out as a libation at the sacrifice of animals, and in later Judaism wine was, and still is, drunk according to a prescribed ceremony at the Passover meal. Paul Gordon notes that "the fact that the familiar name for banquet among the Hebrew was mishteh (drinking) indicates the significance which attached to wine. Its use was pre-supposed as a necessary part of every meal. It was used and served in moderation, and wine and grain represented the major produce of the land."

Catholics believe that Christ at his last Passover meal changed bread and wine into his body and blood. We also believe that Christ gave this same power to his apostles and their successors and that this power is exercised during the central act of Catholic worship, the Mass. As Rabbi Leo Trepp puts it, "Catholic as well as Jewish tradition makes it impossible to establish a community of religious people where wine cannot be obtained. Wine is part of worship, symbol and expression of the human and the divine."

Among the Christian churches, wine is essential for the religious services of the Episcopal (in England, Anglican) Church, the Lutheran Church, the Greek and Russian Orthodox churches, and the Roman Catholic Church. In California the Lutheran Church prefers white or amber altar wine to red altar wine to avoid any representational connotation. The Episcopal Church seems to prefer red altar wine. Both red and white altar wines are used in the Roman Catholic Church. Altar guilds have sometimes requested a switch from red wine to white because the red stains are harder to remove from altar cloths.

In the early centuries of Christianity, winemaking was simple, unsophisticated, and ordinary. Wine was almost as common as bread. Wine was unam-

This essay is based in part on "The Making of Mass Wine," an address by the author to the Ninetieth Quarterly Dinner Meeting of the Society of Medical Friends of Wine on 27 May 1970.

biguously wine, and the Church simply prescribed that bread and wine be used in the Mass. In the fifteenth century, however, the Council of Florence specified that the bread for Mass be wheat bread and the wine for Mass be grape wine. Evidently wine was also being made then from fruit other than grapes.

Wine grapes, the *Vitis vinifera* Mission variety, were first brought to California by the Spanish Franciscan priests and brothers. For their daily religious service, they needed both bread and wine. As soon as possible each Franciscan mission in California had its wheat field and vineyard. The grapes were used to produce wine for Mass and for the padres' table. If the wine was plentiful, some of it might be fortified by the addition of brandy to make sweet wine, some of it distilled to produce brandy. Such fortified wines would resist spoilage better than dry wines, especially at the warmer missions, or when wine was used at any of them in small quantities over a long period of time.

In the early days of the state, California wineries producing altar wine for the Roman Catholic clergy would give the nearest Roman Catholic bishop a description of their winemaking procedures. If they met the requirements of Roman Catholic altar wine regulations, the bishop would certify their acceptability for Roman Catholic Masses. Several early California wineries, such as the vineyard and winery at the Santa Clara mission, began as producers of altar wine. When the Jesuits took over the mission in 1851 and began Santa Clara College, they continued the mission vineyard and winery to produce altar wine. Later, when the college needed the vineyard and winery space, the Jesuits planted a vineyard and built a winery west of Cupertino to produce altar wine. Other early producers of altar wine in northern California were Christian Brothers at Martinez and Concannon at Livermore. In 1888, the Jesuits moved their novices from Santa Clara College to Los Gatos and began producing altar wine at the Novitiate winery there. In southern California, Brookside winery near Ontario was another early producer, marketing its wines under the Guasti Altar Wine label. Beaulieu Vineyards, Beringer Brothers, Cribari, and Louis M. Martini all produced altar wine before and during Prohibition. The government did not interfere with its production and its sales helped a number of California wineries survive. After Repeal these wineries continued to produce some altar wine, but significantly increased their production of commercial wine.

In California, even in a bad year, vinifera grapes require little modification. California wine law is stricter than Roman Catholic Church law with regard to the nature and amount of additives permitted. In fact, it is so strict that any dry California wine is perfectly acceptable as Mass wine on any occasion. When this became widely recognized in the middle of the 1960s, there was a decrease in the sale of altar wine. Some California wineries discontinued their production altogether and concentrated on increasing the sale of their commercial wines. For others, altar wine is still a significant segment of their total business. For the industry, altar wine kept the vineyards alive and the winemakers working throughout the drought of Prohibition.

Canon law requires that altar wine be made from grapes, and not from other fruit, that it not be notably modified by additives, that it not be produced synthetically or from unripe grapes or concentrated grape juice thick enough to qualify as food. It cannot be turned to vinegar, although wine on the verge is permissible, though offensive. It cannot be made by fermenting only the grapes and stems with water once the juice has been removed. It can neither contain more than 20 percent alcohol nor be without any at all. The Roman Catholic Church requires that any alcohol used in fortifying altar wine also come from grapes.

In winemaking there is no substitute for ripe, well-balanced grapes. The main reason for adding notable extraneous material to must or wine is some deficiency in the grape. For example, grapes in cold climates have low sugars and high acids. Wine made from them is unpalatable and sometimes unstable owing to low alcohol concentration. In Church regulations the preferred method for raising the sugar concentration of the must is to add raisins, but on some frontiers raisins may be unavailable. This is probably the reason that in the last century some Canadian bishops received permission to add five kilograms of sugar to every 100 liters of grape juice.

In the eastern part of the United States, wine made from the typical hybrid grapes also tends to be high in acid and low in sugar. Commercial wine is made from these grapes after water is added to reduce the acid concentration. If significant amounts of water and sugar are added to the grape juice, the resulting wine may not be used for Mass wine in ordinary circumstances.

A friend of mine, a priest in Katmandu, Nepal, had the problem of trying to make wine from grapes that would not ripen properly at 5,000 feet above sea level. Even the best hybrids from the Davis campus produced less than 14 percent sugar in Katmandu. With enormous effort, however, my friend managed to produce quite palatable dry and sweet Mass wines from grapes and raisins. In fact, he wrote an excellent booklet for missionaries in prohibitionist countries describing methods for making Mass wine from raisins. Within the past two years, my friend has obtained permission to add as much as twelve kilograms of sugar to every 100 liters of grape juice, the most lenient permission I am aware of in the matter of adding extraneous material to grape juice in making Mass wine. It amounts to approximately 11 percent of the final mixture. (More lenient regulations are in effect in prohibitionist countries where there is missionary activity and in countries where Roman Catholics are severely persecuted.)

In warm climates, grapes tend to be high in sugar and low in acid. Wine made from them often has residual sugar, which with the low acid makes a wine that easily sours or spoils. These wines can be stabilized by adding enough alcohol to raise the total alcohol concentration to 18 or 19 percent. Yeast and acetobacter (a vinegar-making bacterium) do not thrive in that concentration of alcohol. In making such wines for Mass wine, the Catholic Church requires that the alcohol added be grape alcohol and that it be added during the original fermentation. To minimize the amount of water added, it is customary to use 190-proof grape alcohol. The same procedure is used in making sweet Mass wines. The addition of the 190-proof grape alcohol during fermentation kills the yeasts before they can ferment all the sugar into alcohol. The normal maximum alcohol concentration in Mass wine is 18 percent. In emergency situations, wines with up to 23 percent alcohol are tolerable. California commercial sweet wines have an alcohol concentration of 18 percent.

Differences in method of crushing grapes have no significance with regard to Mass wine, but care must be taken to minimize the casual pickup of water where the crushing equipment is frequently hosed off. Wineries often leach the pressed solids with water and press again. The results of these pressings must be kept out of Mass wine. They are usually used for distilling material. Some wineries, especially those using eastern grapes, may heat the must before pressing. This process, employed to promote the extraction of juice and color, is comparable to mild pasteurization and is permissible in making Mass wine. The use of pectin-splitting enzymes before pressing to promote juice extraction is also permissible, because the federal wine regulations limit the amount of enzyme used to 0.15 percent. For similar reasons, the practice of sterilizing the must with sulfur dioxide or a bisulfite compound is also permissible in making Mass wine. The initial sulfur dioxide concentration seldom exceeds 0.02 percent, and much of this is dissipated before fermentation begins.

Fermentation is begun with the addition of pure yeast culture, usually about 2 percent of the total volume. To avoid diluting the must with sugar and water, the yeast is grown on grape juice rather than on a sugar and water solution. The rate of fermentation is usually controlled by refrigeration. This presents no problem in the production of Mass wine. When sulfur dioxide or sorbic acid is used to slow or stop fermentation, the quantities involved are very small and make no significant difference in the final composition of the wine. Although a considerable portion of the solids suspended in a new wine eventually settle out, it is usually necessary to assist this natural clarification by adding various fining agents, such as bentonite, gelatin, albumen, and casein. Their action on the wine is physical rather than chemical. In settling out themselves, they bring down various other suspended solids. Since they add nothing to the wine and remove only suspended solid impurities, their use is not only permissible but also advisable. Charcoal, however, is one fining agent that will remove much of the natural color and flavor of wine if used in large amounts. To reduce the natural color and flavor of wine notably would make that wine illicit for use as Mass wine. The use of water in preparing fining agents is a practical problem. Producers of Mass wine must make certain that their fining procedures do not add notable amounts of water to the wine.

Since Americans are often suspicious of deposits in bottled wine, most American wineries do their best to avoid the precipitation of potassium bitartrate in their bottled wine. Many wineries chill their wines before bottling so that the bitartrates will precipitate in their cold room rather than in their customers' refrigerators. The wine is then filtered cold to remove the bitartrate deposits. This is an acceptable procedure in making Mass wine, as is the newer and less expensive method of ion exchange. Most wines are filtered several times between fermentation and bottling. Here again, it is important to prevent the addition of water to the wine at the beginning or the end of the filtering procedure. White wines and rosé wines are susceptible to deterioration because of oxidation. Frequently they are handled in the cellars under a blanket of nitrogen or carbon dioxide, which are also added at the time of bottling to remove oxygen and to minimize the oxidation during aging. These procedures are acceptable in the production of Mass wine because these gases are not part of the wine. Sulfur dioxide is commonly used to prevent spoilage of wine during aging. It may also be used with Mass wine because the concentration is usually below 0.015 percent.

BIBLIOGRAPHIC NOTE

Sources include Paul Gordon, ''The Bread and the Wine,'' *American Wine Merchant*, July 1943, and Rabbi Leo Trepp, ''The Role of Wine in the Shaping of Western Culture,'' an address to the Society of Medical Friends of Wine, San Francisco, 25 March 1970. The regulations of the Roman Catholic Church regarding altar wine become more sophisticated and precise as winemaking becomes more sophisticated and precise. This can be seen by comparing the article ''Mass Wine'' by Arthur McNeil, S.J., with ''Altar Wine'' by Joseph Farraher, S.J., and Thomas Terry, S.J., *American Ecclesiastical Review* 99 (1938): 19–45 and 146 (1962): 73–88 respectively.

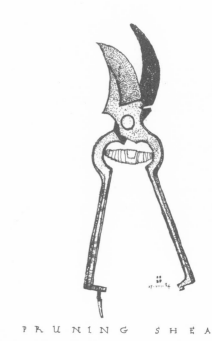

PRUNING SHEARS

This agricultural hand tool of great antiquity long defied drastic alteration in design. Models resulting from new metal technologies and improved compound lever design, markedly less fatiguing to the operator, have appeared in the past few decades, but the pattern illustrated is still in common use.   E.B.

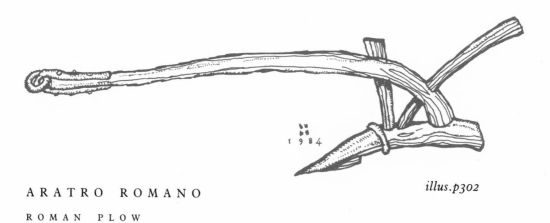

illus.p302

ARATRO ROMANO
ROMAN PLOW

VII

ART, ARTIFACTS, & SOCIETIES

1. ROY BRADY 2. DORIS MUSCATINE

3. DAVID LANCE GOINES, ADRIAN WILSON, ANDREW HOYEM

4. DORIS MUSCATINE 5. ROY BRADY

6. BROTHER TIMOTHY DIENER, F.S.C. 7. PAUL SCHOLTEN, M.D.

8. JOHN BENDER 9. MARK SAVAGE

10. WILLIAM B. FRETTER

VII.1

THE LITERATURE OF CALIFORNIA WINE

by ROY BRADY

A LOOK IN THE CATALOG OF A LARGE LIBRARY UNDER "WINE, CALIFORNIA" DOES NOT BEGIN TO REVEAL THE EXTENT OF THE LITERATURE OF CALIFORNIA WINE. It is widely scattered and often appears in obscure or unexpected places. It is found in various popular magazines, trade papers, and technical journals, frequently in the company of unrelated subjects. Some books have had very limited distribution, and some early publications have become rare almost to the point of extinction. Numerous publications have been issued by societies, universities, viticultural organizations, and nurseries.

This essay is divided into four parts: Pre-Prohibition Literature; Post-Repeal Literature; History; and Periodicals, Newsletters, and Ephemera. It touches but lightly on the extensive technical literature, and, on the whole, is of a historical bent. Pre-Prohibition works are noted when they are worth reading today, as is Agoston Haraszthy's lively account of his vine-gathering trip to Europe in 1861, or when they are historically significant. When recent reprints exist, they are cited. Post-Repeal works are chosen largely for their quality and promise of lasting interest, criteria that rule out various compendia of ephemeral opinion. Periodicals and newsletters are analyzed in general rather than listed in detail. Ignored are the many that resemble the mayfly in longevity as well as intellect. Ephemera are lightly sampled as an indication of what they offer.

PRE-PROHIBITION

The literature of wine in California began with Agoston Haraszthy's nineteen-page "Report on Grapes and Wines of California" in 1858. It was asked for by the State Agricultural Society as practical and up-to-date guidance for the state's winegrowers. It set the pattern for the great bulk of pre-Prohibition literature in being directed at the winegrower rather than the consumer. Haraszthy's major work, *Grape Culture, Wines, and Wine-Making, with Notes upon Agriculture and Horticulture* (New York: Harper, 1862), was in the same direction. It was an account of his vine-gathering trip to Europe in 1861, a sort of early vineyard tour, with only one chapter in the nine actually about California. A large part of the book was taken up by appendices drawn from European sources. Apart from those, it is entertaining reading today. In Dijon train whistles kept him awake all night, and he was irritated by the American minister in Turin, who required that Haraszthy come in person to have his passport visaed.

The pamphlet has become very rare, while the book is fairly common as such things go. That is to say that anyone willing to spend several hundred dollars can probably find a copy of the original within a few years. It has been reprinted twice in facsimile, first as a complete facsimile by Booknoll Reprints, Hopewell, New Jersey, in 1971; next under the title *Father of California Wine: Agoston Haraszthy*, edited by Theodore Schoenman (Santa Barbara, Calif.: Capra Press, 1979). The latter edition includes a twenty-five-page historical introduction but drops 279 pages of appendices and plates.

The first wine book published in California was T. Hart Hyatt, *Hyatt's Hand-Book of Grape Culture; or, Why, Where, When, and How to Plant and Cultivate a Vineyard, Manufacture Wines, Etc.* (San Francisco: H. H. Bancroft, 1867), an ambitious work for the time and again directed at producers rather than drinkers. It was successful enough to be reissued with a new appendix in 1876. Two other practical handbooks from the early days were E. H. Rixford, *The Wine Press and the Cellar, a Manual for the Wine-Maker and Cellar-Man* (San Francisco: Payot, Upham & Co., 1883), and George Husmann, *Grape Culture and Wine Making in California: A Practical Manual for the Grape-Grower and Wine-Maker* (San Francisco: Payot, Upham & Co., 1888). Rixford and Husmann were the most scholarly winegrowers of their time. Rixford owned La Questa Vineyard at Woodside, famous for its Cabernet. Husmann was a leading authority on American grapes at the University of Missouri when he decided to move to California because it was "the true home of the grape." He first managed a winery near the Talcoa estate (now René di Rosa's Winery Lake). Then he founded his own Oak Glen Vineyard, whose very location was to be long forgotten, though his book was signed from there. Then, in the 1960s, Louis P.

Martini bought land for a vineyard high in the hills east of St. Helena and found on it the ruins of a stone winery with the keystone reading "Glen Oak—Husmann Winery—1890." Compared with their more febrile contemporaries, both Rixford and Husmann were temperate in their views of the California wine industry.

The state of scientific knowledge of winegrowing in the mid-1870s is suggested by remarks of George C. Blanchard, president of the California Vine Growers and Wine and Brandy Manufacturers' Association, who attributed the attack of phylloxera to "the large amount of magnetism which had been thrown out through the solar system by the sun for the two years past." He did not detail the connection. In contrast with Blanchard was E. W. Hilgard's scholarly "Lecture on the Phylloxera or Grapevine Louse," the first systematic report on the problem in California. It appeared as University of California Bulletin no. 23 in January 1876.

The conviction that more and better information on winegrowing was needed grew and culminated in the Act for the Promotion of the Viticultural Industries of the State passed by the legislature in 1880. The act created the nine-member board of State Viticultural Commissioners to be composed of members specially qualified by practical experience, and it ordered the University of California to begin research in viticulture. There was great industry on both sides, resulting in two highly important series of publications.

The viticultural commissioners were charged with gathering and disseminating information, a task they did so well during the fourteen years of their existence that in 1937 the California State Library was able to compile a list of about 120 of their reports in its possession. Some are very short, but many are substantial volumes. They survey conditions and problems in California, report investigations, and include translations from European sources.

On the university side, responsibility happily fell to the talented and scholarly Professor Eugene Woldemar Hilgard. In all he published 1,250 pages of viticultural reports, and in addition started a series of bulletins in 1884. His list of sixty-four viticultural publications is too long to give here, but his work is summed up in two University of California viticultural reports: *Report of the Viticultural Work during the Seasons 1887–89, with Data Regarding the Vintage of 1890*, Part I: *Red-wine Grapes* (Sacramento, 1896); and *Report of the Viticultural Work during the Seasons 1887–92, with Data Regarding the Vintages of 1894–95* (Sacramento, 1896).

A thorough study of the raisin side of the grape industry appeared as Gustav Eisen, *The Raisin Industry, A Practical Treatise on the Raisin Grapes, their History, Culture and Curing* (San Francisco: Crocker, 1890). Of considerable interest is Bulletin no. 72, Bureau of Chemistry, U.S. Department of Agriculture, H. W. Wiley, *American Wines at the Paris Exposition of 1900: Their Composition and Character with a Monograph on the Manufacture of Wines in California by Henry Lachman*

(Washington, D.C.: Government Printing Office, 1903). It points up the controversy over the use of European names on California wines. Shortly before the California entries were to be judged, the jury suddenly adopted a resolution against judging wines bearing a "false" designation of origin. That was interpreted to eliminate many of the California entries. They were later readmitted, but it was a shock.

A landmark of California printing was *Grapes and Grape Vines of California* (San Francisco: Edward Bosqui & Co., 1877), published under the auspices of the California State Vinicultural Association; it consisted of seventeen leaves oleographed by Wm. Harring from the original watercolor drawings by Miss Hannah Millard. It is much sought after both as a wine book and as a splendid example of early California color printing. Unfortunately, many copies were broken up for the sake of the plates. Until twenty or so years ago, it was by no means unusual to find individual plates in antiquarian bookshops for $20 to $30, but in thirty years of searching I have seen only one complete copy appear on the market. That was in 1979, when a New Jersey dealer cataloged it at $13,500. The only copy I have actually seen was doing duty as a doorstop at the Wine Institute. In recent years, it has been reprinted twice. The more accessible edition is a faithful reproduction brought out by Harcourt Brace Jovanovich in 1980 with two added sections, a history of fine printing in California, and a historical note by Leon Adams. It was published at $29.95. John Windle of San Francisco brought out a sumptuous edition of 300 copies in 1980. Of these, 200 were issued as loose sheets in a gold-stamped portfolio and 100 were bound in Moroccan goatskin. The prices were, respectively, $850 and $1,250. Windle could locate only six surviving complete copies of the original edition of 1877.

Frona Eunice Wait's *Wines and Vines of California, or a Treatise on the Ethics of Wine Drinking* (San Francisco: Bancroft, 1889), was the first comprehensive description of the California wine industry for the general reader. Its easygoing, if dated, style betrays the newspaper background of its young author. Many things were different in those days. At Inglenook she found wines to be held in the barrel from two to five years. As to the author,

> *She had*
> *A heart—how shall I say?—too soon made glad,*
> *Too easily impressed; she liked whate'er*
> *She looked on, and her looks went everywhere.*
> *(Robert Browning, "My Last Duchess")*

Still, it gives an engaging firsthand account of California wine almost a century ago, and may conveniently be found in a facsimile edition with an introduction by Maynard A. Amerine published by Howell-North Books of Berkeley in 1973.

A quaint little book is Major Ben C. Truman's *See How It Sparkles* (Los Angeles: Geo. Rice & Sons, 1896). His richly mannered style is still a delight to read. His favorite Champagne was "the monarch of all potations," and Château d'Yquem was "nectarous and blissful." Nevertheless, the widely traveled major obviously knew his wines. A facsimile edition was issued by *Wine World* magazine in 1973 with a biographical foreword by Roy Brady and two portraits of Truman.

A book that should be reprinted is Thomas Hardy, *Notes on Vineyards in America* (Australia, 1885). It is a unique glimpse of early California wine through the eyes of a foreign winemaker. The California chapters were reprinted sporadically in *Wines & Vines* magazine between September 1966 and September 1968. The editor thought the copy he used was the only one in existence. Hardy did not suffer from Wait's timorousness. He wrote of the United States, "There is a fearful lot of sham and humbug in this country."

The last gasp as the incubus of Prohibition descended on the country was Sara Bard Field's *The Vintage Festival: A Play Pageant & Festivities Celebrating the Vine in the Autumn of Each Year at St. Helena in the Napa Valley* (San Francisco: John Henry Nash, 1920), a little book more important for its printer than for its contents.

One nineteenth-century book not primarily about wine must be mentioned anyhow because it has been—and doubtless will continue to be—quoted ad nauseam. That is Robert Louis Stevenson's *Silverado Squatters*, which exists in many editions, the first being issued in London by Chatto and Windus in 1883. One chapter is about Napa wine because Stevenson spent his honeymoon on the slopes of Mount St. Helena. A notable California edition of the single chapter was issued by John Henry Nash under the title *Napa Wine* in 1924. No one seems ever to have seen the "four-color engraving of the famous old Napa Winery from a painting by Girard Hale" said to accompany it. *The Silverado Squatters* has been quoted because a famous writer said nice things in it about California wine, a habit famous writers did not widely acquire until very recently. Actually, Stevenson tells us very little and clearly had little experience with wine of any kind. One does not have to look it up. If one reads anything about California wine one will inevitably read it.

POST-REPEAL LITERATURE

In the feeble dawn of California wine writing after Repeal, the first book to reveal itself was Horatio P. Stoll's *Wine-Wise: A Popular Handbook on How to Correctly Judge, Keep, Serve and Enjoy Wines* (San Francisco: Crocker, 1933). Stoll was a pre-

Prohibition wine industry publicist and trade journal editor whose fossilized views had been frozen for the duration, warmed over in the first burst of optimism after Repeal for the delectation of a bemused public, and served forth under a title that split infinitives seriatim. On the first page he said, "I have read almost every work that has been written about wine." It is well he thought to tell us, for he carried his scholarship so lightly that it made no discernible impress upon any other page.

The fact is that little could be said about California wine in 1933. It was years before the winemakers could lift themselves out of the wreckage of Prohibition, make some good wines—few did—and age them long enough to reach the market. The first real book to deal with California wine was Frank Schoonmaker and Tom Marvel's *American Wines* (New York: Duell, Sloan and Pearce, 1941). The authors had been importers of European wines and turned to American wines when the war shut off European sources. In view of that, the book must be regarded as special pleading, but special pleading with verve and literary grace. The engaging style (pure Schoonmaker; Marvel, a former San Francisco *Chronicle* reporter, is believed to have edited it) holds together, with considerable success, a rather fragile fabric of fact.

Schoonmaker is the most felicitous writer on wine that America has produced, and for a long time he was the most influential one, more influential than any individual could be today. He fell into wine writing by accident when he was already well launched into a career as a travel writer with several books to his credit, including one with Lowell Thomas as co-author. In that role, he was known to Harold Ross, editor of the *New Yorker*. Reasoning in his own fashion, Ross concluded that if Schoonmaker knew France, he must needs know French wine. Having gained that illumination, he at once engaged Schoonmaker to write a series of articles on French wine for the newly moistened republic. That was a momentous thing for both Schoonmaker and American wine writing, for he wrote with a grace denied all others. In 1951 he wrote: "A California Cabernet is a Médoc in another octave, played, if you like, by different instruments, and less well played, but the basic theme is there." He ceased writing about travel, took up wine, presently became an importer, and set about becoming the expert he very much was not at the start.

Schoonmaker's career was interrupted by military service. Soon after the war, he was importing again, and the connection with California was to last. In 1948 he started *News from the Wine Country*, described as "A Quarterly Newspaper for the Delectation, Instruction and Divertissement of Bibbers, Sutlers, Oenophilists, Wine Tasters, Poetasters, Gastronomes, Epicures, *Feinschmecker*, *Fines Gueules*, and *Catadores de Vino*," the subtitle reflecting some of the languages in which he was fluent. It was unabashedly commercial, but with Schoonmaker's easy style, the reader seldom noticed. It was quarterly only to the uncertain degree that he felt the urge to produce quarterly. If Schoonmaker's writing about California wine sometimes sounds patronizing or hortatory, it must be remembered that he wrote mostly during the dark age of wine in America, when California wines had a minute, doctrinaire claque rather than today's large, somewhat informed following.

The Schoonmaker-Marvel book began a thin trickle of books on California wine. The trickle became a freshet as Americans began to discover wine in the latter sixties, and everyone had to have his say. The next volume was Mary Frost Mabon's *ABC of America's Wines* (New York: Knopf, 1943), a less deft propaganda piece but written with professional gloss and useful in rounding out the picture of the early forties, providing the opinions of wines are ignored. She tasted a Beaulieu Private Reserve Cabernet at the winery but neglected to tell us the vintage. It must have been the first one of 1936.

The modern personal style of writing about wine in terms of people, incidents, and individual wines first appeared in Robert Lawrence Balzer's *California's Best Wines* (Los Angeles: Ward Ritchie, 1948). It describes visits to thirteen leading wineries. Five more were added in a new preface in a second edition also dated 1948 (though the colophon says 1949 and the preface is dated June 1950). The encyclopedic approach was introduced by John Melville's *Guide to California Wines* (Garden City, N.Y.: Doubleday, 1955), with its bland descriptions of almost a hundred wineries and their wines. A good many were of no interest to the wine lover. Reading the book today, the most startling thing is that a good 40 percent of the wineries are no more, and almost as many survive in little but name. Extensive revisions appeared in 1960 and 1968, the latter one done by Jefferson Morgan.

Frank Schoonmaker had announced preparation of a California book in 1956, but, alas, it never materialized. For many years he wrote a newsletter, "News from the Vineyards," for Almadén Vineyards, but otherwise he was more concerned with European wines. His later comment on California was confined largely to the relatively minor California entries in his *Encyclopedia of Wine* (New York: Hastings House, 1964, and several later editions).

The most important book of the sixties was M. A. Amerine and V. L. Singleton's *Wine: An Introduction for Americans* (Berkeley and Los Angeles: University of California Press, 1964). It is by no means confined to California, but is what the subtitle says it is, and it is the only place where the Davis viewpoint is available to the nontechnical reader: emphasis is on fact rather than fancy. The first half of the book is a clear account of modern wine technology. The second is a concise summary of the world's wines. A second edition appeared in 1977, when the title was shortened to *Wine: An Introduction*. Somewhere toward the other end of the scale is *The Fred Beck Wine Book* (New York: Hill and Wang, 1964), but it is endearing for such remarks as, "When I visit wineries, I am sometimes inclined to say to myself, 'There is less here than meets the eye.' "

The seventies and eighties have seen a great increase in the production of books on wine, but no commensurate increase in solid books of lasting value. Books on wine evaluation abound and have created no small population of advice-dependent unfortunates. One sees them in wine shops, clutching the latest volume of clothbound connoisseurship and nervously asking one another, "Martha, what does he say about this one?" With the publishing lag, the short time many wines are available, and the fleeting lifespan of many wines, such books fall obsolescent from the press, and what little value they do have soon dissipates. Also to be dismissed are the numerous rehashes of the basic facts and the works of naive enthusiasm. One gentleman was in print with a volume of confident counsel eight months after he first discovered the wonders of wine.

A highly significant book is Leon D. Adams's *The Wines of America* (1973; revised ed. New York: McGraw-Hill, 1978). It is primarily a compendium of wineries and their histories, policies, personnel, and tangled relations. Nobody knows the latter as well as Adams. About half of it is devoted to California; the remainder covers the other states, Canada, and Mexico. Since it appeared, Adams has been roaming the continent in preparation for a third edition—a large task, since it came just as California entered its period of frenetic growth.

Hugh Johnson, who understands California wine better than any other European and wine in general better than almost anybody, joined Bob Thompson, California's indefatigable seeker of vinous fact, to produce *The California Wine Book* (New York: William Morrow, 1976). The book contains a wealth of information that could be gathered only through long and close association with the wine industry. But it is not content with being merely informative, for it does not hesitate to generalize and interpret. In his preface Johnson says, "This book . . . is our report on a formative stage in the early life of one of the world's great vineyards." It has some fine photographs.

Robert Benson got an idea that a lot of people wished they had got earlier. He took a tape recorder around the state to interview twenty-eight winemakers and winery proprietors. The result was *Great Winemakers of California* (Santa Barbara: Capra Press, 1977). Many of the questions were conceived in the technophilia of the times.

In the midst of a sea of foolishness about evaluating wines stands the rock of Maynard A. Amerine and Edward B. Roessler's *Wines: Their Sensory Evaluation* (San Francisco: W. H. Freeman, 1976). It takes the classic as opposed to the romantic approach. It covers the scientific background, questions some shibboleths, and explains what really causes "legs" in a wine. Only the hardier reader will penetrate the second half of the book dealing with the statistical procedures needed for the analysis of sensory data.

An important source for the history of wine in California since Repeal, and a little before, is the series of interviews conducted by the Regional Oral History Office of the Bancroft Library in the California Wine Industry Oral History Series. There are twenty-three interviews in nineteen volumes. The project was initiated and financed by the Wine Advisory Board beginning in 1969. Most of the interviews were conducted by Ruth Teiser and most of the introductions written by Maynard A. Amerine. They were not published in the usual sense, but copies are available to research libraries that wish to have them, and they must be consulted in a library (Regional Oral History Office, Room 486, Bancroft Library, University of California, Berkeley, California 94720). Interviewed were Leon D. Adams, Maynard A. Amerine, Philo Biane, Burke H. Critchfield, Carl F. Wente, Andrew C. Frericks, William V. Cruess, Maynard A. Joslyn, Horace O. Lanza, Harry Baccigaluppi, Louis M. Martini, Louis P. Martini, Otto E. Meyer, Harold P. Olmo, Antonio Perelli-Minetti, Louis A. Petri, Jefferson E. Peyser, Lucius Powers, Victor Repetto, Sydney J. Block, Edmund A. Rossi, Brother Timothy (Diener), Ernest A. Wente, and Albert J. Winkler.

Between 1974 and 1980, Vintage Image, a publisher in St. Helena, brought out a series of paperback regional wine books on Napa, Sonoma, Mendocino, and the Central Coast by various hands. The heart of each book is a series of uncontroversial descriptions of wineries and a drawing of each by Sebastian Titus, and there is a section on restaurants, shops, and lodgings in the wine country for travelers. Sometimes the winery and tour sections were issued separately. Some are illustrated with old cuts and current labels. The winery descriptions for Napa and Sonoma also appeared in two large folios with additional material and many old photographs. They are attractive and, with the exception of some shaky history, useful books. There were plans to cover other parts of the state and to issue updated volumes, but now all rights have been sold to the Wine Appreciation Guild of San Francisco. They intend to have revisions made and to publish them at some future time, but there are no definite plans yet.

A very convenient and often revised single-volume guide to the wineries of the state is *California Wine Country*, prepared by the Sunset Editorial Staff and edited by Bob Thompson (Menlo Park, Calif., 1968); it was expanded, updated, and retitled *Guide to California's Wine Country* in 1979, with a second edition appearing in 1982. There are firsthand descriptions of the wineries, regional maps, and some very good color photographs.

HISTORY

Writers on California wine often like to bring in fragments of history, but too often they treat them as a variety of literary decoration. If a story is entertaining, use it;

ask not whence it came. That has resulted in much romanticized and plain bad history. Idwal Jones's *Vines in the Sun* (New York: William Morrow, 1949) is a prime example of the genre. He has the wine commissioners dash down with their fastest horses to investigate the Anaheim disease. Their chemist examines a bit of sap from a vine, and this exchange takes place:

> *"A virus," he said.*
> *"Now what is to be done?"*
> *"Nothing, gentlemen; nothing. This is the end."*

The story falls short of perfection on two points. Since the incident would have been in the 1880s, it was before viruses were discovered. Second, viruses could not be seen in the optical microscopes of the time. One can have no confidence in a book with such stories. The absence of dates and sources makes it worse history.

Only just now do we have a real history of wine in California. That is Ruth Teiser and Catherine Harroun's *Winemaking in California* (New York: Mc-Graw-Hill, 1983). It is very attractively written and displays both an appreciation of wine and a knowledge of California history in general. In many writings, early figures are wooden or mere wraiths. Here they come alive. The portrait of Jean Louis Vignes is especially good. The most important part of the book deals with the pre-Prohibition era, but the Prohibition period and the complex history of the following generation are deftly summarized. Although the book is based on a great deal of research in all the relevant libraries of the state, resulting in important new material, it is written as a straightforward narrative without footnotes. The large number of illustrations, many never published before, is a strong feature of the book.

The major previous effort at a history was Vincent P. Carosso's *The California Wine Industry, 1830–1895: A Study of the Formative Years* (Berkeley and Los Angeles: University of California Press, 1951). It is exceedingly valuable for its extensive bibliography and notes on sources, and it is full of newly discovered facts, but it holds reader interest about as compellingly as the Reykjavik telephone directory. A treatise on pork bellies could generate more passion. The author is indifferent to wine as an aesthetic object, which greatly lessens the reader's interest, and, more important from a scholarly point of view, Carosso's indifference vitiates his interpretations of nineteenth-century opinions of contemporary wines. It was reissued as a California Library Reprint Series Edition in 1976.

Charles L. Sullivan's *Like Modern Edens: Winegrowing in Santa Clara Valley and Santa Cruz Mountains, 1798–1981* (Cupertino, Calif.: California History Center, 1982) is a thoroughly researched local history, and it is to be hoped that scholars in other areas of the state will follow its example. It is well-written wine history by a wine lover. A little book that contains a lot of painstakingly discovered facts about defunct wineries is Irene W. Haynes's *Ghost Wineries of the Napa Valley: A Photographic Tour of the 19th Century* (San Francisco: Sally Taylor & Friends, 1980). Photographs are included whenever possible, even though the buildings are ruinous or used for something else. Two very slim volumes by Ernest Peninou and Sidney Greenleaf under the overall title *Wine Making in California* (San Francisco: Peregrine Press, 1954) cover history to 1894 in the first volume and the history of the California Wine Association before Prohibition in the other. The same authors compiled *A Directory of California Wine Growers and Wine Makers in 1860, with Biographical and Historical Notes and Index* (Berkeley: Tamalpais Press, 1967). It is not so much a history as a compilation of facts, but most interesting nonetheless.

The best discussion of E. W. Hilgard's viticultural work is in Maynard Amerine's "Hilgard and California Viticulture," *Hilgardia* 30 (1962): 1–23. It covers Hilgard's controversy with C. A. Wetmore and includes some spirited quotations. As a guide to historical sources, there is Amerine's "An Introduction to the Pre-Repeal History of Grapes and Wines in California," *Agricultural History* 43 (April 1969): 259–68. Maynard A. Amerine and Louise B. Wheeler's *A Check List of Books and Pamphlets on Grapes and Wine and Related Subjects, 1938–1948* (Berkeley and Los Angeles: University of California Press, 1951) includes all countries and languages. Amerine's later checklists of 1959 and 1969 carry English language listings through 1968. Also useful is Guy J. Guttadauro's *A List of References for the History of Grapes, Wines, and Raisins in America* (Davis, Calif.: University of California Agricultural History Center, July 1976).

PERIODICALS, NEWSLETTERS, AND EPHEMERA

The periodical literature of California wines is widely scattered through popular magazines, newspapers, trade journals, proceedings of societies, wine magazines, numerous specialized periodicals, house organs of wineries, and, lately, that most curious genre, the wine newsletter. The first California periodical to take a substantial interest in viticulture was *The Southern Vineyard*, a newspaper published in Los Angeles by Colonel J. J. Warner from 24 March 1858 to 8 June 1860. Popular magazines took a limited interest in California wine before Prohibition and, indeed, for a long time after it, except for a brief flurry of interest immediately after Repeal. Both before and after Prohibition, the popular press tended to be superficial except for a very occasional article of substance. The earliest in an important magazine was the anonymous "California as a Wineland" in the *Atlantic Monthly* of May 1864. Two months later, Agoston Haraszthy published his characteristically optimistic "Wine-making in California" in *Harper's*. One of the most substantial articles was Arpad Haraszthy's "Wine Making in California," published by the *Overland Monthly* in four parts during the winter of 1871–72. He was too optimistic, but foresaw important things like the development of appellations and the choice of better varieties. These articles were gathered into a small book under the same title by the Book Club of San Francisco in 1978. Ruth Teiser and Catherine Harroun contributed a very useful biographical introduction.

Much of the old periodical literature would be difficult for the average reader to find and, for the most part, would little reward him if he did find it, but a few things deserve resurrection in a small book or two. Certainly Professor Hilgard's biting response to the question of what was wrong with the wine industry is one. It appeared in the San Francisco *Examiner* on 8 August 1889 under the title "Plain Talk to Winemen . . . Sharp Words on the Methods of Ignorant Makers and Dishonest Dealers."

Standing in today's washy torrent of wine commentary, it is difficult to realize how recent a phenomenon it is. For a generation after Repeal, the wine lover had very little recourse in trying to discover the relative merits of currently available wines. What little comment there was tended to be either interested, incompetent, or, more likely, both. During the thirties and forties, there were a couple of provincial trade journals in California, but they were in no way useful to the wine lover. The better trade journal, *Wines & Vines*, became a good trade journal under the editor Irving Marcus in the fifties and sixties. In 1969 Marcus sold it to Philip Hiaring, who has made it into a sophisticated monthly. It is still a trade journal, but it is aware of the wide world, and, though it does not evaluate wines, no one serious about California wine can afford to be without it. The annual directory gives the basic facts on every winery in the country, as it has since 1940, and in recent years Canada and Mexico have been included.

The *California Wineletter*, founded in 1948, brings current news of the industry twenty-three times a year and sometimes comments on a limited number of wines. Though primarily directed at the trade, it has interest for the serious amateur. The *Wine Spectator* is a biweekly in tabloid format covering all the world's wines. It features current news and commentary, profiles, tasting reports, and it is much devoted to wine as a collectible. The former *Redwood Rancher* has become *Wine West* and devotes itself entirely to wine, with articles of much wider appeal than before. Its area of coverage has been expanded to include all the western winegrowing states, as well as British Columbia. The most consumer-oriented is the four-color *Wine Country*, which describes itself as "the magazine from the heart of California's Wineland." It includes articles on some non-California wines and on food.

California material appears in greater or lesser quantity in numerous wine or wine and food magazines. The quality varies exceedingly. The magazines are too numerous and too changeable to discuss individually. One might suppose that the bounding interest in wine of recent years would support several general wine magazines, but it is not so. Big advertisers do not like small wine magazines.

Accordingly, such magazines usually limp along if they do not founder at the launching. They cannot afford to pay much and therefore fail to attract good writers. Their only salvation is in having staff members who can produce adequate copy, and there are not many of them. Otherwise the impecunious editor turns to friend, relative, or complaisant member of the trade. The first two are generally disasters. The complaisant member may know what he is talking about, but selling is likely uppermost in his mind. A magazine supported by a society may be more stable, but the editor comes under pressure to accept contributions from members whose talents are not commensurate with their own perception of them. The desperate editor begins to print public relations stories (in the normal course of events he gets about six pecks of these a day), he reprints "selections from the classics" (i.e., anything old enough to be out of copyright), and every letter to the editor of which any sense whatever can be made. The results are not happy.

If an editor cannot get advertising, he does not need to worry about offending advertisers. When he piously announces that he is eschewing advertising for the greater good of his readers, it may be assumed that he has abandoned all hope of getting any. Since he can't afford good solid articles, they too go by the board. Fearless evaluations of wines become his principal product. Thus is born that popular journal of vinous *virtù*, the wine newsletter. It tells its readers what wines to buy, how good they are on a scale of 1 to 20 or 1 to 100 or whatever, when each wine will "reach its peak," how long they should be aired, where to buy them, and much more. Presumably, psychic powers allow those determinations, for their wellsprings are never revealed.

The newsletters evidently satisfy a great need. To catalogue those organs of the advice industry would be to catalogue the autumn leaves. In addition to the many subscription newsletters, there are those put out by organizations for their members, those from retail merchants, and even some by individuals for their favored friends. At least one MENSA chapter has its own advisor, as does a major aerospace company. Another subscription newsletter is available by computer display.

The wine-buying public seems ready to believe the judgments of anyone with access to a Xerox machine. That readiness to believe would seem to open the way to a good deal of chicanery, but the fact is that most writers of newsletters are honest—grimly honest, and grimly objective as they see it. But that does not always make up for limited experience and a load of preconceptions about wine.

With some notable exceptions, the newsletters are a literature without personality, its lack being supplied by juiceless, and generally useless, technicality. There is much of "peachy/spicy/apricot flavors," "full strength varietal aromas with hints of late-harvest characteristics," "precisely defined stony/mineral fruit aromas wrapped around botrytis/honey/cedar aromas," and "harmonically governed counterpoint with melodies of floral Merlot." Much of it sounds as if it were written by engineers, educators, and bureaucrats. The slash is the principal ornament of the style. The pretentious plural abounds. Does such balderdash tell anybody anything?

Then there are the winery house organs. In recent years they have multiplied along with the wineries. Some of them merely tout the wines, some prickle with technical detail, some sound like the newsletters, but others are full of useful and interesting information. The oldest are the *Mayacamas Bulletin*, begun ca. 1948 (early issues were not dated), and Charles Krug's *Bottles & Bins*, started in 1949. Early followers of Mayacamas suffered and triumphed with the Taylor family as they struggled to establish the winery. *Bottles & Bins* was edited for thirty years by courtly Frank "Paco" Gould almost until his death at ninety-four. Beaulieu Vineyard had a go at it about the same time with the *Napa Valley Gazette* but did not stay the course.

Finally, there exists a large body of wine ephemera, varying from yesterday's junk mail to items of great interest, some of them beautifully printed. Because little effort has been made to collect and catalogue such materials, it is not possible to say with any confidence what exists. Having long been on their trail, I have collected quite a few wine ephemera. A few examples will suggest the kinds of things they are.

Old wine lists show what wines were being drunk and what they cost, and occasional comments can reveal surprisingly different attitudes of another day. The 112-page 1912 catalogue of H. Jevne Company of Los Angeles shows what the wealthy of that city were drinking almost three-quarters of a century ago. The 1940 wine list of the Bohemian Club shows what the members were drinking then, and it was handsomely printed by the Grabhorn Press. There were a good many such lists when printing was relatively cheap and inventories changed slowly.

Also by Grabhorn were the programs of earlier vintage tours of the San Francisco Wine and Food Society. They run a dozen or two pages and include some attractive essays on vinous topics as well as itineraries and menus.

There are many things like the 27-page pamphlet, "Views of the Vintage," published by the Sonoma Wine and Brandy Company, with photographs of the vintage ca. 1913. Such things trickle through the antiquarian bookshops, but they no longer trickle cheaply. The vintage tour programs of 1946, 1950, 1955, and 1957 are probably worth more today than the tours cost.

VII.2

Note: The Wine Museum of San Francisco

by DORIS MUSCATINE

THE WINE MUSEUM OF SAN FRANCISCO WAS THE FIRST OF its kind in the Western Hemisphere; according to its original director, the late Ernest G. Mittelberger, it was "a place where people could share and learn about . . . the rituals, history, and folk tales of wine." Through its collections it demonstrated the diversity of art created over the centuries in celebration of the grape. Assembled over the past forty-five years, the collections contain over one thousand rare books in seven languages; artifacts in porcelain, wood, bronze, pewter, and silver; and original drawings and prints by such artists as Daumier, Picasso, Chagall, Maillol, Kokoscha, and Currier and Ives. The Franz W. Sichel Glass Collection of drinking vessels from the Roman era to the present includes a glass dating from 1590, one of the nine in existence attributed to Verzelini, notable because he was the only Venetian glassblower licensed by Queen Elizabeth I to produce glass in late sixteenth-century England.

The exhibits were arranged by theme to treat the grape and the vine, the vintage and the harvest, and winemaking and the vintner. Art and objects related to Greek and Roman festivities honoring Dionysius, or Bacchus, the god of wine, fertility, and agriculture, dominated a section on mythology and legend. Another display contained works of art devoted to the conviviality historically associated with wine. Two graphic history panels told the stories of wine and civilization and wine in California, and changing exhibits explored the connection between wine and the opera, examined the cooper's art, displayed a collection of mid-nineteenth-century caricatures with "Daumier on Wine," traced the development of the common container with "2,000 Years: The Evolution of the Bottle," and looked at the humorous side of wine with "Fifty Years of Wine Cartoons from *The New Yorker*."

The museum and its collections were created by Alfred Fromm and his family, the late Franz W. Sichel, and the Christian Brothers of Mont La Salle in Napa, California, for whose wines and brandies Fromm and Sichel, Inc., were

318

formerly worldwide distributors. Franz W. Sichel, from Mainz in the upper Rhine-land of Germany, was active in his grandfather's wine firm of Sichel and Sohne in both Europe and the United States until he and Alfred Fromm joined forces to establish Fromm and Sichel, Inc., in 1945. Alfred Fromm, the firm's chairman of the board, was born into a family of vintners and shippers in Kitzingen in the Franconian wine district of Germany, and graduated from the Viticultural Academy in Geisenheim. His wine career shifted from Europe to California in 1938. From that time until 1983 he represented the Christian Brothers, a religious order founded in 1680 in Reims, France, and dedicated to teaching. Although they take vows of poverty, chastity, and obedience, the Brothers are not priests. Members of the order first came to the United States in 1840, established themselves in California in 1868, and have made wine there since 1882. The profits from their California vineyards and wineries support the fourteen Christian Brothers' schools and colleges in the western United States. Mont La Salle Vineyards has handled the marketing since September 1983.

Some forty-five years ago, under the direction of Alfred Fromm and his brother Norman, the Brothers began collecting wine-related art objects, books, drawings, prints, engravings, and sculptures. In the 1960s the collection went on tour to twenty U.S. museums. For a decade from January 1974, it made its home in newly designed quarters, built in modern mission style and executed with the care for fine materials and handicraft consonant with its collections and dedicated, according to its second director James R. Lucas, to the continued celebration of wine as a joyful human experience. Several years ago, Joseph E. Seagram and Sons acquired the museum with the purchase of Fromm and Sichel. Although Seagram subsequently sold Fromm and Sichel in September 1983, it kept the museum, closing it in November in favor of developing the property for other uses. As this book went to press, major parts of the collections were being transferred to the Seagram Museum in Waterloo, Ontario, Canada.

VII.3
Note: The Art of the Label

by DAVID LANCE GOINES, ADRIAN WILSON, ANDREW HOYEM

The label on a bottle of wine is the transitional communication between maker and drinker, the merchant's guide to an orderly stocking of shelves, a means of identification of the bottle in storage, a discreet advertisement, and in some splendid instances, a work of art. In spite of the importance of the function of labels, not enough is said about them in print. Certainly books with pictures of wine labels abound, providing historical illustrations, or reproducing specially commissioned works of major artists, or offering a decorative means of cataloguing wineries; but not many writers discourse on their purpose, or the collecting of them, or the aesthetics of their design. Gathered here, then, are the comments of three California designers, David Lance Goines, Adrian Wilson, and Andrew Hoyem, who have given thought to the refinements that make a good label.

DORIS MUSCATINE

I

WINE labels are, by comparison with other packaging, somewhat conservative, tending toward the typographic rather than the pictorial. This may be due, in part, to three factors. First, there is not much room on a wine label, and quite a bit of information needs to be on it. Second, byzantine government regulations firmly, but vaguely, specify what must and must not be on a label (in theory, almost nothing is acceptable), how large or small it should be and in what range of contrast, and so on and so forth. This contributes to an aesthetic of reduction and an adherence to the tried and true. Last, and perhaps most interesting, no other product is allowed in its original container on the genteel table. This position of trust no doubt exerts a considerable influence on the designer. Although the label must be sufficiently distinctive to prevent confusion among competing wines and to an extent convey to the purchaser some notion of the quality of the contents, it need not compel attention in the usual sense of commercial packaging. Indeed, to do so might be to lose wine's privileged position, and cause it to be decanted like some humbler substance into a more harmonious container.

DAVID LANCE GOINES

7.

Wine label designed by Adrian Wilson for private bottling. Wood engraving by Mallette Dean. Typeface: Jessenschrift handcut by Rudolf Koch. Reproduced in same size as original.

II

THE enormous variety of labels for bottles of wine extends from those carrying only the signature of the maker (and some fine vintages have borne no other identification) to the most lavish, gilded, bemedalled, embossed, ornately lettered, and even seductively shaped pieces of paper to pass through printing presses. Their appearance does not necessarily reflect the quality of the wine they announce. Some bottles that wear the gaudiest dress contain the plainest of beverages.

Between the extremes, there is the possibility of encountering the traditional virtues of fine design and fine printing. Textured papers, subtly modeled typefaces, handlettering in classical styles, rich inking, and deep impression into the paper, with ample surrounding space to increase legibility, are the elements of

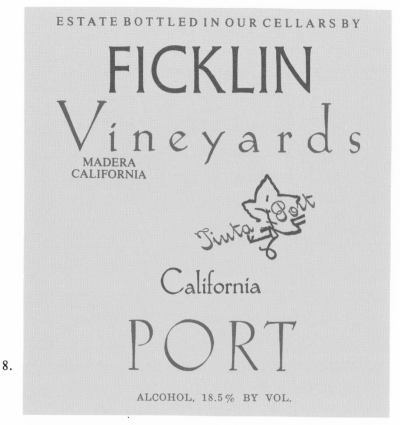

Wine label designed for Ficklin Port in 1951 by Robert Grabhorn and handset and printed at the Grabhorn Press. Typefaces: Weiss Titling, Koch Antiqua, and a nineteenth-century script. Reproduced in same size as original.

the art of the label. An image of the source of the wine—the vineyard, château, cellar, or region—when executed in a strong graphic technique such as woodcut or wood engraving, can enhance the beauty of the label. Full-color paintings are less successful. Large initials, or flourishes, or a flash of color may impart a suggestion of the robustness, lightness, or sparkle that is contained within the bottle. A striking trademark or device can be attractive. Above all, the design and materials should suggest the care and craftsmanship that produced the wine.

Some wineries have commissioned independent designers and printing craftsmen, who occasionally create labels that are works of art. My own venture into winemaking with a friend who was a graduate chemist led inevitably to my printing a

73 Zinfandel, Lytton Springs, bottled May 1975
This old hill vineyard produced two tons per acre in 1973. Many Zinfandel vineyards in deep valley soils produce several times that amount. The intensity gained through low production is evident in the richness and varietal character of this superb wine. The secondary fermentation and aging in small oak cooperage has softened the wine sufficiently for tasting this fall; however, it will need several years of bottle age to approach its potential.   PD (5/75)

RIDGE wine is made with an emphasis on quality and naturalness that is rarely attempted. Our grapes are grown in select vineyards (usually identified on the label), where they are left to ripen to peak maturity, often at some loss of quantity. We let the wine settle and age in small barrels, with only rare cellar treatment other than racking. Varieties are not blended unless so indicated on the label. Near Black Mountain on Monte Bello Ridge, our main vineyard is 10 miles south of Palo Alto, 15 miles inland from the ocean, and over 2000 feet in elevation. For requesting information on ordering wines or visiting the winery for tasting, please send us a note or call (408) 867-3233.   DRB (1967)

RIDGE
CALIFORNIA
ZINFANDEL
LYTTON SPRINGS
1973

GRAPES APPROX 96% ZINFANDEL, 4% PETITE SIRAH
BOTTLED MAY 1975 ALCOHOL 12.8% BY VOLUME
PRODUCED AND BOTTLED BY RIDGE VINEYARDS
17100 MONTE BELLO RD, CUPERTINO, CALIFORNIA

9.

Wine label designed for Ridge Vineyards in 1964 by James Robertson and Bruce Montgomery. Typeface: Optima designed by Hermann Zapf. Front and back label joined. Original 4⅝" × 7".

label. We bought grapes from a grower in the Napa Valley and processed them in the barn of our old country house in Nicasio, north of San Francisco. Facing us across the village green was a quaint, peak-roofed, white clapboard church with a golden cross surmounting the spire. Viewed from our back yard through the driveway, it was perfectly framed by the house on one side and the barn on the other. This touch of New England made a charming paradox set against the bare, rolling California hills that are velvet green in winter and bleached gold in summer. The barn had no back wall, so the wine press, crusher, tank, and barrels were visible.

   When the bottling began, I asked the artist Mallette Dean to create a wood engraving of the scene in exchange for some of that year's vintage. The cut he

IO.

Wine label designed for the Robert Mondavi Winery in 1966 by Mallette Dean and James E. Beard. Wood engraving by Dean. Typeface: Kennerley capitals designed by Frederic W. Goudy. Reproduced in same size as original.

created perfectly captured the atmosphere of this unspoiled valley, the tiny church, and our rustic winery. I chose a rugged typeface called Jessenschrift, handcut by the renowned Rudolf Koch, which seemed to me to harmonize with the process of making wine by hand (and by foot, at first) and to combine well with the vigor of Mallette's block. For the first vintages to be produced in that valley I printed the labels with the wood engraving and the name of the grape in black, the winery and year in red. The makers and location were in small, black capitals. No revelation of alcoholic content was required of amateurs, but it was high enough! For the red wines, a deep gold stock called Tweedweave was used, and for the whites, the same paper in a green tint. I cannot say how this design would have fared on the shelves

See FIGURE 7
p. 321

of a wine store or supermarket or in the in-house shops set up by industrial designers to test consumer acceptance. I do know that it has enhanced many a table, and
the bottles it adorned were emptied with pleasure. Many of our labels have been
soaked off as souvenirs, the ultimate test of a good design and a happy occasion.

ADRIAN WILSON

III

PIECES of printed paper glued to wine bottles are advertising. But wines
are sold by the fluid ounce, not by the label. The reputation of a variety, locale, a
vineyard, winery, or a particular vintage is earned by the contents of a bottle, not by
its trappings. When consumers are entrapped by "design," by the designs of a pack-
ager to "position" a product in the marketplace, they should beware of wine meant
to be sold rather than sipped. Yet how doubly gratifying it is to drink a good wine
from a bottle with a beautiful label.

Identification of contents is the primary function of a label. This information is transmitted typographically or calligraphically, with recognition often
reinforced by pictorial or decorative elements. The arrangement of letters and
words on a wine label is complicated by curvature, for the surface of the bottle to
which the label is applied is a cylinder, exposing only a narrow column to view. The
perceptible area of a label is really quite small: the sides of labels recede from view;
pictures and ornamental patterns in reduced scale should succeed as miniatures (re-
production of art conceived on a larger scale is usually unsuccessful); the lettering
must be readable at a distance and in the round.

Three labels produced in California are exemplary. The first graces
Ficklin Port and was designed in 1951 by Robert Grabhorn. Setting types by hand
from the large collection of leaden alphabets at the Grabhorn Press, he selected an *See* FIGURE 8 p. 322
unlikely combination of letterforms. Perhaps only a fellow printer can appreciate
the subtleties of Grabhorn's choices of type styles and sizes, but by the use of Weiss
Titling, Koch Antiqua, and a nineteenth-century back-sloping script, this master
created the most unusual American wine label in my opinion.

The second is that of Ridge Vineyards, designed in 1964 by James Robertson and Bruce Montgomery, to my eye the most enduringly modern label in
the country. The designers picked the contemporary type of Hermann Zapf, called
Optima. Listings of the maker, variety of grape, location or name of vineyard, and *See* FIGURE 9 p. 323
date are stacked vertically in the same size of sans serif capitals. These entries are
separated into a grid system by colored rules, forming boxes, with the words justified on the left margin, ragged on the right, allowing for entries of differing lengths

to be inserted, depending upon the kind and source of the wine. This was a brilliant solution to the problem of adapting one label to the full line of a vintner. Another innovation of Robertson and Montgomery was the joining of the front and back label, which nicely balances the strong bracket of stacked capitals with a simple line drawing of a basket of grapes.

See FIGURE 10 p. 324

   The third label is from the Robert Mondavi Winery, designed in 1966 by Mallette Dean and James E. Beard. I consider this the most classically beautiful label in the United States. The striking architecture of the then new winery is shown in perspective, and the artist was licensed to add tall trees that later grew to conform with his rendering. Dean's expertise as a wood engraver provided an image appropriate to the scale of a label. Likewise, his experience as a book illustrator and printer assured the compatibility of pictorial and typographic segments. Beard set the type, certainly the smallest used by any of the major wineries. Twelve- and fourteen-point Kennerley capitals are employed for the company and varietal names. Only three sizes of this Goudy typeface appear (including one size of italic). Yet this very economy, the wide letterspacing and leading between lines, and the surrounding white space give clarity and distinction to the Mondavi label.

ANDREW HOYEM

VII.4

UNDERSTANDING A CALIFORNIA LABEL

by DORIS MUSCATINE

FOR WINEDRINKERS WHO CAN UNDERSTAND THE SIGNIFI-CANCE OF THE LANGUAGE, THE STRICT LEGAL REQUIRE-MENTS FOR LABELING IN THE UNITED STATES PROVIDE practical information about what they are drinking. In general, labels contain the following information, of which several statements are mandatory.* (Since new

---

 * For a more detailed description of label regulations, see Chapter 9.

legal requirements took effect on 1 January 1983, currently available wines have been bottled under two sets of regulations, the later usually the more stringent.)

First, the wine must bear a *brand name*. Second, the label must give the *class* or *type*. Class includes grape wine, table wine, dessert wine, sparkling wine and champagne, wine from fruit and other agricultural products, aperitif wine, retsina, and imitation wine, all of which must bear certain qualifying designations. Type includes varietal wine, that is, one named after a grape, such as Sauvignon Blanc or Zinfandel; or generic, such as red or white table wine; semi-generic, such as burgundy or rhine; or proprietary, with an invented name such as Ripple, Thunderbird, or Emerald Dry. If named after a grape, the wine must contain a minimum of 75 percent of that variety (51 percent before 1 January 1983). Any blend can go into the others.

Third, nearly all wines must give some *appellation of origin*; it is mandatory for varietal and semi-generic wines. For wines that use the designation "California," 100 percent of the wine must be from grapes grown and finished in the state. If the appellation is a county, the percentage is 75. In cases of "established viticultural areas," such as Napa Valley, the figure is 85 percent. Where the label names more than one state or county, all of the grapes must come from the places listed and the percentage from each be given.

Fourth, the label must provide the *name and address of the bottler*, or the name and actual bottling location, or (until 1 January 1985) the name and the bottler's principal place of business. The modes of listing the bottler are more confusing than revealing to the average label reader. "Bottled by" means no more than that, giving no clue to the source of the wine itself. However, "cellared and bottled by," "vinted and bottled by," "perfected and bottled by," or "blended and bottled by" means that the bottler may also have blended, or otherwise put the finishing touches on, wine produced elsewhere. In cases where the bottler has fermented at least 10 percent of the wine, the label may read "made and bottled by." If the bottler has fermented and finished 75 percent (formerly 51 percent), the label wording is "produced and bottled by."

In general, table wines (grape wines with an alcohol content of not more than 14 percent) have the option of giving the *alcohol content* on the label (and legally it may vary by as much as 1.5 percent of the amount stated) or of using a type designation, such as light table wine or red table wine. Wines containing more than 14 percent alcohol must state the percentage (which in this case can vary by 1 percent). Although for tax purposes these are designated dessert wines, they include many table wines with higher than normal alcohol. If grape brandy has been added to a dessert wine, it may be designated as follows: sherry (17 to 24 percent alcohol); and angelica, madeira, muscatel, or port (18 to 24 percent alcohol). The tastes and aromas must also be typical of their kind. Twenty-four percent alcohol is the upper limit for dessert wines.

It is mandatory to give the *percentage of any foreign wine* named on a label and blended with an American wine. Otherwise, all other information on a label (beyond that already described) is optional. However, a term such as "estate bottled," optional though it may be, must meet legal requirements when it is used. "Estate bottled" refers to wine made entirely on the premises of a winery from grapes grown on its own land in the same viticulturally defined area. "Vintner grown" or "proprietor grown" is used by wineries that do not technically now meet the requirements for "estate bottled," possibly for no more significant a reason than that their vineyards span two areas, or that they grow grapes in one and make wine in another. If the name of a special vineyard appears on the label, another optional but increasingly popular designation, it must include a geographic appellation and the wine contain grapes at least 95 percent from that property. Naming a vintage year is also optional, but should it be used, 95 percent of the grapes in the wine must have been grown in that year (with a 5 percent allowance for "topping"—replacing wine lost by evaporation during aging).

Many wineries add descriptive terms or provide information, sometimes encyclopedic, on the amount of sugar at picking or the residual sugar at bottling, or give the total acidity, or tell whether the wine was fined or clarified. Although most such additions are not regulated specifically, no label can give false or deceptive statements, and the contents of every label are subject to approval before use and to subsequent verification by the government during unannounced audits. Since there is no legal sanction for such terms as "private reserve" or "special selection," they have no reliable meaning but are often used, especially by small wineries, to distinguish a special lot of wine. When the letters "B.W." plus a figure appear after the bottler's name, they indicate the federal bonded winery identification number and, until 1 January 1985, are not mandatory. Foreign wines sold in the United States must comply with similar requirements, as well as the requirements of their country of origin.

Besides regulating information given, the Bureau of Alcohol, Tobacco and Firearms (BATF) also has regulations governing the design of the label. Among them are specifications for the size of type (for example, all mandatory information on containers of more than 187 millimeters, except the alcoholic content, must be in script, type, or printing not smaller than 2 millimeters and must be substantially more conspicuous than descriptive matter). Other requirements concern the language used (in most cases it must be English, but the exceptions are many); the physical location of the label (it must not obscure government stamps); the manner of affixing it to the bottle (*very* firmly); and the prohibitions governing designs, devices, graphics, and pictorial or emblematic representations that appear on it. Bureaucratic interpretations of these rules sometimes produce comic results, as, for instance, in the following case of the Goines/Kenwood label.

Every year since 1978, Kenwood Vineyards of Sonoma has released a limited bottling of a fine varietal wine with a special label presenting an original work by an outstanding California artist. To launch the series, they selected a 1975 Cabernet Sauvignon from Alexander Valley grapes, and commissioned a design by David Lance Goines, a Berkeley artist whose posters reside in the permanent collections of New York's Museum of Modern Art, Washington, D.C.'s Smithsonian, and the Musée des Arts Decoratifs in Paris. The design he submitted, an innocent art nouveau nude female recumbent in a bucolic hillside vineyard, was rejected by the BATF, which ruled that "the drawing of the young lady must be deleted. More specifically, the Bureau regards the picture as 'obscene or indecent' under the regulations 27 CFR (a)(3) which are attached." The relevant sections of 27 CFR, the federal regulations concerning labeling and advertising of wine, read:

Prohibited practices—(a) Statements on labels. *Containers of wine, or any label on such containers, or any individual covering, carton, or other wrapper of such container, or any written, printed, graphic, or other matter accompanying such container to the consumer shall not contain:*

. . . (3) Any statement, design, device, or representation which is obscene or indecent.

In response to the BATF's ruling, Goines wrote to Marty Lee, vice-president and co-owner of Kenwood:

27 April 1978
Dear Mr. Lee:
Well, this keeps my batting average at a thousand. I've never gotten anything past those blue-nosed bastards the first time yet. I will of course do another design—that's part of the deal. It's nobody's fault that we're stuck with these turkeys, so I'll get another design to you a.s.a.p. It really burns my butt that the design can't be used, as I am very proud of it. Maybe we can come up with some other application. Just to comfort you, they're all going to hell when they die.
　　　　　　　　　　　　　　　　　　　Yrs faithfully,
　　　　　　　　　　　　　　　　　　　David Lance Goines

II.

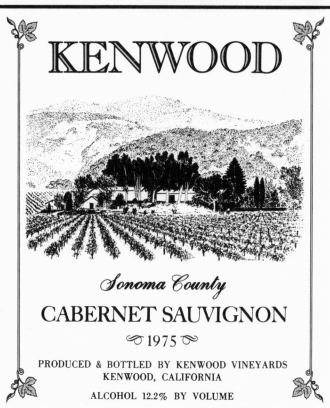

Three versions of a special Kenwood Vineyards label with watercolor linoleum cut in the upper portion designed by David Lance Goines in 1978. This label introduced Kenwood's California Artist Series of wines, a limited annual bottling of Cabernet Sauvignon with an original label designed by a California artist of renown. Goines produced these three renditions of his design before the third received the official approval of the Bureau of Alcohol, Tobacco and Firearms. The first two versions are reproduced full size; the third version is photo-reduced.

In the new design, Goines painted the same scene with the offending female's flesh removed, but her recumbent skeleton in the same position. The new label did not pass this time around either. "Rejected—particularly in light of current opinion on the fetal alcohol syndrome and alcoholism." When the third version, a similar landscape with all figures removed, gained BATF approval, Goines remarked, "In the final 'accepted' version, we'll just have to imagine that the girl is still on the hill, but on the other side where we can't see her and be morally offended by her pretty figure."

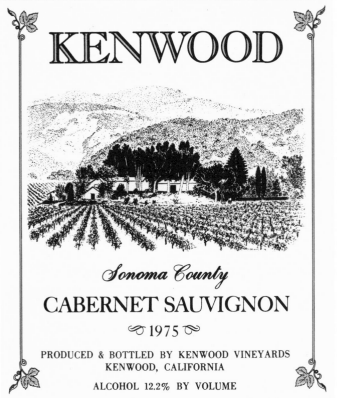

12.

13.

BIBLIOGRAPHIC NOTE

There are two sources for information on federal laws on the labeling and advertising of wine: United States Treasury Department, Bureau of Alcohol, Tobacco and Firearms, *Federal Labeling and Advertising of Wine* (Washington, D.C.); and *Liquor Control Law Reports* (Chicago: Commerce Clearing House). The Commerce Clearing House publishes the reports as quickly as they come out in the *Federal Register*; the official government reports are generally issued sometime later.

VII.5

COLLECTING WINE LABELS

by ROY BRADY

THOUSANDS OF PEOPLE COLLECT BOTTLES AND HOLD VAST MEETINGS. FEW COLLECT LABELS, AND THEY IN FURTIVE ISOLATION. THAT SEEMS ODD TO ME since labels are far more informative, varied, and interesting (to a rational mind) than bottles. That is particularly true of wine labels. It seems only natural that anyone interested in wine, and by nature a collector, would gravitate toward wine labels. Collectors of every variety of paper collectible are so numerous that there are ephemera societies in this country and Britain, but no label collector societies. Are not labels more interesting than bookmarks, calling cards, streetcar transfers, or (heaven help us) the autographs of politicians? People do collect all of those things. I collected labels for thirty years before discovering another devotee, and he was in England. In the four years since, I have compiled a list of about forty collectors worldwide.

Labels can be collected at any level of seriousness, from the desultory saving of the label from an interesting wine or from a momentous occasion (though accumulating streaked labels shakily inscribed "Drunk on Boopsie's birthday '82" argues a certain frivolity of mind) to the determined collecting of every possible label in some particular category, e.g., the Napa Valley, as serious stamp collectors do. The serious collector seeks long vintage runs, every sort of variant, special purpose labels, and whatever else can reasonably be discriminated. These have not been worked out with any detail compared to, say, coin collecting.

I collect California labels and several other smaller categories seriously, and all labels to some degree. California labels have been pullulating even faster than wineries, because the new wineries seem more disposed to frequent and sweeping redesign than were the old. And many of the old have caught the redesign fever. It cannot, alas, be said with any conviction that new is better. After Repeal most wineries contented themselves with uninspired job printer labels, some drab, some garish in purple and gold. Among the few wineries that went to original label designs before World War II were Wente Bros., Beaulieu Vineyard, and Louis Martini. Until Martini's recent program of redesign, their label alone remained unchanged after forty years. Wente and Beaulieu labels have been modified, but are recognizably descended from their predecessors. Everything else has changed.

California wineries used to be reluctant to give any more information than the law demanded, and the law demanded little. They did not have to reveal so much as their true name or address. The paucity of information can make identification of the sources of old labels difficult. The wineries took a name-rank-and-serial-number approach to informing the public. Few wineries wanted to disclose vintage years, and by the late fifties only a handful still did. Even Martini and Wente dropped vintages on some wines. Brother Timothy said Christian Bros. wines would be vintage-dated only over his dead body. Now they are vintage-dated and Bro. Tim is just fine.

Back labels were usually no more than bits of empty puffery about the winery or its eponymous founder. Occasionally they put on lot, bin, cask, or blend numbers. Mostly those were a tribute to the invention of the winemaker rather than descriptive of any character of the wine. Now winemakers are panting to tell all—and deadly accurate all at that. They time the induction of the malolactic with signals from the Naval Observatory and insist upon telling you the pH to eight significant figures though hardly anybody knows what it means. Their labels are informative to the point of garrulity, nay yet unto logorrhea. The new labels, despite their not uncommon excesses, are much to be preferred to the old in giving an abundance of accurate (with the notable exception of founding dates) information. A large collection will come to have historical value, and future scholars will doubtless be able to deduce much history from it.

DESIGN OF LABELS

Labels can also be collected for their designs. Most new wineries make an effort to get attractive labels, and frequent changes argue a continuing effort. A few have engaged recognized artists, a trend probably started by Château Mouton-Rothschild with its 1945 label and continued to the present with names like Chagall, Dali, Picasso, and Warhol. In California Sebastian Titus is perhaps best known. Earl Thollander did the Conn Creek label and some for Domaine Chandon. David Lance Goines did the famous trio for the 1975 Kenwood Cabernet Sauvignon. Some wineries try too hard for novelty with bizarre shapes slotted, skewed, notched, knobbed, tapered, and tortured. Some are too wide and some are too tall. No one has improved on a simple rectangle of pleasing proportions.

WHERE TO GET LABELS

According to the English publication *The Ephemerist*, Clive Bingley's recent book on printed ephemera says that they "are generally distinguished by being difficult to arrange and to find." As to finding wine labels, there is scarcely any market in them as there is for established collectibles like stamps and coins. There are two disadvantages to that. First, no scale of values for labels exists. Second, the collector has no systematic way to add to his collection. Great rarities apart, the stamp collector can get within a reasonable time almost anything he wants, and he will have a good idea of the cost. The label collector has no such recourse. It would be very difficult to get all the Gallo labels used in 1970, but trifling to get all American stamps issued in 1970. But the very difficulty of collecting labels is one of its peculiar charms.

Most collectors begin by taking labels from bottles they have drunk, a very limited source. And even if they get sympathetic friends to save large numbers of bottles for them, they presently find it takes too much time to remove, clean, and press labels. In addition, the growing use of new non-water-soluble adhesives greatly increases time of removal and causes a lot of damage. That and the increasing use of soft papers result in a lot of sorry-looking labels.

Diligence in writing to wineries will yield a considerable number of labels, but the collector has little control over what they will be. Some obdurate wineries will not accede to the most impassioned of pleas, even if duly accompanied by a self-addressed return envelope decked with the gayest commemoratives the post office has to offer. Wineries that do respond most often ignore specific requests such as for complete sets, separate vintage labels, back labels, and private labels. Even if you know the winemaker and visit him personally, you may miss something. I was once at Stony Hill with Fred McCrea who set about getting together all his labels for me. He picked up one and started to put it back saying, "You wouldn't want that." Would I not? It was a delightful label in green and black on textured beige paper he had made for his own use. Writing for labels is worthwhile, but it is not sufficient for achieving completeness or balance.

Some winemakers resent requests for labels. They feel that anyone who wants their labels should buy bottles and take them off. To the collector that does not appear so luminous a method. It would entail buying a great deal more wine than he could drink, and not a little he would not want to drink. It would take much time and much money. The lamentable condition of labels so obtained has been noted above. Getting friends to save labels can be effective if one has the right sort of friends—kindly and willing as a start. Drinking interesting wines is a further step. A habit of visiting wineries and remembering to gather labels is another. Such friends are to be treasured. Though they are not methods I myself favor, I know collectors who poke through dumps for bottles (the condition of their labels attests to that), and others who, with permission or surreptitiously, cut labels from cases in wine shops. Trading with other collectors is an excellent, if supplementary, method. To trade one must already have labels obtained by some other device. One must also find other collectors. That may be slow at first, since in this country there are no collectors' clubs as there are in Europe.

While few stamps or coins of the country can have eluded the collectors' cunning nets, wine labels remain uncharted and unknown. Labels are evanescent. It is their normal destiny to be thrown out with the bottle after the wine is drunk. A few bottles are kept as mementos, but they usually elude the dust bin only until some other whim-borne keepsake usurps their place. Long-cellared labels often decompose, and indications are that few labels have been deliberately kept in the past. We will not have much idea of how many old labels exist until they begin to acquire enough value to coax them from their hiding places. My guess is that, apart from a few special cases, old labels are very scarce. As a rule, wineries do not keep labels long after a bottling run, but occasionally they survive through neglect. At the end of Simi's somnolent period, in about 1972, I was given free run of the label room. Apparently nothing had been discarded in forty years. I came away with several complete sets. In a similar case, the new owners of a winery put the old labels in little packets for the idly curious in the tasting room.

The only time a historically significant collection of labels can be formed is while the labels are current. The principal reasons that many old stamps exist are probably that people began to collect and value them at an early time and because people are inclined to keep old letters indefinitely. Neither condition applies to labels.

We shall doubtless never know what California's first label was. The earliest known reference to a California label dates from 1819, when the governor of California sent a request to Mission San Diego:

His Excellency, Viceroy Count de Venadito, desires to have a dozen bottles of wine from your mission in order to send them to the king, our august monarch, Don Fernando VII. Let each bottle be labeled thus: Wine of New California from Mission San Diego. *

If the request was granted, as doubtless it was, the labels would have been hand-written, for the nearest printing press was far away in Mexico.

The earliest known reference to what certainly was a printed label occurs in *A Yankee in the Gold Rush*, a collection of letters from Franklin A. Buck to his sister. A letter of 1852 written in Weaverville, Trinity County, says, ". . . we are able to indulge occasionally in the vintages of California in the shape of bottles of wine beautifully put up by Keller of Los Angeles."† The earliest surviving label is from the mid-fifties.

* Teiser and Harroun, *Winemaking in California*, pp. 3–4.
† Peninou and Greenleaf, *A Directory of California Wine Growers and Wine Makers in 1860*, p. 19.

COSTS

It has been said that the label is an ideal collectible because it costs nothing. I knew a man who said that wine is an ideal hobby because it doesn't take any time—you do it while you are eating. That is not the only foolish thing he said.

Beyond the most rudimentary level, collecting labels does cost money. It costs, to be sure, nothing but time to soak labels off bottles that happen to come to hand. It costs a few pennies each to put them in some sort of binder. Handsome binders can cost quite a few pennies each. That is the beginning. From the moment you allow a label to influence your choice of a wine, your foot is set on the road to perdition. How tempting it is to buy a dozen different wines rather than a dozen of one. You will pay more for some of the wines and some will be less good. You give up quantity discounts. Upon receiving a merchant's catalog, I have sent off an order for a hundred single bottles with, incidentally, a hundred enticing labels. In restaurants I have ordered a $25 bottle knowing a $15 bottle was better. At the extreme, I have bought a bottle knowing the wine to be no good.

You find yourself driving to distant wineries you probably would not otherwise have visited. You drive miles to pick up bottles saved by friends. You tip waiters to save bottles and bus boys to carry them to the car. If you are completely crackers, you have expensive stationery printed for label requests. Postage on requests mounts up. So does international airmail for trading. The costs of collecting become so entangled with other costs that there is no saying what it really costs. I have always liked to explore the widest possible range of wines, a taste that cannot be neatly separated from the quest for labels. Similarly, I have long enjoyed visiting wineries quite apart from the label possibilities. The costs of serious collecting surely exceed a dollar a label. Costs in time are formidable too, and yet more difficult to estimate.

Actually, there is a minuscule market in labels. Once in a great while, an antiquarian bookseller or a dealer in paper ephemera will offer a small group of labels. In the past, prices have averaged 25¢ to about $1 a label, with one extreme exception. In Montpellier I paid about $18 for an ornate, embossed 1842 Champagne label. Much less frequently, an old album of labels shows up. I have found two in thirty years. One was of California labels from the thirties. The more exciting contained about 300 labels from wines that had apparently been sold in Germany, though some were French. The German labels were from vintages from 1846 through 1868. The price was $300. In recent years, a number of lots have been sold at auction in London and Paris. If a market for labels develops, it will certainly increase the cost of collecting, though it will probably reduce some of the incidental costs now incurred.

CARE OF A COLLECTION

I have become convinced that organization and presentation of a collection are of the highest importance. Maintenance is no problem, the main requirement being a clean dry dark storage place. The space required becomes a consideration with large collections—more than 10,000 labels, say. Good organization is needed for satisfaction in viewing or using a collection. It is essential for rapid determination of what is, or is not, in a collection. It should be possible to find a given label in a large collection about as quickly as the card for a given book can be found in the catalogue of a large library. (The comparison is between card and label, not between book and label, because they are much of a size.) The laws, geography, and structure of the wine industry in each producing country provide a basis for organization. Beyond that the individual collector has to devise his own organization, which will be affected by the size, growth rate, area of specialization, and numerous special circumstances.

French and German labels are easily classified compared with Californian ones. California lacks a close connection between wine and geography. My collection is classified first by county and second by winery in alphabetical order. Within each winery there is a more or less complex classification depending on the particular circumstances of each. With important wines, e.g., Beaulieu Private Reserve Cabernet Sauvignon, the labels are mounted in chronological order in their own section.

The many peculiarities of the California wine industry require many judgments, and no classification is entirely satisfactory. A common problem is that names once attached to wineries now pass freely from hand to hand as brand names. The once proud name of Fountain Grove has become a brand owned by Martini & Prati Wines. Perhaps most curious is the series of transactions by which the Perelli-Minetti Winery, a name itself scarcely known to the public, became the owner of some 200 once independent names, including Greystone. The original Greystone Winery in St. Helena is owned by Christian Brothers (whose own legal name is Mont La Salle Vineyards), but they cannot use the name.

There is the strange case of the various Souverain wineries and their derivatives. The California wine industry is in a ceaseless and bewildering state of change that would have given Heracleitos fits. To complicate things, there are free-floating names attached to no particular winery; a person is free to set up a label and sell under it wine gathered hither and yon. Round Hill was such a name, but now it has become attached to an actual winery in St. Helena. Several new wineries began by using one name for the winery and another for the label and then took the label name for the winery name. Such goings-on make classification difficult. The name as entity seems the best approach—with numerous exceptions, of course. Changes of ownership and other details can be explained in annotations.

For mounting labels, I went to plastic protector sheets in three-ring binders about twenty-five years ago. They have various advantages—protection, flexibility, ease of mounting, moderate cost, and so on. Whether they are suitable in the very long run I do not know. Much of the oldest plastic has warped. Now I have gone to the thinner and more expensive mylar plastic, which the manufacturers say will never warp. Hitler built a thousand-year *Reich*—heigh ho.

Over the years I have come to have strong feelings about the physical arrangement of labels, enough to have remounted all the older labels. The appearance of a well-mounted collection is infinitely more agreeable than that of a carelessly mounted one. Labels should be mounted vertically, except in rare cases where size makes that impossible. They should never overlap or be crowded. A pleasing balance should be struck between borders and spaces between labels. Good arrangement requires more plastic sheets, but the aesthetic difference between that and a hodgepodge is well worth it.

PROBLEMS OF COLLECTING

Collecting labels is for the venturesome because nearly all the rules remain to be defined. What is a label? Presumably it is all printed paper affixed to a bottle by the producer or bottler. That would include main label, back label, separate vintage label, and so forth. If any of those are missing, the label must be regarded as incomplete and accordingly worth little, as would be a damaged or dirty label. In either case, if the label were very rare, or unknown in better state, its value would be much greater. The use of multiple labels is a problem for the collector because once they are off the bottle they may become confused unless he annotates them on the back at once. If a main label turns up without a vintage there are three possibilities: (1) it was a nonvintage wine, (2) a separate vintage label is missing, (3) the vintage was somehow left off, making the label defective. Even having a bottle in hand is no guarantee that one knows what labels were intended to be on it. I had two bottles of Girard Chardonnay 1981 without back labels, yet I subsequently got back labels from the winery.

Separate vintage labels make possible the creation of ghost wines. I have been told that there was no regular B.V. Cabernet 1964 because all of it was declared Private Reserve, but one could readily bring together a main label from another vintage and a 1964 vintage label from another wine. There would be no way of detecting the deception without special knowledge of the situation.

Collectors will doubtless seek variant labels as stamp collectors seek variants. There are many. Labels exist with some having the vintage printed in black, others in red. There are many variations in typefaces. Wineries sometimes adopt a new label design when a particular wine is partly sold, so that the label exists in both new and old forms. A few years ago, Rutherford Hill decided to choose between two new designs by test marketing. The design that lost out is scarce. Another winery printed 35,000 of a new design, did not like it, and destroyed all but the few hundred I got. There are many other such cases to be catalogued.

Some overly cautious producers stamp "specimen" or an equivalent to indicate that the label is not to be used on a bottle. Are they to be regarded as less valuable because they are not quite the real thing, or more valuable because they are probably scarcer than the real thing? When bottles are numbered, there may be extra labels lacking numbers. They are incomplete and, presumably, less valuable. Labels with conspicuous errors are rare and should be worth a great deal more. I treasure a Weibel label reading "Grey Reisling." Some producers print advertising on the backs of their surplus labels, which are handed out at wine tastings and included in promotional mailings, creating another variant. Some have printed the label on a larger sheet and added advertising on the front. What of those?

Once in a while, a winery has a different label made for use on the outside of cases. There were barrel labels when people bought small barrels of wine. Some labels are stamped, handwritten, or overprinted with such phrases as "Sample—not for sale" and "For analytical purposes only." Moving further afield, there are bottles with the labels printed, painted, or stenciled on the glass. Do we keep those? And wine cans? My oldest label is a clay amphora handle from second-century A.D. Palestine with the identity of the wine stamped in Greek. There are a lot of questions to answer and a lot of information to gather if labels are to become a mature field of collecting. And one could write at enormously greater length on the practical aspects of forming and maintaining a collection.

BIBLIOGRAPHIC NOTE

There is little literature on wine labels and their collecting—a small book in German, a small book in French. I have seen only the first, despite years of looking. Articles about labels are also scarce, and those about California labels are mostly frothy stuff. An exception is the handsomely printed little booklet by Yolande Shephard, *Mallette Dean, Artist & Printer, His Influence on Napa Valley & California Wine Labels* (San Francisco: Richard A. Gleeson Library, University of San Francisco, 1982). Though few wine lovers will likely recognize the name of that quiet man, they will recognize his work. He designed the Robert Mondavi, Mayacamas, Inglenook Cask, Heitz, and Chateau Montelena labels. One could write a good many thousands of words about the history of the wine label.

VII.6

Note: Corkscrews

by BROTHER TIMOTHY DIENER, F.S.C.

IN THE DAYS WHEN ALL EDUCATED GENTLEMEN WROTE IN Latin, such a common thing as a corkscrew was handled by their servants. It was beneath the dignity of any proper author to study, mention, or record the history of so plebeian an instrument. At least it seems that way to me when I look for, and find, so little information about the history of this small tool. No one knows for sure the name of the inventor, the country of origin, or even the century when the first corkscrew appeared on the world's stage.

A rare passage in Roman literature is a mention by Horace of corks "used for closing the mouths of wine jars."[*] If the corkscrew did not exist at that time, it may be presumed that loosely fitted corks were allowed to project above the bottle neck so that they could be pulled with the fingers. In 1530, John Palsgrave said "corke" was in use "for stopping the necks of bottles."[†] In 1676, J. Worlidge reported that cider was tightly corked, the bottles stored on their sides or "noses downward" to keep the corks moist and therefore maintain their tight fit.[‡]

A first cousin of the corkscrew is the gun cleaning screw, either double or single pointed, that, attached to a ramrod, removed unfired charges or other materials from muzzle-loading guns of all sizes, up to and including cannon. There was mention of a bullet extractor in a publication titled *Gun Makers' Rates* in England in 1631.[§] Anyone who could make such a bullet extractor could also make a corkscrew. Did the gun cleaning tool come before the corkscrew, or vice versa? No one knows.

Earliest mention, that I have found, of a screw for pulling corks was made by W. Morice in *Coena Quasi* in 1657.[**] As with many novelties in the development of our language, this new thing had many names. It was called a "worme,"

[*]   Charles R. Beard, "Corkscrews," *The Connoisseur* 84 (1929): 28–34, quotation at p. 29.
[†]   Ibid.
[‡]   J. W. Gent [J. Worlidge], *Vinetum Britannicum; or, A Treatise of Cider . . .* (London, 1676), pp. 107–8.
[§]   Watney and Babbidge, *Corkscrews for Collectors*, p. 13.
[**]   Beard, "Corkscrews," p. 30.

"corkdrawer," "bottle-screw," "bottlescrew," "bottle scrue," "corkscrue," "bottle screw," and finally a "corkscrew." Samuel Henshall, an English parson, received the first patent for improved corkscrew design in 1795. He placed a "button" just above the screw so that when the screw was entirely in the cork, the button would press down on it. With further turning of the handle, the cork would rotate, breaking its adhesion to the bottle neck, making it more easily pullable. His idea worked. Some modern corkscrews are made with such a button.

A most handsome and sophisticated new stroke of genius was the 1802 invention of Edward Thomason, who sought to make cork pulling easier while also avoiding the necessity of using one's fingers to remove the cork from the screw. He said in his *Memoirs*: "I produced a combination of the three screws working together, and following each other, so that, on piercing the cork with the point of the worm, and continuing to turn the handle, the cork was drawn out, and by turning the handle the contrary way, the cork was discharged from the worm."* The beautiful workmanship and the efficiency of operation of a Thomason can only be properly appreciated by someone who has pulled a cork or two with it. Incidentally, it appears that Thomason produced the first patented corkscrew with a brush on the handle for removal of dust, cobwebs, and particles of sealing wax from the neck of the bottle. The Thomason corkscrew may be called automatic in that the turning of the handle penetrates the cork and pulls it, and the reverse turning removes the cork from the screw. No upward pull is required of the operator. A modern version, said to be an exact copy, is made in Bristol, England and called "The Vulcan."

Lund's London Rack corkscrew of 1855 incorporated rack and pinion gears. After the corkscrew was in the cork, turning the pinion gear caused the cork to rise out of the bottle neck into an open bell or neck stand. Some modern single lever and double lever corkscrews use gears to raise the cork. There is a two-piece puller, consisting of a simple corkscrew with a small hole in the handle and a pair of levers fitting into the hole and onto the bottle neck in such a way that when squeezed together, the handles raise the cork. Called Lund's Lever, this was also patented in 1855. The popular waiter's corkscrew, made like a pocket knife, has a folding corkscrew and a folding fulcrum (also called a "boot" or "jack-lever") and is often equipped with a knife blade or curved hook-blade for cutting the lead foil or other neck capsule that covers the cork. Folding neatly and fitting in the pocket comfortably, it has been accepted by most waiters as an indispensable tool of their trade. Carl F. A. Wienke, a German civil engineer, is the father of all such waiter's corkscrews, having obtained German, English and American patents in 1883.†

* Watney and Babbidge, *Corkscrews for Collectors*, pp. 51–52.
† Ibid., pp. 69, 111.

A modern double lever corkscrew called the "Brevetto" lifts the cork about an eighth of an inch each time the spring-loaded handles are squeezed.

Some corkscrews have an open-sided bell, or neck stand, and a long screw that penetrates fully through the cork. This allows the cork to climb up the screw and into the bell as the handle is turned. One such, the "Surprise," was registered by George Willetts in 1884.[*] "Screwpull," patented in 1979, works in the same way. This invention of Herbert Allen of Houston, Texas, incorporates several improvements. The screw is a well-designed, sharp-pointed helix, coated with a teflon-like, antifriction material. The bell, or neck stand, is flexible but strong plastic, with bottle rests and bottle grips that allow one hand to hold both corkscrew and bottle while the other turns the handle. Comfortable in the hand and very efficient, "Screwpull" is highly recommended.

A long-term favorite is a two-handled corkscrew that seems to be a distant relative of the Thomason. A smaller, upper handle inserts the screw into the cork; a larger handle, fastened to a threaded shaft, which turns inside the threaded top of the bell, pulls the cork when rotated. The working parts, except for the steel screw, may be made of wood, metal, horn, or other materials. Very rare and smooth working is an antique brass windlass that fits over the bottle neck and helps to pull the cork by the turn of a crank, which winds up a cord looped around the corkscrew handle. The only device of this kind that I have seen is in my possession. Bought in London in 1979, it was patented by J. E. Walton in England in 1884.

Bottles for perfume, medicine, mouthwash, hair color, cider, root beer, soda water, mineral water, sparkling water, beer, mead, wine, distilled spirits, and many other liquids were closed with corks prior to the invention of the metal crown cap in 1892. So it is not surprising to find small and large corkscrews, some designed for ladies and others for men, and some made of precious metals, occasionally set with jewels such as rubies. Artists who worked with gold and silver and other skilled workers competed for the favor of their customers with ornamental and artistic designs as varied as their makers and buyers.

Frustration with bad corkscrews that ripped holes in good corks drove me to study the function and efficiency of this necessary tool. My studies motivated me to collect some object lessons, the good and the bad. The great diversity of interesting things to collect led me on from one thing to another in what may be an endless search for every kind and style, every form and shape of corkscrew. Whether collecting is a good or bad habit, it tends to become addictive.

The one definitive book on the subject in English,[†] an out-of-print article,[‡] and the study of patent office records help the collector to understand cork-

---

[*]   Ibid., p. 135.
[†]   Ibid.
[‡]   Paul Frederickson, "Corkscrews That Work," *Wine Review*, May 1946.

screw function and to learn what was once made and, therefore, may yet be found at some antique shop, garage sale, swap meet, or flea market. For readers of German, there is Manfred Heckmann's *Korkenzieher, Einführung in den höheren Genuss*, which the Wine Appreciation Guild of San Francisco is in the process of preparing for publication in English translation under the title "Corkscrews: An Introduction to Their Appreciation." The Wine Institute, a trade association of California wineries, deserves credit for initiating the first scientific analysis of corkscrew design and function. *Wine Review* published the results in an eight-page, illustrated paper, "Corkscrews That Work," in May 1946.* It gave proof that many corkscrews with a central metal core will damage considerable cork tissue as they go into the cork and then rip the broken fragments out when pulled, leaving the damaged cork in the bottle. Obviously, these are bad corkscrews. A good corkscrew will have a true helical blade that is open centered. Its point will be sharp so that it will penetrate the cork with very little breakage of tissue, and all of the remaining screw will follow the path of the point. Examination of a cork pulled and removed from such a good corkscrew shows a minimum of damage. By gluing the cork into the bottle neck and then trying to pull it, the Wine Institute discovered that a good corkscrew could exert up to a 300-pound pull before ripping a hole in the cork. Regular everyday corks may sometimes require a pull of more than 100 pounds. This is why it is important to have some leverage device to multiply muscle power.

There are cork removal devices that are not corkscrews. Highly esteemed among port fanciers is the port tongs, an instrument like a large pair of pliers, designed to remove the cork of a valuable old crusted port without disturbing the contents of the bottle. A wine cradle or basket is used to hold the bottle so that the cork is above any contact with the wine. The jaws of the tongs are heated red hot and placed around the bottle neck just below the cork to heat the glass. As soon as the tongs are removed, a cold, damp towel is squeezed around the bottle neck, cooling the hot glass so quickly that it cracks, and the bottle neck, with cork, falls into the towel. Any jarring or shaking of the bottle could cause the crust, adhering to the walls of the bottle, to come loose and float freely in the wine.

In 1879 Lucian Mumford took out an American patent for what is today a popular cork puller. It has two flat blades that go between cork and bottle neck. Inserting it with a rocking motion makes one blade move at a time; rotating it while pulling gently draws out the cork without damaging it at all. Mumford named his unit the "Magic Cork Extractor." Today it is commonly called "Ah-So" after one trade name on the market. Humorously referred to as the "Butler's Friend," it could be secretly used and the cork replaced without evidence of damage. This

* Ibid.

would enable a disloyal butler to steal some good old wine and replace it with an inferior product. The shortcoming of these two-pronged cork pullers is their tendency to push a very soft, old cork down into the wine as the operator tries to get the blades between cork and bottle neck. It is a frustrating experience to have the cork drop into the wine.

In my collection, I have a little gadget with three short pins to push down into a cork. Then the entire thing is rotated to remove the cork. Amazingly, it works. But I am always fearful that the pins will bend or break. Called "U-NEEK," it was registered in the United States on 30 December 1947 by Edgar V. Phillips.* Another odd design is the "E-Z Cork Puller." It has a single flat blade with four barbs on one edge. Slipped down between cork and bottle neck and turned 90°, it forces the barbs into the cork, then pulls it straight up. Usually it works. But occasionally it will simply rip a small hole on the side of the cork.

A number of removers on the market are hollow needles with a hole near the point. All are modern. They push through the cork and use a propellant gas to blow it out of the bottle. Carbon dioxide was the first gas used, then hand-pumped air, and lastly Freon. All can work satisfactorily. The gas does not seem to harm the wine. But I do not care for these things: two types frequently run out of gas and all three are susceptible to needles bending, breaking, or falling out of the sockets.

After reading all the above, it will not be a surprise to learn that the author belongs to the International Correspondence of Corkscrew Addicts, a group of fifty people who collect, classify, and research corkscrews and communicate with one another about them. The group's bylaws require members to exchange photos of corkscrews every year. The word "correspondence" in the name means that members must correspond with one another. Founded mainly by Dr. Bernard M. Watney of London in 1974, the society now has members in eight countries. Sorry, there are no vacancies at the moment.

Hugh Johnson, the greatly respected English author, has said: "The invention of the cork is the most important event in the history of fine wine. . . . However well our ancestors may have been able to make their wine . . . it could never have reached anything like the point of soft, sweet perfection which a claret or burgundy can, if it is given the chance, today."† Naturally, I agree with Mr. Johnson. But, if the cork is important, so, too, is the corkscrew, the key needed to unlock the bottle so that the precious liquid imprisoned therein may be enjoyed.

---

* Watney and Babbidge, *Corkscrews for Collectors*, pp. 148–49.
† Johnson, *Wine*, p. 26.

BIBLIOGRAPHIC NOTE

In addition to sources cited in the footnotes, this essay draws on three articles by Bernard M. Watney: "Corkscrews for Collectors," *The Antique Collector*, June 1974; "Corkscrews," *Christie's Wine Review*, 1977; and "Corkscrews Rare and Strange," *Antique Collecting and Antique Finder*, June 1977. See also Brother Timothy Diener, "Corkscrews: An Armory of Gear to Open the Wine," in *The Encyclopedia of Collectibles* (Alexandria, Va.: Time-Life Books, 1978). The German original of Manfred Heckmann's *Korkenzieher, Einführung in den höheren Genuss* was published in 1979 by Mitchell Beazley, London. Those interested in pursuing the subject further may also wish to consult the following: Philos Blake, *Guide to American Corkscrew Patents*, vol. 1, *1860–1895*, vol. 2, *1896–1920* (New Castle, Del.: Bottlescrew Press, 1978, 1981); Donald Bull, *Beer Advertising Openers* and *Beer Advertising Corkscrews* (Trumbull, Conn.: Donald Bull, 1978); Bernard R. Levine, *Knifemakers of Old San Francisco* (San Francisco: Badger Books, 1977); and Evan Perry, *Corkscrews and Bottle Openers* (Aylesbury, Bucks.: Shire Publications, 1980).

VII.7

SOCIAL ORGANIZATIONS

by PAUL SCHOLTEN, M.D.

WINEDRINKING IN GROUPS IS AS OLD AS RECORDED HISTORY: THE BIBLE AND ANCIENT GREEK AND EGYPTIAN MANUSCRIPTS ARE REPLETE WITH TALES OF WINE PARTIES and tastings. Indeed, the word symposium comes from the original Greek custom of pairing wine and conversation, a far cry from the very dry conferences presently held under the same title. But while people have always gathered over wine to enjoy life and exchange ideas, it is a fairly recent idea that a social group actively study wine rather than just sample its pleasures. In the United States, social organizations formally devoted to wine really date only from the end of Prohibition in 1933, and their widespread proliferation and popularity only from about 1960, when wine became a fashionable drink. This coincided with the coming of age of the California wine industry and the production of many world-class wines. Suddenly, a subject that had been confined to a handful of connoisseurs became the hobby of thousands of

Americans. It was only natural that California, as the largest and one of the oldest vinifera grape growing areas in the United States, should produce the largest number of wine enthusiasts, interested in learning more about wine, its production, and its pleasures. Five major types of wine interest groups emerged: the Gourmet Societies, the Professional Organizations, the Robed Brotherhoods, the Special Interest Groups, and the Winetasting Groups.

THE GOURMET SOCIETIES

First on the U.S. wine scene was the International Wine and Food Society. Its founder and patron saint was André Louis Simon of London, a French-born Champagne salesman and journalist, who attributed his long life (he died in 1970 at the age of ninety-three) to good parentage and the daily consumption of wine. In 1933, with French wine sales in the Depression doldrums, Simon, encouraged by the French wine trade, joined with A. J. Symonds in founding the Wine and Food Society of London as a means of stimulating interest in wine and its consumption. The next year, following the repeal of Prohibition, Simon came to the United States on the same mission, visiting New York, Boston, Chicago, Los Angeles, and San Francisco, meeting with knowledgeable winedrinkers, and encouraging the formation of branches of the society. He was successful in all five cities. By early 1935, all of them had formed chapters. Growing to its present size of 144 chapters in twenty-one countries, the society serves as a model for many other American wine groups. Chapters vary in size from Muncie, Indiana's 5 members to New York's 410. In the United States, 32 chapters accept women as full members, 30 do not. The branches are loosely linked to London headquarters by dues and the society's quarterly magazine, which prints all dinner menus of the far-flung affiliates, as well as articles related to wine and food. Of the 62 U.S. branches, 23 are in California.

The San Francisco Wine and Food Society is fairly typical of the California chapters but different from the International Wine and Food Society's London original. San Francisco's 165 male members come from the city's financial district, professional ranks, and Social Register. Some are owners of fine California vineyards and wineries. Membership is by invitation only, with a waiting list of up to two years. Members of the London Society join by simply signing up and paying dues. In San Francisco, new members go through an extensive apprenticeship, first learning about wine as sommeliers at the group's dinners, then graduating to meal planning as members of dinner committees. The highest aspiration is a position on the Board of Governors, whose 15 members meet monthly to plan events and assign dinner chairmanships.

As with most chapters, the main activity of the San Franciscans is a monthly black-tie dinner, usually consisting of six to eight courses accompanied by five or six harmonizing wines. Months of planning, testing, and preparation go into a single evening's dining. First, the committee selects a basic menu, usually French-inspired, often with a regional theme such as Norman or Provençal cooking. Despite this French preference, the San Francisco society has covered the globe in a gastronomic sense, holding numerous Italian, Chinese, Spanish, Greek, and English banquets, as well as dinners honoring other cuisines. A recent Japanese dinner recreated a historic banquet served to the emperor and empress of Japan. Each of the ten courses was presented as a Zen work of art, with the food arranged for visual effect on Japanese plates of collector's quality, a different design for each course. Dinners featuring regional American foods have recreated an 1820s New England feast and an early California barbeque featuring an entire wild boar roasted on the spit.

The society's cellarmaster aids in selecting wines that complement the menu. In their early days, both the Los Angeles and San Francisco societies served only French or German wines, with an occasional port or sherry, but today at least half the wines served are Californian. Sometimes a single historic winery is the theme of a dinner at which its great vintages are served. The San Francisco chapter draws on an extensive cellar, started in 1940, when the fall of France alerted the Board of Governors to an approaching dry spell. They collected a purse and bought up whatever good Bordeaux and Burgundy was available locally. Added to a selection of the best California had to offer, these wines kept the San Francisco society drinking very well throughout World War II and became the nucleus of a 400-case cellar featuring the finest European and American wines. The wine committee, typical of most societies, meets regularly to taste what is best in the current market. Buying young and relatively inexpensive wine, then aging it properly, allows the San Francisco society to serve red wines that are mostly eighteen to twenty years old at much less than current market prices.

When they have completed a tentative menu and wine list, the dinner committee selects a restaurant and discusses food preparation and service with its manager and chef. Generally, only a handful of top-flight restaurants are proud enough of their ability and staff to undertake producing a meal to the demanding specifications of gourmet societies. Most often, the larger wine groups go to hotels or private clubs. An average meal starts at $30 or $40 per person, but can easily climb to $150 or $200 when many wines from great châteaux or their equivalents appear on the menu. Once an establishment accepts the society's challenge, the dinner committee holds a trial dinner aimed at achieving harmony between the wine and food courses and the perfect timing of service. Not infrequently, the pilot dinner reveals that some highly-touted establishment is simply not up to a really elaborate meal. Occasionally, the restaurant is appalled by what is expected of it and backs out after the test. Recently, one meticulous committee only presented its dinner after five trials at three separate establishments. As the dinner draws closer, announcements go out to the society's members. Since a superb meal can only be served to a limited number of diners, larger clubs limit the number who can sign up. Many wine organizations restrict their membership to twenty or thirty-six so that everyone can attend. Another task during the final weeks is preparing the printed menu that accompanies the dinner. The San Francisco society's are usually costly examples of fine printing, typography, and illustration. Traditionally printed in French, the menus are often hand-set by small custom presses, at times hand-lettered and illuminated. Many have become collectors' items.

The night of the dinner arrives. Before dinner cocktails are unthinkable, since they blunt judgment and palate. Smoking before the service of the coffee and liqueurs is sternly discouraged, as is ice water as a routine table item. Dinner is served, course by course, over a period of three to four hours: appetizers and Champagne, soup, fish course, entrée, salad, cheese, dessert, each accompanied by harmonious, and often outstanding, wines. Then comes a regular feature of serious wine dinners: the critique. Knowledgeable members selected for the task frankly discuss the preparation of the meal, the origins of the wine, and any shortcomings in either. Usually, the test dinners have eliminated major disappointments, but occasionally wines do not harmonize with food or the chef has changed the seasoning or preparation of a dish. Comments can be caustic, and over the years several establishments have asked the Wine and Food Society not to return. Conversely, on one occasion five years ago, the criticism was so devastatingly accurate that the directors of one of San Francisco's most exclusive clubs fired the chef early the next morning.

Most wine groups sponsor educational wine tastings and tours for their members. At least three or four times a year, tasting committees stage formal comparisons of carefully selected wines, which members and their guests conscientiously evaluate on a rating sheet. Tastings might compare Bordeaux and California Cabernets or French and California Chardonnays. Every other year since 1936, the San Francisco society has embarked on a two-day vintage tour of California vineyards, banqueting twice daily en route. Over the years, there have also been three society vintage tours to European wine areas.

The Beverly Hills, La Jolla, and Southern California Wine and Food Society chapters are quite similar to San Francisco's: exclusive, male, fairly social, usually dining in formal garb and staging about one event a month. Other chapters tend to be more informal and many accept women members. Some have just two or three events a year, while others, such as the Marin society, are highly active, orchestrating as many as three affairs each month. The Berkeley Wine and Food

Society, in spite of its name, draws members from a wide area, but is no longer affiliated with the International. Its membership includes many professional winemakers, wine sellers, restaurateurs, and wine and food writers. More academic and intellectual than most, its emphasis is on tastings rather than on more social events. It limits itself to thirty-six men and women members, a multiple of nine, the number that can conveniently taste from a bottle of wine, and—in its original day—fit into a member's home for its formal monthly tastings. Meetings now take place most often in a private room in a restaurant. The group holds just two elaborate dinners a year, two wine-country tours and picnics, and other more casual entertainments.

Southern California chapters of the Wine and Food Society are similar to their northern brethren, using the dinner and tasting format, but each emphasizes its own interests and style. The differences in the eleven chapters in the Los Angeles basin have prompted some enthusiasts to belong to two or three. For example, the Pasadena chapter presents only three dinners a year, almost always with traditional *haute cuisine* French menus, but spends much time on planning and trial dinners to ensure a perfect final presentation. The Southern California chapter, located in Los Angeles, on the other hand, likes to stage events with a historical theme. About once a year, it recreates a fiesta banquet as it might have been served almost two hundred years ago on one of the great Spanish or Mexican ranchos. The chapter has gained access for these fiestas to still existing Spanish land grants such as the Bixbee ranch, scene of a recent outing. The Hollywood Wine and Food Society chapter is unique in demanding that members be passable chefs, knowledgeable about food selection and preparation, rather than just interested in wine and good fellowship. Each year some of the members cook and present a very elaborate dinner for their fellows. For many years, they used the kitchens of member Ken Hansen's Scandia restaurant, but since his death in 1981 they have cooked their banquet at the Santa Monica Chronicle restaurant.

Many members of the La Jolla Wine and Food Society chapter are avid duck hunters and proud that they have always been able to bag enough to present a lavish game dinner each fall. The chapter possesses an exceedingly fine cellar of older French wines, which they acquired when a member died and left instructions for his widow to sell his treasures to his friends at prices very advantageous to them. La Jolla also stages a yearly outdoor "picnic," open to female guests, at which a blind tasting of wine and food is presented as a learning experience. At a recent picnic, French Champagnes and American sparkling wines were evaluated, as well as caviar from China, Iran, Russia, and the United States.

Another prominent Los Angeles wine and food group is the Jonathan Gourmet Society, consisting of some forty-five members of the Jonathan Club, one of the area's older and more exclusive downtown men's clubs. It was organized in

1955 and is still guided by the Jonathan's resident gourmet, Joe Vaida. The society puts on a monthly event at the club or one of the Southland's finer restaurants. Occasionally, the members cook at a private home. A special interest is in copying historic or regional dinners, with all appropriate embellishments: setting, costumes, music. Recent dinners of this type have included a Czarist Russian banquet, a Javanese rijsttafel ("rice table"), a Viennese extravaganza, and a night at the Gritti Palace in Venice. The Jonathan members, avid tourists, have visited many California and French wine districts as well as less heralded areas in Sweden, Alaska, and Mexico. On their journeys, they study the region's food and wine, collecting recipes and menu ideas to reproduce in Los Angeles. Another southern California original is W.I.N.O., which began in 1969 when wine writer Jerry D. Mead held cooperative wine tastings in his Garden Grove living room. The tasters referred to themselves as "the old winos" and as the group became more formally organized, they took W.I.N.O. as an acronym for "Wine Investigation for Novices and Œnophiles." W.I.N.O. now has forty chapters with a total of 3,000 men and women members, who meet regularly to taste and evaluate wine and food. Most chapters are in southern California and the Sacramento/San Joaquin Valley, but some are as far away as Texas, Oklahoma, Florida, and Alaska. Members may belong to several chapters. They pride themselves on being devoted to the appreciation of wine and food in an unpretentious atmosphere, but do put on one superlative dinner a year: a nine-course meal featuring fifteen to seventeen wines, in the city of Orange's Hobbit restaurant. Members of all the chapters are invited on a first-come, first-served basis. Mead continues to be W.I.N.O.'s chief executive, editing and publishing two periodicals for members: the *W.I.N.O. Newsletter*, which reports on chapter activities and the general wine scene; and *W.I.N.O. Trader*, which, along with regular commercial wine advertisements, prints free classified ads, including members' offers to trade wines from their cellars.

There are dozens of types of "gourmet" wine clubs in California, most smaller and more informal than the Wine and Food Societies described. The Zodiac Club of San Francisco is one such. Patterned loosely after a Zodiac Circle that flourished in New York City in the 1890s, it consists of twelve dedicated wine drinkers with good cellars who have been meeting for a formal dinner two or three times a year since 1963 at one of the city's private clubs. There is no astrological significance other than the membership of twelve. Indeed, there are no rules or bylaws save one: each dinner chairman names his successor, who schedules, plans, and executes the next dinner. When he has decided on a menu, he solicits his fellows for suitable wines, which are usually uncommon and old. If some members cannot attend, guests fill out the dinner up to twelve.

THE PROFESSIONAL ORGANIZATIONS

These are groups of wine and food lovers who also happen to belong to the same profession. Some are strictly interested in wine, and, other than the shop talk before and during meals, are no different from any other gourmet group. Others link their profession and their hobby. The oldest group in the latter category is the Society of Medical Friends of Wine of San Francisco, founded in 1939, and composed of 325 physicians, dentists, and other medical scientists. The group's purpose is to "stimulate scientific research on wine, develop an understanding of its beneficial effects, and encourage the conviviality and good fellowship that follows its proper use." The society sponsors two annual social events: a wine tour and a huge tasting at which 800 to 1,200 people sample as many as 100 California wines from the state's finest wineries.

However, the principal interest of the Medical Friends of Wine is in serious scientific research. At dinner meetings, guest speakers from the fields of either wine or medicine discuss medical uses of wine and its nutritional and pharmacological properties. Since 1939 the Medical Friends of Wine have sponsored studies of the medical and nutritional values of wine at scientific institutions in the United States and abroad. The society gives a biennial research award of $1,000 for original work "identifying the effects of wine components or indicating appropriate clinical applications of wine in the treatment or prevention of disease." Members were also in many cases responsible for initiating the use of wine as a regular part of the American hospital diet. The society has spawned a number of similar medical wine and food groups: the Physicians' Wine and Food Society of California, the Physicians' Wine Appreciation Society, and the Tamalpais Medical Research Foundation. The Pan American Medical Association is a group with comparable interests.

Doctors are not the only group interested in wine and food. Lawyers, restaurateurs, and military personnel have formed their own wine societies. For example, the Lawyer Friends of Wine of San Francisco, founded in 1965, offers male attorneys the opportunity to "stimulate and increase the knowledge and appreciation of wines" as well as enjoy their convivial effects. The group has a red-wine aging cellar, tastings, an annual vintage tour, and periodic black-tie dinners. All of these groups invite women on their visits to wineries and on vintage tours abroad. Restaurant and food service professionals have their own wine group, the Society of Bacchus. Organized in New Orleans in 1955, the society now has chapters in most major U.S. cities. Its membership includes owners and managers of hotels, clubs, and restaurants. The chapters annually select a local bon vivant to crown "Mr. Gourmet" of the year. The Order of Military Wine Tasters dates from 1959, when a group of officers at Hamilton Air Base in Marin County banded together to taste, study, and appreciate wine. In their initial enthusiasm, the order established branch chapters in Germany, Greenland, San Antonio (Texas), and southern California, but in recent years has confined its activities to the San Francisco Bay Area. It stages regular vintage tours to California's wine regions and monthly tastings and dinners, usually at military bases. Its current 318 members, some retired and some on active duty, are drawn from all of the U.S. armed services.

THE ROBED BROTHERHOODS

In medieval Europe, when most artisans banded together in guilds for mutual protection, the vintners organized regional wine brotherhoods and over the years adopted distinctive robes and rituals. Suppressed at the time of the French Revolution, the brotherhoods reappeared in the 1930s as purely promotional groups for the various wine regions of Europe, mainly in France, Germany, and Switzerland. In this role they often attract less well-versed members whose wine aspirations are largely social. There are now some seventy-five brotherhoods in France, twelve in Bordeaux alone, and a number of the robed and chained groups have spread to America. The Confrérie de la Chaîne des Rôtisseurs reverently traces its origins to 1248 as a guild devoted to roasting meat on a carefully turned spit, although its modern revival dates only to 1950. It is now international, with some eighty chapters in the United States, eleven of them in California. Its dinners tend to be extremely lavish and expensive. The group's glory is its badge of office and membership: a heavy chain and medal hung around the neck and mounted on a broad ribbon whose color matches the grade of the member—Conseiller, Chevalier, Écuyer, or Cadet. Women are admitted to membership as Dames de la Chaîne. Rôtisseur neophytes are initiated with a symbolic tap from a large skewer. Another prominent group, the Confrérie de Chevaliers du Tastevin, founded in France in 1934, has since become a highly social worldwide organization with elaborate robes and rituals. It enjoins its members to drink only Burgundy wine at their dinners. The San Francisco chapter, at least, does not. At initiation rites, officers don purple and gold medieval vestments, dub new members with a wine stock and drape around their necks a silver *tastevin* (wine-tasting cup) hung on a broad silken ribbon. The Los Angeles Chevaliers usually dine in white tie and tails, while the San Francisco chapter prefers black tie dinners. Several other European robed societies have American chapters.

Along with importing robed fraternities, California has produced one native group, the Brotherhood of the Knights of the Vine. Its grand commander, Norman Gates of Sacramento, founded the organization in 1971. A supreme wine enthusiast who worked for sixteen years for the U.S. government in Europe, he was inducted there into some thirty regional wine brotherhoods. On his return to Sacramento, he organized his own group, arraying the members in a proper robe with ermine trim, plumed hats, and golden *tastevins*. The knights, who have since grown to eighteen chapters, hold quarterly dinners and tastings and give yearly awards to those who have advanced the cause of wine.

SPECIAL INTEREST GROUPS

There are a number of small "First Growth" claret clubs wherein groups of eight enophiles undertake to become expert in the eight *Premiers Crus* of Bordeaux.★ They pool their funds to buy a case of each of the eight *Premier Cru* wines from a single year; for instance, all eight 1978s. Then, after a time, they buy all eight of another year, and so on. After they have acquired a sufficient stock, they hold a dinner at a member's home or a restaurant every three months, drinking a single bottle of wine from each of the *Premiers Crus* of a single year. The wines are first tasted blind, without food, and then paired with an elegant dinner. The group keeps careful records and comparisons. As the years go on, the members taste the same wine every several years, becoming experts on this small but important group of Bordeaux. There are similar Burgundy groups of eight: here, rather than buying one year blindly, they first hold tastings of great red Burgundies of several years to see what they want to purchase and cellar. Thereafter, the progressive tasting procedure is the same. Lovers of German wines have similar groups of eight, and there is a German Wine Society with ten chapters that holds tastings and dinners to show off the great German wines. Most members are graduates of a one-week state-operated course given at the German Wine Academy at Kloster Eberbach on the Rhine. In a like manner, Bordeaux-lovers have banded together in La Commanderie de Bordeaux.

     The California Vintage Wine Society started in Los Angeles in the early 1960s, with a San Francisco branch following in 1963. The two branches have aging cellars, tastings, dinners, and vintage tours like other wine organizations but are distinctive in concentrating on well-aged California wines. The North Coast Prestige Wine Society has a similar emphasis and program. The Napa Valley Wine Library plays a distinctive role as a wine appreciation and educational social group. Founded in St. Helena in 1961, its membership has reached 2,500. Its collection, housed in the St. Helena Public Library, includes a wide selection of wine books, periodicals, and ephemera. The association also has an oral-history project, conducts annual large-scale tastings of wines made by Napa Valley wineries, and sponsors heavily subscribed weekend wine courses.

★   In the original 1855 classification, there were only four *Premier Cru* red Bordeaux wines. Present-day usage has expanded this list to eight, adding Mouton, Cheval-Blanc, Pétrus, and Ausone to the original Lafite, Latour, Margaux, and Haut-Brion.

Wine societies were once almost exclusively male, but no more. Women take an active part in many wine groups and are now forming their own all-female societies. The Napa Valley Women's Wine Society includes vineyardists and winery owners who meet regularly for tastings, dinners, and educational sessions. Women on Wine (WOW), a similar group with chapters in the Napa Valley, Modesto, and other California wine regions, plans to expand nationally. The Dames de Champagne flourished in San Francisco for a number of years, but is quiescent at present. For all their focus on rituals, robes, and formal dinners, these wine social organizations have played an important part in the ever increasing interest in California wine. By educating American palates, they have encouraged the production of better wine, and its acceptance as a popular beverage and normal accompaniment of good food.

BIBLIOGRAPHIC NOTE

This essay draws on a number of articles on the subject: Leon D. Adams, "The Critical Gourmets," *San Francisco* 6 (October 1963): 30–31, 48–50; William J. Dickerson, "Confessions of a Wine and Food Society Chapter," *Wine and Food*, no. 129 (Spring 1966): 59–61; Chauncey D. Leake, "The Gourmet Scientist Dines with the Society of Medical Friends of Wine," *Nutrition Today* 5 (Summer 1970): 22–25; and Frances Moffat, "A Jug of Wine, a Loaf of Bread—and Thou Beside Me in a Tuxedo," *San Francisco* 16 (April 1974): 48–51.

VII.8

Note: Tasting Groups

by JOHN BENDER

THE SIT-DOWN "BLIND" TASTING OF EIGHT TO TWELVE WINES, an institution at once derided and feared by foreign visitors, is the most distinctive feature of California connoisseurship.

The sight of a dozen or more wine enthusiasts, merchants, journalists, winemakers, and winery owners bearing down on a table forested with glasses and studded with bottles in brown bags can strike any uninitiated participant with terror. More daunting still is the hushed concentration the celebrants may sustain for up to an hour while they study the wines, taking notes by systematic methods of observation and evaluation. Then comes the exacting discussion of virtue and vice in each liquid, during the course of which one may witness awesome displays of technical, geographical, and terminological knowledge. Finally, the dread moment of the ratings, when every wine but one is sacrificed on the altar of supremacy, though several may have competed boldly with performances of the highest caliber. Now participants will disperse into society, reporting the outcome to friends, merchants, vintners, and—in the case of retailers or journalists—to the public at large. The reputations of the finer wineries, not to mention their inventories and prices, rise and fall in part according to the outcome of these strange rites.

The cult remains largely unofficial, though at the Los Angeles County, Orange County, and San Francisco County fairs, which hold blind tastings on an enormous scale, the opinions of experienced judges are backed by medals in gold, silver, and bronze. But elite wineries participate unevenly at fairs, and so the collective impact on fine wine of the numerous contests held by small groups may surpass that of the few large competitions.

Tasting groups throw winemakers, winery owners, and tradespeople into close contact with vocal consumers, while providing occasions on which those who produce and sell wine can benefit from the friendly exchange of information. Perhaps more significantly, groups consisting largely of winemakers and growers, which exist in most of the regional locales of California, contribute to the formation of consensus about the character of the land and the performance of grapes in different sectors. They tacitly ratify what might be called the "golden mean" of winemaking style for each area. Tasting groups generate considerable pressure toward consensus. This pressure, when superadded among winemakers to the tendency (under the influence of the University of California at Davis) to define quality in largely varietal and chemical terms, may work against distinct individuality of approach. In Bordeaux, by contrast, the tasting societies are made up largely of *négociants* and people in the trade, while growers and winemakers pursue their individual courses in contact chiefly with immediate neighbors.

The very nature of the better California growths has been shaped to a degree by the habit of methodical evaluation at blind tastings. The organization of virtually all tastings around varietal and regional types places a premium on typicality. Truly eccentric wines tend to sink because they cannot be meaningfully placed in context: at best, their admirers and detractors cancel one another, producing an average ranking. On the other hand, a wine within the range of typicality yet possessed of some pronounced trait will often prevail. This works against balanced wines that draw their subtle distinctiveness from soil, climate, and grape; it works for wines with prominent features arising from winemaking choices. Thus we get some Cabernet Sauvignons that invariably stress resinous, minty flavors, while others seek the maximum of berrylike fruit; expensive new French oak is the hallmark of some, while spicy American oak jumps forth from others; the quest for supreme ripeness produces scents of chocolate and raisins, while purplish black colors express faith in long, highly extractive fermentation. For all their quality and interest, California wines may be too prone to stride up with slogans rather than waiting to be known for their inner strength and true individuality. Competitive blind ranking enforces basic standards, but it can tend to reward ostentation at the expense of depth and complexity.

     Blind tastings certainly are not peculiar to California, but their prestige has been consolidated here through the advocacy of statistically analyzed blind judging by Amerine and Roessler in a series of studies emanating, since 1959, from the University of California at Davis. Paradoxically, the most available of these works argues that the failure to analyze rankings, not to mention the self-qualification of judges (tasters), severely undermines the validity of most tasting results. But the message is clear from first to last. Serious judging is done blind under controlled conditions; if not in a laboratory, at least in absence of food. After all, "a dinner is a dinner, but a sensory examination of wines is something else."★

     The technical analysis of wine has little in common with the practice of connoisseurship, but tasting, no less than laboratory testing, enters at crucial junctures in production and marketing. Little of this tasting is strictly blind. Technical evaluation aims to discover faults that emerge in the course of production with a view to correcting or avoiding them. The specialized, largely chemical, vocabulary that suits this purpose is taught in schools of enology. Once safely bottled, however, the wine is described the world over, by vintner and connoisseur alike, in traditional terminologies that include technical words along with many that have been condemned as entirely relative. But the very survival of subjective terms over strenuous scientific protest suggests that they, too, serve a purpose. Their function is to enable subtle discriminations among the elusive traits that distinguish the very finest wines. In this complex terrain, issues of relative quality are far more intricate than judgments concerning the soundness and integrity of wines during production. The ideal winemaker possesses technique, which can be learned, and practices connoisseurship, which must arise from devotion.

     When experts subject themselves publicly to the risks of blind tasting, the outcome can be startling. In 1976, for example, the English merchant Steven Spurrier staged a series of blind tastings in Paris for leading French growers, writers, restaurateurs, and wine officials. The results, which ranked several California

★   M. A. Amerine and E. B. Roessler, *Wines: Their Sensory Evaluation*, p. 56.

wines above the French classics, shook the wine world and provoked the first commercial attention to California wines in Europe since the nineteenth century. The blind format works to the advantage of newer areas and no doubt has served to widen the circle of those who believe California capable of producing wines to equal the best of Europe. The ratings in Paris came as no surprise to the many groups in California that regularly stage comparative blind tastings of varietal wines from different regions of the world.

Full instructions on how to stage tastings of every type, from the introductory showing for beginners to elaborate trade displays, appear in *Michael Broadbent's Pocket Guide to Wine Tasting* (New York: Simon and Schuster, 1982). Broadbent, the English chief of Christie's Wine Department, advocates blind evaluation with missionary fervor and advises adherence in tones usually reserved for articles of faith. In California, where blind tasting in absence of food so dominates connoisseurship that dining seems at times a mere adjunct, neither Broadbent's advocacy nor his tone would be called for. The few basics necessary to informal yet serious tasting are easy to arrange: enough table space for each person to sit down before eight to twelve glasses; good incandescent lighting; a white cloth or place mats; markers for glasses and bottles; bags to conceal the identity of the wines or, better still, standard bottles into which the wines are decanted just prior to tasting; an agreed upon system of ranking. Some tasters prefer the Davis score card, with its stress on the identification of faults, but experts who concentrate on fine wines in bottle (as do most tasting groups) often rate by methods that place more points in the category of overall quality. They believe that this allows latitude for close discrimination among similar wines of a generally high standard. (On terminology, methods of tasting, and score cards, see the books mentioned above and the essay on "Sensory Evaluation" in this volume.)

Despite all the qualities that make tasting groups easy objects of satire, they have played a substantial role in the creation of a knowledgeable public for wine. For these are not, in the main, groups of wine professionals but rather of what used to be called, quite positively, *amateurs*—the most devoted and articulate representatives of the market. Most of the specific groups that I might tell of cannot be listed because they are informally constituted and often nameless. But they are legion. I know of several that date back between ten and fifteen years, though of course many more are comparatively recent. Established societies such as the Berkeley Wine and Food Society and the Marin Wine and Food Society often trace their origins to informal tasting groups.

Organizations specifically dedicated to tasting include the Vintners Club of San Francisco, Les Amis du Vin, and the Napa Valley Wine Library Association. Although the Vintners Club has a considerable general membership, from its foundation it has boasted a high percentage of winery owners, winemakers, and growers. Its weekly late afternoon tastings concentrate on a dozen wines, often of closely similar character. Its rankings, though difficult to evaluate because of the group's large, heterogeneous, and shifting membership, are among the most discussed and influential of all. Les Amis du Vin is a national society with local chapters closely tied to the retail trade. Nationally, it publishes a magazine, offers tours, and promotes wine accessories; its local chapters offer open tastings aimed at educating the general public, and wine seminars where the serious consumer can engage in blind evaluation. The Napa Valley Wine Library Association supports the enology collection in St. Helena by offering a valuable series of weekend courses on every aspect of wine from vineyard practice to marketing and cellarage. These courses include training in sensory evaluation and a variety of tests of skill at blind judging. The association also sponsors a huge summer tasting that, perhaps because it is not blind, has become one of the collective celebrations of the winegrowing community. These groups are visible manifestations of a pervasive manner of dealing socially with wine through studied evaluation.

VII.9

Note:

The Zinfandel Club of London

by MARK SAVAGE

FOR MOST OF US IN THE UNITED KINGDOM, CALIFORNIA WINE is a very recent phenomenon. Ten years ago, few had ever tasted anything from the Napa Valley, and even five years ago it was hard indeed to find a British wine merchant with anything from California on his list. It was just this difficulty, in fact, that brought about the Zinfandel Club. Such authorities as Harry Waugh and Hugh Johnson were well aware of what was happening in California and eager to form some kind of association devoted to sharing in the pleasure of tasting and drinking good California wines, to some extent making up for the difficulty of procuring them in Britain.

Thus it came about that one day in the autumn of 1977, a small group met at Harry Waugh's London home for lunch: Hugh Johnson, John Avery, and Paul Henderson, proprietor of Gidleigh Park Hotel in Devon, a house renowned equally for its cuisine and its list of California wines, unparalleled in Europe, if not the United States. Paul became the club's first secretary. No official minutes exist for that inaugural meeting, but Paul does dimly remember an outstanding Chardonnay from the early 1960s and an old Swan Zinfandel.

The Group decided on the name "Zinfandel Club" as being suitably evocative of California wine in general. Harry had for some time nurtured the idea of a United Kingdom chapter of the Knights of the Vine, and an affiliation remains between the two societies. But it was quite rightly felt that the name "Knights of the Vine" would hardly ring true in England. The only problem with the name "Zinfandel Club" seems to be that certain people assume that members are a strange race of pure "Zin-freaks" who pursue this taste to the virtual exclusion of the other varietals. This is not the case, of course, as a look at the list of past tastings proves.

Hugh Johnson arranged the first club dinner at the Garrick Club on 21 February 1978. Brother Timothy of Christian Brothers Winery in California came as guest of honor. The wines, following an aperitif of a 1968 Beaulieu Vineyard sparkling wine, included the Mayacamas 1975 Chardonnay, Freemark Abbey's 1973 Cabernet Bosche, Beaulieu Vineyard's 1970 Private Reserve Cabernet, Heitz's 1968 Martha's Vineyard, and Joseph Phelps's 1976 Johannisberg Riesling Late Harvest. Not a bad start, it would be fair to assume.

Other good dinners were to follow at well-known London restaurants: one at Lockets with Frank Woods, president of Clos du Bois, another at Lafayette with Robert Mondavi. On Sunday, 18 May 1980, an excellent evening was held at Boodle's Club in St. James's, attended by a large gathering, including such distinguished California winemakers and proprietors as John and Janet Trefethen and William Collins of Conn Creek. If I remember rightly, Francis Mahoney of Carneros Creek was in London too but could not make the dinner, although his wines did. In his speech after dinner, Hugh Johnson was keen to say how impressed he was by the 1977 Carneros Creek Pinot Noir, one of the few successful wines he had encountered from that difficult variety in its Californian guise. We had a Gewürztraminer from Grand Cru Vineyards by way of an aperitif and the other wines with dinner included Trefethen's 1979 White Riesling, Carneros Creek's 1978 Chardonnay, Trefethen's 1977 Chardonnay, and Conn Creek's 1976 Cabernet and Zinfandel. By now, it seemed clear that the club was fulfilling its original raison d'être.

In fact, the situation had changed. Although it was the very shortage of California wine that had caused the club's foundation, ironically, by the time of the Boodle's dinner, California wine was becoming widely available; indeed a California wine explosion seemed imminent. At almost every wine trade gathering, lunch, or tasting, California was now a sure topic of conversation. The media gave constant coverage. More and more wines began to appear. Wine trade opinion itself seemed to be taking sides, with enthusiastic protagonists in one corner and the more skeptical and conservative members in the other. Few trade buyers or journalists had been out to discover what all the fuss might be about, but those who had taken the trouble had returned fully converted and joined the protagonists' camp. There was little doubt that Hugh Johnson's estimate of California as the most exciting new wine region in the world was an entirely valid judgment. The diehard brigade, reluctant to believe that fine wine could really come out of the continent responsible for hamburgers and Coca-Cola, remained doubtful that Californians could apparently achieve in a few decades what had taken the French a thousand years. Furthermore, conservative by nature and proud of the part they have played in the history of claret and vintage port especially, many British drinkers could be expected to treat a newcomer with more suspicion than enthusiasm. We are fortunate to have at our disposal a wide, probably unrivaled, range of fine wines from all over the world.

One might wonder why, in fact, it took so long for California wine to establish itself in the British marketplace. My own first acquaintance with Napa Valley wine was at a fascinating tasting presented by John Avery to the Oxford University Wine Circle on 28 January 1969, at which we blind-tasted Cabernets and Chardonnays from France, California, and Australia. My notes tell me that we placed a Beaulieu Vineyard 1962 Pinot Chardonnay above a 1964 Chablis *Grand Cru*, but that a Beaulieu Vineyard 1962 was outclassed by a 1962 Château D'Issan. Even then, it was clear that the French did not necessarily come out on top, and one wonders now what the results would be in a similarly staged tasting. This is no place, however, to discuss the merits of such comparisons; we all know the results and surprises that California wines have achieved in recent years. The question is, if it was clear in the 1960s that California was a force to be reckoned with, why did it take us until 1980 to really discover what was happening?

Three events combined, I suspect, to bring California wine onto the British market: rising prices in France, the explosion of fine wine production in California itself in the early 1970s, and the weak dollar at that end of the decade. It made a lot of sense to investigate California wines seriously, but still remarkably few people did so. But the British trade finally got the message, and within a space of about eighteen months or so, almost every good wine merchant, barring exclusive specialists, found a place for California on his list. Suddenly it became *the* place to visit: there was a delegation from the "Under 40 Club," followed a year later by an official visit from the Institute of Masters of Wine; senior trade journalists, at least those visiting the Napa Valley, returned to England with a healthy respect for what they had seen, heard, and above all, tasted. California wines had, almost overnight, gained public acquaintance and rapid respectability, at both the top and the lower ends of the market, furthermore.

Not only was the Zinfandel Club off the ground, but California wine was now easily obtainable in depth and breadth. The club held comparative tastings at which large numbers of wines were on show. A grand tasting of nearly forty different wines held at the United States Embassy in Grosvenor Square on Monday, 24 November 1980, included Pinot Noir, Cabernet Sauvignon, Zinfandel, French Colombard, Sauvignon Blanc, Chardonnay, Johannisberg Riesling, Gerwürztraminer, sparkling wine, and even California port.

On 28 May 1981 the first of a number of meetings took place at L'Escargot, a newly refurbished restaurant in Soho, whose list is devoted to United States wines. It has now become the unofficial home of the Zinfandel Club, since Jancis Robinson, the club's former secretary, has married Nick Lander, the proprietor. Some twenty-five Chardonnays were tasted, across a wide spectrum, starting with Taylor California Cellars and ending up with Matanzas Creek and a 1976 botrytised Caymus. On 22 September there was a similar comparative tasting of about twenty-seven Zinfandels, held this time back at the United States Embassy. In November, a Thanksgiving dinner at L'Escargot featured the wines of Stag's Leap Wine Cellars, including Chardonnay, Cabernet Sauvignon, and Merlot. The events of 1982 started with a dinner on 22 February at Brooks' Club, with a vertical tasting of Clos du Val Zinfandels from 1972 to 1977, followed on 19 April by a tasting of about two dozen Cabernets from 1971 through to 1979 at the Café Royal, Piccadilly.

The originators envisaged the club's membership reaching around 100. It now stands at 135, including 66 members of the wine trade, a dozen wine writers, and a dozen Masters of Wine. From this one can gauge that the society manages to combine serious wine appreciation and uncomplicated enjoyment. Its success has led in turn to the conception of the Irish Zinfandel Club, founded in late 1980 by the energy of Thomas Whelehan in Dublin; and there is a strong rumor now that even a French Zinfandel Club is being mooted. It is perhaps a satisfactory tribute to the enthusiasm of California wine producers that the Zinfandel Club should so successfully pursue the fruits of their labors.

VII.10

Note: Wine as Art

by WILLIAM B. FRETTER

IT IS COMMONLY SUPPOSED THAT THE IDEA OF TASTE IS
only a metaphor and can be applied chiefly to choices one makes in the arts of sight
and sound. Taste itself, taste literally interpreted, is not supposed to perceive unities
which are art works. Thus wines cannot be works of art. This I dispute. I begin with
some disclaimers and an acknowledgment. I do not intend to discuss the "art of making wine," or the "art of drinking wine"; nor shall I give advice about stocking a wine
cellar or the virtues of an even temperature in a limestone cave; and I shall not write
about the relative merits of California as compared with French or German wines.

Some years ago I bought a copy of Stephen Pepper's *The Work of Art*.★
As a nonprofessional I found it fairly heavy going but yet rewarding. I had been interested in art and music for a long time, and had rather unsuccessfully made a quest
for an understanding of greatness in music and art, partly to light me on my search
for an understanding of greatness in scientific achievement and discovery. Pepper's
book concerns itself more with an analysis of aesthetic communication than with the
reasons why one artistic object is a masterpiece and another is not. The book as it
describes the process of aesthetic communication creates a light of insight that in-
tensifies on successive readings. What is a work of art? Can a judgment of beauty be
true? The dynamics of the masterpiece, the control object, a vehicle of aesthetic
communication, and the concept of fusion are discussed in successive chapters.

Perhaps my comments on wine and its aesthetic qualities will illustrate
in another way Pepper's ideas and will show that their applicability is not limited
to painting, sculpture, music, and literature. Human beings have valued wine for
thousands of years, as they have valued painting and sculpture, and the depiction
throughout history of wine in paintings, drawings, and sculpture† provides beautiful illustrations of the interaction among these arts.

It is particularly important in the case of non-verbal aesthetic communication to be able to look at the object, or hear it, to look at pictures, or listen to a song

Reprinted from the *Journal of Aesthetics and Art Criticism* 30, no. 1 (Fall 1971).
★   Stephen C. Pepper, *The Work of Art* (Bloomington: Indiana University Press, 1955).
†   Hyams, *Dionysus* (New York: Macmillan, 1965).

or a flute or a record. Words are inadequate and particularly so for the aesthetic appreciation of wine. But the basic question is: can wine be considered as a work of art? Before I discuss this in terms of Pepper's question,★ What is a work of art? the question of particularity must be raised. We must consider a particular wine, in fact a particular glass of wine. Just as all paintings are not works of art, so all glasses of wine are not works of art. Paintings can be ordinary and inartistic, commercial music can be "muzak," and wine too can be ordinary. Wine can be spoiled and too old, and paintings can be faded and deteriorated. Thus not all wine is art, any more than all painting or all music or all writing is art. Also some wine, while classifiable as art, is not as good as other wine.

Stephen Pepper discusses the work of art in terms of three objects: the vehicle, the object of immediate perception, and the object of criticism.† In the case of a painting, the vehicle is probably a canvas with oil pigments spread upon it. It is "the instrument for the production, preservation, and control of the object of aesthetic worth." For wine, the vehicle is a mixture of water, alcohol, organic chemicals, and the pigments contained in a glass. The alcohol serves to preserve the rest of the wine and together with the water makes it possible for the observer to sense the qualities of the wine, just as the canvas holds the paint in the position the artist intended it to be and allows the observer to view the painting. The vehicle has in itself no aesthetic worth in either case, although the monetary worth may not be inconsiderable.

The object of immediate perception is described by Pepper as:

the experience a spectator has at any one time when stimulated by the vehicle. This is the object we see and feel and fill with meaning. It has a date and location. Many will set the location within our bodies. Definitely our bodies are much involved in the object of immediacy. Our sense organs, our eyes in this instance [a painting] give us the colors and the line and the shape; and our brains presumably give us the meaning of the represented objects dependent on learning and memory; and our endocrine systems presumably contribute to our emotion. Our bodies are involved in the perceptual response. The duration of an object of immediacy is a certain spread of time, the time that can be taken in intuitively at a single act of attention.‡

For illustration Pepper uses the perception of a painting like Breughel's *Winter*, or of a statue which must be observed from all sides over a period of time. How does this apply to wine?

The object of immediate perception is first observed visually. We look at the wine in the glass for the character of its color, for its clarity, the degree of its vis-

★   Pepper, ch. 1.
†   Pepper, p. 16.
‡   Pepper, p. 17.

cosity, the pattern of the liquid on the inside of the glass above the wine, the gradations of color in the meniscus of the liquid, and the shape and color of the wine as it moves in the glass. The glass is analogous to the frame of a picture and should be consistent with the style and color of the wine in that a fine wine should be served in a beautiful glass, not in a water tumbler.

Next there is the wine's odor. Its aroma and bouquet are a complex of various odors: the smell of the fruit, of the alcohol, of the many organic compounds formed by the vine in the grape and by the winemaker in the processes of vinification and storage. The object of immediate perception depends also on the glass container, the temperature, and sometimes on the length of time the wine has been in the glass. But to appreciate wine as an aesthetic object, the sense of smell is essential.

The third sense used in connection with the object of immediate perception is that of taste. Like the smell of the wine, taste has many components, subtle differences in the development of the flavor caused by time and strong interactions among the olfactory sensations. Flavors may be complex, or simple, or distasteful, and the intensity of the flavor often determines whether or not it is acceptable.

Thus, as with painting and music, in a single perception of a work of art, we run into some unexpected complexities. What is usually called a single perception—say the first time one hears a musical composition or sees a picture—is already not one act of perceptual response but a succession of such acts. Yet somehow we obtain something of an integral perception of the work and of the series of perceptive immediacies.★

Finally, the full appreciation of the object of immediacy requires what aestheticians call "funding," which is the fusion of meanings from past experiences into a present experience.† It implies memory of past experiences, of pictures seen, of symphonies or quartets heard, of books read, and of wines tasted. The experience of hearing a late quartet of Beethoven is enhanced if earlier one has heard it, or other late quartets, or early ones, or anything else Beethoven wrote. And the experience of tasting a Chambertin is enhanced if earlier one has tasted Chambertin, or Chambertin of another year or from another vineyard in Chambertin, or even a Gevrey-Chambertin from the region. Past experience is essential, and the continual renewing of the experience is desirable, especially where the memory of subtle flavors, odors, and colors is not always reliable.

We now come to the object of criticism, the third of Pepper's objects following the vehicle and the object of immediate perception: "The object of criticism

★   Pepper, p. 19.
†   Pepper, p. 21.

is the totality of relevant material based on the perceptions stimulated by an aesthetic vehicle. . . . It is the object perceived by a person who has become a competent spectator."* Relevancy has two components: first, the direct stimulus, the sensory quality calling up a normal response. Wine should not taste like lemon juice, and it should not have even a strong component of lemon flavor. Nor should it taste like vinegar or smell like sulfur dioxide. Second, the internal components must be relevant to each other. A white wine should not have a strong tannin flavor, which is consistent with and relevant to the complex of flavors in a red wine. This concept of relevancy is similar to one invented in physics by R. T. Birge,† that of internal consistency and external consistency of the data resulting from a scientific experiment.

A competent spectator, also, is needed to perceive the object of criticism. Competence implies discrimination, intelligence, and a certain cultural conditioning for the perception of a style of art or a type of wine. The competent spectator can observe internal consistency in a painting, the consistency of style, form, line, or representation. Consistency of style is particularly important in painting, music, or wine. A particular sweet wine may be considered a great wine, but sweetness is inconsistent in other styles of wine and is recognized by the competent spectator as undesirable. The development of sensory discrimination is thus essential in the education of the competent wine spectator. He notes whether or not the wine has the quality of aesthetic relevancy—internal consistency; flavors must not clash, colors must be consistent with odor and flavor, and all must be determined by fully funded impressions.

But can wine be beautiful? The aesthetic satisfaction gained from what Pepper calls the consummatory response with respect to the stimulating aesthetic vehicle determines whether or not we call the object beautiful. Experiences "controlled by the craftsmanship of artists through an aesthetic vehicle"‡ give us aesthetic satisfaction and lead us to call the object "beautiful." Saying a wine "is beautiful" implies that we find a fully funded aesthetic satisfaction. The winemaker or the winegrower is a craftsman. He may also be an artist, but unless he is skilled at his craft, he will not produce a work of art. Control of the vehicle is as important in winemaking as it is in painting.

Is wine an abstract art? I suspect that most people will concede that abstract art can be beautiful. In a sense all art is abstract, and nonrepresentational art can be beautiful. A certain painting by Hans Hofmann, for instance, brings to my mind the thoughts and feelings I have when I taste a certain German wine of a

---

*   Pepper, pp. 37–38.
†   R. T. Birge, "Calculation of Errors by the Method of Least Squares," *Physical Review* 40 (15 April 1932): 207–27.
‡   Pepper, p. 66.

type called Trockenbeerenauslese (literally, selected dry berries). It suggests farms or vineyards in autumn, ripe yellow wheat, sweet grapes, orange and red leaves, the richness of life. Both the painting and the German wine seem to abstract from a large accumulation of memories, perceptions, emotions, certain ones, and bring them together in relevance and internal consistency. Both give me great aesthetic satisfaction, and to me both are beautiful, abstract art. A fine champagne gives me the same feelings as the scherzo in Beethoven's string quartet in C sharp minor: in both cases a kind of practical joke seems to be played on the spectator. Both abstractly evoke internally consistent emotions, the components of the aesthetic vehicle being fully relevant.

Then there is the *control* by the winemaker. He must be a craftsman; he must grow the vines properly, pick the grapes at the right time, vinify properly, and store the wine in appropriate containers. As he creates an object of abstract art, the winemaker, like the abstract painter, also deals with accidental qualities. Each year the weather is different, or the vines grow old, or rain molds the grapes before they are picked (some of these contingent factors add desirable flavors). Somewhere there is the artist, however, who may be the winemaker, or the proprietor, or the wineseller who insists on a certain type of wine. The artist chooses the basic components: the variety of grape and soil, the exposure to the sun, the type of barrel used, the age of the bottling, and even to some extent the vinification process itself (e.g., the length of time the juice ferments on the skins of the grapes). The artist controls these factors whenever he can to produce the work of art he has conceived. The beauty of the wine is not like the beauty of an autumn leaf on the vine, or of vineyards on rolling hills, or of the girl who is always in the advertising posters picking the grapes. The beauty of wine is a controlled abstract beauty expressing the intentions of the artist.

To call the winemaker an artist is to pose practical problems. One rarely knows his name, but one can be sure that associated with every glass of great wine is an artist. Rarely does his name appear on the bottle. Usually it is necessary to visit the winery to ascertain his identity, and even then it may not be easy to do so because the true artist and the skilled craftsman in winemaking may not be the same person.

James Zellerbach was an artist of a California wine. He made a wine he wanted to be similar to, but distinct from, a great French white burgundy, Montrachet. He studied the components necessary to such a wine, hired a competent winemaker, bought grapes from growers in the best parts of California, and imported barrels made from oak grown in the region of Limousin, in France. With these materials he produced his work of art, a rich white wine made from Pinot Chardonnay grapes. It was stored in the barrels long enough to acquire a slightly oaky taste. Its color is pale, the wine is clear. The color is consistent, a part of the beauty of the wine, but is not itself beautiful. The bouquet is strong and characteristic of the Chardonnay grape having a touch of oak. The taste of the wine is consistent with the bouquet; it is rich and heavy in body, as a white burgundy should be, but it has a flowery aroma that distinguishes it from other French burgundies. The aromas of French white burgundies also differ from each other within the type: the point is to make a wine characteristic of the type but distinguishable in itself. It is a beautiful wine, a great success. James Zellerbach is dead and his wines and winery are dispersed, but in this wine he exhibited artistry.

The second wine I should like to mention is a French red burgundy from Chambertin made in 1959, a great year in Burgundy. The artist in this case was Ronald Avery, a wine merchant in Bristol, England. His conception of what a Chambertin should be is fully achieved in this wine. Made of Pinot Noir grapes of the type that produce a heavy-bodied wine, this wine on Avery's insistence was produced from grapes picked late in the year, sugar possibly being added. The wine is a dark purple, perfectly clear, slightly brownish where the wine meets the glass, and streaks of glycerine stream down the glass after it is swirled. The bouquet is strong and rich in the Pinot character, and in the mouth it is unctuous, rich, not very acid, enough tannin giving it good balance. A wine that matured early, it is in contrast with another Chambertin from the same year that is still not quite ready to drink. It is a typical Avery Burgundy within the Chambertin type.

I do not hesitate to call these wines beautiful. They give me maximum aesthetic satisfaction. They are complex and rich in the varieties of sensual impressions they make. As abstract art, they bring to the spectator a stimulus that evokes in him emotions and thought according to his previous experiences and inclinations. And for full appreciation they require a competent observer who can fuse the meanings of past experiences into a present experience. They illustrate what Stephen Pepper means when he defines a work of art.

CHAMPAGNE BURGUNDY BORDEAUX RHINE CHIANTI

1.   2.   3.   4.   5a.   5b.

10 CM

SOME WINE BOTTLE PROFILES ★

The wine bottles shown above were created to package the wines of different regions in Europe. Long association and tradition have imparted such stature to certain regions, such as Bordeaux, that the name may denote a wine, the design of its package, a city, a harbor, or a color. For a century, all the bottle profiles illustrated have been seen on display wherever wine was on sale, in fine wine shops or supermarkets (and many not so super). In the early years of the century, the Italian Swiss Colony Winery marketed its wines in straw-wrapped fiaschi, a practice that was discontinued during the hostilities of World War II. Its label read "Tipo–chianti roso" or "bianco," and as "Tipo" it was ordered in fine restaurants and hotel dining rooms. Illustration 5b shows a fiascho without the straw wrapping. E.B.

★All bottles are illustrated at the same scale, 1:4.

MEDICAL VALUES & ECONOMIC
PERSPECTIVES

1. WILLIAM J. DICKERSON, M.D.

2. KIRBY MOULTON

3. DORIS MUSCATINE

VIII.1
MEDICAL & THERAPEUTIC VALUES

by WILLIAM J. DICKERSON, M.D.

WINE HAS A LONG HISTORY AS A FRIEND OF MAN, AND FOR ALMOST AS LONG HAS BEEN REVERED FOR ITS MEDICAL AND THERAPEUTIC VALUES. FROM THE PAPYRI OF ANTIQUITY AND THE EGYPTIAN PICTOGRAPHS of 4000 B.C. to current medical journals and texts, this tradition has been richly documented, especially in the writings of Dr. Salvatore Lucia. Yet the medical benefits of wine go unrecognized by most Americans today and are little known even to recent generations of conscientious medical students. This brief review may help in understanding this paradox and in giving a glimpse into the rich treasure of accumulated medical knowledge. Dramatic progress in pharmacology and medical research have diminished, but not eliminated, the role of wine in the modern medicine chest, where even the most time-honored remedies do not gain admission without scientific proof. But because of the diversity of its components, wine can serve both the science and the art of health care, as definitive treatment when there is a proven therapeutic advantage, or, perhaps more importantly, as solace when a specific treatment is lacking or a cure doubtful.

PHARMACOLOGY

To use wine to our best purposes and to avoid its serious pitfalls, we must know something of how the body reacts to it and to the ethyl alcohol (ethanol) it contains. Even today the pharmacology of wine is often mistakenly reduced simply to the pharmacology of ethyl alcohol. This is so despite recognition more than a century ago that the effect of wine on the body is different from the effect of ethyl alcohol.

In 1812, Dr. Benjamin Rush, "The Father of American Psychiatry," a signer of the Declaration of Independence, and a medical professor and clinician of international reputation, wrote, "Unlike ardent spirits [defined as distilled liquors of any kind] which render the temper irritable, wine generally inspires cheerfulness and good humor. It is to be lamented that the grape has not yet been sufficiently cultivated in our country to afford wine for our citizens." Twelve years later, A. L. Henderson made a more distinct differentiation between wine and spirits and alcohol: "If the same quantity of brandy, however, be drunk, diluted with water to the strength of wine, it will produce intoxification more speedily than when taken in the form of wine, and the effect of a mixture of alcohol will be still more injurious. On what principle these differences are to be explained, is altogether unknown. Champagnes intoxicate very speedily." Today we know this "principle" to be attributable to multiple factors.

PHYSIOLOGY

Various factors influence the body's absorption of ethanol, and therefore its effects:

1. *the rate of consumption, perhaps the time of day (morning drinking producing a higher peak in blood alcohol concentration);*

2. *size, sex, and to some degree, ethnic differences;*

3. *the concentration of alcohol in the beverage consumed (the higher the concentration, the more rapid the absorption: thus, alcohol is absorbed most rapidly from distilled spirits, less so from dessert wines, still more slowly from table wines, and most slowly from beer);*

4. *the type of beverage (alcohol is absorbed more slowly and the maximum blood alcohol is less from table wine than from distilled spirits, even when the concentrations of alcohol are equalized);*

5. *the individual's previous experience with alcoholic beverages; and*

6. *the absorbing surface and the flow of blood in the region.*

Food, when present in the digestive tract, conspicuously slows alcohol absorption and reduces the blood alcohol peak by from 15 to 50 percent. Although this is probably the greatest influence on alcohol absorption, the exact mechanism is unknown, but it is variously attributed to buffering action, to a direct alteration of absorption,

DIAGRAM **2**

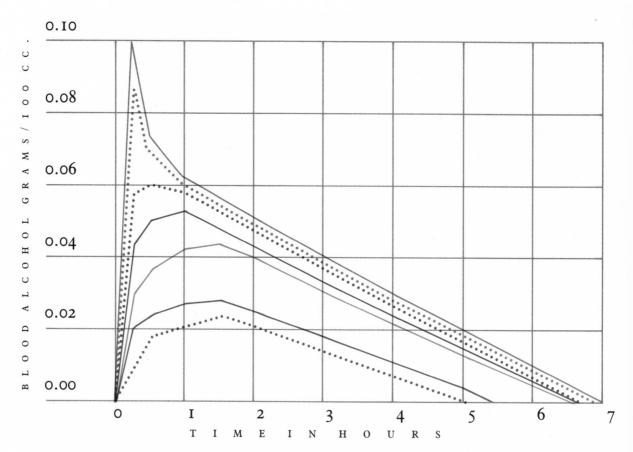

BLOOD ALCOHOL CURVES

LEGEND

—————	Gin, vodka
··············	Whiskey
············	Dessert wine
—————	Table wine
—————	Beer
—————	Table wine with meals
············	Beer with meals

Alcohol is absorbed rapidly from the digestive tract and distributed readily and uniformly through the body by the blood. Blood alcohol concentration, a reliable measure of alcohol in the blood, reflects the alcohol level in the brain. Several factors influence blood alcohol concentration: a person's weight (the rise is slower in heavier individuals), the ingestion of other foods and beverages with the alcohol, and the time allowed for the body to metabolize and excrete the ingested alcohol. Different beverages produce differences in blood alcohol concentration, as depicted in this diagram. When equal total amounts of alcohol per kilogram of body weight are administered to normal volunteers, much higher peaks result from gin and vodka than from table wine and beer taken on an empty stomach. Even lower concentrations result from table wine and beer ingested with meals. Thus one who wishes to enjoy an alcoholic beverage but avoid in-toxication might choose beer or table wine to enjoy with meals rather than a preprandial cocktail of spirits.
SOURCE: C. D. Leake and M. Silverman, *Alcoholic Beverages in Clinical Medicine*, p. 54.

or to slowing the passage of the beverage through the stomach. After a person drinks an alcoholic beverage, the absorption of ethanol into the bloodstream varies from different sections of the gastrointestinal tract. Before it reaches the stomach, there is a minimum of absorption. Absorption occurs slowly through the stomach wall. When the stomach empties its contents into the adjoining sections, the duodenum and jejunum, the remaining alcohol is rapidly absorbed. Should any ethanol remain to move on through the ileum and colon, its absorption is slow. The overall speed depends primarily on the time required for the stomach to empty. This process can be slowed by drugs, but especially by food in the stomach, which may delay complete absorption from two to six hours. Carbonated beverages cause an acceleration, which produces an earlier rise in blood alcohol level, a phenomenon that would have explained to Dr. Henderson why Champagne intoxicates so speedily.

Once absorbed, alcohol is rapidly distributed by the blood and diffuses quickly and uniformly to all tissues (with the ratio depending on their water content). That is why an analysis of urine or expired air can be used to calculate blood alcohol levels. The accompanying diagram shows the combined rates of alcohol absorption, distribution, metabolic breakdown, and excretion and compares the differences in response to various beverages. *See* DIAGRAM 2 p. 372

About 90 percent of the alcohol absorbed is completely oxidized by enzymes produced in the liver. The final step apparently occurs at sites where energy is needed, and produces carbon dioxide and water. This metabolism differs from that of most substances by remaining fairly constant over time, rather than increasing as more ethanol is absorbed or as more calories are required, and occurs at an average adult rate of about one four-ounce glass of table wine an hour (more than one and one-half times as great as that of alcohol). Therefore, to avoid intoxication—legally a blood alcohol level of 0.1 percent—one's intake must not exceed the rate of metabolism and excretion. Driving skills may become impaired at the level of 0.04 percent and aberrant behavior begins at concentrations above 0.05 percent. Ethanol levels above 0.5 percent are generally lethal.

Leonard Goldberg has calculated that the "maximal daily intake" that can be disposed of in twenty-four hours by an "average" person of 154 pounds is two and two-thirds bottles of table wine (two liters), but only half a liter of whiskey. Drinking patterns are important. Three cocktails containing six to seven ounces of distilled spirits consumed in one hour cause a peak blood alcohol level of 0.14 percent, well above presumed intoxication, whereas three glasses of table wine (13 ounces) with a meal produce a maximum of 0.04 percent. Put another way, twice the volume of wine produces less than one-third of the blood alcohol peak of spirits. For most people, three glasses of table wine at dinner should neither impair their driving skills nor alter their social behavior significantly and should produce a level well below intoxication.

In addition, it is possible to estimate a "safe dose of alcohol"—one that avoids the long-term harmful effects of excessive drinking. As alcohol is oxidized, four atoms of hydrogen are released for each molecule of alcohol, a quantity that far exceeds the normal capacity of the body's various hydrogen-accepting systems. The most prominent alterations are to fat and carbohydrate metabolism. When the body's metabolic ability to process alcohol is oversaturated beyond recovery time, irreversible anatomical changes occur. Ample time for recovery is unknown, but A. W. Childs estimates a "safe" dose to be one-fourth of a liter of table wine daily by using an average rate of oxidation and a conservative guess of 3.6 hours a day free of alcohol. Experiments have shown that some tolerance to the effects of alcohol occurs. Even when drinking equal amounts of alcohol and measuring equal blood levels, abstainers show the greatest impairment, heavy drinkers the least.

DIET AND NUTRITION

Technically a food, wine provides approximately 95 calories in four ounces of red table wine (90 calories in four ounces of dry white wine) and, in quantities normally consumed, a negligible contribution of nutrients. From a nutritional standpoint, according to J. T. McDonald, a reasonable limit of alcohol—about three glasses of table wine—would be 10 percent of the total daily calories required to maintain ideal body weight. Through indirect action, wine contributes to nutrition by enhancing the appetite and reducing tension and by its interaction with other foods and physiological functions. In a carefully controlled metabolic study, moderate doses of Zinfandel, compared with both an alcohol solution and deionized water, improved the absorption of calcium, phosphorus, magnesium, iron, and zinc. Wine contains vitamins and a wide variety of minerals in quantities of limited physiological value, except for iron. Four ounces of table wine provide about 5 percent of the Recommended Dietary Allowance of iron for adult males, less for premenopausal females. Most wines have a low sodium and a high potassium content, and are compatible with low sodium diets. Wines that have undergone an ion-exchange treatment would be exceptions and can be identified by the winery.

As an aperitif, four ounces of wine of not more than 20 percent alcohol provide the most desirable stimulation of gastric secretions and movement (motility), aiding the digestion of food consumed within twenty minutes. How this action is triggered—whether directly by alcohol or organic acids or indirectly—is uncertain. Some clinicians report success in using wines to help patients with poor appetites gain weight, even those with anorexia nervosa.

Whether for psychological or physiological reasons, wine seems to aid in the proper regulation of diet. Added to the menus of hospitalized and geriatric patients, wine adds interest to their food, stimulates social interaction, aids relaxation, and improves morale. Some physicians report obese patients have decreased their night raids on the refrigerator and lost weight by substituting wine calories when dieting. They attribute this weight loss to the little-understood "satiety effect of wine" (the feeling that one's hunger has been satisfied). When dry wine is used in cooking, the calories may be ignored because the alcohol evaporates. The new light wines, which contain only one-third the calories, offer an advantage to the weight conscious.

DIABETES

Dry wine may benefit diabetics by brightening restricted diets and by providing energy without the use of insulin. Slightly sweet wines may often be enjoyed by those who do not depend on insulin. Dry wines on an empty stomach, however, cause some diabetic patients taking certain medications (sulfonyl derivatives) to develop facial flushing, heart palpitations, nausea, and low blood pressure. SO_2 in white wines is not recommended for diabetics.

INFECTIOUS DISEASES

Hippocrates' admonition that only wine should be used to moisten wounds may be related to recent scientific findings that various polyphenolic components (which wines contain) have direct bactericidal properties. Recent discoveries have demonstrated that white wines have a synergistic effect with some antibiotics, enhancing their effectiveness against bacteria.

PULMONARY DISEASE

Recent studies have demonstrated that wine's beneficial effects for asthmatics, long recognized by clinicians, may be due to a dilation of the bronchial tubes, making the exchange of air into the lungs easier. In patients with chronic breathing obstructions, ethanol brings improvement by reducing breathlessness and increasing the maximum amount of inhaled air, not through psychological effects, "but by improving lung function."

CARDIOVASCULAR DISEASE

Perhaps the area of greatest current therapeutic interest is the value of the moderate regular consumption of wine in the prevention of coronary disease. Again there is a centuries-long history of the use of alcoholic beverages as tonics or cardiac stimulants and for prompt relief from anginal pain. Similarly, wine has seen regular use in preventing anginal attacks and in aiding patients with high blood pressure. Statistical studies have demonstrated a lower incidence of coronary disease in those European countries distinguished by regular wine drinking; among certain Italian-Americans whose diet includes wine (and fat) in relatively large amounts; in Japanese men who drink moderately; and among other moderate drinkers as compared with heavy drinkers and with abstainers. It should be noted, however, that "alcoholics," those who regularly use large amounts of alcohol, have a two to three times greater death rate from cirrhosis, accidents, infections, certain cancers, and cardiovascular disease. Almost all recent population studies nevertheless agree that abstainers are at greater risk of major heart attacks than moderate or light drinkers.

Some recent studies suggest the possibility of physiological alterations of disease and the possible direct role of wine in lowering the risk of heart disease. For instance, one of the subgroups of cholesterol in the blood, the "high density lipoprotein" faction believed to be the "good" cholesterol that protects against heart attacks, is increased by the use of alcohol. The same lipoprotein may also protect against gallstones. John Kane reports that two glasses of wine a day substantially increase the most protective subgroup, the "scavengers," which remove the "bad" compounds (low density and very low density lipoproteins) that bond to blood vessel walls and interfere with the blood flow to the heart muscle, causing coronary artery disease.

ALLERGIES

Frequently people report being "allergic" to wine, specifically to red wine. Wine is not highly allergenic and is not a hospitable solvent for proteins, the usual culprits in allergic reactions. A computer-based search of the past fifteen years of medical literature reveals only three reports, none proven. Possible allergenic substances in wine might be grape constituents, yeasts, or products of fermentation, but Vincent Marinkovich has shown that even patients known to be highly allergic to the proteins of wine reacted mildly, if at all, to wines with extremely high concentrations of these substances added. He concluded that the various allergenic substances in wine, even when highly allergenic in themselves, are "just not present in sufficient quantity in finished wine to cause any problems." In a further study of another possible culprit, the highly allergenic proteins used to clarify or finish wines, Marinkovich concluded, "Allergic reactions to the finishing agents added to wine must be extremely rare." He believes, therefore, that most individuals can drink wine without fear of an allergic reaction. The possible exception for asthmatics is white table wines with high sulfur dioxide contents.

It is now known that wines contain some histamine and various vasoactive amines, small molecules that possess extreme ability to affect blood vessels. Allergic symptoms occur when histamine is released from the body's own mast cells. The body reproduces even greater numbers of mast cells in allergic people when they are having symptoms. If they drink wine at that time, it may aggravate their discomfort not through an allergic reaction but through the direct influence of ethanol on the cell membrane. When the symptoms subside and the number of mast

376

cells returns to normal, the allergic individual may again be able to tolerate wine without showing symptoms. Antihistamines taken before drinking wine can block this ethanol reaction by binding receptor sites, and thus permit one to drink without developing the symptoms. Alcohol, and especially red wines, may provoke migraine-type headaches in specifically sensitive people. The responsible substance remains unknown. S. W. J. Shaw has excluded pyramine as the agent provoking such attacks in dietary migraine sufferers. Some wines and many other foods, either naturally or by addition, may contain sufficient SO_2 to affect highly sensitive individuals; but aeration of the wines—either through agitation or by decanting—accelerates the natural process of dissipation of this highly volatile compound and ameliorates or virtually eliminates its effect.

ALCOHOL AND GLAUCOMA

Recent studies have demonstrated that when patients with open-angle glaucoma drink alcohol, there is an abrupt fall in their intraocular pressures. Although of little clinical use, this finding can affect diagnostic testing and is another example of the diversity of the physiological effects of wine that can be identified.

WHEN IT IS INADVISABLE TO DRINK WINE

Even moderate consumption of wine with meals may be harmful when there is inflammation of the mouth, throat, esophagus, or stomach, or when a person is suffering from epilepsy. In all such cases, one should seek medical advice. Alcoholic beverages of all kinds are generally forbidden with most conditions where there is hyperacidity of the stomach, when there is bleeding in the upper digestive tract, and when there is cancer of the stomach, as well as with infections of the pancreas, acute kidney infections, liver disease or hepatitis, severe heart damage, and chronic congestive heart failure. Moreover, since ethanol may interact synergistically with other drugs—that is, increase the effects of sedatives/hypnotics, tranquilizers, narcotics, and certain antidepressants—it is essential to have proper supervision when they are used together.

Heavy use of alcohol during pregnancy, especially binge drinking (more than three glasses of table wine daily), is a risk to the fetus, sometimes resulting in Fetal Alcohol Syndrome, a combination of growth retardation, congenital malformations, and mild mental retardation. Some specialists advise total abstinence during pregnancy, believing alcohol to be a direct toxin, causing fetal abnormalities. Katherine Christoffel has reported a case in which one fraternal twin developed severe F.A.S. abnormalities while the other, with obviously equal exposure to the toxin, was only minimally affected. Some specialists believe that alcohol is only one of many factors and that two glasses of table wine with meals each day are harmless.

ABUSIVE DRINKING

Alcoholism, though not within the scope of an essay on the medical and therapeutic values of wine, nevertheless is a problem of such medical, social, economic, and personal magnitude that it must not be ignored. Ten percent of the drinking population, the problem drinkers, comprise a heterogeneous group of people whose diversities follow no pattern but whose shared tolerance of, and dependence on, alcohol set them apart. Their disparities make universal statements difficult, but certain kinds of behavior that foster unsafe drinking are present with fair regularity in most alcoholics. Family studies reveal an increased incidence of alcoholism among relatives of alcoholics, 25 percent in males and 5 to 10 percent in females. Further, when compared with alcoholics with no family history of alcoholism, they were more likely to develop alcoholism of greater severity and more frequently to exhibit behavioral problems, to perform poorly in school and at work, and to have more financial and health problems. Studies of twins and adopted children confirm these findings and attest to a complex genetic susceptibility. A family history of alcoholism should signal a strong warning of possible vulnerability.

Of even greater significance than heredity is the influence of the environment in molding our early development and attitudes, in selecting our friends and cronies, and in forging our social and personal emotional identities. When there is stress in any of these areas, alcohol often softens it. Its analgesic and euphoric qualities, combined with the psychological escapes of denial and rationalization, can form a lethal chain, binding the alcoholic to an exclusive means of dealing with stress. But this form of "dealing," far from solving problems, is merely a way of delaying and accumulating them. Drinking patterns are programmed by the symbolic meanings that each person acquires and nurtures as part of his mental attitude. Our frontier culture produced hard-drinking, macho men who gulped down alcohol as a combined pressure-relieving elixir and social lubricant and viewed drunkenness as humorous or acceptable. G. Lolli has demonstrated that Italians in Italy consumed more wine but became drunk less often than a matched group of Italian-Americans in the United States. The Americans drank less total alcohol (less wine but more beer and spirits), yet reported more intoxication progressively over three generations of Americanization. Lolli concludes, "The custom of using alcoholic beverages separately from other food items—notable at the cocktail hour—is linked with a search for the psychological, rather than physiological, effects of alcohol," a difficulty he attributed to the Americans' lack of learning about the use of wine. This risk factor, unlike heredity, can be reduced by personal efforts, by proper family indoctrination, through group education in such affiliations as wine and food societies, and by the media.

The ability to understand and apply sound principles of prevention, treatment, and rehabilitation depends directly on the extent of knowledge in these fields. To this end, Ernest Gallo, one of the owners of California's largest winery, in April 1983 gave $3 million to the University of California and San Francisco General Hospital to establish the Ernest Gallo Clinic and Research Center devoted to the study of tolerance, addiction, and neurologic responses to alcohol and to the appropriate treatments of alcohol-related diseases.

EMOTIONS

Moderate drinking offers positive rewards to 90 percent of all users of alcohol. Wine's greatest contribution has been its service as man's oldest and safest tranquilizer, having been prescribed for relief of fatigue, distress, pain, and sorrow more than 2,700 years ago. It is this gentle, natural relief from tensions and travails of the day that best serves mankind physically, nutritionally, socially, and psychologically. Wine has an individual meaning to each user. A few moments of personal introspection may provide insights into its role for you. Wine has enhanced the quality of my own life by helping slow a busy pace, stimulating interest in the complexities and enjoyment of food, and deepening the shared pleasures of companionship and old friendships. The role of medicine today is generally conceded to include not merely the combating of diseases but also the prevention of illness and the maintenance of the highest level of fitness of body and mind. Wine may yet find its greatest role in the future search for the highest quality of life.

BIBLIOGRAPHIC NOTE

The high esteem in which wine is held in traditional European medicine is comprehensively documented in S. P. Lucia's *A History of Wine as Therapy*. The use of wine occupied a similar position in early American medicine, but underwent a dramatic decline with Prohibition and has been reinstated only after proven effective by scientific experimental verification of the sort documented by C. D. Leake and M. Silverman in *Alcoholic Beverages in Clinical Medicine*. Excellent summary articles, including a study of the physiological effects of wine, are contained in *Fermented Food Beverages in Nutrition*, edited by C. F. Gastineau, W. J. Darby, and T. B. Turner (New York: Academic Press, 1979). This essay represents a search through current scientific literature, especially journals, for hard data to replace anecdotal accounts of benefits and clinical case reports, utilizing the subject index of the cumulative medical index. An accessible summary of some of the primary material may be found in *Wine and Medical Practice* (San Francisco: Wine Institute, 1980). On specific subjects, see also G. Lolli et al., *Alcohol in Italian Culture* (Glencoe, Ill.: Free Press, 1958), and S. Cohen, "The Blood Alcohol Concentration," *Drug Abuse and Alcoholism Newsletter* 10 (July 1981): 6.

VIII.2
THE ECONOMICS OF WINE IN CALIFORNIA

by KIRBY MOULTON

See TABLE 4
p. 382

THE PRODUCTION OF GRAPES AND WINE IN CALIFORNIA IN-
VOLVES EXTENSIVE USE of the state's fertile land resources and requires the
skills of thousands of workers. It generates revenues that exceed half a billion dollars
for growers and two billion for vintners. In the world context, however, this activity is
dwarfed by that of the major European production countries. When one flies over
the San Joaquin Valley and views the vineyards that stretch in a virtually unbroken
string from north to south, it is difficult to imagine that other regions could be more
extensively planted. Yet they are. In Spain, vineyards occupy 4.2 million acres, six
times the area planted in California. Italian vineyards reach from the cool elevations
of the far north to the sun-baked hillsides of Sicily and cover 3.4 million acres,
slightly more than are allocated to vineyards in the USSR. In France, grapes are
planted to 2.9 million acres. The difference is obviously reflected in production
differences between the major winemaking countries. California produced 439
million gallons of wine in 1980, which was 90 percent of U.S. production but only 5
percent of world wine output. Italy, France, and Spain are the major winemakers.
Italian vintners alone produced 2.2 billion gallons of wine in 1980. A slight blip in
their production represents more wine than most countries drink in an entire year.
France ranked second behind Italy with an output of 1.8 billion gallons, mostly ordinary table wines.

 Worldwide wine consumption in 1980 totaled 7.7 billion gallons. France
and Italy accounted for 35 percent of this and the USSR, Spain, the United States,
and Germany quaffed an additional one-third. Some wide divergences appear when
these volumes are converted to a per capita basis. For example, per capita wine consumption in France and in Italy was approximately 25 gallons per year. Consumers
in Argentina drank 20 gallons and those in Spain about 17 gallons. These levels are
very high indeed when compared to the United States (2.2 gallons), the United
Kingdom (2 gallons), and the USSR (3.8 gallons). Wine consumption is affected by
a wide array of cultural, economic, and political factors that differ among countries.

As a result, per capita consumption levels in one country (France, for example) may be entirely inappropriate as a marketing goal in another country (the United States, for example). The particular set of factors influencing U.S consumers has held per capita consumption to the lowest level among all major wine-producing countries except Algeria. The United States ranks fifth in world wine production but only twenty-seventh in per capita consumption.

A HISTORICAL PERSPECTIVE

The current situation in California's vineyards and wineries parallels that of the industry's earlier days. Its economic history is a fabric of high and low profits, vineyard planting and removal, wine surplus and shortage, and shifting consumer preferences. The industry has become robust and exceedingly complex, but has never really resolved the problem of profitably coordinating vineyard planting with winery shipments.★

THE EVOLVING STRUCTURE

California vineyards expanded enormously between 1880 and 1980 and much of this growth occurred relatively early. Vineyards covered 56,000 acres in 1880, twice that amount in 1885, and six times the 1880 area by 1910. The acreage in that year, 350,000 acres, required seventy years to double again. Almost all of the additional vineyards were devoted to winemaking. Production from this expanded acreage created economic havoc for growers and wine sellers alike. Grower prices tumbled from over $20 per ton in the early 1880s to less than $10 per ton by the end of the decade. Imports posed serious market threats, as they did a hundred years later, and dishonest selling practices eroded grower and winery revenues.

Some marketing problems, described by Professor E. W. Hilgard in 1880, included the practice of selling California wines under foreign labels "after two trips across the Atlantic, or even perhaps only across the Bay." Blending was left chiefly to the wine merchants of San Francisco, with somewhat uncertain results in quality. Hilgard noted, however, that neutral spirits, logwood, glycerine, and sulphuric acid played relatively small roles in the blending practices of these merchants. The Mission grape common in California's early vineyards was believed by Hilgard and others to contribute to marketing problems: the low-quality wines made from it encouraged the production of sweet wines that masked the grape's defects.

It is difficult to place a reliable value on total annual shipments of California wine in the nineteenth century because they included a large number of

★   This section draws on my article "Wine: A Multibillion-dollar Industry," *California Agriculture*, July 1980, pp. 9–11.

TABLE 4

A COMPARISON OF WINE PRODUCTION, TRADE, & CONSUMPTION (1982)

| | Vineyard Area | W I N E | | | |
| | | Production | Imports | Exports | Consumption per Capita |
	1,000 ACRES	MILLIONS OF GALLONS			GALLONS
CALIFORNIA	730	513	. . . . .	. . . . .	4.5
UNITED STATES	826	555	122	9	2.2
FRANCE	2,801	2,092	199	235	22.7
WEST GERMANY	252	407	263	59	6.6
ITALY	3,312	1,919	4	547	21.9
UNITED KINGDOM	0	0	119	0	1.9
SPAIN	4,011	984	0	132	15.1
USSR	3,394	915	179	14	3.8★
BULGARIA	417	129	3	78	5.8★
HUNGARY	393	179	17	68	7.8★
OTHER	8,599	1,977	383	243	. . . . .
WORLD	24,735	9,670	1,289	1,385	. . . . .

★Previous year.

SOURCE: Office Internationale de la Vigne et du Vin, *Ordre du jour et documents* (Paris, 1983), pp. 13–25.

different wines with different prices. Based on estimated average wholesale prices of 65 cents for dry wine and $1.00 for sweet, the value in 1880 was $7 million, or an average of about 70 cents a gallon. A corresponding estimate for 1980 is $1.9 billion, or an average of $5.79 a gallon. Winedrinkers in the United States consumed about 28 million gallons of wine annually during the 1880s, a level stimulated by improved marketing and augmented production. Over 80 percent of this wine was supplied by domestic producers and the balance was imported. During the period when consumption was expanding in the 1870s and 1880s, U.S. producers were able to cut in half the market share held by foreign wines. Even so, the market share of imports was always significant in the pre-Prohibition U.S. wine market. It dropped to an unimportant 3 percent only in the immediate post-Repeal period.

Overall wine consumption averaged over 50 million gallons annually by 1913. Even during Prohibition, per capita wine consumption was sustained as thousands of consumers became home winemakers. This desire to consume wine partly explains the expansion of California's vineyards to 650,000 acres by 1928, a level not again reached during the succeeding fifty years. Wine production surged after Repeal. California production in 1935–39 was 50 percent higher than its pre-Prohibition average, but was dominated by sweet wines, a distinct shift from the 1880s, when dry wines were preferred. One viticulturist opined that though sweet wines might be appropriate for some of the more hearty immigrants, they were definitely unsuitable for the Anglo-Saxon stomach.

ECONOMIC RELATIONSHIPS

Production costs and sales revenues changed significantly between 1880 and 1980 in response to improved technology and vastly different price levels. The scope of these changes can be appreciated by using a common dollar for comparisons between the two time periods. The following comparisons were made by expressing 1880 values in terms of 1980 dollars. Changes in the Consumer Price Index between 1880 and 1980 indicate that 1880 prices should be multiplied by 8.5 to convert them to 1980 dollars.

Land values have increased dramatically over the past century. In 1880, land suitable for vineyards could be bought for from $10 to $125 per acre, and the average was probably $50 per acre. In 1980 dollars, the average price was the equivalent of $425 per acre. There were no bargains like that in 1980, when vineyard sites ranged in value from $3,000 to $10,000 per acre. This radical escalation in land prices helped convert grape growing into the highly capital-intensive activity it is today. It also reduced growers' flexibility in meeting grape price fluctuations and motivated a search for more stable pricing arrangements.

This change is also apparent in vineyard establishment and production costs. Complete development costs in 1980 were about $6,000 per acre, depending on location and characteristics. Even discounting potential differences in cost accounting, such costs far exceed the modern equivalent of 1880 costs, currently estimated to be from $600 to $1,000 per acre. Cultural and harvest costs also increased more rapidly than general prices between 1880 and 1980. They averaged approximately $950 per acre in 1980, excluding depreciation, interest, and overhead, as compared to $100 per acre, the current equivalent of 1880 costs.

Grape prices rose at a slower rate than did production costs. Wine grape prices ranged between $10 and $21 per ton during most of the 1880s, the equivalent of $85 to $180 per ton in modern terms. Comparable prices during the 1970s ranged from $164 to $428 per ton. Thus, prices rose two or three times beyond the level of a century earlier, while costs increased by six to ten times.

Improved yields helped growers survive the cost-price squeeze. Revenue per acre during the 1880s averaged about $80, the equivalent of $650 per acre in modern terms. This was half the average revenue per acre received by California wine grape growers in 1980. More significantly, however, the money that growers had left over after paying labor and other cash costs was greater in the 1880s ($550 per acre) than in 1980 ($310 per acre). The leftover money could be applied against depreciation, interest costs, and returns to the owner's labor and investment. In spite of difficulties in evaluating the accuracy of 1880 statistics, it is clear that growers have had to run very fast just to keep up. The remarkable stability in grower numbers and the substantial increase in grape acreage suggest that they have been successful.

Bulk wine prices actually declined in real terms between 1880 and 1980. The earlier price was 25 cents a gallon, or the equivalent of $2.00 in 1980. Bulk table wine prices in early 1980 were almost one-third lower than this at $1.30 a gallon. Increased winemaking efficiency accounts for an important part of this price restraint.

Wholesale wine prices have changed relatively little over the past century when expressed in 1980 dollars. Restaurant prices, on the other hand, are quite a bit higher today. The cost of a half carafe of house wine was about 13 cents in 1880, the equivalent of $1.10 in 1980 dollars. This is probably half of what an equivalent wine cost in 1980.

VINEYARDS

PHYSICAL ASPECTS

The quality, variety, and quantity of grapes produced from California's vineyards are essential to the economic success of the state's dynamic wine industry. As one winemaker has put it, "Eighty percent of my wines' quality is determined in the vineyard; my influence in the winery is small by comparison."

Grapes are planted to over 700,000 acres in California, making them the preeminent fruit crop in the state. The acreage is divided among three principal types: raisin, table, and wine, indicating the principal, but not the exclusive uses of the grapes. Wine varieties, the principal type cultivated, were planted to 364,000 acres in 1983. Raisin varieties, principally Thompson Seedless, occupied 292,000 acres, and table grapes 90,000 acres. Acreage was up 15 percent from 1975 levels for all three classes.

Prior to 1970, California wine vineyards, planted heavily to black varieties such as Carignane, Barbera, Grenache, and Zinfandel, reflected the orientation of table wine production toward red wines. When consumer preferences began to switch toward white table wines in the 1970s, it required a long time for the proper planting signals to reach grape growers. Plantings between 1970 and 1975 maintained the preponderance of black over white varieties.

Grape prices plummeted in 1974 and 1975 as the supply of black grapes surpassed industry requirements. This initiated a period of vineyard removal and a subsequent period of grafting over from black to white varieties, a change that raised the proportion of white wine grapes from one-third of varietal acreage in 1975 to 48 percent in 1981. As a result, the varietal mix of the crush came much closer to matching wine shipments in 1982 than it did in 1975. This gap closed further after 1982 as newly planted white varietals reached maturity.

Grape varieties are very difficult to distinguish to the untrained eye. Consequently, the array of varieties in California's vineyards is often surprising to the casual observer. State reports list sixty different wine grapes produced commercially, plus a miscellaneous category comprising varieties of very limited planting. A few varieties constitute a major part of the state's vineyard acreage, although their individual importance has changed over time.

French Colombard covered 73,000 acres and was the most widely planted wine variety in 1983. Its high yields and low prices generated little profit in many of California's producing regions. New plantings from 1980 through 1983 almost doubled the acreage and provided a massive expansion in production in subsequent years. Chenin Blanc, the second most popular variety, accounted for 45,000 acres. New plantings, less than half those of French Colombard, nevertheless increased the production capacity of Chenin Blanc vineyards by 50 percent. The third-ranking variety, and first among the black grapes, was Zinfandel. Plantings, relatively heavy in the early seventies, tapered off quickly after 1975. They covered 27,000 acres in 1983. Among the other significant varietals, Cabernet Sauvignon covered 22,000 acres; Carignane, 19,000; and Chardonnay, 24,000.

Economic success in a vineyard depends on many factors, but certainly production per acre (yield) is a critical one. Yields vary enormously according to climatic conditions, geographic location, grape variety, and management practices. Yields of three tons per acre might be considered good on a hilly vineyard in Napa County, while eight tons per acre could be a disappointment on a well-irrigated vineyard in Kern County. These differences are illustrated by comparing yields calculated from state reports of wine grape crush and wine grape acreage in 1983. Mendocino County vineyards produced 4.2 tons per acre of Carignane and 4.9 tons per acre of Chenin Blanc, while vineyards in Kern County produced 8.4 tons and 8.5 tons respectively. Cabernet Sauvignon yields were 3.2 tons in Mendocino County, 3.9 tons in Sonoma County, and 3.5 tons in Napa County; the respective Chardonnay yields were 2.7 tons, 2.8 tons, and 3.3 tons. Yields also vary considerably from one year to another. Wine grape yields reached a high point of 7 tons per acre in 1973, sank to a low of 4.5 tons in 1976, and climbed to a record level of 8.3 tons in 1982.

The existence of two dozen large vineyard operations in California has created the impression that grape production is the exclusive preserve of corporate giants. This is not the case. There were about 9,700 grape producers in California in 1979.* The average size of their individual vineyards was 68 acres. Most of the growers (88 percent) operated units of less than 100 acres—in fact, the average size was 26 acres.

At the other end of the scale, 7 growers reported ownership of vineyards exceeding 5,000 acres. The average size was 6,900 acres, with the largest individual vineyard comprising almost 10,000 acres. In aggregate, 72 growers with operations of over 1,000 acres cultivated 28 percent of California's vineyard land in 1979, and 9,600 growers cultivated the balance. The production of grapes for crush involves 4,500 wine grape growers and the perhaps 2,400 producers of raisin and table varieties who allocate part of their production to the crush market. This market thus influences the income of a large majority of California grape growers.

The pattern of wine grape holdings varies throughout the state. The average size is smallest in the North Coast district (41 acres) and largest in the Central Coast district (403 acres). The range of average sizes among the major producing counties goes from 36 acres in Mendocino to 1,506 acres in Monterey.

ECONOMIC ASPECTS

The profits earned from wine vineyards depend on costs, production, and prices. Between 1970 and 1982, costs increased at a rapid rate, production was highly variable, and prices fluctuated significantly. Viticulture is tremendously capital intensive. The investments required for the acquisition of existing vineyards

---

* The tabulation of grape acreage and number of growers for 1979 was provided by the California Crop and Livestock Reporting Service. Some duplication exists in the grower count because of growers who operate in more than one county or produce two or more classes of grapes.

or for the development of new ones are substantial. In 1982, a year of poor grape prices and soft wine markets, the prices for bearing vineyards ranged from $8,000 to $13,000 per acre in the San Joaquin Valley and up to $25,000 per acre in the North Coast region. Buying land and developing a new vineyard cost from about $10,000 per acre in the former area to $21,000 in the latter.

Investment costs vary considerably according to the specific characteristics of individual operations. Typically, they include site conversion (such as removing trees or vines, ripping the soil and fumigating), irrigation and frost control installations, cultural equipment, and miscellaneous tools and supplies. Investment and development costs escalated rapidly between 1970 and 1982. Sample development budgets estimated by the University of California for the southern San Joaquin Valley showed costs of $2,200 in 1970, $5,500 in 1976, and $10,000 (preliminary) in 1982. Costs in other areas moved in a similar fashion.

The high level of investment costs creates a substantial fixed cost component for vineyard operations. This component, comprising depreciation and real or imputed interest on investment and working capital, accounts for 40 to 60 percent of the full costs of operating a vineyard. The costs of producing grapes vary considerably from vineyard to vineyard, depending on location, cultural practices, size of the operation, and management skill. These costs also increased rapidly during the seventies and reached a level of $3,500 to $4,200 per acre in the North Coast area and $2,000 to $2,300 per acre in the San Joaquin Valley, according to University of California budget worksheets.

At such costs, a Napa Valley grower would need a yield of four tons per acre and a grape price of $1,000 per ton in order to break even. This price exceeds the average price paid in 1982 for all grape varieties in Napa County except for Chardonnay and Cabernet Franc. The cost figures do not provide an accurate measure of a grower's ability to survive, however, because of differences in investment cost. As noted previously, a substantial portion of the university-estimated costs are for depreciation and interest (either actual or imputed) charged at current rates against the replacement value of assets. These fixed costs are lower for established vineyards than for new ones because of inflated land values, interest rates, and development costs. Typically, established operators do not account for imputed interest or changes in replacement value. This situation has created a significant difference between new and older enterprises in ability to survive.

The following example, based on 1979 costs, illustrates the point. In that year, full production costs in the sample region were $2,724 per acre. A vineyard bought in previous years with a land value of $5,000 and an interest rate of 8 percent on real property and 16 percent on operating capital would have a production cost of $609 per ton in 1979. A new vineyard with costs reflecting a land value of $8,000 per acre and an interest rate of 12 percent on real property and 16 percent on operating capital would have a cost of $795 per ton. This difference of almost $200 per ton implies a substantial difference in viability between the two vineyards.

The extreme in short-run economic strength is the grower who has no out-of-pocket interest expenses and puts nothing aside for amortization. His cash costs in the North Coast region for cultivation, harvest, taxes, and overhead would have been about $1,500 per acre or $375 per ton at a four-ton yield in 1979. His survival capacity over heavily leveraged newly established vineyards was considerable. The lesson from this is that California has a split wine grape industry with one part having a far greater ability to weather economic storms than the other. The cost is great, however, in terms of financial loss to others whose production may be required in the future. The orderly development of the grape and wine industry suffers.

Grower prices vary according to the conditions of supply and demand affecting the different grape varieties, qualities, and end uses. Wine grape prices are influenced by the structure of the wine industry, the expected production of grapes for crush, the rate of wine shipments, the level of wine inventories, and conditions in the raisin and fresh grape markets. Grape prices behave like those of other agricultural commodities. They fluctuate significantly from year to year. In some vineyards, they more than cover the costs of production; in others, they are significantly below costs.

Price fluctuations are partially determined by variations in production and tend to offset them. When production expands, prices will drop, and when production declines, prices will increase, unless other factors intervene. Consequently, fluctuations in revenue are less severe than those in price but still remain significant. This leads to irregular cash flows and considerable distress for agricultural bankers.

Plenty of this distress was evident in the 1970s. Average revenues per acre for wine grape production peaked in 1973 at $1,435, dropped to a nadir three years later at $603, and climbed to a record level of $1,696 in 1981, only to fall again in 1982. Similar experience was recorded in earlier years as well. Revenues increased by one-third between 1960 and 1961, declined by 22 percent the following year, then jumped 38 percent in 1964. Revenues per acre and production costs changed at different rates between 1952 and 1982. The divergence in growth rates altered the profit position of growers from one period to another. Between 1950–52 and 1960–62, average revenues per acre of wine grapes increased by three-quarters while costs increased by one-quarter. Net returns to wine grape growers were better at the end of the period than at the beginning. Revenues surged by 150 percent over the next ten years. Costs grew by a relatively modest 50 percent, hence farmers benefited again, compared to a decade earlier. However, the tide turned in the seventies. Although revenues doubled between 1970–72 and 1980–82, costs quadrupled and left many growers in precarious financial situations. During the thirty-year period starting in 1950–52, average revenues per acre increased almost nine times and costs about eight times. Revenues grew faster than costs, even during the shorter period beginning in 1960–62. Thus, net returns to growers in the early eighties were better in real terms than they were twenty or thirty years earlier, but not as large as ten years before.

Aggregate cost figures tend to obscure much detail. For example, growers of white grapes fared better than those of black grapes because the white wine "boom," starting about 1975, stimulated demand. The average price for white varieties in 1981 was $338 per ton. It generated an estimated return per bearing acre of $2,387, which was above the average costs of production. On the other hand, the average black grape price of $213 per ton returned $1,218 per acre, which was below estimated total production costs.

Grape quality influences pricing, although by different amounts according to the needs of individual wineries. These needs are generally determined by the characteristics of the wines produced. However, in years of abundant grape supplies, standards may be tightened in order to restrict grape deliveries to match wine production requirements. Standards may be relaxed when grape supplies are short to assure an adequate volume of deliveries. Price reports by the state of California reveal the great range of quality-based prices for individual grape varieties, but do not identify the quality specifications (other than sugar level) on which the prices are based. These specifications may take into account sugar level, sugar-acid ratio, other components believed related to wine quality, defects such as mold, foreign materials delivered with grapes (leaves, dirt, and so on), and the weight loss in Late Harvest grapes.

The range of prices was greater in the North Coast districts than in the San Joaquin Valley. For example, prices for French Colombard ranged from $375 to $500 per ton in the former districts, and from $210 to $265 in the latter districts. Generally, the lower prices were paid without regard to sugar content (within reasonable limits), while the higher prices stipulated a minimum sugar level with penalties for degrees below the level. The range of prices paid for Chardonnay grapes from Napa County provides some idea of the complexity of quality-based pricing. Prices started at $500 per ton and increased to $2,000 per ton. Since both prices were paid for grapes without a stated minimum sugar content, it is likely that other quality characteristics dominated the pricing scheme. Some observers feel that demand was so great, sugar was ignored.

The link between crush and other grape markets is primarily through Thompson Seedless grapes. Thompsons are used for raisins, marketed fresh, and sold for crush. Typically, from a production level of 2.6 million tons, about 1.6 million tons would be dried, 750,000 tons crushed, and 250,000 tons shipped fresh. A certain flexibility exists in the allocation of these grapes between the raisin market and the crush market. Consequently, the supply of raisin variety grapes influences the price of wine varieties competitive in crush use. This situation was particularly evident in 1982, when a surplus of dried raisins combined with a slowdown in wine shipments to depress Thompson Seedless and wine grape prices.

The link between fresh market grapes and the crush market is not very strong because cultural practices between the two end uses differ and are considerably more expensive for fresh market varieties. Consequently, it is usually only damaged fruit from fresh market vineyards that finds its way to the crush. An important exception is the Tokay variety, which is mostly crushed. By and large, switching between end uses is not very easy and requires a price differential sufficient to justify the effort.

WINERIES

PHYSICAL ASPECTS

The wineries of California are a diverse lot. They range in size from very small to gigantic. Small wineries, such as Ahlgren Vineyard, are tucked into hillsides at the end of winding gravel roads. There a family winemaker, often moonlighting from a full-time job, handcrafts a few hundred or thousand cases, which find their way to friends and a limited number of outlets. It is of these wineries that the romance of California wines is generally written.

At the large end of the scale stands E. & J. Gallo Winery. The main winery covers acres of the flat Modesto countryside with huge storage tanks, modern buildings, and a complex network of roads. Highly skilled winemakers there, and in the Livingston and Fresno plants, produce a wide array of wines to serve extended markets, an estimated 62 million cases in 1983. It is of these and other large wineries that the business of California wineries is generally written.

In between the largest and smallest wineries are an increasing number of wine producers. There were 639 bonded winery premises and wine cellars in California in 1983 and an additional 445 in other states. After adjusting the California figure for inactive wineries and for firms with more than one bonded premises or cellar, it is likely that the number of active winery firms in California was about 550. Napa County was the location of more wineries (131) than any other California county in 1983. There were 120 in Sonoma County, 46 in Santa Clara County, and the balance were spread among thirty-six other counties, led by Mendocino, Alameda, and San Joaquin.

The number of wineries is only one dimension of structure. The size distribution is also important. The ten largest California wineries accounted for 81 percent of the state's wine shipments in 1983. The total shipped by the rest was less than half that shipped by Gallo. Consequently, each county's share of the winery population is unrelated to its share of wine shipments.

Ownership patterns are complex. The majority of California wineries are privately held by individuals or families, prominent among whom are Mirassou Vineyards, Sebastiani Vineyards, E. & J. Gallo Winery, and J. F. J. Bronco Winery. For the most part, they carry on a history of family winemaking in California that reaches back to the 1930s and earlier.

Major corporations with other non-wine-related businesses control an important part of California's wine production. In 1983, shipments by their subsidiaries amounted to 84 million gallons, 23 percent of the state's total shipments. Corporations with foreign headquarters or owned by foreign corporations controlled 52 million gallons (62 percent) of this amount.

The most important conglomerate ownership in terms of California wine volume was that of the Seagram Company, with 1983 wine shipments of 41 million gallons, 11 percent of California's total. This volume was attained through the consolidation of the former Coca-Cola subsidiary, the Wine Spectrum, with Seagram's Paul Masson Winery and other wine operations.

Seagram, with headquarters in Montreal, Canada, had a sales volume of about $2.4 billion in 1981. The largest distiller in the world, it operated wineries in Germany, Israel, Spain, Portugal, France, Italy, Canada, Australia, Brazil, and the United States. It marketed 150 brands of wine and spirits in 175 countries.

The ownership of Almadén Vineyards by National Distillers and Chemical Corporation resulted in the control of 27 million gallons of shipments. National acquired Almadén in 1967 (although a complete buyout was deferred until after 1975). Well regarded as a producer of quality wines, with shipments of 3.6 million gallons when it was bought, Almadén's aggressive marketing policies after that time raised it to third place among all California wineries in 1983.

The second major foreign entry was by John Labatt, a Canadian brewery that acquired the almost defunct Bear Mountain (or LaMont) Winery in the late 1970s. Labatt had sales of about $2.5 billion in 1981. In addition to beer, it produces wine, food, and chemicals, and processes corn, wheat, and other agricultural commodities. Shipments from the LaMont Winery were 6.2 million gallons in 1983.

Nestlé, the giant Swiss-based multinational conglomerate, owns Wine World, Inc., which in turn controls the Beringer Vineyards Division. Shipments of Beringer wines were 4 million gallons in 1983. It was acquired in 1971.

Other proprietary or partnership arrangements involving foreign firms have been prominent because of the character of the wines or of the principals. The establishment of Domaine Chandon in 1974 by Moët-Hennessy of France linked 220-year-old Moët et Chandon, a famous producer of Champagne, with a prestigious California producing region. Moët expanded its entry into California wine production with its subsequent purchase of Simi Winery in Healdsburg, a winery established in 1876.

In 1980, Piper-Heidsieck of Reims, Renfield Imports of New York, and Sonoma Vineyards formed a joint venture to produce and market sparkling wines, the second major infusion of foreign capital and experience into that segment of California's wine industry. Their first releases were in 1982.

Also in 1980, Robert Mondavi and the Baron Philippe de Rothschild, owner of the celebrated Château Mouton-Rothschild, announced a joint venture to produce a world class wine in California. The plan combines the grapes and facilities of Mondavi and the specialized winemaking skills of both wineries. The first release, a red wine Opus One, contained Cabernet Sauvignon and Cabernet Franc from the 1979 vintage.

Other ownerships of interest in the North Coast area include that of Buena Vista by A. Racke Company of West Germany; Franciscan Vineyards by Peter Eckes Company of West Germany; Cambiaso Winery by Four Seasons Corporation, with ownership interests from Thailand; and Cuvaison, with Swiss connections. Woltner & Co., a firm with French connections, has over 400 acres in Angwin and plans to produce wines in the style of its parent, Château la Mission Haut-Brion.

Conglomerate ownership of wineries does not fit well with all corporate strategies. Coca-Cola Company, R. J. Reynolds, Coca-Cola Bottling Company of New York, and Schlitz Brewing Company all divested themselves of California wine properties. Coca-Cola's purchase of the Monterey Vineyard and Sterling Winery in California and Taylor Wine Company and Great Western Winery in New York in 1977 received a great deal of publicity because it marked the entry of the world's largest soft drink company into the world's most traditional beverage industry. The entry was a short-lived affair that ended with the sale of Coca-Cola's subsidiary, the Wine Spectrum, to the Seagram Company in 1983. In another major move, R. J. Reynolds sold most of its California wine properties, excluding Inglenook and Beaulieu Vineyards, back to Allied Grape Growers, a growers' cooperative. The resulting new organization, I.S.C. Wines, was California's fifth-ranking winery in 1983.

A cooperative form of winery ownership, quite important in the major European wineproducing countries, is less significant in the structure of California's industry. Allied Grape Growers (I.S.C. Wines) and Guild Wineries and Distillers, the largest cooperatives producing wine in California, accounted for 8.3 percent of California wine shipments in 1983. Both organizations are strongly dependent on San Joaquin Valley grapes. I.S.C. shipped about one-third more wine than did Guild, but Guild's nearly one thousand members provided up to 8 percent of the state's crush. Their returns to members provide one indication of the value of grapes in wine production and thus become a reference point for evaluating other pricing arrangements.

Other wineries with cooperative ownership are smaller and some have exclusive sales arrangements to supply wines for other wineries. Bonded wineries with cooperative ownership include Delano Growers, East-Side Winery, Gibson Wine Company, Konocti Cellars, Napa Valley Cooperative Winery, Sonoma County Cooperative Winery, Sun Maid Growers, and Woodbridge Vineyard Association.

The degree of concentration in the U.S. wine industry depends on how the market is defined. Of all wines entering U.S. wine distribution channels in 1983, Gallo accounted for 28 percent and Seagram (from all wine operations) for 11 percent. Other top wine shippers were Villa Banfi (5.7 percent, almost all foreign wines), Almadén (5.1 percent), Heublein Wines (4.1 percent), and I.S.C. Wines (3.3 percent). The concentration ratios obviously increase if foreign wines are ignored, but such a comparison is meaningless in the face of competitive market conditions. The top ten California wineries accounted for 81 percent of the state's shipments in 1983; the top twenty, 91 percent; and the remaining 550 (estimated), the other 9 percent.

The structure of California's wine industry is dynamic. The structural changes that occurred in 1983 will not dictate the future any more than the changes of the sixties and seventies did. The rapid increase in the number of California's wineries from 1980 through 1983 diluted the dominance of the state's top twenty wineries, reversing a trend toward concentration. Within the space of 1983, the enthusiastic public reception of a new wine-based beverage, California Cooler, propelled its makers into the tenth spot among California's established wineries. Changes in the popularity of sparkling wines also added significant new firms to California's spectrum of wineries and altered traditional structural relationships.

Bulk wines have an important role in wine production. Figures for shipment within California are not available but appear to be substantial, with large volumes provided by Sierra Winery, California Growers, and others. Almadén, Sebastiani, and Gallo all purchase wines produced by others for blending, bottling, and distribution. Rail shipments of bulk wine out of California were almost 5 million gallons in 1981, 4.5 percent destined for wineries in Pennsylvania, 30 percent for New York.

Bulk wines provide a means for arbitrage in the wine market. They establish an economic relationship between grape growers in all regions, since major wineries are able to substitute bulk wine for grapes as economic conditions dictate. This has been important in enabling New York wineries to expand their output without a corresponding increase in vineyard acreage or an explosive increase in grape prices.

The number, location, ownership, and importance of California wineries changed during a period of remarkable growth in wine consumption. The growth between 1971 and 1983 was characterized by some important elements:

1. *Adult per capita consumption of wine grew by 36 percent to a level of 3.3 gallons.*

2. *Consumer preferences shifted sharply in favor of table wines and away from dessert wines. Per capita consumption of table wines doubled and that of dessert wines diminished by one-half.*

3. *The consumption of white wines moved from 25 percent of total table wine consumption to 61 percent.*

4. *California's wine shipments increased by 61 percent but its market share declined, while that of imported wines more than doubled.*

A background for viewing the wine industry is helpful. Drinkers consumed an estimated 527 million gallons of wine in the United States in 1983, based on shipment figures. About 67 percent of it originated in California, 8 percent in other states, and 25 percent in foreign countries. New York, the second major wine producer, accounted for only 5 percent of U.S. production in 1983.

Most descriptions of the U.S. wine market use shipment figures that are classified according to federal standards for the production, taxation, or importation of wine. These provide a reasonable overview, but are not adequate for a detailed market analysis. Because these classifications are so frequently used, it is worthwhile defining them. The wine classes used—table, dessert, vermouth, other special natural, and sparkling—have very specific meanings, which may be different from those used in Europe or commonly understood by many American consumers.

"Table wines" include naturally fermented still wines of under 14 percent alcohol to which no additional flavoring has been added. Since they may be made from grapes or apples and other fruits, they include wines that some consider "pop" wines. They may also include some with an effervescence below that required for sparkling wines. Table wines entering U.S. distribution channels from all sources in 1983 amounted to 402 million gallons, an increase of 146 million gallons from 1971.

The "dessert wine" class describes still natural wines of over 14 percent and up to 21 percent alcohol (the law allows up to 24 percent, but such high-alcohol wines seldom appear on the retail market) without flavor additives. These include generically labeled wines such as sherry, port, and muscatel, as well as some varietal wines such as Zinfandel, which are occasionally produced with an alcohol level

394

higher than that in table wines. The volume of dessert wines shipped in 1983 was 38 million gallons, a decline of 36 million gallons from 1971.

"Vermouth" was considered a "special" wine by regulatory authorities because it included special flavoring that differentiated it from traditional table and dessert wines. A relatively minor category, it accounted for only 7 million gallons in 1983, a drop of about 3 million from 1971. Shipment figures compiled by the California State Board of Equalization incorporate vermouth into the dessert wine category because the two classes are not distinguished for taxing purposes. This can cause some difficulty in casual comparison of state and federal shipment reports.

"Other special natural wines" also have flavor additives, but for some administrative reason are kept separate from vermouth, hence the added qualifier "other" to distinguish the two. About 66 percent contain less than 14 percent alcohol. Shipments in this class declined from 41 million gallons in 1971 to 36 million gallons in 1983. In California tax data, shipments of other special natural wines are included with table wines or dessert wines, depending on alcohol content.

The "sparkling wine" class is self-descriptive, although it excludes a certain number of wines carbonated at less than the minimum pressure required for that category. Shipments in 1983 were 43 million gallons, up from 24 million gallons in 1971.

Wine consumption is estimated in this chapter by the volume of wine entering distribution channels because more accurate measures of aggregate consumption are not reported. These estimates are reasonable over the long run, but less reliable on a year-by-year basis because of inventory fluctuations and the lag between shipment and consumption.

Some interesting comparisons can be made between the changes noted in each wine class. The consumption of all wines in the United States increased at an average annual rate of 5.9 percent between 1961 and 1971 and then grew by 5.2 percent a year during the following decade. Table wine consumption was the star of this expansion, with average annual growth rates of 10.5 percent and 9.5 percent over the respective decades. Table wine shipments in 1983 were 345 million gallons greater than in 1961.

Sales of other special natural wines grew spectacularly until 1972, then commenced a decline that persisted at least through 1982. It is not clear what happened to the preferences of "pop" wine consumers, although many observers believe that a substantial portion shifted to table wines. "Pop" products accounted for 8 percent of the wine market in 1961, 14 percent in 1976, and 7 percent in 1983.

Dessert wines dominated the U.S. market until the 1960s, but their fall from favor was rapid. Between 1961 and 1983, consumption dropped by 55 percent, to a level of 38 million gallons, only 7 percent of the market. The alcohol content of most dessert wines was lowered in the early seventies in an attempt to make them more compatible with consumer preferences. The diminished production and alcohol reduced the requirement for grapes by perhaps 440,000 tons over a twenty-year period. Increased table wine production took up some of this slack. However, the grapes were not necessarily the varieties perferred for table wines, and not as many were required per gallon, contributing to their relatively poor prices.

Sparkling wine consumption grew rapidly between 1965 and 1971, then backed off for a few years before resuming growth in 1976. Cold Duck was a major contributor to the early growth and subsequent decline. More traditional sparkling wines were the focus of growth in the later years. Premium sparkling wines, those made by the traditional Champagne method, constitute less than 10 percent of total domestic production.

Wine markets ought to be divided up according to how consumers, rather than tax collectors, make their decisions. Such a task is not easy on an industry scale because price-volume-quality figures tend to be proprietary. It is possible to make estimates of market shares according to price specification and brand, from the public sales data of states with government wine monopolies, although such states may not be representative of nationwide markets.

ECONOMIC ASPECTS

Winemaking, like grape growing, is a capital intensive activity. The row upon row of glistening stainless steel tanks, sturdy racks of oak barrels, and computers for fermentation, blending, aging, and flow control provide visual testimony of the extensive investments required by most large wineries. The relatively few available data concerning winery construction and operating costs provide some insights about cost relationships, but must be used cautiously in generalizing about the entire industry.

Several estimates and a survey of winery costs are reported in *The Economics of Small Wineries.** Construction costs vary widely according to winery specification, location, and the time of construction. The group of surveyed small wineries reported construction costs, generally incurred during the period 1975–78, that averaged $35 per case of capacity. Estimates of more current (1982) construction costs for wineries producing fewer than 25,000 cases annually ranged from $72 to $84 per case of capacity. Costs can be quite a bit higher for wineries of unique specification.

---

* See Kirby S. Moulton, ed., *The Economics of Small Wineries*, particularly pp. 2–12, which report the results of a survey of small wineries. An analysis of construction and operating costs for wineries with capacities ranging from a 6,000-gallon capacity to a 100,000-gallon capacity is presented in C. C. Vreeland, J. R. Brake, and G. B. White, *An Investment Analysis of New York Small Premium Wineries* (Ithaca, N.Y.: Cornell University Agricultural Experiment Station, Agricultural Experiment Station Research Paper No. 82–42, December 1982).

There are several observations to make about the differences between the costs reported by wineries responding to the survey and those calculated for current construction. First of all, the difference in values is partly explained by differences in construction dates and the price inflation that occurred between them. Secondly, smaller wineries have great flexibility in "making do" with non-winery structures and in substituting the owner's labor for capital equipment. As a winery increases in size, this adaptive ability decreases. Finally, some construction estimates include prudent reserves for contingencies or for supplies and salaries during the construction period, reserves that may not subsequently be capitalized and carried in the depreciation account. A prudent construction cost analysis should allow an additional 20 to 25 percent for supplies and contingencies.

The wide range in reported costs also reflects considerable differences in individual preferences for buildings and specifications for equipment. In some cases, buildings express personal feelings, in others they are solely utilitarian. Equipment may be made from mild or stainless steel, be oversized to meet future expansion needs, or in the case of a particular piece, such as a centrifuge, not be included at all.

An analysis of several cost studies provides an indication, but not conclusive evidence, of economies of scale in winery construction. The indicated pattern is as follows: if unit construction costs for a 5,000-case winery are considered as 100, then unit costs at the 12,000- to 25,000-case level would be about 89; they would drop to approximately 60 at 100,000 cases and to 33 at 3 million cases. While these estimates are highly tentative, they suggest the possibility of substantial construction economies as size is increased beyond that normally associated with "small" wineries.

Small winery production costs are difficult to interpret because they often exclude the value of unpaid owner or family labor. Those small wineries that were surveyed and provided comprehensive labor input data reported an average of 9.25 minutes of labor per gallon of production, a rate that would require 9,250 labor hours a year for a 25,000-case winery.

Smaller wineries responding to the survey reported average labor figures considerably higher than those for the large respondents. The average for those wineries in the lower half of the size range (that is, making 15,000 gallons or less) was 14.3 minutes of labor per gallon. The average for larger wineries was 8.2 minutes, a savings of 42 percent.

Other production costs were more significant than labor costs. The value of grapes used for winemaking averaged $600 per ton, which is the equivalent of $4.00 per gallon of wine. Bottles and related accessories cost an average of $1.45 per gallon, or about 30 cents for the bottle, cork, label, capsule, and carton. The reported range was from 23 cents to 34 cents. By 1982, such costs for a 100,000-case premium winery had increased to 50 cents. Expenses for chemicals, filters, and other supplies amounted to 91 cents per gallon. As might be expected, the range in values was rather large, 35 cents to $2.36.

Total production costs averaged $7.49 a gallon, the equivalent of $1.50 for a 750 ml. bottle. The range, reflecting the wide difference in practices noted in the previous sections, was defined by a low of $3.85 and a high of $12.89 per gallon, before the calculation of sales and overhead expenses. After adjusting for the general inflation rate, these costs are $5.00 and $17.00 per gallon in 1982 dollars. Expenses for winery sales and overhead, including sales cost at the winery, averaged $2.87 per gallon ($6.89 per case). The range was $1.40 to $5.22, or approximately $2.00 to $7.00 per gallon in 1982 dollars.

Total costs estimated by survey respondents averaged $10.36 per gallon ($25.00 per case). When adjusted for general inflation, the average cost becomes about $14.00 per gallon ($33.00 per case) in 1982 dollars. The difference in reported values, from one-half of the average to 50 percent above it, suggests the extreme difficulty in assessing competitive positions based on average cost information. Quite clearly, some wineries are in a better position to weather competitive price conditions than others.

Estimated costs for new wineries appear higher than those reported by respondents to the winery survey. Production costs cited in the *Economics of Small Wineries* range between $48.00 and $57.00 when converted to 1982 dollars. An analysis of production practices in New York reported costs of $40.00 per case for a 20,000-case winery.

Production costs per case generally go down as winery size expands. However, the surveyed wineries did not show that pattern. As a matter of fact, there were some economic disadvantages when family facilities and labor were superseded by purchased inputs. Other costs cited in the survey of small wineries give an indication of economies of scale. For example, if production costs for a 5,000-case winery are considered as 100, then costs for 17,000 cases would be 85; for 100,000 cases, 73; for 500,000 cases, 54; and for 3 million cases, a unit cost of 47. The variability of survey results should be adequate warning that specific economies of scale can be determined only after very careful analysis of the relevant winery specifications.

Because most wineries are privately held and do not publicize their operational results, it is difficult to obtain information concerning their finances. Others, such as Heublein Wines, Almadén, and Paul Masson, are subsidiaries of larger organizations that publish only consolidated financial results. Comparable information about returns on investment for a cooperative such as Guild is extremely limited. One thus needs to use past data for ideas about financial results.

Stock in Almadén and Taylor Wine Company was publicly traded, and basic accounting data were reported, until 1977. Between 1968 and 1976, return on shareholder equity averaged 13 percent for Almadén Vineyards and 15 percent for Taylor Wine Company. Returns as a percentage of sales averaged 10 percent and 12 percent respectively. The companies were not entirely comparable because Almadén owned several thousand acres of vineyards, while Taylor owned less than one thousand. Almadén was also larger by one quarter in terms of shipments. Nevertheless, both companies were believed to be well managed during the period and to have financial results representative of better operators in the wine industry.

These returns were less than could be earned in food processing or manufacturing. If they were industry norms, then wineries were not making enough money. However, the expansion of Gallo, Almadén, and Masson and the wine acquisitions by Coca-Cola, R. J. Reynolds, and Moët-Hennessy suggest that current or prospective returns are adequate. The entrants exceed the drop-outs and convey the expectation of favorable returns.

Wineries have several choices in establishing channels of distribution. As production increases, however, the emphasis placed on various channels changes. Small wineries may choose to sell all their wine at the winery either in a retail sales room or by mail order. The Sattui Winery in St. Helena, for example, does both. Or they may sell directly to retailers or restaurants, the strategy adopted by Dry Creek Winery when it was first established, and used extensively by smaller wineries. Ridge Vineyards, for example, concentrated a large part of its sales effort on direct selling to consumers—their goal was to sell about 40 percent directly to the public—and to retailers and restaurants.

Other wineries sell to wholesalers in order to establish wide-scale distribution, a necessity as output increases and the sales network expands. Large producers such as Gallo, United Vintners, and Almadén depend on such wholesale distribution systems. Some wineries sell through brokers who undertake the full responsibility for marketing strategy. McDowell Valley Vineyards' association with Vintage Wine Merchants is an example of this type of arrangement. Most wineries, however, find that a combination of distribution channels is most effective.

Most wine in the United States moves through the traditional three-tier distribution system: winery to wholesaler to retailer to consumer. The development of a coordinated sales program in this system requires considerable cooperation because individual wineries have no legal basis in most states for requiring wholesalers and retailers to follow a specified sales strategy. Consequently, wineries select a distribution network with an eye to its probable compatibility with winery marketing objectives.

A variation on the three-tier system involves the participation of a marketing company that assumes the entire responsibility for the output of a winery. These companies, such as Fromm and Sichel, which marketed Christian Brothers products, or Vintage Wine Merchants, which markets for a selected group of smaller wineries, utilize wholesalers and retailers, as appropriate, just as do wineries that sell directly to the trade.

Retail distribution is through food stores, liquor stores, specialty wine shops, drug stores, and other licensed outlets. Large retail organizations buy wine directly from both domestic and foreign producers or from national sales organizations, bypassing the traditional wholesalers, where legally permissible, and performing the wholesaler's functions. The bulk of wine distribution is performed by relatively few wineries, sales organizations, wholesalers, and retailers, even though license figures show numerous organizations are authorized to carry out these functions.

Market margins vary somewhat throughout the United States. Those states that stipulate marketing margins for wine distribution allow a mark-up of about 20 percent for wholesale distribution and 33 to 50 percent for retail distribution. Some states do not segregate wholesale and retail, but set a minimum total mark-up of 75 to 85 percent.

Some states report the financial results of state-owned retail stores, figures not necessarily compatible, because costs of wholesaling and retailing may be commingled. Four states reported retail operating margins (revenues from wines and spirits less cost of goods sold) ranging between 25 and 40 percent of revenue. When considered with a wholesale margin of 20 percent, this is compatible with a frequently used rule of thumb that the retail price is double the price at the winery.

At the retail level, margins vary according to the type of outlet. Discount retailers work on a mark-up of about 15 percent, supermarkets at 25 percent, conventional retailers at one-third to one-half. Exclusive stores may establish mark-ups of higher than 50 percent. Margins on individual items vary considerably depending on turnover, competition, advertising, and cost.

Wine distribution is still suffering a hangover from the effects of Prohibition. Tax laws and state monopolies tend to restrict its free movement in many states. Wine is viewed as an evil by some—hence the large number of persons who do not drink it; as an excellent revenue source by others—hence the proliferation of taxes on it; or as a necessary and pleasurable accompaniment to food—hence the strong drive for wine sales in food stores.

States gained the right to regulate the sale, distribution, and taxation of wines with the repeal of Prohibition; although many have local options for Prohibition, very few have exercised them. Several sell wines in state-owned wholesale and/or retail outlets or have other restrictive arrangements. Price posting regulations exist in about half the states. Wine retailing is permitted in food stores in about two-thirds of the states and is excluded in the remainder.

Wine taxes on table wine vary tremendously according to state policy: one cent per gallon in California, ten cents in New York; $1.51 in Georgia and Virginia. Tax rates also vary according to the origin and alcohol content of the wines. Various license requirements, fees, and other regulations make marketing wine in relation to food even more complex.

It is difficult to isolate the impact of state regulations and taxation on wine consumption because of the influence of numerous other factors. For example, New York is a wineproducing state with a high rate of wine consumption in spite of restrictive retail marketing policies. Industry leaders have little doubt that sales of wine would jump significantly if retail food stores could sell it. Several southern states with barriers to wine marketing have low consumption rates, but cultural factors are probably equally important in discouraging the distribution of all alcoholic beverages. Consumption in Alabama, which has fairly restrictive regulations, is about equal to that of Georgia, which has an open marketing policy.

The prices charged for wine form a complex web that is difficult to penetrate. For example, fine Cabernet Sauvignon from Napa Valley may sell for $5.50 a bottle because of an oversupply, while a bottle of run-of-the-mill Zinfandel may command a higher price because of astute marketing.

Specialty auctions, such as the Napa Valley Wine auctions, command the highest and most publicized prices. In June 1982, 1978 Diamond Creek Cabernet Sauvignon at $450 brought the highest price per bottle. A case of Beaulieu Vineyard's 1974 Private Reserve Cabernet Sauvignon sold for $2,500. Other Cabernets attracted prices of $200 and $250 a case.

Prices exhibit a tremendous variability even when auctions are not considered. A substantial portion of California's wine sells at the equivalent of $1.50 to $2.25 for a 750 ml bottle, with "commercial" premium wineries pricing bottles at $2.25 to $5.00. Only 5 percent of shipments retail for more than $7.00 a bottle.

Consumer wine prices have not, on the average, increased as rapidly as the prices for all items. Between 1967 and 1974, all consumer prices including wine increased by the same percentage. However, between 1974 and 1981, the consumer price index increased by 84 percent and the wine price index grew by only 59 percent. Consequently, wine became a better buy relative to other goods.

Price increases were restrained by the extreme pressure from imports, which benefited from currency devaluations in 1980–82, from intense competition between major domestic producers, and from surpluses of some wines (notably California reds). At the upper end of the scale, however, there was less constraint and some new premium wineries set prices close to those of famous French châteaux. In 1982, when many new wineries found that they had more competition and that consumers had become more conscious of the relation of price to quality, there was a noticeable retreat.

THE WINE CONSUMER

Although drinking wine in the United States has a long history, it has not been a popular beverage in the sense that beer or soft drinks have. Over the past twenty years, preferences have changed and wine enthusiasts have increased in number, but they are still a small portion of the population. It is difficult to calculate the number of winedrinkers in the United States, because so many use it infrequently. If one includes all those who drink wine at least once a year, wine users number between 63 million and 114 million (depending on which research result is cited),★ a figure considerably higher than the number of winedrinkers in France, where great quantities of wine are consumed. Obviously, the key factors are how often the consumer drinks and how much.

In France 46 percent of the adult population drink wine every day, or almost every day, usually with meals. This amounts to eighteen million people, who account for 90 percent of wine purchases. The corresponding U.S. consumers—those who drink wine every day, or almost every day—comprise 7 percent of the adult population, or 11 million people, who buy 55 percent of the table wine sold.

Thus, although the United States has a larger number of adult wine users than France, very roughly in the ratio of 3 to 1, it has fewer daily consumers. The French regular consumer averages five and a half (750 ml) bottles weekly. The corresponding drinker in the United States consumes less than one liter (0.9 liters). Comparatively, the American might enjoy a small glass every day to his French counterpart's almost five.

The per capita consumption of table wine by individuals with incomes exceeding $25,000 is double the overall average for adult winedrinkers in the United States. Figures based on 1978 table wine use in homes show these more affluent individuals each averaged 4.8 gallons a year. It is clear that the wealthier group is not made up entirely of heavy winedrinkers.

The relation of income to wine consumption is important because of the expected future growth of income. Projections by the National Planning Association call for an increase in real consumer income equivalent to 2.69 percent a year between 1980 and 1990. Coupled with the increased number of mature adults by 1990, it could more than double the number of families with real incomes over $25,000. If this group's per capita consumption rates remain unchanged, their total table wine demand would exceed 340 million gallons.

Anticipated changes in the age composition of the population of the United States over the next decade will also lead to increased wine consumption if

★ Numerous studies are cited in Kirby S. Moulton, "The Factors Influencing Wine Consumption: A Comparison Between the United States and Europe," *Proceedings* of the International Symposium of the International Office of Vines and Wines, Verona, April 1982.

the various age groups maintain their preferences. The population is expected to mature, with a larger proportion in those groups that typically drink more wine. If the estimated drinking patterns remain constant until 1990 and all other factors hold at their 1980 levels, the aging of the population will result in about a 15 percent increase in wine consumption.

Winedrinking in the United States is significantly concentrated in the professional classes. Households headed by professionals consume an estimated half again as much as other households, about 4.8 gallons a person in 1980. The consumption of families headed by white collar workers is average, while those headed by blue collar workers use about half that of other winedrinking households, about 1.6 gallons a person.

The geographic location of consumers is representative of a number of factors—such as income distribution, occupation, regional culture, and ethnic mix—that directly affect winedrinking. In the United States, those who drink more than the average live in the Northeast and the West (where 18 percent of the population accounts for 30 percent of the wine consumption). They tend to come from urban areas with populations exceeding a million.

The concentration of urban wine consumers has increased wine consumption. Urban audiences are easier to reach with advertising and promotion campaigns. Distribution channels are relatively short, can handle large volumes of products at low cost, and can provide consumers with a wide array of choices. Urban dwellers, generally less conservative than their rural counterparts, are more willing to try new products.

About half the people who choose not to drink wine do so because they don't like it. Another 39 percent abstain as a matter of principle; others cite lack of knowledge about wine or of experience with it. Of those households that have reduced their consumption of wine, 26 percent have found its taste unappealing. Some cited lack of knowledge (23 percent), relatively high price (20 percent), and concerns about health (12 percent).

Brand was the single most important factor influencing wine purchases, according to an important market survey.* If the weighted value of responses concerning brand is assigned a value of 100, then the value of responses concerning other factors were: friends, 88; price, 87; label, 52; area, 44; flavor, 33; and advertising, 31. The remaining factors were given considerably less weight. The industry, which places significant importance on the influence of advertising in establishing brand preferences, increased its advertising expenditures more than fourfold between 1970 and 1980.

---

* Not all studies yield the same ranking. The one cited here is from R. J. Folwell and J. L. Baritelle, *The U.S. Wine Market*.

Color preferences have changed very rapidly in the United States. In 1960 consumers chose red wines for 74 percent of their table wine consumption, white wines for 17 percent, and rosé for 9 percent. By 1983 this pattern had almost reversed itself, with reds accounting for only 22 percent, whites for 61 percent, and rosé for 17 percent. In France, by contrast, 86 percent of consumption was of red wines, a fact that gives rise to some interesting questions about the future for U.S. producers. Of primary concern is the uncertainty as to whether American drinkers of white wine will move back toward red. Does the European market provide a model for future U.S. consumption? Or will the American craze for white wine as an aperitif and as a mealtime beverage spread to Europe and alter traditional patterns there?

North Americans drink very little wine compared to the large volume of soft drinks (39 gallons a year per capita), beer (37 gallons), and milk (28 gallons) consumed. They also drink a considerable amount of water with meals. On the other hand, U.S. consumers use wine more broadly than Europeans. Winedrinking in France is mostly restricted to meals. A study of American consumers reports that they drink 49 percent of their wine with lunch or dinner, the balance during the evening (usually before or after meals), with snacks, or in the morning. Much current advertising stresses the use of wine for occasions other than meals. This diversity could provide a good base for expansion, particularly if use at mealtimes also begins to follow European patterns.

SUMMARY

This essay has considered the economic aspects of California's dynamic wine industry and the wrenching changes it has experienced over the past twenty years. Vineyard costs accelerated at an alarming rate and squeezed the profits of many growers. Varietal preferences changed and required a substantial alteration in the composition of California's vineyards. Large wineries embarked on aggressive selling campaigns to capitalize on newly emerging consumer tastes and to fend off the flood of foreign wines. The number of small wineries more than doubled in ten years and brought a wide array of superb wines to the American consumer. White table wines became the "hot" item in the wine market owing to their vastly improved quality and their particular appeal to American tastes. Wine marketing changed significantly as supermarkets, discount houses, and wine specialty stores replaced whiskey-oriented liquor stores as the primary outlets. Wine brokers or agents began to offer complete marketing services to selected wineries, permitting them to expand their markets, particularly out of state. Advertising expenditures surged in response to intense competition.

Several questions remain unanswered. Export of wines has increased dramatically as the quality of California wines has gained international recognition. Yet the total volume of exports remains very small. Can California serve both domestic and foreign markets adequately? More important, perhaps, will the new European Economic Community agreements ensure that California wines receive treatment in foreign markets equal to that which foreign wines enjoy here? Competition from foreign wines and from those produced in other states could increase substantially and place considerable economic pressure on California producers. Consumer preferences could change, as they have in the past. The question of whether California's wine industry, as presently constituted, can be competitive and still return adequate profits under these conditions deserves intensive study. If the experience of the past century is a guide, however, the future appears bright.

BIBLIOGRAPHIC NOTE

This study draws, in particular, on Kirby S. Moulton, ed., *The Economics of Small Wineries* (Berkeley: University of California Cooperative Extension Service, 1981), a compilation of articles about winery costs, marketing strategies, and other factors affecting winery operations. R. J. Folwell and J. L. Baritelle, *The U.S. Wine Market*, U.S. Department of Agriculture, Agricultural Economic Report no. 417, December 1978, report on an extensive survey of consumer wine preferences. Of relevance, too, is the report of a study conducted by National Family Opinion, Inc., "1980 Beverage Market Demographics Revealed in 'SIP' Study," *Impact Newsletter*, 1 May 1981, which gives a good summary of recent consumer demographics. An excellent description of wine consumption characteristics in France may be found in D. Boulet, J. Y. Huguet, and J.-P. Laporte, *La consommation du vin en France* (Paris: Ministère de l'agriculture, Office national interprofessionnel des vins de table, 1980).

VIII.3

Note: Extravaganzas

by DORIS MUSCATINE

SINCE THE EIGHTEENTH CENTURY, WHEN THE INVENTION
of the cork made aged wines possible, there has been an association of fine wine and
grand establishments. The prototypes of this association, the Bordeaux châteaux,
represent a natural integration of winemaking, hereditary ownership of the vineyard, and a personal residence that reflects the grandeur of aristocratic living. Early
in its history, California—suddenly wealthy but without the same longevity of tradition—tried to emulate that grand style in its wine country properties, just as it copied
European elegance in its city residences. By the early 1860s, on a hillock above his
Buena Vista vineyards, Agoston Haraszthy had built a splendid white Pompeiian
villa styled with columns, porticos, and a playing fountain. He called it a ranch and
had a picture of it reproduced on his stationery. In the 1880s, Leland Stanford spent
several million dollars developing the world's largest vineyard and building the
world's largest winery to accompany it. But for personal reasons he never constructed a million-dollar home planned as part of the 55,000-acre Viña estate. (Nor did
he make more than average-to-good wines there.)

Some of the notable California wineries of the later nineteenth century
represent at least an attempt to perpetuate the architectural grandeur of the châteaux scheme, even if the owners sometimes did not live on the premises. Charles
Krug Winery, much expanded in later years, still centers on the two enormous stone
buildings that date to its founding in 1861. Several memorable stone structures in
the Napa area were designed by Captain Hamden McIntyre, the great winery architect of the 1880s. One of them, the massive Greystone Cellars now owned by the
Christian Brothers, was planned to be the largest stone cellar in the world. Another,
the romantic stone building with the Scottish name Inglenook given to the property
by its original owner, was built for Gustave Niebaum, a Finnish sea captain and
Alaskan fur trader. A huge, three-story wooden building now occupied by Trefethen Vineyards showed McIntyre's versatility in other media. His Far Niente,
built in 1882 with two-foot-thick walls of native stone, was restored in the late
1970s. In the spirit of the great French estates, it is surrounded by manicured
landscaping and its own vineyards, and includes handsome living quarters for the

owners. Although it is closed to the public, it is equipped to entertain privately in the grand manner—its dining room can seat fifty under chandeliers that once hung in the old Seattle Opera House. Chateau Montelena is another of McIntyre's 1880s stone buildings, but the landscape that surrounds it—a lake and two islands replete with tea houses—is the legacy of a former owner who liked Chinese tea gardens.

Several early buildings of equal distinction are executed in a variety of architectural styles. One such is the Beringer Winery's Rhine House, built as a residence by Frederick Beringer, who had it copied in detail after the family home in Mainz, Germany. As he reported in *Silverado Squatters*, Robert Louis Stevenson once visited the handsome Victorian home on Jacob Schram's winery estate, now the residence of Jack and Jamie Davies, the current proprietors of Schramsberg. Another of the splendid Victorians of the 1880s is the Tiburcio Parrot home, which dominates Spring Mountain Vineyards. Restored to its former magnificence as the estate residence, it is familiar to television viewers as the mansion in the series "Falcon Crest." The Chateau Chevalier, refurbished by Greg and Kathy Bissonette, was built a few years after the Parrot Victorian and retains its European turrets, towers, and masonry. It includes substantial living quarters on the top floors above the working winery.

Almost from the first, many of California's wineries were straight-forward wine factories with no attempt at architectural distinction. They carried on their commercial life apart from the principal residence of their owners and often apart from the vineyard ownership as well. Today it is a matter of happenstance whether a winery has its own vineyards, as do the French châteaux, and whether or not they are adjacent. At E. & J. Gallo, for instance, most of the grapes come from elsewhere. Today the largest winery in the world, Gallo is a complex of industrial buildings housing laboratories, winemaking and storage facilities, a glass factory for bottle making, and a trucking headquarters. The only concession to the tradition of elegance is a modern office building whose lobby is an atrium filled with live tropical birds and exotic plants. Along with utilitarian architecture, another characteristic of a substantial number of workaday wineries is that, unlike Gallo, they have few pretensions to elaborate entertainment. The personal hospitality typical of the great houses of Europe, open only to the few, has been converted in California to a public hospitality, open to the many, expressed in the form of tours, tasting rooms, and picnic facilities.

Nearly equal in number, particularly in wineries making boutique or special bottlings, are the efforts to express outwardly through the architecture of the winery something of the graciousness and beauty lavished on a personal residence in the châteaux. At Sterling Vineyards a Swiss aerial tramway transports tourists up to the blazing white Mediterranean buildings of the winery, ornamented with specially designed tiles and commissioned works of sculpture. The architecture of the spreading low-slung building designed by Cliff May for Robert Mondavi Winery is reminiscent of California's early Franciscan missions, while Spanish colonial themes are expressed in the arches, tiles, and bright white walls of Cuvaison near Calistoga. Joseph Phelps, Sonoma Vineyards, and Chappellet's striking pyramidal building are pure examples of modern California architecture; in contrast, Monticello Cellars, a tribute to that early wine enthusiast Thomas Jefferson, plans an office building copied after the original Monticello. A small estate with residences and winery, Hanzell, along with emulating the Burgundian winemaking style, has modeled at least one facade on the Clos de Vougeot. Another winery that strives for a Gallic look, Chateau St. Jean has a French tower straight out of the Middle Ages that provides a view over the whole winemaking process and the rest of the property.

In a few notable cases, California has outdone itself in its interpretation of the winery estate. Jordan, the most grandiose California exponent of the traditional châteaux theme, mimics its French models so faithfully that for all purposes it might be standing on the banks of the Gironde instead of in the hills of Alexander Valley. Some time after Thomas Jordan, the proprietor, made a fortune in oil in Indonesia, he and his wife—intense Francophiles and serious wine drinkers—tried to acquire a first ranked French wine estate and learned that the first growth châteaux are official national treasures, not for sale to foreign purchasers. Their awakening to the possibilities of creating a truly great wine in California came over a bottle of 1968 Beaulieu Vineyard's George de Latour Private Reserve Cabernet Sauvignon made by André Tchelistcheff. Within a year they owned a thousand acres of potential vineyard in an area where the temperatures, like those of Bordeaux, are moderated by nearby ocean masses. They employed Tchelistcheff as consultant. Within a decade they were presiding over a "French" estate that produced a California Cabernet Sauvignon which had been instantly well received.

Their large yellow stucco country manor encloses winery, guest quarters, and facilities for grand entertainments. A private residence stands nearby. The three guest suites, with views from their wrought iron balconies out over the vineyards, are elaborately furnished with fireplaces and antiques and replicas reflecting three different periods of French architecture. The bathroom fixtures are marble, the plumbing gilded, the beams hewn by hand. Every suite has a bidet. Plants abound and bedside tables offer copies of *Réalités* and other such magazines and books of current interest. From the guest wing there is an internal view back over the oak cask storage room of the winery. On the floor below, a glass window-wall separates the formal dining room and the winery and affords dramatic effects when the chandeliers in the cask room are suddenly turned up to reveal the massive oak casks in the room behind. The professionally equipped, restaurant-sized kitchen employs a permanent local staff supplemented, when there are harvest celebrations, birthdays, and other special occasions, by guest chefs from highly ranked restaurants in France and the United States.

The Firestone Vineyard, located in Los Olivos in the Santa Ynez Valley, is a great "château" in scale and elegance, but the French aristocratic tradition has been completely supplanted by California's modern architectural style and spirit of informality. Before he took up winemaking, Brooks Firestone, whose father Leonard had once been United States Ambassador to Belgium and whose grandfather Harvey had amassed a fortune making tires, had spent a dozen years learning that the family business was not where he wanted to be. With his father and Suntory, Ltd., the Japanese whiskey company, as silent partners and with André Tchelistcheff as consultant, he took over a part of his father's 2,850-acre cattle ranch to create a winery estate. The four levels of the new winery building splay out like a deck of cards in the middle of the vineyard. Redwood reinforces the strong simple lines of the architecture, and stained glass windows and red tile floors enrich it. A fountain in the courtyard is the setting for occasional concerts. The Firestone ranch house is a few miles down the way.

Domaine Chandon, the elegant home of a wine conglomerate rather than of a private family, is a unique combination of technical capacity, public hospitality, and beauty of design. The French firm of Moët-Hennessy established the winery, along with a splendid French restaurant, in 1977. Nestled at the foot of the Mayacamas Mountains in the Napa Valley, it performs the venerable French processes of *remuage*, *dégorgement*, and *dosage* in a modern building of striking architectural accomplishment. Visitors can watch the making of sparkling wines, tour a small champagne museum, purchase samples in a salon for tasting, and dine on the *cuisine française*, meticulously prepared by an imported French chef and his team.

The firm's interest in making wine abroad started in 1960, and in 1968 it merged with several other companies. Because of the strict labeling laws in France that limit the quantity of Champagne and the area of its production (the vineyards of the Côte des Blancs, the mountain of Reims, and the valley of the river Marne), the enlarged firm could not take advantage of its combined resources by expansion there. It could, however, send its experts abroad to make Champagne-style wine for foreign markets directly.

Moët-Hennessy acquired 1,500 acres of land in the Napa Valley in the spring of 1973, more than a third of it in an area whose climate and conditions resemble those of Champagne. Edmond Maudière, one of Moët-Hennessy's principal winemakers, is consulting enologist and technical director. The design of the finished building combines vast expanses of glass, concrete, steel, and the most modern technological facilities with traditional features of Moët's French architecture and Napa's bucolic setting. The great vaulted *caves* of Moët inspired the arched roofs and entries; the beamed ceilings of its French wineries are equally at home in California. Typical of both French and Napa masonry, the rubble walls are made of rocks gathered on the site and hauled down from the hills by a neighbor's giant Percheron horse.

With its elegant restaurant and hospitable tasting room, Domaine Chandon is designed to introduce Americans to sparkling wine as an all-around drink, rather than as the traditional beverage uncorked only for special occasions. The cuisine is designed as an agreeable accompaniment. In a striking glass-walled salon or on the adjoining patio, tasters can purchase wine by the flute or bottle and the kitchen sends along trays of complementary savories. The glass walls and terraces of the dining room overlook rolling vineyards and more distant hills. Inside, the profusion of flowers and the elegant napery recall similar outposts of fine cooking found in the French countryside. It would be a splendid development if Domaine Chandon, with its generous orientation toward the public and its emphasis on the connection between food and wine, were to become the exemplar of the great American château of the future.

The LEGAL & POLITICAL HISTORY
OF CALIFORNIA WINE

JAMES M. SEFF AND JOHN F. COONEY

IX

THE LEGAL AND POLITICAL HISTORY OF CALIFORNIA WINE

by JAMES M. SEFF *&* JOHN F. COONEY

THE CALIFORNIA WINE INDUSTRY HAS EXPERIENCED A TUMULTUOUS POLITICAL HISTORY, WHICH HAS FUNDAMENTALLY INFLUENCED THE COURSE OF ITS DEVELOPMENT. From its outset, the industry has been subject to pervasive regulation at the federal, state, and local levels. Government intervention has been prompted by three major concerns: raising revenue through taxation, protecting the health of consumers, and encouraging temperance in consumption of alcoholic beverages. Each of these considerations has been preeminent at different times, and the dominant concern has fluctuated repeatedly over the years.

The political history of California wine before 1918 was dominated by two major issues, its battle to obtain federal legislation defining the terms of its competition with foreign producers and eastern winemakers, and its struggle against the prohibitionist movement. After fifteen years of dormancy during Prohibition, the wine industry emerged in 1933 to address the unfinished business of developing effective consumer protection standards. In the post-Repeal period the wine industry has thrived in an atmosphere of intimate political involvement with all aspects of its operation.

The legal and political history of California wine presents a fascinating case study of the manner in which interest groups organize to use the regulatory process for their own purposes and of the constant changes in fortunes as coalitions of interest groups form and dissolve. Its development illustrates the untidy and pragmatic process by which our political system evolves the basic ground rules that govern the economy.

REGULATION DURING THE FORMATIVE YEARS OF THE WINE INDUSTRY

Prior to the Civil War, the major government interest in wine was as a subject of taxation. The first federal Revenue Act of 1789 imposed a tariff on imported wines, liquors, and beer, and these beverages have remained continuously subject to customs duties ever since. At the time of California's admission to the Union, the tax rate on imported wine was 40 percent of its declared value. Unlike liquor, which was first subjected to an excise tax in 1791, wine made from domestic grapes was exempt from taxation. Congress found adequate sources of revenue elsewhere without taxing this infant industry, which Thomas Jefferson, among others, described with favor.★

Wine was first produced in California by the Catholic missions. In 1823, the Mexican government abolished the mission system, destroying the only large-scale grape-growing enterprises. When California became a state in 1850, the wine industry was entirely in the hands of private producers. Wine production first became significant to the state's economy during the late 1850s, sparked by demand from the growing population around San Francisco. To encourage the development of the industry, the state legislature in 1859 passed a law exempting new vineyards from taxation for their first four years, the period necessary for the vines to begin commercial production.

The California wine industry enjoyed freedom from direct federal regulation until the Civil War. The Union government faced an enormous need for additional revenues to support the armed forces, however. In 1862, Congress imposed a temporary, but increasingly severe, system of internal revenue taxes on many previously exempt activities, including an excise tax of five cents a gallon on all domestic wines. The effective tax rate nearly equaled the price of ordinary wines, and California producers suffered a substantial reduction in sales and profits. The tax on grape brandy, used to raise the alcoholic content of so-called fortified or sweet

---

★   "I rejoice, as a moralist, at the prospect of a reduction of the duties on wine, by our national legislature. It is an error to view a tax on that liquor as merely a tax on the rich. . . . No nation is drunken where wine is cheap; and none sober, where the dearness of wine substitutes ardent spirits as the common beverage. It is, in truth, the only antidote to the bane of whiskey" (*The Writing of Thomas Jefferson*, ed. Albert E. Bergh [Washington, D.C.: Thos. Jefferson Memorial Foundation, 1907], 15:177).

wines, was raised in stages from twenty-five cents to a prohibitive two dollars a gallon. Winemakers and dealers also were required to pay substantial fees to obtain operating licenses. To prevent foreign producers from obtaining an unfair competitive advantage over the U.S. industry during the war, Congress imposed compensating "temporary" tariff increases on foreign wines in 1862 and 1864.

After the Union victory, Congress quickly repealed most of the internal revenue taxes levied during the war. The taxes on distilled spirits, beer, and brandy were such effective revenue producers, however, that they were maintained to help repay the enormous national debt. Throughout the late nineteenth century, these liquor excise taxes generated approximately 50 percent of all federal revenues. But the wine industry was so small and its revenue raising capacity so insignificant that Congress abolished the excise tax on U.S. wine in late 1865. Congress thereby conferred on wine a distinct price advantage over other alcoholic beverages. Despite the often bitter protests of the distilled spirits and brewing industries, the wine industry still pays substantially lower taxes on a relative alcohol basis.

The wine industry's freedom from internal taxation contributed to its growth in other significant respects. Winemakers were spared the limitations on production techniques and close inspections Congress imposed on other alcoholic beverage producers to prevent tax evasion. In addition, winemakers enjoyed much lower capital requirements than the other beverage industries. Liquor and beer producers paid the excise taxes by purchasing special government stamps, which had to be affixed to the containers before the beverages were withdrawn from bonded warehouses for distribution. The producers therefore paid the taxes weeks or months before they could recover the cost from retail customers. The wine industry's exemption from taxation thus conserved its cash flow and substantially reduced its cost of doing business.

THE STRUGGLE FOR SUPREMACY IN THE U.S. MARKET, 1870–1918

In the years after the Civil War, California transformed its industry from an infant to a strong economic and political force. The growing population and return of national prosperity sparked a dramatic expansion in California vineyards. At the start of the 1870s, California replaced Missouri as the largest wineproducing state. The opening of the transcontinental railroad in 1869 greatly expanded California's ability to sell its wines in eastern markets in competition with local and foreign wines. Competition from European wines was particularly keen, because consumers generally preferred them to American wines. As late as 1870, imports accounted for approximately half of all U.S. wine consumption.

Through its congressional delegation, the California wine industry pursued a lengthy campaign to protect its competitive position. The battle was joined in a series of tax and tariff bills. At crucial points, California was able to turn the rising popular sentiment for pure food legislation to its advantage and ultimately obtained a favorable position.

The "temporary" Civil War tariffs, including the duties on wines, were repealed much more slowly than the domestic excise taxes. In 1870, Congress voted a general reduction in import duties, but representatives of the California wine industry argued successfully against lowering the tariffs on wines. This exchange marked the first step in the conversion of the wine tariff from a revenue-raising device to a means of insulating U.S. wineries from foreign competition.* In advocating a protective tariff, California producers parted company from most other western and agricultural interests. Farmers generally wanted low tariffs, because the United States was a food exporter; high tariffs only invited foreign retaliation against U.S. exports, while increasing the price of some products farmers used. California wine exports were negligible, however, and the industry clearly preferred the prospect of capturing the growing U.S. market to the potential for lower costs.

In 1875–76, during a national economic depression, the California wine industry experienced the first of a series of major depressions. Wine prices plummeted sharply to ten to fifteen cents a gallon. One major contributing factor was a large oversupply of grapes as the vines planted during the boom of the late 1860s came into commercial production. Another major cause was consumer resistance to California wines. Many winemakers who had recently entered the field were inexperienced and produced wines of uncertain quality. In addition, most California wines were shipped east in bulk containers; many spoiled or were subjected to adulteration. Good wines often were sold at high prices under fraudulent foreign labels, leaving only the poorest wines to be sold under the California name.

The wine industry sought to recoup its finances by further excluding foreign wines from the market. After extensive lobbying by California interests, Congress passed the Tariff Act of 1875, a piece of special interest legislation explicitly intended to protect the domestic wine industry. Wines imported in casks were taxed at the unprecedented rate of forty cents a gallon, which nearly equaled the market price of ordinary drinking wines. Rates on bottled wines were approximately one-third greater, providing U.S. producers with an extra measure of protection in the especially profitable luxury wine trade. The law also prohibited im-

---

* The situation today, however, is quite the reverse (see p. 431). In the first forty years after Repeal, the U.S. wine industry shifted its focus from protection to free trade, not altogether to its benefit.

portation of wines containing more than 24 percent alcohol, so that merchants could not defeat the tariff by importing high alcohol wines and then stretching them with water or cheap wine after entry. The wine industry's victory was confirmed in 1879, when the Senate refused to ratify a proposed reciprocal trade treaty with France that would have reduced tariffs on its wines and brandies by 50 percent.

The California wine industry returned to profitability at the end of the 1870s as the country recovered from the depression and the devastation of French vineyards by phylloxera diminished competition from foreign wines. In 1880, the California legislature passed two measures that greatly assisted the development of the wine industry. It established a continuing wine and grape-growing research program at the state agricultural college.★ And it created a State Board of Viticultural Commissioners to encourage and regulate grape production.† With the outbreak of phylloxera in California's vineyards, the state, in November 1881, issued comprehensive quarantine regulations, and the board attempted to supervise the fight against the disease. Thereafter, until its abolition in 1894, the board also helped producers improve grape-growing and winemaking techniques. Despite the attack of phylloxera, the wine industry flourished in the early 1880s. By 1881–82, demand for new grape cuttings for planting greatly exceeded supply. The Tariff Act of 1883 contributed to the industry's continued expansion by increasing duties on foreign wine by an additional 25 percent.

The wine industry's vulnerability to fluctuations in the business cycle reasserted itself in 1886. A large crop, swollen by recent plantings, caused a panic in the market and a precipitous drop in prices. Depressed economic conditions and low prices continued to plague the industry into the early 1890s. These problems were compounded by high railroad and steamer rates, which slowed California penetration of eastern markets. The industry gained only a small measure of relief from discriminatory rail rates by passage of the Interstate Commerce Act of 1887.

In one respect, the depression of the late 1880s laid the foundation for the future prosperity of the industry by accelerating growers' conversion from the Mission grape to newly imported European varietals. American consumers strongly preferred European-style wines, but contemporary viticultural practices did not permit the satisfactory growth of *Vitis vinifera* in the states east of the Rocky Mountains. California therefore had a natural monopoly in U.S. production of European-

---

★ Now the Department of Viticulture and Enology at the University of California at Davis, the preeminent institution of its kind in the United States and one of the great centers of wine research and education in the world.

† A forerunner of the Wine Advisory Board and other agricultural advisory boards established in the next century under the California Marketing Act of 1937.

type wines, and high protective tariffs gave the state a substantial price advantage over European countries in marketing ordinary drinking wines. In response to these incentives, plantings of new foreign varietals more than quadrupled during the 1880s, from approximately 20 percent to substantially more than 90 percent of all California wine grapes. Many California wines thereafter were made in the European manner and sold under European names that had become semi-generic, such as burgundy, rhine wine, and champagne.*

The depression also was marked by renewed concern about the adulteration of American wine. Beginning in 1860, many states and large cities had adopted laws against impure food and alcoholic beverages, including wines. Despite these formal prohibitions, the reputation of California wines continued to suffer because of spoilage, adulterations and other deleterious practices. In 1887, after lengthy chemical investigation, the U.S. Department of Agriculture published a finding to the effect that much U.S. wine was subject to watering and contained high levels of preservatives, and that fortified wines contained very little grape juice but were composed primarily of alcohol, sugar, and water.† California and New York, the two major wineproducing states, adopted pure wine laws in 1887. Other producing states soon followed, but these laws had little effect. Indeed, the State Supreme Court rendered the California statute unenforceable in a case brought by a leading merchant.‡

Experience soon proved that adulteration and contamination of wine had to be attacked at the national level, because no state could enforce its laws against producers who shipped illegal products from other states. Furthermore, the states were unable to agree on the standards for determining acceptable wine. The California law defining "pure wine" prohibited addition of any sugar to the wine. This provision reflected California practice, because the growing season is long enough for the grapes to develop enough natural sugar so that the wine, when completely fermented, will have enough alcohol to inhibit its turning sour. Growing seasons in eastern states are shorter. Except for extraordinary years, eastern producers needed to add some sugar to the unfermented grape juice to obtain an acceptable wine. The New York law, for example, defined "pure wine" so that a winemaker could add sugar and water to wine up to a maximum of 25 percent of its volume in order to perfect it.

California producers considered this practice an adulteration or "stretching" of the wine, a fraud on consumers they believed gave eastern wineries

---

*   For a further discussion of the use in California of semi-generic place names, see text and footnotes beginning at p. 440.
†   *Food and Food Adulterants*, part 3 (Washington, D.C.: U.S. Department of Agriculture, 1887).
‡   *Ex parte* Kohler, 74 Cal. Rptr. 38, 15 P.2d 436 (1887).

an unfair competitive advantage. All attempts at a compromise on this question failed in 1886 and 1887. The definition of what constituted a lawful "wine" therefore had to be resolved by federal law. For the next thirty years, the California and eastern wine industries struggled to have Congress adopt their respective definitions of "pure wine."

During the late 1880s, the California wine industry also profited from the next national wave of protectionism. Protective tariffs were the major issue in the presidential election of 1888, and the Republican victory ensured substantial across-the-board increases. The resulting McKinley Tariff Act of 1890 substantially raised the rates on imported brandy and Champagne, but not on table wines. The question of greatest concern to the California wine industry, however, was the "pure sweet wine bill," which after a heated battle was passed as part of the McKinley bill. California producers long had sought relief from the internal revenue law taxing as distilled spirits the grape brandy used to raise the alcohol content of sweet wines. Although grapes fermented into table wine were not taxed, grapes distilled into brandy and later added to wine were taxed at the prohibitive rate of $1.10 per gallon. In addition, the producer had to pay the brandy tax upon its withdrawal for use, months before the resulting sweet wine was sold. The California industry sought to have grape brandy used in fortification declared exempt from tax. California producers argued further that any remedial legislation also should outlaw adulteration of sweet wine by prohibiting introduction of distilled spirits made from products other than grapes.

As finally adopted, the "pure sweet wine bill" was an overwhelming victory for California. The bill allowed winemakers to use grape brandy on a tax-free basis to fortify wines up to a 25 percent alcohol content. Only California grew enough grapes to produce enough grape spirits to permit tax-free fortifying in any appreciable quantity. Producers in other states therefore had to purchase brandy from California if they wished to make sweet wines. Thanks to this legislative preference, California captured 97 percent of the growing sweet wine trade in the years before Prohibition.

The Democratic victory in the election of 1892 produced a narrow congressional majority favoring lower tariffs. The resulting Tariff Act of 1894 reduced some wine duties, but California successfully preserved its favorable position. The duty on table wines imported in casks was reduced to thirty cents a gallon for wines of 14 percent alcohol content or less; for cask wines between 14 percent and 24 percent alcohol, the duty remained at fifty cents. This provision responded to the emergence of a working-class demand for ordinary bulk wines from European countries, prompted by a major wave of immigration from southern European wineproducing countries. The Tariff Act also redressed, in part, eastern producers' dissatisfaction with the pure sweet wine bill. Under the compromise provision, eastern wine-makers were permitted to add up to 10 percent cane or beet sugar to the wine prior to fortification. This amendment had little effect on California's continued dominance of the sweet wine trade.

Upon returning to power in 1897, the Republicans reinstated the highest tariffs yet, but the wine industry benefited only marginally. The duty on bulk table wines was increased to forty cents a gallon, while other rates remained unchanged. The Tariff Act also authorized the president to negotiate reciprocal trade agreements with foreign countries, including a maximum reduction of 25 percent on brandies, Champagne, and table wines. This concession was directed at France, which in 1892 had imposed its own protective tariff in retaliation for American taxation of its exports. In 1898, President McKinley signed a reciprocal agreement allowing importation of U.S. agricultural products into France at minimum rates in return for a reduction in duties on French brandies and table wines (but not Champagne) imported into this country. Despite this agreement and similar protocols with other wineproducing countries, however, European producers could not significantly penetrate the U.S. market. After 1890, the protective tariffs essentially prevented the importation of any wines other than premium products favored by connoisseurs or bulk wines consumed by recent immigrants at holiday time. Between 1870 and 1900, the market share of foreign wine fell from 50 percent to 12 percent.

After its complete success on the tariff issue, the wine industry turned its political efforts to the struggle for a national pure wine law. Congress refused to adopt pure food laws on an industry-by-industry basis; accordingly, the wine controversy became part of a larger battle for a general federal pure food and drug law. The pure food movement was a coalition of consumer groups, professional organizations, and reputable trade interests that sought to eliminate abuses by unethical competitors. Passage of a federal law was long delayed because of strong opposition from patent medicine makers, who were the nation's largest advertisers, and elements in various industries that feared adoption of a federal standard for their product would outlaw their method of production. The dispute over the proper definition of pure wine was one of many instances in which a trade could not agree upon the minimum constituents of a lawful product. Similar disputes persisted for many years between dairy interests, oleomargarine producers, two schools of baking soda manufacturers, and, most importantly, the so-called straight whiskey and continuous distillation branches of the distilled spirits industry. The clash of these well-financed interests resulted in an impasse. The Senate, the citadel of vested interests, refused to pass any bill.

Beginning in 1897, each session of Congress considered a pure food law that had three major provisions: (1) prohibition of adulteration of foods, drugs, and beverages, including wines; (2) authorization for the Department of Agriculture to establish binding standards of identity and quality for these products; and (3) prohibition of "misbranding"—that is, labeling nonconforming goods as if they actually satisfied a standard. In 1902, Congress authorized the department to determine what constituted adulterations and publish advisory standards, which would not have the force of law but would guide the states in enforcing their own pure food laws. The Senate, however, refused to go any further. The mandatory standard of identity provisions were deleted from the Pure Food and Drug Act as finally enacted in 1906. This pathbreaking law succeeded in preventing introduction of toxic substances into wine. But its misbranding provisions were rendered ineffective by Congress's failure to provide any mechanism for determining what the genuine product must contain. False labeling continued to plague the wine industry until after Prohibition.

Frustrated in its search for a legislative solution to the "pure wine" dispute, the California wine industry next sought relief through the administrative process. In 1909, the Board of Food and Drug Inspection of the Department of Agriculture issued a decision declaring that addition of water and sugar to wine prior to fermentation was improper, and that the resulting product could not be called "wine" without further label characterization. Eastern producers immediately sought to have that decision reversed. In 1910 the secretaries of treasury, agriculture, and commerce and labor, in an extraordinary action, issued a joint ruling reversing the board and declaring that, in light of their long history of commercial acceptance, eastern table wines could continue to be called "wine" as long as they did not contain more than 20 percent sugar and water. That decision permitted many adulterations, and in 1913 the Agriculture Department issued a clarifying decision, which held that "wine" must consist only of fermented grape juice, subject to the "usual cellar treatment" the department prescribed. This decision, which was to define appropriate winemaking procedures for fifty years, was the only enduring result of the appeal to the administrative approach. The battle for advantage returned to Congress.

Although foreign wines could penetrate the U.S. market only with great difficulty, the wine industry continued to press for higher tariffs. During the market slump of 1909, Congress accommodated the industry by raising wine duties to the highest levels yet. The reciprocal trade treaty with France was also abrogated. The wine industry lobbied effectively to prevent rate reductions in the Democratic tariff reform of 1913, but its success proved short-lived. In 1914 Congress imposed an excise tax on domestic wines for the first time since the Civil War: eight cents a gallon, to be paid by purchase of a stamp to be affixed to the container when the wine was sold to consumers. In response to the complaints of eastern interests, Congress also imposed a retail tax of fifty-five cents a gallon on grape brandy used to fortify sweet wine, cutting in half the cost advantage California had enjoyed for twenty-five years.

The sudden imposition of these excise taxes sharply curtailed sales of California wines. Consumers refused to pay higher prices, and California distributors accumulated large inventories of unsold wine. Accordingly, merchants had less demand for wines in 1915, and many grape growers could not find a market for their crops. The California wine industry therefore sought relief from Congress in 1916. After forty years of struggle, eastern wine producers had obtained the leverage they needed to force California to sue for peace.

The Internal Revenue Act of 1916 constituted a final victory for the eastern producers on the standard for "pure wine." The bill defined "wine" so that vintners lawfully could add sugar and water to the unfermented grape juice, up to a maximum of 35 percent, to correct natural deficiencies in the grapes. With agreement on this definition, eastern producers obtained permanent legislative validation of their method of operation. In return, the excise tax on table wine was reduced to four cents a gallon, although the tax on sweet wine was raised to ten or twenty-five cents depending upon its alcohol content. Congress also changed the method of collecting the tax. Most wine was sold in bulk in reusable containers, and many consumers had evaded the retail tax by using the same stamp time and time again until it became worn. Congress therefore abandoned the retail tax and imposed the new tax on the producer, as with all other alcoholic beverages. To prevent cheating, Congress also subjected winemakers for the first time to a detailed system of regulatory and production controls. With the entry of the United States into World War I in 1917, Congress doubled the wine excise taxes. In addition, it subjected imported wines to the excise taxes, further disadvantaging their sale with a second level of taxation. By that time, however, the movement for Prohibition was on the verge of success.

PROHIBITION

Legal efforts to control consumption of alcoholic beverages started long before the founding of the California wine industry. During the nineteenth century, liquor control ordinarily was a local or municipal function. The most common kind of control was a licensing system under which wholesalers and retailers were required to obtain permission to operate under conditions imposed by local political authorities. Typical restrictions included limits on the locations and times for liquor sales, the fixing of liquor prices, and the prohibition of sales to entire groups, such as minors, slaves, and Indians. In 1847, the Supreme Court upheld the constitutionality of the first "local option" laws, which gave individual cities and counties the right to prohibit sale of any alcoholic beverages within their boundaries.

Licensing and local option provisions proved ineffective so long as neighboring areas did not enforce similar restrictions on liquor consumption. Reformers therefore attempted to shift responsibility for liquor control to the state level. During the 1850s, a wave of prohibitionist sentiment swept the country. At its height, thirteen eastern states totally outlawed alcoholic beverages. Gradually these laws were repealed, and control of liquor returned to the local level. The prohibition movement reemerged during the Populist agitation of the 1890s, and by 1896 eight states had adopted prohibition laws. Prohibition again lost its political appeal, however, and by 1900 almost all the laws had been repealed and replaced by local option laws.

The third wave of prohibitionist movement, this time primarily southern and western in origin, became a significant political force after 1907. Spearheaded by the Rockefeller-financed Anti-Saloon League, prohibition enjoyed great political success; by 1910 eight states had enacted total prohibition laws. This campaign, however, encountered substantial constitutional obstacles, because state efforts to prevent importation of liquor conflicted with federal laws that allowed interstate transportation of liquor. Encouraged by an activist Supreme Court that used judicial review to strike down state laws hostile to business interests, anti-prohibition forces turned to litigation for relief. The Supreme Court duly held that, absent a special act of Congress, prohibition laws were unlawful to the extent that they prevented consumers from importing liquor from other states for their own use. Congress responded in 1913 by enacting the Webb-Kenyon law, over President Taft's veto. The statute provided that, in this one area of federal jurisdiction, the national law would yield to conflicting state laws, and dry states would be permitted to seal their borders against shipments of liquor from wet states. The prohibitionist victory proved hollow, however, because the automobile soon facilitated interstate smuggling.

World War I enormously increased popular support for prohibition. From 1914 to 1918, the number of states with prohibition laws increased from fourteen to thirty-two. The prohibition forces finally recognized the need for a uniform national solution, because, as with local option laws, as long as consumption remained legal in any nearby area, effective control was impossible. In December 1917, after an unprecedented lobbying campaign, Congress adopted the Eighteenth Amendment, prohibiting the commercial production or sale of any intoxicating liquor within the United States. By January 1919, the necessary thirty-six states had ratified the amendment, which accordingly became effective on 16 January 1920.

In anticipation of ratification, Congress adopted increasingly stringent statutes, which essentially made the liquor trade illegal. The Internal Revenue law of 1918 prohibited the production or sale of wine after 30 June 1918, and until the conclusion of the war, in the certain knowledge that the Eighteenth Amendment soon would become effective. The law permitted merchants to export their inventory, and they responded in 1919–20 by shipping millions of gallons of American wine overseas, leaving only residual stocks in bonded government warehouses. Furthermore, in October 1918, over President Wilson's veto, Congress passed the Volstead Act to implement the Prohibition amendment. The law virtually outlawed the commercial production of wine. Although little noticed at that time, it also left an enormous loophole by permitting home fermentation of grapes (see also pp. 82–83).

Simultaneously with the triumph of prohibition, the war prompted another development that would have long-term effects on the wine industry. The increase in demand from European countries trapped in a war of attrition raised the price of grapes, especially raisin grape varieties, approximately 300 percent between 1914 and 1920. The acreage of raisin grapes under cultivation exploded in response. The price of grapes peaked in 1920–21 and fell throughout the rest of the 1920s to 50 percent of the 1914 level. Production, on the other hand, did not peak until 1926 and remained at a high level thereafter, creating a persistent surplus of raisin grapes. This overhang troubled winegrowers for decades.

Most commercial production of wine in California ceased during Prohibition. The number of wineries gradually dropped from a pre-Prohibition figure of just over 700 to 130 at the lowest point (see pp. 53–54). Some wineries were able to continue operations at a low level by obtaining licenses to make sacramental and medicinal wines, which were legal under the Volstead Act. But legal production averaged somewhat less than 20 percent of the prewar level.

Ironically, while Prohibition crippled the commercial wine industry, Americans drank more wine during that period than at any previous time in the country's history. Homemade wine was legal under the Volstead Act, and large numbers of drinkers switched to wine from liquor and beer. The federal government estimated that wine production from 1920 to 1929 averaged 111 million gallons annually, with a peak of 154 million gallons in 1928, compared to prewar consumption of only 53 million gallons. Home winemaking created an enormous new market for grapes, and California growers greatly increased rail shipments of fresh grapes to the East. This market provided an outlet for a substantial quantity of the raisin grapes flooding the market.

With popular resistance to Prohibition, and the refusal of governments to appropriate sufficient funds for enforcement, consumption of alcohol rose steadily throughout the 1920s. The public ultimately decided that the widespread disrespect for law created by this measure, the involvement of criminal enterprises in the illicit liquor trade, and the health hazards of bootleg alcohol constituted greater evils than regulated control of consumption. Liquor also appeared a tempting source of tax revenues for governments hard pressed by the Depression.

In February 1933, Congress submitted the Twenty-First Amendment to the states for ratification. The amendment repealed national Prohibition and made permanent the awkward situation created by the Webb-Kenyon Act. Each state could adopt whatever laws it wished governing the "transportation" of "intoxicating liquors" (including wines) if the beverages were bound for delivery or use in the state. As subsequently interpreted by the Supreme Court, the Twenty-First Amendment gave the states nearly total power over wine and other alcoholic beverages. The states thus can, and do, enact laws and regulations that, were their subject any other lawful consumer product, would violate the Supremacy Clause, the Commerce Clause, and other sections of the Constitution, as well as the Due Process and Equal Protection Clauses of the Fourteenth Amendment to the Constitution. This constitutional anomaly has forced the wine industry to operate under a multitude of overlapping, and often inconsistent, state distribution laws.

The states ratified the Twenty-First Amendment with unexpected speed, and Prohibition was repealed effective 5 December 1933. The wine industry that emerged upon Repeal had immediately to address the consumer protection issues that had remained unresolved after the compromise of 1916.

REGULATION OF WINE AFTER REPEAL

Full-blown wine and liquor industries sprang into existence on the day Prohibition ended, and the federal government had no mechanism in place to regulate alcoholic beverages. President Roosevelt therefore created a new regulatory body, the Federal Alcohol Control Administration, pursuant to his powers under the National Industrial Recovery Act. In short order, the FACA adopted a series of codes that regulated every aspect of the production, importation, and distribution of wine.

Conditions in the wine market were chaotic. Attracted by the lure of windfall profits, many small firms jumped into the wine industry at Repeal. Often these enterprises were poorly financed and their winemakers lacked experience. Existing stocks of legal wine were quite small. During Prohibition, adulterated, falsely labeled, and dangerous beverages had been freely consumed, and these conditions continued to plague the wine industry. In addition, too many winemakers tried to capitalize on the first surge of demand by rushing improperly made or insufficiently aged wines to market. To combat these evils, the FACA adopted a comprehensive series of standards of identity, which defined the legal composition of various types

424

of wines. The agency also adopted a separate set of regulations prohibiting "misbranding"—that is, labeling wine in violation of the standards of identity.

Upon reconvening in 1934, Congress's first act was to impose stiff new taxes on wine and other alcoholic beverages to help finance the government. Congress followed the pattern of prewar tariffs by taxing table wines at ten cents a gallon and higher alcohol dessert wines at rates of from twenty to fifty cents a gallon. The taxes were deliberately set as high as possible without actually encouraging illegal production or importation. The high tax on fortified wines also was designed to promote temperance by encouraging consumption of less intoxicating wines. As a result of Prohibition, national drinking habits shifted fundamentally from table to higher alcohol fortified wines. For example, table wines accounted for 65 percent of all consumption before World War I. After Repeal, fortified wines outsold table wines by three (some sources say four) to one despite their heavier tax burden.

Heavy state taxes compounded the depressing effects of the federal levies. The rates ranged from a low of two cents a gallon in California to the prohibitive level of a dollar a gallon in some other states. Five of the eleven other wineproducing states imposed discriminatory taxes upon California wines.

Furthermore, wine sales were constrained by a crazy quilt of different laws restricting the sale and consumption of wine, which the states adopted under the powers granted them by the Twenty-First Amendment. Many states tried to deter wine consumption by continuing prohibition or greatly restricting sales. Some states fixed artificially high prices, while others adopted burdensome (and often conflicting) distribution schemes. For example, almost all states except California outlawed sales of wines in bulk and required that wine be sold in bottles. Prior to Prohibition, approximately 95 percent of all wine had been sold in bulk. The new laws disrupted this old consumption pattern and raised prices by requiring more expensive containers. The combined effect of high taxes and complex state restrictions greatly impeded the growth of the California wine industry.

Nor were these the only problems. The California industry itself, on the eve of Repeal, was in an organizational shambles. Whatever its political ability and experience prior to Prohibition, it now lacked cohesion and direction. To counterbalance these defects, the industry had a collective, if unformed, will to improve and succeed, substantial commitment to excellence, and considerable talent. Shortly after Repeal, the California Chamber of Commerce invited interested members of the grape and wine industries and the public to discuss the need for a statewide, closely knit organization to deal with the institutional challenge of returning California to its position of dominance. In October 1934, a committee of California vintners unanimously approved the organization of a voluntary trade association of California wineries, which became the Wine Institute.

The Wine Institute was formed for two principal purposes: to upgrade and to stabilize the industry. It began with a board of directors of twenty-nine vintners elected to give equitable representation to the several wineproducing districts of the state. It accepted for itself a challenging program, but of all its tasks none was more pressing or important than the establishment of quality wine standards insuring that California wine was as good as it should, and could, be. These standards, which under the aegis of the Wine Institute were enacted as state regulations with the force and effect of law, were restrictive and demanding, hard medicine for those who otherwise might have cut corners. They generally adopted federal production and labeling regulations, but further prohibited the use of sugar in still wines, severely limited the use of water (federal regulations continue to permit amelioration with sugar and water of up to 35 percent of the volume of the product), established limits for sweetness and fixed acidity, and even set alcohol minimums substantially higher than those permitted under federal law.★

The Wine Institute set to work to reduce taxes and license fees, eliminate or reduce bureaucratic red tape, open new markets, help educate consumers and the trade about wine and its proper uses, and provide numerous kinds of information to its members, including industry statistical and market research data. The institute also began collecting, analyzing, and explaining the wine laws and regulations of the federal government and the several states, which were contradictory, lacking in uniformity, and nowhere gathered in one place. It started programs to obtain reasonable insurance and transportation rates for the grape and wine industries, contracted for medical and enological research at the University of California, attempted to develop uniform taxation and production regulations, and, in general, sought to aid, develop, and protect the California wine and grape industries. The institute was a voluntary trade association, however, and money was tight. By the end of 1934, only forty-two wineries had joined, and the future of the organization seemed uncertain. But by the end of the following year, membership had tripled.

★   After Repeal, California produced substantial quantities of wine that contained just over the federal alcohol minimum of 7 percent, but which were unstable and spoiled in shipping. The problem received considerable notice within the eastern trade and led to a diminution of the reputation of California wine. California winemakers realized that much of this spoilage would not occur if they increased minimum alcohol levels. They therefore established minimum alcohol requirements for red wine at 10.5 percent by volume and for white and rosé wine at 10 percent. These minima were removed in the late 1970s after modern production technology had obviated the possibility of spoilage, and because wines of lower alcohol, particularly Late Harvest and other similar German-style sweet table wines, were freely sold in California but could not be produced there, placing the California industry at a competitive disadvantage. However, the other original California wine production standards still remain in place and continue to be among the strictest in the world.

Even so, funds were still insufficient to address all of the serious problems plaguing the industry. Since several important California winegrowers declined to join the voluntary trade association, others committed to the future of such an organization began a movement toward a mandatory program.

This movement culminated in the approval, almost three years to the day after the formation of the Wine Institute, of the Marketing Order for Wine, an order administered by the California Department of Agriculture (now the Department of Food and Agriculture). To become effective, 65 percent of the total number of wineproducers in the state, or the producers of at least 65 percent of the total amount of wine, had to approve the order. Winegrowers who chose not to approve nonetheless had a legal obligation to contribute to its financial support, the levy being based on the number of gallons of wine each grower produced. Some of them, who later were to take very significant leadership roles in the industry, resisted the assessment until ordered to pay by the courts. The Marketing Order for Wine was administered by the California Director of Agriculture and a fifteen-member Wine Advisory Board whose members were appointed by the director. The Wine Advisory Board's principal responsibility was to conduct "advertising and sales promotion" of California wine. While the board had its own staff and conducted many of its own programs, it contracted with the Wine Institute to conduct several of the more ambitious functions. Thus, four years after its founding, the Wine Institute represented, through its contract with the Wine Advisory Board, every winery in California. But the institute itself never relinquished its noncompulsory status as a voluntary association. Thus, although most winegrowers joined the Wine Institute, even those who chose not to do so supported it indirectly until the abolition of the Wine Advisory Board in 1975.

Meanwhile, the wine industry began to develop along the lines marked out by the FACA's regulations. In May 1935, however, the Supreme Court ruled that the entire National Industrial Recovery Act was unconstitutional. That decision undermined the legal basis for the FACA's existence. Congress responded in August by passing the Federal Alcohol Administration Act, which ever since has formed the basis for federal regulation of the wine industry.

THE FEDERAL ALCOHOL ADMINISTRATION ACT (FAAA)

The FAAA enacted into law much of the FACA program, with changes to reflect lessons learned after Repeal. The FAAA does not directly regulate how wine may be made. What constitutes a lawful wine is determined by definitions in the Internal Revenue Code and by the provisions of the Pure Food and Drug Act prohibiting adulteration of wine or use of harmful additives. Rather, the FAAA controls wine-

427

making through two other kinds of controls, a mandatory licensing scheme and prohibitions against improper trade practices.

The FAAA requires each winemaker to obtain a federal permit to operate. In order to obtain that permit, winemakers must prove good character and financial and technical qualifications. These tests were intended to prevent criminals and people without adequate capital or prior experience from entering the wine industry. The act also prohibits certain trade practices, such as a winery's requiring a retailer to buy and sell its products to the exclusion of the products of another supplier. The most important of the trade practice provisions required the enforcement agency to adopt regulations that would prohibit false, misleading, or deceptive statements on wine labels and provide consumers with adequate information about the identity and quality of the wine. The FAAA also prohibits false and misleading wine advertisements and authorizes the agency to review and approve in advance every wine label.

In December 1935, the government adopted standards of identity for wine and required that all wine labels and advertising thereafter comply with those definitions. Some of the proposed standards, especially the rule defining the minimum alcohol content of port wine, threatened to rekindle the battle between eastern and California winemakers. The dispute, in which principle and economic self-interest were inevitably combined, involved whether certain practices traditionally followed in the East—but illegal in California—were proper or constituted adulteration. The government ultimately modified the final regulations to establish a compromise all sections could accept. With minor modifications, those standards remain in effect today.

The standards authorized winemakers to continue the traditional pre-Prohibition practice of selling American wines under European geographic or type names, such as champagne, burgundy, and rhine wine, that had become semi-generic in this country. This practice, which was widely followed for many years after Repeal, created a substantial trade barrier to the export of California wines, since all major European producing countries had adopted the Madrid Convention of 1891, which prohibited trade in wines that appropriated European geographic names.

Although of little significance at the time, the standards also permitted wines to be labeled and sold under a varietal name if 51 percent or more of the wine was derived from the grape variety indicated on the label. The proposed standard sparked a lively controversy. A few producers considered the names of some grape varieties, particularly Riesling and Zinfandel, to designate a *type* of wine and argued that their wines should be able to be sold under those names even though they contained few grapes of the designated variety. The government, however, insisted on following the established trade practice that a varietal name indicated that at least 51 percent of the grapes in the wine were of the named variety. This rule became of increasing importance in the late 1930s, when Frank Schoonmaker promoted the practice of selling quality wines under varietal names.

The original FAAA standards also permitted wines to be sold under geographical names if 51 percent of the grapes came from the area designated on the label. At that time, wines traditionally were sold under state names rather than those of smaller areas within a state. The standard was intended to impose an upper limit on the practice of eastern vintners who increased their output by blending California wines with their own production but continued to use an eastern state name. Again, this regulation was unimportant when first adopted, but became increasingly significant over the years, as winemakers began adopting narrow geographic appellations within a state, and consumers demonstrated their willingness to pay premium prices for wines with select local appellations.

RECOVERY OF THE WINE INDUSTRY

In the years following adoption of the FAAA, the California wine industry struggled to recover from the twin blows of Prohibition and Depression. The industry was repeatedly aided by the sympathetic assistance of the federal and state governments. Although this assistance was accompanied by increased government regulation of many aspects of wine production, the industry evolved methods of operation that permitted it to prosper under increased political supervision.

FEDERAL ECONOMIC ASSISTANCE

Despite high expectations in 1933, the wine industry generally did not prove profitable after Repeal. Prices for grapes dropped steadily in 1934 and 1935 owing to a grape surplus, depressed economic conditions, the high level of excise taxation, and competition from tax-free homemade wines. Following the lead of the Wine Institute, the industry therefore petitioned Congress for relief in the form of a reduction in wine excise tax rates. In June 1936, Congress responded by cutting all wine excise taxes in half, while maintaining the high level of taxation on all other alcoholic beverages. This legislation materially increased wine's historical competitive price advantage. The spirits in sweet wines, which could contain up to 24 percent alcohol, were taxed at between one-tenth and one-third the rate of the same amount of alcohol in liquor and beer.

Congress also supported the wine industry through continued high protective tariffs. At Repeal, the effective tariff on foreign wines was approximately 80 percent of their value. Reversing the prewar pattern, the law imposed higher rates on ordinary wines imported in bulk than on the finer bottled wines. Combined

429

with state laws prohibiting sales in bulk and the efficient production practices of American winemakers, the tariff effectively excluded ordinary foreign wines from the U.S. market. Although Congress in 1936 ratified a reciprocal trade treaty with France that reduced wine duties by 35 percent, European winemakers still could compete with California only in expensive, prestige wines. The high rate of duty on Champagne particularly encouraged U.S. production. In 1914, imports of Champagne accounted for 97 percent of U.S. consumption, but by 1951, almost 80 percent of all sparkling wines consumed in the United States were produced here.

PRICE SUPPORT PROGRAMS OF THE 1930S

In the late 1930s, the wine industry was affected by two major disputes between the federal and state governments concerning their relative authority to regulate the economy. In both cases, the federal government elected to defer to state control while preserving the principle of federal dominance.

The first dispute involved state efforts to protect small retail shops, including liquor stores, from being put out of business by competition from larger, more efficient outlets. Since the late nineteenth century, small retail businesses had tried to compel manufacturers to establish a minimum price at which all retailers must sell their product, thereby denying large stores the opportunity to undersell smaller competitors. The Supreme Court had ruled that such minimum resale price maintenance agreements were illegal, at least when undertaken solely through private contracts. In 1933, however, California became the first state to pass a law authorizing creation of a so-called "fair trade" system of governmentally endorsed, uniform statewide resale prices. Retail wine sales quickly became subject to such an agreement. Other states promptly adopted similar laws, even though they appeared to contradict the Supreme Court's ruling. In the face of heated debate as to a state's authority to overrule the federal antitrust laws and the extent of its power under the Twenty-First Amendment to regulate alcoholic beverages, Congress compromised. In 1937, it passed the Miller-Tydings Act, which for the time being exempted state "fair trade" statutes from the reach of the federal antitrust laws.

The second major dispute concerned the California Prorate Order of 1938, another state attempt to avoid the federal antitrust laws. The oversupply of California grapes, especially raisin varieties, persisted throughout the 1930s. Various federal credit agencies extended loans to allow producers to stabilize prices by withholding excess supplies, but the relief was only temporary.

In 1938, California's grape growers, acting under authority of state law, adopted a marketing order that required producers to keep 45 percent of their crop off the market until 1941 and crush those grapes into brandy. Dissenting growers sued under the federal antitrust laws, claiming that the Prorate Order was an illegal price-fixing scheme. The Supreme Court agreed that the order would be illegal if it were simply a private agreement, but upheld it in order to avoid the difficult constitutional question of whether the state's power under the Twenty-First Amendment preempted the antitrust laws.★ The Court improvised a solution, creating a new "state action" exception to the antitrust laws. It held that as long as a state was actively involved in the formation and implementation of the anticompetitive practice, the antitrust laws would not apply unless Congress expressly stated that they overruled state law.

The legality of the Prorate Order had ceased to be of immediate practical concern by the time the Court ruled in 1941. The Prorate Order was not renewed for 1939 due to objections from coastal winegrowers, and World War II soon provided an interim solution to the oversupply problem. This temporary diversion of raisin and other grapes to distilleries did, however, prove to be the genesis of the modern California brandy industry.

WARTIME EMERGENCIES

During the Second World War, Congress "temporarily" tripled the excise taxes on wine to help finance the armed forces. California growers responded to the government's request and expanded grape production, especially of raisin varieties, both to feed displaced persons and to provide an additional source of industrial alcohol.

With the return of peace, these outlets for raisin grapes disappeared, and the grape industry again faced a persistent oversupply. During the late 1940s, the federal government officially certified the grape industry as depressed, entitling growers to favorable tax treatment. The impoverished condition of the grape market adversely affected the wine industry, because the overhang of grapes suitable for production of brandy or low-quality white wines maintained a ceiling on prices for grapes for other wines. And this time the wine industry was unable to obtain government relief. Indeed, the only significant regulatory development increased competitive pressure on the wine industry. In October 1947, as part of its European recovery program, the federal government ratified the General Agreement on Tariffs and Trade, which substantially reduced U.S. tariffs on many products including wines. As a consequence, U.S. tariffs on foreign wine today are the lowest of any wineproducing country: $0.375 per gallon on table wines, $1.00 per gallon on most dessert wines, and as little as $0.25 per gallon on certain specialty wines such as Japanese sake and Spanish sangria. By contrast, the members of the European Economic Community impose a table wine tariff that fluctuates between about $1.00 and $0.75, depending on various factors, and the tariff on most U.S. table wine entering Japan is more than ten times the U.S. tariff on Japanese sake.

★   Parker v. Brown, 317 U.S. 341 (1943).

In 1951, during the Korean War, the government again imposed temporary increases in the excise tax on alcoholic beverages. The Treasury Department, with the strong support of the brewing industry, sought to triple the wine excise taxes in order to eliminate the historic advantage wine had enjoyed over other alcoholic beverages. Approximately 75 percent of all wines consumed at the time were high alcohol dessert wines, and wine had made noticeable inroads on the market shares of other beverages. After intensive lobbying by the industry, wine's privileged tax status was preserved. Congress raised all alcohol excise taxes by 15 percent; the tax on table wine thus rose to $0.17, on dessert wines to $0.67, and on sparkling wine to $3.40 per gallon.

The struggle with the brewers ended the debate about the proper level of wine taxation. The 1951 wine excises, although initially considered temporary, were extended from year to year and finally made permanent in 1965. Since 1951, sparkling wine producers have tried to obtain reductions in the discriminatory tax on their product, which is twenty times the rate on still wines, but Congress has consistently refused to respond to their pleas.

By the mid-1950s, the wine industry returned to its customary political effectiveness. In addition to defeating all attempts to raise wine taxes, Congress aided the wine industry in 1954 by substantially liberalizing the provisions of the Internal Revenue Code governing the methods by which wine may be produced. In particular, Congress amended the law, left over from the early years of the pure food movement, that prevented winemakers from employing production techniques that were not considered "usual cellar treatment" in 1916. The industry had long chafed under this restriction and lobbied vigorously to have the law updated. The 1954 amendment resolved the question once and for all by allowing winemakers to use any production technique that received general acceptance in the trade. This technical change gave American vintners great flexibility in developing new wine styles.

THE POLITICS OF WINE DURING THE BOOM YEARS

As the wine industry entered the era of growth and prosperity that began in the 1950s, the political environment changed. With the legal and economic foundations for its development firmly established, the focus shifted from such basic questions as tariffs and taxes to more complicated issues such as reducing marketing restrictions, the appropriate level of detail on labels, the development of a sophisticated geographic appellation of origin system and the increasingly complex relationship with wine producers in other nations.

In California, the Wine Institute and the Wine Advisory Board contributed richly to the industry's success in the boom years. Many of their programs played key roles in the increasing understanding and acceptance of wine by U.S.

consumers. The Wine Institute continued to perform many of the Wine Advisory Board's statutory responsibilities under its annual contract with the board. The Marketing Order for Wine, under which the board operated, was renewed twenty-one times. But in 1975 the industry turned its back on the Wine Advisory Board, voting not to renew the Marketing Order and to make the Wine Institute once again fully dependent upon the voluntary association of winegrowers.

The elimination of the Marketing Order did not result from industry dissatisfaction with the board. To the contrary, the industry showed every indication of being well pleased with both the board and the institute. Rather, overt political interference caused the industry to reject further participation of the state in its internal affairs.

In 1974 Edmund G. ("Jerry") Brown, Jr., was elected governor of California. Among his most important supporters was a coalition of agricultural workers that had an ongoing feud with certain powerful members of the California wine industry. In early 1975 the governor asked his new director of the Department of Food and Agriculture, Rose Bird (now chief justice of the California Supreme Court), who was responsible for the administration of the Marketing Order for Wine, to audit the contract between the Wine Advisory Board and the Wine Institute. Administration officials stated informally at the audit's outset that they intended to prove that senior officers of the Wine Institute were using state money for illegal purposes and were otherwise involved in criminal conduct. To their disappointment, however, the audit produced absolutely no damaging evidence.

The Wine Advisory Board and the Wine Institute were both pleased that the audit found them blameless. In their view, the administration's activities were motivated by political considerations that had nothing to do with either organization. But the audit publicized the fact, which the industry had never hidden, that the Wine Institute was vigorously involved in a campaign to remove or reduce trade barriers erected by other states to the sale of California wine. In order to do this, the institute had assembled a highly qualified government relations staff whose responsibilities were to lobby for the interests of the California industry throughout the United States. Although the California Marketing Act of 1937 explicitly authorized expenditures of state funds "for the prevention, modification, or removal of trade barriers which restrict the free flow of . . . [wine] to market" including "negotiations with state . . . agencies," the Brown administration indicated its unwillingness to permit money collected under the Marketing Order for Wine to be used to attempt to influence the laws and regulations of other states.

The wine industry greatly resented the administration's interference for obviously partisan political reasons in the legal activities of its trade association. The industry therefore voted not to renew the Marketing Order and thus closed the door to state government intrusion in its internal affairs. The Wine Advisory Board, which for nearly forty years substantially assisted the Wine Institute in promoting California wine, ceased operation on 30 June 1975. The Wine Institute remains as the industry's trade association, supported 100 percent by the dues of its voluntary members. And while the Wine Institute no longer can say that it represents, through the Wine Advisory Board, every winery in California, it can at least conduct its work free of political interference.

At approximately the same time that the Brown administration was attempting to discredit the Wine Institute, the federal government reasserted its power to regulate interstate commerce in order to eliminate state restrictions on the distribution of wine and other alcoholic beverages. In 1975 Congress repealed the exemption that permitted states to maintain "fair trade" laws. This action substantially increased price competition among retail liquor dealers in many states.

Furthermore, in the *Midcal* case of 1980, the Supreme Court greatly liberalized the wine trade by declaring unlawful a California statute that allowed wine suppliers to fix the retail price of wine.★ The Supreme Court considered explicitly the long-unsettled question of the relationship between the state's power to regulate liquor under the Twenty-First Amendment and the federal antitrust laws. The Court concluded that the Twenty-First Amendment protected only a state's right to prohibit the importation or sale of liquor, but did not give the state power to throw its protective cloak over dealers who managed to capture the legislative process and obtain permission to engage in collusive, anticompetitive practices. Although this decision hardly spelled an end to the tangle of post-Repeal state laws regulating wine distribution, it constituted an important landmark in the effort to introduce a more uniform system of regulation and reduce the burden of conflicting local laws on wine producers.

Another powerful stimulus to uniformity in state wine regulation is a recent study by the Columbia University Legislative Drafting Research Fund, concluded in 1983. Based on a comprehensive analysis of all state liquor laws, the report identifies the underlying public policies and proposes a model state alcoholic beverage law. The movement to enact uniform state laws has met with only limited success. Although no student of alcoholic beverage control law expects the Columbia proposal to be widely adopted, it is a giant step forward. Those most familiar with the tangle of contemporary alcoholic beverage laws hope the study will provide a logical system to guide legislators who must deal with the problem in the future.

★ California Retail Liquor Dealers v. Midcal Aluminum, Inc., 445 U.S. 97 (1980).

THE LABELING REGULATIONS TODAY

The state and federal legal and regulatory systems are certainly more complicated than they need to be, but, as this chapter has suggested, they are the logical outgrowth of a complex ebb and flow of social and economic factors. To the uninitiated, whether attorney or layman, they present a formidable barrier. "Curiouser and curiouser," as Alice said. Not only does each state have its own set of laws and regulations, but even those federal laws and regulations that establish overriding policy, and thus control what the states can and cannot do, are subdivided in ways comprehensible only in historical perspective.

　　The Internal Revenue Code, for example, not only governs taxation (which one might expect) but also controls winemaking practices (which one might not) in painstaking detail, reflecting the political belief that the only proper response to a social problem is direct government regulation of every aspect of production. The winemaking regulations are so complete, in fact, that they prescribe the means of winery ingress and egress, and establish requirements for the location and capacity of tanks, pipelines, catwalks, and other details of construction. While some construction and equipment requirements could be justified as necessary "to protect the revenue," it is impossible to understand others. Minute data regarding the use and care of the burette and pipette for the determination of the acidity of juice, or details of ebulliometers designed to determine the percentage of alcohol in wine may be interesting to the chemist or enologist, but one may justifiably wonder about their inclusion in a federal regulation.★

　　As previously indicated, the Federal Alcohol Administration Act of 1935 is as important and complex a wine law as the Internal Revenue Code. The FAAA is perhaps of most interest to people who drink wine, because it establishes wine labeling standards that prohibit consumer deception and require labels to provide the consumer with adequate information as to the identity and quality of the wine. Since Repeal, an agency of the U.S. Treasury Department has enforced the federal alcoholic beverage laws and regulations. At first, logically enough, this agency was a unit, then a division, of the Internal Revenue Service. In 1972, however, the agency obtained full bureau status and is now known as the Bureau of Alcohol, Tobacco and Firearms (ATF). The fact that the agency responsible for guns, bombs, and cigarettes is also responsible for wine tells volumes more about the political mind than about the nature and quality of any of these commodities.

　　While the FAAA establishes the broad guidelines and minimum requirements of the wine labeling and advertising law, its implementing regulations

★   As this book is prepared for publication, the Bureau of Alcohol, Tobacco and Firearms is considering the elimination of these and similar production minutiae from these regulations.

provide the detail. California, as the principal winegrowing state in the nation, has adopted almost all of the federal regulations by reference, with a very few exceptions. Because so many people are interested in wine labeling, these regulations are frequently described and explained. Unfortunately, because of their detail and complexity, even very knowledgeable commentators sometimes confuse and misstate the requirements. In addition, like any law or regulation, those dealing with wine labeling are organic—that is, changing, whether as a result of new rule making in response to evolving needs or requirements, or of lawsuits that may derive solely from the personal vagaries of those who bring them rather than from any societal imperative. Thus, the student of wine labeling must always understand that even if yesterday's dicta become today's dogma, by tomorrow they may have become nothing more than interesting historical facts.

Because the ability properly to read and understand a wine label is so important, we include a description of some of the most important labeling rules as of 1 January 1983. Some of these rules are scheduled to be modified in 1985, and other unanticipated changes will certainly occur. Since 1975, in accordance with the requirements of the federal Administrative Procedures Act, ATF has conducted numerous informal rule-making procedures directed at the first significant modification of the wine labeling rules since their promulgation in 1935. Most of the new rules that resulted from this process became effective for wine *bottled* on or after 1 January 1983. But, because there will be plenty of wine around for years bottled under the prior regulations, we explain both sets of rules.

VINTAGE WINE

At least 95 percent of a wine labeled with a vintage year must be derived from grapes harvested in that year. Until the early 1970s, U.S. regulations required that 100 percent of the wine come from the stated year. Wines used to top casks containing other wines had to be of the same vintage, creating obvious problems for winemakers who aged wine in small oak barrels, where it was subject to evaporation. Winegrowers successfully petitioned ATF to lower the requirement and permit a 5 percent leeway for topping.

All vintage labeled wine must bear an appellation of origin other than a country.* Why a wine simply labeled "American," or "France," should not be vintage labeled is unclear, although this follows the practice in the European Economic Community. At one time, vintage labeled wine had to come from grapes 95 percent of which were grown in the designated viticultural area. This has not been true since 1978, although it still confuses some people.

---

* At press time, ATF is also considering eliminating this requirement.

VARIETAL WINE

Few terms are as abused as "varietal wine." Some people, for example, laud a Chardonnay as "an excellent varietal wine," but disdain a wine made from Thompson Seedless grapes as something less elegant than a "genuine" varietal wine. But, since Thompson Seedless is a recognized grape variety, just as is Chardonnay, a wine that derives the requisite percentage of its volume from Thompson Seedless grapes is as much a "varietal" wine as is a Chardonnay, even if it may not be quite as interesting. Under ATF regulations, a "varietal" wine is *any* wine named after a specific grape variety that derives not less than 75 percent of its volume from that variety and is labeled with an appellation of origin. In addition, a minimum of 75 percent of the grapes of the specified variety must have come from the appellation of origin area on the label.

Before 1983 the regulations imposed a twofold varietal requirement. The wine had to derive both at least 51 percent of its volume and its "predominant taste, aroma, and characteristics" from the designated variety. The second test was functionally unenforceable because it was entirely subjective, and whatever ATF may be, it is not a collection of specialists trained in sensory wine evaluation. The California wine industry urged ATF to eliminate the subjective portion of the test and to raise the minimum varietal requirement from 51 percent to 75 percent, in the belief that wines made with the higher percentage would perforce have the taste, aroma, and characteristics of the named grape.

The requirement that the entire minimum 75 percent of varietal grapes be grown in the appellation of origin area closed a loophole with which some industry critics tried to embarrass winegrowers. Theoretically, the regulations had permitted a "Sonoma County Chardonnay" to derive only 26 percent of its volume from Chardonnay grapes grown in Sonoma. Although 51 percent of the grapes had to be Chardonnay, and 75 percent of the grapes had to come from Sonoma County, 25 percent of the Chardonnay grapes could have come from elsewhere. Thus, an unscrupulous (and irrational) winemaker could have loaded the wine with 49 percent of an undistinguished white grape, such as Burger, from Sonoma County. Of course, a Sonoma County Chardonnay that contained 49 percent of Sonoma Burger grapes probably would not taste very good, and so would enhance neither the winemaker's reputation nor his pocketbook. But the potential for mischief existed, and the 1983 regulations quite properly removed it.

The regulations provide certain exceptions to the current 75 percent rule. For example, wine made from any *Vitis labrusca* (eastern) variety may contain not less than 51 percent of the named grape, provided the label discloses this fact. This is so because many winemakers believe that wine from labrusca grapes has such an overpowering varietal character that it would not be pleasant to drink at

75 percent. A similar exception exists for any wine ATF, on a winemaker's application, finds to be "too strongly flavored at 75 percent." No one had invoked this exception, designed for as yet undeveloped or undiscovered vinifera varieties or hybrids, by 1 January 1983, but someone may do so in the future.

Wines may be labeled with two or three grape variety names if the percentage derived from each appears and all of the wine is made of the labeled varieties.

APPELLATIONS OF ORIGIN

Until 1983 a wine was entitled to bear an appellation of origin if at least 75 percent of its volume came from the indicated place; if it had been fully manufactured and finished within the state in which the place was located (thus prohibiting a "Napa Valley" wine further blended or otherwise treated in New York, South America, or Australia before bottling); and if it conformed to the laws and regulations of the named place governing consumption, manufacture, and designation of wines for home consumption.

The reference to local law and regulation, while generally ignored by most writers, became an important enforcement tool for ATF. For example, in the early 1970s, the U.S. market was inundated with Spanish "burgundies" selling for sixty-nine cents a bottle and Spanish "Cabernet Sauvignons" selling for ninety-nine cents. ATF, prodded by the Wine Institute, determined that only about forty acres of Cabernet Sauvignon grew in all of Spain (and this was entirely owned by an American who made high-quality wine from his vineyards and imported it directly to his Beverly Hills restaurant). The Spanish Cabernet thus had to have been mislabeled in violation of the FAAA. With regard to the Spanish "burgundy," it was clear that while Australia, Canada, and the United States were all permitted to label wines with semi-generic designations such as burgundy, because they had not signed the Madrid and Lisbon treaty agreements concerning the repression of indications of false or fallacious origin, the Spanish, who were protected under these treaties with regard to Spanish Sherry, among other things, most certainly had subscribed. The production of "burgundy" therefore violated Spain's obligations under the Madrid and Lisbon Agreements and failed to conform to local law regarding designation of wines for home consumption. Thus, because the wine was mislabeled in Spain, it was mislabeled in the United States, and U.S. Customs, at ATF's request, forbade its further importation.

Political Subdivisions

Many California winemakers view the 1983 appellation of origin rules as the most important amendment to the wine labeling regulations since their promulgation in 1935.* The 75 percent production requirement continues for wine labeled with a political subdivision as the place of origin. Political subdivisions, according to the regulations, include not only nations, states, or counties, but two or three contiguous states (e.g., "Washington-Oregon") and two or three counties in the same state. In the case of multi-state or multi-county appellations, all of the wine must come from the indicated areas, and the label must state the percentages from each. But for the other political appellations, as in the past, at least 75 percent of the wine must come from the indicated political subdivision area, and it must be fully finished (except for cellar treatment and blending) in this country (for "American" wine) or within the labeled state or an adjacent state (for a state appellation) or within the state (for a county appellation). Additionally, as in the past, the wine must conform to the laws and regulations of the named area covering the composition, method of manufacture, and designation of wines made in the area. Again, this requirement allows ATF to enforce state or other local regulations against bottlers in those states when the state lacks the interest or resources to do so.

    For example, although under the federal regulations a wine would be entitled to the appellation of origin "California" if only 75 percent of the grapes came from California, California regulation requires that any wine bearing the appellation of origin "California" (or any political subdivision of California) must derive virtually all of its volume from California grapes. If California did not become aware of a violation of this rule or move to stop it, ATF could certainly discover it during one of its unannounced, routine "post-audit" winery inspections. Because the practice would violate California rules, it would also violate federal regulations and, after informing the state, ATF could move against the winery on its own.

    U.S. appellation of origin rules for imported wine continue the requirement that the wine must conform to local law. When the 1983 regulations were first announced in 1978, this requirement was notably absent with respect to foreign wines. This omission was an oversight, however, and ATF reincluded it without additional public hearings. As in the case of the Spanish "burgundy," the rule is designed to ensure that foreign winemakers do not produce a product for sale in the United States which would be unlawful under their own regulations.

---

*   The increase in varietal percentage from 51 percent to 75 percent may seem more dramatic, but, with the exception of a few large wineries, general practice has been to include considerably more than 51 percent of the named grape in the blend. In fact, it is unlikely that very many winemakers were inconvenienced by the higher varietal percentage since they were using close to, or more than, 75 percent of the named grape all the time. On the other hand, although the increase in the percentage from political subdivisions at 75 percent to viticultural areas at 85 percent is not nearly so dramatic, the designation and delimitation of viticultural areas within the United States is a new departure.

Semi-generic Names

The whole question of the use, by the United States and some other countries, of what are technically known here as "semi-generic" names is both nettling and controversial.* Under its regulations, ATF must make a finding that a geographical name has become semi-generic before it may be used as a designation of a type of wine. The list of permissible semi-generic wines has become exclusive in practice and includes only the following types:

angelica	*malaga*	*rhine wine (synonym, hock)*
burgundy	*marsala*	*sauterne*
claret	*madeira*	*haut sauterne*
chablis	*moselle*	*sherry*
champagne	*port*	*tokay*
chianti		

The regulations also include, as another category of geographic names, those that are not generic or semi-generic and that do not designate a wine type. The regulation includes, as examples of such appellations, American, French, California, Napa Valley, and Lake Erie Islands (but, with regard to the latter two, see below).

The regulations do provide, on the other hand, an extensive list of non-generic names that *are* distinctive designations of specific grape wines (including Bordeaux Blanc and Rouge, Graves, Médoc, Château d'Yquem, Château Margaux, Château Lafite, Pommard, Chambertin, Montrachet, Liebfraumilch, Schloss Johannisberger, and Lacryma Christi) and an even more extensive list of distinctive designations of specific natural table wines, which are supposed to be qualified by the word "wine" or its French or German equivalent (Bordeaux, Médoc, Margaux, Graves, Pomerol, St. Émilion, Côte de Nuits, Bourgogne, Gevrey-Chambertin, Vosne-Romanée, Nuits St. Georges, Côte de Beaune, Puligny-Montrachet, Beaujolais, Côte du Rhone, Loire, Anjou, Saumur, Alsace or Alsatian, Mosel-Saar-Ruwer, Mosel, Swiss or Suisse, to name a few).

Accordingly, U.S. winemakers can produce a burgundy but not a bordeaux, a moselle but not a mosel. And the regulations that permit these anomalies seem to have just grown, like Topsy. U.S. labeling practices before Prohibition took a good deal more liberty with European names than is the case today. Califor-

---

* The regulations require that a geographic name that is the designation of a type of wine "shall be deemed to have become generic only if so found by the . . . [ATF]." The regulations give only two examples: vermouth and sake.

nia produced not only burgundy, but its own "Chateau Yquem,"* its own "Medoc," and, by far most troubling to the French, its own "California Cognac." After Repeal, the United States and France conducted a series of discussions on the question of American wine and spirits labeling. The French demanded that the use of all semi-generic names by American producers cease forthwith. But they were only partially successful. The regulations in this area are a result of political and economic compromise, rather than of internally coherent philosophy or public policy.

Of course, the United States has never signed the Madrid or Lisbon Agreements (which protect appellations of origin). But a number of wise friends, and even a few members of the American wine industry, have urged the elimination of names like burgundy, chablis, and champagne, whether these words are perceived as "generic," "semi-generic" or, as has often become the case, some peculiarly hybrid regulatory combination. But, with the exception of the State Department, almost every agency of the federal government to which the issue has been presented (including ATF, the Foreign Agricultural Service of the Department of Agriculture, the Patent and Trademark Office, and the U.S. Trade Representative) has vigorously and successfully resisted any change. So also has the U.S. wine industry on the whole, although some producers, usually of more expensive wines, may privately take the other approach. For the foreseeable future, the semi-generics are here to stay. But how did they get here and why are they so important?

When the first European pioneers from the "Old Country" made wine in California from *Vitis vinifera* grapes that looked like, smelled like, and tasted like what they knew at home, they called it by Old Country names. Certainly, by the early 1880s, names like chablis, champagne, and burgundy were commonly used in California to describe wines *similar to* those grown in France. As wine historian William Heintz has noted, French varieties, in any case, were probably grown in small

---

*   But, according to at least one writer describing the state of wine labeling in 1891, the fault even then lay in Bordeaux: "The merchants of Bordeaux have been largely responsible for this apparent robbery of local fame. . . . Sweet Sauternes after the style of this great vintage [Château d'Yquem] have been labeled Château Yquem, the true marks of the genuine Château wines being avoided; the name of the wine having become in a measure typical" (Daniel O'Connell, *The Inner Man: Good Things to Eat and Drink and Where to Get Them* [San Francisco: Bancroft Co., 1891], quoted by William Heintz, "Heintz on History," *Wines & Vines*, November 1982, p. 121). And, O'Connell notes, the term sauterne "as a distinction has . . . lost much of its local significance and become, as is true of Port, from Oporto, Sherry from Xeres, Burgundy from Bourgogne, *expressive of a typical characteristic of a class of wines*" (O'Connell, p. 88, cited by Heintz in "The Production and Marketing of 'Chablis'-Type Wines in California and, Incidentally, in the United States, circa 1880s to 1940," a private study for the Wine Institute [1982], hereafter cited as "Heintz Study," p. 4, emphasis supplied).

quantities as early as the 1860s in California's Santa Clara Valley. And by the 1880s, "California chablis" was freely sold. As Heintz points out,

nearly all wine sold in California and in many other parts of the U.S. in . . . the 1880s, used the common French names, the names internationally known. Wine lists attached to restaurant menus commonly advertised "Champagne," "Claret," "Sauterne," "Burgundy," and "Riesling," "Moselle" or "Hock" (for white German-type wines). There was no other nomenclature which the general public or even the wine trade understood.★

The French objected then, as they do now, and the controversy continues to flourish. It has shown up periodically over the years, fanned by one critic or incident and then another. The French producers, especially, continue to do their bit by filing lawsuits around the world against the use, for example, by Canadians of "champagne" (the French lost but continued to press the battle); and against the sale of "California chablis" in Bermuda (the specific company involved agreed

★   Heintz Study, p. 3. After California semi-generics won important awards at the Chicago World's Fair of 1893 and the San Francisco Mid-Winter Fair and international wine competition of 1894, California wines began to acquire an international reputation. As Heintz notes, at the Paris World's Fair of 1900, "the French directors apparently decided that it was time to halt completely the practice in California of labeling wines with French names," by barring such wines from the judging (Heintz Study, p. 16). The California wines in question bore labels plainly, perhaps even proudly, indicating that they were California, not French, wines. But the French were adamant and, after all, it was their fair.

 Still, their actions touched off a heated controversy in the far west. Andrea Sbarbono, president of Italian Swiss Colony Winery in Sonoma County, believed the French rejected California's wines out of fear, not principle (Heintz Study, p. 16). Sbarbono asked, apparently with some heat,

Now I ask you in all common sense, what are you going to call that but California Burgundy? The trade knows the wines by the names used in commerce. What are you going to call port, or sherry, or sauterne when it is grown from the identical cuttings grown in those countries, and which makes the same class of wine? A wine merchant, when he desires a Burgundy or a Sauterne, cannot order a "Fresno" or a "Sonoma." Custom has made these names familiar to the trade. [Pacific Wine & Spirits Review, 31 December 1900, p. 8, quoted in Heintz Study, p. 18]

 Nor was the controversy over. In 1904, Charles Bundschu, of the prestigious Gundlach-Bundschu of Sonoma (which was granted a gold medal in Paris in 1900), noted that "English Ale and Port are famous in all countries" and that "Caviar," "Sardines," and "Frankfurters" are commonly accepted food classifications (*Pacific Wine & Spirit Review*, 24 February 1904, pp. 8–9, quoted in Heintz Study, p. 19). Bundschu continued,

As long . . . as the word "California" is faithfully connected with the designation of the wine, no duplicity is intended. . . . When we have a "Cape Colony Port," an "Australian Sherry," a "Chile Burgundy," before us, we are challenged to comparison and no particular deception is contemplated. [Pacific Wine & Spirit Review, 24 February 1904, pp. 8–9, quoted in Heintz Study, p. 19]

to stop importing the product rather than try the suit to an uncertain conclusion), and "champagne" in parts of the Caribbean.

But, for all of the heavily articulated concern, it is very hard to imagine how any U.S. winery that bottles semi-generic wines could seriously be accused of attempting to perpetrate a deception upon the consumer. The ATF regulations for semi-generic wines permit such designations "only if there appears in direct conjunction . . . [with the semi-generic name] an appropriate appellation of origin disclosing the true place of origin of the wine." ATF enforces this requirement with particular vigilance and vigor.

Viticultural Areas

One of the most important changes under the 1983 appellation of origin regulations is the creation of a new appellation category besides political subdivisions: the viticultural area. Although the term "viticultural area" had appeared in the regulations before, it had never been specifically defined. The 1983 regulations define it as follows:

A delimited grape growing region distinguishable by geographical features, the boundaries of which have been recognized and defined [by ATF, and listed] in part 9 of this chapter [i.e., in another section of the regulations].

ATF itself "recognizes and defines" viticultural areas. The regulations contain detailed criteria the bureau uses in the defining process. Any interested party may petition the bureau, in the form of a letter, for designation of a viticultural area. If the request fits within the established criteria, the bureau is likely to grant it with a minimum of fuss. But if the request becomes controversial, ATF is certain to conduct at least one hearing to gather testimony on which to base a decision.

ATF announced its viticultural area rules in September 1978. By 1 January 1983, the bureau had received nearly a hundred petitions to establish viticultural areas and had taken final action on only about twenty of them. ATF has discovered that the motive force behind most viticultural area petitions is economic rather than geographical; viticultural area designation confers upon growers and wineries within such areas a cachet of quality that may well raise the price of their grapes and wine. And, as the reader will discover, without viticultural area designation, wine-growers are precluded from using "estate bottled" on their labels.

Once the bureau "recognizes and defines" a viticultural area, the requirements for its use on a label are quite straightforward. Not less than 85 percent of the wine must come from grapes grown within the viticultural area (rather than the 75 percent required for political subdivision appellations of origin). Additionally, the wine must be fully finished within the state, or one of the states, within which the area is located, and must conform to the laws and regulations of all of the states concerned.

The latter requirement clearly contemplates viticultural area designations that overlap state lines (for example, the Columbia River Basin). The regulations also contemplate, at least implicitly, viticultural areas that themselves overlap other viticultural areas (nothing in the regulations precludes the winegrowers on Mayacamas Mountain to petition for and obtain a viticultural area designation, even though Mayacamas Mountain is partly in Sonoma County and partly in the Napa Valley viticultural area), or smaller viticultural areas completely contained within the boundaries of larger ones (several are now in the planning stages). And ATF, the wine industry, and many observers anticipate that the process of defining and establishing new viticultural areas will continue for a long time. The wine industry, after all, is still in its formative stage in California, and will probably continue to experiment with various grape types and different growing locations indefinitely.

ESTATE BOTTLED

Before 1983, "estate bottled" on a U.S. wine label meant only that the wine in the bottle was grown from grapes under the ownership or control of the winery, located in the vicinity of the winery. Unfortunately, no regulation existed defining "ownership or control," or "vicinity." Initially, ATF permitted "estate bottled" only on wines produced from a vineyard contiguous to the producing winery. But a vintner then argued that his vineyard lost contiguity only because of its bisection by a public road, and the bureau acquiesced in his use of the term. Subsequently, other winegrowers pointed out to the bureau that contiguity was not nearly as important or relevant to quality as combined growing and bottling conditions. Their vineyards, they said, were "just over the hill from the winery," "just a few miles from the winery," "within the same county as the winery," or, in at least one case, "in a different county but under the ownership or control of the winery." While the bureau would not go so far as to permit "estate bottled" to appear on the label of the latter winery, they did permit the others to use it, and, ultimately, the term lost much of its significance. The tough new 1983 rules remedy this situation.

The new "estate bottled" rule is based on the existence of a viticultural area. In order to use the term on the label, a bottling winery must be located in the same viticultural area that produced all of the grapes (naturally, the label must show the viticultural area). The winery must have grown 100 percent of the grapes on land it "owned or controlled." And the winery must have crushed, fermented, finished, aged, and bottled the wine "in a continuous process (the wine at no time having left the premises of the bottling winery)." This time, the regulation defines "control." If the winery does not actually own the land itself, it must have the legal right to perform, and must actually perform, "all of the acts common to viticulture under the terms of the lease or similar agreement of at least 3 years duration."

The rule permits estate bottling of wine made from grapes grown by members of a cooperative, as long as the winery and the grapes come from the same viticultural area and the wine meets the other requirements of the rule. Finally, the rule prohibits use of any term other than "estate bottled" on a label to indicate combined growing and bottling.

The estate bottled rule, undeniably tougher than its predecessor, closes many of the asserted and real prior loopholes, but it does create other problems. For example, the requirement that the wine never leave the bottling winery's premises means that a winery that grows grapes in the Napa Valley, crushes them at one Napa Valley facility and then ships them to another for bottling cannot claim to have estate bottled the wine, even though the winery complies with all of the classic requirements for combined growing and bottling. Likewise, wineries that comply but for the fact that the grapes and winery are located in different viticultural areas are prohibited from using the term. Moreover, ATF, abrogating its prohibition against any other similar term, has already informally agreed to permit such wineries to use descriptions such as "proprietor grown" and "vintner grown." Note, however, that while "estate bottled" wine must meet certain strict technical requirements, the regulation cannot, and does not try to, assess or guarantee the wine's intrinsic quality. In fact, a wine could comply with all of the strictures for use of "estate bottled" and be terrible. And, obviously, some splendid wine will not be able to use the term for technical reasons that have nothing to do with its potability.

U.S. wine labeling regulations probably require more detail and provide more valuable information to those who know how to use them than do the rules of any other country, but unlike those of many foreign countries, they do not address quality. At one point in the mid-1970s, ATF flirted with a system that would have permitted it to award an "ATF Seal" to wine that met certain specified criteria, but when the bureau sought comment on this proposal at public hearings, it noted a startling uniformity of opposition among all members of the public and the industry who testified.

Inherent in the U.S. labeling system is the notion that the American consumer, and only the consumer, is the final judge of a wine's quality. Neither the regulatory agency, the industry, nor the retailer is in as good a position to make final decisions about a wine's acceptance or the price it should command. Ultimately, if the wine is sound and the price fair, it will find a ready market, no matter what its label says. Conversely, if the equation is out of balance, the wine will not sell. No matter how sophisticated the consumer or how detailed the label, the question will always be, is this a good wine for the price? And only the consumer can decide.

BIBLIOGRAPHIC NOTE

The following specialized studies have been of use in the preparation of this essay: C. Byse, "Alcoholic Beverage Control before Repeal," *Journal of Law and Contemporary Problems* 7 (Autumn 1940): 544–69; K. Farrell and O. Blaich, *World Trade and the Impacts of Tariff Adjustments upon the United States Wine Industry* (Berkeley and Los Angeles: University of California Press, 1964); B. Gaguine, "The Federal Alcohol Administration," *George Washington Law Review* 7–8 (1939): 844–65; F. P. Lee, "The Jurisdictional Aspects of Federal Regulation of Adulteration and Misbranding of Alcoholic Beverages," *Food, Drug, and Cosmetic Law Quarterly* 3 (March 1948): 82–93; and J. O'Neill, "Federal Activity in Alcoholic Beverage Control," *Journal of Law and Contemporary Problems* 7 (Autumn 1940): 570–92. See also U.S. Congress, House Committee on Ways and Means, *Pure Wine: Hearings on H.R. 12868*, 59th Cong., 1st sess., 1906; House Committee on Ways and Means, *The Kent Wine Bills: Hearings before a Subcommittee on Wine Legislation*, 64th Cong., 1st sess., 1916; Senate Committee on Finance, *Tariff Schedules: Hearings before a Subcommittee*, 63d Cong., 1st sess., 1913; Federal Alcohol Administration, *Hearing with Reference to Proposed Wine Misbranding and Advertising Regulations* (Washington, D.C., 1935); Federal Alcohol Administration, *Regulation No. 4 Relating to Labeling and Advertising of Wine* (Washington, D.C., 1935); Federal Alcohol Control Administration, *Regulations Relating to Standards of Identity and Quality for Wine (Misbranding Regulations, Series 6)* (Washington, D.C., 1935); Federal Alcohol Control Administration, *Regulations Relating to the Labeling of Wine (Misbranding Regulations, Series 7)* (Washington, D.C., 1935); Federal Alcohol Control Administration, *Legislative History of the Federal Alcohol Administration Act* (Washington, D.C., 1935); U.S. Tariff Commission, *Report on Whiskey, Wine, Beer and Other Alcoholic Beverages and the Tariff*, Report no. 90, 2d ser. (Washington, D.C., 1935); U.S. Tariff Commission, *Grapes, Raisins and Wines: A Survey of World Production*, Report no. 134, 2d ser. (Washington, D.C., 1939).

APPRECIATIONS & EVALUATIONS

1. MAYNARD A. AMERINE 2. JAMES LAPSLEY 3. ROY BRADY

4. HARVEY STEIMAN 5. ALICE WATERS

6. BOB THOMPSON

X.1

SENSORY EVALUATION, OR HOW TO TASTE WINE

by MAYNARD A. AMERINE

IF WINES ARE MADE TO BE ENJOYED, WHAT IS THE NEED FOR FORMAL SENSORY EVALUATION? PROBABLY NONE. HOWEVER, IF IT LEADS TO A FULLER APPRECIATION OF THE WINE, THERE is a point. Furthermore, any artistic creation of man develops styles and degrees of artistic perfection. The artist creates, but the consumer appreciates. Appreciation is a personal and *learned* response. Some sort of evaluation of quality must develop. Everyone who drinks a glass of wine consciously or unconsciously makes an evaluation of it. That evaluation, to a degree, determines whether we consume more or less of the wine and, more important, whether we order it in the future. How do we make this distinction?

There are, of course, many levels at which this evaluation may be made. The wine may be simple and intended for quenching the thirst. Little sensory evaluation occurs, except that the wine must not be disagreeable or spoiled. Or, it may be a more complex product deserving of a more complete sensory appraisal. Here the consumer begins to verbalize his opinion of the wine's flavor and other sensory characteristics. With more and more experience, the appraisal becomes more complex and complete and, surely, less erratic. These reactions require some training, unless one wants to drink only lesser quality wines.

Those lucky enough to be raised in an environment where wines are regularly consumed and appreciated almost automatically acquire not only a taste for them but a great deal of information on their sensory evaluation and relative quality. Our preferences for certain styles of wine may thus be formed in the home. Young adults learn the language of wine appreciation, that one wine is better than another, by comparing their personal reactions with those of more experienced tasters. Most of us are not, however, raised in such a fortunate home environment. We may still be lucky enough to have knowledgeable friends who share their wines and experience and help us acquire familiarity and greater appreciation. Nowadays one may attend classes in wine appreciation and, if the instructor is practiced and unprejudiced, learn a good deal. Experience, not reading, is what is needed. All that books can do is tell you how to acquire a skill. Accepting someone else's sensory values robs you of the exquisite pleasure of developing and enjoying your own. No two people see the quality of a wine from the same point of view. Don't feel wrong about not having the same opinion as someone else (no matter how enologically prestigious the other person may be). But do try to understand why the other person arrived at such an erroneous evaluation!

What one can acquire is a familiarity with the visual (appearance and color), odor, taste, and tactile sensations of various types and qualities of wine and their proper limits. A brief outline of these follows.

VISUAL

After fermentation the new wine is cloudy, mainly with yeast. With time the yeast cells precipitate, and, with aging and the normal cellar operations, at bottling the wine will be brilliant, with no suspended solids. If the cellar operations have not been properly performed, the wine may stay, or again become, cloudy. Cloudiness may reflect undesirable growth of microorganisms, excess metal or tartrates, and similar problems, and, whatever the cause, reduces the sensory and aesthetic value of the wine. In some cases, cloudy wines also have undesirable colors and odors. The terms brilliant, clear, dull, and cloudy represent a sequence of increasing turbidity—and decreasing quality from the point of view of appearance. They are about all we normally need to say about the wine's appearance.

Wines have a color varying from the lightest yellow to dark amber, to rosé, to medium to dark red. Every wine type has its appropriate color. Deviations from this color often reflect some chemical or microbial problem and involve a reduction in quality and also in color appreciation. There is no shortcut to acquiring knowledge of the appropriate color for a given type of wine. Too little color in a white table wine may indicate that too much sulfur dioxide has been used. Too amber a color indicates that it has been aged too long, has been exposed to air, or lacks sufficient sulfur dioxide. Some white dessert wines may, however, properly have an amber color because of treatment or age.

449

Too purple a color in a red may indicate a high pH, which could be due to harvesting too late or an excessive malolactic fermentation. Besides being off-color, such a wine may taste flat. Too little color in a red wine may indicate a wine made of grapes from a very warm region or season, an excessive use of sulfur dioxide, or some other defect. Old red dessert wines may acquire an amber-red (tawny) color.

The consumer gains considerable aesthetic value from the brilliant red or white color of the wine. Cloudiness or off-colors reduce one's appreciation. Furthermore, from the specific cloudiness or color, the drinker may be able to determine the cause of the deficiency. Similarly, with experience, one learns to associate the proper color with the relative quality of the wine. This does not preclude personal preference, but a brown tint in a red table wine is an indication of long, and generally excessive, aging. The consumer soon learns to associate the color with aldehyde or sherry-like odors and reduced quality.

ODOR

No doubt the appearance and color of a wine are important aesthetic values. But it is what we smell that is the major aspect of the wine's quality. To get the maximum odor from a wine, swirl it in a glass filled about 30 percent and sniff quickly and deeply—once. Then rest a moment before repeating. Otherwise, continuous sniffing reduces olfactory sensitivity.

What can one expect? First, aroma—the odors from the grapes: aromatic Muscat in muscatels, grassy-smoky Sauvignon Blanc in less alcoholic wines of that variety, green-olive Cabernet Sauvignon in its wines. Second, bouquet—the odors resulting from fermentation, processing, and aging: an (undesirable) yeasty smell in newly fermented wines, acetaldehyde in *flor* sherries, caramel in baked sherries, an ester-champagne odor in bottle-fermented sparkling wines, and a slight woodiness in cask-aged red wines. And many, many more. Our olfactory apparatus is incredibly sensitive. The number of identifiable odors is well over 1,000, and for experts surely many more. With more than 400 organic compounds present, many interactions between odors can, and do, occur. The odors of the different compounds may be simply additive, $2 + 2 = 4$. Some interact synergistically—that is, $2 + 2 = 5$. In other cases, the odors at least partially mask each other—that is, $2 + 2 = 3$. The wine without a distinctive odor is the least interesting wine.

Of course, not all the odors may be desirable. Wines unduly exposed to air may acetify and a vinegar odor develop. This is now rare, thanks to modern technology and the legal limits imposed by the pure food laws and regulations. Sulfur dioxide is used as a mild antiseptic agent, particularly in white table wines. When properly used, its odor need not be noticeable or notable. But a careless winemaker may add more than is necessary and a wine with the off-odor of sulfur dioxide is born. Its recovery is by no means certain. Red wines are often aged in 50-gallon oak barrels—but too much woodiness is objectionable. On rare occasions, wine will smell "corked." This unpleasant odor occurs when corks are defective. Obviously it is found mainly in wines that have been in contact with the cork for some time.

There are other off-odors, but fortunately the careful winemaker either prevents their occurrence or reduces the odors to below their olfactory threshold by fining or blending.

TASTE

The third step is to taste the wine. Surprisingly, the sense of taste, exclusively located in the mouth, and in adults on the tongue, is simple and limited. There are only four primary tastes: sweet, sour, bitter, and salty. Since very few wines have a salty taste, we can usually forget it. Most wines are not sweet. Obviously sweetness is only a factor in those with more than about 1 percent sugar, which is more than half the population's threshold for sweetness in wines. The desirable level of sweetness depends on the type of wine and the preference of the consumer. Most rosé wines have a modicum of sweetness—about 1.5 percent sugar. Tests show that more than half the population prefer these slightly sweet wines. But Sauternes and ports may have 14 percent sugar and Malagas 20! Who would say that a sweet port does not have its place?

All wines must have some sourness. Without acidity, the wine would taste flat, its color would be atypical, and it would spoil easily. But wines should not be painfully sour. Wines range from about 0.5 percent acid in dessert wines to about 1 percent for table wines. Wines made from grapes grown in very cool climates or seasons, or picked too soon, may be excessively sour. One of the winemaker's tasks is to be sure the acidity does not produce too little or too much sourness. Bitterness, due to various polyphenolic compounds such as some tannins and related substances, is occasionally noted in young red table wines. Most consumers find it objectionable.

TACTILE

A few young red wines may give a puckery sensation in the mouth. This astringency is produced by substances similar to those producing bitterness. Few consumers find astringency a desirable quality. On the other hand, sparkling wines contain excess carbon dioxide, which produces a mild tactile sensation in the mouth. Most people find this attractive, at least for a glass or two!

TEMPERATURE

Why do we prefer to drink white wines cool and red wines less cool? For one thing, it is what we expect. Possibly, because white wines have less aroma and, generally, less bouquet, the coolness offers another sensory quality. Or would red wines be too bitter or astringent if served cold? Do we need the extra warmth to release the greater aroma and bouquet of red wines? Or is it just an outmoded custom?

SUMMING UP

We drink wines because of their pleasant sensory qualities and effects. Because of the infinite diversity of these qualities in wine, it is a true aesthetic object. One can cultivate an appreciation of it. The rule is very simple: look, smell, taste, and contemplate. If the wine doesn't please your palate, it is not a good wine for you. If it pleases someone else, you might ask yourself, "What am I missing?" Or if it pleases you and doesn't please someone else, you might ask, "Why does it displease the other person? Am I missing some undesirable sensory quality?"

It is a good idea that you commit yourself to some qualitative opinion about a wine. And write it down in your own words: good, not good, too sour, too sweet, bitter, astringent, purple color, flat, whatever. *Then* compare your notes with those of your peers. Where were you imperceptive? Where did you accent the positive too much? Or not enough?

We are, of course, greatly influenced by the opinions of our peers. But we should not blindly accept the opinion of another person on aesthetic values. No one can predict the subtle degrees of appreciation that someone else may have for a particular wine. The opinions of writers on specific wines must therefore be taken with caution. Likewise, if you attend a tasting where someone comments on wines, listen and learn, but don't blindly say you agree unless you do. Accepting someone else's opinion over your own is to commit the psychological error of the "halo" effect. With experience, our sensory values may change, but after a few years most connoisseurs arrive at relatively stable aesthetic standards for themselves and in comparison with one another.

THE NEXT STEP

This book is not for professional enologists. People who make wines, or blend wines, or sell wines need to make command decisions to determine differences among wines. They use (or should use) an array of sensory tests to reach conclusions: score cards, ranking, paired tests, and so on. And, if they are wise, they analyze the results by appropriate statistical procedures for their significance. If you read that one wine has an average score of 14.2 and another of 14.1, don't conclude that the first is better than the second unless some statistical measure of the difference between the wines is given. Or if, according to an advertisement, one wine ranks better than others, without some statistical measure of the significance between the ranks you will never know whether that is true or not.

BIBLIOGRAPHIC NOTE

For a full discussion of the professional sensory evaluation of wine, see Amerine and Roessler, *Wines: Their Sensory Evaluation*. Other references include Broadbent, *Wine Tasting*; Peynaud, *Le Goût du Vin*; and Yoxall, *Enjoyment of Wine*.

X.2
Note: Popular Courses in Wine Appreciation

by JAMES LAPSLEY

IN THE SPRING OF 1951, DR. MAYNARD AMERINE'S NEW COURSE, Viticulture 1, at the University of California at Davis introduced formal instruction in wine appreciation designed for the interested layman rather than the future wine-industry professional. From that beginning over thirty years ago, serious wine appreciation courses have multiplied in number and spread to every state. Today, over 8,000 Davis students have passed through the basic course, and, since 1960, University Extension has offered a slightly altered version to the general public on several of its campuses. In 1977 the *Chronicle of Higher Education* estimated that over 1,000 academic institutions offered wine-related courses, reaching over 200,000 individuals. While the University of California cannot claim responsibility for the dramatically increased interest in wine that has occurred since 1970, the Department of Viticulture and Enology at Davis can point to its seminal role in creating a formal curriculum in wine appreciation and in training many members of the wine industry who have gone on to teach wine appreciation classes in other parts of the United States.

Of course, wine appreciation is probably as old as winemaking and many books or classes predate the basic course taught at Davis. For instance, in

1888, Arpad Haraszthy, the son of the founder of Buena Vista, lectured the State Viticulture convention on "How To Drink Wine," counseling his audience to "select what is pure and pleases your palate best," good advice in any era. In the 1940s, the Wine Institute of San Francisco, representing the industry, initiated both a home study course and a training program for retailers and restaurant employees, with the obvious purpose of building a domestic interest in American wine. The institute's effort paralleled that of the now defunct Wine Advisory Board, which promoted comparative tastings of European and California wines in selected retail markets and distributed information on the use of table wines. These latter efforts helped to spur interest in American wines, but they were not intended as an objective overview of winemaking and appreciation such as is taught at Davis.

The major goal of most wine appreciation classes is to broaden the student's understanding and knowledge of the variety of wine types by introducing the major factors in wine production and composition that cause wines to differ. The student is made aware of how wine is perceived by the senses; learns to evaluate it in an objective manner; gains experience in tasting; and leaves the course with an understanding of the difference between personal preferences and the generally recognized objective quality. Finally, instruction given in a setting that demystifies wine encourages students to expand their personal knowledge of wine. The courses on the Davis model accomplish this through a series of lectures on such topics as grape varieties, viticultural regions and practices, wine production methods, sensory evaluation techniques, and domestic and foreign wine types. Regular tastings are an integral part of these courses, often with wines adjusted for sweetness or acidity.

The first University Extension course, held in San Francisco in 1960, drew over forty students plus some unwelcome attention from temperance advocates, one of whom wrote requesting information on "alcoholic appreciation courses," inquiring "other than a hip flask, what other special equipment is required?" The success of the first class led to three courses the following year, instructed by Amerine and George Cooke, the Cooperative Extension enologist. All three classes were well received and would have been followed by additional classes but for pressure brought to bear by the temperance movement on George Alcorn, the director of Agricultural Extension. Using the logic that Agricultural Extension did not "put on cauliflower appreciation courses," Alcorn forbade Cooke to be involved in the future with any that dealt with wine appreciation. A letter from Amerine to Alcorn succinctly explained the need for such courses, arguing that the Department of Viticulture and Enology was charged with improving wine quality in the state and that "a high quality product cannot exist in a vacuum. We must also be concerned with developing a critical consumer." Despite the letter, Alcorn directed Cooke to avoid future classes, with the unfortunate consequence of fewer such offerings through the university.

454

During the 1960s, other wine appreciation courses drawing on the Davis model filled the demand for information on wine. One of the best known is still sponsored by the Napa Valley Wine Library Association. The first class, taught by Dr. Amerine in St. Helena in 1964, was limited to sixty students. Over thirty-five had to be turned away, creating the need for a second class in the fall with an augmented faculty from Davis. In 1966 the association started drawing on local winemakers as lecturers, maintaining the original class format and employing Amerine and Vernon Singleton's *Wine: An Introduction* as the class text. First published in 1965 as an outgrowth of the authors' experience in teaching wine appreciation at Davis, it is now used in most wine appreciation courses throughout the United States. To date, over 5,000 students have gone through the association's weekend classes, currently offered several times a year.

Since 1970 wine has become an accepted part of the good life. This is seen in the switch from dessert to table wines, the growing number of small wineries, the growth in per capita consumption of wine, and the increase in the number of wine appreciation courses offered throughout the nation. Indeed, the increased interest in wine led to the creation of the Society of Wine Educators in 1977. Founded at Davis, it is a national nonprofit educational organization directed toward the improvement of the teaching of wine appreciation, winemaking, and wine culture. Headquartered in Salt Lake City with over eight hundred members, the society promotes education for wine writers and teachers through its annual meeting, regional conferences, and its newsletter; with its comprehensive listing of wine education aids, resources and classes, it assists wine merchants, instructors and industry members. The society is proving to be an important force in the standardization and upgrading of wine education in the United States and is a logical outgrowth of the wine industry's trend toward improved technology and higher wine quality.

As the general public's knowledge grows, so does the level of wine appreciation courses. More and more classes stress the use of odorant samples, component tastings, and alternate scoring systems, or emphasize particular varieties, regions, or wine styles. Still, the basic purpose remains constant: to help the individual learn more about the nuances of wine in order to expand the area of personal choice. What Arpad Haraszthy said in 1888 remains true today: "No one can dictate to another what wine will please him best or what wine he should drink. In this matter everyone has to be his own judge."

Wine appreciation classes do not give final answers but provide the context in which the individual can refine his or her own questions.

X.3

SECRETS
OF WINE TASTING

by ROY BRADY

A WINE EXPERT IS SOMEONE WHO CAN TASTE A WINE ABOUT WHICH HE KNOWS NOTHING AND UNERRINGLY NAME THE VINTAGE, VINEYARD, AND VINTNER. There are many wonderful stories about such experts, most of whom are French. There is, for instance, the case of M. Grandgousier, sommelier at a famous Paris restaurant. Being late for work one day, the master tried to cross the Place de la Concorde on foot during the rush hour. He was struck down by a 1948 Citroën driven by an unemployed Bulgarian couturier. Traffic ground to a halt. One of the vehicles that stopped was a van belonging to Établissements Nicolas, the famous wine merchants.

As luck would have it, the van was carrying a carton of *les prestigieuses bouteilles* to a *réveillon* on the Île St. Louis. Surveying the damage and knowing his duty, the driver of the van jumped out, crying, "Stand back! That man is badly injured! He must have *le bon vin de France*!" He snatched a bottle from the carton, yanked out the cork, dashed some wine into a Baccarat goblet (the Haut Brion design), and held it to the stricken man's lips. As a few drops of the fluid dribbled down his throat, the great sommelier roused himself enough to murmur, "Château . . . Lestage-Darquier-Grand-Poujeaux . . . 1956. . . ." Then he expired. All of Paris exclaimed, "Vive la France!" and burst into "La Marseillaise," the ladies weeping uncontrollably as they tore the Bulgarian to shreds.

A heartwarming scene to imagine, isn't it?

It is also poppycock, balderdash, and twaddle.

The identification of wines is largely a parlor trick. It is not something serious judges of wine ordinarily do. It is a sort of sleight of hand—and I believe that those who practice it are bound, at least occasionally, to explain their tricks to the public or risk slipping into outright charlatanry.

The late Henry French Hollis was one of the most distinguished tasters of his day—and he was also probably the first person to write openly about how

Reprinted, with minor alterations, from *New West*, 9 October 1978.

wines really are identified. Hollis was a Democratic senator from New Hampshire from 1913 to 1919, and he was also, in his earlier days, a staunch Prohibitionist. Happily, he discovered the glories of Burgundy in time. He was born again, divorced barren Abstinence from his bed, and took the daughter of the vine to wed. In practical terms, he quit politics, went to France and became a respected wine shipper and a particular expert on the wines of the Bourgogne.

Hollis once explained that identifying a wine was seldom like recognizing Lloyd George walking down the street. It is not sudden and unambiguous. Rather, it is an exercise in Sherlockian deduction. The taster gathers all the clues he can and probes for more as he goes along. He must always be ready for the bold guess or the big bluff. And if luck is with him, he might come up with the name of the wine.

Challenged to identify a wine about to be served, the smart taster can learn much from details that have nothing to do with the wine itself. He will watch the cork being drawn, for instance, noticing its length, shape, firmness, and branding. The shape of the neck and color of the glass of the bottle are also useful. So is the shape of the bottle.

A good example of this process occurred at one of the weekly tasting sessions I attend. One member presented a bottle from which cork and capsule—usually good hints to a wine's identity—had already been removed, and the label had been soaked off. It looked bad. But then I noticed that the label had left faint traces of glue on the bottle and that this glue had been applied in broad horizontal bands. I knew of only one winery doing that at the time. The outline of the glue showed that the label had been both tall and wide. Same winery. Finally, the bottle was of a dark tint not then widely used. Those three clues made it almost certainly a wine from Ridge Vineyards.

The wine itself was not much help. It was fairly dark but not particularly distinctive. It could have been any of half a dozen grape varieties. I began to think about the man who had brought the wine. He liked oddities. He always tried to get new wines as soon as they came out. What was the newest and oddest Ridge wine? Nineteen-seventy-one Carignane. That had to be it. It was the winery's first attempt with that grape, and the grape itself is rarely used as a varietal.

After a bit of purely ceremonial peering, sniffing, and tasting, I named the wine. Cheers all around! I had identified the wine "blind." But tasting had had little to do with it. I would have made the same guess without it.

Another time I was at the table of a professor of rhetoric and a prolific wine talker. He prided himself on making great wine buys and, as usual, one evening he delivered a flowery exordium on the red wine to come. Another guest declared that he would like to see just how a *wine expert* like me (emphasis his) identified a wine. A glass was put down. I lifted it under the unwavering gaze of seven pairs of eyes.

As I feared, the wine was a thin mediocrity that could have been made in any backward winery anywhere in the world. Going through the usual sniffing and slurping act, I hastily sifted through the clues I had. The neck of the bottle sticking out of the napkin wasn't American, Italian, or French. It was from some minor wine country—but which? I knew that the professor bought all his wine from one shop—luckily, one in my own neighborhood. I had noticed a big display of two 99 cent Chilean wines there, a Riesling and a Cabernet. The wine was red, so it had to be the latter, which happened to be, I recalled, a Tocornal Cabernet 1962. A few words from me on the effects of the Pacific slope on the Cabernet vine, and I recorded another triumph.

Once in a great while, of course, a wine *is* recognized in a flash. At one time Ficklin Vineyards made a highly distinctive Ruby Cabernet that I used as a daily table wine at home. After hundreds of drinkings, it became tolerably familiar. One evening a friend put a glass of wine before me and asked what I made of it. A single sip put the answer beyond doubt. It was the same Ruby Cabernet—a fact I was doubly sure of because Walter Ficklin was sitting across the table.

No one who really knows wine would seriously expect a taster to regularly and reliably identify every wine he is given to taste.

Professionals who are evaluating wines to buy and sell or for scientific reasons do not work in the dark. They may or may not know specific details of the wines they are tasting, but they do know that they are dealing with, say, red Burgundies, or, to be more specific, with wines of the Côte de Nuits, or, to be more specific still, with wines of Gevrey-Chambertin.

Social wine affairs are usually ridiculous. Suppose you were a music lover and were invited to enjoy an evening of music at a friend's house. Would you expect your host to sit you down and play snatches of this and that and ask you to identify composers, conductors, and soloists while other guests held their breath expectantly? And what if he asked you who had made the piano being played, and when it was last tuned, and by whom?

And even if you could make at least some of these identifications, what would this have to do with the enjoyment of music? The amateur of music will listen to a good deal of music and he might happen to know things about its history. But nobody expects him to be able to identify every piece he hears or to give a lot of irrelevant details about it.

Wine merchants tasting wines with a view to buying are not interested in parlor tricks. Neither are judges at official wine competitions, nor winemakers deciding on what treatment their own wines need, nor scientists studying winemaking.

Such people are interested in making objective judgments about wines —judgments that can be reproduced. To the general public, "wine tasting" has always been tinged with romance and obscurity. But serious, professional wine judging is, in fact, a highly systematized procedure. Any person with normal senses and the persistence to complete an arduous course of tasting can become a competent judge—and one whose results will generally agree with those of other trained judges. Wine tasting is not as exact a science as astronomy—but, as the late Frank Schoonmaker, the most eminent American wine man of his time, always argued, wine can be evaluated more accurately than music or painting can.

Yet, even the most highly skilled evaluators are not the "wine experts" the public fancies them to be. There are probably no wine judges anywhere in the world to surpass those at the University of California at Davis. These men and women are highly trained scientists whose business is the analysis and improvement of grape growing and winemaking. They taste wines constantly, working without the distractions of noise, extraneous odors, conversation, phone calls, and other nuisances. They work alone. When they taste, physical details of lighting, glassware, and serving temperatures are all rigidly controlled.

An exceedingly interesting experiment was conducted with nine of these judges not long ago to determine just how well they really could identify not specific wines, but simply the grape varieties from which certain wines had been made. Here was an experiment conducted under the best conditions, with some of the best judges in existence. These were no "wizard palates" on TV talk shows or "guest experts" performing at riotous public tastings. They were university professionals with an average of nineteen years of daily tasting experience each. Their task was simplified by the fact that all the wines in each group they tasted were of the same year. All the wines had been made at the university. Grape variety was the only variable.

The judges failed. The only variety identified correctly more than half the time was the Muscat—one of the most distinctive and easily recognizable grapes there is. Cabernet Sauvignon was identified a bit more than a third of the time and Chardonnay less than a quarter of the time. Zinfandel was correctly identified about a third of the time, but it was called Cabernet almost as often. Cabernet wasn't called Zinfandel as often, but it *was* called Pinot Noir, Petite Sirah, and several other things.

These sobering results show how limited is the success to be attained when wine judges are rigorously denied all information about the wines they are considering. It is undoubtedly true that there are a few people with an extraordinary ability to identify wines, but this ability, as Schoonmaker also pointed out, is a matter of the elusive gift of taste memory and of specialization and luck—and, he might have added, of the opportunity to sample vast numbers of wines.

A person who tastes, say, dozens of white burgundies of the Côte de Beaune every day will become adept at identifying these wines—but he still will not recognize them as one would recognize Lloyd George. He will have learned the personalities of each vintage, the characteristics of each district, the quirks of each producer, even details as specialized as the influence on the wine of various kinds of barrels. Faced with a sample, he begins to decide what it may be and what it may not be. Successively eliminating, he narrows down the possibilities to a few, or, with luck, to one. But take him to Bordeaux and he is as helpless as thee and me.

The American wine experience is unlike nearly all others, except the British, in the enormous variety it offers. In most parts of the world, one finds local wines, if such there be, or a limited selection sanctioned by the government, or nothing at all. In America's major cities, on the other hand, it is possible to find and purchase good (and bad) examples of the wines of almost every winemaking area of the world, from Beaujolais to the Barossa Valley, from St. Helena to Siena.

All that variety is fine. We can try almost any wine we may hear about, given a little patience and persistence. The drawback is that we are never likely to become really expert with any one kind of wine. Our experience is too diluted. Though we might buy every white Burgundy on the market, we could never develop the kind of intimate knowledge that comes to a Burgundian who tastes wine every day in the cellars of the growers and shippers of the region. We can't even really know California's wines in that way, because California wine is still half-tamed, wild, runaway stuff. French wines are defined by Appellation Contrôlée laws that tell them exactly what they must be. In its youthful exuberance, California wine refuses to be thus tied down. Every year, Château Lafite is made from much the same vines in much the same way. That is true of very few California wines.

The distinguished English wine taster Harry Waugh—himself a director of Château Latour—notes that he has been to many blind tastings in Bordeaux and elsewhere at which vineyard proprietors failed to pick out their own wines—and they had a great advantage over a true blind taster because they knew that their own wines were present. And once asked if he had ever confused Bordeaux and Burgundy, Waugh ruefully replied, "Not since lunch." That's the way an honest wine taster sounds.

Though we may be wrong when tasting and attempting to identify wine, there is no shame in it. Rather, there is shame in pretending to superhuman talents that we do not possess. Often, a person with a reputation as a wine taster will confront this situation: Someone will walk up, thrust a glass under his nose and demand an opinion. Such behavior is unfair at best. At worst, it is rude and boorish. It asks a wine judge to do something he never claimed he could do.

The expert should exclaim, "Begone, oaf!" But he never does. Instead, he temporizes and equivocates, which legitimizes the approach of the oaf.

There are more would-be experts than real experts, of course. Real experts work quietly and slowly. They write down their opinions before speaking, and they stand behind them later. The would-be expert starts talking at once but is adroit at avoiding being pinned down.

But wine has become overexperted anyway. It should be drunk by a mountain stream in summer or in front of a good fire when winter grips the land. It deserves better than to be reduced to a column of numbers under the direction of a grim expert—even a real one—at a seminar.

Wine is made to be swilled by amateurs, not to be analyzed by experts.

X.4

Note: Wine with Food

by HARVEY STEIMAN

THE FIRST THING THAT MUST BE SAID ABOUT MATCHING food and wine is that almost any wine can be drunk happily with any food—within reason, of course. I'm not sure I care for the idea of port with scallop mousse—although I have had port wine sauce on lobster that was extraordinary—but by and large any table wine will be pleasant to drink alongside any food. On the other hand, it is no secret that a bite of food with any wine changes the apparent character of the wine. When things are going splendidly, the wine also elevates the character of the food. Any cheese with any wine will provide ample evidence of that. When the food and wine match up just right, the effect is like adding woodwinds to the strings of an orchestra. The sensations enhance each other, sometimes dramatically, occasionally with breathtaking clarity.

Much of the fun of winedrinking is how to find those combinations. My advice is the same as that given to novice winedrinkers who wish to learn more about the beverage—practice. Pay attention to what you're eating as well as to what you are drinking, and think about what makes a special combination wonderful. I do this whenever I dine, mentally evaluating the way each wine and each morsel of food match up, often with several wines on the table. One conclusion that emerges rather quickly is that no wine and food rules are carved in stone. Moreover, and this is critical, certain elements of each wine emerge as key factors in choosing which wine to serve with a particular dish.

Most important is balance, the internal balance of the wine itself as well as the balance of the wine with the food. If a wine is too low in acidity, it tastes flat next to food. Food, especially cheese, also seems to soften wines that have high levels of tannin. I also find that the lightness or heaviness of the wine is more important than whether it is red or white. True, reds are generally heavier than whites, but there's a significant overlap; Chardonnay is usually heavier than Beaujolais. Alcohol content is a fairly reliable indicator of the weight of a wine.

Aside from the structure of a wine—its body, sweetness, acidity, tannin, and intensity of flavor—the most important element to consider is the wine's flavor. Somehow, in discussions of matching food and wine, this usually is ignored, but the characteristic flavors of a wine can make the difference between a matchup that brings you pleasure and one that is simply pleasant and not memorable.

Among white wines, the hierarchy of taste intensity runs from wines with strong flavors, such as the Muscats, to almost nonexistent, such as Chenin Blanc. Beginning with the strongest flavors, there is the Muscat grape. The most famous of these wines is Italy's Asti Spumante, but there are also some still Muscats made in California, Italy, and France that are usually sweet and extremely spicy. The sparkling Muscats are wonderful poured over fresh berries at the peak of their ripeness. I can only match these wines with fruit.

Gewürztraminer can be almost as assertive, its spiciness balanced with a floral character. The dry Alsatian versions are less obviously varietal than their California cousins, and the Alsatians are a classic pairing with a strong-flavored dish such as *choucroute garni* (wine kraut with sausages). The sweeter California versions are nice with fruit and nuts. I've had them with spice cake and carrot cake, to advantage.

White Riesling comes in several levels of sweetness, and the flavors range from the intensely floral character of the dry (Alsace, California) to the peach-like, apricotlike, and even honeylike flavors that appear in the sweeter ones. Dry Rieslings match up nicely with poached fish in simple sauces. Another extraordinary mating is a dry Riesling with buttered corn on the cob as an appetizer. I like slightly sweet Rieslings with fish in nut sauces (such as trout amandine) and with pear desserts. They also mate well with ham, as do most fruits. The sweet Rieslings, such as the German *Auslesen* and *Beerenauslesen* and the California Late Harvests, are a wonderful match for almond tarts or nut tortes, especially those that also contain peaches or apricots. As for the very sweet Rieslings, the *Trockenbeerenauslesen* and the sweetest wines from California, these are so rich and complex that I can't imagine drinking them any way but by themselves, with awe.

Sauvignon Blanc and Sémillon grapes produce wines similar in flavor to each other: grassy, weedy, sometimes floral, often herbaceous. They tend to be light to moderate in body but moderate to strong in flavor. These Sancerres, Pouilly-Fumés, dry Graves, and their American counterparts are the perfect wines to serve with garlicky chicken dishes, spaghetti in garlic butter, or dishes with strong herb flavors that seem to want a dry white wine. Sweet wines made from these grapes (Sauternes, Barsacs) I have a hard time matching up with fruit desserts. Chocolate by itself seems to clash with these wines, but if you put the chocolate on fruit, the combination works better.

Most of these white wines, especially such light, sippable varieties as those made from White Riesling, Chenin Blanc, Gewürztraminer, and Muscat grapes, have the balance and temperament that puts one more in mind of cocktail hour than dinner. These wines can be consumed to advantage with food, as suggested, but they are often a good deal more fun by themselves. Chardonnay, on the other hand, has been called the white wine for red wine drinkers. As it is often made in California, it has the added complexity one expects from red wines—vanilla and wood smells from barrel-aging, the additional bite from some tannin, although not as much as red wine—and heavier body. As it is made in France, it ranges from light and steely (Chablis) to rich and fat (the expensive white Burgundies of the Côte d'Or). Elsewhere, winemakers gravitate to one of the above styles. In all cases, however, the object is food. No white wine is so geared to food as those made from Chardonnay grapes. The best ones simply are not as good by themselves.

The tart, lemony taste of the light, steely wines of Chablis, most Oregon Chardonnays, and the few from California not aged in oak (Parducci, Sebastiani) suggests fish, especially white-fleshed fish with light butter sauces. As you get toward the buttery, rich, spicy flavors of Meursaults and Cortons, or most California Chardonnays, I think of fat fish like salmon, sturgeon, shad, and tuna. Veal in rich sauces (but not meaty ones) matches up surprisingly well with a fat Chardonnay. A pleasant surprise is a Chardonnay drunk with a classic Italian *osso buco Milanese*.

Red wines, like Chardonnay, are almost exclusively made with food in mind. Most need food to bring out their best qualities, even if it's only a hunk of cheese. In red wines, distinctive tastes suggest certain foods. Bordeaux wines get their personality mainly from Cabernet Sauvignon and Merlot grapes, which often have the taste of herbs, currants, berries, olives, green peppers, and mint. I don't know about you, but these flavors are not the ones that come to my mind in thinking about beef. Yet individuals otherwise knowledgeable about wine persist in serving these wines with beef. Lamb, yes. Duck, game birds, venison, even wild boar, yes. For me, however, the tastes of Cabernet Sauvignon clash with beef. Burgundy, on the other hand, made from the Pinot Noir, is often described as meaty, with flavors of cherry, mushrooms, and spices. All of these suggest beef, although they are certainly fine with other meats and poultry, too. The Pinot Noir is a much more versatile grape than the Bordelais varieties.

I find it helpful to think of these two types as anchoring two ends of the flavor spectrum of red wine. In between are wines of varying richness, body, and intensity, but the flavors are seldom as strong or specific. Zinfandel, for example, is a great all-purpose wine. Its berry, vanilla, and spice flavors will match up with any food that calls for a red wine, even such unlikely possibilities as grilled salmon. (It's true; don't dismiss the notion without trying it.) Chianti, especially the oak-aged Classicos and Reservas, fall into roughly the same class. So do the wines of the Côtes du Rhone, Italian Barberas, and California Petite Sirahs. Flavor is not a prime consideration with these wines. They are not distinctive enough to clash with most foods that call for red wine. Weight on the palate is most important. The lightness and suppleness of Italian Barbarescos and Nebbiolos and the subtle flavors of most Spanish reds lend themselves to the Pinot Noir/Burgundy end of the spectrum.

The heaviest red wines of them all are ports. The wines carry a wallop of alcohol (in the neighborhood of 20 percent to table wine's 11 to 13), a high level of fruit flavor, and the tastes of aging in oak barrels, not to mention enough sugar to satisfy anyone's sweet tooth. Although these wines are lovely to drink by themselves after a meal, there are certain foods that are a classic match with port—any of the blue cheeses, especially Stilton, and nuts, especially walnuts. The fruit flavors typical of port are cherries and berries. Does that remind you of any other wine? They are the same flavors as Zinfandel. If you have been wondering what foods to serve with those Late Harvest Zinfandels, try Stilton and walnuts. Some find it almost as satisfying as port.

SOME UNEXPECTEDLY GOOD FOOD AND WINE COMBINATIONS

A full-bodied, oak-aged Chardonnay with osso buco *made the Milanese way with stock, white wine, onions, garlic, celery, bay leaf, lemon and parsley. The* osso buco *seems to "butter up" the Chardonnay, bringing out its richness, while the Chardonnay smoothes out the rough edges of the veal shank preparation.*

A fruity, medium-bodied Zinfandel with baked salmon fillets. It's especially excellent if the salmon is prepared with sorrel. The youthful fruit of the red wine is a bold and exciting match for the salmon's slightly fatty richness. Even if the wine has some evident tannin, the combination still works.

A medium-sweet or medium-dry sherry with spicy Indian food. Something about the combinations of spices used in Indian cooking sets off resonances with the nutty tastes of the sherry. The wine's sweetness tames the hot pepper tastes.

A youngish, full-bodied Cabernet Sauvignon with bittersweet or semisweet chocolate. The Cabernet must show some youthful fruit, but it need not be very rough to make a smooth pairing with not-too-sweet chocolate. Doesn't work with milk chocolate, although chocolate truffles are fine.

X.5

Note: Memorable Menus

by ALICE WATERS

Chez Panisse restaurant in Berkeley, California, has been acclaimed over the past several years for its special kind of cooking: at the same time derivative and innovative, it is, in essence, a celebration of the quality and freshness of local products. The menu and techniques that have evolved in its kitchen are refinements of its early inspiration from the French in much the same way that the styles of California winemaking are self-confident departures from their largely European inheritance. Behind the efforts in both the kitchen and the winery, one belief remains constant: that food and wine are better enjoyed together. Alice Waters, the best-known proprietor of Chez Panisse, describes her way of thinking.

DORIS MUSCATINE

At Chez Panisse, we use a lot of wine in cooking. It takes experience to know which combinations make a perfect balance, but even so, because there are so many variables, so many unexpected possibilities, the result is never absolutely predictable. Wine is a living, breathing, changing thing, which affects its own taste, the way it tastes with food, and the way it changes the nature of a dish in which it is cooked. For instance, a *beurre blanc*—a simple sauce of shallots, butter, and white wine boiled down until it is well reduced—changes greatly according to the wine you put in. A Gewürztraminer gives quite a different sauce than a chablis. Or a Zinfandel or a burgundy in a beef stock makes it as different as those red wines are from each other. At the restaurant we often vary a classic dessert like zabaglione by making it with, say, Late Harvest Riesling instead of the standard Marsala. Even the wine-based vinegars used to dress the same basic greens make very different salads.

On practically every menu we have some dish that is cooked with wine. We use a lot of Zinfandel. We poach figs in it, marinate birds and everything else in it—it gives a beautiful color—and we do a lot of fish with Zinfandel butter. Another marinade we use for birds is a California sweet Riesling or a French Beaumes-de-Venise. When the birds are grilled, they get a beautiful color from it and a sweet

Some of this material appeared in different form in Alice Waters's *The Chez Panisse Menu Cookbook* (New York: Random House, 1982).

honey taste instead of the usual charcoal. We have also done variations on Richard Olney's blancmange. That simple pudding—especially, to my own taste, the hazelnut one—is a wonderful complement to Sauternes and Late Harvest Rieslings.

Besides the way wine changes dishes you cook it with, it changes the taste of food you drink it with. Some wines seem perfect matches: Chalone Pinot Noirs, for instance, with pork slightly marinated in a sugar brine with coriander seeds, peppercorns, juniper berries, bay leaves, a few sprigs of fresh thyme and marjoram, then spit roasted—it's a wonderful combination. Sometimes a food can overwhelm a wine. I'm thinking of something strong in the way of meat taking over the delicate flavors of an older vintage, say of a 1968 Beaulieu Vineyard Cabernet, which would be delicious, however, with grilled quail and a wild mushroom risotto.

I have learned a lot about pairing food and wine at the teaching lunches given by Shirley Sarvis each week at the Stanford Court Hotel in San Francisco. She presents five different wines with a meal of several courses and fills all of the glasses at the beginning so you can taste each wine separately without food. Then you taste them all with each course, and it never turns out the way you expect. For instance, on one occasion, a slightly sweet Late Harvest Riesling was just right with lightly smoked salmon, and on another, a 1970 Cabernet was perfect with the same rich oily flesh grilled over charcoal.

For several years, Chez Panisse has featured special dinners celebrating wine. Many of them have centered on the foods and wines of Burgundy, Provence, Alsace, Périgord, Champagne, or northern Italy. But there have also been many that focused on California. One of these, "A Toast to Great Wines and Great Friends," started with the choice of wines and was built from there. It began with 1967, 1972, and 1973 Ridge Monte Bello Chardonnays, with which we served a country-style Roquefort cheese tart. We followed that with a salt cod bouillabaisse—it was the first time we had made the recipe, which came from Lulu Peyraud, our Provençal friend from Domaine Tempier in Bandol. It's made with lots of garlic, saffron, tomatoes, fresh basil, and good olive oil, and it was wonderful with three different Ridge Cabernet Sauvignons. We had a charcoal-grilled rack and saddle of spring lamb with a compote of leeks, fresh mint, a Zinfandel sauce, and four Ridge Zinfandels, one from 1968 and three from 1970. We ended with assorted cheeses paired with a 1971 and a 1974 Ridge York Creek Petite Sirah, and, along with coffee, a 1971 Ridge Lodi Zinfandel Essence.

Perhaps the starting point of the special wine celebrations was a dinner Jeremiah Tower cooked featuring the regional foods and wines of northern California. It started with bluepoint oysters from Tomales Bay served with a 1973 Schramsberg Cuvée de Gamay. Then there was a cream of fresh corn soup, Mendocino style, with crayfish butter, and after that, Garapata Creek trout from Big Sur smoked over California bay leaves and paired with a 1973 Mount Eden Chardonnay that also served to go with Monterey Bay prawns sautéed in garlic butter. The main course was preserved Sebastapol goose accompanied by a 1970 Beaulieu Private Reserve Cabernet Sauvignon. The cheese course, Vella dry Sonoma Jack, had a 1974 Ridge Fiddletown Zinfandel to go with it. With the caramelized fresh figs, Jeremiah served a 1974 Harbor Mission del Sol; and there were also walnuts, almonds, and pears from the San Francisco Farmers' Market. Jeremiah cooked another great wine dinner, revolutionary, most extreme, in which he paired everything—even roast beef—with French Sauternes. It was brilliant. Magnificent.

In 1975, when the Joseph Phelps Winery started making Zinfandel for the restaurant, we thought of a week of menus that would go well, really well, with the wine. It is surprising how adaptable Zinfandel is, how so many different dishes go well with it. For that week, and every year since, we served menus designed so that you could drink the fruity *nouveau* Zinfandel all the way through the meal. The food was typical, robust, bistro-style cooking. The first menu was marinated squid with roasted red and green peppers, entrecôte of beef grilled over grapevine cuttings and sauced with Zinfandel and shallots, followed by a salad of romaine lettuce, anchovies, and croutons. Grapevine cuttings add something special because they burn very hot and make a very aromatic smoke that penetrates whatever is cooking over them. Over the years, we have served the new Zinfandel with such very different foods as beef marrow on toast; fresh sautéed Dungeness crab; duck livers in a sherry vinegar, walnut oil, shallot and parsley sauté; oysters cooked with Muscadet and fennel butter; cassoulet; rabbit terrine with hazelnuts and Chartreuse; buckwheat crêpes filled with wild mushrooms; roast suckling pig; and braised oxtails with a five-onion sauce. We have poached sausages in it and made a version of *coq au vin—coq au* Zinfandel—chicken cooked with the wine, bacon, mushrooms, and pearl onions, with a garnish of garlic croutons. One year we paired spring lamb from the Dal Porto Ranch with Zinfandel made by Joseph Phelps from Dal Porto Ranch grapes. Maybe it was just psychological, but it really worked!

X.6

THE CRITICS LOOK
AT CALIFORNIA WINES

by BOB THOMPSON

IN THE MOST PERFECT OF ALL POSSIBLE WORLDS, A WINE
BIBBER WOULD LIVE BY THE COUNSEL OF A WISE WINE
MERCHANT. Glimpses of the ideal may be had from old literature, above all
Saintsbury's *Notes on a Cellarbook*, the most gentlemanly record of wine buying
and winedrinking to be found anywhere. At each of his posts, Saintsbury found
a merchant he trusted and with whom he could deal man to man. The merchant,
for his part, did his homework at both ends. He learned which were the reputable
producers, learned Saintsbury's preferences, and put the two together. Merchants and merchants alone stood between the good professor and the men who
made the wines.

As Saintsbury also records, in some parts of the world hierarchies of
consumers and producers have sometimes gotten so rigidly established that buyers
need only ask for a correct label to keep their social feathers preened. Check the vintage charts for a superior year, check the roster of Firsts, Seconds, and Thirds (or
Grands and *Petits*), check the wallet for maximum allowable expenditure, and bingo!
The best money can buy. If anyone drinks with long teeth, it is the drinker's fault,
not the wine's. Sooner or later the reluctant learn to like what they are supposed to
like, and the hierarchy grows stronger.

In the 1950s and 1960s, California was something like that. Form players
could, and did, coast through the era knowing to a surety that a baker's dozen of labels yielded every fully pedigreed bottle a collector had to have. Beaulieu Vineyard,
Inglenook, Charles Krug, and Louis M. Martini had all the Napa Cabernet Sauvignons one needed until Souverain Cellars and Heitz Cellars joined the lists. Almadén,
Buena Vista, Concannon, Hallcrest, Paul Masson, and Martin Ray had to be watched
for an occasional memorable example of Cabernet. For Chardonnay the knowing
bibber went to Hanzell, Heitz, Charles Krug, Stony Hill, Wente Bros., and, toward
the closing hours of the sixties, Chalone. On the occasions when Pinot Noir rose to
the heights, the bottles came from Beaulieu, Chalone, Hanzell, Heitz, and Mar-

tini. Even less often, Martin Ray would join the list. Oh, the rare surprise would come from elsewhere, but a collector could earn full marks for thoroughness as well as skill by sticking with that short list year after year. A true believer would round out the cellar with some Johannisberg Rieslings, Zinfandels, and the odd Barbera, but not at the expense of adding any different labels. The ultimate hobbyist knew enough to harbor some Livermore Sauvignon Blancs from Wente and Concannon.

By 1982 Napa's 15 wineries had become 110, and its 10,000 acres of vineyard 25,000. Sonoma nearly paralleled that growth. Monterey County had gone from a single, episodic winery to a dozen, and from 30 acres of vineyard to 32,000. And so on, through San Luis Obispo, Santa Barbara, Mendocino, Lake, the Sierra Foothills, Temecula, and, I fear, someplace I have yet to hear about.

Where does the confident collector of 1968 turn fifteen years later? In circles. The old certainties were based on a stagnant market rather than mature development of the state's vineyard lands, and they have been drowned by a single wave of new optimism. In the turbulence, a newcomer wins a competition against a well-regarded older hand, and puts his price up accordingly. Sometimes a price is set because somebody has built a jewelbox winery full of state-of-the-art equipment using money rented at 24 percent. Sometimes it is only the wish to be one of the best that causes a fledgling proprietor to position himself at the top, as the marketing people say. The old hands must elect to play in the new game, or sit tight and wait for the bubble to pop.

A high-school track coach I knew once launched tryouts by lining up all his new hopefuls and firing his starter's pistol without a word of explanation. He thought the natural sprinters would take off while the distance men hung back, thus sorting themselves out on the first day. What he learned was that in a race of no known distance, the only place people feel safe is in touch with the leaders. Like the novice trackmen, California's wineries find themselves running in an uncertain, but wildly hopeful, bunch. While would-be connoisseurs wait for class to tell in the various distances, the question will not go away. Which are the wines to buy? The question before that is, what advice to heed?

The answer ought not to be hard, but it is. Prohibition decimated the ranks of wise wine merchants to such a degree that there are not yet enough to go around. The good ones that do exist cannot keep up with the scores of new labels that have appeared in each of the past several years. But this is not the main difficulty. With wine more than with most products, people with guests want to do the right thing, which is to say bring to their dinner tables only the best. In a winner-take-all society, that means Number One, the Super Bowl winner. (I have heard a restaurant diner reject a bottle of Third Growth Médoc on grounds that he was not having any third-rate anything.)

The truth is that at least a hundred California Cabernet Sauvignons, about the same number of Chardonnays, and smaller numbers of each of the other varietals and the generics are perfectly acceptable. If all were right with the world, huge numbers of people would buy a dozen or so cases of wine a year, more or less as Saintsbury did. The roster would include several bottles each of a pricey Cabernet Sauvignon or Pinot Noir for grand occasions and slightly larger supplies of a less costly one for regular company. There would be a similar pair of Chardonnays or Sauvignon Blancs, some White Riesling or Chenin Blanc for weekend sipping, some sparkling wine, a few bottles of a dry sherry-type for evenings, and a few bottles of a port-type for the winter fire. (In addition, there would be considerable amounts of a daily red and daily white. Saintsbury took his regular meals in a common room, and did not need to lay in daily stocks.) All would be bought on the advice of a merchant, who would suggest an occasional trial bottle to see if greater satisfaction might be found with something different. Smaller numbers—those of us who use wine more as a hobby than as a beverage—would buy more widely so we could fret over nuances in the wines and the critics.

This is not going to happen soon, if ever. It has gotten into the national psyche that there can be a Super Bowl wine. Even before the Super Bowl syndrome developed, it had gotten into the national mind that wine is a matter for experts. The question thus remains, what advice to heed? For those who will not, or cannot, put their trust in a good merchant (or, better yet, themselves), the fragile choices are three: the laws governing labels, which are decades away from defining much; awards from county fair and other competitions, which only point to benchmarks; and published critics, who also only point to benchmarks, and who are a growth industry themselves and thus extremely uneven as advisers.

LAWS

Whenever Americans are bewildered by choice, the reflex is to turn to Europe for guidance from the comforting petrifactions of history. Among domestic wine fanciers, the siren call comes from Bordeaux, which has not only the *appellation d'origine contrôlée* (AOC) laws, but the iron-hard recommendations of 1855 to keep presumed quality sorted to a fine point.

French regulations define a formidably complicated ladder of quality in wine. *Vins de pays* serve as the base. These wines come from large areas, legally defined but not lavishly praised. *Vins délimités de qualité supérieur* (VDQS) come from regions recognized as rather better than those yielding *vins de pays*. Regions entitled to an *appellation d'origine contrôlée* are the pinnacle of the basic system, but are subdivided in their turn when the appellation encompasses famous properties. Taking Bordeaux as an example, the appellation Bordeaux is more general and less prestigious than Médoc, which in turn carries less prestige than Pauillac or the other three famous communes within it. Beyond the AOCs there is a fourth layer, the château. Any château is assumed to outweigh anything bottled merely as Pauillac, and as for Château Lafite, it brings us to the pinnacle of the classification of 1855, which divides not regions but properties into the five *Grands Crus Classés* and the lesser *Cru Exceptionnel* and *Cru Bourgeois*, and which predates the AOC laws by eighty years. What the AOC laws really do is guarantee the privileges of properties that had earned fame before Napoleon, let alone 1855, and not only in Bordeaux but Burgundy, Champagne, and the Rhone. On the other side of the coin, the laws make life very difficult for those left ouside the pale when the system was devised. Alsace, a source of delicious wines, could not gain AOC status until 1962. Cahors could not clamber into the first rank until 1971, even though its grapes may have been in some degree responsible for the greatness of some of the pre-phylloxera clarets.

As much as it is true that the French appellation laws only formalized recognition of properties that had stayed on the peak throughout a long history, the system can be said to have evolved from the specific to the general. It does not appear to be an accident that the great properties have a comfortable margin between themselves and the boundaries of their communes, and that there is a commune for every great property. However, the chap barely outside such a communal boundary is in a very different economic realm because his best wines seldom or never challenged the bottlings of properties inside it when a challenge would have counted.

In California, the nascent Viticultural Area program of the Bureau of Alcohol, Tobacco and Firearms is going at the task the other way about, formalizing boundaries of the unknown. The Napa Valley, long the most famous vineyard in California, was delimited in 1981, the first region in the state to achieve the status of Viticultural Area. Two proposals were offered. One included only the watershed of the Napa River, a territory that more than encompassed the vineyards to which Napa owes its reputation. The other, winning proposal took in nearly all of Napa County, including a broad expanse east of a 2,000-foot-high range of hills forming one wall of the Napa River drainage area. The growers in these eastern vales candidly argued economic hardship as much as, or more than, kindred growing conditions, but appear to have won the battle on the grounds that grapes from their area had gone into "Napa Valley" wines since pre-Prohibition times. Perhaps, but not in the sense of 1855. I have seen no record of a vineyard in that part of the county being singled out as extraordinary in any era, and in any event grapes from all over the state had gone into "Napa Valley" wines under earlier regulations. For the valley to keep its current stature in a more mature appellation system, there will have to be second and perhaps third levels of discrimination, bounded more closely to the vineyards that have given Napa its fame.

Other regions delimited since Napa have less history to give them shape, sometimes much less. Two, Edna Valley and Santa Maria Valley, have had post-Prohibition vineyards only since the 1970s, and wineries only since 1977. Two others, Guenoc Valley and McDowell Valley, encompass only a single, young winery each, although McDowell's vines have a consistent history to support its distinctiveness. Of thirteen districts approved by the end of 1982, only Livermore Valley, Santa Cruz Mountains, and Sonoma Valley have a substantial number of wineries and histories as long as Napa's. Another thirty-nine districts were pending, a mere handful of them with long history and demonstrated edges. All are, or will be, equal in the eyes of the law, which—rightly—has not yet proposed any *vins de pays* or VDQS districts, since none has proven itself that much better or worse than the others.

A second aspect of the French appellation laws is their limitation on grape varieties permitted in the making of AOC wines. In Bordeaux, to keep that region as the example, reds may be made only from Cabernet Sauvignon, Cabernet Franc, Malbec, Merlot Noir, and Petit Verdot. AOC whites must be made of Sauvignon Blanc, Sémillon, and Muscadelle de Bordelais, plus seven obscure and little-planted varieties such as Mauzac Blanc. In California, there is not a single restriction on grape varieties, nor should there be at this point. Considering that vineyard acreage in Napa increased from 10,000 in 1962 to 24,000 in 1982, there must be a good deal of exploration yet to be done in the most mature district in the state. In comparison, the others have hardly begun to understand which varieties will profit them most. In place of permitted varieties, some law-oriented consumers have pressed for strict interpretation of the regulation on varietal naming. For most of these people, 100 percent of the named variety is none too much. The standing regulation has required 75 percent of the named grape in wines bottled since 1 January 1983, as against 51 percent prior to that date. So far, the net effect has been very difficult to taste in varietally labeled wines, but has led to any number of proprietary names that almost certainly will confuse the average consumer more than the old, permissive regulation did.

The legalists hope, I suppose, that laws were what made wine so reliable for Saintsbury, not mature land use. Meanwhile, the new appellations are a very dim guide. The most telling geographic information on current California wine labels is the name of a vineyard. Vineyard-designated wines are increasing steadily in numbers. As clusters of praiseworthy vineyards begin to point toward meaningful sources of quality, California will have some boundaries worth formalizing.

Although California is a lifetime or two short of its 1855, common sense has not kept two American critics from offering their personal judgments as counterparts to the accumulated wisdom of those rankings. One, in a tone that sounded rather pious in print, announced that his selection of Cabernet Sauvignons had not been affected in the slightest by price, thereby missing the exact point of 1855. The

472

other did not specify which wines accounted for his choices. At least their efforts pointed out two crucial facts. First, both overlooked the crucial underpinning, which is that the clarets nominated as *Grand Cru Classé* were not just labels. They represent vineyard properties as well as wineries. These critics' California nominations included large proportions of what the French would call assembled wines—that is, blends from several vineyards. A few more have come from single vineyards, but not always the same ones from one year to the next. Only a handful qualified as estate wines in the Bordeaux sense. Secondly, the basic foolishness of definitive categorizing of wineries in a rapidly expanding industry may be seen at a glance later in this essay, in the lists of changing favorites between the 1950s and now.

WINE COMPETITIONS

In the absence of refined appellation laws, competitions at county and other fairs operated by quasi-governmental boards come as close as California does to legalized judgments on wine quality. The gap is a very great one.

California's several statewide wine competitions assess currently available wines. There are few or no distinctions as to region of origin, vintage, or other detail, only separation into classes by wine types. For award winners, no prestige or privilege carries over from one year to the next, or one fair to the next. Still, fair awards are useful sources of guidance, particularly to knowledgeable consumers, and especially if taken in the aggregate. In effect, they offer the trial bottles that might otherwise be recommended by a wise merchant.

The current era of explosive growth may also be a golden age of California wines, as some have claimed. It certainly is a golden age of wine competitions. At present, Los Angeles and Orange counties maintain well-established, widely supported annual statewide competitions. San Francisco and Riverside counties have newer ones. Sonoma, Mendocino, and Amador counties, and the Central Coast districts sponsor regional contests each year. In addition to these eight fair-sponsored competitions, there is a ninth conducted by a newspaper, the *San Jose Mercury-News*. More loom on the horizon.

Like all forms of criticism, wine competitions flourish in times of rapid change, and dwindle when their subject is stable. Statewide competitions were annual, or nearly so, during the first period of great growth in California winemaking, from the 1880s until Prohibition in 1919. They were popular again from the mid-1930s through the 1950s as a huge wave of post-Prohibition winemakers struggled to find their footing. In this era, both the California State Fair at Sacramento and the Los Angeles County Fair at Pomona sponsored major annual competitions. The Sacramento fair dropped its wine competition after 1967, leaving Los Angeles to carry the banner. Los Angeles had sagged to small entry lists by the late 1960s, when the vigorous chairmanship of Los Angeles lawyer and connoisseur Nathan Chroman began to revive the fortunes of not only his own contest, but the breed.

The small-panel sensory evaluation system used at fairs has come to dominate wine evaluation in California, not only at fairs, but by wine tasting clubs and critical publications as well. For this reason, the mechanics are worth some exploration. The commonest small-panel format uses four or five judges who taste coded samples in separate booths. Wines are presented in flights of no more than fifteen, usually fewer. After each flight is tasted, the judges gather to be polled for recommendations. Where there is no clear majority, panel members talk a wine in or out of further contention. In small classes of twenty wines or less, the process tends to be quick. Elimination and awards rounds almost always are consecutive. The elimination round simply retains wines for medal consideration, or dismisses them. Once a class is trimmed to medal candidates, judges taste new samples and rank the wines by medal value, then gather to average their results and make joint medal recommendations. In larger classes of a hundred or so candidates, eliminations are done on one day, and awards given on a later day. This system, developed at the University of California at Davis for the State Fair at Sacramento, is in use at the Los Angeles, Riverside, and San Francisco county fairs.

The Orange County system is much different. In fact, the judges do not quite judge. There panel members taste separately, score each wine on the famous UC Davis twenty-point system, and recommend an award. Then a separate panel called the Awards Committee feeds the point totals into a computer to establish a curve, compares the statistical profiles with the judges' written comments, and makes the awards on a sliding scale.

The *San Jose Mercury-News* competition is radically different. It has no set panels, but rather individual judges who taste a series of mixed-bag flights that may include several different wine types each. Six judges taste each wine and give it a score on a twenty-point system less rigorously analytical than the Davis one. Point totals are averaged and winning wines given awards on a fixed point scale.

Other differences distinguish the fairs as well. San Francisco uses only consumers as judges, each tested for ability to reproduce results—to rank the same group of wines in the same order repeatedly in spite of changed codes and changed sequence of service. Orange County uses only winery owners and winemakers. Los Angeles uses a combination of consumers and winemakers, as does San Jose. All of the fairs except Orange County have voluntary participation by the wineries. Orange County automatically enters all wines commercially available in the county.

How well these fairs do their work is a subject of endless debate among winemakers and consumers alike. Maynard Amerine, one of the inventors of small-panel tasting, has cataloged four principal procedural dangers. Time-order error is the damaging of one wine by its place in a sequence, usually by following a poor

474

wine. Stimulus error is the response of one judge to reactions by another judge, or response to some false clue such as packaging. These are nicely countered by the fairs in one way or another: separate booths for each judge, varied orders of presentation, varied orders of tallying results, and complete disguise of packaging and other such visual clues. Two other procedural problems depend on the caliber of the judges for their solution. The error of leniency is what it says, the forgiving of real flaws. The error of central tendency is, in plainer language, sticking to the middle of the scorecard out of timidity.

The fact is that these procedural questions affect every wine tasted in a judgmental way, whether at a fair or by a critic, whether individually or in comparison with other wines. For a number of reasons, I believe fairs do the best job of minimizing errors of judgment of any critical forum using the small-panel system.

Judges have no control over any field they are judging. There is no playing it safe by looking only at wines with such credentials that one's expertise cannot be compromised by voting some $4.99 unknown well ahead of something famous and expensive. As a corollary to the above, the fairs see to it that judges have no chance to adjust the results to fit their prejudices, a temptation to which I have succumbed in reporting some of my private tastings, and a guilt I do not think I bear alone among the wine critics of the world.

Any wine that gets a medal has passed muster with three-fourths or more of the members of a panel of skilled tasters. Those that win in several fairs are particularly valid choices. Such (near) unanimity is no idle notion. Four- to six-member panels rub out the mistakes a single taster is sure to make, but do not fall victim to the monotony of mass judgment. The more skilled the panelists, the more this is true. A panel of judges accustomed to working together may be absolutely unanimous in choosing twenty-five wines out of a hundred for medal consideration, and rarely will have more than three or four differences of opinion. However, and this is useful for the uncertain to think about, the same judges may make four radically different individual rankings of the final twenty-five. Differences in quality among the finalists may be minimal. In well-defined classes, they often are. However, quality and style are separate subjects, and style causes personal preferences to take over in the stretch run.

For reasons of common sense, judges must reward a variety of styles. Although awards lists carry no notice of the fact, judges should, and do, give gold to a perfect example of an inexpensive wine meant to be drunk now, and bronze to an expensive wine, superior, but still some time away from its finest hour, or otherwise a stride or two off a perfect pace. Any buyer who just searches for gold medal winners is ignoring the fact that bronze and honorable-mention table wines rank in the top 20 to 30 percent of their classes in major fairs. Dessert wines, more equal in quality, pull down larger percentages of medals. Whatever the percentages, almost any medal winner is likely to be one of the favorites of one or another of the judges.

None of this is to say fairs are perfect, even at the limited task of finding some current benchmarks. Good wines slip through the cracks, while poor ones sometimes sneak onto the honors lists. Also, judges have been accused, probably rightly, of giving bales of hardware to overweight wines that make a great first impression but wear out their welcome before anyone is halfway through dinner. However, any sober reading of the lists of repeat winners of the past five years will show that the bombastic wines are matched, at least one for one, by delicate, even whimsical ones. Further, an impressive percentage of the heavyweights that have won fair medals also have shown up atop the listings in other critical forums. Finally, in defense of all wine critics in an era of aesthetic chaos, more and more of the durable voices are learning to doubt the exceedingly showy stuff.

THE CRITICS

Criticizing critics is less rewarding than criticizing anything or anybody else because they all have weapons with which to return the fire, and, by the nature of their calling, the will to do it. My co-editors have pushed me onto this parapet for having sinned in most, if not all, of the available critical forums, and not once but repeatedly. Who, they asked, should know sin better than a sinner? Who better to cast stones, and, unspoken but clearly implied, who better to stop them when they come back? Besides, they had the votes, and so, on to pariahhood.

Critics come in such diverse forms as newspaper columnists, magazine writers, newsletter publishers, and authors of books. They struggle not only with their own strengths and weaknesses, but with those of their vehicles. Newspapers are blessedly immediate. Local columnists can deal well with wines in neighborhood shops while they are in stock. However, most are hard pressed by time and budget to provide much more than that kind of shopping-list information. Especially hard put are those who are far away from the wineries. General interest national magazines lose the intimate contact with a specific market, and also can be less than timely. In compensation, they are able to send their writers to the source to dig into a subject deeply enough to help those who want to see beyond their local horizon. Books—real books, not annual shopping lists—have little or no immediacy, but such good ones as Hugh Johnson's *Wine* or Gerald Asher's *On Wine* provide the kind of perspectives that help readers develop critical standards of their own.

In spite of its overall impact on information peddling in modern America, television is largely silent about wine, save for annual incursions into the vineyards at harvest time to explain in thirty to sixty seconds that the sun is shining and everything is wonderful, or that it is raining and the vintage faces doom. The silence should, and probably will, last. The massive audiences of network television fit only a handful of large producers, who advertise. Broadcast media in general are not suited to discussing a subject that often turns on such fine points of memory as whether the voice of authority is recommending Cabernet Sauvignon from Rutherford Hill rather than Rutherford Vintners or Rutherford Ranch, or Chateau St. Jean Chardonnay 1978, Beltane, as opposed to Chateau St. Jean Chardonnay 1979, Belle Terre.

All of the general interest publications leave room for a relatively new development, a special interest wine press that digs so deep into the subject that only hobbyists care to follow. This press includes a fortnightly newspaper, several monthly magazines, and a substantial number of monthly or bimonthly newsletters. The stock in trade of all of these is the comparative tasting, sometimes personal, more often by a small panel. Because they are oriented to hobbyists, these publications tend to be elitist. Many of the newsletters are almost painfully so.

Whatever their forum, three generalities characterize the new wave of critics. The frame of judgment has shifted from wineries to specific wines. California criticism has changed from hedonistic to technical criteria, as evidenced by the predominance of small-panel blind tastings with Davis-type scorecards. And, lastly, the old gentility of fond amateurs has given way to testy, even forthrightly hostile, consumerist types.

The main problem with the current crop of critics in whatever medium is that they have multipled as fast as the wineries. One telling measure of growth in the advice game is that the Wine Institute's public relations department received 2,347 clippings in 1978 and 10,256 in 1982. Maynard Amerine has said it takes ten to twenty years to develop a competent judge for wine competitions. Since critics are subject to time-order error, stimulus error, and all the other hazards that plague judges, but are not required to work under the constraints of a competition, they can be presumed to need at least the same amount of time as a judge to develop.

Against that requirement, critics need to be swift. One of the reasons for wine's current popularity in print is its evident novelty, the stuff on which the periodical press lives. The recent explosion of interest has its positive side: wine gets its name in the papers. Long term, though, the pressure to be novel has its perils. First, newcomers in quiet times have great difficulty finding current information, as anyone who tried to study California wine during the 1950s will recall. Second, when the subject is hot, the emphasis is on who is hot this season, or this month, or even this week. Brand-new wineries receive intense attention, while backbone wineries have a hard time making themselves heard. As an example of this aspect of novelty, one newsletter has ranked twelve Chardonnays as outstanding during the past five years. Three came from one well-established winery, one from a five-

year-old cellar. The remaining eight were from labels three years old or less.★
The proportions are not atypical. The Paris tasting staged by Stephen Spurrier in
1976 offers a different measure of novelty as a virtue, real or perceived. It was not so
much that somebody staged an international tasting, or that expert tasters placed
some California Cabernet Sauvignons and Chardonnays on an equal footing with
some of their French counterparts. That had been happening for several years. The
Spurrier tasting became important because *Time* reported it. When Gault-Millau
staged their much more informative Wine Olympiad a few years later, the news
magazines had already spent their interest in the comparative tasting story. The
Gault-Millau results went ignored by all but special interest wine publications and a
few newspapers. Annual results from the California fairs are reported even less.

The pressure to be novel has its most embarrassing perils when it results
in rushing to judgment. Something in wine makes its novitiates anxious to spread
the revealed truth faster than they learn it. This anxiety leads to astonishing wines
from new winemakers, and astonishing advice from new critics. One critic early
in his career had the following to say about a fledgling winemaker's Cabernet Sauvignon, which he rated "Very Good": "It has a dark color with an amber edge and a
ripe, fruity nose with an earthy quality and a hint of volatile acidity—complex and
attractive. . . . A bit short on the palate, nonetheless with 3–4 years bottle age the
wine should be quite attractive."† Readers who know that oxidation and vinegar
augment themselves with time are entitled to ask why anyone should invite them to
buy such a wine, let alone advise them to cellar it until it gets worse (as the one in
question indeed did).

One of the most difficult obstacles critics—new or old—put in the way
of their audiences is erratic use of the language of evaluation. "Forward," a coinage
by the English wine trade, is used there to describe a wine that is aging more rapidly
than its peers. A San Diego critic regularly uses it to identify prominent characteristics in any wine. Several have used the word, I believe, to identify wines that are immediately pleasing, although the closest reading of the contexts leaves room to wonder. A second example has to do with the emotional or aesthetic value put upon a
term of agreed definition. The University of California literature chooses "herbaceous" as a flavor association for Cabernet Sauvignon of correct varietal character.
In this usage, the flavor should be there whether the observer cares for it or not.
The writer of a southern California newsletter uses "herbaceous" only to disparage
Cabernet Sauvignons he does not like, reserving "cherry-like" as the flavor association of praise.

★   John Tilson, *Underground Wineletter*, vols. 1–4.
†   Tilson, *Underground Wineletter*, vol. 2, no. 2, p. 23.

The scrupulous definitions of descriptive terms by researchers at the University of California at Davis can seem narrow and fusty until they are pitted against the bewildering images of unbridled critics. The middle ground, where synonym and allusion enliven scrupulous observation, is not trodden often enough to make a case against the Davis insistence on precision. Proof may be found in any of the newsletters that attempt to slog through descriptions of a hundred or more wines of a type. As examples of the perils: "Rather intense yet narrowly defined stony/mineral fruit aromas are wrapped around spicy, slightly toasty barrel aged qualities" and "Light to medium intensity aromas offer tight, sleek fruit suggestive of green apples along with soft, oaky elements. In the mouth the wine is tart, narrow and a little bit bland."* These images, purporting to describe Chardonnays, are impossible to follow. How does one wrap stone around wood? How does a tart, green apple become either sleek or bland?

Then there is the school that eschews shapes and spatial relationships in favor of such infinitely precise flavor association that there is no recipe to test the mélange: "It [the wine] has a light gold yellow color with a deep, fruity/vanilla/spicy/buttery/lemony nose with hints of toast and eucalyptus. Very nice in the mouth, the flavors are round with a fruity/vanilla/spicy/citric/toasty complexity, yet the wine has a firm underlying acidity."† At least the vocabulary leans on fruit and wood flavors. Incidentally, this is a Chardonnay, too.

Another problem of elaborate descriptions is that they often belie the evaluation. " A very likeable wine offering bright direct fruitiness in nose and flavors but also containing an underlying grass note. The balance is towards the lively, tart side with the fruit following through into a lingering, slightly brusque finish" describes a wine I would buy, but it got only an "average" rating, maybe for having the contradictory finish.‡ Meanwhile, another wine got an "outstanding" from the same critics in the same review: "Toasty, butterscotch aromas of ripe fruit and extensive oak influence also exhibit spicy and somewhat fumey, alcoholic character. The full bodied fleshy feel on the palate leads to ripe, heavy, oaked flavors and a good deal of glycerine richness that all combine to subjugate the fruit to a minor role in the wine. It follows that the flavors should be oaky, hot, and slightly bitter. Size and depth carry this wine; a bit more fruit could have brought it more harmony." The discussion still is of Chardonnays.

Dancing in these mine fields is hard for critics and readers alike. One longs for observers who can reveal more by saying less, but the gift seems reserved

---

*   Charles Olken and Earl Singer, *Connoisseur's Guide to California Wine*, vol. 7, no. 1, pp. 7, 19.
†   Tilson, *Underground Wineletter*, vol. 4, no. 2, p. 33.
‡   Olken and Singer, *Connoisseur's Guide to California Wine*, vol. 7, no. 1, p. 17.

for Hugh Johnson, Gerald Asher, and one or two other Britons moved by unabashed affection for the drink rather than intellectual suspicion of it.

Seekers of advice about wine also will have a steady diet of scorecard results in place of, or as supplements to, muzzied literature. While the U.C. Davis twenty-point scorecard and many of its derivatives are useful analytic tools, they also have become an aesthetic calamity as great as, or greater than, any caused by words. In place of affectionate description, one gets 17.5 as the final verdict on 23° Brix, .78 TA, and 3.21 pH. Perhaps it is logical that California wine critics should adopt precise numbers in place of uncertain words, just as California winemakers elect for scientific technique over empirical wisdom. California is a technological society far more than a literary one. Numbers are more comfortable symbols than adjectives for many of the electronics and aerospace wizards who make up so much of the home audience for California wine, and no small part of the critical apparatus. Still, when I become Minister of Truth, scoring wines will be permitted to all and encouraged among apprentices, but publishing or broadcasting numerical evaluations of wine quality will be punishable by fine and imprisonment.

Literary quality aside, long-lasting critics are prone to two diseases. One is boredom by overexposure, the other a tendency to develop minor megalomania. Boredom is revealed by an extreme fondness for novelty, or, oppositely, by endless repetition of the same advice. Megalomania surfaces in frequent exhortations to hurry out and buy exactly what the adviser suggests while there is still some left. The implication that other readers are rushing out to empty shelves is often couched in phrases heavily laden with the first person.

At root, useful criticism of wine, like useful criticism of architecture or theatre or movies, depends on solid reporting. Skilled reporters are always around, though never numerous. Solid reporters willing to act as critics are rarer still. Among those with books, national exposure, or both, Alexis Bespaloff (*New York Magazine* and several books) and Frank Prial (*New York Times* and several magazines) epitomize the reporter/critic, the kind who provides factual background that allows, and even helps, the reader to form an independent opinion, one that is perhaps contrary to the critic's own.

THE CRITICS' CHOICES

Having noted all the weakness in critics that I can think of, it is time to say that comparisons of the handiworks of a cross-section from the craft will yield an instructive list of California wines, at least the more expensive ones.

The tables that follow list critical favorites among Chardonnays, Pinot Noirs, Cabernet Sauvignons, Johannisberg Rieslings, and Zinfandels, and are organized to show both consensus choices and individual quirks of some mainline critics.

To give the exercise form, several conditions guide the selection of both wines and critics. Concerning wines, only the five varietals noted above are used because they have earned the clearest records. Only wineries active for a span of five years are included, on the assumption that five vintages is the barest minimum time needed to create a reputation. (The span of years slides for each type, ending with the last vintage for which all or nearly all wines had been released for sale as this piece was being researched and written.) Concerning critics, criteria vary by type of publication. Lists of favorite wines drawn from books are of no fixed length because lists in books cited were of no fixed length. In the case of the books, mention on a list is the only requirement for inclusion. In the case of the fairs, the wines listed are those of the ten wineries receiving the largest number of medals for the vintages stated. The minimum number of awards is two, which caused some lists to stop short of ten. In the case of the newsletters, the wines listed are those from the ten wineries winning the highest average score for the vintages stated. The minimum number of mentions is two. Lists stop short of ten when average placings fall short of better than average rating. In the cases of both fairs and newsletters, ties for tenth place may yield longer lists.

Less specific conditions apply to the critics chosen as representative. The earlier decades of the 1950s and 1960s are represented only by authors of books, since books are almost the only accessible record from that period. The handful of major magazine pieces written then echo the selections in books so closely that their inclusion would change nothing. Because books emerge more slowly, most of the critics of wines of the 1970s are publishers of monthly or bimonthly newsletters and panels of judges at statewide fairs. Copyright date or other indication of time is given with each list. By way of further introduction:

THE SOURCES

BOOKS AND AUTHORS:

Evaluations of wines from the 1950s are by John Storm in *An Invitation to Wines* (New York: Simon and Schuster, 1955); John Melville in *Guide to California Wines* (Garden City, N.Y.: Doubleday, 1955); and Lindley Bynum in *California Wines and How to Enjoy Them* (Los Angeles: Home H. Boelter Lithography, 1955). Storm was a Los Angeles resident who wrote familiarly of California wines in a book covering the world. The latter two authors wrote only of California wines from close vantages in northern California. Bynum, incidentally, was a highly regarded judge at fairs. *The Consumers Union Report on Wines & Spirits* (Mount Vernon, N.Y.: Consumer Reports, 1962) came from a specific set of comparative tastings, and as such is the forerunner of several later cross-section reports. The tasters were mostly from the wine trade in New York. These books represent virtually the entire published record. Wines of the 1960s are evaluated by a more diverse list of authors. Nathan Chroman, author of *The Treasury of American Wines* (New York: Crown Publishers,

1973), is a Los Angeles lawyer, chairman of the Los Angeles County Fair wine competition, and a regular wine columnist of the *Los Angeles Times*. Hurst Hannum and Robert Blumberg's *The Fine Wines of California* (Garden City, N.Y.: Doubleday, 1971) is included for three reasons: because the authors wrote as novices in their twenties, because their book is a cross-section something like the one by the Consumers Union, and because they launched sharp criticism of individual wines in print. They were resident in San Francisco at the time. William Massee, in *McCall's Guide to Wines of America* (New York: McCall Publishing Co., 1970), produced a superficial book, but one reflecting views close to those of the New York wine trade. James Norwood Pratt, at the time he wrote *The Winebibber's Bible* (San Francisco: 101 Productions, 1971) with the collaboration of Jacques de Caso, was an amateur of wine in the old and best sense of the word. He was then a resident of San Francisco. Two authors represent the early to mid-1970s. Jefferson Morgan (three revisions of Melville's *Guide to California Wines*) was an investigative reporter on the *Oakland Tribune* and its wine columnist when he made the judgments cited here from the fifth edition (New York: E. P. Dutton & Co., 1976). He since has become a hotelier and free-lance travel writer in the British Virgin Islands. The other is, or are, Peter Quimme (*The Signet Book of American Wine*, 3d ed. [New York: New American Library, 1980]). Quimme is a nom de plume belonging to a husband-wife writing team based in New York. Their interest in California wine is that of the outsider, both occupationally and geographically. Their research is exhaustive.

FAIRS:

The lists come from all three statewide fairs with at least five years in the record books. Their modes of operation are described in the section on Wine Competitions.

NEWSLETTERS:

These, devoted primarily to comparative tastings, are a phenomenon of the 1970s. All of the ones used here are by Californians, because only the locals seem to have both access to the whole waterfront and the will to cover it, so only they produce consistently complete results. All have been publishing long enough to cover the five-year span of vintages for each wine type. The balance is even between northern and southern California. Robert Finigan (*Finigan's Private Guide to Wine*) covers a fairly broad range of California wines as well as European ones. The emphasis is on expensive varietals. His base is San Francisco. Charles Olken and Earl Singer (*Connoisseur's Guide to California Wines*) devote almost all of their space to California, focusing closely on varietals. They also work from San Francisco. John Tilson (*Underground Wineletter*) deals almost exclusively in pricey Cabernet Sauvignons and Chardonnays among California wines, which share space with equally pricey clarets and Burgundies. The publication is written from Orange County. From San Diego, Nicholas Ponomareff (*California Grapevine*) devotes 90 percent of his space to a broader range of California wines than any of his peers. All four newsletters work with tasting panels of varying formality. Only Ponomareff prints the results of his panel's deliberations as well as his own. In the case of his newsletter, the panel results are the ones used.

THE WINES

AFTER SO LENGTHY A PROLOGUE, IT IS TIME TO TAKE NOTE OF THE WINES THAT PROVOKED IT. *Only one more preliminary point need be made, and that is that the notes will have to do with what Californians used to call the Big Four—Chardonnay, White Riesling, Cabernet Sauvignon, and Pinot Noir—plus Zinfandel, because they have earned the clearest records. It would be easy to add a section on champagnes, and possible to add ones on Sauvignon Blanc, Gewürztraminer, and dessert wines. However, they would not illuminate the process of evaluating wine any more than the chosen five.*

The tables following my notes on each varietal are offered with a certain reluctance. The intention is to allow readers to test a sampling of critics by the wines those critics prefer. But human nature is going to creep in here. Lists offer a beguiling way to work through a wine card or winnow the field at a wine shop, so there will be a certain amount of dot-totting followed by engraved-in-the-rock conclusions that the wine with the most dots is the best one in the field, the Super Bowl champion. Take a grain of salt right now. These tables are not—emphatically NOT—offered as anything like a judgment on which wines are best.

For a first fact, a number of critics I admire do not have a voice.

For a second, a number of my favorite wines do not appear, whereas some others that appeal to me very little are included prominently.

No list with those kinds of failures can be the last word on wine, can it?

CHARDONNAY I

Students of French wines have no trouble accepting Chardonnays called Chablis, Le Montrachet, and Pouilly-Fuissé as different, not only because they are, but also because they have different names to announce the changes. Students of California Chardonnays face at least as broad a range of character and style, but with the handicap of an almost complete lack of signposts. Every label reads "Chardonnay," or, in the old mode, "Pinot Chardonnay." (No difference is implied.) So drinkers struggle to learn what to expect label by label, and struggle even more to decide which labels ought to occupy the top rungs of the ladder . . . or ladders . . . and why.

Most of the dilemma is new. Until the early 1960s, the handful of Chardonnays made in California were pretty much of a style, and critics treated them that way. Books and magazines of the era gave a generalized description of what Chardonnay ought to be, followed by a list of wines that lived up to the notion. Melville was more voluble than most: "Chardonnay yields in the cooler wine-growing districts of California an eminently distinguished wine, golden, full-bodied and fragrant, flavorful and smooth, reminiscent of still champagne."★

Such evaluations worked perfectly well until the oft-cited Hanzell 1957 Chardonnay added the flavors of new French oak barrels to deliberations on character and quality. For a time the question was, wood or no wood? Since 1971 or 1972 the question has not been if, but rather how much wood? In fact it is much harder to find a bottling without a solid smack of oak than it is to find one in which wood distinctly outweighs fruit, and this in spite of efforts by winemakers to counterbalance wood with more intense fruit flavors from riper grapes. For these turns of events, the critics can lay no blame at other doorsteps. Ripe, woody wines have won a great majority of all the prizes and plaudits since criticism turned from general comment to descriptions of individual bottlings. In summarizing the California dream as "I

★ John Melville, *Guide to California Wines*, p. 35.

484

CHARDONNAY TABLES ON PAGES 488–93

can out-Chardonnay any kid on the block," Frank Prial was almost the only critical voice begging for some restraint until he made the point.*

The other new factor in judgment is regional character, far more diverse with 13,700 acres in twenty-three counties than it was when Napa, Alameda, and Santa Clara shared fewer than 100 acres among them. Napa, Sonoma, and Mendocino are unified by more characteristics than divide them. Monterey, San Luis Obispo, and Santa Barbara also have several threads in common, threads that separate them from the more northerly counties, sometimes to a remarkable degree, sometimes by the subtlest of margins. The picture is complicated much more by the fact that every region produces as wide a range of styles as all of Burgundy.

All of these changes have not caused contemporary critics to be in any more doubt about what makes a superior Chardonnay than their predecessors were. In fact, their selections are more consistent than the lists show. The first ten choices vary somewhat, but first twenties come close to being identical. Sometimes the descriptions are remarkably consistent. One universal favorite has, according to one critic, "a perfumed, fruity, vanilla/spice/tropical fruit nose" and "good, firm structure and lingering aftertaste. With age the wine should develop a round, buttery texture."† Another view of it: "Rich, assertive, concentrated, forward fruit flavors; lingering aftertaste. . . . Some tasters found the wine to be a bit overdone and overstated in character."‡ Yet a third: "Intense varietal nose with oak well balanced to the leafy, green olive and apple aromas. Lush, full impression on entry. Lots of varietal fruit here in spite of high (14.5%) alcohol. Rich, powerful wine showing good depth and room for development."§ But there is always at least one dissenter: "lovely indeed, elegant and purely varietal, but for me the earth simply didn't move as I might expect it to for $17."** Again and again with wines rated at or near the top, the adjectives of approbation are "big," "fat," "assertive," "vari-

---

*   Frank Prial, "A Dissenter's View of California Wines," *New York Times*, 16 September 1981, p. C–1.
†   Tilson, *Underground Wineletter*, vol. 2, no. 6, p. 111.
‡   Nicholas Ponomareff, *California Grapevine*, vol. 7, no. 4, p. 54.
§   Olken and Singer, *Connoisseur's Guide to California Wine*, vol. 6, no. 2, p. 30.
** Robert Finigan, *Finigan's Private Guide to Wines*, vol. 8, no. 11, p. 83.

485

CHARDONNAY *continued*

etal," and "well-balanced oak." Most of the wines earning these descriptions are presumed to be excellent agers.

While Prial has a point about some California Chardonnays on the lists of favorites being overblown, his comment was made in the context of pairing them with French food. If the idea of regional compatibilities has virtue in the first place, then Californians are more right than wrong in pursuing the path they are on. In the reverse of Prial's experience, I recently had an excellent Meursault with a typically Californian chicken dish involving avocado and sesame seeds. The Meursault crumbled under the assault, while two heartier California Chardonnays performed with distinction. Neither, it should be said, could out-Chardonnay half the kids on the block.

In the absence of a firm geographic scale such as the French have, it is possible to string California Chardonnays, like beads, along a line based in the major elements of style. At one end of the string are the supple, silken, fruit-dominated Chardonnays. A useful benchmark would be Trefethen. Next come equally silky wines with more prominent flavors of oak. Robert Mondavi is an example. Then follow wines with subtle to distinct flavors of the grape, but consistently austere textures that evoke such descriptives as "structured," or any of the geometric shapes used by the spatial relationship school. Freemark Abbey is representative. Finally come the austerely textured and distinctly oaky wines, of which Chalone and Mayacamas are examples separated by distinct regional characteristics. All the others listed here fit somewhere along the strand, but never all in the same places for everybody.

The ageworthiness expected of fine Chardonnay can come with any style. However, with few exceptions, it will be a while before the world learns which

CHARDONNAY TABLES ON PAGES 488–93

of the highly praised wines of the past few vintages will age as well as the critics have predicted. Not only are most of the wines still young, so are many of the wineries that produced them. Evidence in favor of the high hopes comes from Hanzell, Stony Hill, Heitz Cellars, and Charles Krug Chardonnays from the 1960s, many of which continue to be splendid company to dinner. During the 1970s, Freemark Abbey and Trefethen joined Hanzell, Heitz, and Stony Hill in producing particularly ageworthy Chardonnays. Whatever threads tie them together contain at least some of the keys to longevity, and also to the complexity and harmony that mark superior Chardonnay.

While the newcomers of the mid-1970s finish proving themselves, dozens of newer newcomers clamor at the gates. Some cellars with fewer than five years on the record books seem likely to challenge current favorites. From Napa County, Acacia, Monticello, St. Andrews, and Vichon have drawn lavish praise for their early efforts. The Russian River region has similarly well-regarded newcomers at Balverne, DeLoach, Iron Horse, and Sonoma-Cutrer. The Central Coast counties of Monterey, San Luis Obispo, and Santa Barbara are more enigmatic for lack of track records in vineyard and winery alike. At Jekel, on the Salinas Valley floor far below Chalone, a young winemaker named Dan Lee made several delicious Chardonnays before moving on to establish his own label, Morgan. In their succulent, almost sweet youth, his wines make me think that this is what would happen if the Germans could get Chardonnay to ripen, but it would be rash to anticipate what will come of them with time. Nearby Ventana shows somewhat similar character. And none of these lists take into account resurgent old-timers like Beringer, the most recent wines of which have fared extremely well in competitions and critical publications alike.

TABLE 5, CHARDONNAYS, turn leaf ▶

487

TABLE 5

CHARDONNAYS from the 1950s and 1960s

| WINERY | 1950s | | | | 1960s | | | KEY ▶ |
	A	B	C	D	E	F	G	H
1. ALMADÉN	●	●	●	●		●		
2. BEAULIEU VINEYARD	●	●	●	●	●	●	●	●
3. DAVID BRUCE								●
4. BUENA VISTA							●	
5. CHALONE								●
6. FREEMARK ABBEY								●
7. HANZELL					●	●	●	●
8. HEITZ CELLARS						●	●	●
9. INGLENOOK	●	●	●	●		●		
10. CHARLES KRUG				●	●	●	●	●

The symbol ● *indicates a critic's choice.*

The symbol ● *indicates that the winery does not enter the competition in question.*

A . John Melville
B . Lindley Bynum
C . John Storm
D . *Consumers Union Report on Wines & Spirits*
E . William Massee
F . Hurst Hannum and Robert Blumberg
G . James Norwood Pratt and Jacques de Caso
H . Nathan Chroman

| WINERY | ▲ KEY ◆ | | | | | | | |
| | A | B | C | D | E | F | G | H |
			1950s			1960s		
11. PAUL MASSON	●	●	●					
12. MAYACAMAS	●		●			●	●	●
13. MIRASSOU						●	●	
14. ROBERT MONDAVI						●		●
15. MARTIN RAY	●		●				●	
16. SOUVERAIN★								●
17. STONY HILL					●		●	●
18. WEIBEL	●	●	●			●		
19. WENTE BROS.	●	●	●	●	●		●	●

CHARDONNAY

★ *Reference is to the defunct Napa Valley Souverain, not the active one in Sonoma County.*

◆ *Key to alphabetic sequence A–H shown here is abridged. For unabridged key see page 535.*

TABLE 6

CHARDONNAYS from the 1970s (I) *continued* ▶

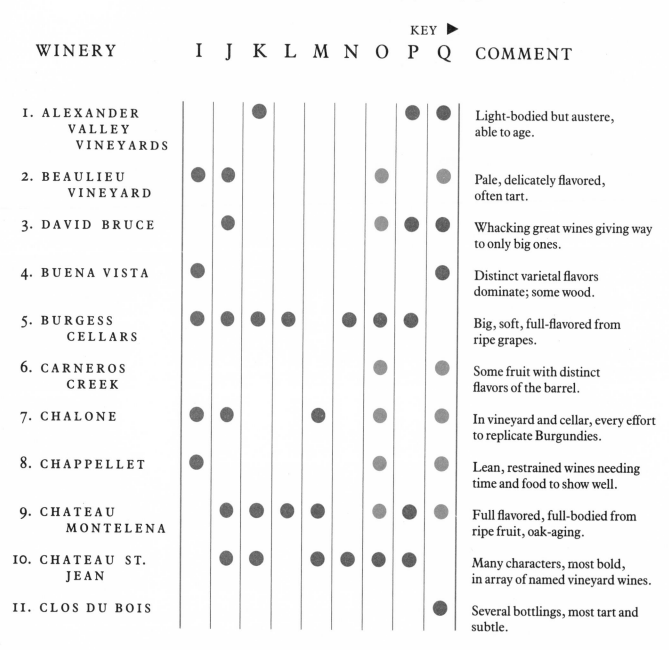

WINERY	I	J	K	L	M	N	O	KEY ▶ P	Q	COMMENT
1. ALEXANDER VALLEY VINEYARDS			●					●	●	Light-bodied but austere, able to age.
2. BEAULIEU VINEYARD	●	●					●		●	Pale, delicately flavored, often tart.
3. DAVID BRUCE		●					●	●	●	Whacking great wines giving way to only big ones.
4. BUENA VISTA	●								●	Distinct varietal flavors dominate; some wood.
5. BURGESS CELLARS	●	●	●	●		●	●	●		Big, soft, full-flavored from ripe grapes.
6. CARNEROS CREEK							●		●	Some fruit with distinct flavors of the barrel.
7. CHALONE	●	●			●		●		●	In vineyard and cellar, every effort to replicate Burgundies.
8. CHAPPELLET	●						●		●	Lean, restrained wines needing time and food to show well.
9. CHATEAU MONTELENA		●	●	●	●		●	●	●	Full flavored, full-bodied from ripe fruit, oak-aging.
10. CHATEAU ST. JEAN		●	●		●	●	●	●		Many characters, most bold, in array of named vineyard wines.
11. CLOS DU BOIS									●	Several bottlings, most tart and subtle.

The symbol ● indicates a critic's choice.

The symbol ● indicates that the winery does not enter the competition in question.

I . John Melville
J . Peter Quimme
K . *California Grapevine*
L . *Connoisseur's Guide to California Wines*
M . *Robert Finigan's Private Guide to Wines*
N . *Underground Wineletter*
O . Los Angeles County Fair Wine Competition
P . Orange County Fair Wine Competition
Q . *San Jose Mercury-News* Wine Competition

▲ KEY ◆

WINERY	I	J	K	L	M	N	O	P	Q	COMMENT
12. DRY CREEK							●			Straightforward flavors of the grape dominate.
13. ESTRELLA RIVER							●			Soft, gentle, almost whimsical compared to typical giants.
14. FRANCISCAN							●			Soft, polished, easy to drink early.
15. FREEMARK ABBEY	●	●	●	●	●				●	Richly textured, complex; one of the best agers.
16. HACIENDA									●	Tart, lean, needing time and food to show best.
17. HANZELL	●	●	●	●		●	●		●	Rich, ripe, unctuous. Fine agers.
18. HEITZ CELLARS	●	●					●		●	Individualistic style based in intense flavors of the grape.
19. HUSCH VINEYARDS									●	Style emerging under new owner; has been richly fruity.
20. CHARLES KRUG	●									In recent seasons light, easily drinkable.
21. LANDMARK							●			Discreet balance of fruit and wood in nicely made wines.

CHARDONNAY

◆ *Key to alphabetic sequence I–Q shown here is abridged. For unabridged key see page 535.*

TABLE **6**

CHARDONNAYS from the 1970s (II) *concluded* ▶

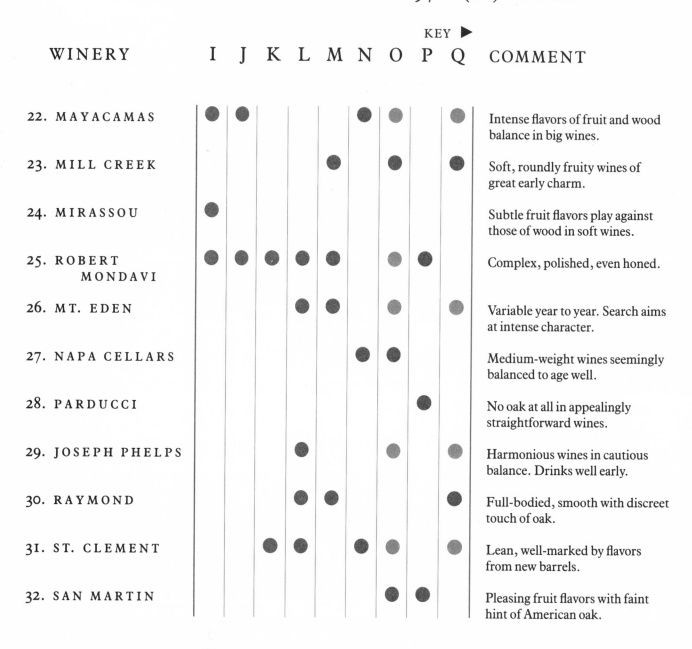

KEY ▶

WINERY	I	J	K	L	M	N	O	P	Q	COMMENT
22. MAYACAMAS	●	●				●	●		●	Intense flavors of fruit and wood balance in big wines.
23. MILL CREEK				●			●		●	Soft, roundly fruity wines of great early charm.
24. MIRASSOU	●									Subtle fruit flavors play against those of wood in soft wines.
25. ROBERT MONDAVI	●	●	●	●	●		●	●		Complex, polished, even honed.
26. MT. EDEN				●	●		●		●	Variable year to year. Search aims at intense character.
27. NAPA CELLARS						●	●			Medium-weight wines seemingly balanced to age well.
28. PARDUCCI								●		No oak at all in appealingly straightforward wines.
29. JOSEPH PHELPS				●			●		●	Harmonious wines in cautious balance. Drinks well early.
30. RAYMOND				●	●				●	Full-bodied, smooth with discreet touch of oak.
31. ST. CLEMENT			●	●		●	●		●	Lean, well-marked by flavors from new barrels.
32. SAN MARTIN							●	●		Pleasing fruit flavors with faint hint of American oak.

The symbol ● *indicates a critic's choice.*

The symbol ● *indicates that the winery does not enter the competition in question.*

492

I . John Melville
J . Peter Quimme
K . *California Grapevine*
L . *Connoisseur's Guide to California Wines*
M . *Robert Finigan's Private Guide to Wines*
N . *Underground Wineletter*
O . Los Angeles County Fair Wine Competition
P . Orange County Fair Wine Competition
Q . *San Jose Mercury-News* Wine Competition

▲ KEY ◆

WINERY	I	J	K	L	M	N	O	P	Q	COMMENT
33. SANTA YNEZ VALLEY					●				●	Lush, thoroughly ripened fruit flavors.
34. SIMI		●					●		●	Evolving style balances oak and fruit.
35. SONOMA VINEYARDS	●	●						●		Pleasant in a lighter, softer style.
36. SPRING MOUNTAIN	●	●					●		●	Rather on the lean side for fruit and texture.
37. STAG'S LEAP WINE CELLARS						●	●		●	Complex. Skillfully polished, easy to drink early.
38. STERLING				●						Another adroit, subtle balancing act between fruit, wood flavors.
39. STONY HILL	●	●	●	●		●	●		●	Pure original. Profound fruit flavors. Elegantly complex with age.
40. STONY RIDGE									●	Soft, straightforwardly fruity.
41. TREFETHEN			●	●		●	●		●	Remarkably silky on the palate. Delicious for its fruit.
42. VILLA MT. EDEN					●			●		Of the bigger school, and well marked by wood-aging.
43. WENTE BROS.	●	●								Little or no wood masks subtle tastes of Chardonnay.
44. ZACA MESA						●				Full-bodied, ripely full-flavored, deft touches of oak.

CHARDONNAY

◆ *Key to alphabetic sequence I–Q shown here is abridged. For unabridged key see page 535.*

CABERNET SAUVIGNON **II**

In another color, in another key, the story of Cabernet Sauvignon is the same as Chardonnay's. Because the wines can be extraordinary, and because they can compare favorably with French models, they have been the darlings of both the critics and the marketplace for the past twenty years.

Interestingly, critics seldom yield to the temptation to describe Cabernet Sauvignons in terms of Bordeaux, a near reversal of the way they think about Chardonnay. One nearly universal favorite was described in very similar terms by four newsletter writers. "The wine has a dark color and lovely fruity/cedary/cherrylike nose. It has ripe, fruity flavors and nice balance with medium body and nice depth," wrote one.★ "Medium-dark ruby color; fairly rich, fruity, spicy, elegant aroma of medium-full intensity; balanced; medium-full body; rich Cabernet flavors; moderate tannin; lingering aftertaste" was a second view."† A third impression was "a handsomely rich color and an admirably defined varietal nose introduce those superb Cabernet flavors of the Rutherford area. . . . I would like to look again at this gem in three years, although it should continue to improve for at least double that time."‡ Finally, "Fairly dark garnet color. The somewhat closed-in nose offers cedary, herbaceous varietal aromas. Attractive flavors, soft tannins, and a round, supple entry provide immediate appeal. A few years of bottle age will draw out even more interest and resolve the bitterness in the finish."§ A difficulty for readers is

★ Tilson, *Underground Wineletter*, vol. 2, no. 3, p. 40.
† Ponomareff, *California Grapevine*, vol. 4, no. 4, p. 1.
‡ Finigan, *Finigan's Private Guide to Wines*, vol. 9, no. 2, p. 10.
§ Olken and Singer, *Connoisseur's Guide to California Wines*, vol. 5, no. 6, p. 113.

CABERNET SAUVIGNON TABLES ON PAGES 498–505

that only a handful of wines have such defined styles as to elicit this kind of consistent description, while very different wines may cause almost identical responses. For example, a much darker and more tannic wine than the one noted above caused one of the same critics to write, "Dark garnet color. Slightly closed-in nose offers almost perfumy oak esters and attractive currant-like fruit with just a touch of mint. Medium-bodied and well structured, the wine shows . . . stylistic elegance. Excellent balance promises good aging potential and development of the closed-in flavors. Should improve for six to ten years."* It should not be difficult to decide in advance of consulting the footnotes which of the four critics is quoted twice. Neither would it be hard to substitute one description for the other, but it could be a problem to substitute one wine (Caymus) for the other (Ridge) at any number of meals.

It is exactly on such points of style that Cabernet Sauvignon is one wine type that makes me wish to take issue with my colleagues in the criticism game. A good many bottlings on their lists of favorites—however described—are almost opaquely dark, incurably tannic, and overtly oaky, though they are much exceeded in these characteristics by others not on the lists.

Somehow the idea got implanted among a number of new entrants to winemaking and no few critics that, because first-rate Médocs can be undrinkable

---

* Olken and Singer, *Connoisseur's Guide to California Wines*, vol. 5, no. 6, p. 122.

495

CABERNET SAUVIGNON *continued*

for their first few years, so California Cabernet Sauvignons should be. Throughout the 1970s, impassioned newcomers to winemaking drowned us in inky juices with enough tannin to cure a cow's hide, and they were egged on by critical acclaim. If such wines change with age, it has not been for the better, or at least not enough to suit me. Among these ill-proportioned brutes are a majority of the healthy, sound wines in the world I would rather add to the burdens of the next generation than drink myself.

When I grope around the darker corners of my cellar to pull out one of the splendid survivors from the 1960s or 1950s, keen anticipation always has a companion recollection of how appealing and harmonious the wine was as a youngster. The 1969 Heitz–Martha's Vineyard, the quintessential California Cabernet Sauvignon, presently is as plump and intricate as a statue of Buddha. It has been so since its beginning. The 1955 Louis M. Martini Special Selection now has a limpid grace as close to the texture of claret as this state has come. It arrived on the market that way. The 1973 Stag's Leap Wine Cellars Cabernet Sauvignon that did so well at Spurrier's tasting in Paris spent a mannerly youth, too. When I grope around my wine merchant's for new wines to squirrel away, these are the kinds I seek. For purposes of establishing a scale, Caymus, Chappellet, Clos du Val, Conn Creek, and

CABERNET SAUVIGNON TABLES ON PAGES 498–505

above all Louis M. Martini are others thus far reliably at the gentler end of the scale, while Diamond Creek, Mt. Veeder, Ridge, and Villa Mt. Eden have tended to stay toward the darker and more tannic end. (It is not wise in these experimental times to categorize wineries too firmly on points of style and assume they will stay put. Some have leaned toward more tannin over the past few years, while others have pulled back. It keeps the game interesting.)

For all my plaints, Cabernet Sauvignon still is California's finest red, and more classics and neoclassics come from this variety than any other. Not surprisingly, in view of the span of years it takes an ageworthy red to lay down a record and the brevity of the grape variety's history in the rest of the state, nearly all of the highly praised bottlings come from Napa and Sonoma wineries. (Some of them, I shall undoubtedly be taught after a few years, started out inky dark and relentlessly tannic.) One true measure of Napa's dominance in local perceptions of what Cabernet should be is that three of four medals awarded Ridge Cabernets at major fair competitions were for wines from a Napa vineyard, York Creek. Another measure is that, aside from Ridge, no other winery south of San Francisco has managed yet to carve out a solid reputation for home-grown Cabernet or any of its kin. That may change after only a few years more, although where, and at whose hand, is not yet clear.

TABLE 7, CABERNET SAUVIGNONS, turn leaf ▶

TABLE 7

CABERNET SAUVIGNONS from the 1950s and 1960s

| WINERY | 1950s | | | | 1960s | | | KEY ▶ |
	A	B	C	D	E	F	G	H
1. ALMADÉN	●	●	●	●	●			
2. BEAULIEU VINEYARD	●	●	●	●	●	●	●	●
3. BERINGER		●		●				
4. DAVIS BYNUM								●
5. CHRISTIAN BROTHERS					●			●
6. CONCANNON			●		●	●		●
7. CRESTA BLANCA							●	
8. GEMELLO								●
9. HALLCREST	●	●	●					
10. HEITZ CELLARS					●	●	●	●
11. INGLENOOK	●	●	●	●	●	●	●	●
12. CHARLES KRUG		●		●	●	●	●	●

The symbol ● *indicates a critic's choice.*

A . John Melville
B . Lindley Bynum
C . John Storm
D . *Consumers Union Report on Wines & Spirits*
E . William Massee
F . Hurst Hannum and Robert Blumberg
G . James Norwood Pratt and Jacques de Caso
H . Nathan Chroman

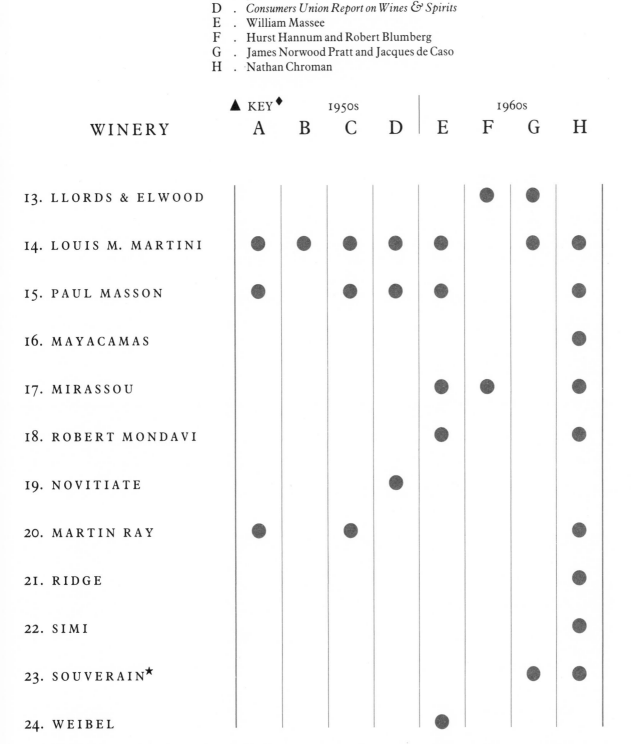

| WINERY | ▲ KEY ◆ 1950s | | | | 1960s | | | |
	A	B	C	D	E	F	G	H
13. LLORDS & ELWOOD						●	●	
14. LOUIS M. MARTINI	●	●	●	●	●		●	●
15. PAUL MASSON	●		●	●	●			●
16. MAYACAMAS								●
17. MIRASSOU					●	●		●
18. ROBERT MONDAVI					●			●
19. NOVITIATE				●				
20. MARTIN RAY	●		●					●
21. RIDGE								●
22. SIMI								●
23. SOUVERAIN★							●	●
24. WEIBEL					●			

CABERNET SAUVIGNON

★ *Reference is to the defunct Napa Valley Souverain, not the active one in Sonoma County.*

◆ *Key shown here is abridged. See unabridged key, page 535.*

TABLE **8**

CABERNET SAUVIGNONS from the 1970s (I) *continued* ▶

KEY ▶

WINERY	I	J	K	L	M	N	O	P	Q	COMMENT
1. AHLGREN									●	Tiny producer of intense wines.
2. ALEXANDER VALLEY VINEYARDS									●	Conventional style for light to delicate wines.
3. BEAULIEU VINEYARD	●	●					●	●	●	De Latour distinctive after long wood-aging.
4. BERINGER									●	Resurgent. Recent wines complex, harmonious.
5. BURGESS CELLARS		●					●	●		Leans toward dark, intense wines.
6. DAVIS BYNUM	●									Conventional stylist.
7. CAYMUS		●	●	●	●	●	●		●	Consistent producer of supple, polished wines.
8. CHAPPELLET					●		●		●	Refined but austere wines, slow to mature.
9. CHATEAU MONTELENA			●	●		●	●		●	Supple earlier; increasingly dark, tannic.
10. CLOS DU VAL		●			●		●		●	Lean, polished wines demand time, food.

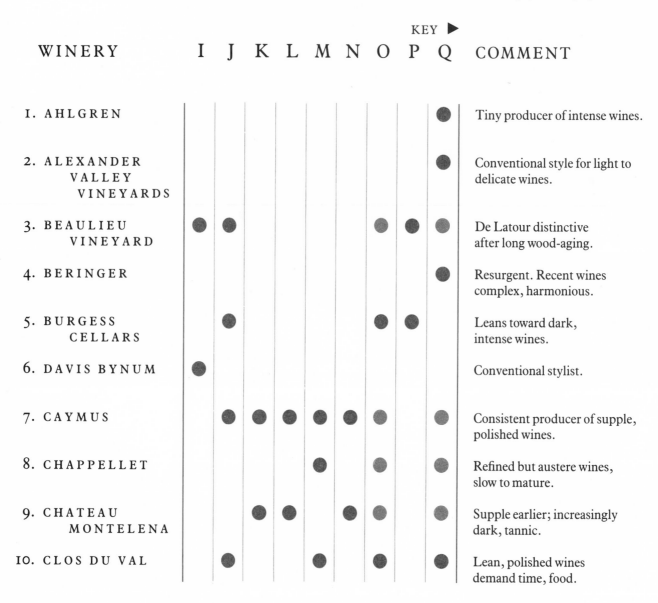

The symbol ● *indicates a critic's choice.*

The symbol ● *indicates that the winery does not enter the competition in question.*

I . John Melville
J . Peter Quimme
K . *California Grapevine*
L . *Connoisseur's Guide to California Wines*
M . *Robert Finigan's Private Guide to Wines*
N . *Underground Wineletter*
O . Los Angeles County Fair Wine Competition
P . Orange County Fair Wine Competition
Q . *San Jose Mercury-News* Wine Competition

▲ KEY ◆

WINERY	I	J	K	L	M	N	O	P	Q	COMMENT
11. CONN CREEK							●	●		Always soft, rich, distinctly fruity.
12. CONCANNON	●	●								Lightly rigged, ageworthy.
13. DEHLINGER					●		●		●	Conventionally styled; need some time.
14. DIAMOND CREEK			●	●		●	●	●	●	Dark, tannic, intensely varietal.
15. DRY CREEK								●		Consistent wines of some intensity.
16. EDMEADES							●			Straightforward varietal flavors mark the brand.
17. FETZER		●						●		Consistent, soft, having early appeal.
18. FREEMARK ABBEY	●	●					●		●	Light to delicate wines of considerable finesse.
19. GEYSER PEAK							●			Steady commercial wines.
20. HACIENDA								●		Intense variety but not austere. Always in contention.

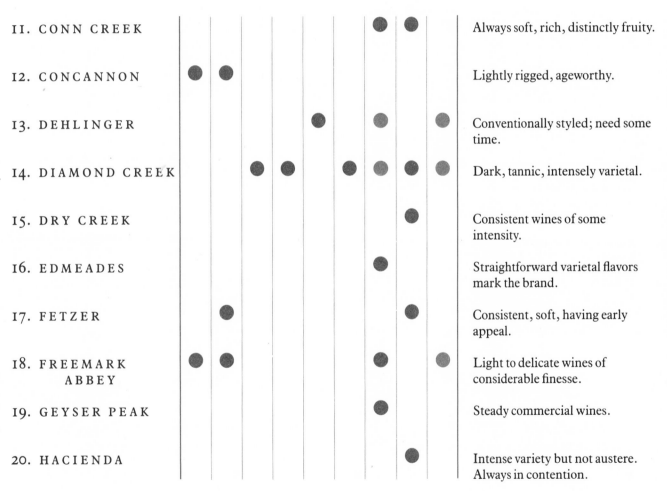

CABERNET SAUVIGNON

◆ *Key to alphabetic sequence I–Q shown here is abridged. For unabridged key see page 535.*

TABLE 8

CABERNET SAUVIGNONS from the 1970s (II) *continued* ▶

WINERY	I	J	K	L	M	N	O	P	Q	COMMENT
21. HEITZ CELLARS	●	●	●	●		●	●	●	●	Complex, distinctively personal wines of great charm.
22. HMR								●		Straightforward; some regional character.
23. INGLENOOK	●	●							●	Steady, conventional, usually with early appeal.
24. JOHNSON'S ALEXANDER VALLEY							●		●	Straightforward varietal wines.
25. KENWOOD									●	Straightforward varietal, often intensely so.
26. CHARLES KRUG	●						●			Steady, sound, easy to drink early.
27. LLORDS & ELWOOD	●									Variable in detail but consistently conventional.
28. LOUIS M. MARTINI	●	●								Always balanced, stylish, age-worthy, and fine value for money.
29. MAYACAMAS	●	●					●		●	Intensely flavored, slow to mature.
30. MILL CREEK					●				●	Supple, straightforward, appealing early.

The symbol ● indicates a critic's choice.

The symbol ● indicates that the winery does not enter the competition in question.

I . John Melville
J . Peter Quimme
K . *California Grapevine*
L . *Connoisseur's Guide to California Wines*
M . *Robert Finigan's Private Guide to Wines*
N . *Underground Wineletter*
O . Los Angeles County Fair Wine Competition
P . Orange County Fair Wine Competition
Q . *San Jose Mercury-News* Wine Competition

▲   KEY ◆

WINERY	I	J	K	L	M	N	O	P	Q	COMMENT
31. MIRASSOU	●									Conventional style, distinct regional character.
32. ROBERT MONDAVI	●	●					●	●	●	Evolving toward supple elegance. Always in contention for honors.
33. MONTEREY PENINSULA								●	●	Variable approaches to individual vineyard bottlings.
34. MONTEVIÑA									●	Fat, soft wines from a warm region.
35. MT. EDEN				●			●		●	Of the dark, tannic school.
36. MT. VEEDER					●		●		●	Another of the dark, tannic school.
37. PARDUCCI		●								Reliably appealing, sometimes complex and refined.
38. PEDRONCELLI		●						●		Good with food, good value for money, often distinctive.
39. JOSEPH PHELPS			●	●		●	●	●	●	Style varies with vineyard from supple to tannically austere.
40. RAYMOND					●			●	●	Velvety, complex, individual, appealing.

CABERNET SAUVIGNON

◆ *Key to alphabetic sequence I–Q shown here is abridged. For unabridged key see page 535.*

TABLE **8**

CABERNET SAUVIGNONS from the 1970s (III) *concluded* ▶

KEY ▶

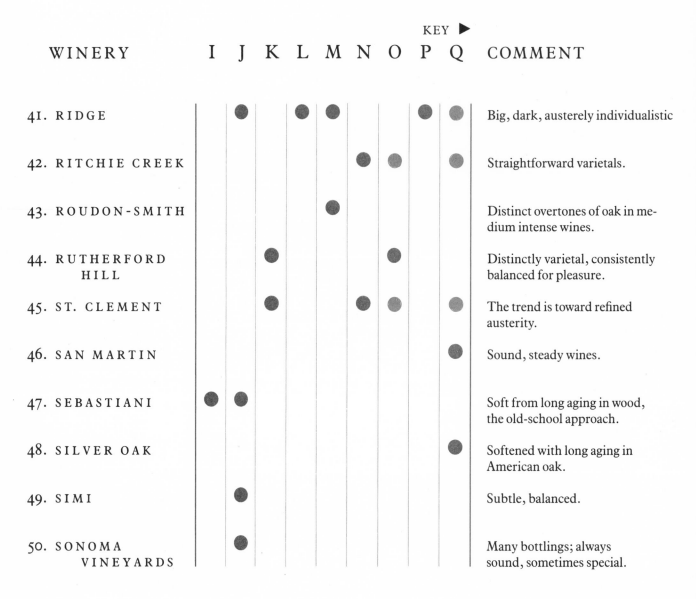

WINERY	I	J	K	L	M	N	O	P	Q	COMMENT
41. RIDGE		●		●	●			●	●	Big, dark, austerely individualistic
42. RITCHIE CREEK						●	●		●	Straightforward varietals.
43. ROUDON-SMITH					●					Distinct overtones of oak in medium intense wines.
44. RUTHERFORD HILL			●				●			Distinctly varietal, consistently balanced for pleasure.
45. ST. CLEMENT			●			●	●		●	The trend is toward refined austerity.
46. SAN MARTIN									●	Sound, steady wines.
47. SEBASTIANI	●	●								Soft from long aging in wood, the old-school approach.
48. SILVER OAK									●	Softened with long aging in American oak.
49. SIMI		●								Subtle, balanced.
50. SONOMA VINEYARDS		●								Many bottlings; always sound, sometimes special.

The symbol ● indicates a critic's choice.

The symbol ● indicates that the winery does not enter the competition in question.

I . John Melville
J . Peter Quimme
K . *California Grapevine*
L . *Connoisseur's Guide to California Wines*
M . *Robert Finigan's Private Guide to Wines*
N . *Underground Wineletter*
O . Los Angeles County Fair Wine Competition
P . Orange County Fair Wine Competition
Q . *San Jose Mercury-News* Wine Competition

▲ KEY ♦

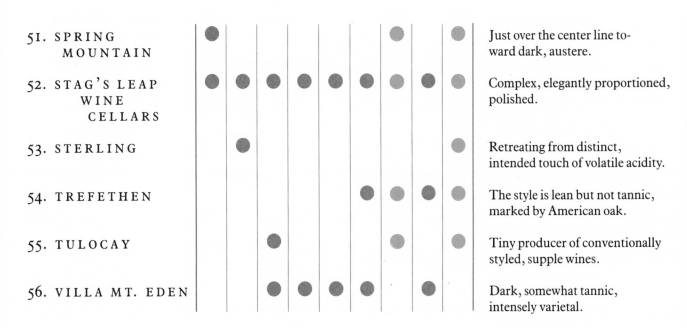

WINERY	I	J	K	L	M	N	O	P	Q	COMMENT
51. SPRING MOUNTAIN	●						●		●	Just over the center line toward dark, austere.
52. STAG'S LEAP WINE CELLARS	●	●	●	●	●	●	●	●	●	Complex, elegantly proportioned, polished.
53. STERLING		●							●	Retreating from distinct, intended touch of volatile acidity.
54. TREFETHEN						●	●	●	●	The style is lean but not tannic, marked by American oak.
55. TULOCAY			●				●		●	Tiny producer of conventionally styled, supple wines.
56. VILLA MT. EDEN			●	●	●	●		●		Dark, somewhat tannic, intensely varietal.

CABERNET SAUVIGNON

♦ *Key to alphabetic sequence I–Q shown here is abridged. For unabridged key see page 535.*

WHITE RIESLING III (JOHANNISBERG RIESLING)

The rapid evolution of California White (Johannisberg) Riesling from universally dry to erratically sweet between 1968 and 1973 has been chronicled in the section on "Other White Wines." While it was happening, the critics, including me, went bananas. We showered praise and heaped medals on the new breed, with the general view that sweeter was better. The winemakers were not unmoved by the same wines, or the prospects of winning a share of the laurels. Dry was forgotten as a style before sweet was defined, or mastered, and certainly before it was described on labels. (It still is not.) In the end, there is room to believe that favorable criticism helped injure the object of affection. Too many of the wines, it would seem, were too sweet for dinner but not sweet enough for dessert. In any case, the public did not follow the critics' lead. After the public was heard saying nay, the search for a successful style shot off in more directions rather than fewer, and blame began to be laid in all quarters.

An almost perfect picture of White Riesling's declining critical fortunes is in *Robert Lawrence Balzer's Private Guide to Food and Wine*. Balzer maintained his enchantment long enough to approve of the 1977s and 1978s. In summarizing a blind tasting of a mixed field of German and California White Rieslings, he wrote, "The truly wine-wise know that as recently as five years ago, any such competitive tasting would have been ridiculous." However, he continued, "We're happy we intermixed the wines. It appraises the improved stature of California viniculture in this department. It would allow us the prediction that the lines of difference will become even less perceptible in years to come, and barring price factors, make competition even keener. Maybe our report, to the legions of white wine fans, will put the bloom back on the 'riesling-types.' "[*] The bloom did not come back, and the

---

[*] Robert Lawrence Balzer, *Robert Lawrence Balzer's Private Guide to Food and Wine*, vol. 8, no. 12, pp. 126–27.

WHITE (JOHANNISBERG) RIESLING TABLES ON PAGES 510–15

1979s and 1980s brought forth no such praise. Rather, Balzer's overall judgment was, "It did not take us long to realize why the category was lacking in popularity. While the 1980s young wines made in dry finish were good, the one year older wines were sad indeed, underscoring the advice to drink Riesling young. Moving into those with residual sugar, they seemed better."★ Results from other tastings do not suggest that the wines had lost that much charm in two years, but sales figures show that public desire for them had diminished even while the hosannas were ringing. The consolation, if any, is that the sales of German wines fell off as fast as those of the Californians.†

In his lament for the 1979s, Balzer raises one valid point that may have contributed to White Riesling's downfall. It is the latter-day fragility of those styled dry or just off dry. Many such wines from recent vintages, perhaps a majority, have faded quickly even when well cellared. It is easy to imagine many disappointing bottles that stayed over-long in poorly conditioned stores or warehouses. This fragility has not always been a part of White Rieslings. Charles Krug, Louis M. Martini, the old Napa Valley Souverain, and Stony Hill all come to mind as 1950s and 1960s makers of White (Johannisberg) Rieslings that would keep at good, even peak form for three to five years, and from almost any vintage. Martini and Stony Hill still are such producers.

With or without fragility as a consideration, the conventional wisdom puts most of the blame for White Riesling's troubles on unpredictable sweetness at levels ranging from a mere whisper to a saturating 25 percent, and especially on wines that try to reach the pinnacle of Late Harvest, but fail. Any diligent reader of recent reviews of the varietal class will come across dozens of comments in the fol-

★   Balzer, *Robert Lawrence Balzer's Private Guide to Food and Wine*, vol. 10, no. 2–3, p. 139.
†   German sales quickly rebounded.

WHITE (JOHANNISBERG) RIESLING *continued*

lowing vein: "Light peach-like aroma. Soft wine with simple, pallid flavors. The sweetness counters the dullness of the flavors."★

The two factors of uncertain aging ability and wildly variable degrees of sweetness might help explain a small enigma. In any one competition, White Riesling is one of the easiest classes for judges to agree about. Even in large fields, judgment is quick and close to unanimous. However, except for a handful of consensus favorites, aggregate opinion is in less agreement than for other types. Rapid maturity in the bottle could be one source of the confusion. Another possibility is that, with sugar levels so variable, a wine that appears excessively sweet in one field would seem better balanced in another.

Whatever the cause of White (Johannisberg) Riesling's diminished popularity, the quest wineries face now is to preserve Late Harvest wines as a specialty, and to find a way back to 1968 for the rest before even the diehards lose interest. The critics may or may not be of help. They continue to show a predilection for 2 to 3 percent of residual sugar rather than the 1 percent or less generally held to be preferred in table wines. One critic described a much-favored bottle thus: "Pleasing, ripe apricot and honeysuckle aromas telegraph the extraordinary appeal of this unusually successful wine. Lush, sweet entry to the mouth." The comment ends with "nice as either an afternoon sipping wine or with food."† A similar ambivalence about whether to have food or drink the wine for itself runs through appreciations of many top-rated wines in most critical reviews, along with fondness for concentrated fruit flavors and detectable sweetness.

There is no gainsaying the deliciousness of many of the sweeties, but the fascination is hard to sustain for more than one glass. A more revealing test of con-

---

★   Olken and Singer, *Connoisseur's Guide to California Wines*, vol. 3, no. 3, p. 45.
†   Olken and Singer, *Connoisseur's Guide to California Wines*, vol. 3, no. 3, p. 47.

WHITE (JOHANNISBERG) RIESLING TABLES ON PAGES 510–15

ventional White (Johannisberg) Riesling than the tasting table is its ability to play
in perfect harmony with the sweet meat of Dungeness crab. An alternate test, necessary in this era of dwindling supplies of crab, is a bucket of steamed rock cockles,
also a sweet meat though not so succulent as crab. If a table wine of White Riesling
cannot meet these tests, it has not fulfilled its potential. The Napa Valley Souverains
Lee Stewart made in 1968 and 1969 caused irreparable losses to local crab populations, but the cause seemed, and seems, just. The shock produced by those unprecedented and well-nigh perfect wines lingers now only in the memories of fogies, and
is not to be repeated because there are several bottlings each vintage that are in much
the same vein and probably just as good. The names that leap to mind are Chateau
St. Jean, Grgich-Hills, Joseph Phelps Vineyards, Raymond Vineyard and Winery,
Stag's Leap Wine Cellars, Stony Hill, and Trefethen. Others with less than five vintages on the critical record, but bidding to join this elite, include Balverne, Jekel,
Smith-Madrone, and Ventana. Not all of them are quite as low in residual sugar as 1
percent, but that is mutable from one vintage to the next. Not all of them stay
healthy as long as the Souverain did, but that is a mystery a long way from solution.

  The Late Harvest wines are a separate matter. Chateau St. Jean and Joseph Phelps Vineyards own the inside track for the superbly concentrated styles
equivalent in sweetness to German *Beerenauslesen* and *Trockenbeerenauslesen*. They
have been joined from time to time by Burgess Cellars, Felton-Empire, and Raymond, and frequently by Freemark Abbey, to which all the others owe a bow for
proving that the deed was possible with the memorable Edelwein of 1973. The
country only needs a few hundred cases of such wines a year, but, my, how it needs
them as a nectar and a tribute to greatness in craftsmanship.

TABLE 9, WHITE RIESLINGS, turn leaf ▶

TABLE 9

WHITE RIESLINGS from the 1950s and 1960s

WINERY	1950s				1960s			KEY ▶
	A	B	C	D	E	F	G	H
1. ALMADÉN	●	●	●			●	●	
2. BEAULIEU VINEYARD	●		●		●	●		
3. BUENA VISTA	●	●	●	●				
4. CHAPPELLET								●
5. CHRISTIAN BROTHERS								●
6. CONCANNON					●			●
7. HALLCREST	●		●					
8. HEITZ CELLARS					●	●	●	●
9. INGLENOOK						●		
10. CHARLES KRUG		●	●	●	●	●		●

The symbol ● indicates a critic's choice.

The symbol ◉ indicates that the winery does not enter the competition in question.

A . John Melville
B . Lindley Bynum
C . John Storm
D . *Consumers Union Report on Wines & Spirits*
E . William Massee
F . Hurst Hannum and Robert Blumberg
G . James Norwood Pratt and Jacques de Caso
H . Nathan Chroman

▲ KEY ◆   1950s   1960s

WINERY	A	B	C	D	E	F	G	H
11. LLORDS & ELWOOD						●	●	●
12. LOUIS M. MARTINI	●	●	●	●				
13. PAUL MASSON					●			
14. MIRASSOU	●	●	●				●	
15. ROBERT MONDAVI						●		
16. NOVITIATE					●		●	●
17. SOUVERAIN★	●	●	●		●	●	●	●
18. STONY HILL								●
19. WEIBEL					●			

WHITE RIESLING

★ *Reference is to the defunct Napa Valley Souverain, not the active one in Sonoma County.*

◆ *Key to alphabetic sequence A–H shown here is abridged. For unabridged key see page 535.*

TABLE 10

WHITE RIESLINGS from the 1970s (I) *continued* ▶

KEY ▶

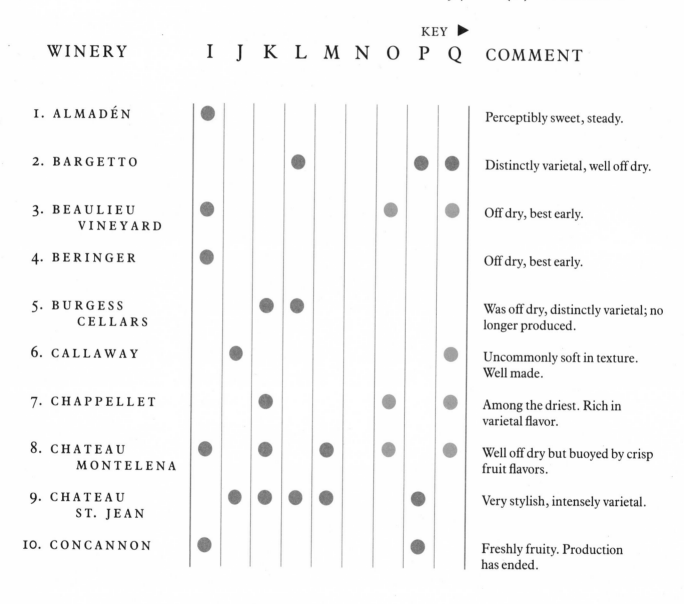

WINERY	I	J	K	L	M	N	O	P	Q	COMMENT
1. ALMADÉN	●									Perceptibly sweet, steady.
2. BARGETTO			●					●	●	Distinctly varietal, well off dry.
3. BEAULIEU VINEYARD	●						●		○	Off dry, best early.
4. BERINGER	●									Off dry, best early.
5. BURGESS CELLARS			●	●						Was off dry, distinctly varietal; no longer produced.
6. CALLAWAY		●							○	Uncommonly soft in texture. Well made.
7. CHAPPELLET			●				○		○	Among the driest. Rich in varietal flavor.
8. CHATEAU MONTELENA	●		●		●		○		○	Well off dry but buoyed by crisp fruit flavors.
9. CHATEAU ST. JEAN		●	●	●	●			●		Very stylish, intensely varietal.
10. CONCANNON	●							●		Freshly fruity. Production has ended.

The symbol ● *indicates a critic's choice.*

The symbol ○ *indicates that the winery does not enter the competition in question.*

I . John Melville,
J . Peter Quimme
K . *California Grapevine*
L . *Connoisseur's Guide to California Wines*
M . *Robert Finigan's Private Guide to Wines*
N . *Underground Wineletter*
O . Los Angeles County Fair Wine Competition
P . Orange County Fair Wine Competition
Q . *San Jose Mercury-News* Wine Competition

▲ KEY ◆

WINERY	I	J	K	L	M	N	O	P	Q	COMMENT
11. FELTON-EMPIRE					●		●			Intriguing balance of sweet and tart in finest bottlings.
12. FETZER							●	●		Affable, perceptibly sweet sipper. Good varietal character.
13. FIRESTONE			●		●					Straightforwardly fruity, well off dry.
14. FRANCISCAN			●				●			Soft, pleasant, sweet. A sipper.
15. FREEMARK ABBEY	●	●							●	Was weighty, powerful in fruit flavors. Production ended.
16. GRGICH-HILLS				●						Stylish balance of sweet and tart. Fine varietal.
17. HACIENDA				●			●			Lush textures, intense varietal, off dry.
18. HEITZ CELLARS	●	●								Was weighty, powerful of its fruit. Production ended.
19. CHARLES KRUG	●		●				●		●	Reliably attractive as sweet sipper.
20. LLORDS & ELWOOD	●									Light, fairly crisp in most editions.

WHITE RIESLING

◆ *Key to alphabetic sequence I–Q shown here is abridged. For unabridged key see page 535.*

TABLE **10**

WHITE RIESLINGS from the 1970s (**II**) *concluded* ▶

KEY ▶

WINERY	I	J	K	L	M	N	O	P	Q	COMMENT
21. J. LOHR							●		●	Soft, sweet, a well-made sipper.
22. LOUIS M. MARTINI	●									Dry, with floral scents. Lasts well. Needs food.
23. ROBERT MONDAVI	●	●	●	●			●	●		Impeccable, delicate varietal, sweet, a sipper.
24. MONTEREY VINEYARD		●		●						Soft, off dry.
25. NICASIO	●									Style seems variable. Usually dry, sturdy.
26. JOSEPH PHELPS		●	●				●		●	Two styles, one tartly dry, the other more lush and aromatic.
27. RAYMOND			●				●	●		Rich, ripe fruit flavors precede a crisp finish. Fine.
28. SAN MARTIN		●							●	"Soft" style is intensely varietal and very sweet.
29. SEBASTIANI	●									Dry, in the old California style. Well made.
30. SONOMA VINEYARDS		●					●			Off dry, delicately varietal.

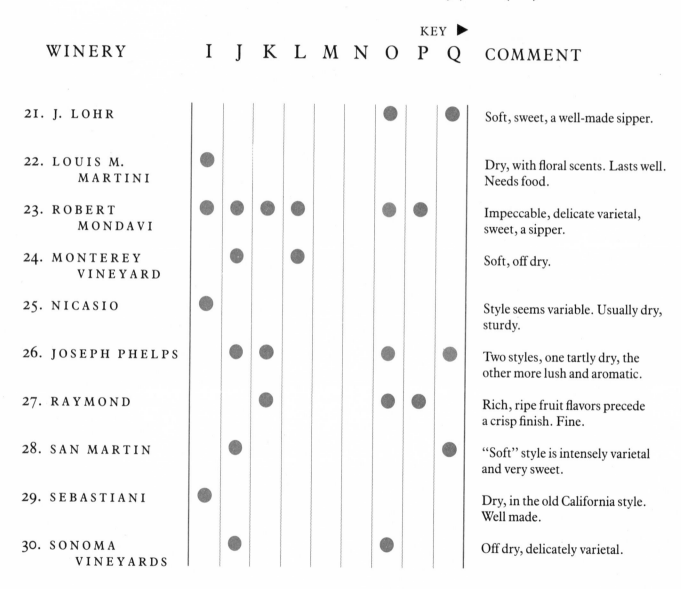

The symbol ● *indicates a critic's choice.*

The symbol ● *indicates that the winery does not enter the competition in question.*

I . John Melville
J . Peter Quimme
K . *California Grapevine*
L . *Connoisseur's Guide to California Wines*
M . *Robert Finigan's Private Guide to Wines*
N . *Underground Wineletter*
O . Los Angeles County Fair Wine Competition
P . Orange County Fair Wine Competition
Q . *San Jose Mercury-News* Wine Competition

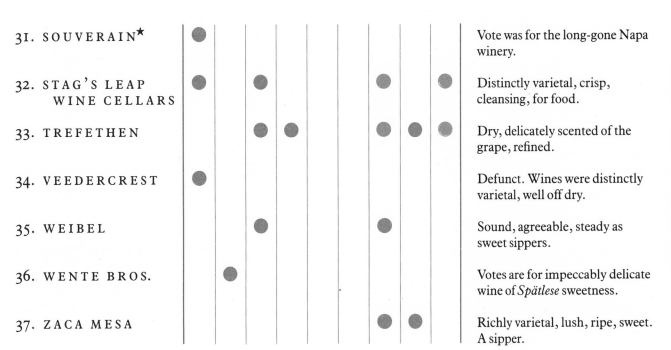

WINERY	I	J	K	L	M	N	O	P	Q	COMMENT
31. SOUVERAIN★	●									Vote was for the long-gone Napa winery.
32. STAG'S LEAP WINE CELLARS	●		●				●		●	Distinctly varietal, crisp, cleansing, for food.
33. TREFETHEN			●	●			●	●	●	Dry, delicately scented of the grape, refined.
34. VEEDERCREST	●									Defunct. Wines were distinctly varietal, well off dry.
35. WEIBEL			●				●			Sound, agreeable, steady as sweet sippers.
36. WENTE BROS.		●								Votes are for impeccably delicate wine of *Spätlese* sweetness.
37. ZACA MESA							●	●		Richly varietal, lush, ripe, sweet. A sipper.

WHITE RIESLING

★ *Reference is to the defunct Napa Valley Souverain, not the active one in Sonoma County.*

◆ *Key to alphabetic sequence I–Q shown here is abridged. For unabridged key see page 535.*

PINOT NOIR   IV

As long ago as 1895, the legendary scientific researcher E. W. Hilgard wrote off Pinot Noir in California. And still growers and winemakers fight the brave fight, winning just often enough to find another thread of hope, tatter of courage, stroke of inspiration.

The critics keep the same faith as the winemakers, finding just enough rarities to offset all their disappointments. Printed remarks of the past few years sound like a broken record. "I know how assiduously vintners are trying to crack the riddle of this most temperamental of varieties, and from time to time I come upon a truly admirable bottle. Over the last year or two I found just enough first-rate bottles to engender some excitement," wrote one.★ "There is increasing reason to be enthusiastic," wrote another.† "Pinot Noir has never quite made good in California. The status of California Pinot Noir is, however, changing quite rapidly, as proved by this tasting of new releases," wrote yet a third.‡ But the writers do not stop there. "Unfortunately," continued the first, "California Pinot Noirs are still a pretty sad lot overall." The second went on to note that "this is not to say that the problems in handling the grape have disappeared overnight. In point of fact, no such great breakthrough has occurred."

The breadth of their disappointment is reflected accurately in the brevity of their lists of favorites. Where selections of Chardonnay and Cabernet Sauvignon run well past the allotted maximum of ten because of ties, few lists of Pinot Noirs reach ten. Short or long, the lists obscure the fact that newsletters and magazines pay much less heed to Pinot Noir than to Cabernet Sauvignon, less even than to Zinfandel and Merlot. The lists also fail to reflect the fickleness of the observers. Hope lurks on the frontier far more for Pinot Noir than for any other variety. Each

---

★   Finigan, *Finigan's Private Guide to Wines*, vol. 8, no. 1, p. 4.
†   Olken and Singer, *Connoisseur's Guide to California Wines*, vol. 5, no. 3, p. 1.
‡   Ponomareff, *California Grapevine*, vol. 4, no. 5, p. 1.

PINOT NOIR TABLES ON PAGES 520–25

new seeker of the grail gets high scores for a vintage or two, then the ratings start to sink as attention shifts to still newer names. This is painfully true of a number of wineries that did not rank quite high enough to make the rolls of honor. It is almost as true of several names on the lists. Fair judgings, while their lists are also brief, are not quite so revolutionary. A majority of the most frequent winners are represented at both ends of the time span. What comes of detailed looks at fair medal winners is a sense of the importance of vintages to Pinot Noir. Of the five years surveyed, wines from 1975 and 1979 won disproportionate shares of the medals. No other variety shows such a clear pattern.

Pinot Noir's specific failure in the eyes of critics would seem to be its inability to be Burgundian on demand. A San Francisco critic spells it out most clearly: "Almost as annoying [as 'Every year is a vintage year'] is the venerable contention that California simply cannot produce Pinot Noir to rival at least very good French Burgundy. In fact, the best California Pinot Noirs of my experience reach a quality level exceeded only by the very greatest contemporary Burgundies. . . . I suppose what bothers me the most in considering California Pinot Noirs is the disparity between what some are achieving and what others could if they either tried harder or were more talented."★ In tasting note after tasting note, he praises wines by ranking them against Burgundian models. Chalone is "very varietal and Beaune-like." Others have a "fine young Nuits style." And so on. At the other end of the critical spectrum, a Los Angeles writer, an unfettered admirer of Burgundies, rarely reviews California Pinot Noirs, praises them more rarely still, and hardly ever for being Burgundian. But the supreme accolade, given along with 18.5 points, went to a Santa Cruz Mountains Vineyard Pinot Noir: "This wine is very much like

★ Finigan, *Finigan's Private Guide to Wines*, vol. 6, no. 11, p. 1.

PINOT NOIR *continued*

powerful young Burgundy at this stage and seems destined to improve with five or more years bottle age.''*

The same two writers are on opposite sides of the question of the variety's ageworthiness. The San Franciscan has come to believe that California Pinot Noir should be made for early consumption, and then consumed early. The southern Californian, in one of his few tests of Pinot Noir, was astonished that older vintages were indistinguishable from fine Burgundies in a blind tasting, and of the opinion that several dramatic wines from the mid-1970s might be better than their forebears. In spite of that optimism, he returned to the variety only once between 1979 and early 1983, and then only to look at current releases. Of such contradictions is the critical reputation of Pinot Noir made.

The search for what fine California Pinot Noir should be has caused winemakers to produce such exaggerated efforts as the Santa Cruz Mountains Vineyard wines (14.6 percent alcohol or more) during the past few years. There have been scores of experiments with extra-ripe grapes, superheated fermentation, fermentation with this or that proportion of stems tossed into the pot, and I don't know what else, but surely some unusual approaches to barrel-aging. Revolutionary ideas be damned. Pinot Noir must be coaxed more than other wines, but the durably good ones indicate that the future lies with conventional winemaking. It may also lie, as a few brave souls have suggested, with ignoring Burgundy as a model.

Of those with long records, Chalone has stayed on course, perhaps the closest echo California has to Burgundy. Hanzell, on the other hand, continues to

* Tilson, *Underground Wineletter*, vol. 1, no. 1, p. 5.

PINOT NOIR TABLES ON PAGES 520–25

make splendid Rhone-types from the grape, many vintages distinctly ageworthy. Louis M. Martini rises to the occasion more often than many realize, primarily using grapes from the Carneros district at the cool, Bay end of the Napa Valley. What is most interesting about the Martini wines is that they are made for themselves and not to a model, and still manage to be both stylish and noticeably varietal. They, too, have aged particularly well. Still, as the past would have it, a majority of hopes are with newer cellars, especially those—antithesis of Burgundy—with vines close to salt water. Among the Napans with fewer than five vintages in the marketplace, Acacia stands out. The winery uses only grapes grown in the Carneros. Three neighbors near the western Sonoma County town of Forestville have signalled that their district just might be a right place. Dehlinger, DeLoach, and Iron Horse all have made wines that have the earmarks of durable excellence, and at least some of the signs of greatness. An exception to the sea air theory, tiny Calera, on the opposite slope of the Gavilan Mountains from Chalone, has produced its first few hundred cases of Pinot Noir, and haunted palates with the harmonies.

While there is some evidence that Pinot Noir should be drunk fresh out of the fermentor, and other evidence that it should be tucked away for a decade or more, the wines mentioned here all beg their drinkers to have only modest patience. If they can be seen as typical, then it takes fine California Pinot Noirs about five to seven years to compose themselves. The subtle flavors of the grape variety seem to hide until the more prominent tastes of fermentation and wood subside a bit. Those who drink and dismiss Pinot Noirs earlier miss their point.

TABLE 11, PINOT NOIRS, turn leaf ▶

TABLE **II**

PINOT NOIRS from the 1950s and 1960s

WINERY	A	B	C	D	E	F	G	H
		1950s				1960s		KEY ▶
1. ALMADÉN	●		●	●		●	●	
2. BEAULIEU VINEYARD	●	●	●	●	●	●	●	●
3. BERINGER			●					
4. BUENA VISTA				●		●	●	
5. HANZELL						●	●	
6. HEITZ CELLARS						●	●	
7. INGLENOOK	●	●	●	●	●			●
8. CHARLES KRUG		●						
9. LLORDS & ELWOOD						●	●	
10. LOUIS M. MARTINI	●	●	●	●	●	●	●	●

The symbol ● *indicates a critic's choice.*

The symbol ◐ *indicates that the winery does not enter the competition in question.*

A . John Melville
B . Lindley Bynum
C . John Storm
D . *Consumers Union Report on Wines & Spirits*
E . William Massee
F . Hurst Hannum and Robert Blumberg
G . James Norwood Pratt and Jacques de Caso
H . Nathan Chroman

▲ KEY ◆   1950s   1960s

WINERY	A	B	C	D	E	F	G	H
11. PAUL MASSON	●	●		●				
12. ROBERT MONDAVI								●
13. PARDUCCI							●	
14. MARTIN RAY	●		●			●		●
15. SOUVERAIN★			●					
16. WEIBEL						●		
17. WENTE BROS.						●		

PINOT NOIR

★ *Reference is to the defunct Napa Valley Souverain, not the active one in Sonoma County.*

◆ *Key to alphabetic sequence A–H shown here is abridged. For unabridged key see page 535.*

TABLE **12**

PINOT NOIRS from the 1970s (I) *continued* ▶

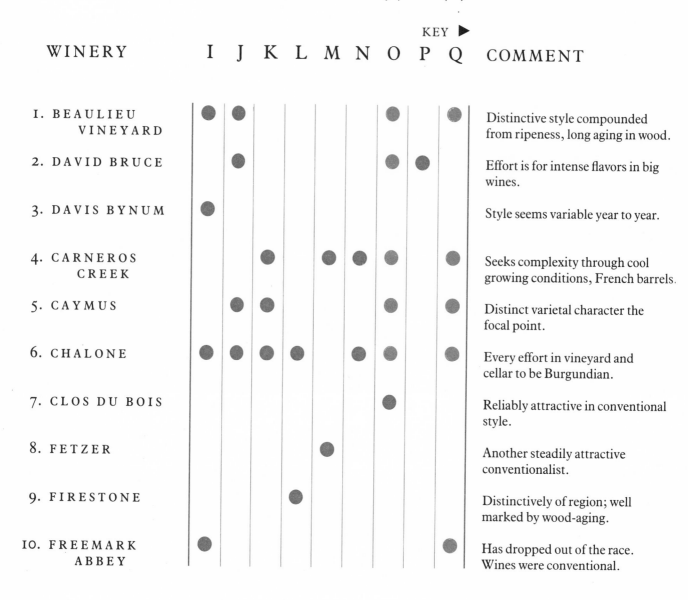

WINERY	I	J	K	L	M	N	O	P	Q	COMMENT
1. BEAULIEU VINEYARD	●	●					●		●	Distinctive style compounded from ripeness, long aging in wood.
2. DAVID BRUCE		●					●	●		Effort is for intense flavors in big wines.
3. DAVIS BYNUM	●									Style seems variable year to year.
4. CARNEROS CREEK			●		●	●	●		●	Seeks complexity through cool growing conditions, French barrels.
5. CAYMUS		●	●				●		●	Distinct varietal character the focal point.
6. CHALONE	●	●	●	●		●	●		●	Every effort in vineyard and cellar to be Burgundian.
7. CLOS DU BOIS							●			Reliably attractive in conventional style.
8. FETZER					●					Another steadily attractive conventionalist.
9. FIRESTONE				●						Distinctively of region; well marked by wood-aging.
10. FREEMARK ABBEY	●								●	Has dropped out of the race. Wines were conventional.

The symbol ● indicates a critic's choice.

The symbol ● indicates that the winery does not enter the competition in question.

I . John Melville
J . Peter Quimme
K . *California Grapevine*
L . *Connoisseur's Guide to California Wines*
M . *Robert Finigan's Private Guide to Wines*
N . *Underground Wineletter*
O . Los Angeles County Fair Wine Competition
P . Orange County Fair Wine Competition
Q . *San Jose Mercury-News* Wine Competition

▲ KEY ◆

WINERY	I	J	K	L	M	N	O	P	Q	COMMENT
11. GUNDLACH-BUNDSCHU			●				●			Distinctively varietal, consistently appealing.
12. HACIENDA			●							Husky, intensely flavored from ripe grapes, barrel age.
13. HANZELL	●	●					●		●	Very ripe, lush textured wines of individual character.
14. HEITZ CELLARS	●						●		●	Ripe grapes and long aging in wood are hallmarks.
15. HMR				●		●				Ripe, regionally distinctive wines.
16. INGLENOOK	●									Steady, conventionally styled wines.
17. LLORDS & ELWOOD	●									Have seemed variable in character from year to year.
18. LOUIS M. MARTINI	●									Subtle, supple, consistently ageworthy.

PINOT NOIR

◆ *Key to alphabetic sequence I–Q shown here is abridged. For unabridged key see page 535.*

TABLE **12**

PINOT NOIRS from the 1970s (II) *concluded* ▶

KEY ▶

WINERY	I	J	K	L	M	N	O	P	Q	COMMENT
19. MILL CREEK							●			Soft, appealing wines focused on fruit flavors.
20. MIRASSOU	●									Complex, soft, regionally distinctive.
21. ROBERT MONDAVI	●		●				●		●	Ripe, well marked by wood, but curiously lean in texture.
22. J. W. MORRIS							●			Soft to fat feeling and smacking strongly of oak.
23. MT. EDEN		●	●		●		●		●	Big, richly flavored, with more tannic austerity than common.
24. NAVARRO							●			Well-balanced mixture of fruit and oak in pleasant wines.
25. PEDRONCELLI								●		Gentle, harmonious, with early appeal.
26. JOSEPH PHELPS				●			●		●	Ripe, soft wines with distinct flavors from barrel-aging.
27. SANFORD & BENEDICT		●	●	●			●		●	Individualistic; perhaps from technique, perhaps region.
28. SANTA CRUZ MOUNTAINS			●			●	●		●	Heavy, high-alcohol (14 to 15 percent), rather short-lived.

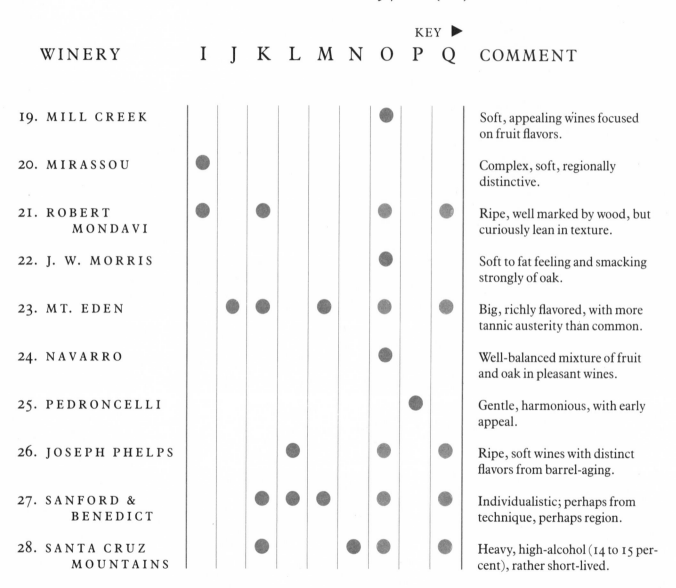

The symbol ● indicates a critic's choice.

The symbol ● indicates that the winery does not enter the competition in question.

I . John Melville
J . Peter Quimme
K . *California Grapevine*
L . *Connoisseur's Guide to California Wines*
M . *Robert Finigan's Private Guide to Wines*
N . *Underground Wineletter*
O . Los Angeles County Fair Wine Competition
P . Orange County Fair Wine Competition
Q . *San Jose Mercury-News* Wine Competition

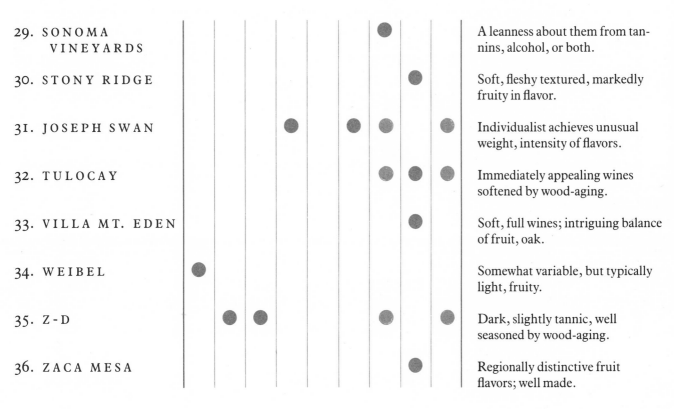

▲   KEY ◆

WINERY	I	J	K	L	M	N	O	P	Q	COMMENT
29. SONOMA VINEYARDS							●			A leanness about them from tannins, alcohol, or both.
30. STONY RIDGE								●		Soft, fleshy textured, markedly fruity in flavor.
31. JOSEPH SWAN				●		●	●		●	Individualist achieves unusual weight, intensity of flavors.
32. TULOCAY							●	●	●	Immediately appealing wines softened by wood-aging.
33. VILLA MT. EDEN								●		Soft, full wines; intriguing balance of fruit, oak.
34. WEIBEL	●									Somewhat variable, but typically light, fruity.
35. Z-D		●	●				●		●	Dark, slightly tannic, well seasoned by wood-aging.
36. ZACA MESA								●		Regionally distinctive fruit flavors; well made.

PINOT NOIR

◆ *Key to alphabetic sequence I–Q shown here is abridged. For unabridged key see page 535.*

ZINFANDEL V

During the past decade, the always versatile Zinfandel has been stretched to new limits. What once was a conventional red capable of being anything from America's Beaujolais to a good claret has gone on to become a sweet wine of as much as 16 percent alcohol, a dry wine of as much as 16 percent alcohol, and a frivolous confection produced by carbonic maceration. Somewhere along the line, the public appears to have thrown up its hands in the same way and for the same reason it did over White Riesling: the name means too much or very little at all, and Zinfandel is very hard to sell in the early 1980s.

During these rapid developments in style, critics took themselves down the primrose path. There was the first rush to praise brave new tries, followed by a period of milling about in search of a trend, then a growing disenchantment.

The carbonic maceration wines, usually identified as Nouveaux, Nuevos, or similar, had only a brief hour in the sun before their lack of character did them in. The high-alcohol ones, sometimes labeled Late Harvest whether sweet or dry, have had a longer run. The sweet Ridge Zinfandel Essences of the early 1970s won applause from a rich variety of sources. So did the equally sweet Mayacamas Zinfandel Late Harvest from the same era. They should have done. They were splendid, something like vintage ports without the fiery distilled alcohols. Unfortunately, they proved to be the products of rare chance. The more winemakers tried to imitate them, the drier and harsher the wines that came along as would-be successors. It appears to be these harsh wines that have gotten thumbs down from the public.

Throughout the mid-1970s, ever fainter choruses of praise attended winemakers such as Louis P. Martini, John Parducci, and John Pedroncelli, who

ZINFANDEL TABLES ON PAGES 528–34

persisted with steady, well-proportioned red table wines. In fact, it would appear from the recent lists of critical favorites that they have all but been lost in the shuffle during the last three or four years. One telling measure is in the fact that such high-alcohol, high-extract Zinfandels as those of Lytton Springs and Carneros Creek got twelve reviews between them from the newsletter that pays the greatest attention to Zinfandel, while Martini, Parducci, and Pedroncelli managed one among them. ⋆ It is too bad the balance is not more even, because the latter three and a few more like them continue to make the kind of Zinfandel the public used to drink a good deal of, wines of medium color, with a clear smell of berries, and oak so far in the background as to be hard to find and harder to identify. They have enough tannin to notice, but not enough to glue lips to teeth, and they have a light freshness of texture that will cleanse away thick tomato sauce. That is plenty of virtue for a wine of modest dimensions.

As in the case of White Riesling, the trick for wineries now is to preserve (and, in my view, improve) Late Harvest Zinfandel as a specialty, whilst regaining some sort of footing for conventional, foodworthy Zinfandels. A clear nomenclature on the labels will help.

By now it should be abundantly clear that I have the touch of megalomania required of all critics. It should be equally clear that my critical arteries are hardening in the direction of conventional, conservative style rather than novelty. High-alcohol Zinfandels have an audience in this world, mostly of people in wine clubs who taste them comparatively. But that audience does not, and will not, include me, because inky colors, searing tannins, the fires of 14 and 15 percent of alcohol, and dense aromas of raisins and wood too often have come, all of them at once,

Text concluded on page 536

TABLE 13, ZINFANDELS, turn leaf ▶

⋆ Ponomareff, *California Grapevine*, vols. 3–8.

TABLE 13

ZINFANDELS from the 1950s and 1960s

| WINERY | 1950s | | | | 1960s | | | KEY ▶ |
	A	B	C	D	E	F	G	H
1. ALMADÉN		●						
2. BERINGER			●	●				
3. DAVID BRUCE								●
4. BUENA VISTA	●	●		●	●		●	●
5. CADENASSO	●							
6. CHRISTIAN BROTHERS						●	●	
7. CONCANNON	●	●						
8. CUCAMONGA WINERY	●							
9. DIGARDI	●							
10. FETZER								●
11. GEMELLO								●
12. ITALIAN SWISS	●							

The symbol ● indicates a critic's choice.

528

The symbol ● indicates that the winery does not enter the competition in question.

A . John Melville
B . Lindley Bynum
C . John Storm
D . *Consumers Union Report on Wines & Spirits*
E . William Massee
F . Hurst Hannum and Robert Blumberg
G . James Norwood Pratt and Jacques de Caso
H . Nathan Chroman

WINERY	▲ KEY ◆	1950s			1960s			
---	A	B	C	D	E	F	G	H
13. CHARLES KRUG		●	●	●	●	●	●	●
14. LOUIS M. MARTINI	●	●		●	●	●	●	●
15. MIRASSOU						●	●	●
16. ROBERT MONDAVI						●		●
17. NOVITIATE			●	●				
18. PARDUCCI			●		●			
19. RIDGE							●	●
20. SAN MARTIN						●		
21. SEBASTIANI					●			●
22. SOUVERAIN★	●	●			●			
23. WEIBEL		●	●					
24. YORK MOUNTAIN	●	●						

ZINFANDEL

★ *Reference is to the defunct Napa Valley Souverain, not the active one in Sonoma County.*

◆ *Key shown here is abridged. See unabridged key, page 535.*

TABLE 14

ZINFANDELS from the 1970s (I) *continued* ▶

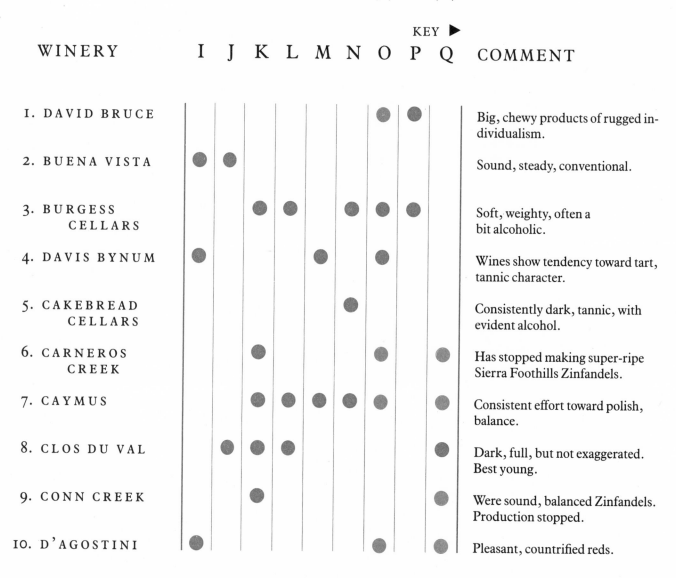

WINERY	I	J	K	L	M	N	O	P	Q	COMMENT
1. DAVID BRUCE							●	●		Big, chewy products of rugged individualism.
2. BUENA VISTA	●	●								Sound, steady, conventional.
3. BURGESS CELLARS			●	●		●	●	●		Soft, weighty, often a bit alcoholic.
4. DAVIS BYNUM	●				●		●			Wines show tendency toward tart, tannic character.
5. CAKEBREAD CELLARS						●				Consistently dark, tannic, with evident alcohol.
6. CARNEROS CREEK			●				●		●	Has stopped making super-ripe Sierra Foothills Zinfandels.
7. CAYMUS			●	●	●	●	●		●	Consistent effort toward polish, balance.
8. CLOS DU VAL		●	●	●					●	Dark, full, but not exaggerated. Best young.
9. CONN CREEK			●						●	Were sound, balanced Zinfandels. Production stopped.
10. D'AGOSTINI	●						●		●	Pleasant, countrified reds.

The symbol ● indicates a critic's choice.

The symbol ● indicates that the winery does not enter the competition in question.

I . John Melville
J . Peter Quimme
K . *California Grapevine*
L . *Connoisseur's Guide to California Wines*
M . *Robert Finigan's Private Guide to Wines*
N . *Underground Wineletter*
O . Los Angeles County Fair Wine Competition
P . Orange County Fair Wine Competition
Q . *San Jose Mercury-News* Wine Competition

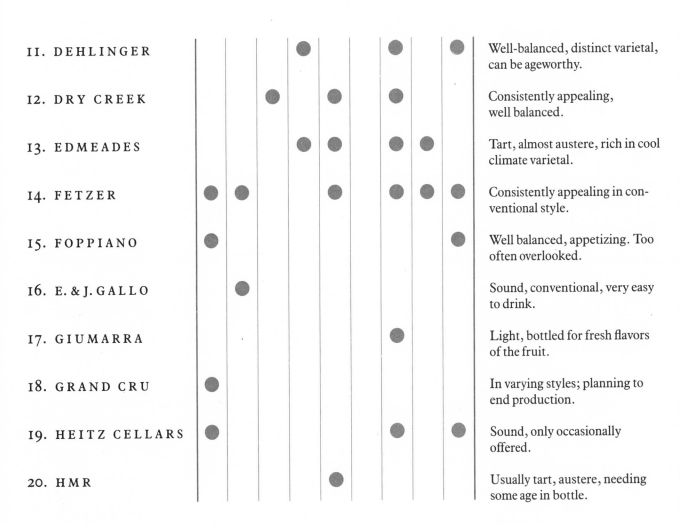

WINERY	I	J	K	L	M	N	O	P	Q	COMMENT
11. DEHLINGER				●			●		●	Well-balanced, distinct varietal, can be ageworthy.
12. DRY CREEK			●		●		●			Consistently appealing, well balanced.
13. EDMEADES				●	●		●	●		Tart, almost austere, rich in cool climate varietal.
14. FETZER	●	●			●		●	●	●	Consistently appealing in conventional style.
15. FOPPIANO	●								●	Well balanced, appetizing. Too often overlooked.
16. E. & J. GALLO		●								Sound, conventional, very easy to drink.
17. GIUMARRA							●			Light, bottled for fresh flavors of the fruit.
18. GRAND CRU	●									In varying styles; planning to end production.
19. HEITZ CELLARS	●						●		●	Sound, only occasionally offered.
20. HMR					●					Usually tart, austere, needing some age in bottle.

ZINFANDEL

◆ *Key to alphabetic sequence I–Q shown here is abridged. For unabridged key see page 535.*

TABLE I4

ZINFANDELS from the 1970s (II) *continued* ▶

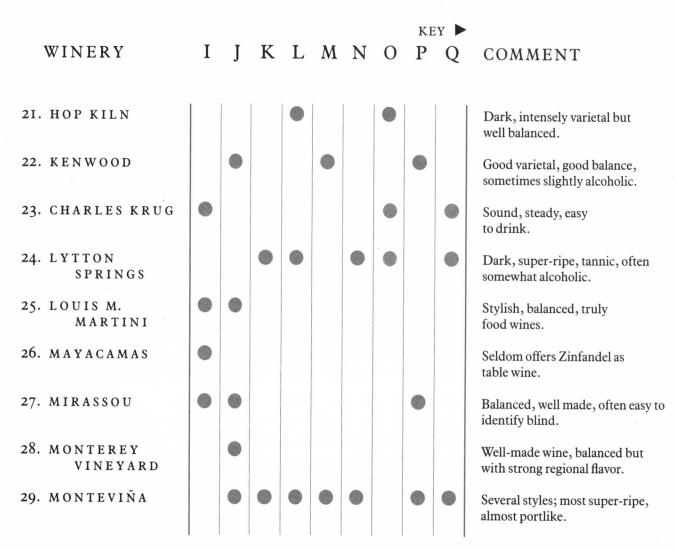

WINERY	I	J	K	L	M	N	O	P	Q	COMMENT
21. HOP KILN				●			●			Dark, intensely varietal but well balanced.
22. KENWOOD		●			●			●		Good varietal, good balance, sometimes slightly alcoholic.
23. CHARLES KRUG	●						●		●	Sound, steady, easy to drink.
24. LYTTON SPRINGS			●	●		●	●		●	Dark, super-ripe, tannic, often somewhat alcoholic.
25. LOUIS M. MARTINI	●	●								Stylish, balanced, truly food wines.
26. MAYACAMAS	●									Seldom offers Zinfandel as table wine.
27. MIRASSOU	●	●					●			Balanced, well made, often easy to identify blind.
28. MONTEREY VINEYARD		●								Well-made wine, balanced but with strong regional flavor.
29. MONTEVIÑA		●	●	●	●	●		●	●	Several styles; most super-ripe, almost portlike.

The symbol ● *indicates a critic's choice.*

The symbol ● *indicates that the winery does not enter the competition in question.*

I . John Melville
J . Peter Quimme
K . *California Grapevine*
L . *Connoisseur's Guide to California Wines*
M . *Robert Finigan's Private Guide to Wines*
N . *Underground Wineletter*
O . Los Angeles County Fair Wine Competition
P . Orange County Fair Wine Competition
Q . *San Jose Mercury-News* Wine Competition

▲ KEY ◆

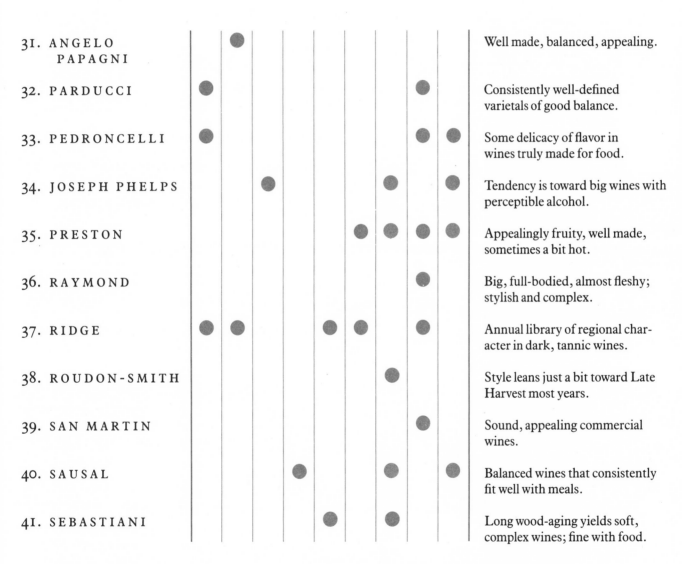

WINERY	I	J	K	L	M	N	O	P	Q	COMMENT
31. ANGELO PAPAGNI		●								Well made, balanced, appealing.
32. PARDUCCI	●							●		Consistently well-defined varietals of good balance.
33. PEDRONCELLI	●							●	●	Some delicacy of flavor in wines truly made for food.
34. JOSEPH PHELPS				●			●		●	Tendency is toward big wines with perceptible alcohol.
35. PRESTON						●	●	●	●	Appealingly fruity, well made, sometimes a bit hot.
36. RAYMOND								●		Big, full-bodied, almost fleshy; stylish and complex.
37. RIDGE	●	●			●	●		●		Annual library of regional character in dark, tannic wines.
38. ROUDON-SMITH							●			Style leans just a bit toward Late Harvest most years.
39. SAN MARTIN								●		Sound, appealing commercial wines.
40. SAUSAL				●			●		●	Balanced wines that consistently fit well with meals.
41. SEBASTIANI					●		●			Long wood-aging yields soft, complex wines; fine with food.

ZINFANDEL

◆ *Key to alphabetic sequence I–Q shown here is abridged. For unabridged key see page 535.*

TABLE **14**

ZINFANDELS from the 1970s (III) *concluded*

KEY ▶

WINERY	I	J	K	L	M	N	O	P	Q	COMMENT

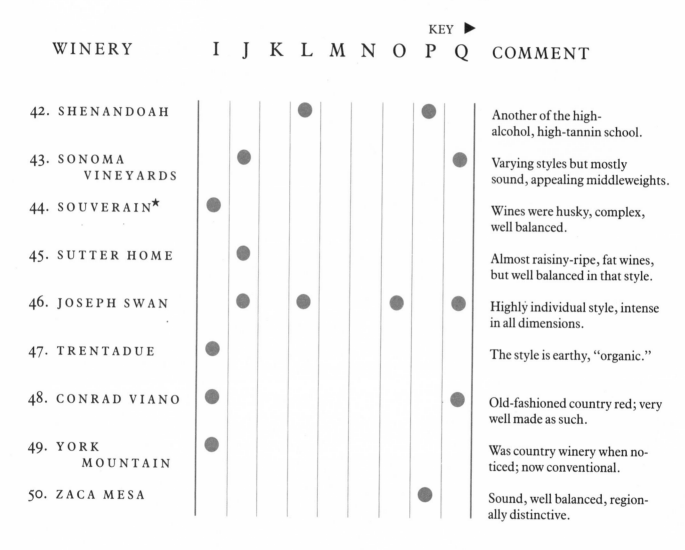

WINERY	I	J	K	L	M	N	O	P	Q	COMMENT
42. SHENANDOAH				●				●		Another of the high-alcohol, high-tannin school.
43. SONOMA VINEYARDS		●							●	Varying styles but mostly sound, appealing middleweights.
44. SOUVERAIN★	●									Wines were husky, complex, well balanced.
45. SUTTER HOME		●								Almost raisiny-ripe, fat wines, but well balanced in that style.
46. JOSEPH SWAN		●		●			●		●	Highly individual style, intense in all dimensions.
47. TRENTADUE	●									The style is earthy, "organic."
48. CONRAD VIANO	●								●	Old-fashioned country red; very well made as such.
49. YORK MOUNTAIN	●									Was country winery when noticed; now conventional.
50. ZACA MESA								●		Sound, well balanced, regionally distinctive.

★Reference is to the defunct Napa Valley Souverain, not the active one in Sonoma County.

The symbol ● *indicates a critic's choice.*

The symbol ● *indicates that the winery does not enter the competition in question.*

KEY TO SOURCES OF CRITICS' CHOICES AND COMMENTS
LISTED IN TABLES 5–14 INCLUSIVE.

*   A.   John Melville, *Guide to California Wines* (1955): list of selections.

*   B.   Lindley Bynum, *California Wines and How to Enjoy Them* (1955): list of selections.

*   C.   John Storm, *Invitation to Wines* (1955): list of selections.

*   D.   *Consumers Union Report on Wines & Spirits* (1962): list of selections.

†   E.   William Massee, *McCall's Guide to American Wines* (1970): list of selections.

†   F.   Hurst Hannum and Robert Blumberg, *Fine Wines of California* (1971): wines with highest average rankings in 4-star system.

†   G.   James Norwood Pratt and Jacques de Caso, *Winebibber's Bible* (1971): list of selections.

†   H.   Nathan Chroman, *Treasury of American Wines* (1973): wines with highest rankings in 4-star system.

‡   I.   John Melville, *Guide to California Wines*, 5th ed., revised by Jefferson Morgan (1976): list of selections.

‡   J.   Peter Quimme, *Signet Book of American Wine*, 3d ed. (1980): list of selections.

§   K.   *California Grapevine*, ed. Nicholas Ponomareff, vols. 3–8 (1977–83): highest average rankings.

§   L.   *Connoisseur's Guide to California Wines*, ed. Charles Olken and Earl Singer, vols. 2–7 (1977–83): highest average rankings.

§   M.   *Robert Finigan's Private Guide to Wines*, ed. Robert Finigan, vols. 5–10 (1977–83): highest average rankings.

§   N.   *Underground Wineletter*, ed. John Tilson, vols. 1–4 (1979–83): highest average rankings

§   O.   Los Angeles County Fair Competition: largest number of awards.

§   P.   Orange County Fair Wine Competition: largest number of awards.

§   Q.   *San Jose Mercury-News* Wine Competition: largest number of awards.

*   A, B, C, D: Vintages of the 1950s.

†   E, F, G, H: Vintages of the 1960s.

‡   I, J: Vintages of the 1970s.

§   K, L, M, N, O, P: Vintages of 1975–79 (Tables 8, 12, 14), of 1976–80 (Table 6), and of 1977–81 (Table 10).

ZINFANDEL *concluded*

in wines that age gracelessly in my cellar when they are not overwhelming good food on my dinner table. My only standard in wine is how well it fits what I eat. We critics, all of us, are transparent, easier to solve than commuter crossword puzzles.

Some of us look at wine only as a food. Some only want the tasting game. Most want a little of each. In any case, for critics and normal people alike, wine comes down to a handful of points that make us each and every one an open book. Those points, a majority of them common to many foods, are: alcohol, sugar-acid balance, tannin, fruit flavors, and, latterly, wood flavors. Alcohol is prominent enough to light its characteristic little fire in the back of the throat, or not. A good many people want the sensation. A good many do not. Most lean one way or the other consistently. Sugar can be tasted as sweet, or it cannot. It may be the number one factor in the choices of a majority of all wine drinkers, who, again, tend to be habitual in liking a little or not wanting any in their dinner wines. Because of wine's acids, it may remind one of the feel of grapefruit juice at one extreme, or be as flat as yesterday's cola at the other. Some people like tart, some like bland, most like the middle road. The puckering powers of tannin divide the world of red wine drinkers into two camps in the same way as sugars and acids. Forcible amounts of oak evoke yes or no responses, too. This much is simple and steady. Fruit flavors are harder to be categorical about. Some pungently aromatic varieties—Gewürztraminer and Sauvignon Blanc—are sought or shunned on their basic character. In most cases, though, the sum of the parts wins or loses on tongues of critics, connoisseurs, and beginners. The excuses all come later.

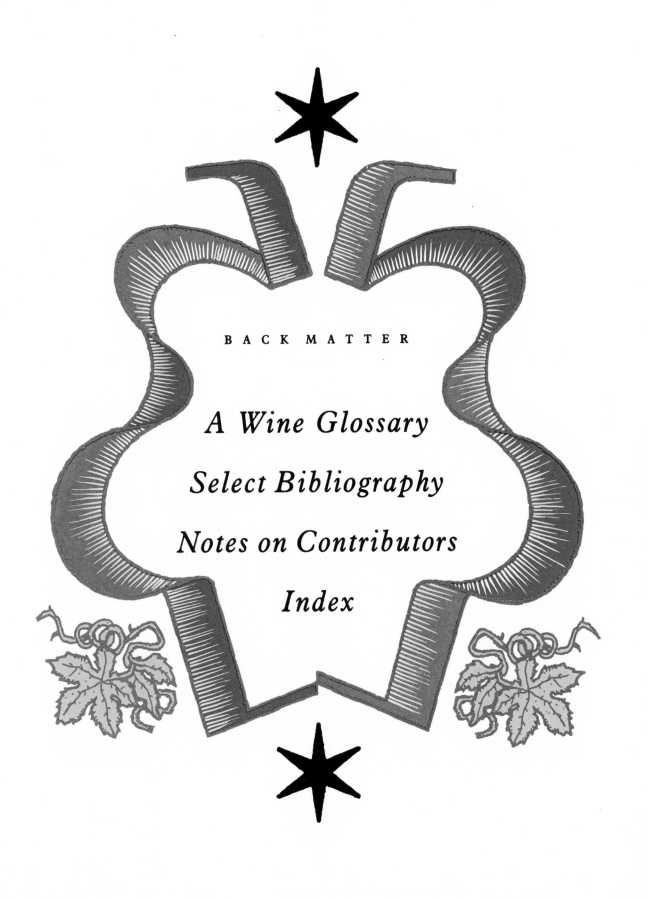

BACK MATTER

A Wine Glossary

Select Bibliography

Notes on Contributors

Index

A WINE GLOSSARY

THIS GLOSSARY DEFINES PARTICULAR WORDS AND TERMS found in the book and provides a general wine vocabulary that includes common foreign terms and the language most frequently employed in wine tasting and sensory evaluation.

DORIS MUSCATINE

A

Acetaldehyde: The most important of the aldehydes produced in the course of fermentation, a distinctive and favorable component of sherry, but undesirable in other wines.

Acetic: Vinegary in smell due to excessive acetic acid, the main component of vinegar. See VOLATILE ACIDITY.

Acetobacter: The microorganism that produces acetic acid (vinegar).

Acid: A component of grape juice and wines. The most important acids present are malic, tartaric, succinic, lactic, and citric.

Acidic: See SOUR.

Acidity: The total of the natural acids contained in wine. Wines low in acid taste flat; those high in acid taste sharp.

Aeration: The deliberate addition of oxygen during the winemaking process.

Aftertaste: The flavor that lingers in the mouth after tasting a wine.

Agglomerated cork: A champagne cork made of pieces glued together and finished at the end with a round of high-quality cork.

Aging: The final process in winemaking of holding wines for a period of time to allow some of the components to mature and change beneficially.

Alcohol: Ethanol, or ethyl alcohol, formed during fermentation, one of the major components of wine. Other alcohols can also be present in lesser concentrations, generally recognizable by their fusel oil odor, an undesirable quality when in excess.

Alcohol by volume: The percentage of alcohol contained in a wine by volume, declared by law on the label. Table wines cannot contain more than 14 percent; dessert and fortified wines (legally the same) contain more than 14 percent but not more than 24 percent, although wines of more than 21 percent are not normally found on the market.

538

Alcoholic: High in alcohol, causing a slightly burning sensation in the mouth usually described as hot.

Aldehydes: Produced during the fermentation of sugar to alcohol, aldehydes contribute to the flavor and quality of wine, but in excess are undesirable.

Altar wine: Those wines made exclusively for sacramental use according to laws set down by the church.

Amelioration: The legal addition of sugar, water, and/or acid to balance deficiencies in wine.

Amino acids: Constituents of proteins (sometimes called "nature's building blocks") present in grape musts; they provide nutrients in the metabolism of yeast during fermentation.

Amontillado: An aged dry sherry.

Ampelography: Scientific description or classification of grape vines.

Anaheim disease: The old name for Pierce's disease, caused by a bacterium that attacks grapevines.

Anion exchange: A method of stabilizing wine by the exchange of ions for undesirable constituents.

Anthocyanins: Red pigments.

AOC: See APPELLATION D'ORIGINE CONTRÔLÉE.

Aperitif: A wine generally drunk before a meal, also called appetizer wine.

Appearance: One of the categories by which a wine can be judged by sensory evaluation, generally including an assessment of clarity, cloudiness, deposits, dullness, and similar conditions.

Appellation d'origine contrôlée (AOC): The label term for French wines that guarantees their geographic delimitation and standard of quality.

Appellation of origin: In the United States, a general term for the label designations that indicate geographic origins of bottled wines that meet specific legal requirements. Any wine, at least 75 percent of which is made of grapes grown in the area designated on its label and that conforms to the laws and regulations relevant there, is entitled to a country, state, or county appellation. In the case of multistate or multicounty appellations, all of the grapes must come from the areas named and the percentages noted on the label. Wines made at least 85 percent from grapes grown in delimited viticultural areas of distinguishable geographic features and defined boundaries are entitled to an appellation naming that region. Imported wines must conform to the local laws in force in their place of origin.

Appley: A descriptive term for a smell and flavor generally associated with white wines, particularly burgundy types, and derived from malic acid.

Arginine: An amino acid, the presence of which can be monitored for the nutritional information it gives about the vine.

Aroma: The smell that derives from the grapes.

Aromatic: A spicy, abundant aroma.

Ascescence: Acetic acid and ethyl acetate, which produce a vinegary smell.

Ascorbic acid: Vitamin C, sometimes used as an antioxidant in the winemaking process to prevent browning.

Astringent: Harsh and puckery in the mouth, an effect generally caused by excessive tannin.

ATF: The Bureau of Alcohol, Tobacco and Firearms (also BATF).

Auslese: (Literally, selection); a German designation for wine made from specially selected grape bunches high in sugar.

Austere: Lacking modulation and softness.

Autolysis: The self-digestion of yeast by enzymes contained in it.

B

Baked: An acceptable odor characteristic of such wines as sherry, but a negative quality in table wines or sweet wines that have been overcooked. Also, in California, a process for making sherry by storing the wine for several months in large vats kept at high temperatures either by heating the cellar in which they are stored or by circulating hot water through coils in the containers. Baking can also be achieved by leaving the containers in the sun over an extended period.

Balance: An equilibrium among the taste and odor components of a wine in which no characteristic is disharmonious.

Balling: A system for measuring the sugar content (as dissolved solids) of juice or wine, expressed as degrees Balling. Called after the man who devised it, the name is pronounced as in "balance." For all purposes the same as BRIX.

Balthazar: An enormous bottle containing the equivalent of sixteen normal bottles, used for champagne.

Barrel-fermented: Wine that has undergone fermentation in small casks as opposed to very large ones.

BATF: The Federal Bureau of Alcohol, Tobacco and Firearms (sometimes ATF).

Beerenauslese: (Berry-selection); in Germany, overripe, high-sugar grapes selected individually from choice bunches, and the wine made from them.

Bench-grafted: Vines grafted to rootstock, then developed in greenhouses and field nurseries, and planted while still dormant.

Bentonite: A type of clay used in fining or clarifying wine by settling out solid substances through adsorption.

Berrylike: A term used to describe the aroma and flavor of some red wines.

Big: Full-bodied, robust wines, often high in alcohol.

Binning: Storing premium bottled wine (before its release for sale) for six months to several years to obtain the benefits of aging in the bottle.

Bitter: A taste that when excessive is a detraction, but which in moderation can add agreeable complexity and balance to wines of strong fruity flavors; usually derived from the stems and seeds.

Black grapes: Same as red or purple grapes.

Blanc de blancs: Usually sparkling wine made entirely of Chardonnay (occasionally of other whites) rather than the more traditional blend of black and white grapes.

Blanc de noirs: A white wine made from black grapes, with a blush, or deeper tone than a white wine from white grapes. Frequently used for sparkling wine.

Blend: To combine wines of different varieties or lots to add interest or harmony to the finished product; or a wine so made. Many winemakers also blend the free-run with the pressed juice for balance and complexity.

Bloom: The white, slightly waxy coating of the mature grape.

Bocksbeutel: A somewhat squat bottle traditionally or exclusively used for the wines of Franconia (Germany); similar bottles are used in Chile and Portugal.

Body: The amount of fullness or substance perceived as a tactile experience, dependent on alcohol: the higher the alcohol, the more viscous the wine.

Bonded: Legal winemaking or warehousing facilities under bond to the government for payment of taxes on the wine made or stored there.

Bone dry: Containing no residual sugar, in contrast to some wines labeled "dry," which often do. See NATURAL.

Botrytis cinerea: A mold, usually natural but sometimes induced, that pierces the skin of the grape, causing dehydration and a concentration of sugar. The intensity and richness of flavor that result are highly prized in some white dessert wines but disastrous in red wines. Also called noble rot, noble mold, and *pourriture noble*.

Bottle age: The mature characteristics of a wine attributable to the length of its stay in the bottle.

Bottle-aging: Keeping bottled wines for a period of time to allow some of the components to mature.

Bottle-fermented: A champagne or sparkling wine made either by the *méthode champenoise* or the transfer method.

Bottle sickness: A temporary condition following bottling, particularly of some white wines, which produces an unpleasant oxidized odor.

Bouquet: The part of the smell derived from the winemaking processes and aging, often developed in the bottle.

Boutique wineries: Those making premium, generally expensive, varietal wines, often from designated vineyards, on a relatively small scale of production.

Briary: A term used to describe a stemmy character in a wine.

Bright: When used to describe appearance, a clear wine.

Brilliant: Absolutely clear and free of particulates.

Brix: A measure of the sugar content. See BALLING.

Browning: A sign of aging, most often indicating that a wine has oxidized and is about to go, or has already gone, over the hill.

Brut: Champagne or sparkling wine that is very dry but may still contain a trace of sweetness.

Budwood: Well-developed canes bearing buds suitable for use in grafting or budding.

Bulk process: In making sparkling wine, a technique (also called "Charmat process") that uses large, covered containers for the secondary fermentation, a less expensive method for production in large quantities.

Bulk wine: Generally, less expensive wines sold in large containers or jugs. Some large producers buy bulk wines from other wineries and blend, bottle, and distribute them under their own labels.

Bung: A plug for stoppering a wine cask.

Bung hole: A small opening in a cask through which wine can be put in or taken out.

Burnt: An odor characteristic of wines that have been baked too long.

Butt: A wine barrel or cask of moderately large capacity.

Buttery: An odor in wine reminiscent of butter.

Butyric: An off, or slightly spoiled, odor produced by bacterial action.

C

California bottle: Also called composite bottle, designed for universal use for wines made in California.

Candle: To test the clarity of wine by looking at it with a candle or other light held behind the bottle.

Cane: The woody, mature state of the shoot (new growth) of the vine.

Canopy: The "umbrella" formed by the foliage of the vine.

Cap: The crust consisting of skins that forms on top of the juice during fermentation. In order to extract the color and to prevent spoilage, the cap must frequently be submerged by punching down or by covering with juice pumped from the bottom.

Capsule: The molded plastic or metallic material that fits over the cork and part of the neck of a wine bottle.

Caramel: A cooked odor in sweet sherries or similar wines, produced by baking.

Carbonated: Wines infused with carbon dioxide to make them bubbly.

Carbon dioxide (CO_2): A gas formed during fermentation, but undesirable when remaining or recurring, except in sparkling wines or those meant to be effervescent.

Carbonic maceration: The fermentation of uncrushed whole grapes, which takes place partly inside the berries, some of which break down by their own weight, others by the action of the internal fermentation. The resulting light, intensely fruity, low tannin wines are mildly effervescent, an effect of the carbon dioxide produced in the process, and are meant for early drinking. Nouveau-style wines are made by this process.

Casse: An undesirable opaque or cloudy quality.

Cation exchanger: A long column, used in the ion exchange process to replace potassium with sodium or hydrogen as a means of stabilizing wine.

Cave: In France, a wine storage cellar.

Centrifuge: A machine used to clarify wine or must.

Chai(s): A French term for above ground areas for wine storage.

Chambrer: To allow red wines to come up to room temperature.

Chamfered corks: Those with beveled ends.

Chapitalization: The addition of sugar to must, legal in such areas as Burgundy, but not permitted in California.

Charmat process: The same as bulk process for making sparkling wines.

Chateau-type: A term without legal definition but sometimes used in the United States to indicate a sweet, dessert-style table wine.

Chewy: A term for big, heavy-bodied wines, viscous enough to seem almost chewable.

Citrusy: Having a taste and odor reminiscent of citrus fruits.

cl (centilitre): 1/100th of a litre.

Clean: A wine without obvious faults.

Clear: A wine of good clarity but not quite brilliant (without any suspended solids).

Clone: (1) The propagation of a group of plants from a single source to perpetuate selected characteristics or special attributes; (2) the variety so produced.

Closed-in: A wine that has yet to release its potential qualities.

Closures: Materials such as corks or metal screw-on caps used to close bottles.

Cloudy: A hazy appearance indicating the often unwanted presence of suspended matter, sometimes resulting from poor winemaking techniques, but characteristic also of some unfined or unclarified wines.

Cloying: Having an exaggerated sweetness, unbalanced and unpleasantly excessive.

Coarse: Rough, without finesse.

Cold-fermented: White wines fermented in containers whose temperatures are controlled internally or with jackets.

Cold stabilization: A technique of chilling wine before bottling to cause the precipitation of harmless potassium acid tartrate crystals or other sediment that might later cause haziness or deposits.

Colloid: A substance that may produce haze in a wine that has not been colloid-stabilized.

Color: A component of wine derived primarily from the grape, typical and describable for each variety. The color sometimes indicates too high pH, certain metals, excessive aging, too much or too little sulfur dioxide, or underripe grapes. White wines vary from pale straw to yellow to gold to amber; reds from pink to claret to ruby to purple.

Complex: Containing varied components or having nuances not usually found in ordinary wines.

Composite bottle: A recent design intended for use in California for all varieties, but not yet widely adopted; also called the California or universal bottle.

Concentrate: A reduction of grape juice by evaporation often used in home winemaking or in areas where fresh grapes are unobtainable.

Controlled fermentation: A fermentation whose progress is altered by adjustment of temperature or pressure.

Cooked: An odor in wine similar to baked.

Cooperage: Containers for storing wine, usually barrels, casks, and tanks of wood or steel.

Corky: A faulty smell or flavor derived from a fungus-infected or chemically tainted cork.

Crackling: A wine produced by the bulk, or Charmat, process or by artificial carbonation, that is bubbling but not as vigorously as champagne or sparkling wine.

Cradle: A device for holding a bottle of wine to allow pouring without stirring up any sediment.

Cream: A full-bodied, usually golden, sweet sherry used mostly as a dessert wine.

Cream of tartar: Potassium bitartrate, sometimes the cause of cloudiness or harmless crystalline deposits in wine.

Cross: A hybrid of two grapes of the same or different species.

Cru(s): In France, the designation for an outstanding vineyard (literally, growth).

Crush: The specific process of breaking the grape skins to begin fermentation. Used generally, as "the crush," it designates the total procedure of winemaking steps preceding fermentation.

Crusher: Usually a stemmer-crusher, a machine that macerates the grapes after destemming them.

Cruvinet: A French invention now coming into use in the United States, installed as part of the back bar; it displays and dispenses a variety of bottled wines, keeping them at the proper temperature and preventing their spoilage by replacing the wine withdrawn with nitrogen gas.

Cultivar: A variety of grapevine.

Culture: A growth of organisms such as yeast that may be used to inoculate crushed grapes to aid fermentation.

Cutting: A segment of a cane or shoot that will develop into a new plant when grown under favorable conditions.

Cuvée: A specific blend of wines, often of different varieties, combined in the final lot; generally used in making sparkling wine but occasionally also in producing table wine.

D

Decant: To pour the clear wine off the sediment or deposits in a bottle, generally necessary only for older wines and those made without fining or clarifying.

Delicate: Lighter, less assertive wine.

Demi-sec: Moderately to medium sweet, generally applied to sparkling wines.

Demijohn: A large glass container often of about 5-gallon size, sometimes with a wicker wrapping.

Deposit: The sediment in a wine that precipitates with age.

Depth: Intensity.

Dessert wine: Wine of more than 14 percent but not more than 24 percent alcohol, fortified with grape brandy or neutral grape spirits; also commonly any sweet wine used to accompany dessert, such as high-sugar Late Harvest wines, those from grapes infected with *Botrytis cinerea*, and those made from raisined grapes.

Diatomaceous earth: A light, friable material derived from fossilized microscopic algae (diatoms) used as a filter in clarifying wine.

Dirty: Off-flavors and odors resulting from a faulty winemaking process or poor equipment.

Disgorge: In the making of sparkling wine, to eliminate the accumulated sediment in the neck of the bottle by freezing it, uncorking the bottle, and using the pressure of the gas in the wine to eject the sediment.

dl: Deciliter, one-tenth of a liter.

Dosage: In the making of sparkling wine, usually brandy and wine, or wine, mixed with sugar, used to replace the wine lost in the disgorging of sediment.

Dry: Generally, without a sweet taste, but technically fermented to less than 0.2 percent residual sugar (the label term indicating totally dry is "bone dry").

Dull: When used to describe appearance, a hazy character, usually attributable to suspended matter in the wine.

Dumb: Used of a young wine whose attributes are not altogether released; the same effect is sometimes found in wines served too cold.

E

Earthy: An undesirable flavor suggestive of earth or soil.

Elegant: A term based on purely subjective criteria, generally used to imply that a wine is harmonious and has finesse and complexity.

Enology (also spelled oenology): The science of viniculture or winemaking.

Enzyme: An organic compound produced by a living organism (such as yeast) that causes fermentation and other chemical changes.

Essence: A red wine of very high sugar content, usually from Late Harvest grapes.

Estate bottled: A wine produced solely from grapes grown on land owned and controlled by and in the same viticultural area as the winery making it, as well as being made entirely on the premises.

Ester: A volatile compound, produced by the interaction of alcohol and acid, that adds nuances to the taste and smell of wine.

Ethyl acetate: A component of the vinegary smell in acetic wines.

Ethyl alcohol, ethanol: A product of the conversion of sugar by yeast enzymes during the process of fermentation.

Extraction: In winemaking, drawing out and dissolving the pigments and other solubles in the skins, seeds, pulp, and occasionally stems, which are kept in continuous contact with the juice.

Extra dry: A champagne or sparkling wine that is, contrary to its designation, generally sweet, containing 1.5 to 2.5 percent sugar.

Eye of the Partridge: The rose color of some wines such as Blanc de Noirs, white wines made from black grapes.

Eye of the Swan: A proprietary name for Eye of the Partridge.

F

Faded: A wine with a somewhat oxidized character.

Fat: A tactile quality of a wine that is full-bodied and rich.

Fermentation: The conversion by yeast enzymes of the grape sugar in the must or juice into alcohol and carbon dioxide.

Fermentor: A large container in which fermentation takes place.

Fiasco (fiaschi): A type of wine bottle, often covered with raffia.

Field-budded: See FIELD-GRAFTED.

Field-grafted: Budwood grafted to rootstock in the vineyard in late summer or early fall. Also called field-budded.

Field sampling: Checking the sugar level, acidity, and other factors relevant to maturity in a representative selection of grapes, to determine when the fruit in a vineyard is ready to harvest.

Fifth: A wine bottle containing one-fifth of a gallon, or 25.6 ounces, the most widely employed size in the United States until 1 January 1979, when new regulations made it mandatory to use liter measures.

Filter: To clarify wine after fermentation by removing suspended matter such as yeast cells with the aid of porous membranes; also the porous material used in the process. Filtration is the process of clarifying wine with filters.

Finesse: A nonspecific but complimentary term that conveys general elegance, balance, and good winemaking, among other subjective judgments.

Fining: The process of clarifying wine by employing such agents as gelatin, egg whites, bentonite (clay) and, more rarely, isinglass, that adsorb or carry along most of the other suspended matter with them as they settle to the bottom.

Finish: The lingering aftertaste of a wine, varying from long to short to none, smooth to rough, hot (alcoholic) to flat (low acid) to puckery (tannic).

Finishing: The processes involved in clarifying wine before it is bottled.

Fino: A type of sherry, light and on the dry side, produced by the *flor* method of growing a film of yeast on the wine's surface that gives the wine a distinctive aroma and flavor.

First-growth: A designation applied to Bordeaux clarets from the Médoc that ranked highest in the 1855 official French classifications. The same as PREMIER CRU.

Flat: Lacking sourness in the taste; characteristic of low acid wines.

Flavored wines: Aperitif wines such as vermouth that are flavored with spices, herbs, and other pungent substances.

Flor: A yeast of the species *saccharomyces fermentati*, *Saccharomyces capensis*, or *Saccharomyces bayanus*, that produces a filmy cap or "flowering" during the production of sherry, and imparts a distinctive flavor. Wine so flavored is called *flor* sherry.

Flowery: Aromas and flavors, usually in white wines, that are reminiscent of flowers.

Flûte: (1) Tall, long-necked green bottle obligatory for wines from Alsace, but also used, in clear glass, for rosé from France; (2) the traditional tall, narrow glass for serving sparkling wine.

Foil: See CAPSULE.

Fortified: Any wine, but most frequently sherry, port, and so-called dessert wine, in which, by the addition of spirits or brandy, the alcohol content has been increased to more than 14 percent and not more than 24 percent and the fermentation halted before all of the sugar has been converted. Normally, wines on the retail market are well below 24 percent.

Foxy: A flavor associated with native American grapes of the *Vitis labrusca* species, such as Concord.

Fractional blending: The solera system, a process that blends wines of several years so that each receives a wine from a younger year, the finished wine finally containing some of all of them.

Free-run: In pressing, the crush juice that runs free from the press before force is used.

Fresno odor: Also called "rubber boot" odor, typical of high pH wines, particularly from the Central Valley, in which bacterial spoilage may be less inhibited.

Fructose: Along with glucose, one of the principal sugars in wine.

Fruity: A flavor or aroma that is strongly of the grapes, usually characteristic of young wines.

Full-bodied: Feeling full in the mouth, a measure of the viscosity contributed by a wine's high alcohol content.

Fusel oils: Certain higher alcohols that, in excess, contribute an undesirable odor to wine.

G

Gassy: An undesirable bubbly effect usually produced by the carbon dioxide from an unwanted secondary fermentation that takes place after bottling.

Gelatin: A protein used in fining or clarifying wine.

Generic: Wines named after general categories (red or white table wine) and place-names (Burgundy, Rhine, Sherry [Jerez], Champagne), although the latter are technically known in the United States as semi-generic.

Geranium: An undesirable odor resembling that of geraniums; it comes from the action of bacteria on sorbic acid.

Glucose: One of the two principal sugars in wine, the other being fructose.

Glycerol (glycerine): A component of wine.

Graft: To splice a varietal vine to a rootstock of another type, usually one that is resistant to particular predators or diseases; sometimes used to change the variety. Also, the union or spliced portion of a plant so treated.

Grassy: A characteristic flavor or aroma of some wines, which, in moderation, adds interest.

Green: A color sometimes present in pale-colored whites; a flavor generally associated with young wines made from underripe fruit.

Green-olive: The odor widely associated with Cabernet Sauvignon.

Gris, vin gris: A rosé wine.

Gun-flint: A somewhat metallic taste or smell.

H

Hardening: When applied to canes, the state of dormancy.

Harsh: A wine high in astringency.

Hazy: See CLOUDY.

Heat summation: A University of California, Davis, system for measuring seasonally the cumulative average daily temperatures above 10°C (50°F) in the grape-growing regions of California, a useful gauge in making decisions on the best locations for varietal plantings. Also called temperature summation.

Herbaceous: An agreeable odor reminiscent of herbs, generally associated with Sauvignon Blancs and Cabernet Sauvignons, but sometimes an excessive off-odor indicating faulty winemaking.

Hock bottle: Used for German and Alsatian wines; or a bottle of that tall, long-necked style.

Hot: High in alcohol, producing a slight burning sensation on the palate, generally undesirable except in dessert-style wines.

Hybrid: A new grape variety developed by crossing two or more varieties or species.

Hydrogen sulfide: Responsible for the undesirable odor of rotten eggs in a wine.

Hydrometer: An instrument used to measure the amount of sugar in grape juice.

I

Imperial: An oversized bottle with the capacity of eight normal bottles, used for red wines.

Inoculation: The addition of a yeast starter to wine must to begin fermentation; or of a bacterium to cause a malolactic fermentation.

Ion exchange: A method used when there is excessive potassium that may cause the formation of crystals (bitartrate precipitates) after bottling. The potassium is replaced by cations, which have more soluble acid tartrates.

IPM: Integrated pest management of a vineyard, using a multilevel attack.

Isinglass: A gelatinous material, obtained from the air bladders of sturgeon and other fish, that is used in clarifying wine.

J

Jammy: A fruity, berrylike aroma or taste, usually in high-sugar Late Harvest grapes, concentrated enough to suggest the flavor of jam.

Jeroboam: An oversized bottle containing the equivalent of six normal bottles, generally used for red wine. A jeroboam of champagne, however, is four-bottle size.

Jug wines: Generally less expensive, generic wines sold in large containers, although varietals are more and more frequently included.

K

Kcal: Kilocalorie or kilogram calorie.

Kick: See PUNT.

Kosher wine: Sacramental wine certified by an official council to have been harvested and produced according to specific rules under rabbinical supervision.

L

l: Liter.

Labrusca: *Vitis labrusca*, the common grape species native to America and found on the East Coast.

Lactic acid: Produced in wine as a conversion of malic acid during a secondary, or malolactic, fermentation, generally lowering the total acidity and adding to the complexity of red wine.

Lactone: A component of the aroma of wines derived from barrels of oak and other woods.

Late Harvest: Most often, but not exclusively, a white wine whose high level of sugar at harvest is the result of *Botrytis cinerea*; usually drunk as a dessert wine. Also used of some Zinfandels from grapes picked at high levels of sugar.

Lees: The yeast residue that settles to the bottom during fermentation. Wines that are left too long before racking can pick up the odor of lees.

Legs: The same as "tears," the weeping or drops that have inched up the inside surface of the glass above the wine and run slowly back down.

Lignins: Components of oak including vanillin, one of the products of oxidation, that contribute to the aromas of wines aged in barrels.

Linalool: The flowery odor associated with Muscat grapes.

Long: A term to describe the desirable finish of a wine.

M

Made and bottled by: Legally only designates that at least 10 percent of the wine in the bottle was fermented at the winery.

Maderized: Wines oxidized to the point of browning, with a Madeira-like odor not desirable in table wines.

Magnum: A bottle that contains the equivalent of two normal bottles.

Malic acid: The acid in wine that converts to lactic acid during a secondary, or malolactic, fermentation.

Malolactic fermentation: A secondary fermentation, often occurring naturally, that converts malic to lactic acid and carbon dioxide, adding complexity to red wines and to some Chardonnays; undesirable if it occurs or continues in the bottle, trapping gas and off-odors.

Marriage: A blending, or marrying, of two or more lots of still wine.

Matchstick: A term used to describe the burnt match odor of excess sulfur dioxide, most often found in young white wine.

Mercaptan: An offensive off-odor of methyl and ethyl sulfides.

Metallic: A taste suggestive of, but not necessarily caused by, metal.

Méthode champenoise: The classic method of making Champagne by completing the second fermentation, clarification, and other processes in the same bottle in which it is marketed.

Methuselah: A large bottle for Champagne containing the equivalent of eight ordinary bottles.

mg/l: Milligrams per liter.

Microclimate: The climate within a small area that differs from the climate in the larger area around it.

Mildew: A fungus that is a major problem in quality vineyard control. The odor from heavily mildewed grapes is often transmitted to the wine.

Mist propagation: A recently introduced technique to speed up the growth of vine cuttings that depends on temperature control and humidity (mist).

ml: Milliliter, one-thousandth of a liter.

MOG: Material other than grapes, such as leaves, weeds, and insects, that becomes mixed with them during the harvest.

Mold: A fungus growth usually detrimental to grapes. The major exception is *Botrytis cinerea*, the noble mold or noble rot, which is responsible in moderation for the great sweet French Sauternes, German Rieslings, and Late Harvest California white dessert wines.

Moldy: Grapes, containers, and corks that have become moldy usually transmit that unpleasant odor to the wine with which they are in contact.

Mousy: In wine, a disagreeable odor suggestive of something spoiled.

Must: The juice and pulp produced by crushing or pressing grapes before fermentation.

Musty: A dank, old-attic smell, attributed to unclean storage containers and sometimes to grapes processed in a moldy condition.

N

Natural: In sparkling wine, the driest designation; given to wine made without the addition of the usual *dosage* of sugar and brandy.

Nebuchadnezzar: A giant bottle containing the equivalent of twenty regular bottles.

Négociant: A shipper of wine.

Nematodes: Vineyard pests that in their larval form attack vine roots, stunting the growth of the plant.

Noble mold, noble rot: Botrytis cinerea, a fungus that attacks grapes causing a loss of moisture and a concentration of sugar that increases the intensity of flavor. Advantageous in moderation in white grapes but undesirable in red.

Nose: The smell of the wine, including both the aroma and the bouquet.

Nouveau: A young wine meant for immediate drinking, generally produced by carbonic maceration.

Nutty: A madeira, or baked, flavor, desirable in dessert or appetizer wines such as sherry, but unpleasant in table wines, where it occurs as a result of oxidation.

O

Oaky: Toasty and vanilla smells and flavors contributed during barrel aging by the oak.

Odors: Among the terms used to describe the odors of wine are flowery, fruity, yeasty or beerlike, rancio, leafy, green, vegetative, herbaceous, like sauerkraut, wet straw, wet wool, caramel, sunburned, peppery, nutty, oaky, woody, moldy, cigar boxy, mousy, musty, minty, geraniumlike, citrusy, raisiny, like eucalyptus, green-olive, fusel oil (higher alcohols), rubber boot (Fresno), and like berries, apples, peaches, figs, melons, truffles, and violets.

Oenology: See ENOLOGY.

Off-dry: Very slightly sweet.

Off-odors: Generally unpleasant odors, such as the tanky or moldy smells from unclean storage containers, that suggest a problem in the finished wine. Common off-odors include green, vegetative, or leafy ones, and sauerkraut, rotten egg, mousy, wet straw, wet wool, rubber boot, and excessive sulfur dioxide ones.

Oïdium: Powdery mildew.

Oloroso: A type of sherry, from light to dark in color, according to age, and usually sweetened and grapey, produced without the use of *flor* (a growth of yeast on the surface). The sweeter styles are called "cream" sherries.

Onion skin: The deep, tawny pink of some rosé wines; also the slight browning of old red wines; *pelure d'oignon* in French.

Overcropping: In viticulture, encouraging too large a yield per acre.

Own-rooted: Vines that have not been grafted but are on their own rootstock.

Oxalate: One of the constituents of wine that can form a precipitate by combining with other components, causing cloudiness.

Oxidation: The changes in wine caused by exposure to air, sometimes beneficial, but often undesirable, especially when excessive.

Oxidized: Wine that has changed by contact with air, usually producing undesirable browning and sherrylike flavors (chemically, largely acetaldehyde).

P

Particulates: Solid matter in suspension in wine, often contributing to a hazy or cloudy appearance.

Pétillant: Another term for spritzy, bubbly, effervescent, or crackling.

Petiole: The leaf stem.

Petiole analysis: A test to determine the nutritional needs of a given vine.

pH: The measure of hydrogen ions, or active acidity; the lower the pH, the higher the acidity.

Phenols: A group of compounds occurring naturally in wood and extracted from oak cooperage during aging that includes tannins, flavonoids, pigments, and colorless compounds.

Phylloxera: A highly destructive root louse that infests *Vitis vinifera,* but not some of the native American stock, most of which is resistant to it.

Pierce's disease: A disease of grapevines caused by a bacterium and spread by insects. Formerly called Anaheim disease.

Polyphenols: Tannins and related compounds.

Pomace: The solid residue after pressing.

"Pop" wines: Proprietary wines made from fruit bases, such as Ripple, Boone's Farm, Thunderbird, and others.

Potassium bitartrate: Cream of tartar, a by-product obtained from the pomace, or cake, left after pressing; also found in the crystals that sometimes precipitate in bottled wine.

Powdery mildew: Oïdium, one of several fungi that can cause severe damage to grape crops.

ppm: Parts per million.

ppsi: Pounds per square inch.

Precipitates: Substances separated from a solution in the form of solids.

Premier: See NOUVEAU.

Premier(s) cru(s): In France, the first-growth, or highest-ranked, vineyards in the Médoc region of Bordeaux, according to the official classification of 1855.

Press: To exert pressure on crushed grapes to extract their juices. Also, a hand-operated or mechanical device used in the process. The four common types are a vertical, hand-operated, wooden basket press; a horizontal, mechanical, metal basket press; a horizontal, pneumatic air-pressure (or bladder) press, including a tank press; and a continuous press that allows uninterrupted feeding and juice removal.

Press wine: The wine obtained by pressing in a machine.

Pricked: The sensation associated with the vinegary taste of acetic acid.

Primordia: The initial stages of the fruiting flowers in a grape bud.

Private reserve: Because there is no legal definition, this term on a label generally, but not necessarily, indicates that the wine is of special quality, above the ordinary run. Same as PROPRIETOR'S RESERVE and SPECIAL SELECT.

Produced and bottled by: Legally designates that 75 percent or more of the wine was fermented and clarified at the winery named on the label.

Proprietary wines: Those bearing fanciful names such as Rhine Castle, Rubion, or Ripple, usually registered as a trademark by the brand owner.

Proprietor's reserve: See PRIVATE RESERVE.

Pruning: Cutting back the vegetative part of the vine after it has become dormant, a process that affects the size, and therefore the quality, of the next year's crop. In California, the three most frequently used systems are head training (with spurs), cane pruning, and cordon pruning.

Puckery: A tactile sensation in highly tannic wines.

Pulp: The flesh of the grape or other fruit.

Pump over: To circulate wine from the bottom of the container over the top of the cap, or crust, that forms during fermentation, thus ensuring optimal extraction from the grape solids and inhibiting bacterial spoilage.

Punch down: To push the cap that forms on the surface of fermenting wine down into the juice.

Puncheon: A large wooden cask for storing wine.

Punt: The indentation in the bottom of some wine bottles. Also called kick.

PVPP: Polyvinylpolypyrrolidone, a synthetic proteinlike material, used in removing substances in white wines that cause browning.

R

Racking: Syphoning or pumping wine from one container to another to clarify it by leaving the sediment behind.

Raisiny: Tasting like raisins, often the result of a wine being made from overripe grapes.

Rancio: In sherry, a desirable odor that develops with age and oxidation, but not an attribute in table wines with the exception of some sweet red wines with a high alcohol content.

Refractometer: An instrument for measuring the sugar content of grape juice by refraction.

Regions I–V: A classification by the University of California at Davis of the winegrowing areas of the state by their measure of heat during the growing season.

Rehoboam: An outsized bottle with a capacity of six regular bottles, used for champagne.

Residual sugar: Sugar that remains unconverted in the wine after fermentation.

Rhine bottle: A tall, long-necked bottle used for German and Alsatian wines, and in the United States for wines made in those styles.

Riddler: A person who turns, or riddles, bottles of sparkling wine to accumulate the sediment in the neck for removal before final corking.

Riddling: A method used at the end of the bottle fermentation of sparkling wine to encourage the yeast sediment toward the cork for later disgorgement. The process, which can take between a week and a month, consists of placing the bottles neck down in special racks and spinning them individually about an eighth of a turn daily. Now often done mechanically.

Riddling rack: The rack designed to hold bottles of sparkling wine in the proper position for riddling, or turning. Also called A-rack, after its shape.

Rootstock: The part of the grapevine that is planted directly in the soil. A different bearing variety is often later grafted to rootstock resistant to disease.

Ropy: Wines with an undesirable gelatinous quality.

Rotten egg: The term most often used to describe the odor of excessive hydrogen sulfide.

Rough: The tactile experience applied generally to young tannic red wines before they have begun to round out.

Rubber boot, or rubbery: See FRESNO ODOR.

Ruby: A style of port, generally on the young side and rather sweet.

S

Saccharometer, saccarometer: A device for measuring the percentage of sugar in crushed grapes.

Saccharomyces cerevisiae: One of the two predominant species of yeasts found in grapes and wines throughout the world (the other being *Kloeckera apiculata*), embracing most of the strains used or occurring in wine fermentations. Among the yeast strains used commercially in California are Burgundy, Champagne, Montrachet, Tokay, and Steinberg.

Sacramental wine: See ALTAR WINE.

Salmanazar: A very large bottle with a capacity of twelve normal bottles.

Sauerkraut: An off-odor from the growth of lactic acid bacteria following excessive malo-lactic fermentation.

Scion: A cutting used in grafting, containing a bud of the desired vine.

Seasoning: Conditioning barrels either by washing with mildly neutralizing solutions or by first using them to process other than premium wines.

Sec: Somewhat dry, except in sparkling wines, where it means medium sweet to sweet.

Secondary fermentation: A fermentation that takes place either spontaneously or by design after the completion of the primary fermentation. In the making of sparkling wine, the gas produced gives the wine its bubbles. In dry red wine, the malolactic fermentation lowers the total acidity and adds desirable nuances to the flavor, unless it occurs spontaneously after bottling. In most white wines, it is a fault.

Second crop: The less-ripe fruit that matures after the first crop has been picked. Also called second picking.

Sediment: Particulates that form deposits in some wines stored in containers, or, with age, in some bottled wines.

Select: Generally implying something special about a wine, but meaningless since there is no precise description.

Selected Late Harvest: Generally meaning a table wine made in a sweet dessert style. By law, the label must list the percentage of sugar at harvest and the amount of residual sugar, and it must state that the wine is "Late Harvest."

Semi-generic: Wines named after a geographical designation such as burgundy, moselle, or rhine.

Sensory evaluation: The systematic assessment of wine by sight (color and appearance), smell (aroma, bouquet, off-odors), taste (sweet, sour, bitter), and feel (viscosity, temperature, "pain" [burning, tingly, or prickly sensations]).

Settling: The natural precipitation of the solid matter in wine.

Shermat: The base wine used in making sherry by baking, by the submerged *flor* method, or by the surface process. From "sher" for sherry and "mat" for material.

Sherrified: See MADERIZED and OXIDIZED.

Shoot: A new growth of the vine.

Short: A term that suggests that the finish of a wine disappears too quickly or is not discernible.

Silky: Smooth.

Skin contact: The process of holding grapes and juice together for a period of time before pressing to obtain an extraction of color.

Slightly sweet: Containing a barely perceptible amount of residual sugar.

Slip skin: Grapes of the *Vitis labrusca* type common to the eastern United States, in which the skin separates or slips easily from the flesh.

Smoky: A smell and taste most often found in white wines.

Smooth: Wine without harshness on the palate.

Sodium bisulfite, sodium metabisulfite: In winemaking, sources of sulfur dioxide used as sterilants to prevent undesirable bacterial growth and unwanted oxidation.

Soft: Generally, a wine lacking tannin.

Solera: A system, used in the production of sherry and port, of continuous blending of wine of several years, employing tiers of casks arranged so that the amount of the oldest wine withdrawn from the bottom rank is replenished with the next oldest wine from the barrel above it, and so on to the youngest wine on the top. The finished wines are consistent in quality and age, and contain some wine from each year in the solera.

Sommelier: A wine steward.

Sorbic acid: Used as a sterilizing agent to prevent the growth of unwanted molds, and to inhibit secondary fermentations. When attacked by bacteria, its by-products are detectable as an undesirable geraniumlike odor.

Sour: A tart or acidic taste, often causing a sharp sensation in the mouth, desirable in small amounts but unpleasant in such abundance as is characteristic of wines very high in acid or made from underripe grapes.

Spalling: The pocking or erosion of uncoated or unlined concrete tanks.

Sparkling wines: Wines whose effervescence is produced by carbon dioxide captured during a second fermentation in the bottle or container in which it is made. The term applies to all champagne-style wines made outside the Champagne district in France.

Spätlese: (Late picking); in Germany, a designation for very ripe, sweet grapes picked at the end of the normal harvest; also the wine made from them.

Special natural wines: Made pursuant to formula, they must contain only natural ingredients. Sometimes referred to as "pop" wines.

Special select: See PRIVATE RESERVE.

Spicy: Smells and tastes akin to aromatic spices.

Spirits: Distilled alcohol used to fortify some wines, such as sherries, ports, and other dessert wines, by increasing their alcohol content.

Split: A wine bottle containing 6.4 ounces.

Spritzy: Wines with a minor amount of sparkle from carbonation, most often undesirable.

Spumante: Italian sparkling wine.

Stabilization: The process of causing the precipitation of unwanted substances, either by chilling or ion exchange in unbottled wine, so that they will not cause haziness or form crystals in the finished product.

Starter: Yeast used to start or ensure fermentation.

Stemmer: A machine that separates the stems from the grapes; when combined with a crusher, it is called a stemmer-crusher.

Stemmy: An odor of stems.

Still wines: All wines made without effervescence.

Stomates (stomata): The pores on the under part of a leaf through which carbon dioxide, air, and water are exchanged.

Stuck fermentation: An incomplete fermentation that stops before all the sugar has been converted to alcohol.

Sulfide: The same rotten egg odor as hydrogen sulfide.

Sulfur: Used to dust vineyards as a control for powdery mildew (oïdium).

Sulfur dioxide: A gas used to inhibit the growth of fungi on grapes. It gives an unpleasant odor to wine when present in noticeable quantities.

Sulfury: The smell of wines that have been treated during their production with excessive sulfur; it frequently dissipates.

Sweet: A flavor in wine, the appropriate intensity of which depends on the type of wine.

T

Table wine: In general, still, dry wine meant to accompany food, as opposed to special wines such as sparkling, appetizer, or dessert wine.

Tanky: An unpleasant musty odor and taste in a wine aged, stored, or left too long in an unclean tank.

Tannin: A polyphenolic compound derived from the skins, seeds, and stems of grapes, which gives young red wine an astringent, puckery quality, but contributes to its longevity and normally ameliorates as the wine ages. In excess, it causes a bitter taste.

Tart: Characterized by a desirable sour taste derived from the wine's acidity.

Tartrates: Salts of tartaric acid that can form harmless crystals in unstabilized bottled wine.

Taste: Technically limited to four categories: sour, bitter, sweet, and salt (seldom in wine). Many of the terms used to describe "taste" in wine are actually odors.

Tastevin, tâte-vin: Burgundian-style silver tasting cup.

Tawny: The amber or brownish color characteristic of some appetizer and some dessert wines, such as port, that have been aged in wood.

T-budding: A method of grafting a new variety to an existing plant.

Tears: See LEGS.

Temperature summation: See HEAT SUMMATION.

Thermovinification: In California, an experimental method of crushing red wine grapes and heating them to a high temperature to extract skin color and tannin, then cooling, pressing, and fermenting without the skins.

Thief: A tubular glass, plastic, or wooden instrument for withdrawing a sample of wine from a cask or barrel.

Thin: A wine lacking body because it is low in alcohol; sometimes described as watery.

Threshold (or absolute threshold): The concentration of any single component of wine at which it can be recognized by a taster.

Tinta: A style of California port, named after the "Tinta" grape, much the same as ruby—sweet and bright red in color.

Tirage: In making sparkling wine, the mixture of still or *cuvée* wine, yeast culture, and sugar drawn off into bottles or larger containers to undergo the secondary fermentation and allow the spent yeasts to settle out.

Tired: An oxidized wine.

Toasting: The caramelization of the staves of barrels, which affects the flavors of the wine aged in them.

Topping: A technique to control oxidation in containers by replacing wine lost through evaporation.

Total acid: Usually expressed as tartaric acid, the measure of total acid aids in such decisions as when to harvest, whether to blend to ameliorate tartness, and whether to clarify or stabilize the wine to prevent later crystallization.

Transfer process: A champagne and sparkling wine process that removes the wine from the bottle after fermentation for filtering in pressurized tanks before rebottling. Such wines are labeled "bottle fermented" or "fermented in the bottle," as opposed to "fermented in this bottle," often used on the more expensive *méthode champenoise* wines.

Trockenbeerenauslese: In Germany, individually selected Late Harvest grapes of the highest concentration of sugar and consequently the most expensive quality. Sometimes referred to as TBA.

Turbidity: Clouding because of suspended sediment, ranging from cloudy, the most affected, to dull, to clear. Brilliant is the term used for a wine with no suspended solid material.

U

Ullage: Leakage or evaporation of wine from its container, resulting in oxidation and often spoilage.

Unctuous: See CLOYING.

Unfiltered: A wine that has not gone through a filtering process to clarify it.

Unfined: A wine that has not gone through a fining process (the use of egg whites, bentonite, or gelatin) to clarify it.

Universal bottle: See COMPOSITE BOTTLE.

V

Vanillin: An extract of the oak used in aging wines, present in the smell and flavor.

Varietal wine: Since 1 January 1983, any wine named after and containing 75 percent or more of a *Vitis vinifera* grape variety, and grown in the appellation of origin appearing on the label (51 percent for native varieties and hybrids); prior to that date, any wine containing 51 percent or more of the named grape.

VDQS: See VIN DÉLIMITÉ DE QUALITÉ SUPÉRIEURE.

Vegetal: Containing such tastes and smells as bell peppers and asparagus, adding to the complexity of a wine in small amounts, but undesirable when excessive.

Velvety: Wine that is thick, soft, and smooth on the palate.

Vigneron: French term for a vineyardist.

Vin délimité de qualité supérieure: A designation that guarantees that the area of production and grapes used for certain French wines comply with strict legal definitions. Used for wines generally of less fine quality than those entitled to an *appellation contrôlée.*

Vinegary: The unpleasant odor produced by acetic acid.

Viniculture: The science of winemaking.

Vin ordinaire: A French term for wine for everyday drinking.

Vinous: Winelike.

Vin santo: An Italian-style dessert wine produced from dried or raisined grapes.

Vintage: Applied in the United States to wine in which at least 95 percent of the grapes come from the harvest of the year designated on the label. A vintage year is also one worthy of being specified on the label ("1976 was a vintage year"). In England, however, the vintage is the equivalent of the harvest. Vintage port is one that is aged in bottles rather than in wood.

Vintner: A person who makes or sells wine.

Vintner grown: Like "proprietor grown," a label designation informally approved for wineries that, through such technicalities as having facilities in two viticultural areas, are not entitled to use the term "estate bottled."

Virus disease–free: When applied to rootstock, free of obvious virus symptoms, although possibly not free of latent infection.

Virus-free: When applied to rootstock, entirely free of any virus disease as revealed by presently known indicators.

Viticultural area: Since 1 January 1983, a region described as having distinguishable geographic features and governmentally recognized and defined boundaries. Wines bearing a viticultural area designation on their labels must contain 85 percent of the grapes from that area.

Viticulture: The science of growing grapes.

Vitis labrusca: A native American grape whose wines are most commonly described as foxy or resembling Concord grape juice.

Vitis riparia: A native American grapevine resistant to the phylloxera louse and therefore used as rootstock for *Vitis vinifera* scions.

Vitis rotundifolia: A native American grape common to the South Atlantic coast; also known as muscadine.

Vitis rupestris: A native American grapevine used as disease resistant rootstock onto which European varieties can be grafted.

Vitis sativa: Any of the cultivated varieties of the *Vitis vinifera* species.

Vitis silvestris: A native American wild grape.

Vitis vinifera: The European–Middle Eastern grapevine from which most of the world's fine table wines are made.

Volatile acidity: A component derived from acetic acid along with ethyl acetate; in noticeable amounts, it gives the wine a vinegary quality.

W

Watery: See THIN.

Weeper: A bottle that has leaked because of an old or faulty cork, an indication that the wine inside may be spoiled.

White grapes: Without any red pigments.

Woody: Similar to oaky, the term applies to qualities derived from the barrel that can add nuances to wine in moderation but can overwhelm it when excessive.

Y

Yeasty: The smell of the yeast used in fermentation, attractive in modest amounts in young wines, but more often undesirable and frequently an indication that the wine is still undergoing a mild fermentation.

Select BIBLIOGRAPHY

LISTED BELOW are writings of a general nature that have been used in the preparation of this book, as well as some important works on wine, California and other, that are suggested for further reading. Specialized references and those relevant only to a particular section are given in the footnotes or in the bibliographic notes following individual essays. Several contributors to this volume have supplied annotations.

A

ADAMS, Leon D. *Revitalizing the California Wine Industry*. Berkeley: Regional Oral History Office, Bancroft Library, 1974. Early days of the industry by a very old hand. *R. B.*

ADAMS, Leon D. *The Commonsense Book of Wine*. 3d ed. Boston: Houghton Mifflin Co., 1975.

ADAMS, Leon D. *The Wines of America*. 1973. 2d ed., rev., New York: McGraw-Hill, 1978.

ALLEN, H. W. *A History of Wine*. London: Faber & Faber, 1961. An agreeably idiosyncratic account by a journalist, classical scholar, and connoisseur. *R. B.*

AMERINE, M. A. *The University of California and the State's Wine Industry*. Berkeley: Regional Oral History Office, Bancroft Library, 1972. Reviews the impact of the university's research. *M. A. A.*

AMERINE, M. A., ed. *Wine Production Technology in the United States*. American Chemical Society Symposium Series, no. 145. Washington, D.C.: ACS, 1981. Pre- and post-World War II technological advances. *M. A. A.*

AMERINE, M. A.; BERG, H. W.; KUNKEE, R. E.; OUGH, C. S.; SINGLETON, V. L.; and WEBB, A. D. *The Technology of Wine Making*. 4th ed. Westport, Conn.: AVI Publishing Co., 1980. Originally published as M. A. Amerine and W. V. Cruess, *The Technology of Wine Making* (1960), 2d ed., M. A. Amerine, H. W. Berg, and W. V. Cruess, *The Technology of Wine Making* (1967). The standard U.S. text. *M. A. A.*

AMERINE, M. A., and JOSLYN, M. A. *Table Wines: The Technology of Their Production*. 1951. 2d ed. Berkeley and Los Angeles: University of California Press, 1970. For the enologist. *M. A. A.*

560

AMERINE, M. A., and OUGH, C. S. *Methods for the Analysis of Musts and Wines.* New York: John Wiley & Sons, 1980. Up-to-date analytical procedures. *M. A. A.*

AMERINE, M. A., and ROESSLER, E. B. *Wines: Their Sensory Evaluation.* San Francisco: W. H. Freeman & Co., 1976. Rev. ed. in press. How to make sense of sensory data. *M. A. A.*

AMERINE, M. A., and SINGLETON, V. L. *Wine: An Introduction.* 1964. 2d ed. Berkeley and Los Angeles: University of California Press, 1977. An introduction for college students. *M. A. A.*

AMERINE, M. A., and WINKLER, A. J. "Composition and Quality of Musts and Wines of California Grapes." *Hilgardia* 15, no. 6 (1944): 493–675. A report on the research that led to the classification of five heat-summation regions. *M. A. A.*

AMERINE, M. A., and WINKLER, A. J. *California Wine Grapes: Composition and Quality of Their Musts and Wines.* California Agricultural Experiment Station Bulletin no. 794. Berkeley, 1963. An up-date on the preceding entry. *M. A. A.*

AMERINE, M. A., and WINKLER, A. J. *Grape Varieties for Wine Production.* California Agricultural Experiment Station Leaflet No. 154. Berkeley, 1963. A summary of the preceding item. *M. A. A.*

ANDERSON, O. E., Jr. *The Health of a Nation.* Chicago: University of Chicago Press, 1958.

ASHER, Gerald. *On Wine.* New York: Random House, 1982. A collection of sensitive and insightful essays on wine, many of which are based on the author's articles written for *Gourmet* magazine. *D. M.*

B

BALZER, Robert Lawrence. *California's Best Wines.* 2d ed. Los Angeles: Ward Ritchie, 1949. Visits to the best wineries of the time. *R. B.*

BALZER, Robert Lawrence. *Wines of California.* New York: Harry N. Abrams, 1978. An enormous, handsome volume on California wine and wineries, lavishly illustrated with maps and photographs, most in color. *D. M.*

BERTI, Leo A. "A Review of the Transfer System of Champagne Production." *American Journal of Enology and Viticulture* 12, no. 2 (April–June 1961): 67–68.

BESPALOFF, Alexis, ed. *The Fireside Book of Wine.* New York: Simon & Schuster, 1977. A charming anthology for wine lovers, embracing selected wine writings from Chaucer to A. J. Liebling. Illustrated with occasional graphics. *D. M.*

BLOUT, Jessie Schilling. *A Brief Economic History of the California Wine Growing Industry.* State Department of Agriculture, Bureau of Marketing, 1943. With many references. *M. A. A.*

BOULET, D.; HUGUET, J. Y.; and LAPORTE, J.-P. *La consommation du vin en France.* Paris: Ministère de l'agriculture, Office national interprofessionel des vins de table, 1980.

BOWMAN, Jacob N. "The Vineyards in Provincial California." *Wine Review*, April, May, June 1943.

BRADY, R. "California Wine, A.D. 2000." *Journal of the International Wine & Food Society* 5 (February 1979): 35–38. One observer's view of the future. *R. B.*

BROADBENT, Michael [J. M. Broadbent]. *Wine Tasting: Enjoying, Understanding*. 6th ed. London: Christie Wine Publications, 1979. The way the English look at wine. *M. A. A.*

BROADBENT, Michael [J. M. Broadbent]. *The Great Vintage Wine Book*. New York: Alfred A. Knopf, 1980. An English expert, the head of the wine department at Christie's, records the rare and famous wines tasted during his career, and discusses vintages good and bad, including the effects of weather and aging on wine quality, with a section devoted to California. *R. B.*

BROADBENT, Michael [J. M. Broadbent]. *Wine Tasting: A Practical Handbook on Tasting and Tastings*. 1968. London: Christie, Manson & Woods, 1982.

BUENA VISTA VINICULTURAL SOCIETY. *Report of the Board of Trustees and Officers— 1866*. San Francisco: Alta California Book and Job Printing Office, 1866.

C

CALIFORNIA WINE CLIPPINGS. Special Collections. University of California, Davis.

CAROSSO, Vincent P. *The California Wine Industry, 1830–1895: A Study of the Formative Years*. Berkeley and Los Angeles: University of California Press, 1951. A definitive history of the young California wine industry. *M. A. A.*

CHEN, Jack. *The Chinese of America, 1785–1980*. San Francisco: Harper & Row, 1980. With a section on the contributions of the Chinese to the wine industry. *D. M.*

CHROMAN, Nathan. *The Treasury of American Wines*. New York: Crown Publishers, 1973.

COHEN, S. "How to Become an Alcoholic." *Drug Abuse and Alcoholism Newsletter* 8 (October 1979): 8.

D

DE GROOT, R. A. *The Wines of California, the Pacific Northwest, and New York*. New York: Summit Books, 1982. A premature attempt to classify some American wines. *R. B.*

DIENER, Brother Timothy, F.S.C. *The Christian Brothers as Winemakers*. Berkeley: Regional Oral History Office, Bancroft Library, 1974. History of the Christian Brothers' winemaking and their several wineries. *R. B.*

F

FADIMAN, Clifton, and AARON, Sam. *The Joys of Wine*. New York: Harry N. Abrams, 1975.

FESSLER, Julius H. *Guidelines to Practical Winemaking*. 3d ed., rev., Oakland, Calif.: Julius H. Fessler, 1971.

FISHER, M. F. K., and YAVNO, Max. *The Story of Wine in California*. Berkeley and Los Angeles: University of California Press, 1962. In lyrical text and stunning photographs, the authors give a history of wine in California and describe its production from the planting of the vine to the bottling of the wine. *D. M.*

FLAHERTY, Donald L.; JENSEN, Frederick L.; KASIMATIS, Amand N.; KIDO, Hiroshi; and MOELLER, William J. *Grape Pest Management*. University of California Agricultural Sciences Publications, no. 4,105. Berkeley: Division of Agricultural Sciences, University of California, 1981. Essential for California viticulturists. *M. A. A.*

FOLWELL, R. J., and BARITELLE, J. L. *The U.S. Wine Market*. U.S. Department of Agriculture, Agricultural Economic Report no. 417. Washington, D.C., 1978. A study of where and to whom wine is sold. *M. A. A.*

FOSDICK, Raymond B., and SCOTT, Albert L. *Toward Liquor Control*. New York: Harper & Bros., 1933. Foreword by John D. Rockefeller.

FRANCIS, A. D. *The Wine Trade*. New York: Barnes & Noble, 1973. A learned history of the trade, particularly with respect to England. *R. B.*

FREDERICKSEN, Paul. "The Authentic Haraszthy Story." *Wines & Vines* 28 (1947), no. 6, pp. 25–26, 42; no. 7, pp. 15–16, 30; no. 8, pp. 17–18, 37–38; no. 9, pp. 17–18, 34; no. 11, pp. 21–22, 41–42. Reprinted in booklet form.

G

GEIGER, Maynard J. *The Life and Times of Fray Junípero Serra, O.F.M.* 2 vols. Washington, D.C.: Academy of American Franciscan History, 1959.

GORMAN, Robert. *Gorman on California Premium Wines*. Berkeley: Ten Speed Press, 1975. A personal philosophy on wine quality. *M. A. A.*

GROSSMAN, Harold J. *Grossman's Guide to Wines, Spirits, and Beers*. 6th ed., rev. Harriet Lembeck. New York: Charles Scribner's Sons, 1977. A complete general reference work including a section on California wines, with maps and photographs. *D. M.*

H

HANSEN, Harvey J., and MILLER, Jeanne Thurlow. *Wild Oats in Eden: Sonoma County in the 19th Century*. Santa Rosa, Calif.: n.p., 1962.

HARASZTHY, Agoston. "Report on Grapes and Wines of California." *Transactions of the State Agricultural Society*. Sacramento, 1858.

HARASZTHY, Agoston. *Grape Culture, Wines, and Wine-Making, with Notes upon Agriculture and Horticulture*. New York: Harper, 1862; Hopewell, N.J.: Booknoll Reprints,

1971; Santa Barbara, Calif.: Capra Press, 1979, as *Father of California Wine: Agoston Haraszthy*, edited by Theodore Schoenman, with a foreword by Robert Balzer. A report of Haraszthy's trip to Europe, particularly interesting for grape and wine information. *M. A. A.*

HARASZTHY, Arpad. *Wine-Making in California*. San Francisco: Book Club of California, 1978. Originally published in four parts in the *Overland Monthly* (Winter 1871–72). How it was done in the 1870s in California. *M. A. A.*

HARRISON, L. V., and LAINE, E. *After Repeal: A Study of Liquor Control Administration*. New York: Harper & Bros., 1936.

HEINTZ, William F. "The Role of Chinese Labor in Viticulture and Wine-Making in 19th Century California." Master's thesis, Sonoma State University, 1977.

HEUBLEIN PREMIÈRE NATIONAL AUCTION OF RARE WINES XIII. Farmington, Conn.: Heublein, 1983. Annual since 1969. Lyrical descriptions and photographs of wines to be auctioned. *R. B.*

HILGARD, E. W. *Report of the Viticultural Work During the Seasons 1887–93, with Data Regarding the Vintages of 1894–95*. Sacramento: A. J. Johnston, State Printer, 1896. Hilgard's last publication on his research. *M. A. A.*

HINE, R. V. *California's Utopian Colonies*. San Marino, Calif.: Huntington Library, 1953. Includes Fountain Grove. *R. B.*

HOUSTON, James D. *Californians: Searching for the Golden State*. New York: Alfred A. Knopf, 1982. Contains a valuable profile of Paul Draper and Ridge Vineyards, as well as remarks on Zinfandel. *D. M.*

HU, T. Y. *The Liquor Tax in the United States, 1791–1947*. New York: Columbia University Graduate School of Business, 1950.

HUSMANN, George. *Grape Culture and Wine Making in California: A Practical Manual for the Grape-Grower and Wine-Maker*. San Francisco: Payot, Upham & Co., 1888. A very good treatise for its time. *M. A. A.*

HUSMANN, George. *American Grape Growing and Wine Making*. 4th ed., rev., New York: Orange Judd, 1895.

HUTCHISON, John N. "The Wines of the Americas." In *Wines of the World*, edited by André Simon. New York: McGraw-Hill, 1967.

HUTCHISON, John N. "The Astonishing Hungarian." *Wine & Food Magazine* (London), Spring 1968. A popular account of Agoston Haraszthy. *M. A. A.*

HYAMS, Edward. *Dionysus: A Social History of the Wine Vine*. New York: Macmillan Co., 1965.

HYATT, T. Hart. *Hyatt's Handbook of Grape Culture; or, Why, Where, When, and How to Plant and Cultivate a Vineyard, Manufacture Wines, Etc.* San Francisco: H. H. Bancroft, 1867. 2d ed., 1876. For its time, a fine text on grape growing and winemaking. *M. A. A.*

J

JACKSON, D., and SCHUSTER, D. *Grape-Growing and Winemaking*. Orinda, Calif.: Altarinda Books, 1981. From the New Zealand point of view, but with good comments on climate, etc. *M. A. A.*

JOHNSON, Hugh. *The World Atlas of Wine: A Complete Guide to the Wines and Spirits of the World*. 1971. 2d ed., rev., New York: Simon & Schuster, 1977.

JOHNSON, Hugh. *Wine*. New York: Simon & Schuster, 1974.

JOHNSON, Hugh. *Hugh Johnson's Pocket Encyclopedia of Wine*. Rev. ed. New York: Simon & Schuster, 1979. Precise information on many wines. *M. A. A.*

JOHNSON, Hugh. *Hugh Johnson's Modern Encyclopedia of Wine*. New York: Simon & Schuster, 1983. Published in Great Britain by Mitchell Beazley as *Hugh Johnson's Wine Companion: The New Encyclopaedia of Wines, Vineyards, and Winemakers*. *D. M.*

JONES, Idwal. *Vines in the Sun*. New York: William Morrow & Co., 1949. A romantic view of the California grape and wine industry. *M. A. A.*

JOSLYN, M. A. *A Technologist Views the California Wine Industry*. Berkeley: Regional Oral History Office, Bancroft Library, 1974. A good account of the post-Repeal industry by a participant. *R. B.*

JOSLYN, M. A., and AMERINE, M. A. *Dessert, Appetizer and Related Flavored Wines: The Technology of Their Production*. Berkeley: University of California Division of Agricultural Sciences, 1964.

K

KING, Norton L. *Napa County: An Historical Overview*. Napa, Calif.: Office of the Napa County Superintendent of Schools, Piercy C. Holliday, 1967.

L

LAMB, Richard, and MITTELBERGER, Ernest G. *In Celebration of Wine and Life*. 1974. Rev. ed. San Francisco: Wine Appreciation Guild, 1980. Lavishly illustrated from the Wine Museum of San Francisco. *R. B.*

LEAKE, C. D., and SILVERMAN, M. *Alcoholic Beverages in Clinical Medicine*. Chicago: Year Book Medical Publishers, 1966.

LEGGETT, Herbert B. "The Early History of Wine Production in California." Master's thesis, University of California, 1939. San Francisco: Wine Institute, 1941. Mimeographed.

LICHINE, Alexis. *Wines of France*. 1951. 5th ed., rev. in collaboration with William Massee, New York: Alfred A. Knopf, 1969.

LICHINE, Alexis. *Alexis Lichine's New Encyclopedia of Wines & Spirits*. 1967. 3d ed., rev., New York: Alfred A. Knopf, 1981. Includes an expanded section on U.S. wines with several pages and maps devoted to California. *D. M.*

LICHINE, Alexis, and PERKINS, Samuel. *Alexis Lichine's Guide to the Wines and Vineyards of France*. New York: Alfred A. Knopf, 1979.

LONG, Z. R. "White Table Wine Production in California's North Coast Region." In *Wine Production Technology in the United States*, edited by M. A. Amerine, pp. 29–57. Washington, D.C.: ACS, 1981.

LUCIA, S. P. *Wine as Food and Medicine*. New York: Blakiston Co., 1954.

LUCIA, S. P. *A History of Wine as Therapy*. New York: J. B. Lippincott Co., 1963.

LUCIA, S. P. *Wine and Health*. San Francisco: Fortune House, 1969.

LUCIA, S. P. *Wine and Your Well-Being*. New York: Popular Library, 1971.

LUCIA, S. P., ed. *Alcohol and Civilization*. New York: McGraw-Hill, 1963.

M

MABON, Mary Frost. *ABC of America's Wines*. New York: Alfred A. Knopf, 1942. Interesting period propaganda. *R. B.*

MACARTHUR, Mildred Yorba. *Anaheim: "The Mother Colony."* Los Angeles: Ward Ritchie Press, 1959.

McKEE, Irving. "The First California Vines." *California, Magazine of the Pacific* 36 (September 1946): 22, 46.

McKEE, Irving. "The First California Vineyards." *California, Magazine of the Pacific* 36 (September 1946): 20, 46.

McKEE, Irving. "Beginnings of California Winegrowing." *Historical Society of Southern California Quarterly* 29 (March 1947): 59–71.

McKEE, Irving. "Early California Wine Commerce." *Wine Review* 15 (January 1947): 12–13.

McKEE, Irving. "Early California Wine Growers." *California, Magazine of the Pacific* 37 (September 1947): 34–37.

McKEE, Irving. "The First California Wines." *Wines & Vines* 28 (April 1947): 47–48.

McKEE, Irving. "Three Wine-Growing Senators." *California, Magazine of the Pacific* 37 (September 1947): 15, 28–29.

McKEE, Irving. "Jean Louis Vignes: California's Pioneer Wine-Grower." *Wine Review* 38 (July 1948): 18–19, (September 1948): 12–13.

McKEE, Irving. "Jean Paul [*sic*] Vignes, California's First Professional Wine-grower." *Agricultural History* 22 (July 1948): 176–80.

McKEE, Irving. "Mission Wine Commerce." Distributed by the Wine Institute as a "preprinted" article from *California, Magazine of the Pacific*, dated December 1948, but evidently never published in the magazine itself.

McKee, Irving. "Vallejo—Pioneer Sonoma Wine Grower." *California, Magazine of the Pacific* 38 (September 1948): 16–17, 28–29.

McKee, Irving. "Red Mountain: Historic Vineyard of Stanislaus County." *California, Magazine of the Pacific* 39 (September 1949): 18, 29.

McKee, Irving. "Early California Wine Dealers." *Wines & Vines* 31 (February 1950): 12.

McKee, Irving. "Historic Wine Growers of Santa Clara County." *California, Magazine of the Pacific* 40 (September 1950): 14–15, 32–34.

McKee, Irving. "Historic Napa County Wine Growers." *California, Magazine of the Pacific* 41 (September 1951): 14–15, 22–24.

McKee, Irving. "The Oldest Names in California Winegrowing." *California, Magazine of the Pacific* 41 (September 1951): 17, 34.

McKee, Irving. "Historic Fresno County Wine Growers." *California, Magazine of the Pacific* 42 (September 1952): 12–13, 23.

McKee, Irving. "Historic Alameda County Wine Growers." *California, Magazine of the Pacific* 43 (September 1953): 20–23.

McKee, Irving. "George West: Pioneer Wine Grower of San Joaquin County." *California, Magazine of the Pacific* 44 (September 1954): 17–18.

McKee, Irving. "Historic Sonoma County Wine Growers." *California, Magazine of the Pacific* 45 (September 1955): 17, 33–34.

McKee, Irving. "Historic Wine Growers of Sacramento County." *California, Magazine of the Pacific* 46 (September 1956): 17, 29.

Mark, E. L., and James, K. M. *Drinking in America.* New York: Free Press, 1982. An illustrated history of American drinking habits and attitudes. *R. B.*

Martini, L. P. "Red Wine Production in the Coastal Counties of California, 1960–1980." In *Wine Production Technology in the United States,* edited by M. A. Amerine, pp. 59–84. Washington, D.C.: ACS, 1981.

Melville, John. *Guide to California Wines.* 1955. 5th ed., revised by Jefferson Morgan. New York: E. P. Dutton & Co., 1976. An excellent buyer's guide in its original version, intelligently revised in keeping with the late author's format. *D. M.*

M'Kee, Andrew. *Grape and Wine Culture: The Grape and Wine-Culture of California.* Report of the Commissioner of Patents for the year 1858. Washington, D.C., 1859.

Moulton, K. S., ed. *The Economics of Small Wineries.* Berkeley: University of California Cooperative Extension Service, 1981.

Muscatine, Doris. *Old San Francisco: The Biography of a City.* New York: G. P. Putnam's Sons, 1975. Includes early history of wine, winemakers, and the wine industry in San Francisco and the vineyard country. *D. M.*

N

National Family Opinion, Inc. "1980 Beverage Market Demographics Revealed in 'SIP' Study." *Impact Newsletter* 11, no. 9 (1 May 1981).

NEGRUL, A. M. *Vinogradarstvo s osnovami ampelografii i selektsii* [Viticulture and principles of ampelography and selection]. 3d ed. Moscow: Gos. Izd-vo Selkhoz. Lit-ry, 1959. A partial English translation by J. W. Ballou is filed at the University of California, Davis.

NESFIELD, David W. C. *The Vine Land of the West; or, Champagne and Its Manufacture*. San Francisco: Bosqui Engraving & Printing Co., 1883. Includes an article by Arpad Haraszthy. *M.A.A.*

NEWMARK, Harris. *Sixty Years in Southern California, 1853–1913.* 3d ed. Boston: Houghton Mifflin Co., 1930.

O

OLKEN, Charles; SINGER, Earl; and ROBY, Norman. *The Connoisseur's Handbook of California Wines.* 2d ed., rev., New York: Alfred A. Knopf, 1982. A pocketsized guide to the wines and wineries of California and the West Coast. *D.M.*

OLMO, H. P. *Plant Genetics and New Grape Varieties.* Berkeley: Regional Oral History Office, Bancroft Library, 1976. An engrossing account of Olmo's work, with many anecdotes of Davis. *R.B.*

OSTRANDER, Gilman M. *The Prohibition Movement in California.* Berkeley and Los Angeles: University of California Press, 1957.

P

PANUNZIO, Constantine. "The Foreign Born and Prohibition." *Annals of the American Academy of Political and Social Science* 163 (September 1932): 147–154.

PENINOU, Ernest P., and GREENLEAF, Sidney S. *A Directory of California Wine Growers and Wine Makers in 1860.* Berkeley: Tamalpais Press, 1967.

PEYNAUD, E. *Le Goût du Vin.* Paris: Dunod, 1980. A French enologist looks at wine evaluation. *M.A.A.*

PIJASSOU, René. *Le Médoc.* Paris: Tallandier, 1980. Relevant to Cabernet. *D.M.*

PUISAIS, J.; CHABANON, R. L.; GUILLER, A.; and LACOSTE, J. *Precis d'initiation à la dégustation.* Paris: Institut Technique du Vin, 1969. Reprinted as *Initiation into the Art of Wine Tasting.* Madison, Wis.: Interpublish, 1974. Useful on the physiology of the senses. *M.A.A.*

Q

QUIMME, Peter [pseud.]. *The Signet Book of American Wine.* 3d ed. New York: New American Library, 1980.

R

RAMEY, Bern C. *The Great Wine Grapes, and the Wines They Make*. Burlingame, Calif.: The Great Wine Grapes, Ltd., 1977. A brief ampelography. *M. A. A.*

ROBARDS, Terry. *The New York Times Book of Wine*. New York: Quadrangle/New York Times Book Co., 1976.

ROBÈRGE, Earl. *Napa Wine Country*. Portland, Ore.: Graphic Arts Center Publishing Co., 1975. A photographic and personal view. *M. A. A.*

ROBINSON, Jancis. *The Great Wine Book*. New York: William Morrow & Co., 1982. An English wine writer focuses on the great wines of the world; with detailed descriptions, profuse color photographs, and regional maps. Robert Mondavi, Chateau St. Jean, Joseph Phelps, and Ridge are the four California wineries included. *D. M.*

S

SAINTSBURY, George. *Notes on a Cellar-Book*. London: Macmillan & Co., 1920.

SALVATOR, Ludwig Louis. *Los Angeles in the Sunny Seventies: A Flower from the Golden Land*. Translated by Marguerite Eyer Wilbur. Los Angeles: Bruce McCallister and Jake Zeitlin, 1929.

SCHOONMAKER, Frank. *Frank Schoonmaker's Encyclopedia of Wine*. 6th ed., rev., New York: Hastings House, 1978.

SCHOONMAKER, Frank, and MARVEL, Tom. *American Wines*. 2d ed. New York: Duell, Sloan and Pearce, 1941. Includes some historical material about California wines. *M. A. A.*

SIMON, André L., ed. *Wines of the World*. 1967. 2d ed., by Serena Sutcliff. New York: McGraw-Hill, 1981.

SINGLETON, Vernon L., and ESAU, Paul. *Phenolic Substances in Grapes and Wine and Their Significance*. New York: Academic Press, 1969. All that was known then on the subject. *M. A. A.*

STOLL, Horatio P. *The Grape Districts of California*. San Francisco: H. P. Stoll, 1931. Long since outdated, but useful for its time. *M. A. A.*

STOLL, Horatio P. *Wine-Wise: A Popular Handbook on How to Correctly Judge, Keep, Serve and Enjoy Wines*. San Francisco: H. S. Crocker Press, 1933. A popular post-Repeal text, mainly on California. *M. A. A.*

STONE, Frank H., ed. *Catalog of Wine Education Materials*. 1982. 2d ed., rev., Salt Lake City: Society of Wine Educators, 1983.

STONE, Irving. *Men to Match My Mountains: The Opening of the Far West, 1840–1900*. Garden City, N.Y.: Doubleday, 1956. Romantic California history. *M. A. A.*

SULLIVAN, Charles L. *Like Modern Edens: Wine Growing in Santa Clara Valley and Santa Cruz Mountains, 1789–1981*. Cupertino, Calif.: California History Center, De Anza College, 1982. A fine historian traces the development of grape growing and winemaking from the days of the Spanish to current times. Many photographs of historic interest and an excellent modern map locating contemporary vineyards. *D. M.*

T

TAYLOR, Robert Lewis. *Vessel of Wrath.* New York: New American Library, 1966. A biography of Carry Nation, temperance agitator. *D. M.*

TEISER, Ruth, and HARROUN, Catherine. *Winemaking in California.* New York: McGraw-Hill, 1983. An excellent history with revealing illustrations of the California wine industry. *M. A. A.*

THOMPSON, Bob. *California Wine.* 2d ed., rev., Menlo Park, Calif.: Lane Publishing Co., 1977.

THOMPSON, Bob. *Guide to California's Wine Country.* 3d ed., rev., Menlo Park, Calif.: Lane Publishing Co., 1982.

THOMPSON, Bob. *The Pocket Encyclopedia of California Wines.* New York: Simon & Schuster, n.d.

THOMPSON, Bob, and JOHNSON, Hugh. *The California Wine Book.* New York: William Morrow & Co., 1976. A pioneering effort to describe regional and style variations of the major table wine types. *B. T.*

TROOST, G. *Die Technologie des Weines.* 5th ed. Stuttgart: Eugen Ulmer, 1980. The standard German text on grape growing and winemaking. *M. A. A.*

TRUMAN, Major Ben C. *See How It Sparkles.* Los Angeles: George Rice & Co., 1896. Colorful opinions of many wines by a connoisseur of the time. *R. B.*

W

WAGNER, P. M. "Wines, Grape Vines and Climate." *Scientific American* 230, no. 6 (1974): 106–15.

WAGNER, P. M. *Grapes into Wine: The Art of Winemaking in America.* New York: Alfred A. Knopf, 1976. 5th ed., 1982. Especially good on making wine from native grapes and hybrids. *M. A. A.*

WAIT, Frona Eunice. *Wines and Vines of California; or, a Treatise on the Ethics of Wine Drinking.* San Francisco: Bancroft Co., 1889; Berkeley: Howell-North Books, 1973. An early state-of-the-art record of California wineries. *M. A. A.*

WARBURTON, Clark. *The Economic Results of Prohibition.* New York: Columbia University Press, 1932.

WATNEY, Bernard M., and BABBIDGE, Homer D. *Corkscrews for Collectors.* London and New York: Sotheby Parke Bernet, 1981.

WEAVER, Robert J. *Grape Growing.* New York: John Wiley & Sons, 1976. A text for lower-division college students and home grape growers. *R. B.*

WEBB, A. Dinsmoor, ed. *Chemistry of Winemaking*. Washington, D.C.: American Chemical Society, 1974. A series of essays on various aspects of winemaking. *M. A. A.*

WEBB, Edith Buckland. *Indian Life at the Old Missions*. Los Angeles: Warren F. Lewis, 1952. Includes a good account of mission winemaking. *R. B.*

WENTE, Ernest. "Reminiscences." Extract by John N. Hutchison from an original typescript at Wente Bros. winery. *Wines & Vines* 63 (December 1981): 38–41.

WILLEBRANDT, Mabel Walker. *The Inside of Prohibition*. Indianapolis: Bobbs-Merrill Co., 1929.

WINKLER, A. J., and AMERINE, M. A. "What Climate Does: The Relation of Weather to the Composition of Grapes and Wines." *Wine Review* 5 (1937), no. 6, pp. 9–11; no. 7, pp. 9–11, 16.

WINKLER, A. J. "Color in California Wines. II. Preliminary Comparisons of Certain Factors Influencing Color." *Food Research* 3 (1938): 429–47.

WINKLER, A. J.; COOK, James A.; KLIEWER, W. M.; and LIDER, Lloyd A. *General Viticulture*. 2d ed., rev., Berkeley and Los Angeles: University of California Press, 1974. Originally published as A. J. Winkler, *General Viticulture* (1962). The standard text on grape growing. *M. A. A.*

Y

YOUNGER, W. *Gods, Men, and Wine*. London and Cleveland: The Wine and Food Society in association with World Publishing Co., 1966. A scholarly and original history of wine from the earliest times, with many illustrations. *R. B.*

YOXALL, H. W. *The Enjoyment of Wine*. London: Michael Joseph, 1972. An exemplary book on the subject. *M. A. A.*

Notes on Contributors

MAYNARD A. AMERINE, Professor of Enology Emeritus at the University of California, Davis, and currently a consultant to the Wine Institute, San Francisco, is a worldwide authority on winemaking, a connoisseur and collector of fine wines, and a prolific writer on wine and winemaking, having published almost four hundred books and articles. He is the co-author of *Dessert, Appetizer and Related Flavored Wines*; *Table Wines: The Technology of Their Production*; *The Technology of Wine Making*; *Wines: Their Sensory Evaluation*; and *Wine: An Introduction*. He has traveled widely and is the recipient of numerous national and international awards, among them the French Mérite Agricole and a Guggenheim Fellowship. He is a member of the Accademia Italiana della Vite e del Vino. In 1978 the Gallo Foundation established in his honor the Maynard A. Amerine Professorship of Enology and Viticulture at the University of California, Davis.

★

GERALD ASHER was trained in the wine trade in France, Germany, and Spain. Over the past twenty-five years he has specialized in European and California wines as the managing director of Asher, Storey & Co., London; as the vice-president of Austin, Nichols & Co., New York; as the president of Monterey Bay Company, California; and, currently, as the president of Mosswood Wine Company, San Francisco. He has chaired the New York Champagne Importers Committee and the Geographic Appellations Committee of the Wine Institute, San Francisco; he currently chairs the annual California Barrel Tasting dinner, New York, and was a member of the Board of Directors of the New York Wine and Food Society. He is a Chevalier du Tastevin, Compagnon du Beaujolais, a member of the Alsace Order of St. Étienne, and an Eschanson of Châteauneuf-du-Pape, and he has been decorated with the French Mérite Agricole. His regular column appears in *Gourmet Magazine*, and his book *On Wine* is based on those writings.

★

JOHN BENDER was born in Tulsa, Oklahoma, where, during his youth, wine tasting was confined to the altar rails of the more ceremonial churches. He was introduced to claret by fellow students at Princeton and began comparative tastings while earning his doctorate at Cornell. His interest expanded during visits to major European wine districts and during several periods of residence abroad and travels since. In 1967, shortly after he joined the faculty in English at Stanford University, enthusiasts from Esquin Imports introduced him to California-style blind tasting. He is still an active member of that group and an officer of the Berkeley Wine and Food Society. He is the author of *Spenser and Literary Pictorialism* and a number of articles and reviews on the literature and art of the Renaissance and the eighteenth century.

★

DAN BERGER, wine columnist and editor for the *San Diego Union* since 1978, was previously wine columnist for the *Los Angeles Herald-Examiner* and for ten years a reporter with the Associated Press. His syndicated column appears nationally in more than one hundred papers of the Copley News Service. He is a contributor to numerous wine publications, writes a regular column for *California Grapevine*, and is the wine and spirits editor and restaurant reviewer for the *San Diego Home/Garden Magazine*. A judge at such competitions as the San Francisco Fair and Exposition, the Sonoma County Fair, and Central Coast judgings, he became the director of wine judging at the Riverside County Farmers' Fair in 1983. He currently teaches two advanced wine seminars at the University of San Diego and lectures privately.

★

ERNEST BORN, a native of San Francisco, received his B.A. and M.A. degrees from the University of California at Berkeley. He spent several years studying abroad and working as Art Director for *Architectural Record* and *Architectural Forum* in New York, where he first began an architectural practice. In 1936 he established architectural offices in San Francisco, was for many years a member of the faculty of the School of Architecture at the University of California, Berkeley, and served as a consultant to the San Francisco Bay Area Rapid Transit District. His long collaboration with Walter Horn culminated in two books: *The Barns of the Abbey of Beaulieu at Its Granges of Great Coxwell and Beaulieu St. Leonards* and *The Plan of St. Gall*. He is the co-author with Lorna Price of "Architectural Models: A Note," the closing chapter of *The Plan of St. Gall: In Brief*. His awards and honors include a Taussig Traveling Fellowship and a Guggenheim Fellowship, and he is Fellow of the American Institute of Architects and Academician of the National Academy of Design.

★

ROY BRADY received an M.S. in mathematics and philosophy from the University of Chicago, taught for some years at the Illinois Institute of Technology, then went into systems analysis at Ramo-Wooldridge, Rand Corp., and others. He became interested in wine while in college and published his first article in 1951 ("Wine in the Novels of Thomas Love Peacock"). He has written on wine in numerous magazines both in the United States and in England and has edited a wine magazine of such obscurity that he does not recall the name. He has collected a large wine library, now in the Department of Special Collections, California State University, Fresno. He is currently working on a book about the changing aspect of the wine culture based partly on thirty-five years of notes in as many volumes.

★

JACK CHEN, an artist and historian, is currently the director and coordinator of a research and exhibition project entitled "The Pear Garden in the West: America's Chinese Theatre, 1852–1983." He has been a consultant on Chinese studies to the New York State Education Department; Senior Research Associate on Chinese and Peace Studies at Cornell University; and a contributor to such publications as the *New York Times* and *Foreign Policy*. He is the author of eight books, including *The Sinkiang Story*, *The Chinese of America*, and *America's Chinese Theatre*. For many years he lived and worked in China: in 1926, when his father, Eugene Chen, was Foreign Minister in the Wuhan government; and between 1950 and 1971, when he also served as consultant-editor to *People's China* and *Peking Review*. A year spent on a rural commune in Hunan province resulted in the book *A Year in Upper Felicity*. His efforts made possible the first exhibits of modern Chinese graphic art in the United States and modern American graphic art in China.

★

JOHN F. COONEY, an administrative lawyer in Washington, D.C., graduated from Brown University with highest honors, and received a J.D. from the University of Chicago Law School, where he was editor of the *Law Review*. He has maintained a private practice in Washington and served as Assistant to the Solicitor General of the United States in the Department of Justice. After writing this article, he became Assistant General Counsel of the Office of Management and Budget. He has represented the Wine Institute before the United States Court of Appeals for the District of Columbia Circuit in *Wawszkiewicz v. Department of the Treasury*, a case involving the legality of amendments to the department's wine labeling and advertising regulations.

★

DARRELL F. CORTI has for eighteen years been associated with Corti Brothers, a major purveyor of fine wines and specialty foods in northern California. His formal education included study at the University of Madrid, and he is fluent in several European languages. He has been a frequent taster at national and international wine judgings, is an associate of the American Society of Enologists, a member of the Medical Friends of Wine, a Corrispondente Straniero of the Accademia

574

della Vite e del Vino, and a member of various wine and food societies. His interest in the Sierra Foothills has been credited as a moving force in its reevaluation as a major viticultural area.

★

JACK L. DAVIES has been Managing Director of Schramsberg Vineyards and a producer of premium champagne since 1965, when he acquired and began the restoration of the vineyards. Previously he had received an M.B.A. from Harvard and had held a variety of executive posts in corporate management and consulting. From 1962 to 1965 he was a vice-president of Ducommun, Inc. He has been an officer and director of the Wine Institute and the president of Napa Valley Vintners; and he is a member of the San Francisco Wine and Food Society and the Society of Bacchus. He has traveled widely, has written on wine and on management, and has been a wine judge at the Los Angeles County Fair. His newest venture, R & S Vineyards, is an operation to produce a superior brandy in Napa County in partnership with Rémy Martin of France.

★

WILLIAM J. DICKERSON, M.D., Associate Clinical Professor of Psychiatry at the University of California, practices psychiatry north of San Francisco and has served as Chief of Staff of Ross General Hospital. He owns vineyards in the Napa Valley and is a member of the faculty of the Napa Valley Wine Library Association's Wine Appreciation Course. He has been a wine judge at the California State Fair, is a home winemaker, has published articles about medicine and enology, and has lectured on wine to lay and professional groups. He has traveled extensively in Europe and conducted tours in Canada, Europe, and the United States, with particular interest in the wine country. He is a member of the American Society of Enology, the Napa Valley Wine Technical Group, the Berkeley and San Francisco Wine and Food societies, and the Medical Friends of Wine, and is one of the founders of the First Growth Group, dedicated to tasting the best wines of Bordeaux.

★

BROTHER TIMOTHY DIENER, F.S.C., is the vice-president and cellarmaster of the Christian Brothers, Mont la Salle Vineyards, overseeing production in five operational sites. His first contact with wine was as a student Brother, helping to move large wine casks from the old winery at the Christian Brothers novitiate in Martinez to the present location near Napa. After attending St. Mary's College, he taught chemistry in the Christian Brothers' schools and started winemaking in 1935 as Mont la Salle's wine chemist. He is curator of a corkscrew collection of more than fifteen hundred pieces.

★

PAUL DRAPER, winemaker and partner at Ridge Vineyards, grew up on an eighty-acre farm in the Chicago suburb of Barrington. After receiving a degree in philosophy from Stanford University and studying Italian at the Monterey Language School, he served in the Army in liaison in northern Italy. Later he studied French at the University of Paris and traveled extensively in France and Italy, gaining practical experience in traditional winemaking. In the mid-1960s, with his closest friend, the owner of York Creek Vineyards, he set up a small winery in the coast range of Chile, where they produced a number of vintages of Cabernet Sauvignon until the economic situation forced them to return to California in 1969. At Ridge's Monte Bello estate vineyards, he has continued working with Cabernet Sauvignon and with his new love, Zinfandel.

★

MARY FRANCES KENNEDY FISHER (M. F. K. Fisher), one of the most distinguished prose writers in the United States, was born 3 July 1908 in Albion, Michigan. In 1911 she came with her family to Whittier, California, where her father edited and published the *Whittier News* for the next forty-two years. She has lived for long periods in France and Switzerland, at one time running a small vineyard in Vevey. Her work has appeared in a wide variety of publications and she is a steady contributor to the *New Yorker*. Among her books are *The Art of Eating*, a collection of five gastronomical writings; *Not Now But Now*; *Here Let Us Feast*; *A Cordiall Water*; *Map of Another Town*; *The Cooking of Provincial France*; *With Bold Knife and Fork*; *As They Were*; *Among Friends*; *A Considerable Town*; and, with photographer Max Yavno, *Wine in California*. She is the translator and annotator of Brillat-Savarin's *The Physiology of Taste*. Her newest book is *Sister Age*.

★

WILLIAM B. FRETTER, a native Californian, is Professor of Physics and former Vice-President of the University of California. He has been a Guggenheim Fellow, has lived and worked in France, has been a Lecturer in the Collège de France, and has been decorated with the Legion of Honor. He is Grand Officier of the Confrérie des Chevaliers du Tastevin. A home winemaker since 1950, he has cultivated a vineyard in the Napa Valley for thirty years.

★

DAVID LANCE GOINES, a printer, designer, and author, was born 29 May 1945 in Grant's Pass, Oregon. His book *A Constructed Roman Alphabet* received the 1983 American Book Award. His graphic work is represented in numerous public and private collections.

★

CATHERINE HARROUN, a Stanford graduate, was for many years in charge of the Wells Fargo Bank History Room. A freelance writer, researcher, and photographer since 1950, she has worked mainly in collaboration with Ruth Teiser. She has been an interviewer and editor for the Regional Oral History Office of the Bancroft Library at the University of California, Berkeley, since 1965. She is co-author with Ruth Teiser of numerous articles on books, printing, and the wines of California and Italy; co-editor of two books published by the Book Club of California, *Printing as a Performing Art* and Arpad Haraszthy's *Wine-Making in California*; and co-author of an illustrated history, *Winemaking in California*, awarded the Commonwealth Club's 1982 Silver Medal for the best book on Californiana by a resident author.

★

SUE EILEEN HAYES is a fourth-generation Californian, a member of a ranching family that settled in the Mattole Valley in 1849. She was educated at Stanford University and received a Ph.D. in agricultural economics, specializing in agricultural labor, from the University of California, Berkeley. She is the author of several studies of agricultural labor in California and the United States and is presently Professor of Economics at Sonoma State University. As an exchange student, she lived with a wine-producing family in Calabria, Italy, and participated in winemaking.

★

WALTER HORN, Professor of the History of Art Emeritus, University of California, Berkeley, was born in Waldangelloch near Heidelberg, Germany, and received his doctorate at Hamburg University under Erwin Panofsky. After three years of post-doctoral study in Italy, he came to the United States in 1938 and joined the faculty at Berkeley. He is the author in collaboration with Ernest Born of *The Barns of the Abbey of Beaulieu at Its Granges of Great Coxwell and Beaulieu St. Leonards* and *The Plan of St. Gall*. He founded the monograph series California Studies in the History of Art, helped to establish the University Art Museum, and is a member of the Board of Trustees of the Fine Arts Museums of San Francisco, a Fellow of the Medieval Academy of America, and a recipient of a Guggenheim Fellowship.

★

577

ANDREW HOYEM, a typographic designer and director of the Arion Press, is noted for the printing and publishing of deluxe limited-edition books. A partner in the Grabhorn-Hoyem Press from 1966 to 1973, he has also published four volumes of his poetry, including *Articles* and a translation from Middle English of *The Pearl*. He has given public poetry readings in England and the United States. In 1975, the Palace of the Legion of Honor presented a one-man exhibition of his drawings. He produced *Picture/Poems*, an illustrated catalogue, to accompany it.

★

JOHN N. HUTCHISON was born in Iowa in 1911. He received a degree in journalism from the University of Arkansas and served as an editor and reporter for a number of newspapers. A retired lieutenant colonel in the United States Army Reserve, he is the holder of the Bronze Star. As a diplomat, he spent a long career in the Foreign Service, assigned to Paris, London, Manila, Washington, and Wellington, and was awarded the Superior Service Award of the United States Information Agency. He wrote "Wines of the Americas," a section for the first edition of *Wines of the World*, edited by André Simon. He has been a contributor and, since 1973, a contributing editor, to *Wines & Vines Magazine*. For ten years he has served as the California correspondent for four New Zealand daily newspapers. He has lived or traveled on every continent but South America and is now settled in Sebastopol, California.

★

HUGH JOHNSON has divided his career between wine and horticulture. He was born in London in 1939 and was educated at Rugby and King's College, Cambridge. He worked for the late André Simon and has written over the years for many magazines and newspapers, including *Vogue*, the *Sunday Times*, and *Queen*, which he also edited from 1968 to 1970. He is currently Editorial Director of *The Garden*, the journal of the Royal Horticultural Society, and of its sister paper, *The Plantsman*. He is Wine Editor of *Cuisine* and the president of the *Sunday Times* Wine Club. His books include *Wine*, *The World Atlas of Wine*, *The International Book of Trees*, *The California Wine Book* (with Bob Thompson), *The Pocket Encyclopedia of Wine*, *The Principles of Gardening*, and *Hugh Johnson's Modern Encyclopedia of Wine*. Besides being a lover of wine, he says, he is a mad keen gardener with twelve acres of rare trees in Essex, England.

★

AMAND N. KASIMATIS has been Extension Viticulturist at the University of California, Davis, since 1955. He was previously employed by the University of California Cooperative Extension as Farm Advisor for horticulture in Kern County. The author of numerous technical and practical publications on California grape-growing practices, he is also the assistant editor of *The American Journal of Enology and Viticulture*. He is a consultant to the California Raisin Advisory Board and the Vinicultural Research Committee of the Wine Institute and has been a director of the American Society of Enologists. His work has taken him to Mexico, Australia, South America, and South Africa.

★

JAMES LAPSLEY, a native of northern California, received a degree in history from the University of California, Santa Cruz, in 1971, after which he began graduate work in American history at the University of California, Davis. Since 1977 he has been the head of the Agricultural Unit of University Extension, responsible for planning and administering continuing education programs in agriculture—including viticulture, winemaking, and wine appreciation—for the Davis campus. A home winemaker since 1973, he bonded his own thousand-case winery in Woodland in 1980. In his spare time he works on his doctoral dissertation, a history of winemaking in the Napa Valley.

★

ZELMA LONG has been vice-president and winemaker at Simi Winery since 1979. After studying chemistry, microbiology, and nutrition at Oregon State University and serving a one-year dietetic internship at the University of California Medical School in San Francisco, she enrolled in the masters program in enology at the University of California, Davis. She went on to work for Robert Mondavi Winery as a laboratory technician for two years and as the head enologist for eight. She is a past president of the Napa Valley Wine Technical Group, a current director of the American Society of Enologists, and past president of the American Vineyard Foundation. She travels frequently to Europe to study traditional winemaking techniques and is the owner of Long Vineyards, a small winery in the Napa Valley.

★

ELEANOR McCREA, born 9 December 1907 in Buffalo, New York, has lived in California since 1916. Educated at Wellesley College and later in business school, she worked as a legal secretary. In 1943 she and her husband Fred purchased Stony Hill, began planting vineyards there in 1948, built the winery in 1951, and bonded it a year later. They moved to Stony Hill to live on a year-round basis in 1962. After her husband's death in 1977, she took over the running of the winery with the help of her son Peter and the winemaker Michael Chelini. She has two children, two foster children, ten grandchildren, and one great-grandchild.

★

CAROLE P. MEREDITH, Assistant Professor in the Department of Viticulture and Enology at the University of California, Davis, received her undergraduate degree in biology and her doctorate in genetics from that campus. Her previous employment as a research biologist for Stauffer Chemical Company was preceded by a year at Michigan State University as the recipient of a National Science Foundation Postdoctoral Fellowship. She has also served at the University of California, Davis, as a research assistant in the Vegetable Crops Department, a teaching associate in the Genetics Department, and a research assistant in the English Department, where she developed a new course in scientific writing. She is a member of a number of professional societies, including the American Society of Enologists, the International Association for Plant Tissue Culture, and the American Association for the Advancement of Science.

★

TIMOTHY J. MONDAVI was born and raised at the Charles Krug Ranch in St. Helena, California, where his family operated the winery. While studying Viticulture and Enology at the University of California, Davis, he worked in the cellar and laboratory at the Robert Mondavi Winery between school sessions. After graduation, he worked on experimental programs at the Stellenbosch Farmers Winery in South Africa. Since 1979, he has been Executive Vice-President in charge of production at Robert Mondavi and is currently in charge of all winemaking and related activities. He is a member of the Napa Valley Vintners, Napa Valley Wine Technical Group, and several Wine Institute committees.

★

KIRBY MOULTON is an economist for the University of California Cooperative Extension and the Giannini Foundation of Agricultural Economics at Berkeley. His research centers on issues of agricultural marketing and international trade. He has written extensively about the economics of the U.S. grape and wine industry and lectured about this subject in the United States and abroad. He edited the book *The Economics of Small Wineries*, which has been distributed widely. While a visiting professor at Institut Agronomique Méditerranéen de Montpellier, France, during 1977–78, he commenced an intensive study of European Common Market policies affecting trade in wine and other horticultural products. Dr. Moulton completed his undergraduate education at Yale University and earned his M.B.A. and Ph.D. degrees at the School of Business Administration, University of California, Berkeley.

★

DORIS MUSCATINE writes on food, wine, and cultural history. Her articles have appeared in numerous magazines and newspapers in the United States and abroad. She has written three books: *A Cook's Tour of San Francisco*, *A Cook's Tour of Rome*, and *Old San Francisco: The Biography of a City*, for which she received an Award of Merit from the city and county of San Francisco. She owns a vineyard in the Napa Valley and has been a home winemaker for a number of years.

★

THOMAS PINNEY is Professor of English at Pomona College, Claremont, California. He was introduced to California wines while a graduate student at Yale University, and migrated from Connecticut to California shortly thereafter. In the twenty years since, he has made the study of Californian and other American wines a hobby. He is currently at work on a comprehensive history of winegrowing in the United States since the beginning of settlement. Apart from his work on wine, he has published on Lord Macaulay and George Eliot and is presently preparing an edition of the letters of Rudyard Kipling.

★

MARK SAVAGE, M.W., was born in 1949 in Uganda, a country in which viticulture is nonexistent. His earliest recollection of drinking wine is of a bottle of La Gratitude imported from South Africa. He was educated in England, reading classics, ancient history, and philosophy at University College, Oxford, joining the Wine & Food Society, and serving as the president of the Oxford Wine Circle. The Oxford Tasting Team, never beaten in this period, in later years went down to defeat by an Exeter team coached by Mr. Savage. His early experience in the wine trade was with Moët et Chandon (he reports a bottle of Champagne a day is the best preventative of the common cold), Harrods, El Vino's of Fleet Street, O. W. Loeb & Co., and Tanners of Shrewsbury. In 1975, as the Vintners Scholar, he won a year of travel abroad, and in 1980 he became a Master of Wine. In 1976 he established Windrush Wines Limited, which includes on its list some thirty-six wines from the smaller fine wineries of California and the Northwest. He conducts his business from a Victorian castle in Cirencester.

★

PAUL SCHOLTEN, M.D., is a native of San Francisco. A past president and the current historian of the San Francisco Medical Society, he practices obstetrics and gynecology, is Director of Women's Services at the San Francisco State University Student Health Service, and is Associate Clinical Professor of Obstetrics and Gynecology at the University of California Medical School in San Francisco. He has served as the president of the Society of Medical Friends of Wine and the San

581

Francisco Wine and Food Society, and has been a frequent wine judge at the Los Angeles County Fair. He is the author of some 150 articles on medicine, wine, food, history, and travel.

★

WALTER SCHUG is consulting winemaker, viticulturist, ranch manager, and vice-president of Joseph Phelps Vineyards. Born in Germany into a family with a long tradition of grape growing and winemaking, he grew up on the state-owned vineyard and winery estate of Assmannhausen in the Rheingau. He served a six-year work and study apprenticeship in several well-known German vineyards and wineries and, in 1959, received a degree in engineering from the College of Viticulture and Enology in Geisenheim. That same year he came to the United States and subsequently held several responsible positions in the California wine industry. In 1973, when he joined Joseph Phelps Vineyards as Principal Winemaker, he was responsible for laying out and developing the vineyards, designing and selecting equipment and cooperage, and participating in the design of the winery building. Since 1980 the Schug family has also been making wine under the Schug Cellars label.

★

JAMES M. SEFF, Managing Counsel in San Francisco of the New York alcoholic beverage law firm of Buchman, Buchman, and O'Brien, was senior San Francisco Counsel for the Wine Institute from 1978 to 1983 and its Staff Counsel from 1969 to 1978. An English honors graduate from the University of Michigan, he later received a J.D. from the University of California (Boalt Hall). From 1967 to 1969, he was legal and supply officer on the *U.S.S. Davidson*, and retains the rank of commander in the United States Naval Reserve. He has been the president of the Barristers' Club of San Francisco, a director of the Bar Association of San Francisco, vice-president of the California Young Lawyers Association, and has served on committees of or as delegate for numerous professional and community organizations. He has edited three professional legal journals and written for many more, often on the subject of the Bureau of Alcohol, Tobacco and Firearms' regulations regarding wine.

★

HARVEY STEIMAN, the former food and wine editor of the *San Francisco Examiner* and now Managing Editor of *The Wine Spectator*, was born in Massachusetts, grew up in Los Angeles, majored in music at California State University, Los Angeles, and started his career in journalism as a sports writer. He later gave up sports to become the food editor and restaurant critic of the *Miami Herald*. He is the author of *Great Recipes from San Francisco* and, with Ken Hom, of *Chinese Technique*.

His one-hour radio program "The KCBS Kitchen" is broadcast daily. Chairman of the wine judging for the San Francisco Fair and Exposition, he has also served as a judge for major California wine competitions. He reports that his six-hundred-bottle wine cellar seems to be growing at the same alarming rate as his five-year-old daughter Katherine.

★

FORREST R. TANCER is a partner in and winemaker for Iron Horse Vineyards. A San Franciscan, he was educated at the University of California, Berkeley, and studied viticulture at Fresno State University. Before becoming involved in the wine industry, he spent a year and a half in Brazil as an agricultural extension agent in the Peace Corps. In 1971, he began work as vineyard manager at Iron Horse, then leased by Sonoma Vineyards, planting Pinot Noir and Chardonnay. During the fall and winter he worked in the Sonoma Vineyards' cellar, learning the art of wine-making. In 1976, when new owners took over Iron Horse, he continued as the manager, became the winemaker there and the cellarmaster for Sonoma. When Iron Horse expanded in 1979, he joined as a full-time partner. He lives on a 450-acre ranch in the foothills of the Alexander Valley, where he has planted Cabernet Sauvignon, Sauvignon Blanc, and Zinfandel for Iron Horse wines.

★

RUTH TEISER is a freelance researcher, writer, and photographer who works mainly in collaboration with Catherine Harroun. After obtaining her undergraduate and M.A. degrees from Stanford University, she did additional graduate work in California history. Since 1965 she has been an interviewer and editor for the Regional Oral History Office of the Bancroft Library at the University of California, Berkeley, working principally on interviews concerning books, printing, and California winemaking. Until 1974, she contributed book reviews and articles on fine printing and small presses to the *San Francisco Chronicle*; since then she has written occasionally on books and wine for the *San Francisco Examiner*'s *California Living* magazine. She is the author of histories of the Society of California Pioneers and the Ghiradelli Company; and with Catherine Harroun, of an illustrated history, *Winemaking in California*, which won the Commonwealth Club's 1982 Silver Medal for the best book on Californiana by a resident author. With Catherine Harroun, she edited *Printing as a Performing Art* and Arpad Haraszthy's *Wine-Making in California*, both for the Book Club of California. She has published a number of articles on books, printing, and the wines of California and Italy.

★

THOMAS D. TERRY, S.J., an educator and wine chemist, was born in Pittsburgh, Pennsylvania, in 1922. He joined the Jesuit order in Los Gatos, California, in 1939, and picked grapes in the vineyard there. He was educated at the University of Santa Clara and St. Louis University and obtained a Ph.D. in wine chemistry from the University of California at Davis. He was ordained a Roman Catholic priest in 1952. After two years as wine chemist for the Novitiate winery in Los Gatos, he became Dean of the College of Arts and Sciences at the University of Santa Clara. He was for two years Academic Vice-President at Loyola University of Los Angeles, before serving as President of the Novitiate of Santa Clara from 1968 to 1976. From 1978 to 1982 he was President of the Novitiate winery in Los Gatos. At the time of his death in February 1984, he was chaplain of the University of Santa Clara Law School. He was a member of the American Chemical Society and the American Society of Enologists and wrote numerous articles for journals and for the *Catholic Encyclopedia*.

★

BOB THOMPSON is a freelance editor and writer whose books on wine include *The Pocket Encyclopedia of California Wine*, *California Wine Country*, *Guide to California's Wine Country*, *California Wine*, *American Wines and Wine Cooking* (with Shirley Sarvis), and *The California Wine Book* (with Hugh Johnson). He worked in the public relations office of the Wine Institute from 1966 to 1968 and wrote a weekly column for the *San Francisco Examiner* from 1970 to 1978. He has been the California Wine Country Tour study leader for the Smithsonian Institution since 1976 and is a judge at the wine competitions of the Los Angeles County Fair, the San Francisco Fair and Exposition, the Sonoma Harvest Fair, and the Tri-Cities Pacific Northwest Wine Fair. Since 1982 he has been a member of the teaching staff of the California Sommelier Academy.

★

PHILIP M. WAGNER, a writer born in New Haven, Connecticut, 18 February 1904, served as editor of the *Baltimore Evening Sun* from 1938 to 1943, after a number of years as its editorial writer and London correspondent; then as editor of the *Baltimore Sun* until his retirement in 1964. He is an *officier* of the French Ordre du Mérite Agricole and was the American delegate to the Fédération Nationale de la Viticulture Nouvelle. He is the author of numerous articles and books, among them his first book, *American Wines and How to Make Them*, twice rewritten and twice retitled, and still in print after fifty years; and his latest, *Grapes into Wine*, now in a fifth printing. He is best known for introducing and popularizing French hybrid vines, the basis for a new winegrowing industry in areas east of the Rockies where the classic *Vitis vinifera* does not succeed. As a consequence of his work with hybrids, he established the Boordy Vineyard nursery and winery, the latter now passed on to old friends; he still retains his interest in the nursery.

*

ALICE WATERS, cook, restaurant proprietor, and author, graduated from the University of California, Berkeley, as a student in French culture, studied education in London, and taught for a time in a Montessori school. Her serious interest in cuisine developed at nineteen during an extensive trip to France. Her professional commitment began in 1971 with the opening of the restaurant Chez Panisse in Berkeley, California. She is the author of *The Chez Panisse Menu Cookbook* and, with David Lance Goines, of *Thirty Recipes Suitable for Framing*. Her newest book, written in collaboration with Patricia Curtan and Martine Labro, is *Chez Panisse Pasta, Pizza and Calzone*.

*

JEAN R. WENTE, a native Californian, has since 1977 served as Vice-President, Chairman of the Executive Committee, and Chief Financial Officer of Wente Bros., the winery founded by her late husband Karl's family. She has also been a director of New Parrott & Company since 1977 and a director of Wente Bros. since 1970. In 1980–81, she was President of the Monterey Winegrowers Council and is still a director. She graduated with a B.A. degree in history from Stanford University and spent the following year as a graduate student there in the department of history. Among the community groups for which she has been, or is now, an officer are the Oakland Museum Association, the Alameda County Art Commission, the California College of Arts and Crafts, and the California Council for Humanities in Public Policy. Her children, Eric, Philip, and Carolyn, are now president, vice-president, and vice-president for public relations at Wente Bros.

*

ADRIAN WILSON is a book designer, printer, author, and lecturer on typographic design and on the history of the book. He became interested in wines and their labels when he designed and printed a series of keepsakes, *The Vine in Early California*, for the Book Club of California. He has been a partner in, and produced labels for, a private California winery. He is the author of *Printing for Theater*, *The Design of Books*, and *The Making of the Nuremberg Chronicle*, among other books. He is the first San Franciscan to have been awarded a MacArthur Prize Fellowship. On occasion he sits in as jazz clarinetist at the Washington Square Bar and Grill in San Francisco.

INDEX

NOTE: Page numbers printed in italic type refer to information found in illustrative material (figures, diagrams, or maps).

A

Acacia Winery: Chardonnay, 487; Pinot Noir, 217, 218, 219, 519

Acidity: of grapes, 105, 114, 145, 161, 177, 215; and temperature, 99; of wine, 183, 451, 461. *See also* pH

Act for the Promotion of the Viticultural Industries of the State (1880), 306

Adams, Leon D., 47, 68, 71, 78, 307, 311, 312; on dessert wine, 280–81, 283–84

Adulteration of wine and fraudulent labeling, 37–39, 417–18, 419–20; of altar wine, 299–300; during Prohibition, 57. *See also* Labels and labeling; Standards of identity

Advertising, 71, 73–74, 403

Aesthetic qualities of wine, 362–67, 449–52. *See also* Qualities of good wine; Styles of wine; Tasting wine

Affenthaler grape, 134–35

Aging wine, 159, 161, 165–67, 221. *See also* Barrel-aging; Barrels; Bottle-aging; Oak aging; Oak barrels; *and names of specific wines*

Aguardiente. See Brandy

Ahlgren Vineyard, 390; Cabernet Sauvignon, 500

Alabama, 401

Alameda County, 19, 37, 45, *94*, *98*, 101, *102*, 390; Chardonnay in, 485; vine acreage in, *106*

Alcohol absorption and metabolism, 371–73; and blood alcohol curve, *372*; long-term effects of, 374

Alcohol content of wine, 163, 327–28, 363, 426n, 462

Alcoholism, 376, 378–79

Alcorn, George, 454

Aleatico, 234

Alexander Valley Vineyards: Cabernet Sauvignon, 500; Chardonnay, 490; Pinot Noir, 216

Algeria, 381

Alhambra, 8

Alicante Bouschet, 57–58, 59, 60, 234–35

Allen, Herbert, 342

Allen, J. Fiske, 225

Allergies and wine, 376–77

Alley, Curtis, 150

Allied Grape Growers (I.S.C. Wines), 74, 80, 392

Allier oak. *See* Oak barrels

Almadén Vineyards, 19, 80, 391, 392, 398–99, 468; Cabernet Sauvignon, 498; champagne, 269, 270, 271, 275, 276, 279; Chardonnay, 488; newsletter, 310; Pinot Noir, 520; White Riesling, 510, 512; Zinfandel, 528

Almeria grape, 60

Alpine County, *94*, *98*, *106*

Alsace, 440, 462, 471; bottles, 169; heat summation for region of, *112*

Alta California, 265

Altar wine. *See* Sacramental wine

Alvarelhão grape, 288

Amador County, 16–17, 37, *94*, *98*, *102*; vine acreage in, *106*

Amelioration. *See* Sugar added to wine

American Champagne Company, 270

Amerine, Maynard A., 57, 72–73, 76, 209, 228, 234, 308, 310, 311; and California

M

N

S

COLOPHON

Type for the text of this volume was set on a Mergenthaler Linotron 202, using a Mergenthaler digital adaptation of PLANTIN. Even in notes as brief as these, it is proper to interrupt myself to say that the Linotron Plantin font yields a notably agreeable interpretation of MONOTYPE PLANTIN 110 (something that cannot be said for many digital adaptations from the hot-metal era of typography). The body text was set in the 12 point size, 3 point leaded. Footnotes were set in 10 point, 3 point leaded. Extended captions, such as notes for maps, were set in 12 point italic, 3 point leaded. The rapturous burst of joy by M.F.K.F. in her Preface quite undid me, and got specified as 17 point, 4 point leaded. It was so set, not without several trials. Digital composition is by LeRoy Wilsted, Christine Taylor, Brenda Becker, Henry Mooney, and Jane-Ellen Long of Wilsted & Taylor Publishing Services, Oakland, California.

Display type for article headings, with names of authors, was set in 30 point digital PLANTIN. The display type for chapter headings, in PERPETUA TITLING 258, was set in foundry type of various sizes (48 point, 60 point, etcetera) by Othmar Peters of Mackenzie-Harris, San Francisco, California.

The jacket and endpapers were printed by Max Strassman, Mastercraft Press, San Francisco, on Thistle Multicolor, a paper manufactured for and distributed by Process Materials Corporation, Rutherford, New Jersey.

The book was printed and bound by KINGSPORT PRESS, an Arcata Graphics Company, Kingsport, Tennessee. Printing was by offset lithography on a six-color web-fed press. The web-fed printing technique uses paper in rolls (as opposed to sheet-fed printing, which uses cut sheets). One roll of paper may be twenty-three- to twenty-four-thousand feet long (about $4\frac{1}{2}$ miles). The technique demands great care in inking and ink formulation, particularly when adapted to work of superior character, requiring a black of densest opaque quality. Kingsport Press has its own ink compounding and formulation facilities to provide positive assurance in ink matters.

Text paper stock, milled for this book, is PENN TEXT LAID, 70 pound weight, manufactured by the Penn Tech Mill, Johnsonburg, Pennsylvania.

Book-binding cloth is BUNTGEWEBE 300, made by Vereinigte Göppinger-Bamberger Kaliko GmbH of Bamberg, Germany, and distributed in the United States by Whitman Products Ltd. of West Warwick, Rhode Island.

Book design is by Ernest Born, who drew the large roman numbers in chapter headings and several items of ornamental and geometric character that are found scattered throughout the volume, sometimes in association with incidental illustrations and supportive technical captions.

A FEW COMMENTS

Publishing in the present day is an extremely complex endeavor that is closely keyed to schedules at every phase in the creation of a book. Bookmaking procedure is so involved that it seems impossible to conceive of a "simple" book. Such an entity cannot be more than a wistful fantasy in these times, to book designer or director of production or typesetter.

This colophon might in theory be included as part of the "Acknowledgments" (page v), of which it is in many respects merely an extension, but since it concerns matter of a technical and particular nature, it seems more appropriate to collect it under a separate rubric. Historically, I believe, the colophon was preempted by the volume's printer, when the printer might have been publisher, entrepreneur, and sometimes even author and editor of the book the reader held in hand. The colophon might perhaps have been irrelevant to the subject of the book, yet still hold a position of prime importance in its makeup.

The colophon, whatever its place may once have been, retains a singular importance in publishing practice today; it can assist the reader in gaining a small understanding of the many-faceted expertise required to make a book of quality with the aid of a breathtaking technology that sometimes complicates at a faster rate than it simplifies our lives and work.

Preparation of illustrations, maps, page layouts, and the like requires quite extensive use of photographic services, much of which is very involved and complicated, requiring rare expertise and long experience of a particular kind. Bill and Mary Sander, General Graphic Services, San Francisco, from the inception of this volume gave photographic support of impeccable quality, often delivered under stressful conditions. Their excellent work contributes much to this volume.

My gratitude to David Paulson of San Francisco, Warren Weber of Sacramento, and, in particular, Kenneth Galt of Sacramento. These men, all of the Department of Transportation, Division of Mass Transportation, promptly made available to me information of great detail and importance in my preparation of the maps for the article "The Wine and Its Environments," by Maynard A. Amerine and Philip Wagner. Mr. Galt is Transportation Planner to the State of California.

These reflections summon the need to acknowledge an unstinting willingness by Professor Thomas Pinney, Pomona College, Claremont, California, to provide caption copy for a map that had suddenly become an urgent requirement of book design and of decent editing, at a stage when it was "too late for that kind of thing." Yet, get done it did, and in a twinkle.

Similarly, I am grateful for the press-button promptness of Mr. John W. McConnell of the Acquisitions Department, Shields Library, University of California, Davis, who provided bibliographic information essential to the completion of page design and cohesive editorial policy.

To John Hogan, Wine Merchant, John Walker Co., San Francisco, who never was so busy he could not give generously of his time and discuss countless issues and share his background of encyclopedic scope, my grateful thanks.

The pages of this volume comprise a vivid testimonial to an exceptionally successful collaboration between its designer and his typesetting services.

The book designer specifies every piece of type in a volume by means of a vocabulary of utmost simplicity confined almost entirely to units of measurement (point, pica, quad, etc.). Yet a typographic composition may present a graphic pattern of utmost complexity, possessed and governed by an aesthetic of infinite extent. How then, in such a muddling quandary, do designer and typesetter talk to each other? I do not know. I suppose more by signal or vibration than by sensible terrestrial phenomena that respond to explanation by sane and rational language. Telephones help. And the pencil studies of the designer's layouts and sketches facilitate communication. Furthermore, when the designer is reputed to be of fastidious habit and meticulous in too many ways, and when, as here, the typesetters are designers themselves, clearly the chances for rapport in collaboration are very small. Consequently, a joint effort so felicitous as this has been seems explicable only as a phenomenon of divine origin. I am, besides being grateful to higher powers, grateful to LeRoy Wilsted and Christine Taylor for their never-failing enthusiasm and brilliant interpretation of my hundreds of sketches and scribbles and inscrutable doodles, and for imparting a prevailing coherence and ease in reading.

Too, it is fitting that I tell of the fund of patience seemingly bottomless that resides within Czeslaw Jan Grycz, production manager of the Press, who has piloted this volume through tumultuous seas, passing between many a Scylla and Charybdis en route to California Vintage 1984, yet he still appears fresh and cheerful. Double miracle.

E.B. ▶

615

to those who have been able to last so long and
to read so far,

SALUTE A TUTTI, AMICI

WINE IS LIFE

M F K F p. xxii

UNIVERSITY OF CALIFORNIA PRESS / SOTHEBY PUBLICATIONS

BERKELEY

LOS ANGELES

LONDON

1984